DE 59 .C55 1988

Civilization of the
ancient Mediterranean :
30660000084884

FOR REFERENCE

Do Not Take From This Room

ART INSTITUTE OF DALLAS

3 0660 00008488 4

LEARNING RESOURCE CENTER
THE ART INSTITUTE OF DALLAS
2 NORTHPARK 8080 PARK LANE
DALLAS, TX 75231

DEMCO

Civilization of the
Ancient Mediterranean

GREECE AND ROME

DE 59 .C55 1988

Civilization of the
ancient Mediterranean :
30660000084884

Civilization of the Ancient Mediterranean

GREECE AND ROME

3 0660 00008488 4

EDITED BY

Michael Grant and Rachel Kitzinger

LEARNING RESOURCE CENTER
THE ART INSTITUTE OF DALLAS
2 NORTHPARK 8080 PARK LANE
DALLAS, TX 75231

VOLUME II

CHARLES SCRIBNER'S SONS
MACMILLAN LIBRARY REFERENCE
New York

Simon & Schuster Macmillan and Prentice Hall International
LONDON · MEXICO CITY · NEW DELHI · SINGAPORE · SYDNEY · TORONTO

Copyright © 1988 Charles Scribner's Sons

Library of Congress Cataloging-in-Publication Data

Civilization of the ancient Mediterranean.
Includes bibliographies and index.
1. Civilization, Classical.   I. Grant, Michael,
1914–   . II. Kitzinger, Rachel, 1948–   .
DE59.C55   1987   938   87–23465
ISBN 0–684–17594–0 (set)

ISBN 0–684–18864–3 (vol. 1)
ISBN 0–684–18865–1 (vol. 2)
ISBN 0–684–18866–X (vol. 3)

Charles Scribner's Sons
An Imprint of Simon & Schuster Macmillan
1633 Broadway, New York, NY 10019-6785

All rights reserved. No part of this book
may be reproduced in any form without the
permission of Charles Scribner's Sons.

9 11 13 15 17 19 Q/C 20 18 16 14 12 10 8

Printed in the United States of America

The paper in this book meets the guidelines for permanence and
durability of the Committee on Production Guidelines for Book
Longevity of the Council on Library Resources.

Contents

VOLUME I

Chronological Table · xvii

Introduction · xxv

HISTORY

Historical Summary of Greece
A. R. Burn · 3

Historical Summary of Rome
Arther Ferrill · 45

LAND AND SEA

Land and Sea
J. Donald Hughes · 89

POPULATION

Races and Physical Types in the Classical World
Peyton Randolph Helm · 137

Early Greek Migrations
Ronald A. Crossland · 155

Late Roman Migrations
E. A. Thompson · 171

Languages and Dialects
David Langslow · 183

AGRICULTURE AND FOOD

Farming and Animal Husbandry
K. D. White · 211

Foodstuffs, Cooking, and Drugs
Don R. Brothwell · 247

TECHNOLOGY

Theories of Progress and Evolution
G. E. R. Lloyd · 265

Greek Building Techniques
J. J. Coulton · 277

Roman Building Techniques
James E. Packer · 299

Engineering
John G. Landels · 323

Transportation
Lionel Casson · 353

Crafts and Craftsmen
Alison Burford · 367

Calendars and Time-Telling
Alan E. Samuel · 389

Alphabets and Writing
Rachel Kitzinger · 397

Book Production
Susan A. Stephens · 421

GOVERNMENT AND SOCIETY

Greek Forms of Government
Oswyn Murray · 439

Alternative Paths: Greek Monarchy and Federalism
Michael Grant · 487

Roman Forms of Government
E. Stuart Staveley · 495

Greek Class Structures and Relations
Stanley M. Burstein · 529

Roman Class Structures and Relations
Richard P. Saller · 549

Slavery
Thomas E. J. Wiedemann · 575

CONTENTS

Greek Law

Douglas M. MacDowell · 589

Roman Law

Alan Watson · 607

Greek Administration

Chester G. Starr · 631

Roman Administration

John Ferguson · 649

Interstate Relations

Shalom Perlman · 667

Wars and Military Science: Greece

J. K. Anderson · 679

Wars and Military Science: Rome

Graham Webster · 703

VOLUME II

ECONOMICS

Greek Trade, Industry, and Labor

M. M. Austin · 723

Roman Trade, Industry, and Labor

Keith Hopkins · 753

Mines and Quarries

John F. Healy · 779

Greek Taxation

Robert J. Littman · 795

viii

CONTENTS

Roman Taxation
Brent D. Shaw · 809

Insurance and Banking
Wesley E. Thompson · 829

Piracy
Lionel Casson · 837

RELIGION

Divinities
John Ferguson · 847

Myths and Cosmologies
Michael Simpson · 861

Magic
John Ferguson · 881

Greek Cults
Susan Guettel Cole · 887

Roman Cults
John Ferguson · 909

Greek Priesthoods
Judy Ann Turner · 925

Roman Priesthoods
Mary Beard · 933

Divination and Oracles: Greece
John Pollard · 941

Divination and Oracles: Rome
John Ferguson · 951

ix

Sacrifice and Ritual: Greece
Michael H. Jameson · *959*

Sacrifice and Ritual: Rome
John A. North · *981*

The Afterlife: Greece
Emily Vermeule · *987*

The Afterlife: Rome
John A. North · *997*

Ruler Worship
J. Rufus Fears · *1009*

Judaism
Seth Schwartz · *1027*

Christianity
Helmut Koester and Vasiliki Limberis · *1047*

PRIVATE AND SOCIAL LIFE

Greek Education and Rhetoric
Carolyn Dewald · *1077*

Roman Education and Rhetoric
Cecil W. Wooten · *1109*

Folklore
William F. Hansen · *1121*

Athletics
David C. Young · *1131*

Greek Spectacles and Festivals
Robert Garland · *1143*

Roman Games
John H. Humphrey · 1153

Greek Associations, Symposia, and Clubs
Nicholas R. E. Fisher · 1167

Roman Associations, Dinner Parties, and Clubs
Nicholas R. E. Fisher · 1199

Medicine
John Scarborough · 1227

Greek Attitudes Toward Sex
Jeffrey Henderson · 1249

Roman Attitudes Toward Sex
Judith P. Hallett · 1265

Images of the Individual
Peter Walcot · 1279

Prostitution
Werner A. Krenkel · 1291

VOLUME III

WOMEN AND FAMILY LIFE

Women in Greece
Helene P. Foley · 1301

Women in Rome
Sheila K. Dickison · 1319

Greek Marriage
Sarah B. Pomeroy · 1333

Roman Marriage
Susan Treggiari · *1343*

Birth Control, Childbirth, and Early Childhood
Valerie French · *1355*

Houses
Alexander Gordon McKay · *1363*

Clothing and Ornament
Larissa Bonfante and Eva Jaunzems · *1385*

LITERARY AND PERFORMING ARTS

Epic Poetry
Bryan Hainsworth · *1417*

Greek Lyric and Elegiac Poetry
Joseph Russo · *1437*

Roman Lyric and Elegiac Poetry
Gordon Williams · *1455*

Bucolic Poetry
David M. Halperin · *1467*

Drama
Peter D. Arnott · *1477*

Epigrams and Satire
J. P. Sullivan · *1495*

Music and Dance
Edward Kerr Borthwick · *1505*

Literary Criticism
Frederick T. Griffiths · *1515*

Greek Historiography and Biography

Stephen Usher · 1525

Roman Historiography and Biography

Ronald Mellor · 1541

The Novel

John J. Winkler · 1563

Letter Writing

Robert Glenn Ussher · 1573

PHILOSOPHY

Greek Philosophy

G. E. R. Lloyd · 1585

Roman Philosophical Movements

Elizabeth Asmis · 1637

THE VISUAL ARTS

Greek Architecture

J. J. Coulton · 1653

Roman Architecture

Roger Ling · 1671

Urban Planning

Thomas D. Boyd · 1691

Greek Sculpture and Gems

Jerome J. Pollitt · 1701

Roman Sculpture and Gems

Richard Brilliant · 1727

CONTENTS

Greek Painting and Mosaic
Jerome J. Pollitt · 1749

Roman Painting and Mosaic
Roger Ling · 1771

Coins
R. A. G. Carson · 1795

EPILOGUE

The Progress of Classical Scholarship
R. R. Bolgar · 1819

Maps · 1833

List of Contributors · 1845

Index · 1851

ECONOMICS

Greek Trade, Industry, and Labor

M. M. AUSTIN

SOURCES: ANCIENT AND MODERN APPROACHES

The sources for Greek economic history are by and large the same as for Greek history in general: they include literary works (historical and other), documentary texts (inscriptions, and in the case of Ptolemaic Egypt, papyri), and the evidence of physical remains of all kinds. That is to say, apart from a few surviving literary texts that have a more specifically economic content, no ancient Greek source provides any attempt at a description or analysis of economic life as a whole. The evidence is of a fragmentary and random kind, dependent on chance allusions in literary sources or the accidental survival of documentary or archaeological material. Most serious for the economic historian is the shortage of reliable and detailed statistical data, even on such an essential aspect as population figures. The total size of the population of classical Athens, for example, and the relative proportions of citizens, metics (free noncitizen residents), and slaves, remain to this day matters of conjecture and controversy. A modern economist approaches his subject quantitatively and with precise figures; a historian of the ancient Greek economy can only aim at approximate qualitative evaluations.

This does not mean that Greek thought was unaware of or indifferent to economic factors. First, Greek society had from the archaic period onward an openly materialistic and acquisitive streak. Wealth was a much discussed theme throughout Greek ethical and political writing. Many different views were expressed about the proper limits of wealth, about the various ways of acquiring it, and about its uses. But it was generally assumed that wealth as such was not only worth having, but that it was indispensable for the good life. Poverty was reckoned an evil, and was the object of distaste or contempt, or at best of pity: "Blessed are the poor" was a sentiment alien to Greek society. Second, the Greeks of the classical period and later were well aware that their civilization had started from modest beginnings and had grown considerably in wealth. In this process economic factors were assigned a positive role: trade, economic differentiation, and the invention of basic techniques were all part of civilization and an essential precondition for it. Third, from the fifth century onward Greek political literature shows an increasing interest in the financial management of states as war made growing demands on state resources. Two works reflecting this interest have survived: Xenophon's *Ways and Means* of *ca.* 355 B.C., prompted by Athens' financial distress after a disastrous war with her allies; and a collection of fiscal stratagems employed by cities and rulers in financial difficulties in Book Two of the *Financial Management* (*Oeconomica*), by an anonymous Aristotelian writer of the late fourth or early third century B.C.

Yet none of this ever led to economic analysis as such. What was missing was the realization that there was such an entity as "the economy," which existed in its own right and was susceptible of analysis for its own sake. Our word "economy" is derived from the Greek *oikonomia*, which did not mean economy in our sense, but rather denoted management of the household (*oikos*) or management in general. Among Xenophon's works is a treatise entitled the *Household Management* (*Oeconomicus*) concerned with the functions of the head of a household; it discusses many topics, economic and noneconomic, that are part of his role, but it does not give any systematic discussion of economic life in general or of different kinds of economic occupation. Similar in spirit is the Aristotelian *Financial Management* already mentioned, of which Book One discusses in a very literal way various levels of financial management, from that of the household, through the city level, to that of a satrap in the Persian Empire, and finally that of the king. That was the limit reached by Greek economic thinking.

In practice, to use the terminology of Karl Polanyi, the economy remained "embedded" in Greek society and social relations; it did not develop or become thought of as an autonomous sphere in its own right. Hence

the lack of any systematic inquiry into it. (Technical treatises on specific aspects, such as existed from the fourth century onward—Aristotle, *Politics* 1.1258b37–1.259a5—are another matter.) Hence too the difficulty facing the modern historian, used to thinking in specifically economic terms. Can modern economic concepts be properly applied to the ancient Greek world? The terms "trade," "industry," and "labor" conjure up precise associations in the reader's mind, and he will recognize these entities in the Greek world. Yet they are not concepts that translate readily into ancient Greek. Thus there is a double danger: to apply modern economic concepts unthinkingly to the Greek world can result in serious distortion by making the Greek world seem closer to our own than it really was. But to reject them altogether leaves a gap and can lead to another kind of distortion through underestimation of how far the Greek world did develop economically.

This dilemma lies at the heart of the modern study of the subject, and the character of Greek economics has been a matter of scholarly controversy ever since the subject began to be studied in the nineteenth century. At issue was the question whether in its economic life the Greek world should be conceived as having developed along "modern" lines, or whether it had remained more or less "primitive" in character. Particular attention was paid to Greek trade and its relations with politics. The debate can be seen as part of a much wider issue, the more or less explicit equation of the classical ancient world with that of western Europe. As regards the Greek economy, the alternative "either modern or primitive" is not a satisfactory one. The best modern research, under the influence of sociological and anthropological studies (the work of Max Weber and of Karl Polanyi, to name only these), has discarded it in favor of a wider, functional approach that seeks to understand Greek economics within the context of Greek society as a whole.

Greek economics cannot be considered in isolation but must be related to Greek society, its institutions and values. No less controversial has been the question of slavery and its place in the Greek (and Roman) worlds. How far was Greek civilization dependent on the institution of slavery? As with the controversy on Greek economics, the debate has ideological implications about both the ancient and the modern worlds. It is not just a matter of facts, but of rival conceptions of Greek society. Any analysis of Greek economic life is therefore partial, since it presupposes a view of Greek society as a whole that is open to challenge, and provisional, since further research and debate may cause it to be modified.

THE ECONOMIC DEVELOPMENT OF THE GREEK WORLD

Between the eighth and the third centuries B.C. the Greek world grew considerably in size, population, and total wealth, so much so that the historian is tempted, with some justification, to describe the development in terms of economic growth. But this calls for immediate qualification. First, it will be seen that economic growth in the Greek world was subject to many limitations. Second, the development was due only in part to economic growth proper (the development of commodity production and commercial exchanges) and owed much to other factors as well. Factors that seem to us purely economic in character, such as the invention and diffusion of coinage, were not in the Greek world considered purely economic. Conversely, factors we might see as primarily noneconomic, such as war, had in the Greek world an economic function among others. Third, it goes without saying that increase in total wealth did not mean equal

distribution of new wealth among all members of society. The contrast between wealth and poverty runs throughout Greek history and, if anything, increases during and after the fourth century. Fourth-century political writers were much concerned with the issue of social conflicts between rich and poor, an issue the Hellenistic age did not solve. Rather, it accentuated the contrast: the great and ostentatious wealth of the new royal dynasties and their courts dwarfed the largest private fortunes of the classical period.

Land

Territorial expansion was the first aspect in the economic development of the Greek world. This happened largely in two major waves of settlement, the first the colonization of the archaic period, a long and piecemeal process that scattered new Greek cities widely around the coasts of the Mediterranean and the Black Sea, the second the inland penetration and settlement of Asia in the wake of the Macedonian conquest, a faster and more deliberate operation. Acquisition of new land in the first instance benefited the new settlers, not the communities they left behind. Nevertheless, despite its political fragmentation, the cultural unity of the Greek world ensured a continuity of communications between its far-flung members. And continuity of communications assisted the development of exchanges between different parts of the Greek world as well as with non-Greeks.

Population

Territorial expansion was partly responsible for the second aspect, increase in total population. Increase in territory made possible an increase in the size of the population sustained. But beyond the increase in the size of the free population, there was an equally important increase in the dependent population under the control of Greeks. In the absence of any major technical changes in the conditions of production, growth in commodity production came chiefly in the form of increase of dependent labor. The Greek world knew concurrently several different forms of dependent labor, but two may be singled out. First, acquisition of land for colonial settlement often went together with the reduction of the local non-Greek population to a dependent status. This is true in various ways of both main periods of Greek colonial expansion. Second, the political and social evolution of Greek society in the archaic period resulted in the development of chattel-slavery as the Greeks' most distinctive form of dependent labor. Chattel-slavery presupposed trade and stimulated its growth. Although chattel-slavery was by no means restricted to purely productive economic functions, it had a large effect on economic development by making possible an increase and diversification of commodity production.

Urbanization

Territorial expansion went virtually hand in hand with the third aspect, urbanization. Urbanization is part of the wider history of the Greek city-state, but whereas the city-state as an autonomous political unit declined from the fourth century or even earlier, urbanization was a continuously expanding process. Even before the Macedonian conquest of Asia, the Greek city provided a model for the development of a Greek-style urban culture in areas on the fringe of the Greek world. The economic significance of urbanization, however, needs careful assessment. Urbanization should not be taken to imply a large-scale shift of population from the countryside to the cities. Even in classical Athens, the largest urban concentration in the Greek world of its time with the twin centers of Athens and Peiraieus, the majority of Athenians still lived in the countryside of Attica at the outbreak of the Peloponnesian War (Thucydides, 2.14–17). Only the largest Hellenistic royal capitals may have had urban concentrations numbering into six figures. A few dozen cities may have numbered into five figures; the majority of smaller towns remained below this. Further, the causes of urbanization were not economic but political and social. The prosperity of cities and of states in general, where it was not based on imperial power, is regularly derived by ancient sources from the possession of good territory, sometimes some special natural resources (such as mines), and occasionally indirect revenues and benefits derived from international trade. What is regularly missing is the ascription of the growth and prosperity of a town to manufacturing activity. Urbanization reflected the conviction of the wealthier classes that the city was the center of political, religious, and cultural activity, and of civilized life in general.

Nevertheless, the growth and spread of cities had consequences for economic life in general. In the *Education of Cyrus* (7.2.5) Xenophon writes:

> In small cities the same workmen make couches, doors, plows, tables, and often the same person actually builds the house and is thankful if he finds enough employers to make a living. . . . In large cities, because of the great demand for each particular trade, a single trade is enough to provide a living, sometimes even only a fraction of a trade.

Urban life required at the very least the development of urban crafts and a degree of economic differentiation. The demands of the wealthy created new needs. Even the smallest town was a center of exchange for locally made goods and local produce. The agora was a distinctive Greek institution, found in every city however small and felt by the Greeks to be one of the characteristics of their civilization. In the Homeric poems the agora is only a meeting place for political and social activity; it soon acquired a commercial function as well, a function that often spilled beyond the limits of the civic agora proper, as in the agora of classical Athens. The Greeks "have a meeting place in the middle of their city where they gather together, swear oaths, and deceive each other"; this is the hostile view of the Greek agora ascribed to the Persian king Cyrus in Herodotus (1.153). In the larger cities, the function of the agora as a marketplace for exchanges could embrace wider areas. The Athenian agora was visited by traders from neighboring towns, as is charmingly illustrated in Aristophanes' *Acharnians.*

Above all, larger cities that were well placed for maritime communications and possessed good harbor facilities became virtual centers of international trade: Peiraieus in the classical period and Byzantium, Rhodes, or Alexandria in Hellenistic times are examples of this. Thus trade, traders, and trading places early became part of the scene of Greek history, and freedom of trade was the normal pattern except for special cases of state intervention. Of all branches of trade, the grain trade became the single most important one in the Greek world. In theory, any town had to be able to sustain itself from its own territory: self-sufficiency was the ideal. In practice, the unpredictability of climatic conditions and the incidence of war created a permanent risk of local shortages and so stimulated the development of trade in staple foods. Local exchanges of agricultural produce are already attested in the Homeric poems and in Hesiod. From there it was a slow but natural development toward an import trade in grain from countries farther afield, such as Egypt or the north shore of the Black Sea, as well as within the Greek world. By the mid fifth century at the latest, the growth of Ath-

ens' population forced her to rely on regular grain imports from abroad. Even smaller cities were likely to require intermittent imports. By the classical period, the grain trade had become a familiar part of economic life in the Greek world.

RELIGION AND THE ECONOMY

Many of the largest surviving physical remains of the Greek world are of buildings that were religious in character, more so than in the Roman world, which developed early an individual tradition of large-scale public works of a purely utilitarian character (roads, bridges, aqueducts). This by itself gives some idea of the impact of religion on economic activity in the Greek world. The construction of temples and other religious buildings (theater and athletics were under the patronage of religion) was a matter of considerable civic pride and religious feeling and probably absorbed greater resources than any other activity except, in some cases, war. This in turn provided work for craftsmen and a challenge to their skills, as did the provision of dedications such as statues. The larger religious festivals involved much expenditure for sacrificial animals and competition prizes. Fairs also regularly grew up around the more important festivals, and religious celebrations of a more than local character fostered the movement of Greeks over wider areas. In the Hellenistic period, even more lavish sums were spent on these celebrations, and the number of festivals multiplied.

But in other ways religion acted as a brake on economic activity by indirectly withdrawing a great deal of wealth from circulation. The practice of costly dedications by states, rulers, or private individuals dates to the archaic age and continued vigorously thereafter. The gifts of Croesus of Lydia at Delphi and elsewhere were famous (Herodotus,

1.50–52, 92). Many more followed. It was also the practice to dedicate in some form a tithe of war booty in temples as an offering of thanks for victory in war. Thus over the years the larger sanctuaries accumulated considerable resources in wealth, including gold and silver, on a far larger scale than was normally the case with Greek cities, which were chronically short of funds save for exceptional cases, such as that of fifth-century Athens. Yet moneylending by temples was limited in scope. Most of the time this wealth was not put back in circulation, except for occasional cases of forcible seizure of temple funds by rulers or states short of money, invariably for military purposes.

WAR AND THE ECONOMY

War was a constantly recurring activity of Greek states, from their emergence in the archaic period until Roman conquest put an end to war in the Greek world. Over the period as a whole, war gradually increased in scale, complexity, and frequency, and thus in the demands it placed on all the resources of the Greek world, human and material, and in the impact it had on Greek society and the economy. From the small-scale, fragmented, intermittent, nonspecialist warfare of the archaic period, to the large-scale, almost permanent, specialized, and technical warfare of the major Hellenistic kingdoms is a long step, but in retrospect the development can be seen to have progressed steadily.

War was so much part of Greek life that it is difficult to isolate the impact it had on economic life specifically. War absorbed considerable financial resources, increasingly so from the fifth century onward with the development of military pay, larger fleets and armies, and from the fourth century with the use of mercenary soldiers. The growing inability of the Greek cities in the

fourth century to finance the conduct of war effectively is one of the factors in their political decline and in the shift of power toward larger, monarchical states with greater resources at their command. War was destructive of human and material resources and thus in some ways was an obstacle to economic development. Ravaging of agricultural land remained a universal practice of Greek warfare throughout this period; although the long-term effects on agriculture were probably limited, the immediate effects could be severe, which encouraged at least temporary reliance on imports of food from outside and hence stimulated trade. War could also disrupt normal economic activity; it was common for cities at war to close their markets to each other.

In other ways war also acted as a stimulus to economic activity by necessitating the provision of weapons and equipment. In the early world of predominantly hoplite warfare this would have been modest in scale. Subsequently it developed, with the growth of larger naval forces beginning in the sixth century, the development of increasingly large and elaborate fortification works beginning in the fifth century, and the invention of artillery and siege engines beginning in the fourth century. The complex armaments of the Hellenistic age, on land and at sea, were but the culmination of older trends. Diodorus Siculus (14.41.3–4) has preserved a vivid description of the massive preparations organized by Dionysius I of Syracuse in 399 B.C. on the eve of launching a war against the Carthaginians in Sicily:

He assembled skilled craftsmen by command from the cities under his control and by attracting others from Italy, Greece, and the Carthaginian-controlled territory in Sicily with the promise of high wages. His intention was to manufacture a large number of weapons and missiles of every description, and also quadriremes and quinqueremes. No ship of the size of a quinquereme had ever been built before. Having assembled many craftsmen, he divided them into groups according to their skills and placed over them the most distinguished of the citizens, promising great gifts to those who manufactured weapons.

War necessitated manufacture; war also necessitated trade. The growth of long-distance and long-term campaigns, beginning in the fifth century, created a need to supply troops in the field. The practice of opening special markets outside towns for this purpose is attested from this time onward. Traders in fact followed armies as a matter of course and not only sold supplies to the troops but also bought booty and captives from them. Without traders a victorious army would soon have become encumbered with the fruits of its own success. Coinage, often issued specifically for the payment of troops, was put back into circulation by them. Thus in many ways war and trade went hand in hand, each assisting the other.

Indeed, war was itself a recognized mode of acquisition, taken for granted from the time of the Homeric poems to the Hellenistic age and beyond. War was a form of economic activity. Writes Xenophon: "It is a law established for all time among all men that when a city is taken in war, the persons and the property of its inhabitants belong to the captors" (*Education of Cyrus* 7.5.73). Plato also asserts: "In war all the possessions of the vanquished become the property of the victors" (*Laws* 1.626b). War accounts for a large part of the increase of wealth for Greek states, and in some cases for individual Greeks. It was through conquest that much of the land available to the Greeks for settlement was acquired. The conquest of Asia was preceded by a propaganda campaign, known chiefly through the writings of the Athenian Isocrates, who urged the Greeks to abandon wars against each other and turn instead to the far more rewarding task of invading the Persian Empire. The idea was in fact an old one (Herodotus, 5.49). As previously noted, the acquisition of new land often entailed the reduction of the non-Greek population to some form of servitude. Victory in battle also meant booty and captives, and war thus assisted the growth of chattel-slavery. The largest single influx of precious metals into general circulation came as a result of the capture by the Macedonians of the vast accumulated treasures of the Persian Empire (334–330 B.C.), much of which was coined by Alexander and the Successors.

From the early fourth century onward a few successful military leaders acquired large private fortunes from warfare as freelance officers in foreign service or as independents working for their own interests. The founders of the great Hellenistic royal dynasties and their followers were simply the most conspicuously successful of such war leaders. It is in general a simple observation that the outstandingly prosperous states in Greek history owed their fortune not to commercial or industrial activity, but in the first instance to the fruits of superior military power and imperial revenues. This holds good in different ways for Sparta down to the early fourth century, the fifth-century Athenian naval empire with its tribute-paying allies, Macedon under Philip and Alexander, the major Hellenistic kingdoms, all of them military in character, and even Hellenistic Rhodes, although in her case prosperity also depended on benefits derived from international trade.

THE STATE AND THE ECONOMY

Private Ownership and Private Enterprise

Economically, the Greek world was largely one in which the means of production and of private enterprise were privately owned. In the world of the city-states (and also in the less developed ethnos—statelike tribal groups)—the state itself was not a direct participant in economic activity proper, and this had important consequences both for the functioning of economic activity and the state's attitude to it.

As regards land, most agricultural land was in the hands of individual citizens. The normal Greek pattern was that ownership of land within the state was a prerogative of the citizen and one of the privileges that marked him off from all those who were not members of the political community. Despite the unusually extensive development of urban crafts and trades, a majority of the citizens in classical Athens (perhaps some three-quarters in all) owned land in some form. The proportion must have been even higher in other, less developed cities. Some land was owned by temples and religious associations, but always on a modest scale and in practice it was treated in the same way as privately owned land, being let out to tenants. The only land that was not privately owned was marginal land, fit only for communal grazing. Ownership of mines, at least of precious metals, was normally asserted by the state, yet here too their exploitation was left in practice to the private enterprise of citizens. That at least was the case with the silver mines of Laurium in eastern Attica in the fourth century and possibly earlier, the only mines in the classical period for which there is detailed evidence. The Athenian state's participation was limited to collecting rents from leases of mining concessions and other dues.

As regards dependent labor, some of the larger and wealthier Greek cities did own a number of public slaves, but they were invariably used solely for political and administrative functions, as secretaries, minor functionaries, assistants to magistrates, and even as a special police force; such was the case with the corps of Scythian slaves used by Athens in the classical period to patrol political meetings. They were never used by the state for economically productive purposes. Xenophon in *Ways and Means* suggested that the Athenian state acquire slaves to work in the silver mines (4.14–52); but this was to be achieved by renting them to individual entrepreneurs, and the proposal was in any case not adopted. There were no state factories: all the economically productive slaves were privately owned by individuals. The Spartan Helots may appear to present an exception in that they were collectively owned by the community of the Spartiates and could only be freed by it, not by individual Spartiates. Yet in practice they paid dues to individual Spartiate masters whom they sustained in this way.

In trade, too, the Greek state was not a direct participant. Characteristic of the Greek world was the distinction that grew up by the end of the archaic age between the fast and mainly oar-driven warship, not well suited to carrying larger loads nor to remaining at sea for long periods, and the slow and mainly wind-driven merchant vessel, suitable for the transport of heavier cargoes over long distances. The distinction went beyond technical characteristics. In the early archaic age, warships probably were at first built and owned by the wealthy, and the connection between the wealthy and the provision or maintenance of warships never totally disappeared. At Athens, for instance, it was institutionalized in the form of the trierarchy, whereby the state provided the ships and the crews' pay while the wealthy trierarch commanded and paid for the maintenance of the ship. Occasionally a wealthy man might provide a ship of his own for the state as a demonstration of civic generosity. But the state asserted control over the organization and use of war fleets, and this remained the norm in Greek history. The same never happened with merchant vessels, which remained throughout in private hands. Strictly speaking, there were no merchant fleets in the Greek world, only merchant vessels that were privately owned; the only fleets were military and state controlled. International maritime trade was thus in the hands of private individuals from many Greek and non-Greek states. This fact and the consequences that followed are well illustrated in the case of the grain trade in the classical period.

Classical Athens was unusually dependent on regular imports of grain from abroad to feed her large population. It was a matter of state concern and policy and was regularly discussed in the Athenian Assembly. The means used by Athens to try to ensure her supplies (detailed below) rested on the assumption that the trade was ultimately in the hands of foreign merchants, private individuals over whom Athens had no permanent control. It never occurred to Athenians or to the leaders of any other Greek state that it might be a practical proposition for the state to build a merchant fleet of its own in order to guarantee the community's food supply.

Regulation of Economic Activity

Strictly speaking, Greek states did not have any economic policy at all, since they did not recognize the existence of "the economy" as an entity in its own right, the functioning of which could be influenced by state initiatives and interventions. On the other hand, the state had certain functions and needs that impinged in various ways on economic life. Religion and war have been mentioned; to these should be added an interest in essential supplies, the policing of markets, the collection of public revenues, and the issuing of coinage.

Supplies

The ideal of self-sufficiency had a long history in the Greek world. There is something of a paradox in this, given the unequal endowment of Greek lands with essential re-

sources and given the fragmentation of the Greek world into many small units with necessarily limited resources, a fragmentation that continued in the Hellenistic world despite the growth in the East of larger monarchical states. Essential resources that were random in their distribution included metals and timber which, together with linen and pitch, were essential for shipbuilding and other military purposes. Export bans on these and on essential grain produce are frequently attested, sometimes on a permanent basis, sometimes as a special wartime measure. Solon, for example, is said to have banned the export of all agricultural produce from Attica except olive oil (Plutarch, *Parallel Lives*, "Solon" 24.1–2). States that had the need for supplies from abroad tried wherever possible to control both their sources of supply and the flow of traffic, partly to maintain their own advantage, partly to deny the sources to other hostile states. Fifth-century Athens made open and effective use of her naval power for that purpose:

> For if a city is rich in timber for shipbuilding, where will it export it if it does not reach an understanding with the rulers of the sea? Again, if a city is rich in iron, copper, or linen, where will it export these if it does not reach an understanding with the rulers of the sea? Now these are the materials from which I build my ships. . . . In addition, if our rivals wish to export these materials elsewhere than to Athens, they will be prevented by us from doing so or will have to avoid going by sea. (Old Oligarch, *Constitution of Athens* 2.11–12)

It goes without saying that few states were ever in the position of using direct naval power to such effect as fifth-century Athens. For many, political and diplomatic action was required to try to secure the right to import certain resources from foreign states or rulers who controlled their export. The kings of Macedon, for example, exercised a monopoly control over the export of timber from Macedon and used this asset for political purposes in their relations with Greek states. The Spartocid rulers of the Cimmerian (Crimean) Bosporus (438–*ca.* 110 B.C.) similarly controlled the export of grain from their territories and granted preferential conditions to Athens.

Most crucial was the food supply of Greek states. Ideally, a town had to be able to feed itself from its own territory. In practice, food shortages, if only of a temporary character, were a recurring difficulty for even small cities due to unpredictable climatic conditions, crop diseases, or the ravages of war. The ability of states to control their supplies of imported grain varied greatly. The magistrates of the small city of Teos in the fifth century could only pronounce annual curses against those preventing imports of grain— perhaps wealthy local landowners hoping to make a profit (Meiggs and Lewis, *Selection of Greek Historical Inscriptions* no.30). Maritime states with war fleets of their own would occasionally bring to land merchant ships with cargoes of grain, forcing them to dispose of them on the spot. Convoys of warships to protect merchantmen are occasionally attested.

Athens' dependence on imported grain was reflected in several fourth-century laws. No citizen or metic was allowed to transport grain to any destination other than Athens, nor was he allowed to lend money on a ship that was not commissioned to import grain. All grain brought to Athens had to be sold there, one-third at the grain market in Peiraieus, and the remaining two-thirds at the grain market in Athens. The grain markets were policed by special officials. Most of the traders who imported grain, however, were foreigners over whom Athens had no permanent control. The most she could do was to speed up judicial procedures in the case of trials over maritime loans in order to enable the traders to take to the sea again with little delay. The case of Athens was excep-

tional, but the problem was a recurring one and there is much scattered inscriptional evidence to illustrate it. The temporary appointment of special grain commissioners (*sitonai*) was a frequent device. Some states went further. A Samian law of the second century B.C. records in detail the setting up of a permanent fund by public subscription for the purpose of making regular purchases of grain through special annually elected officials. Grain was then to be distributed on a monthly basis to all Samian citizens free of charge (Dittenberger, *Sylloge Inscriptionum Graecarum* no. 976).

It will be seen that all such interventions were a matter of controlling essential supplies and do not constitute a proper commercial interest. Given the organization and personnel of trade in the Greek world and the nature of state interest in trading activity, commercial rivalries and conflicts, all too casually projected back onto the Greek world by some modern historians, are conspicuous for their absence from interstate Greek politics.

Policing of Markets

The instances of state intervention in economic activity that have been mentioned were directed at certain essential supplies, not at the traders who brought them. Rather, traders themselves were welcome; access to markets was normally open and unrestricted, except in wartime, and it was in the interests of states to allow this. Xenophon's observation that "all states welcome those who import something" (*On the Cavalry General* [*Hipparchicus*] 4.7) aptly summarizes the Greek attitude. (Spartan xenophobia was an exceptional case.) The foreign trader was an indispensable element in economic life. He brought foreign goods, purchased local produce in return, and during his stay benefited the state through the payment of dues and individuals through rents for accommodation. It was therefore essential to make him feel welcome, as Xenophon argued at length in *Ways and Means*, when insecurity caused by Athens' war against her allies caused many traders to desert Peiraieus. Very occasionally a whole category of foreigners might be excluded by a state in peacetime; such is the case with the much-discussed but obscure Megarian decree issued by Pericles some time before the outbreak of the Peloponnesian War banning Megarians from the Athenian agora (in its narrow sense, the civic center of Athens) and from all ports of her empire.

Yet otherwise Athens could boast of being hospitable to foreigners and of having conferred a "benefaction" on mankind through the opening of Peiraieus as a market for international exchanges in the center of Greece (Isocrates, *Panegyricus* 42). This was a claim others could make. Polybius, for example, mentions the highly strategic position of Byzantium at the entrance to the Black Sea; the Byzantines could have prevented the flow of trade to and from the Black Sea but did not do so, hence they deserved to be considered "the common benefactors of all" (*Histories* 4.38). By the fourth century, if not earlier, the notion grew up that ideally the seas should be free for international traffic and that Greek states should undertake by treaty to recognize this. The first definite instance is in a clause of the Peace of Philocrates between Macedonia and Athens in 346 B.C. This was probably a reaction to growing insecurity on the seas due to developing piracy; after the fifth century there was no naval power strong enough to enforce complete security over a wide area, although Hellenistic Rhodes fought hard to achieve that aim.

As regards markets on its own territory, the role of the state consisted primarily in supervision and policing and in levying dues, not in regulating economic activity as such. The state imposed through special officials the use of its own weights and measures and normally the use of its own coins. It also sought to ensure for the benefit of the citizen consumer (not of the producers) fair trading and fair prices. States concluded judicial agreements with each other for the settlement of disputes between their respective nationals in their courts; traders would have been among these. The state benefited directly through the collection of sundry harbor and market dues and taxes on all imports and exports and on certain sales. Such taxes were universal in the Greek world from the archaic period onward (Corinth under the Bacchiads is an early example) and implied by themselves the development of commercial activity on a more than local scale. The larger maritime states, such as classical Athens or Hellenistic Rhodes, profited most, but inland tolls were also common. A typical tax was the 2 percent duty levied on all imports and exports whatever their origin and nature; it is widely attested in the Greek world. The intention was purely fiscal. The notion of the protective customs barrier was unknown to the world of the Greek cities, as was the notion that taxation as such had an impact on the economy and could therefore be used as an economic regulator.

Coinage

Coinage is one of the Greeks' distinctive and lasting contributions to history. More accurately, it seems to have been invented by the kings of Lydia in the seventh century, but it was the Greek cities' widespread adoption of the new medium that ensured its gradual diffusion and success. By the classical age, most Greek cities that could issued coins at least intermittently; Sparta's deliberate avoidance of coinage was an anachronistic oddity. With the Hellenistic age and the new kingdoms, Greek-style coinage became gradually more diffused in Asia. As will be seen, the adoption and spread of coinage and eventually of a monetary economy in most of the Greek world had important consequences for economic life.

Yet a clear distinction must be drawn between the ultimate effects of the spread of coinage and the aims pursued by the issuing authority. The issuing authority was almost always a state, a political entity, whether a Greek city or an individual ruler; very occasionally a commander in the field, not himself a ruler in his own right, would issue coins for the payment of troops on an emergency basis. Coins were issued by the state primarily for its own purposes, not for those of the users. From the utilitarian point of view, the issuing of coins was a means for the state to make essential state-related payments, as for military expenses (the pay of soldiers and sailors), construction work (religious or military), distributions to the citizen body, and pay for political functions in democratic cities, or as a means of collecting taxes and fines.

But coinage had also a more than strictly utilitarian function: coinage was a symbol of statehood and political identity. When Athens in the fifth century sought to impose on her allies the use of her own silver coinage, the purpose was probably political and psychological, the assertion of Athenian supremacy rather than any hypothetical economic or commercial aim. Coinage was in general a matter of considerable civic pride, and this may help to explain its rapid spread among the majority of Greek cities from the sixth century onward. Coins displayed the heads of patron deities or other distinctive symbols; the Hellenistic royal coinages showed the heads of rulers or of members of their dynasties. Coins also displayed the name of the issuing authority, a community of citizens, or, in the Hellenistic age, an individual king. Much care and artistry was often expended on the engraving of the dies, far more than was necessary for the purely utilitarian functions of coinage. It is not obvious that the issuing authority ever saw a necessary connection between the striking of coins and the functioning of economic activity, or that it had to take that connection into account. The issuing of coinage, in other words, was and remained more a political function of the state than an economic one.

THE PTOLEMIES AND THE ECONOMY

Against this view of the world of the Greek cities may be set the case of the Ptolemies and their attitude to the economy. The Ptolemaic kingdom is the one Hellenistic royal state for which detailed evidence is available due to the survival of documentary papyri. The Ptolemies drew not only on the practices and attitudes of the Greek world from which they came, but also on native Egyptian traditions of royal absolutism, requisition of labor, and a centralized bureaucracy. As kings they could control vastly greater resources, human and material, than any Greek city, and as newcomers to a conquered world they had opportunities for innovation not to be found in the world of the Greek cities. Like other Hellenistic monarchies, Ptolemaic Egypt was in the first place "spear-won" territory, the possession of the ruler through the right of conquest, which he transmitted to his successors as a family inheritance or could even alienate, in part or whole, through sale or bequest. An earlier generation of scholars, impressed by the apparent similarity between Ptolemaic Egypt and contemporary totalitarian states, talked readily in terms of the Ptolemies' planning and control of the economy. Further study and a changed perspective have led to a more restrictive evaluation both of the Ptolemies' direct participation in the economy and of the effectiveness of their control over it.

As regards natural resources, the Ptolemies, unlike classical Athens with the silver mines at Laurium, did control and exploit directly the gold mines in Nubia; the mines were worked by forced labor of condemned criminals. Much of the land of Egypt was technically royal land; large parts of it were assigned by the kings to high officials at court and to military settlers, nominally on a precarious and revocable basis, although in practice land so granted gradually became by the later second century the personal property of the beneficiaries. Royal land was cultivated by native labor, the royal peasants, whose status defies classification according to the classical Greek antithesis between slave and free person. They were not slaves of the Ptolemies, but neither were they free. They were liable for compulsory labor on irrigation and other works and paid dues to the king. They worked his land on a contractual basis, although it was a contract between unequal partners.

In industrial production, there were no royal factories proper despite the resources available to the Ptolemies. The same is true of all the other Hellenistic monarchies. The Ptolemaic kings sought rather to maximize revenues from existing forms of production and introduced to the economy of Egypt a number of monopolies, a fiscal device known already in Greek cities (for example, monopolies in coin-changing). The best-known Ptolemaic example is that of the oil monopoly, in which native labor working under contract produced oil that was retailed by licensed dealers at fixed prices. The whole process was hedged with elaborate safeguards and restrictions, for the intention was purely fiscal, concerned with maximization of royal revenues and prevention of fraud, not with maximization or improvement of production.

Trade with the outside world was for the Ptolemies an important source of wealth and supplies. In some ways they went beyond the practices of Greek cities: taxation of trade by them, as of economic activity in Egypt and in the foreign lands they controlled directly, was heavier and more extensive. For example, they taxed certain luxury imports from the Greek world at varying rates up to 50 percent, and they were the first to introduce the notion of the protective customs barrier to prevent foreign oil from undercutting the Egyptian oil monopoly. Yet in many ways their attitude toward trade was similar to that of the Greek cities. Neither in Egypt itself nor in the Mediterranean did the Ptolemies, the leading naval power of the third century, have any merchant fleet of their own. Grain paid as tax to the king was conveyed to royal granaries in Alexandria by ships owned mostly by private Alexandrian citizens, sailing under contract, not by the king's own ships. It was then exported to the Greek world by a multitude of private foreign traders, not by any Ptolemaic merchant fleets. The foreign traders brought in return a wide variety of goods from the Greek world in demand among Greeks living in Egypt or needed for the running of the country, especially precious metals, which the Ptolemies needed for their coinage and which were always in short supply (*P. Cairo Zenon* 59.021). There is no good evidence that the Ptolemies ever sought to turn their sphere of influence in the Greek world into a commercial empire in which Egyptian produce was imposed on the Greeks on conditions determined by the Ptolemies. The existing mechanisms of trade made this impossible in the first instance.

The coming of the Ptolemies to Egypt profoundly affected the country. Like the pharaohs before them, they extensively reclaimed land for settlement, but they also introduced new plants and breeds of animals, spread the use of coinage, and completed the introduction of ironworking in an attempt to reproduce in Egypt the conditions of life that were familiar to them in Greece. Yet their impact was limited in other ways. There was a built-in resistance on the part of the native peasantry to the introduction of foreign ways; there was inefficiency and corruption in the Ptolemaic bureaucracy, which they could never fully control; and most important, there was a limitation in what they attempted to achieve. They created and financed in Alexandria a research institute, the Museum with the Library, yet it was only in military technology that there was any systematic attempt to put theory into practice. The conditions of production remained in Egypt much the same as before.

The Ptolemies sought through a range of fiscal devices to maximize their revenues but were never concerned with the necessarily negative effect of their heavy taxation on economic activity. The richest and most self-advertising of the Hellenistic monarchies, they spent much of their wealth on conspicuous consumption of many kinds, not on investment for economic growth. For all the differences between Ptolemaic Egypt and the world of the Greek cities, the Ptolemies remained in many ways close to that world and to its attitudes.

COMMERCIAL AND NONCOMMERCIAL EXCHANGES

Enough has been said to show that from an early date trade was an integral and distinctive part of Greek life. Yet at the same time, goods circulated or were exchanged in ways other than purely commercial, and this too is no less characteristic of Greek history. The impacts of religion and war on the economy have already been mentioned. Of

particular importance also was the practice of gift-giving, attested throughout Greek history in many forms from the Homeric poems through to Hellenistic times and beyond. It should be said that gift-giving, whether between individuals, between states, or from individuals to states, was never disinterested but always carried out in the expectation of a return. Gift-giving could serve a multiplicity of functions. It could serve the function of a noncommercial exchange, as in the gift-giving between chieftains described in Homer, which among other things was a means of obtaining metals. Where there was no direct and equivalent material return, gift-giving could bring esteem and influence with one's fellow citizens, and the phenomenon of wealthy individuals playing community benefactors grew in importance during the Hellenistic period. With gifts to foreign states, the aim might be self-advertisement in the wider Greek world and the creation of goodwill or ties of dependence on the part of the receiving community.

Numerous examples are known, particularly in the Hellenistic age when the newly established wealthy monarchies wished to enhance their reputation within the Greek world where the role of kings as bestowers of generosities was appreciated. On many occasions, the donations came from a single state or ruler, for instance, gifts of grain or other supplies to individual cities. Polybius describes in a famous passage (5.88–90) the generosities showered on the island of Rhodes after a severe earthquake in 227/226:

Ptolemy III Euergetes promised them 300 talents of silver, a million artabas of wheat, timber for the construction of ten quinqueremes and ten triremes, consisting of 40,000 cubits of squared pine planking, 1,000 talents of bronze coinage, 3,000 talents of two, 3,000 pieces of sailcloth, 3,000 talents of bronze for the repair of the Colossus, 100 architects with 350 workmen, and fourteen talents every year for their wages, and in addition 12,000 artabas of wheat for competitions and sacrifices, and 20,000 for the supplying of ten triremes. Most of this he gave at once, as well as a third of the money promised.

The donations of other rulers are also listed. Polybius mentions the episode primarily as an example of royal generosity, yet his account shows that the gifts came from cities all over the Greek world as well as from kings. The episode stood in a long tradition of competitive Panhellenic generosities to relieve disasters to other Greeks.

TRADE

The Homeric poems already show the existence of trade proper as well as gift-giving, and to the early Greeks the traders par excellence were the Phoenicians. It may be that early contacts with them stimulated the Greeks to develop maritime trade themselves. At any rate, the archaeological record shows the development of some long-distance trade in the Greek world by the early eighth century at the latest; this is the implication of the discovery of the port at Al Mina on the Orontes in North Syria, where the presence of Greeks from Euboea and the islands is attested not later than ca. 800 B.C. Thereafter trade in the Greek world went on developing and grew in geographical range and in the variety of goods exchanged as the Greek world itself expanded.

As trade developed as an activity in its own right, different words came to be attached to different kinds of traders. By the seventh century, the word *emporos* had acquired its regular sense of the maritime trader who sold abroad goods produced by others but did not own his ship, while in Homer it still meant a passenger in a ship. There was the *naukleros* who, unlike the *emporos,* owned the ship he sailed in. Then there was the *kapelos,* the local small-scale dealer who did not engage in long-distance trade. Local trading was subdivided into various branches dealing with different goods. During the archaic age maritime traders also acquired distinctive ships of their own. It may be that initially warships, owned by the wealthy, were used for the dual purposes of transporting goods as well as warriors. Herodotus describes (1.163) the Phocaeans as the first Greeks to sail on long-distance voyages. They discovered the Adriatic, Etruria, Spain and its southern region and port of Tartessus (the claim is exaggerated), and they sailed in warships (pentekonters), not in round merchantmen. It is therefore of great significance that by the late sixth century, if not earlier, the distinction noted above between warship and merchant vessel should have become clearly established. Trade also developed its own functional locations within cities in the Greek world (agoras) and on the fringes of the Greek world, at meeting points with non-Greek peoples. Al Mina in North Syria is perhaps the earliest of the ports of trade to have been established and many others followed, including Pithecusae on the island of Ischia in the west (*ca.* 750 B.C.); Naucratis in Egypt in the late seventh century; sites on the north shore of the Black Sea from the seventh century; and Spina at the mouth of the Po from the late sixth century.

There is every reason to believe that what led to the development of overseas trade was a demand for goods not available in the Greek world, not a search for markets for Greek goods. Trade thus served import, not export needs. The search for metals, already attested in Homer, may well have been a motive in the earliest ventures at Al Mina in the east and at Pithecusae in the west, where extensive archaeological traces of ironworking have been found; the iron ore was imported from Elba. The growing appetite of the aristocracy for wealth and such luxury goods as fine textiles, jewelry, and rare scents was a further incentive to the development of trade. The rise of chattel-slavery, discussed below, created an increasing demand for the import of slaves. By the sixth century, if not earlier, imports of foodstuffs, above all grain, from Egypt, the north shore of the Black Sea, and possibly Sicily and southern Italy as well, began to develop on a significant scale. By the second half of the fifth century a large maritime center like Athens could boast of having available to it all the produce of the world. Thus Hermippus (frag. 63 Kock) wrote:

From Cyrene come silphium and oxhides, from the Hellespont mackerel and all kinds of salted fish, from Thessaly salt and sides of beef. . . . Syracuse provides pigs and cheese. . . . From Egypt come sails and papyrus, from Syria frankincense. Crete sends cypress for the gods, and Libya provides much ivory for purchase. Rhodes provides grapes and dried figs, while pears and plump apples come from Euboea, slaves from Phrygia, mercenaries from Arcadia. Pagasae provides slaves. . . . Zeus's acorns and shiny almonds come from Paphlagonia. . . . Phoenicia provides the fruit of the palm and fine wheat flour, Carthage furnishes carpets and embroidered cushions.

Traders

The maritime trader is a familiar and ubiquitous figure in Greek literature, a frequent presence in Herodotus' account of the archaic age, and regularly taken for granted in subsequent literature. Yet generally traders appear as both numerous and anonymous as individuals, and references to them are usually of a collective kind (such as to traders from Aegina, Byzantium, Rhodes) or their origins are frequently left altogether unspecified. A few individuals are sometimes singled out for special reasons, but the only substantial body of evidence about the world of maritime traders comes from a specialized source, a group of fourth-century speeches delivered in court in Athens that are concerned with disputes over maritime loans and are preserved in the Demosthenic corpus. A number of individuals from many different Greek states appear there and engage in trading or moneylending or both. They are significantly almost all unknown otherwise in the remaining evidence: they came from circles outside those of the leading political and social figures.

The general anonymity of the trader in Greek literature, despite his ubiquitous presence, is no accident but accurately reflects his status in Greek society. Trade was essential for civilized life and although the trader was normally welcomed for what he imported, he was not high on the social scale or in social estimation. Cases of individuals making fortunes from commercial ventures are unusual and are mentioned as such in literature. Most traders were men of modest means. From the evidence of the Demosthenic speeches it can be seen that many maritime traders did not own their ships and of those who did, only two are known to have owned more than one. Nor did traders combine into larger, institutionalized companies; partnerships were limited in scope and in the possibility of growth. Trading, like economic activity in general, was at once substantial in total volume and fragmented in organization. The classes of wealthy merchants who supposedly exercised a powerful influence on the politics of the Greek world, and the alleged commercial rivalries and wars of Greek states are both fictions of modern historians, conjured up by a misleading identification of ancient Greece with the contemporary world.

Financing of Trade

The typical trader was thus a man of limited means, dependent on financing by others for the undertaking of commercial ventures. A long-distance journey could take weeks and was subject to the hazards of weather and piracy. Even if he had his own ship, the trader had to purchase a cargo for exchange as well as provisions for the journey. It has been plausibly suggested that in the archaic period traders may often have been dependents of the wealthy, who owned the ships and could organize ventures to obtain supplies, although positive evidence for this is lacking and it is not clear that the practice survived into the classical period. However, traders must also have worked independently, able somehow to raise working capital. In the classical period this is attested as a regular institution from the late fifth century, and the practice may be supposed to have been older.

Traders borrowed from moneylenders at a high rate of interest (up to 30 percent or more)—a reflection of the risks involved—on the security of their ship or of their cargo, although they were not bound to repay the loan if they suffered shipwreck or some other unavoidable hazard. The sources for the funds were always noninstitutional, usually from a single lender or a small ad hoc group. The idea of organizing moneylending practices in an institutional form in order to spread the risks over a larger number of lenders does not seem to have arisen; commercial credit was thus as fragmented as commercial activity itself. The evidence for commercial moneylending is almost exclusively of Athenian origin, although the practice was common in the Greek world. In the fourth century at least, Athens imposed limitations on the practice by forbidding Athenians or persons resident in Athens to lend money on ships that were not bound to carry grain to Athens as their return cargo. It is not known whether other Greek states imposed similar restrictions, although this seems unlikely; what Athens did was to give a new twist to a no doubt older institution that had arisen out of the need of traders for capital.

COINAGE AND MEANS OF EXCHANGE

It was argued above that Greek cities introduced coinage for state-related uses, not for the convenience of other users. It does not seem likely that states saw in the new medium a means of facilitating local or long-distance exchanges. The early issues in the sixth century were mostly of large denominations, which would have been of limited use in small-scale local transactions. The large denominations, moreover, tended not to travel in any significant quantity beyond the area of issue, with the exception of coins of Athens and from the Thraco-Macedonian area, found in large quantities in the Levant and Egypt in the late sixth and early fifth centuries. Both were silver-producing areas and could issue silver coins in greater abundance and with greater regularity than other Greek states. The coins were evidently accepted as bullion, that is, as silver by weight, not as coins of specific values. In any case trade, whether local or long-distance, was much older than coinage and could continue without it. The Phoenicians long remained indifferent to the new invention. When Carthage began to strike Greek-style coins in the fourth century, it was for the payment of mercenaries and did not serve any commercial function.

Even in classical Athens, which developed

739

a full range of fractional denominations (although still probably issued primarily for state payments) and which had a fully monetary economy, there is evidence of small-scale barter of local or regional agricultural produce. As regards long-distance maritime trade, coinage was not a necessity either. Polybius, writing in the second century, describes the Black Sea trade of Greece as follows (4.38):

> Those commodities which are indispensable to life, cattle and slaves, are supplied to us by the countries around the Black Sea, as is generally agreed, in greater quantity and of better quality than by any others; and as far as luxuries are concerned, they supply us with honey, wax, and salt fish in abundance. In return they receive from our part of the world the surplus olive oil and every kind of wine. With grain there is interchange; they give us some on occasion and sometimes import it from us.

There is no mention here of coinage as an element in the transactions. Even more explicit is Strabo, writing in the time of Augustus (*Geography* 11.2.3):

> Where the river Tanais [Don] flows into the Bosporus [Lake of Maeotis, Sea of Azov], there is a city called Tanais, founded by Greeks who controlled the Bosporus. It used to be the common place of exchange for the nomadic tribes of Asia and Europe and those who sailed across the Sea of Azov; the former brought slaves and hides and whatever else nomads can provide, while the latter brought in exchange fabrics, wine, and all other things which are part of civilized life.

Finds of Greek coin hoards do not in fact overlap with known trade routes: for instance the large-scale grain imports to classical Athens from the Cimmerian (Crimean) Bosporus are not matched by finds of Athenian coins in that area.

The text of a maritime loan, preserved in a fourth-century speech in the Demosthenic corpus (35, *Against Lacritus* 10–13), gives an indication of how the trade functioned: the main cargo, consisting of a consignment of 3,000 jars of wine from Mende in Chalcidice, was picked up by the trader on his way from Athens to the Black Sea and eventually exchanged for a return cargo of grain. The wine trade is in fact archaeologically the best attested trade in Greek history, thanks to the discovery of tens of thousands of jars (or fragments) from the best wine-producing parts of the Greek world. They come notably from the larger islands of the Aegean and date from the classical and Hellenistic periods with a distribution in the Greek world and on its Black Sea and Levant fringes. The export of wine from the Greek world started in the archaic age, and it is likely that wine and, to a lesser degree, oil were the largest single exports available to the Greeks generally. Finely painted pottery, on the other hand, although preserved in large quantities and found widely in the Greek world from the archaic age to the fourth century and outside the Greek world, notably in Etruria (but not in the Levant), was probably of less economic significance than has often been thought. Even at the height of its success in the fifth century, when the industry had achieved a virtual monopoly position, the manufacture of Athenian pottery involved only a few hundred potters and painters. It is the large-scale survival of fine pottery and the great attention devoted to it for artistic reasons that has created the illusion of the economic importance of the industry.

Coinage and Credit Practices

Coinage was thus not a prerequisite for trade; on the other hand, the spread of coinage in the Greek world did in the long run have an important effect on economic activity, both locally and more widely. Coinage provided in a compact and convenient form a means of reckoning value, a means of storing and transporting wealth, and a means of exchange. Thus Pericles in fifth-century Athens could sell all his crops from his estates in Attica for cash and purchase his daily necessities at the market (Plutarch, *Parallel Lives,* "Pericles" 16). By the fourth century Athens had a fully monetary economy, and all values were expressed in terms of coinage (whereas Solon in the early sixth century had reckoned wealth in terms of agricultural produce). Athenian literature of the classical period contains many references to moneylending in various forms; the institution of coinage evidently facilitated this. All the known commercial loans in the classical period were invariably contracted in the form of coinage. The spread of the practice thus presupposes the spread of coinage, as does also the ubiquitous taxation of trade and economic activity mentioned earlier. All this was further facilitated by the quasi-international status achieved by a few exceptionally prolific coinages that came to be used over a wide area, notably the coinage of Athens in the classical period and the coinage of Alexander with its numerous imitations in the Hellenistic period.

Yet both the amount of coined money that circulated and the character of credit practices in the Greek world were subject to a number of important limitations. As regards coinage, Greek states never went over completely to the idea of purely token currencies but retained throughout a connection between the issuing of coinage and the availability of precious metals. The earliest coins were made strictly of precious metals, at first electrum, a natural alloy of gold and silver, then silver, which became the precious metal most frequently used by Greek cities. Philip II of Macedon introduced an abundant gold coinage, and thereafter the leading monarchies coined in both gold and silver. Token bronze coinages of no intrinsic

metallic value and thus valid only in their area of issue began in the fifth century in Sicily and southern Italy, which had more limited supplies of silver than the Aegean world. In the late fourth century Athens was one of the last Greek cities to institute a regular bronze coinage. Thereafter Greek cities had normally a bimetallic system and so never did away with their dependence on precious metals. There was a lingering feeling that "good coinage" had to be of "good metal," a view the Ptolemies, for example, also shared. Sources of precious metals, however, were very unevenly distributed, and supplies could therefore be very spasmodic and unpredictable. Besides, a great deal of the precious metals in existence never reached the form of coinage. Much remained in private hands, as gold and silver plate and jewelry, a frequent method for the well-to-do to accumulate wealth in a useful and pleasing form. Much also was stored in temples in the form of expensive dedications by individuals, states, or rulers.

As regards credit practices and moneylending, the Greek world never moved beyond certain limits. For a start, all transactions were on a strictly cash basis: the notion of the credit sale was unknown and this fact automatically restricted demand. Institutionalized moneylending only developed up to a point and never superseded personal moneylending by individuals. Temples have been mentioned. Banks proper developed by the classical period, the best known examples being in fourth-century Athens. Most bankers there appear to have been non-Athenians; they served as moneychangers, accepted deposits, and made loans to individuals, but significantly there is no evidence that they took any part in maritime commercial loans, which all came from individual lenders. Banks thus did not serve as institutions to channel private funds into the promotion of economic activity. In the Hellenistic period, inscriptions show the existence of monetary foundations established by private individuals or by states for a variety of purposes (such as the Samian grain fund mentioned above). They provided the founding authority with a steady income from the interest on loans made from them, although it is not known who borrowed the money and for what purposes and thus what impact such foundations had on economic activity.

Moneylending in the Greek world remained predominantly personal and noninstitutional in character, with important consequences. The mechanisms for channeling private funds for credit purposes were limited, and moneylending remained fragmented; this would certainly have limited the capital available for credit. Above all, moneylending remained an expression of social relations whether between equals in the same social class or between unequals in different social classes. There was much lending among the wealthy for a variety of social and political purposes and for conspicuous consumption. There was much lending between the wealthy and the poor, often usurious in character, a recurring problem of Greek society from the archaic age onward as the frequent demand for the reduction or abolition of debts implies. The fear of debt and possible loss of independence was the nightmare of the poor and was voiced in Greek literature as early as Hesiod (*ca.* 700 B.C.). Strikingly missing most of the time are the notion of the economically productive investment and the idea that spare capital should normally be put to economically useful purposes. Individuals and states from the archaic age to Hellenistic times were as one in their belief that wealth should be stored, used, or displayed but not invested for productive purposes. Even maritime loans, the only form of economically productive loans known to Greek history, were productive probably more in effect than in intention.

INDUSTRY

In the material productions of the Greek world the vast majority of goods in daily use were handmade by craftsmen who worked with a few simple tools and mechanical devices, not machines, and a few basic materials, notably metals, timber, stone, clay, leather, and linen. So innovative in many other fields, Greeks added relatively little to the techniques they inherited. With few exceptions, even objects that were produced in repetitive series for mass use, such as coins, were individually struck and not made with techniques of genuine mass production. The limitation of existing techniques affected the quantity of the goods that could be produced, not their quality; the high standard of the best Greek work needs no elaboration. All this is true not only of smaller objects but also of the large material creations of the Greek world. The Parthenon was built by a multiplicity of individual craftsmen working under the supervision of Phidias and Ictinus, who were themselves reckoned as craftsmen. The Greeks did not have separate words for artist and craftsman; a sculptor or a painter was a *technites* as much as a shoemaker—they all practiced a *techne* (skill).

In this respect there is of course much similarity between the Greek world and the ancient Near East, famed for its crafts. Yet the place of the craftsman in Greek society was more complex by comparison. Craftsmen of the Near East are largely anonymous figures; the craftsman in Greek society was an individual with an identity and thus offered a contrast to the trader. Beginning in the seventh century when poets began to speak with individual voices, it became common for craftsmen to sign their work. The craftsman's pride in his work is a recurring theme, and some had achieved lasting individual fame by the archaic age. The craftsman was a necessary part of society, and his work was valued.

Yet at the same time estimation of the work of the craftsman did not lead necessarily to a corresponding estimation of his role as a person in society. In his *Parallel Lives* ("Pericles" 1–2), Plutarch comments:

> We take pleasure in perfumes and purple garments, but we regard dyers and perfumers as men unworthy to be free and as mean artisans. . . . No young man of good birth having seen the Zeus of Pisa or the Hera of Argos desired to become Phidias or Polyclitus. . . . A work may delight us with its charm, but there is no need to regard its creator with admiration.

These sentiments need not be taken as universally representative of every period of Greek history and every class of society, but neither can they be wholly brushed aside. It is no accident that in the divine pantheon Hephaestus the smith was at once a wonderfully skilled craftsman and an ugly and misshapen being, the object of fun and ridicule on the part of the other gods. Nor was this just a matter of attitude. Xenophon writes: "In some cities, especially those with a military reputation, no citizen may pursue an artisan's trade" (*Household Management* 4.1–4; 6.4–8). Xenophon may have been thinking here of Sparta in particular, but cases of such exclusions are known elsewhere.

Classical Athens, it is true, was less restrictive. A craftsman was not debarred from possession and exercise of political rights, and many were seen in the assembly. Yet the point remains purely negative since a craftsman who was an Athenian was not disqualified from enjoying citizen rights, but

his craft did not have any more positive content as regards political functions. However skilled, craftsmanship never constituted an entitlement to political rights; the same crafts were practiced in Athens by citizens, metics, and slaves. The building accounts of the Erechtheum (built 421–407 B.C.) show citizens, metics, and slaves working side by side, doing the same kind of work and receiving the same rates of pay. Yet their work on the same building did not provide a common bond between them; it neither united nor divided them. What divided them was a social and political gulf. The citizen alone had political rights; the metic and the slave did not enjoy personal freedom. There were in Athens and in other cities quarters assigned to particular crafts, as today in the souks of North Africa. But there were no trade guilds grouping together all the different workers in a particular craft. There was no industrial class of artisans, just as there was no class of traders. Economic functions were separate from political ones and were lower in status.

As with trade, manufacturing activity was large and involved many workers, yet industry remained fragmented, individualistic in character, and lacked any larger organization. Industrial establishments varied in size. Those staffed solely by free persons were invariably small-scale family businesses that could not grow for reasons presently to be examined. Those staffed by slaves could grow, yet even here the largest known industrial establishment, the arms factory of the metic brothers Lysias and Polemarchus at Peiraieus during the late Peloponnesian War, reached a total of about only 120 slave workers (Lysias, 12.19). All other cases in Athens in the fourth century never exceeded two-digit figures. For example, the orator Demosthenes inherited from his father two workshops, one with over thirty slaves who made knives, the other with twenty slaves who made beds (Demosthenes, 27.9–11). Besides, all such establishments were just the slave holdings of individuals acting independently for their own account; there were no partnerships and economic activity did not grow into larger associations.

Two examples are illustrative. Temple building was the largest single industrial enterprise undertaken by Greek cities (apart from military expenditure on fleets and fortifications). Contracts for temple building are known from inscriptions. The construction of each temple involved a number of separate contracts with many individual workers. Moreover, the state often had to provide workers with materials, make a substantial advance payment before work started, another at the halfway stage, and a small residual payment on completion of the task. The implication is that workmen, who were often traveling craftsmen, were persons of small means with little capital or resources of their own. There were no large building companies. Second, the silver mines at Laurium in east Attica, by far the largest single industrial enterprise pursued over a long period of time in classical Athens, played a major part in the economy both of the Athenian state and of individual Athenians. Mining activity fluctuated according to conditions, but at peak periods it certainly involved 10,000 or more workmen, and it is in the Laurium silver mines that the largest slave holdings by individuals are known. The Athenian general Nicias had, we are told, a thousand slaves, the wealthy Hipponicus six hundred, and an unknown Philemonides three hundred (Xenophon, *Ways and Means* 4.15). Yet there too industrial activity was fragmented and individualistic in character, and consisted of a large number of Athenian entrepreneurs (non-Athenians were probably excluded) who worked separately and did not combine into larger partnerships.

LABOR

Free and Dependent Labor

Free labor coexisted throughout Greek history with various forms of dependent labor. Both free and dependent labor were often occupied in the same kind of work, and sometimes worked side by side, as the case of the Erechtheum workmen illustrates. It is not possible to distinguish qualitatively between the work of freemen and that of the unfree. Whatever the development of various forms of dependent labor and whatever the numbers involved, dependent labor never displaced free labor, and in practice the majority of free Greeks had to work themselves, with or without the assistance of dependent workmen. Only a minority of the wealthier citizens, who controlled dependent labor on a larger scale and were usually large landowners as well, were freed from the need to have to earn a living through economically productive work. On the other hand, they were the dominant minority, culturally, socially, and politically, through the leisure and influence their wealth gave them. This was equally true of the aristocratic world of archaic Greece, of democratic Athens, and of the court circles of the Hellenistic monarchies.

With few exceptions the distinction between free and unfree labor rested not in the type of work involved but in the conditions under which the work was performed. Only a few occupations that involved particular physical hardship—notably work in the mines—tended to be left to slaves or to other degraded categories. Otherwise, chattel-slaves were virtually everywhere and were found not only in many forms of economic activity (sometimes in positions of responsibility) but also in other functions, as for example the work performed by the public slaves already mentioned.

The ancient world lacked the notion of

labor as a salable commodity separate from the person of the worker. To work for someone else was to be placed in a position of dependence upon him; a freeman therefore wanted to work for himself, not for an employer. An unfree person had to work for someone else, and this was the mark of his dependent status. Writes Aristotle: "The condition of the freeman is that he does not live for the benefit of another" (*Rhetoric* 1.9.1367a32). An Athenian, impoverished by the Peloponnesian War and forced to work, reacted with horror to the suggestion that he might became a wealthy man's bailiff: "I could not bear to endure slavery" (Xenophon, *Memorabilia* 2.8.3). This attitude had profound consequences for economic life. The worker in the modern world seeks security of employment and better wages and working conditions; work itself is judged to have a positive value while unemployment carries a stigma. The free Greek usually had to work for a living, but work for him was a necessity and had little positive value in itself. Above all, he sought the preservation of his own independence and dreaded the thought of having to work on a permanent basis for another. This seemed to him the first step on the road to a loss of free status.

The consequence of this attitude was the limited development of wage labor, with only a few exceptions. Agriculture could not do without hired labor on a seasonal basis at peak periods. Mercenary service was a special case; it emerged in the archaic period, then grew on a very large scale from the late fifth century to Hellenistic times. Work of freemen for the state, a nonpersonal employer, did not carry a stigma. Construction work on temples, previously mentioned, usually took the form of contract labor to do specific pieces of work. Among other state employees, the larger Greek cities also developed the institution of public doctors who were paid a retainer to guarantee their availability, although their services were not free; the position was honorific and could be lucrative. But with exceptions such as these, most labor was not wage labor. Hence the lack of a genuine labor market and the absence of demands concerning wages and working conditions. The economic demands of poor citizens (who alone among the poor could voice such demands) concerned land and debt. Wages proper tended to be both low and restricted in range. All these factors furthered the tendency noted above toward the fragmentation of economic activity. It is an invariable pattern that where workshops grew beyond the limits of a small family business the extra labor used was always slave labor, not that of freemen. Similarly, no free person is ever found employed in domestic service. There could therefore be no competition between free and unfree labor.

Chattel-Slavery

Greeks took for granted and relied on some form of dependent labor throughout their history. This was not peculiar to them but is characteristic of preindustrial societies generally, given the limits of technological conditions of production. What was peculiar to the Greeks, and to the Romans as well, was the exceptional development taken by one particular form of dependent labor, chattel-slavery, which grew from the archaic period onward to become the dominant form of dependent labor in the world of city-states. The chattel-slave's principal characteristic was that he was literally the possession of his master, totally dependent on him, an article of property that could be bought, sold, or bequeathed; he had no control over his person, let alone his labor.

The Greeks were dimly aware of the novelty of chattel-slavery as developed by them. One Greek writer, the fourth-century historian Theopompus, credited the people of his native Chios with having invented the institution of the chattel-slave who was purchased from traders. But generally when Greek writers imagined a world without chattel-slaves, they regularly placed it in utopian contexts of a golden age of effortless abundance when there was no need for work. In practice the growth of chattel-slavery must be seen in the context of the social and political development of archaic Greece. It relates to the momentous development of the notion of the free citizen as a member of a polis, a development that in many Greek cities resulted in the inclusion of the lower classes and the peasantry in the political community for the first time in history. Athens is the best-known case. Until the time of Solon, debt-bondage and hectemorage (tenant farming: the poor worked the fields of the rich and paid them a rent) were accepted Athenian institutions. Solon then abolished the bondage of Athenians in Athens for all time. Dependent labor, no longer available to the wealthy from within the community, had therefore to be brought in from outside. It is no accident and no contradiction that classical Athens was both the most advanced democratic state and probably the largest slave-owning city in the Greek world. Paradoxical as it may seem, the growth of chattel-slavery was a sign of political and social progress, although it was progress for some at the expense of others. The chattel-slave guaranteed the continued freedom of poorer citizens, who thus in a sense had as much interest in the institution as the wealthiest slaveowner.

A captive in war became the property of his victor, who could dispose of him as he wished. This was a standard assumption already evident in the Homeric poems where normally men are put to death and women enslaved. But war was not by itself a sufficient source of supply, and its incidence was unpredictable. The part played by slave breeding is disputed, but in any case the development of chattel-slavery implied the development of slave trading to meet a growing need, following perhaps the example of the Phoenician slave dealing familiar already in Homer. Professional slave traders and established slave markets emerged. In classical Athens, for instance, a monthly slave market was held in the agora. Regular markets appeared on the periphery of the Greek world at the junction with barbarian hinterlands, such as at Byzantium, Tanais on the Don, and Ephesus, and along the major commercial routes of the Greek world. For example, Hellenistic Delos became a major center for this trade in the second and first centuries.

The evidence for what may be called a seamy side of Greek society is less abundant than for trade in general, yet slave trading can be inferred to have been as regular a part of economic activity as trade in staple foods. Slave merchants were active in many places, following in the wake of armies to purchase booty and captives, and actively involved themselves in kidnapping (piracy and the slave trade went hand in hand), or dealing with non-Greek chieftains on the fringes of the Greek world who controlled the sale of slaves from their own tribes. Even Greeks might end up as slaves in other Greek states, depending on the chances of war or capture by pirates. Generally, however, the Balkans, the shores of the Black Sea, and many parts of Asia Minor and Syria provided most of the slave traffic. For example, one Cephisodotus, a metic in Athens in the late fifth century, is known from an inscription recording the sale of his confiscated property to have owned at least sixteen slaves, including five Thracians, three Carians, two Illyrians, two Syrians, and one each from Colchis, Cappadocia, and Lydia (Meiggs and Lewis, *Selection of Greek Historical Inscriptions* no.79 A).

The advantage of chattel-slavery was its

flexibility. Chattel-slaves could be purchased by anyone who could afford them and they could be put to any required use. Paradoxically, a dehumanizing institution that treated human beings as articles of property also gave scope for the employment of individual talents. Hence the great variety of economic and noneconomic functions chattel-slaves performed. Hence too the great variety of statuses enjoyed in practice by different slaves: as public servants in administrative functions, domestics in individual households, workers in factories (some independent and paying a rent to their masters), hired workmen, bankers, agents, mineworkers, or as trusted overseers in managerial positions who supervised the work of other slaves. Such was the slave to whom Pericles entrusted the management of his estates while he devoted himself to politics (Plutarch, *Parallel Lives,* "Pericles" 16). Although chattel-slaves employed in economic activity were frequently found in urban occupations, they were also present in agriculture as workers or as managers of estates. Thus, while chattel-slavery probably developed initially for social and political rather than for purely economic reasons, the flexibility of the institution had considerable economic consequences. Chattel-slavery made possible a degree of economic growth and diversification and increase of commodity production. The large-scale exploitation of the silver mines of Laurium, for example, would not have been possible without chattel-slaves.

On the other hand, the institution had certain disadvantages from the slaveowner's point of view. Although large-scale revolts were not a threat (except for a brief and exceptional period in the late second and early first centuries), and the difficulties of organizing a revolt among large but scattered numbers of slaves of different origins, languages, and statuses are obvious, individual slaves were always potentially resentful and rebellious. As Plato put it, "The animal 'man' is bad-tempered. . . . The slave is no easy chattel" (*Laws* 6.777b). Runaway slaves were a constant problem, especially in times of war; some 20,000 are alleged by Thucydides to have deserted Athens and Attica after the enemy occupation of Deceleia in 413 B.C. (7.27). There was even physical danger to masters from their slaves, hence "all masters act as unpaid bodyguards of each other against their slaves and against evil-doers, to avoid violent death" (Xenophon, *Hieron* 4.3).

The problem evoked various responses. One was simply to rely on coercion and to take security precautions; physical maltreatment was generally assumed to be part of the life of a slave. Another was to provide incentives to slaves for good behavior; the institution of manumission appeared in the late sixth century and was increasingly common thereafter. At the grace of their master, some slaves might obtain freedom, although often of a conditional kind and at a price. Manumission was a means of reinforcing the institution by making it more efficient; the hope of manumission encouraged slaves to good behavior, and the practice enabled masters to capitalize on older slaves to acquire new ones. It should be said that whatever the potential disadvantages of chattel-slavery, no Greek was ever discouraged from acquiring slaves if he could. Still less was there any serious questioning of the institution as such. There are indications of a debate in the late fifth and fourth centuries on whether slavery was "contrary to nature" or not, known in particular from Aristotle's attempt in Book One of the *Politics* to argue for the naturalness of the institution. The debate was conducted only within a limited circle and never led to an abolitionist movement. It came to an end with Aristotle, and the institution continued unchanged.

Other Forms of Dependent Labor

Besides chattel-slavery, Greek society was also familiar with other forms of dependent labor that it shared in common with other contemporary civilizations. Having established a clear-cut distinction between free and slave, the Greeks then had difficulty in categorizing other forms of dependent labor that did not lend themselves to precise classification. One ancient definition tried to group them under the broad category of those "between freedom and slavery," an admission of the conceptual difficulty involved. The forms of dependent labor varied but are best described by reference to their differences with chattel-slavery. They shared a common characteristic with free labor, namely that dependent persons remained members of their community of origin, unlike uprooted and atomized chattel-slaves. They therefore preserved a communal identity, including language, religion, and all-important family rights; they were self-reproducing, whereas chattel-slavery presupposed the development of a trade to ensure a regular supply of labor.

Various types may be distinguished. Individuals or groups could be unfree within their own larger community, such as the debt-bondsmen and hectemors of archaic Athens before Solon. The whole community might be subjected as a group to another community while preserving its identity, as indicated by their collective names, and enjoying a more or less defined status of quasi-contractual subjection on specific terms. On the Greek mainland the Helots of Laconia and Messenia, subjected by Sparta, are the best-known examples, but the institution existed elsewhere, as in Thessaly (the *penestai*) and in Crete. These communities owed their status probably to conquest at an early stage of Greek history, before the large-scale development of chattel-slavery, but the institution was also exported by the Greeks to colonies founded in the archaic age. Individual cases are known both west and east, such as the *killyrioi* of Syracuse, or the Mariandynians at Heraclea in Pontus on the Black Sea, who paid dues to the Heracleans but could not be sold into slavery. The practice was probably more widespread than the evidence suggests. On the Greek mainland, this form of dependent labor was generally characteristic of less politically and socially developed states where the classical distinction between free and slave and between citizen and noncitizen was less clear. Abroad it was possible for cities to combine it with chattel-slavery, as was probably the case at Syracuse and Heraclea.

From an economic point of view, these forms of dependent labor were less flexible than chattel-slavery; they were predominantly rural in character and uses. There is an obvious contrast in the classical period between Sparta and Athens, both imperial states. At one extreme was Sparta, landlocked, introverted, and xenophobic, with a complicated hierarchy of internal subjects (Helots, *perioikoi,* and intermediate grades) and a limited degree of economic and cultural development; and at the other extreme Athens, cosmopolitan and extroverted, open to outsiders and outside influences, free of internal subjects but with many chattel-slaves, economically developed and diversified, and a center of international trade and great cultural achievements.

Another limitation was the recurring threat or reality of large-scale revolts, made possible by precisely those factors that made revolts of chattel-slaves difficult or impossible. Sparta again is the best-known case; the fear of Helot revolt runs through her whole history. The Messenian Helots eventually achieved their freedom after the demise of Sparta at the battle of Leuctra in 371 B.C.; most of the remaining Helots probably obtained freedom in the inner convulsions of Spartan history at the end of the third century. Although less is known about similar groups elsewhere, the Spartan pattern may well have been reproduced in their case by the fourth century. It seems that in the course of the classical period this particular form of dependent labor was on the decline in the Greek world, while chattel-slavery continued unabated.

However, this Spartan-Helot form of dependence also existed in various forms in other countries outside the Greek world, notably in Asia and Egypt, and this fact was well known to the Greeks. The fourth-century plans for a conquest of Asia were explicitly aimed at the acquisition not only of new land for settlement but also of a dependent labor force. The conquered peoples of Asia were to serve "as Helots" to their new masters (Isocrates, *To Philip* 3.5). But not all Greek settlers in the Hellenistic East benefited from this imperial goal or to the same degree. The largest beneficiaries were the members of the new royal establishments, the Macedonian dynasties and their immediate followers. In Asia the evidence is very scanty and consists chiefly of a small number of inscriptions referring to large estates of members of the royal entourage, worked by native dependent labor who owed dues and services to their new masters as they had done before. One crucial gap in the evidence is the conditions of land tenure in the many new Greek foundations and the status of the native peasantry in relation to the Greek settlers, although it would seem that nonintegration was the norm. In Egypt, where the evidence is fuller, the peasantry was deliberately excluded from the few Greek-founded cities of Alexandria, Ptolemais, and the older Naucratis. They continued to provide the Ptolemies, as they had the native pharaohs before, with a large labor force, subject to various kinds of requisition and compulsory labor. But they were working for the benefit of a foreign dynasty and foreign immigrants. Thus the coming of the Greeks to Asia and Egypt did nothing to alter or improve the status of the native dependent labor. They were not reduced to the status of chattel-slaves, but neither were they emancipated. But then that had never been the intention anyway.

BIBLIOGRAPHY

SOURCES

Individual Works

Diodorus Siculus, *Library of History* C. H. Oldfather *et al.*, eds., 12 vols. (1933–1964); Old Oligarch (found in the works of Xenophon), *Constitution of the Athenians*, Glen W. Bowerstock, trans. (1968); Plutarch, *Parallel Lives*, Bernadotte Perrin, trans., 11 vols. (1913–1926); Polybius, *The Histories*, W. R. Paton, trans., 6 vols. (1922–1927); Strabo, *Geography*, Horace Leonard Jones, trans., 8 vols. (1917–1932); Xenophon, *Cyropaedia* (*Education of Cyrus*), Walter Miller, trans., 2 vols. (1914).

Source Collections

Michel Austin, *The Hellenistic World from Alexander to the Roman Conquest: A Selection of Ancient Sources in Translation* (1981); Michael H. Crawford, ed., *Sources for Ancient History* (1983); Michael H. Crawford and David Whitehead, *Archaic and Classical Greece: A Selection of Ancient Sources in Translation* (1983); Wilhelm Dittenberger, *Sylloge Inscriptionum Graecarum*, 4 vols., 3d ed. (1915–1924); C. C. Edgar, *Catalogue général des antiquités égyptiennes du Musée du Caire: Zenon Papyri*, I (1925); Russell Meiggs and D. M. Lewis, eds., *A Selection of Greek Historical Inscriptions* (1969); Thomas J. Wiedemann, *Greek and Roman Slavery* (1981).

STUDIES

Michel Austin and Pierre Vidal-Naquet, *Economic and Social History of Ancient Greece: An Intro-*

duction, Michel Austin, trans. (1977); John Boardman, *The Greeks Overseas* (1964; rev. ed. 1980); *Cambridge Ancient History*, vol. III, 2d ed. (1982–); Paul A. Cartledge and F. D. Harvey, eds., *Crux: Essays Presented to G. E. M. De Ste. Croix on his 75th Birthday* (1985); Moses I. Finley, *The Ancient Economy* (1973; 2d ed. 1985), *The World of Odysseus* (rev. ed. 1977), *Economy and Society in Ancient Greece* (1981), and *Ancient History: Evidence and Models* (1985); Johannes Hasebroek, *Griechische Wirtschafts- und Gesellschaftsgeschichte bis zur Perserzeit* (1931); Robert J. Hopper, *Trade and Industry in Classical Greece* (1979); Sarah C. Humphreys, *Anthropology and the Greeks* (1978); Claude Orrieux, *Le papyrus de Zénon* (1983); Claire Préaux, *L'Economie royale des Lagides* (1939), and *Le monde hellénistique*, 2 vols. (1978); Mikhail Rostovtzeff, *The Social and Economic History of the Hellenistic World*, 3 vols. (1941); Anthony M. Snodgrass, *Archaic Greece* (1980); Chester G. Starr, *The Economic and Social Growth of Early Greece* (1977); Edouard Will, "Trois quarts de siècle de recherches sur l'économie grecque antique," in *Annales: Economies, sociétés, civilisations,* **9** (1954).

War and the Economy

Michel Austin, "Hellenistic Kings, War, and the Economy," in *Classical Quarterly,* **36** (1986); Lionel Casson, *Ships and Seamanship in the Ancient World* (1971); Yvon Garlan, *War in the Ancient World: A Social History* (1975); V. D. Hanson, *Warfare and Agriculture in Ancient Greece* (1983); Arnold W. Lawrence, *Greek Aims in Fortification* (1979); William K. Pritchett, *The Greek State at War,* 4 vols. (1971–1986).

Trade, Traders, and Exchanges

Michel Austin, *Greece and Egypt in the Archaic Age,* Cambridge Philological Society Proceedings, suppl. 2 (1970); Benedetto Bravo, "Remarques sur les assises sociales, les formes d'organisation et la terminologie du commerce maritime grec à l'époque archaïque," in *Dialogues d'histoire ancienne,* **3** (1977); Geoffrey E. M. De Ste. Croix, *The Origins of the Peloponnesian War* (1972); Peter Garnsey, Keith Hopkins, and C. R. Whittaker, eds., *Trade in the Ancient Economy* (1983); Peter Garnsey and C. R. Whittaker, eds.,

Trade and Famine in Classical Antiquity, Cambridge Philological Society Proceedings, suppl. 8 (1983); Lynn Foxhall and H. A. Forbes, "*Sitometreia:* The Role of Grain as a Staple Food in Classical Antiquity," in *Chiron,* **12** (1982); Philippe Gauthier, *Symbola: Les étrangers et la justice dans les cités grecques* (1972), and "De Lysias à Aristote (*Ath. pol.,* 51, 4): Le commerce du grain à Athènes et les fonctions des sitophylaques," in *Revue historique de droit français et étranger,* **59** (1981); Louis Gernet, "L'Approvisionnement d'Athènes en blé aux Ve et VIe siècles", in *Mélanges d'histoire ancienne,* G. Bloch, ed. (1909); Arthur R. Hands, *Charities and Social Aid in Greece and Rome* (1968); Johannes Hasebroek, *Trade and Politics in Ancient Greece* (1933; repr. 1965); Alan W. Johnston, *Trademarks on Greek Vases* (1979); Russell Meiggs, *Trees and Timber in the Ancient Mediterranean World* (1983); Charles M. Reed, *Maritime Traders in the Greek World of the Archaic and Classical Periods* (D.Phil. thesis, Oxford 1981); Julie Vélissaropoulos, *Les nauclères grecs* (1980); Paul Veyne, *Le pain et le cirque* (1976).

Coinage and Credit Practices

Raymond Bogaert, *Banques et banquiers dans les cités grecques* (1968), and "La banque à Athènes au IVe siècle avant J. C. État de la question," in *Museum Helveticum,* **43** (1986); Michael Crawford, *La moneta in Grecia e a Roma,* G. Menci, trans. (1982); Geoffrey E. M. De Ste. Croix, "Ancient Greek and Roman Maritime Loans," in Harold Edey and B. S. Yamey, eds., *Debits, Credits, Finance and Profits* (1974); Moses I. Finley, *Studies in Land and Credit in Ancient Athens, 500–200 B.C.* (1952); Colin M. Kraay, *Archaic and Classical Greek Coins* (1976); Léopold Migeotte, *L'Emprunt public dans les cités grecques* (1984); Keith Rutter, "Early Greek Coinage and the Influence of the Athenian State," in Barry Cunliffe, ed., *Coinage and Society in Britain and Gaul: Some Current Problems,* Council for British Archaeology, Research Report no. 38 (1981).

Industry, Craftsmanship, Labor

Pierre Briant, *Rois, tribute et paysans* (1982); Alison Burford, *The Greek Temple Builders at Epidauros* (1969), and *Craftsmen in Greek and Roman Society*

(1972); Constantin E. Conophagos, *Le Laurium antique et la technique grecque de la production de l'argent* (1980); Geoffrey E. M. De Ste. Croix, *The Class Struggle in the Ancient Greek World* (1981); Moses I. Finley, *Ancient Slavery and Modern Ideology* (1980); Yvon Garlan, *Les esclaves en Grèce ancienne* (1982); Peter Garnsey, ed., *Non-Slave Labour in the Greco-Roman World,* Cambridge Philological Society Proceedings, suppl. 6 (1980); Philippe Gauthier, *Un commentaire historique des Poroi de Xénophon* (1976); Heinz Kreissig, *Wirtschaft und Gesellschaft im Seleukidenreich* (1978); J. G. Landels, *Engineering in the Ancient World* (1978); Detlef Lotze, *Metaxu eleutherōn kai doulōn: Studien zur Rechtstellung unfreier Landbevölkerungen in Griechenland bis zum 4. Jahrhundert v. Chr.* (1959); Claude Mossé, *The Ancient World at Work* (1969); Josef Vogt, *Ancient Slavery and the Ideal of Man,* Thomas Wiedemann, trans. (1975); David Whitehead, *The Ideology of the Athenian Metic,* Cambridge Philological Society Proceedings, suppl. 4 (1977).

Roman Trade, Industry, and Labor

KEITH HOPKINS

MOST ROMANS WERE PEASANTS, laboring primarily for the production of their own food. That is the single most important fact about the Roman economy. Agriculture was the Roman Empire's most important industry. Food was the single most important item of production, consumption, and trade, both in volume and in value. And most of the townsmen, who were engaged in making or in selling goods, spent the great bulk of their incomes on buying food. In sum, labor, industry, and trade in the Roman world, at all periods, were dominated by agriculture, by the need to supply both peasants and townsmen with food.

Peasants typically grew more food than they themselves needed just to keep alive. They produced a surplus, by which is meant anything produced over and above the needs of minimum subsistence. Peasants consumed some of this surplus themselves, either as food or by exchanging it in the local market for goods and services. In this way, some peasants lived above the level of minimum subsistence and so constituted a market for goods made by and for services provided by townsmen; for example, they bought iron-tipped tools, pots, trinkets, love philters, priestly rituals, inscribed contracts, and justice. But peasants surrendered most of their surplus involuntarily as taxes paid to the state and as rent paid to landowners. This transfer of the agricultural surplus from primary producers to consumers by the three channels of trade, taxation, and rent formed the foundation of the Roman economy and of the Roman state.

The basic structure of the Roman economy was determined by several interlocking factors: for example, by the size of its population, its overwhelming dependence on muscular energy, the gradual diffusion of important technological innovations throughout the Roman world, the difficulty and expense of mining for metals on a large scale, the impact of increasing monetization, and the high cost of land transport even on paved roads. These relatively stable factors will have to be discussed in order to understand the constraints within which Roman labor, industry, and trade always operated. Also discussed will be the direction and volume of trade, and a distinction will be maintained between trade in staple foods, in simple and cheap manufactured goods like pots, and in relatively expensive goods like textiles. Understanding trade involves understanding the size and cost of Roman shipping and the involvement of merchants and financiers. It also involves appreciating the sophistication of the consumer market for luxuries and other goods in the Roman Empire and the division of labor and status among free and slave artisans who produced the goods for the consumers. Finally, the impact of a growing empire on the economy of the conquering Italians and the conquered provincials will be considered. Taxes were the sinews and trade was the lifeblood of the empire.

POPULATION

By modern standards, Roman death rates and birthrates were extremely high. Incurable sickness, suffering, and sudden death were endemic. Romans dealt with these human tragedies with a mixture of magic, medicine, and cruelty, and with a variety of religious beliefs, rituals, sacrifices, and prayers by which they hoped to control natural and supernatural forces. The average expectation of life at birth was only about twenty-five years. Many children died in infancy, many adults in their prime. We have to envisage a society and an economy suffused with uncertainty; yet even the uncertainty had a structure. Most women spent their adult lives in child rearing. Most men inherited their status, property, and occupation while they were still young, from their fathers. The turnover of generations was therefore much faster than in modern societies. But opportunities for change were limited by the level of technology, by its predominantly oral transmission, and by the rigidities inherent in a society dominated by inherited status.

The total size of the Roman population set very broad limits to production and to consumption. Unfortunately, only a few population figures are known, and these figures are susceptible to various interpretations. But it seems probable that in 225 B.C. Italy (excluding Sicily and Sardinia) had a population of about five million. In 27 B.C., Italy's population was about seven million. This growth, by about two million over two centuries, was the result of two main processes: the massive import of slaves from conquered territories, and the tremendous growth in the city of Rome. Rome's population at the end of the last century B.C. was about one million, as large as London in 1800 or New York City in 1860. The impact of this metropolitan market on labor, industry, and trade can be readily imagined. In the same period, the number of slaves in Italy had grown to over two million. Seen another way, migration had redistributed labor from conquered provinces to Italy, and within Italy from countryside to town.

The population of the whole Roman Empire at the beginning of the first century A.D. was about fifty to sixty million. In the peaceful conditions secured by Roman rule, it seems probable that the population grew. In the third century A.D., because of barbarian invasions and repeated civil wars, it seems likely that the total population fell, only to recover—at least partially—in the fourth century, and to fall again in the fifth and sixth centuries because of barbarian invasions and plague. We know that significant population swings occurred in western Europe in postmedieval times; in principle, it seems probable that similar fluctuations occurred in the long centuries of Roman civilization, with dramatic implications for Roman labor, industry, and trade. But not enough is known to be able to quantify these changes in total population.

In spite of changes, some important characteristics of the Roman population persisted over centuries. First, as we have already stressed, the great majority, at least 80 percent of the working population, was primarily engaged in agriculture. The preponderance of agriculture reflected low average productivity. It took the work of four peasant households to feed a fifth, nonagricultural household. Second, most large and all very large towns were sited on or near the Mediterranean coast or on rivers. The Roman economy was built up around an internal lake, the Mediterranean Sea. Great cities like Rome, Antioch, Carthage, and Alexandria (the last three had a combined population in the first century A.D. of about one million) drew their food from a large hinterland. Such food had to be brought as great a distance as possible in ships; land transport would have been too expensive for long haulage. Third, the whole Mediterranean basin has a similar climate. There was therefore no systematic specialization in agricultural product by region. The basic foods—wheat, lentils, olive oil, and wine—were grown in all regions, and most people lived off local food. The extent of interregional trade in basic foodstuffs was limited. Finally, when the Romans expanded their empire northward into the Balkans, Germany, northern France, and Britain, they absorbed large tracts of territory with significantly lower population densities than the coastal regions of the Mediterranean. Much traffic was carried along the Rhine and Danube, which were more important as lines of communication than as lines of defense. But behind those rivers lay a large and relatively empty hinterland with few towns and a low density of trade.

TECHNOLOGY, INVENTIONS, AND INNOVATIONS

Another factor limiting Roman labor, industry, and trade was technology. The basic constraint here was that energy in the Roman world was primarily derived from human muscle and from animals, principally oxen, mules, and donkeys. Humans and draft animals can deliver only about 20 percent of their intake in mechanical energy. A well-fed human adult male, consuming 3,200 calories per day, can therefore deliver in one day only about one horsepower per hour (641 calories). A population living at the level of minimum subsistence (less than about 2,000 calories a day per person) can deliver much less mechanical energy.

It is not known how many Romans were well fed nor how many were living at or near minimum subsistence. But it is known, for example, that the access paths and doorways to the granaries at Ostia, the main port of Rome, were too narrow for draft animals. So the huge granaries which fed the city of Rome were filled and emptied by human porters. And river barges filled with grain were dragged twenty-two miles upstream from Ostia to Rome by human haulers. Most Roman labor was performed by sweat of brow. Human energy was the chief fuel of the Roman economy.

Draft animals supplemented human labor. Horses belonged primarily to the rich and were used more often for cavalry in battle, for chariot races, for show, and for rapid travel than for routine agricultural work. This underutilization of horses may seem surprising, given their pervasive use for agriculture and cartage in North America and in European advanced societies right up to the modern period. Three reasons for this were particularly important. First, draft animals are only as good as their hooves. The Romans used horseshoes (*soleae*) made of straw, leather, or metal, but these were only tied or clipped on. They were not nailed on. Second, the Romans apparently used a "throat and girth" harness for their horses that was originally designed for oxen. Because it sat high on the horse's throat, it tended to throttle a horse pulling a heavy load. Instead of being able to pull fifteen times as much as a man, a horse wearing an ox-harness could pull only four times as much, and so seemed better suited for light chariots than for heavy carts. And finally, horses were expensive to feed, especially in regions of the Mediterranean which were short of pasture. In a poor society, all draft animals compete with humans for food. But horses need much more high-quality food than oxen.

Slow-trundling oxen were the prime movers of the Roman economy. They pulled the wooden plows faced with iron which raised productivity in Roman farming well above previous levels. They pulled the carts which took the agricultural surplus to market. Ox carts, donkeys, and mules carried the goods which were sent across country, inland between farms, rivers, and towns. Oxen set the economic tone, sturdy and slow moving. At the first plowing of a season, Roman oxen were expected to cover about seven miles, and at second plowing about eleven miles in one day. They pulled carts at about one and a half miles per hour (less if drawing a heavy load), and eleven miles was about the maximum they could travel in a day. Thus oxen presented a stout barrier both to growth in agricultural productivity and to the easy movement and exchange of surplus produce.

Technology is the science of transcending human (and animal) limitations, allowing humans to do what once seemed beyond their capacity. Compared with the grandeur of Roman civilization, a list of Greco-Roman technical inventions seems puny: the screw and the gear; the direct screw press for crushing olives; the rotary mill for grinding grain; the water mill used for grinding grain and for sawing wood and stone; the fore-and-aft sail and the lateen sail, both of which helped ships to hold their course better in contrary winds; glassblowing; cranes and concrete, used particularly in large-scale

buildings; the torsion catapult, which helped state armies reduce walled towns; the *dioptra,* an optical instrument for surveying; the water clock; the water organ; and steam-powered toys.

Given the sophisticated inventiveness of Romans and of Greeks under Roman rule in other spheres, for example, in law, warfare, mathematics, astronomy, and architecture, the list may seem disappointingly short. At some level it must reflect a lack of concern with, or even a disdain for, mundane techniques of production among the educated and wealthy. Their prime concern, if pressed, was not to increase the richness of the cake, but their share of it: at the international level by warfare between states, and at the personal level, by tightening the screws of exploitation on slaves and free tenants, or by increasing the size of their estates through corruption, remarriage, and inheritance. According to this line of argument, then, the lack of technical progress in the Roman world was largely due to two distinct cultural tendencies among the rich and powerful: the preservation of status by consumption and the preservation of wealth by increased exploitation.

There is another, radically different way of perceiving Roman technical progress. We can concentrate on innovations and on political organization, rather than on inventions. By innovation is meant the adoption of techniques already invented. In the centuries of Roman history these included many improved techniques of agriculture and manufacture and many social arrangements which facilitated the spread of trade throughout the Mediterranean basin. They spread along an axis which went roughly from southeast to northwest, from the Middle East to Greece, through Italy to northwestern Europe. Military conquest promoted this diffusion, not least by providing the overarching political organization, which made agriculture itself and long-distance trade more secure and more profitable.

The Roman Empire was only the latest in a series of kingdoms and empires (for example, Minoan, Punic, Hellenistic) based on conquest, which amalgamated tribes and previous kingdoms into larger entities. The formation of the Roman Empire as a single political system and its preservation for several centuries were made easier by several technical innovations such as the cutting edge of iron weapons, the adoption of coined money, and the spread of writing, the last of which allowed the codification of knowledge, beliefs, and rules.

A list of gradually diffused innovations is impracticable. Let us start instead with a few illustrative examples, such as farming, metals, money, and paved roads. According to the geographer Strabo, conquest by Rome induced "barbarians" in southern Gaul to switch from warfare to urban life and farming (*Geography* 180). The twin development of towns and settled agriculture was widespread in the western provinces under Roman rule. In Gaul, Spain, and Britain, hilltop forts were dismantled and the population was resettled in more accessible and less defensible sites below. In Britain under Roman rule, settled agriculture expanded even to marginal lands, and the total population grew significantly. New crops, such as turnips, radishes, beans, cabbage, and peas were introduced, and had a profound and lasting effect on British cooking. In sum, in order to understand how Roman rule changed labor, industry, and trade, we should look not only at dramatic inventions, but also at the gradual diffusion of improved practices in production and distribution.

METALS, MINING, AND MONEY

Iron swords were in regular use in Greece by about 1000 B.C. Yet in Britain before the Roman conquest, according to Julius Caesar, the inhabitants used iron bars by weight for money (*The Gallic War* 5.12). Archaeologists have confirmed Caesar's observation by finding hoards comprising hundreds of iron bars. Iron in pre-Roman Britain was a suitable object for buried treasure. By contrast, according to a recent careful study of the metal residues in slag heaps at six Roman sites in southern England, average production of iron at these six sites alone totaled 550 metric tons per year during the second century A.D. By that time, iron had become a common metal, in widespread use for agricultural implements as well as for weapons. Unfortunately, we do not know total iron production in Britain, or for that matter in any region of the Roman Empire.

But information does exist which allows estimates of the production of silver and lead mines in Spain. Already by the second century B.C., the silver mines near Carthago Nova (Cartagena) were worked by 40,000 slaves. Conditions, according to Diodorus Siculus (5.38), were as appalling as one would expect:

> The slaves produce incredible profit for their masters, but they themselves wear out their bodies, digging underground by day and by night, and many of them die under the strain of such terrible conditions. They are not allowed any pause or rest from their work, but are forced by the blows of their overseers to endure sheer misery.

The Rio Tinto and Tarsis mines in southern Spain were also very large. Neither has been worked between late antiquity and the early modern period. The ancient slag heaps each had an estimated volume of twenty to thirty million metric tons. Each would have taken the labor of 5,000 miners for 300 years to produce.

The mines at Rio Tinto go deep underground. Several miles of underground galleries were typically only about 36 inches (91 cm) high; clearly men, not animals, were used for haulage inside the mines. Drainage was achieved by an ingenious system of eight pairs of wooden waterwheels, set one above another. Each wheel was 14 feet (4.3 m) in diameter and was powered by a man walking a treadmill. The rim of the wheels was hollow and contained a bucket compartment at the end of each spoke; at the bottom of the turn the bucket filled with water, at the top it emptied into a channel supplying the next wheel with water. In this way, 2,400 gallons (9,085 l) could be raised 97 feet (29.6 m) per hour by sixteen men working on the treadmills. The amount of drainage necessary was also reduced by digging expensive transverse channels deep into the hillside.

The scale of Roman mining operations is amazing, if we consider the technology available and the manpower required. One exploratory mine, again in southern Spain, was unsuccessful. It yielded nothing but 30,000 metric tons of rock—a huge quantity, which indicates the scale of capital investment, available from private entrepreneurs, required to open up new silver mines. In the last century B.C., the Roman mint for a long period consumed fifty metric tons of pure silver a year just for coinage. At the end of the first century A.D. the mint's annual consumption of pure silver was still forty to forty-five metric tons. At that time Roman coins were 94 percent pure silver.

The mining and refining of silver involved a huge amount of work. According to a recent estimate, each metric ton of silver in Roman conditions probably required 500 to 1,000 man work-years. Each ton of pure silver involved digging up roughly 100,000 tons of rock with iron and stone picks, hammers, chisels, and gads, or by fire setting. This immense quantity of rock had to be dragged to the surface in baskets by ropes and human muscle. In deep workings, and

some Roman workings in the Spanish silver mines were over 800 feet (244 m) underground, this labor involved the use of tons of illuminating oil. Once the ore was brought to the surface, it was broken up by hammers, picked over by hand, ground, and washed. Ten thousand metric tons of trees could provide enough charcoal (500–2,000 tons) to smelt the ore at the required temperature, 1,000° C; all this to produce one metric ton of silver. The by-product of one ton of silver production was 400 tons of lead (used for pipes). And large amounts of slag had to be carted away. Behind each issue of Roman silver coins, there were large-scale ramifications: huge investment, much equipment and fuel, a large labor force, and effective social organization.

Coined money was a Greek invention and a Roman innovation. The Roman state produced silver coins in unprecedented amounts, mostly to pay soldiers in foreign and civil wars. One largely unintended consequence was that a mass of money was available throughout the Mediterranean world to finance the long-distance trade which developed in the wake of imperial conquest. As we have just seen, the manufacture of silver coins on a large scale involved a complex process of production. A large volume of coins also helped create and maintain a complex network of trade.

The Latin word for money is *pecunia*, derived from *pecus*, meaning cattle, reflecting Rome's nonmonetized, pastoral origins. The first Roman silver coins were minted only in the third century B.C. By the end of that century, during the long war against Carthage, Rome may have been minting between one and two million denarii per year. A hundred years later, average production was fourteen million denarii per year. It is difficult to give an accurate idea of the value of money in an economy in which most people produced most of what they needed. Roughly speaking, each denarius could buy about 19 pounds (8.7 kg) of wheat at farmers' prices (3/4 denarius per *modius;* one *modius* equaled 14.4 pounds, or 6.55 kg); each denarius was enough to maintain a family of four persons at minimum subsistence for about three days. Between 157 and 50 B.C., the total stock of Roman silver coins in circulation rose over ten times, and almost doubled again by the end of the first century A.D. This massive rise in the supply of money reflected two processes: the growth of trade in the expanded area controlled by Rome and the percolation of money into a myriad of exchange transactions which had previously been embedded in the subsistence economy. Put another way, the technically simple innovation of money increased the proportion of food and goods which people bought. Money changed the nature of Roman labor, industry, and trade.

ROMAN ROADS

Roads, like money, were a simple technical innovation. They required a considerable input of labor to construct and to maintain. They were constructed often for military purposes and to speed communications between Rome and its conquered provinces. The network of paved roads grew with conquest. By the first and second centuries A.D., according to one estimate, there were 56,000 miles of paved highways in the empire as a whole, supplemented by nearly 200,000 miles of secondary and tertiary roads. In several provinces, there were better roads under Roman rule than there were until the late nineteenth century. And as with the growth of money, one unintended consequence of expanding the network of paved roads was the growth of trade.

Roman roads were impressive monuments to Roman power. Within Pompeii, and on the outskirts of Rome itself and in various parts of the empire, one can still see stretches of road with great flat slabs of stone. In Britain, the main roads, 24 feet (7.3 m) wide, were often raised on causeways 4 to 5 feet (1.25–1.5 m) above the level of the surrounding countryside. Ivan D. Margary (1967) has commented: "The amount of apparently unnecessary labor put into the embankments . . . must have been prodigious." Yet as a result of all this labor, Roman roads are still visible, especially in aerial photographs and on maps, running arrow-straight through the countryside.

The alignment of roads was carefully planned. There were, for example, seventeen roads running through the Alps; careful investigation of one road shows that gradients were never more than one in six. In order to overcome natural obstacles, considerable ingenuity, technical skill, and brute force were employed. For example, just outside Rome a road was protected from hot sulfur springs overhead by a concrete tunnel, covered outside with slabs of stone. Another road to the south of Rome was cut 117 feet (35.7 m) deep through solid rock, while another road to the northeast of Rome (Via Cassia) was driven through the crater of an extinct volcano in a cutting 1,625 yards long, 22 yards deep, and 20 feet wide (1,486 by 20 by 6 m). Along the river Danube, in a gorge, the road was built out on wooden supports cut into the rock. There are other examples. It would be pointless to enumerate the Roman bridges, built so well that they are still standing. There are over 350 surviving.

The capital cost of constructing paved roads and their associated bridges, cuttings, embankments, and tunnels was enormous. But merely economic considerations were not primary. Roads were judged partly on aesthetic grounds. They combined use with beauty. Plutarch wrote, "The roads were driven through the countryside, exactly in a straight line, partly paved with hewn stone, and partly laid with impacted gravel. Gullies were filled in, intersecting torrents and ravines were bridged, so that the layout of the road on both sides was the same, and the whole work looked level and beautiful" (*Parallel Lives,* "Gaius Gracchus" 7). Roads symbolized the power of Roman armies. The cost of their construction was therefore not limited by a calculation of economic return. Indeed, it is doubtful that anyone in Roman times thought of roads as economic investments, on which a return had to be made.

Even so, the common method of road construction was extravagant. The total depth of the roadway, from fitted stone slabs or cobbles at the top, through gravel or crushed stones mixed with concrete and then a layer of hardcore mixed with loose mortar, to the foundation layer of stones, was often 3 to 4 1/2 feet (91–137 cm), and so several times thicker and much more rigid than ordinary modern roadways. To be sure, this four-layer construction was not always kept to. It varied with local circumstances and supplies. In one region of Asia Minor, for example, paving stones were placed directly on the ground. In the deserts of North Africa and Syria, the land surface of the desert provided an adequate surface and foundation for Roman roads. On minor roads, the top surface often consisted of gravel. But where Romans did take the trouble to build deep roads, maintenance costs, like those of horizontal walls, were very high.

The Roman invention of concrete constituted a significant technical advance, but Roman concrete, excellent for wall construction, was not plastic enough for roads. Besides, there were no expansion joints between paving slabs, and so in mountains and in the northern parts of the empire, changes in temperature caused considerable distortion. Repair was very expensive just because the method of construction was so thorough: potholes could not be firmly filled

without reworking an entire stretch of the road. Four Latin inscriptions indicate that the cost of relaying a Roman road in Italy in the second century A.D. was about 30,000 denarii per mile. That is the repair cost; it does not make any allowance for the cost of acquiring land in the first instance (if it was bought and not requisitioned), nor for preliminary engineering works and bridges. Let us for the moment assume that paved roads needed repair on this scale only once in forty years (a conservative estimate: in reality, few roads with significant traffic and variable weather would have lasted that long). We shall not take into account routine road maintenance such as running repairs between major refurbishments or the repair of minor roads. Let us suppose that major refurbishments cost 30,000 denarii per mile every forty years in a system comprising 56,000 miles of major roads. The cost would be 42 million denarii, or between one-fifth and one-sixth of probable state revenues. In other words, major road repairs, regularly done, would have cost a quarter as much as the Roman army.

Although these calculations are inevitably crude and speculative, their implications are serious. In interpreting fragmentary evidence, competing interpretations must be weighed. First, there is the apologistic pro-Roman idealistic view that Roman roads were expensive to build and maintain, and were typically kept in good repair. For example, inscriptions on stone survive from Spain in the first century A.D. which show that three roads there were repaired at intervals of sixteen, nineteen, and twenty-three years. A second view, which can be called the primitivist view, is that Roman roads were not expensive to maintain because maintenance was carried out by the unpaid labor of soldiers and convicts and of peasants living in villages near the roadway. And it is clearly true that some roads were built by soldiers and repaired by forced peasant labor. In some sense, it may be misleading to cost all road repairs in money. And yet the problem of regular repair persists, and even grows if we imagine that it was entrusted to the involuntary, taxed labor of unskilled peasants. As one fourth-century law hopefully put it, "Because of the huge length of our roads, we want everyone in eager rivalry and humble devotion to hasten to the repair of the public highways" (*Theodosian Code* 15.3.4).

Finally, there is the pessimistic view that Roman main roads regularly fell into disrepair because the Roman state's budgetary resources and organizational capacities were unable to service its capital expenditure on roads—just as governments in some developing nations today buy expensive, technologically advanced jet fighters, and then find that they have neither the technicians to service the planes nor enough money to let them fly. In support of this pessimistic view, there are numerous inscriptions from several provinces which record that roads were repaired "when they had deteriorated completely through long-term negligence" (*Corpus Inscriptionum Latinarum* 10.6954) or were "restored to public use after long neglect" (Dessau, *Inscriptiones Latinae Selectae* 5888). In A.D. 21, according to a senator, many roads in Italy were pot-holed and impassable because of the negligence of the officials in charge and the dishonesty of the building contractors. If roads in Italy, and even the main road south of Rome, the Via Appia, fell into disrepair (*Corpus Inscriptionum Latinarum* 9.6075), what hope for roads in the provinces?

The correct answer to the question of how well Roman main roads were kept in repair is probably an amalgam of all three perspectives: idealistic, primitivist, and pessimistic. In the long centuries of Roman rule over a vast area, some major roads were maintained, others sometimes neglected; some maintenance work and materials were paid for in cash, some were carried out by unpaid

peasant labor. A sixth-century encyclopedist observed that the Romans "built paved roads over almost the whole world, both for directness of travel and to prevent the populace from being unemployed." The amount of labor required must have been enormous. Seen like this, roads became themselves the objects of manufacture and trade, annually involving thousands of laborers, stonemasons, stone breakers, lime burners, carters, and supervisors. Roads were also channels of trade which brought merchants, travelers, innkeepers, wayside peddlers, and peasants with food to sell and goods to buy together in a continuous and mutually profitable stream.

Roman roads have been discussed at some length because they constitute a paradigm for technical diffusion and for the impact of technical diffusion on Roman labor, industry, and trade. For the most part the roads were technically simple, but planned with great care. Most bridges carrying roads across rivers were similarly well planned, solid, and simple. However, those built deep in fast currents, or over great rivers like the Danube or Rhine, represented very considerable engineering achievements. Above all, road and bridge construction required complex social organization, the integration of labor, and a long-term commitment to a collective good. The purpose of the far-flung road system was primarily military. Roads also provided speedy communications, and by their grandeur symbolized the glory of Roman conquest. But within the limitations of land transport—and those limitations were considerable—paved roads and the social order they symbolized had a significant impact on the volume of overland trade.

LAND TRANSPORT

Land transport was expensive. Roman evidence on prices is fragmentary, but it suggests that in the first few centuries A.D. land transport cost fifty-five times as much per ton mile as transport by sea, and six times as much as transport by river. There was considerable variation around these figures, but these ratios serve as rough guides; they are also corroborated by comparable evidence from other preindustrial societies with better documentation.

Some economic historians have used these ratios to stress the limited importance of trade between inland towns in the Roman world. Transport, in their view, was too expensive for large-volume trade. Paved roads, in good repair or not, were of only marginal significance from an economic point of view. Let us examine this argument. Because of high transport costs it was impossible to move large quantities of wheat or barley overland by ox cart and pack mule unless the transport was organized by the government and the cost of the transport imposed on taxpayers. If there was a famine deep inland, there was little anyone could do about it.

Two classic cases illustrate this point. In the middle of the fourth century A.D. there was a famine around Caesarea (Kayseri, in central Turkey). It is over 200 miles by road from the nearest Mediterranean port and much farther by river from the Black Sea. A local bishop described the problem: "There was a famine, the most terrible in the memory of man. The city languished, but there was no help from any part, no remedy for the calamity. Cities on the seacoast easily endure a shortage of this kind, importing what they are short of by sea. But we who live far from the sea, profit nothing from our surplus, nor can we get what we are short of, because we cannot export what we have nor import what we need" (Gregory of Nazianzus, in Migne, *Patrologiae Cursus, Series Graeca*, vol. 36, 541).

The second case comes from the same period. In A.D. 362–363 there was a serious famine in Antioch (Syria), one of the empire's largest towns. The reigning emperor, Julian the Apostate, brought relief to the city by bringing 2,600 tons of wheat, about 6,700 cartloads, by road from two towns 50 and 100 miles inland where a significant surplus was available. Private entrepreneurs had been unable to tap it. High transport costs were probably not the chief obstacle, since bringing wheat 100 miles would have cost only half the normal farm price of wheat, whereas wheat in famine-struck Antioch cost more than three times the normal farm price. The main problem for private entrepreneurs was probably that they lacked the power to organize land transport on that scale, over that distance, and to protect the convoy through hungry villages on the way to the city. Only the emperor, with the army at his elbow, could commandeer resources on a scale sufficient to meet an emergency.

These two examples show that in normal circumstances it was impracticable to transport a large volume of wheat by road between most towns. The relatively high cost of land transport and lack of entrepreneurial organization contributed, but so did the uncertainty surrounding information about prices, and the limited purchasing power of consumers. But what was true for wheat, bulky and cheap, was not necessarily true for higher-value goods which weighed less.

POTS AS OBJECTS OF TRADE

Two further examples, pots and textiles, can be used to illustrate some basic characteristics of the Roman economy. Pots are the template and the curse of Roman economic history. Their chief characteristic is survival. Archaeologists and economic historians have therefore often used the dispersion of pots around their place of manufacture as an indication of the patterns of trade. At first sight, that may seem sensible and unproblematic. But the conclusions are not as simple as they may seem. First, there is the problem of bias: the pattern of trade derived from surviving pots is as much a map of archaeological activity as it is of trade. Second, pots break into many pieces. Consequently, it is often difficult to gauge the number of pots from the number of finds, especially in old archaeological reports; and it is even more difficult to estimate the volume of Roman trade from the volume of finds. That is the problem of estimating the universe from the sample of finds. Finally, there is the vexed problem of proxies. Pots survive better than cloth, bronzes, wood, or iron. Is it valid to use a distribution map of pots as proxies, or tracers for other items of trade which have long since perished? It seems plausible enough to trace the wine trade from pottery wine containers (amphorae), though repeated reuse is a problem. But it is not certain that a distribution map of wool or iron would look like a distribution map of Italian wine jars. After all, wine could have moved in one direction, and wool or iron in the reverse or in quite other directions. For the moment, it seems sensible to be cautious and to confine conclusions to analogy. Pots, both tableware and containers, were of moderate value, bulky, heavy, and liable to breakage. Yet they were moved in considerable numbers far from their points of origin, in spite of high transport costs. It seems likely that goods of higher value and lower volume were moved even farther and in greater amounts around the Roman world.

The diffusion of pottery can best be illustrated by two distinct yet complementary methods. We first shall examine the origin of pots found at a single site, and then trace the diffusion of pots from particular potteries. The Roman military fort at Burrium (Usk in southern Wales) was occupied for a limited period in the middle of the first century A.D. Four-fifths (82 percent) of the medium-quality pottery cups found there came from Lugdunum (Lyons) in France, in spite of the inconvenience and cost of bringing them by road, river, and sea. The remainder of the cups came from six sources, ranging from the lower Rhine, which was the nearest source, to southern Italy. It is not now possible to rediscover the reasons which explain this diversity. But costs of transport were clearly not a main determinant of the type of cups which Roman soldiers used and bought.

Complementarily, consider Arretine vases. Known for their attractive glossy red glaze, they are perhaps the archetypal Roman pottery. Arretine vases were made in large numbers after about 30 B.C., and they have been found on archaeological sites all over the Roman Empire and as far away as India. Yet Arretium (Arezzo, in central Italy) lies inland, sixty miles from the sea, and although it is near the headwaters of the river Tiber and near a tributary of the Arno, it is some way from a navigable river.

In the early first century A.D., for reasons which no one knows, Arretine pots lost their market predominance. Instead that was won by potteries making similar glazed ware at Condatomagus (La Graufesenque, near Millau in southwestern France). Production there was on a considerable scale. The names of several thousand potters are known: one schedule of production alone listed over 700,000 items. Unlike Arretium, Condatomagus lay near a river, the Tarn, a tributary of the Garumna (Garonne), which flows into the Atlantic Ocean. But its main markets (judged by modern finds) were in the opposite direction, in the Roman military garrisons along the Rhine and Danube rivers. Its products were also sent to Italy, probably via the Mediterranean port of Narbo (Narbonne).

Once again, for reasons unknown, market dominance switched, from the potteries of Condatomagus to Ledosus (Lezoux, in central France near Clermont-Ferrand), on the banks of the shallow Allier, a tributary of the Loire, which flows into the Atlantic. Again, the bulky, fragile, and not particularly valuable pots were sent by river westward in large numbers, even though they were eventually to be sold along the eastern frontier rivers, the Rhine and Danube. Even for such goods, an inland location did not prevent trade. But perhaps a large volume of goods was transported overland, as the geographer Strabo stated (4.1.14), between rivers.

Two further points should be stressed. First, pots were not fundamental goods within the Roman economy. One should not talk, as some have done, of potteries as large industrial centers. But they are indicators of what could happen in the Roman economy. Pots were moved in large numbers over long distances, partly by road. And if pots were moved, what were the effective obstacles against trade in raw wool, cloth, leather, and dyes—goods of lower volume and higher value? Second, the significant differences in cost between transport by land, river, and sea were partly undermined by the fact that much long-distance trade necessarily involved a combination of all three.

TEXTILES

Any economic history of medieval Europe takes the cloth trade seriously. Several important towns in England, France, Flanders, and Italy owed their prosperity principally to their trade in cloth. But few ancient sources mention cloth manufacture, and unlike pots, cloth perishes, so that very few textiles survive archaeologically. And yet the cloth trade must have been important in the Roman Empire. Townsfolk living in cramped multistory blocks in the city of Rome or Ostia, or even in the small two-story houses of Pompeii, had insufficient room for the complex processes of scouring,

combing, weaving, fulling, and dyeing which turned raw wool into cloth. We know that Romans used alum to prepare wool to take dyes, or putrefied human urine, which was collected in vats in the streets of Rome. The ammonia in urine combined with wool's natural grease to form a soapy compound. (The cloth was then washed.) The point is that fulling and dyeing involved the use of expensive and bulky vats; they could not be done at home.

The total demand for cloth in the Roman Empire must have been enormous, both in volume and in value. Everyone, rich and poor, peasant, slave, and artisan, needed clothes. We do not know how much cloth was bought and how much was homemade. But the fragmentary evidence surviving, particularly from Egypt, suggests the widespread existence of professional weavers, not only in small towns but even in villages. For example, there were eight or twelve weavers in one village, seven in another, and according to a tract from a house-by-house census there were at least thirty-seven weavers in the town of Arsinoë (in the Fayum) in A.D. 94. This suggests that many villagers and townsfolk bought cloth. Those who did so had to sell their produce in the market in order to get money to pay clothiers, just as clothiers paid a longish line of associates (spinners, fullers, dyers) for their work and peasants for their food. Cloth was embedded in a nexus of trade between peasants and artisans. And even if only half the empire's population, twenty-five to thirty million people, bought cloth once in every ten years, then the volume of trade was enough to secure the livelihood of many weavers.

Unfortunately, the number of weavers and the average size of workshops concerned in the manufacture of cloth are not known. Double furnaces and large vats can still be seen in workshops at Pompeii, but it is difficult to deduce the number of workers from such archaeological remains, although a recent study speculatively suggested that the largest textile workshops at Pompeii employed twenty workers. In the fourth century A.D., the central government set up some large wool-weaving and linen-weaving "factories" to supply the army. These were probably conglomerates of piece workers simply working together under one roof, without considerable economies of scale. Surprisingly, the normal size of manufacturing units seems not to be critical for productivity, even in industrial economies until the beginning of the twentieth century. So the small size of most ancient workshops was not the chief brake on ancient productivity.

Except in mining, the large integrated factory was unknown in the Roman world. The amount of capital which Romans invested in manufacturing equipment was low. Energy, as we have seen, was muscular. The system of contracting-out a large volume among a number of small family workshops was known, but was never used on the scale familiar in the early stages of textile industrialization in England. Cloth in the Roman world was expensive because it required prolonged labor to make. The typical workshop was probably based on a household, with the occasional addition of a hired hand (*Oxyrhynchus Papyri* 737), a slave, or an apprentice. In one contract, dating from the second century A.D., a man hired out a female slave to work as a weaver for one year. Her clothing was the responsibility of the lessor; the lessee provided her food. She had eight holidays in the year; otherwise she was not to be absent by day or night, except when the lessor needed her overnight to bake bread. The fee was 420 drachmas (enough to buy 1.27 metric tons) of wheat; it was a substantial price, and would have been sufficient to keep a family of four at minimum subsistence for well over a year. It indicates both that the slave worked hard and that her produce was valuable.

The cloth trade dealt in luxuries, but it was not confined to the elite. This is confirmed by the emperor Diocletian's *Edict on Maximum Prices* dated A.D. 301, which listed 450 prices for different types of cloth. The list includes linen shirts in premium qualities from five different specialist centers of production, ranging in price from 7,000 to 20,000 denarii. But the edict also listed much cheaper shirts in qualities "fit for soldiers" and "for the use of commoners or slaves" at 150 to 500 denarii. The wide range of price, quality, and provenance, and the imperial administrators' knowledge about them indicated a firm market pattern in which cloth from different regions competed. In this trade, the costs of transport by road mattered little. The edict names raw wool and woolen garments from all over the empire, from Britain, Gaul, Spain, Italy, Africa, Greece, and the Balkans. To be sure, some of these were premium goods. Lower-quality goods were sold mostly in their region of manufacture. But a pound of the very cheapest wool was worth seven and a half times as much as a pound of wheat, and a journey by mule of nearly 200 miles added only 10 percent to the cost price (*Edict* 1,17,25). And it is known that army units in central Asia Minor in the second century A.D. were supplied with tunics and cloaks levied as tax in kind from Egyptian villages (four cloaks and a tunic from one village, nineteen cloaks and five tunics from another). Distance by sea, river, and road was an obstacle, but an obstacle which was often overcome.

SHIPS AND MERCHANTS

The Mediterranean Sea was the Roman Empire's internal lake. In spite of the Romans' reputation as landlubbers, it was not land routes but the Mediterranean Sea which afforded Rome the main avenues for its imperial expansion. And when the whole of the

Mediterranean basin was unified under Roman rule, the Mediterranean was called "Our Sea" (*Mare Nostrum*). It was effectively cleared of pirates from 36 B.C. until the third century A.D. Prolonged peace brought a decrease of risk and an increase in seaborne trade. Ships carried cargoes of wheat, wine, olive oil, wood, metals, and luxuries, especially to the city of Rome with its large population and unparalleled concentration of wealthy consumers. They also carried soldiers, merchants, migrants, and slaves, to say nothing of government officials, itinerant preachers, and craftsmen, across the sea between Rome and the provinces. Political, cultural, and economic integration proceeded hand in hand. Ease of transport and communication by sea in some degree compensated for low technology and low productivity. In that sense, the Roman Empire was built on water.

The Romans developed the technical capacity to build and sail large ships. The evidence is archaeological, literary, and legal. Underwater archaeologists have discovered about 800 shipwrecks from classical times, of which about 550 can be dated. These dated wrecks provide a convenient index of the frequency of ship sailings in successive periods. They confirm a general supposition that sailings were more frequent between 200 B.C. and A.D. 200 than ever before, and were more frequent then than for the next thousand years. To be sure, this index is only rough and ready; as always, there are technical qualifications. The location of ancient shipwrecks discovered by underwater enthusiasts reflects the relative prosperity of the western Mediterranean today; the eastern Mediterranean is underrepresented. In the last two centuries B.C., many ships were sunk by pirates. In peaceful conditions and as sailing techniques improved, ships kept less to the coast and more to the open sea. Since modern divers in search of archaeological remains keep largely to shallow waters, deep-sea wrecks are less likely to be found. That may be why there are more wrecks dated to the last two centuries B.C. than to the first two centuries A.D. But in spite of doubts and qualifications, the basic correlations hold: the more trade, the more sailings; the more sailings, the more wrecks. There was more seaborne trade in the Mediterranean at the height of Roman power than there was to be up to the fourteenth or fifteenth century.

Very few of these numerous wrecks have been thoroughly investigated, and from them, the size of a typical Roman merchant ship cannot be deduced. Six carefully studied wrecks, dating from the last century B.C. to the third century A.D., all measured over 200 and up to 450 metric tons burden. The consistency of this archaeological evidence suggests that the Romans regularly built ships of this size. On occasion, they also built very large ships of well over 1,000 metric tons burden, but critical examination of the testimony suggests that such ships were white elephants or fantasy. One such monster ship sailed once and was then beached; another built by order of a Roman emperor to carry a huge Egyptian obelisk as booty to Rome proved more useful sunk than afloat, since it served as the foundation for one of the breakwater piers in Rome's new harbor at Ostia. There is no merit in the view that Rome's wheat supply (at least 150,000 metric tons per year) was shipped by a small fleet of very large ships. Very large ships were expensive to build and ruinous to lose by shipwreck; if they were blown off course, they would have had difficulty in finding a port large enough to shelter in.

Even on the empire's main shipping route, which funneled wheat from Sicily, North Africa, and Egypt to Rome, some ships were quite small. This can be seen from a legal text of the second century A.D.; it provided tax immunity to those who built and sailed ships supplying wheat to Rome, provided the owner had one ship of 330 metric tons burden, or several ships totaling 330 metric tons, each of at least 65 metric tons burden. It seems clear that even on this premier route, large ships did not drive small ships out of business. Indeed, the archaeological evidence shows that the Romans regularly built ships of 200 to 450 metric tons burden.

At this point, some comparative evidence may help. Ships of 1,000 metric tons burden and over were regularly built for the transatlantic trade only after 1800. In the eighteenth century, the average size of ships trading from England to India was 440 metric tons burden. However, the ships on these long-distance routes were selected for large size; the average size of all seagoing vessels was much lower. For example, at the beginning of the eighteenth century, the average size of all ships entering Boston, Chesapeake Bay, and Barbados were fifty, ninety-seven, and fifty-seven metric tons, respectively, and in the sixteenth century the average size of ships using the Spanish Mediterranean ports was only about seventy-five metric tons burden. Such evidence casts serious doubt on a modern conclusion, often quoted, that "the smallest craft the ancients reckoned suitable for overseas shipping was seventy to eighty tons burden." This assertion is both intrinsically implausible and weakly based on a single, defective, heavily restored text listing port regulations on a Greek island in the third century B.C. Two points can be quickly made. First, the growth of the Roman Empire transformed the scale of Roman trade and Roman shipping to a level unimaginable in the Greek world. Secondly, the Mediterranean Sea in Roman times always contained a huge variety of ships, large and small.

It is important to appreciate the size of Roman ships, because ships are to transport and trade what factories are to production. Ships were mostly small because ports were

small and because the capital available both for the construction of the ships themselves and for the purchase of the cargo was limited. The size of ships reflected the availability of capital, the size of merchants' stock, and the size of markets. In order to understand the constraints under which Roman labor, industry, and trade operated, these factors should be explored.

No direct evidence exists for the capital cost of Roman merchant ships; once again comparative evidence is helpful, in this case the records of costs of constructing and fitting out merchant ships in fifteenth-century Genoa and in seventeenth-century England. As with all such comparisons, there are several complications and qualifications. First, the cost of ship construction varied considerably in Genoa and in England, as it probably did in Rome. Shipbuilders always have to choose between high capital cost and durability on the one hand, and on the other hand lower capital cost and a shorter life for the ship, just as they have to choose between strength and buoyancy. In light of the evidence, the best that can be expected is a rough order of magnitude, and one that can legitimately ignore this variation in cost and concentrate on average prices. But prices in current coin, in old Genoese lire and English pounds sterling, will not help much.

And so a tactic that has become standard in comparative economic history is adopted. Fifteenth-century Genoese and seventeenth-century English ship construction costs are converted into tons of wheat at prices contemporary to their times. The reason for this conversion is that cereal prices dominated most underdeveloped preindustrial economies to such an extent that the prices of many goods and wages co-varied with wheat prices. As a final step, tons of wheat are then converted into Roman money at a standard farm price, in this case three sesterces per *modius* (one *modius* equals

14.4 lbs., or 6.55 kg; four sesterces equal one denarius). Once again, this Roman wheat price is only a crude guide to reality. The farm price is much too low for the city of Rome and rather high for some regions of the empire.

This long chain of linked speculations must be judged by its results. The average cost of constructing and fitting out a merchant ship of 400 metric tons burden in fifteenth-century Genoa was 772 tons of wheat; in seventeenth-century England, 628 tons of wheat. Converted into Roman money, the cost varied from 288,000 to 354,000 sesterces. But the costs of Roman ship construction were in all likelihood significantly higher than in early modern Europe. Roman merchant ships were built outer shell first, like fine pieces of furniture; external planks were carefully joined together by mortise and tenon and by wooden dowels. The shell was then strengthened by an internal frame. The outside was sometimes protected against marine borers by lead sheathing below the waterline. That was an additional expense. From about A.D. 400 onward, European ships were built more cheaply, skeleton first, to which the outer planks were bolted or nailed, clinker style, one overlapping another; the gaps were caulked to make them waterproof. Overall, the capital cost of European skeleton construction was cheaper because it required much less skilled labor. Roman ships were as labor-intensive as Roman roads.

A Roman merchant ship of 400 tons burden, laden with wheat at the conventional farm price, was worth about 500,000 sesterces. It was worth considerably more when it successfully disgorged its cargo at the ports of Rome, especially if it carried part cargoes of higher value than wheat, such as wine, olive oil, cloth, dyes, or leather. Each such ship was worth more than the minimum fortune of a Roman knight. If all the ships needed to supply Rome with food and basic raw materials were added together, they would be equal to the fortunes of many senators. This can easily be calculated. Rome's population in the first two centuries A.D. was about one million people. At minimum subsistence (484 lbs., or 220 kg, wheat equivalent per person per year), they consumed 220,000 metric tons wheat equivalent per year. That was the minimum. To this minimum must be added all extra (nonwheat) food consumed above the level of minimum subsistence, fodder for draft animals, bricks and stone for building, timber for building and fuel, clothing, shoes, metal for tools, oil for lamps, and luxuries. Only a small portion would have been supplied locally. Even in the sixteenth century, when Rome had a population of about 150,000, it needed to import food by sea.

Supplying Rome was big business. The volume of shipping depends on the number of voyages made, and in this two factors deserve emphasis. First, Roman cargo ships customarily spent four winter months, November to March, in port; the risks of winter sailing were considered too high (Vegetius, *On Military Matters* 4.39). Second, turnaround times were probably quite long (to give some scale of comparison they were 106 and 94 days on average in Maryland and Virginia, respectively, in the late seventeenth century), partly because of weather bunching: sailing ships tended to arrive in a cluster with a fair wind, and that delayed their use of port facilities.

If two voyages on average are allowed per ship per year to Ostia (fewer from Egypt, more from Sicily), then the capital cost of the merchant ships supplying Rome with minimum subsistence was 88 million sesterces. When the volume of nonsubsistence trade, the capital cost of quayside installations, and the cost of river boats taking food and goods the last 22 miles up the river Tiber to Rome are added in, then an estimate of 100 million sesterces (the minimum fortune of 100 senators) invested in merchant shipping seems conservative. And the value of Rome's minimum subsistence alone (once the free wheat distributed to citizens by the state is subtracted) was worth 65 million sesterces per year at farm prices. The value of seaborne trade to Rome must surely have exceeded 100 million sesterces per year. In terms of capital investment and turnover, trade into Rome was very big business.

Shipping food, basic raw materials, and luxuries to the city of Rome was both a paradigm and an exception. Rome was by far the largest city in the empire; the volume and the total value of trade to the city and the capital costs of the shipping involved in that trade were also exceptional. But they were important exceptions, and they suggest a revision of current conventional wisdom about Roman trade, namely that it was virtually the exclusive province of small-time traders, and that if a trader made a fortune, he rapidly switched his fortune out of trade to higher-status landowning.

The enormous scale of trade to Rome and the large amounts of capital at risk in ships must have involved investment by the rich and powerful. (As noted, a fully laden 400-ton grain ship was worth at least 500,000 sesterces; this was more than the minimum fortune of a knight, which was 400,000 sesterces.) Investors probably split risks by taking shares in several ships (Plutarch, *Parallel Lives,* "Cato the Elder" 21). Splitting risks gave some middling investors access to large-scale maritime trade, but it did not diminish the total capital involved. Investment in shipping and in trade was less prestigious and more risky than investment in agricultural land. But because it was risky, it was also more profitable to the successful. Trade to Rome necessarily involved investment by wealthy landowners, either directly or through agents, and it helped make some of them even wealthier.

VOLUME OF TRADE AND DIVISION OF LABOR

Trade is a vital link between production and consumption. Through trade, consumers can get a wide variety of products which they do not grow or make themselves. The distribution of goods through trade allows the specialization of labor, both within a region and between regions. Trade makes possible the growth of towns and an increase in the number of townsfolk who are freed by trade from the need to grow or make all that they need for themselves. The development of trade was vital for the development of towns and of the literary, artistic culture that is associated with Roman civilization. The growth of trade was also vital for the growth in the power of the Roman state. For example, trade enabled the Roman government to buy goods and services in marketplaces distant from where taxes had been raised, just as it allowed Roman soldiers to spend their pay in frontier garrisons. Goods produced in one place were consumed elsewhere. This discussion of Roman labor, industry, and trade will conclude with an analysis of three distinct structures: the volume of trade and the division of labor in towns, the status of labor and the impact of slavery, and the network of taxes and trade.

Large-scale trade was not confined to Rome. The cities of Alexandria, Antioch, and Carthage had a combined population roughly equal to that of Rome. They too were supplied with food, raw materials, and luxuries for their elites from outside their immediate hinterland. And whereas Rome exacted some of its imports as tax in kind, and paid for many others out of tax revenues transmitted to Rome and spent there by generals, emperors, courtiers, and soldiers, the largest provincial cities had to earn money for their imported food and for their raw materials by the manufacture and export of goods, or by the profits that they earned as entrepôts in the transmission of taxes from the richest provinces, both to the frontier armies and to Rome.

The entrepôt trade was important. The trade between India, Arabia, and Egypt, for example, was dominated by merchants from Alexandria. Goods were brought by camel caravans moving across the desert by night from the Red Sea ports to the Nile, and then shipped downriver to Alexandria. They were mostly luxuries: pepper, pearls, ivory, silk, diamonds, sapphires, tortoiseshell, frankincense, spikenard, transparent muslins, ginger, glass, tempered "Chinese" steel blades, cinnabar, and panthers and leopards for slaughter in the Roman amphitheater (*Periplus of the Erythraean Sea* 56 ff.; *Digest* 39.4.16.7).

In the last century B.C., barely twenty ships were involved in the Red Sea trade. By the reign of Augustus, the merchant fleet had grown considerably; 120 ships sailed annually from one Red Sea port alone to India (Strabo, *Geography* 2.118; 17.798). And then in the first century A.D., techniques of sailing and navigation improved, so that instead of coasting, ships went almost 2,000 miles straight across the Indian Ocean with the monsoon winds. They could make the round trip in six months. The total value of the Indian trade alone was estimated at more than 50 million sesterces every year in the middle of the first century A.D. (Pliny the Elder, *Natural History* 6.100–106). That estimate represented the prices paid in India, where many Roman coins and pots have been found. The imported goods were sold inside the empire at many times their cost. The total value of Roman trade with Arabia, China, and India was estimated by the same author at over 100 million sesterces per year, or the minimum fortune of one hundred senators at the time of Augustus' reign (Pliny the Elder, *Natural History* 12.84).

The very large difference in price between buying and selling luxuries allowed substantial profits and covered the costs of transport from India to Rome, the risks of loss, customs duty at the Roman frontier, and the delays implicit in selling luxury goods in a limited market. Potential purchasers of expensive luxuries were concentrated in Rome and the largest cities. There they constituted a profitable market, profitable especially for the financiers who backed the trade, more than for the ship captains, sailors, camel drivers, and retailers, who cared for the goods on their long journey from producer to consumer.

It was the financiers who invested in the construction of ships and who lent money for the purchase of precious cargoes on risky voyages across the Indian Ocean. They hoped that the ship would in due course return with rich and salable cargoes: "worrying, counting the days, working out the months, weighing the principal in his mind, dreaming of the interest, and dreading the expiry date in case it proved unprofitable . . . keeping constant watch on the shore, worrying about strong winds, and continually asking new arrivals at the port whether they have heard of shipwreck anywhere or whether his debtors sailed anywhere dangerous" (Gregory of Nyssa, in Migne, *Patrologiae Cursus, Series Graeca*, vol. 46,441). These financiers were not themselves usually merchants, nor did they constitute a merchant class. They were landowners and social leaders who had financial interests on the side.

Between luxuries and staples, the Roman economy consumed a great variety of goods and raw materials. It is impossible to list all the goods on sale. The emperor Diocletian in A.D. 301 tried to control galloping inflation by fixing maximum prices. His *Edict on Maximum Prices* survives in several versions from different parts of the empire. It lists well over 1,000 goods and services: wines, beer, olive oil, radish oil, fish sauce, ham, smoked sausage, and butter; the wages of a farm laborer, stonemason, carpenter, cabinetmaker, wall painter, blacksmith, shipwright, brickmaker, camel driver, coppersmith, sewer cleaner, parchment maker, scribe, tailor, gymnastic instructor, shorthand teacher, and lawyer. Prices are given for hides, books, shoes, and sandals all in different qualities, saddles, bridles, halters, sacks, whips, packsaddles, lengths of timber, shuttles, spindles, ladders, axles, freight wagons, plows, shovels, picks, tubs, mills, sieves, needles, shirts, and over 300 different types of cloth or clothing. Most of the goods are simple transformations of raw material, but some products such as chemicals (alum and alkali for preparing cloth, pitch for storing wine, glazes and paints for tiles or pots) required considerable labor.

There are no contemporary statistics on the volume of trade within the Roman Empire, and without statistics it is difficult to reconstruct economic history. Nonetheless there are some usable clues. First, a simple calculation provides a rough order of magnitude. Eighty to 90 percent of the population of the Roman Empire in the first two centuries A.D. was primarily engaged in agriculture. For the sake of simplicity, assume that 15 percent of the population was not engaged in agriculture. Immediately it can be deduced that trade in nonfoods amounted to 15 percent of gross domestic production, because townsmen sold that much to peasants in order to buy food. To be sure, there are difficulties in and qualifications which should surround such crude estimates. Rents in kind should be subtracted, and money rents too if we consider that receivers of rent were nonproductive. Against that may be added the volume of trade both among townsmen and between townsmen and peasants, and the probability that the standard of living for many people was above minimum subsistence levels.

The Roman Empire in the first two centuries A.D. was characterized by unprecedented prosperity. This prosperity was induced partly by prolonged peace and partly by the gradual diffusion of technical innovations. It is a common archaeological observation, at least in the western provinces of the Roman Empire, that more artifacts are found at Roman than at pre-Roman levels: more coins, pots, lamps, iron tools, carved stones, and ornaments. In the first 200 years A.D., material culture reached a higher level in a wider area of the Mediterranean basin than it was to reach again for centuries. Archaeological finds comprise not only luxury objects made of gold or silver, but also, for example, simple glazed tableware, relatively expensive blown-glass bowls, sophisticated medical instruments, and everyday items like padlocks, keys, and iron nails.

We must be careful not to exaggerate or to romanticize Roman prosperity. The poor were miserably poor; the grandeur of Rome was built on the backs of sweating peasants. Many, perhaps even most, people lived near the level of minimum subsistence. And yet it is also important to recognize the extent of differentiation that existed even among the peasantry. By chance, an almost complete tax list survives from an Egyptian village, Karanis (in the Fayum), for the year A.D. 172; it indicates the amount of garden land owned by 413 households. The mean-size plot owned by the top twenty-six households was thirteen times larger than the mean-size plot owned by the bottom 242 households. Modern excavations corroborate the existence of a small group of relatively wealthy inhabitants. Archaeologists found some twenty relatively spacious houses in Karanis dating from the second century A.D.; their contents ranged from painted murals and Alexandrian glassware to Syrian perfume flasks and imported wood.

Another complete list from the village of Tebtunis, in the same region of Egypt but dating from the first century A.D., shows that

771

dowries varied considerably in size—from 18 to 1,600 drachmas; if ordered by size, the 25 and 75 percent cutoff points were 40 and 200 drachmas. By this measure, the village contained at least a fivefold variation in its capacity, or willingness, to pay a dowry. Such data help undermine a common stereotype that peasant villages in the Roman Empire were uniformly poor. Instead, they were steeply stratified and internally differentiated. Put another way, the aggregate demand for consumer goods from the thousands of villages spread across the empire must have been enormous: best clothes for brides and grooms, a new cloak for rich peasants or prosperous traders to wear at festivals, or ordinary clothes for the local schoolteacher, bank clerk, doctor, or middling landlord. Somehow in our mind's eye we have to create a balanced picture: general poverty and small units of production on one side, and on the other a varied and sophisticated market for a large variety of goods, concentrated especially in but not exclusive to the largest towns.

The division of labor provides yet another measure of Roman economic sophistication. Tombstones from Rome show the existence of over 200 named occupations. The astrological handbook written by Firmicus Maternus in the fourth century A.D. mentions 264 occupations. This compares with 350 trades listed in Campbell's *London Tradesmen* published in the mid eighteenth century. Such lists should obviously be used with caution; probably none is complete, and some differences may derive more from philological variation than from economic development. Even so, it seems probable that the longer list of occupations in eighteenth-century London reflects the fact that England, northern Europe, and North America had by then reached a level of economic sophistication which classical Rome never reached.

Three more longish lists of occupations from the Roman world deserve attention;

they reflect the division of labor in small towns. Pompeii in the Bay of Naples was covered by volcanic ash from Vesuvius in A.D. 79. Burial inscriptions and election posters daubed on stucco walls reveal eighty-five trades in a population of about 12,000. The second list comes from Korykos, a small and undistinguished town on the coast of Cilicia (southeastern Asia Minor; Turkey) and dates from the third to sixth centuries A.D. A set of tombs had short and simple burial inscriptions; over half of them named the occupation of dead adult males. Surprisingly, for such a small town, 110 different trades were mentioned, some of them very humble: woodcutters, beggars, clothes menders, and cooked-food sellers, and at the other end of the scale, goldsmiths and priests. Thirteen percent of the tradesmen with known occupations were in luxury trades; 18 percent in textiles; 10 percent in pottery; 8 percent in shipping; 15 percent in food sales; 5 percent each in building and smithery. Even in small towns, the urban market served a complex variety of needs. The third list is the least satisfactory; it comes from a house-by-house census in or around the Egyptian town of Arsinoë (in the Fayum). It lists the twenty-four occupations of 253 adult males; almost three-fifths were in agriculture, as farmers, shepherds, or plowmen; 15 percent were weavers, and 9 percent were wage laborers. Once again textile manufacture seems important, and perhaps wage labor was more entrenched in the Roman economy than some modern scholars have allowed.

STATUS AND IMPACT OF SLAVERY

Rome was a slave society. That affected attitudes toward labor in the Roman world, not just for slaves, but for everyone. It affected the attitudes of slaveowners toward slaves and toward free people who performed slavelike labor. Slavery affected attitudes toward work among the free poor. Slavery pervaded Roman society; as a metaphor, it penetrated political philosophy and religion. Early Christians characterized themselves as slaves of God, a fact disguised by English translations of "slave" as "servant." But paradoxically (at least for those who think that evil cannot produce good), slavery elevated the status of free citizens. And so it helped preserve political participation by poor citizens in Rome down to the last century B.C., just as it had helped promote democracy in classical Athens. The political power of poor Roman citizens persisted, because the rich exploited imported slaves instead.

Slavery was cruel. Agricultural slaves typically worked on large estates in chain gangs. The Roman senator and moralist Cato, in the second century B.C., recommended that slaves worn out with work should be sold (*On Agriculture* 2.7). Some masters in the first century A.D. left sick slaves in public squares to fend for themselves, only to reclaim them if they recovered. Conditions for slaves working in the silver mines were terrible; in the quicksilver (mercury) mines, conditions were lethal (Strabo, 12.3.4). Indeed, for most slaves employed in the mines or on agricultural estates, the only escape from hard work and ill treatment was death.

Domestic slaves, whether skilled or manual, were not immune. Roman literature abounds with incidents of arbitrary cruelty by educated masters to their slaves. The famous physician Galen records the frequent outbursts of violent rage and physical attacks on slaves, which he had himself witnessed. He tells of an instance in which the emperor Hadrian in anger stabbed a slave in the eye with a stylus. Hadrian regretted it later and told the slave to choose a gift in compensation. The slave asked for his eye back (Galen, *Opera Omnia* 5.17). Gladiatorial shows, in which slaves were publicly killed for the pleasure of the free, provide further evidence, if evidence is needed, of the Romans' institutionalized violence toward their slaves. As a Roman proverb went: "All slaves are enemies."

There was another side to the coin. A recently published papyrus from Roman Egypt, dating from the first or second century A.D., contains an appeal to the authorities for compensation from a careless driver of a donkey, which had run over and seriously injured a young slave girl on her way to a singing lesson. In her plea, the appellant wrote: "I loved and cared for this little servant girl, a house-born slave (her name was Peina), in the hope that when she grew up, she would look after me in my old age, since I am a helpless woman and alone" (*Oxyrhynchus Papyri* 3555). There can be no doubt that many slaveowners loved particular slaves—an old nursemaid, a slave woman whom the master freed and married, a faithful male secretary, or a bailiff handsomely rewarded in a will. Roman authors were fond of telling stories about a slave's loyalty in a crisis, how this one hid his master from pursuing soldiers, or that one would not betray her mistress even under severe torture.

These stories were part of the mythology that helped blind slaveowners to the misery that they themselves inflicted on the majority of their slaves. And yet for a minority of Roman slaves, the experience of slavery was significantly different from that of slaves centuries later in the American South. First, Romans employed slaves in highly skilled occupations, for example, as doctors, bailiffs, literary agents, palace administrators, and as trading entrepreneurs or bankers, acting on their owners' behalf. Second, many such responsible slaves bought or were given their freedom. And among freed slaves of the Roman emperors, we find some of the most powerful figures of the Roman state. Ex-slaves were also merchants and

773

rich landowners. One ex-slave in 8 B.C., for example, left a fortune of 60 million sesterces, over 4,000 slaves, and 264,000 head of cattle and sheep (Pliny the Elder, *Natural History* 33.135). Finally, there was no color bar, nothing which irredeemably distinguished slaves and ex-slaves from the freeborn. On the contrary, by an old tradition, slaves freed by citizens became citizens themselves. The ample evidence available suggests that Roman slaves were freed in the thousands. The hope of freedom, the expectation, and the realization achieved by so many other slaves must have pervaded and lightened many a slave's perception of his tasks.

Slaveholdings in the Roman Empire were concentrated in Italy. By the end of the last century B.C. slaves probably comprised well over 30 percent of Italy's total population. It seems likely that there also were significant numbers of slaves in Greece and in the large seaboard towns that had once been parts of Hellenistic kingdoms, but the only solid testimony consists of inscriptions listing manumissions in small towns of central and northern Greece, and a passing remark by Galen that there were as many slaves in Pergamum (Bergama, in Turkey) as adult men or women (*Opera Omnia* 5.49). It also seems likely that there were relatively few slaves in the agricultural regions of the West, if only because it made no sense to buy slaves with scarce capital when the rich and powerful could exploit free peasants at lower cost by the exaction of rent and tax.

Census returns for Egypt, outside Alexandria, show that slaves constituted 10 percent of the total population. Surprisingly, slaves were found most often as members of a small household, often when it had been depleted by death (26 percent of such households had one or more slaves). Large households, comprising more than one nuclear family—those that had plenty of their own labor—were least likely (7 percent) to have a slave. This Egyptian evidence suggests that slaves were often supplementary labor, recruited to help a family through a crisis caused by death. Such slaves combined domestic and agricultural labor. Within Egypt, slaves clearly did not constitute a dominant mode of production.

In spite of regional variations in the number and occupation of slaves, slavery had three important functions in the Roman economy. For one, slavery secured the long-distance mobility of labor in a society in which there was no effective labor market. By defining humans as objects of legal ownership—as property—slavery allowed conquering Romans, as their empire grew, to import into Italy an underclass of exploitable aliens. Without slaves, how could rich Romans have realized their wealth? Not that slavery was the only channel of migration. Indeed, in the process of conquering an empire, slavery can be seen as the reciprocal of military expansion and colonization. Vanquished slaves were sent in one direction from conquered provinces to Italy, while in the other direction, conquering soldiers were recruited to leave their Italian farms; they were dispossessed of their land by their own elite, moved into armies of conquest, and were then eventually settled in huge numbers in colonies on the land of the conquered.

Needless to say, the switch between imported slaves on the one hand and exported peasant soldiers on the other hand can be made to sound neater than it was in reality. But reality included decades of violent civil war, which destroyed valuable farmstock, drove thousands of Italian peasants into the army, and led to the eventual resettlement of about 300,000 Italian veterans in colonies outside Italy between 69 and 8 B.C. The reciprocal flows of migrant labor, impoverished slaves, and enriched soldier-settlers were basic ingredients in the peaceful political settlement achieved by the emperor Augustus.

A second function of the growth of slavery

in Italy from the second century B.C. onward was an increase of inequality, a growth in wealth especially for the rich within Roman society, without forcing free Roman citizens into directly exploited roles, except in their traditional role as soldiers. Slavery allowed the myth of notional equality among Roman citizens and basic citizen rights to survive in spite of a tremendous increase in inequality. Slavery defined even very poor free citizens as in some sense superior. Slavery saved free citizens from becoming the obvious servants or direct employees of the rich. The price of this development was the degradation of manual labor by its association with slavery. Cicero in the last century B.C. considered that all wage laborers, retailers, traders, and artisans were sordid (*On Duty* 1.150–151). This view was probably prevalent in the upper classes, but it cannot therefore be imagined that all Romans despised traders, artisans, and manual laborers. Indeed, monuments to craftsmen of all types, bakers, masons, butchers (often depicting the tools of their trade), and to merchants were set up both at Rome itself and in the provinces. Traders and craftsmen were themselves obviously proud of their work.

Finally, slavery contributed to economic growth, partly because it allowed the close coordination of the labor of several workers under the domination of a single owner, and partly because it allowed, or even demanded, more exploitation than free Roman citizens were used to. In modern industrial societies, at least until recently, people worked very hard. They went to work for eight hours or more for six days a week. But free peasants, even on a moderately fertile farm, needed to work only about one hundred man-days per year in order to supply a family of four persons with minimum subsistence. That is perhaps why there were so many festivals, over a hundred days a year, in the old Roman calendar.

Confronted by the free citizens' tradition of sturdy independence, and their resistance to continuous wage labor, it was not surprising that wealthy Romans turned instead to captured slaves. Slaves could be forced to work in chain gangs for long hours and for most days of the year. The inefficiencies of slavery, its high capital cost, the cost of supervision and of sabotage are well known. But no one can doubt that Roman slave gangs on large agricultural estates produced larger surpluses than subsistence farmers. The growth in the population of Rome provided a huge market for the new surplus produced by slaves from farms once cultivated by free peasants. Slavery increased the productivity of labor.

TAXES AND TRADE

The Roman Empire persisted as a single political system for at least six centuries (200 B.C.–A.D. 400). Its integration and preservation rank, with the Chinese empire, as one of the greatest political achievements of mankind. The acquisition of a huge empire transformed a large section of the traditional Italian economy. The influx of imperial profits in the form of booty and taxes changed Rome from a small town to a resplendent metropolis, capital of an empire. It was there that competing politicians, political generals and, later, emperors lavished their largess. By the end of the last century B.C., 250,000 adult male citizens, plus women, children, and numerous slaves, inhabited the city; small tradesmen, artisans, porters, domestic slaves, priests, schoolteachers, merchants, and large-scale entrepreneurs kept this huge preindustrial city going.

Outside Rome, peasant soldiers were dispossessed of their land. Many of them migrated to Rome and to citizen colonies overseas. Their places as agricultural laborers were taken by a smaller number of captured slaves who were forced to produce an unprecedented surplus. This extra surplus represented the slaveowners' profit. It also consisted mostly of food, sold in the newly expanded market created by the city of Rome. Agricultural slavery grew as the urban population grew and as the market for food expanded.

Growth of the empire dramatically changed the volume and direction of trade. This development can best be analyzed by considering the operation of the Roman economy in the first two centuries A.D. We start by tracing the implications of two simple facts. First, the grandeur of Rome rested upon millions of tax payments, made mostly in cash, by small peasants, spread over a huge empire. Second, the empire was defended by a standing army of 300,000 or more soldiers recruited for twenty-five years' service. Half of these soldiers were citizen legionaries; the others were recruited from provincials. All were paid more than enough to maintain a family at minimum subsistence; they were also prohibited from making legal marriages. Legionaries were paid at premium rates, roughly twice a family's minimum subsistence (900 sesterces per year in the mid first century A.D.). Soldiers were the second-largest occupational group in the whole empire, after peasants, and they were paid in cash. Nearly all of them were stationed in permanent garrisons near the frontiers of the empire.

At the risk of oversimplification, the whole Roman Empire can now be envisaged as comprising three spheres: (a) an outer ring of frontier provinces, in which defensive armies were stationed; (b) an inner ring of relatively rich provinces, such as Spain, southern Gaul, northern Africa, Asia Minor, Syria, and Egypt, which were relatively fertile, populous and urbanized, and therefore paid more taxes than other provinces; and (c) the center, comprising Italy and the city of Rome, the seat of the emperors' court and of the central government. Italy was not liable to the empire's chief tax, the tax on agri-

cultural land. But Rome and Italy, like the army, consumed a large volume of taxes.

The frontier armies (a) and the emperors' court at Rome and the central administration of the empire (c) together consumed more taxes than were produced either in the frontier provinces themselves or in Italy. The inner ring of relatively fertile, populous, urbanized, and rich provinces (b), bordering on the Mediterranean Sea, paid much more in taxes than was spent locally. They were tax-exporting provinces. Their taxes were sent to and spent on soldiers along the frontiers and on entertainments and administration in Rome. In order to pay new taxes in cash each year, the inner ring of provinces had to sell and export goods equal in value to the amount of taxes exported. How else could they get their money back? Stated differently, the Roman state's expenditure necessarily stimulated interregional, long-distance trade.

The process was doubtless not as simple as it now seems. Large-scale reciprocal flows of taxes and trade were the cumulative result of myriads of local transactions and transformations. The impact of change was greatest in the western provinces. Peasants were now forced for the first time to produce more food and to sell it in order to pay taxes. They were pitchforked into the money economy. Some of this new surplus was probably shipped direct, relatively unchanged, to tax-consuming regions; for example, Spanish olive oil was exported in huge volume to Rome. The cost of transporting staples was high, as we have seen, but not insuperable. Complementarily, the new surplus was also in part sold locally and consumed by artisans, who paid for it by producing goods of higher value and lower volume, such as textiles or leather, which could also be exported to distant markets. Towns were the nodes in a complex network of industry and trade which together made it practicable for artisans to convert a local surplus of agricultural produce into goods which could be exported and sold in order to earn money, which then, as the wheel came full circle, enabled both artisans and peasants to pay taxes.

The imposition of taxes levied in money thickened the network of exchange throughout the empire. Peasants sold their produce in local markets. Artisans labored in small-scale industries in market towns. Shipowners and haulers transported and merchants traded in staples and higher-value goods between towns, along roads and rivers, and across the Mediterranean. The collection of so much tax in money allowed the central government an unprecedented flexibility. They could spend revenues in Rome and on the frontiers, in places far removed from the peasants who labored to produce a surplus. Tax, trade, labor, and industry were prime ingredients in Rome's enduring political success.

BIBLIOGRAPHY

SOURCES

Cato, *On Agriculture,* William D. Hooper, trans. (1967); Cicero, *On Duty,* Walter Miller, trans. (1975); *Corpus Inscriptionum Latinarum,* Theodor Mommsen, ed. (1863–); *The Digest of Justinian,* Alan Watson, trans., 4 vols. (1985); Diodorus Siculus, *Library of History,* Charles Oldfather, trans., 10 vols. (1933); Firmicus Maternus, *Ancient Astrology,* Jean R. Bram, trans. (1975); Galen, *Opera Omnia,* Karl Kuhn, ed., 20 vols. (1892–1916); *Inscriptiones Latinae Selectae,* Hermann Dessau, ed., 3 vols. (1892–1916); *Patrologiae Cursus, series Graeca,* J. P. Migne, ed., 161 vols. (1857–1866); Pliny the Elder, *Natural History,* Henry Rackham, trans., 10 vols. (1967); Strabo, *Geography,* Horace Jones, trans., 8 vols. (1917); *The Theodosian Code,* Clyde Pharr, trans. (1952).

STUDIES

Peter A. Brunt, *Italian Manpower 225 B.C.–A.D. 14* (1971); Lionel L. Casson, *Ships and Seamanship in the Ancient World* (1971); John H. D'Arms, *Commerce and Social Standing in Rome* (1981); John H. D'Arms and E. C. Kopff, eds., *The Seaborne Commerce of Ancient Rome* (1980); Geoffrey E. M. De Ste. Croix, *The Class Struggle in the Ancient Greek World* (1981); Richard P. Duncan-Jones, *The Economy of the Roman Empire*, 2d ed. (1982); Moses I. Finley, *The Ancient Economy* (1973), *Ancient Slavery and Modern Ideology* (1980), and *Economy and Society in Ancient Greece* (1981); Tenney Frank, *Economic Survey of Ancient Rome,* 5 vols. (1933–1940); Keith Hopkins, *Conquerors and Slaves* (1978), "Economic Growth and Towns in Classical Antiquity," in Peter Abrams and Edward A. Wrigley, eds., *Towns in Societies* (1978), "Taxes and Trade," in *Journal of Roman Studies,* **70** (1980), "Models, Ships and Staples," in Peter Garnsey and C. R. Whittaker, eds., *Trade and Famine in Classical Antiquity* (1983), and "Introduction," in Peter Garnsey, Keith Hopkins, and C. R. Whittaker, eds., *Trade in the Ancient Economy* (1983); Arnold H. M. Jones, *The Later Roman Empire 284–602,* 3 vols. (1964), and *The Roman Economy* (1974); Barry G. D. Jones, "The Roman Mines at Rio Tinto," in *Journal of Roman Studies,* **70** (1980).

J. G. Landels, *Engineering in the Ancient World* (1978); Ivan D. Margary, *Roman Roads in Britain* (1967); Russell Meiggs, *Roman Ostia,* 2d ed. (1973); Walter H. Schoff, ed., *Periplus of the Erythraean Sea* (1912); Geoffrey Rickman, *The Corn Supply of Ancient Rome* (1980); Mikhail Rostovtzeff, *Social and Economic History of the Roman Empire,* 2d ed. (1957); Charles Singer, ed., *The Mediterranean Civilizations and the Middle Ages, c. 700 B.C. to c. 1500 A.D.,* and *A History of Technology,* II Singer et al., eds. (1954–1970); Chester G. Starr, *The Roman Empire, 27 B.C.–A.D. 476* (1982); William L. Westermann, *The Slave Systems of Greek and Roman Antiquity* (1955); John P. Wild, *Textile Manufacture in the Northern Roman Provinces* (1970).

Mines and Quarries

JOHN F. HEALY

MINES

The first flint mines date from the late Mesolithic period. The major impetus to large-scale mining of ore minerals came in the Bronze Age, when native gold had to be supplemented by the exploitation of alluvial deposits, and copper by working deep ore-laden veins in the rock. In Sinai the oxidation zone of copper extended to a depth of 245–260 feet (75–80 m) and mining dates from *ca.* 3000 B.C. At Timna, near the north end of the Gulf of Aqaba, there is evidence of elaborate systems of shafts and galleries, together with processing facilities on the surface. Most early Egyptian gold came from surface alluvial deposits—placers—but the Turin Papyrus, a unique document dated *ca.* 1250 B.C., shows a map of the shaft-and-tunnel gold-mining complex at Wadi al-'Allaqi (Sudan).

With the exception of gold, copper, and mercury, metals are found only as compounds, that is, in chemical combination with other elements, mainly oxygen, sulfur, and arsenic. When a metalliferous deposit occurs on the surface, the ore is often in the form of an oxide, for example cassiterite (SnO_2), or a carbonate, as malachite ($CuCO_3Cu(OH)_2$), the latter having been altered by the chemical action of the atmosphere from an original sulfide state. At greater depths, oxides and carbonates are replaced by sulfides such as galena (PbS). The main ore bodies mined by the Greeks and Romans included gold quartz (gold), argentiferous galena (silver), chalcopyrite and chalcocite (copper), cassiterite (tin), galena (lead), iron pyrites and hematite (iron), calamine (zinc), and cinnabar (mercury).

Greek Mining

Three methods of mining were used in the classical world: placer, opencast (open-cut), and deep vein. Although gold quartz was mined, the primary sources for Greeks and Egyptians alike were alluvial deposits along the course of rivers and streams. Such placer deposits result from the weathering of mineral-bearing rocks where they outcrop, and many agents, including water, wind, and changes of temperature, bring about the disintegration of the quartz matrix. The loose fragments, called detritus, are transported and concentrated by the action of running water, the most effective means of gravity separation. The Greeks collected the heavier grains of metal on the greasy fleeces of sheep, pegged out directly in rivers, or, as Strabo explains (*Geography* 11.2.19), in perforated troughs. The product is aptly termed "white gold" by Herodotus (1.50.2) since all auriferous ore is associated with silver.

The second major source was reef gold—native metal embedded in a solid matrix—which occurs alone either in nests or as finely disseminated particles, or in connection with certain sulfides in the veins. Gold tellurides were unknown, although the presence of tellurium as a trace element is useful in determining the source of gold, as, for example, from Dacia (Romania). Gold may have been mined by simple opencut methods, but Strabo (4.2.1) is more likely to be referring to the practice of digging pits. The gradual exhaustion of alluvial sources led to the development of underground mining in the case of gold. Silver mines on the island of Thasos in the northern Aegean were opened by the Phoenicians and still in operation at the time of Thucydides (4.105), and Herodotus (3.57) records the existence of gold and silver mines on Siphnos in the Cyclades. Early mines on the mainland include those in Attica, in the vicinity of Mount Pangaeus, and others generally in the northern regions of Macedonia and Thrace.

PROSPECTING.   In the absence of any detailed knowledge of the principles of geology, the Greeks were unable to prospect scientifically and relied on identifying the color of minerals at outcrops. Thus the line of the "first contact" in Attica, the junction between adjacent bodies of ore-bearing rock, was revealed by the red color of iron oxide (hematite) found on the surface. Although iron was the initial object of their search, miners must soon have noticed lumps of galena with their shiny facets, less quick to oxidize and too heavy to be swept away by water. Among other signs of mineralization would have been a rich vegetation indicating the presence of phosphorus or potassium, while a denuded surface would have signaled the presence of pyrite or arsenopyrite below the surface. The most serious shortcoming of the Greeks was the failure to apply the geological evidence of one site to another; for example, although the geological formation of the area around Mount Ocha (Euboea [Evvia]) was similar to that of Laurium, no large-scale mining was attempted there.

LAURIUM.   One of the best-known mining regions of the classical world was southeastern Attica, especially the area of Mount Laurium (Laurion), where there are the remains of a Mycenaean citadel on the hill at Velatouri. Pottery shards confirm the existence also of a flourishing Mycenaean urban complex at nearby Thorikos. The discovery of fragments of litharge, the product of the cupellation of lead sulfide—a refining process to separate the metal—indicates that galena was being mined from *ca.* 1350 B.C. and possibly from as early as 1500 B.C. Mining continued with few interruptions into the period of Roman occupation, until the slave revolt in 103 B.C. The mines at Laurium owed their existence to the simplicity of the geological formation of the region, that is, to the occurrence of lead, zinc, and silver deposits on the crystalline basement rocks. Three layers of limestone alternated with two of schist and contained veins of three principal minerals: argentiferous and pyritic galena, and sphalerite.

The first mining at Thorikos was by pitting—digging holes as primitive shafts until ore was found. When the ore ran out the pit was abandoned. This technique was later replaced by digging mine passages (adits) into the hillsides. When miners were successful in discovering a vein, the shapeless exploratory opening was reduced to a small gallery of regular dimensions; otherwise it was abandoned. The first contact at Laurium had been haphazardly exploited and surface lodes became less important as the need for silver increased. This inevitably led the Athenians to mine the deeper sulfide deposits. The loss of the Thracian silver mines to the Persians at the end of the sixth century B.C. provided an added incentive. A "third contact" was opened up and by 483 B.C. was producing 100 talents of silver a year. (There is no definitive evidence regarding the "second contact." Most likely this line did not provide adequate economic returns, and so was not mined.) The mines covered a large area, the richest being concentrated near Maroneia. Analysis of gold trace elements and lead isotope ratios in Athenian coinage distinguishes Attic from Thracian silver.

The generic term for a mine is *metallon,* which may include a processing plant (*ergasteria*) on the surface. There were three broad categories of mines: new operations (*kainotomiai*), mines already in production (*ergasima*), and discontinued workings (*anasixima*). Aristotle, however, refers only to *ergasima* and *anasaxima* that were subsequently reopened (*palaia anasaxima*).

SHAFTS. More than 2,000 shafts are recorded at Laurium, the average depth being 164 feet (50 m), and the deepest, the Puits Francisque, 390 feet (119 m). To excavate a shaft, a central hole was first dug with a long pointed or chisel-like rod. Then the surrounding earth or rock was cut away out to the intended sides of the shaft and down to the hole depth. The process was repeated to go deeper. At Laurium shafts are rectangular or square, the largest being 6.5 feet × 6.25 feet (2.00 m × 1.90 m), and the average about 6 feet × 4 feet. The center line is vertical, but for every 33 feet (10 m) of depth the cross section turns through an angle of

8 to 10 degrees; thus the rectangle at the base of the shaft may be at right angles to the one at the top. Holes found at the sides of a shaft were probably for the insertion of runglike pieces of wood used in place of actual ladders. Medieval mines made use of a similar means of access to and from the bottom of the shaft. The rungs were short enough that the center of the shaft area was left clear for hauling up the ore mineral and spoil. In the Siphnian silver mines, however, the worthless rock in which valuable metals occur (gangue) was separated from the mineral underground and left in heaps. Various attempts have been made to estimate the time needed to dig a shaft. In *Les mines de Laurion* (1897), Edouard Ardaillon suggested that 2,000 man-hours would have been required to dig a shaft to a depth of somewhat more than 300 feet (100 m). Most recently, Constantin Conophagos, in *Le Laurium antique* (1980), gives an estimated extraction rate of 203 cubic feet (5.76 m³) per worker over a thirty-day period, assuming replacement labor and continuous digging day and night. In driving a tunnel (gallery) Conophagos arrives at a rate of about 32 feet (10 m) a month.

GALLERIES. Rectangular, square, or trapezoidal galleries (*huponomos, diorux, diadusis, orugma,* or *syrinx,* all general terms used to describe galleries) were driven out from the base of the shaft. Very occasionally the gallery was irregular where the vein had been followed exactly. Gallery height was never more than 3 feet, 4 inches (1 m), often as low as 2 feet (60 cm), with a width of 2–3 feet (60–90 cm). It was, therefore, impossible for a miner to work other than stretched out on his back. The cramped conditions impaired miners' efficiency since clearly they could not employ their strength to the full in digging. The limited size of the cross section, however, and the fact that the galleries were driven through schist and limestone meant that elaborate roof shoring was generally unnecessary. Where rock and ore minerals were not closely packed—because of chemical changes they had undergone since their original deposition—the unstable masses were shored up by well-cut mortise and tenon joints between props and lintels; the olive wood came from Kamareza (Laurium). Wood for mining is mentioned by Demosthenes (*Against Meidias* 167). The *mesokrineis*—rock pillars left in the ore mineral to support the gallery roof—are more likely to have been boundaries rather than additional roof supports, although this interpretation is open to question. On the Cassandra peninsula (Chalcidice, northern Greece), large abandoned excavated workings (stopes) became underground kitchens and sleeping quarters for the miners. Traces of hearths remain, and holes in the rock walls were used as niches for lamps or as cupboards.

VENTILATION. Metalliferous mines do not have the problem of methane gas (CH_4), although Lucretius (6.810 ff.) and Pliny (*Natural History* 33.98) later refer to poisonous fumes in gold and silver mines. Nevertheless the provision of adequate ventilation was a major problem. Temperature in a mine increases by one degree with every 100 feet (30 m) of depth. This, together with the small size of the galleries, smoke from lamps, and heat generated by the miners and their exhalations, made working conditions appalling. In ancient mines all methods of ventilation depended on the natural circulation of air by draft and convection, assisted by simple devices. One method, described by Pliny (*Natural History* 31.49), but probably used from the earliest period, relied on the agitation of the air by strips of linen, using the same principle as a punkah. At Laurium shafts sunk in pairs, with parallel galleries and frequent connecting crosscuts, were also employed to assist the movement of air. Sometimes fires were lit in one shaft

to cause a down draft in the other. Occasionally a shaft was cut with vertical grooves down two opposite walls to enable it to be divided by boarding (brattice), a chimney being built over one half to increase the draft by convection. Such chimneys are found in the mines at Mount Pangaeus in southern Thrace. Openings at different levels, where the configuration of the terrain allowed, also assisted the flow of air. The remains of suffocated miners at Laurium and elsewhere, however, show that the Greeks were not always successful in providing effective ventilation.

LIGHTING. Two types of lighting were used, simple torches made of resinous wood, and stone and terra-cotta lamps containing olive oil and a floating wick. Examples of the latter exist from mines on the islands of Seriphos and Thasos and at Laurium. There is no archaeological evidence to support the claim made by Diodorus Siculus (3.12.6) that miners carried lamps attached to their foreheads in the manner of modern mining practice.

DRAINAGE. The Greeks did not encounter any serious problems of drainage at Laurium because of the porous rock formations and the fact that they did not mine below the groundwater level. From the evidence of surviving vessels, it would seem that bailing alone sufficed.

MINING TOOLS. Hand tools used by Greeks were simple and few in number. They included a hammer (*typis* or *tykos*) with pointed and flat heads at opposite ends not unlike a modern geologist's hammer. It weighed about 5 1/2 pounds (2 1/2 kg) and could be used in an upward or downward direction. A gad (*xoïs*), a pointed or chisel-like rod, was used with the hammer in breaking up rock and ore mineral. The miners' pick (also *tykos*) had a thick blade about 16 inches (40 cm) long and 6–8 inches (15–20 cm) wide, pointed at one end and with a socket at the other for a handle. Mining coin types from Damastion (near Stageira, in Macedonia) illustrate picks. In addition there was a kind of mattock or shovel (*skalis*), used for raking up dislodged ore and debris or for collecting placers, as described by Strabo (3.2.9).

MINING TECHNIQUES. Ore was extracted by driving a series of passages, generally horizontal, along the strike of a vertical or steeply dipping vein and taking the ore from above or below the gallery (overhand and underhand stoping). Although written in the first century B.C., the account of mining reef gold in Egypt given by Diodorus Siculus (3.12.1–6) provides a good general picture of mining and conditions of work:

> The earth is naturally black and contains seams and veins of quartz which is unusually white and in brilliancy surpasses everything else which shines brightly by its nature, and here the overseers of the labor in the mines recover the gold with the aid of a multitude of workers. . . . The gold-bearing earth which is hardest they first burn with a hot fire, and when they have crumbled it in this way, they continue the working of it by hand.

This is the well-attested practice of fire setting by means of which quartz, if heated to between 560 and 600° C and quenched, undergoes a remarkable molecular change and becomes friable. Diodorus Siculus continues:

> The soft rock . . . is crushed with a sledgehammer by myriads of unfortunate wretches. The entire operations are masterminded by a skilled worker [*technites*] who distinguishes the stone and points it out to the laborers; and of those who are assigned to this unfortunate task the physically strongest break the quartz rock with iron hammers, applying no skill to the task but only force and cutting tunnels through the stone, not in a straight line but

wherever the seam of glistening rock may lead.

HAULAGE OF ORE. Ore mineral, except at Siphnos, was normally carried out of the workings by boys, according to Diodorus Siculus (3.13.1), and hauled to the surface in sacks, or baskets, or handed up the shaft to ground level by a chain of miners.

Roman Mining

Mining continued in the Hellenistic period at most sites, and with the spread of their empire the Romans inherited the basic mining techniques and tools of the Greeks and Egyptians. They also added new methods and developed mining technology, especially in the sphere of engineering. Operations came under the control of the tax collector (*publicanus*) and later of the procurator of mines (*procurator metallorum*).

The provinces of Spain were an important acquisition for the Romans. Strabo (3.2.8) aptly describes the Iberian peninsula as "a country full of metals," and its mineral wealth is confirmed by Pliny the Elder (*Natural History* 33 *passim*). Alluvial sources were still being worked in northwest Spain, under the early principate, although elsewhere most placers had been exhausted. The Romans evolved a new mining technique, hushing (hydraulicking), in which a suitable source of water was brought to the site by aqueducts to supply dams or tanks behind the area being worked. When a sufficient head of water had been built up, it was released to break down the covering soil (overburden) and mineral deposits. The size of such operations was vast: the three major aqueducts at Las Medulas (Asturias) delivered about 9 million gallons (34 million l) of water a day. Tin ore in Spain and Britain was mainly concentrated by rivers or streams, but Diodorus Siculus (5.38.4) states that "tin does not occur on the surface of the earth, as certain writers repeatedly assert in their histories, but is dug out of the ground." This passage undoubtedly refers to buried leads, as in Cornwall, where alluvial tin has sand, peat, or gravel as an overburden, sometimes to a depth of 50 feet (16 m).

OPENCAST. Tin in Gaul and, with one exception, iron on Elba, were mined by extensive opencast (opencut) workings. Copper was similarly mined at Tres Minas (Spain).

PROSPECTING. Romans had a marginally greater knowledge of geology than the Greeks and by the time of Pliny the Elder (A.D. 23–79) understood the physical characteristics of minerals. They continued to rely to a certain extent on surface indications in their search for ore minerals, but they also carried out elementary prospecting. In Spain, so Pliny explains (*Natural History* 33.67), miners looked for "*segullum,* a kind of earth that indicates the presence of gold" and knew, when searching for sources of tin, that "tiny [black] pebbles [cassiterite] occasionally appear in the dry beds of torrents . . . and in certain goldmines [*alutiae*]" (*Natural History* 34.157). In Dacia miners actually tried to discover the parent ore body of rich placers, in the Urba Mountains, by advancing upstream from the alluvium to the diluvium of the side valleys. In Spain they discovered vein copper below layers of silver and alum. More often than not, luck rather than design led them to sources of ore mineral. It is commonly alleged that the Romans did not have any knowledge of faulting, or other geologically based complications, but the evidence of the Bottino lead mines (in Etruria) shows that they were able to trace the continuation of a lode over a fault.

RIO TINTO. Copper was mined in Spain before 2000 B.C., and the Phoenicians exploited argentiferous ores from as early as the seventh century B.C. It seems likely that in some locations mineral veins were visible in the pockets of jarositic earth. Apart from the rich sources of gold quartz in Asturias and Gallaecia (northwestern Spain) which Pliny describes (*Natural History* 33.67 ff.), some of the most important mines were along the Rio Tinto (southwestern Spain). There operations extended between the Baetis River (Guadalquivir), near Seville, and Portugal, along a corridor approximately 106 miles (170 km) wide. The main ore bodies (incorporating the peaks of Cerro Salomon, Cerro Colorado, and Cerro San Dionisio) resulted from two different periods of primary mineralization. The first and more abundant appears to have been pyritic, when the lavas and porous rock sediments throughout the Cerros were fractured and impregnated with pyrite, but without copper. Copper minerals were deposited in the second phase, accompanied by an intense chloritization of the host rocks. Individual ore shoots consist of a ramification of near-vertical veinlets filled with pyrite, chalcopyrite, quartz, and chlorite. The phenomenon known as secondary enrichment leads to a downward migration of valuable metal in the veins so that the upper 200–300 feet (60–90 m) of a vein are usually the richest portion of the deposit. The Cerro San Dionisio lode contains chalcocite (Cu_2S) to this depth and, below this, greater amounts of chalcopyrite ($CuFeS_2$), one of the most important ores of copper. The main phase of exploitation at Rio Tinto dates from the first century B.C.

SHAFTS. Unfinished shafts at Linares (southern Spain) illustrate the method of sinking; shafts were normally rectangular and unlined, but if round, were lined with stone. There are holes in the sides for the provision of wooden foot rungs, as in Greek shafts.

GALLERIES. The Romans often employed more elaborate systems of galleries than their Greek counterparts, which had as many as four levels, with connecting shafts, as on the islands of Andros. Roman galleries were small in cross section, but some were wider at the top to accommodate miners' shoulders as they passed through. Occasionally galleries were of an arched section.

VENTILATION, LIGHTING, DRAINAGE. The Romans appear to have followed Greek practice in matters of ventilation and lighting. It was in mine drainage that the Romans made the most significant developments, since they were often forced by the nature of the mineralization, especially in the case of copper, to mine below the groundwater level. Diodorus Siculus describes (5.37.3) the hazard of underground water in Spanish silver mines: "Now and then, as they go down deep, they come upon flowing subterranean rivers, but they overcome the might of these by diverting the streams which flow in on them by means of channels leading off at an angle." Four main methods of mine drainage were used, according to the depth of the mine and volume of water: crosscuts, bailing, Archimedean screws, and mine drainage wheels.

Numerous examples of crosscuts are found at Minas de Mouros (southeastern Spain), Madenokhorio (Thrace), Rio Tinto (Spain), and Dolaucothi (Wales). Pliny writes (*Natural History* 33.97) that bailing was employed in the mines at Baebelo, where "the tunneling had been carried a mile and a half [2.4 km] into the mountain. Along the whole of this distance watermen [*aquatini*] are posted who all day and night, in spells measured by lanterns, bail out the water and make a stream." Buckets were pointed so that they would tilt over for easy filling. Some were made of esparto grass rendered watertight by tar, others of copper.

Vitruvius (*On Architecture* 10.4.1) describes the basic construction of an Archimedean screw, the helix of which imitates a natural shell (Lat. *cochlea*, Gk. *kochlias*). A number of extant examples survive from Sotiel Coronada near Rio Tinto, Centenillo, and other sites in Spain. In addition an interesting terra-cotta from Alexandria shows such a screw being rotated by a slave treading cleats. The screw has a rotor shaft, with spiral blades attached (eight, according to Vitruvius), and is encased in a wooden cylinder bound by hoops and covered with pitch. Surviving examples appear to have been tilted at an angle of 15 degrees, although Vitruvius suggests 37 degrees as the optimum elevation for maximum efficiency. Estimates based on a screw of 1 foot (30 cm) diameter and just short of 8 feet (2.4 m) long suggest that a man could raise 2,375–3,170 gallons (9,000–12,000 l) per hour to a head of 4 1/4 feet (1.3 m), given a working efficiency of 60 percent. The output is directly related to the pitch of the blades and the elevation of the whole device. Archimedean screws were usually operated in rows, each one filling a tank which would in turn be emptied by the next.

Screws proved inadequate for use in deep mines and were replaced by mine drainage wheels which, although needing more manpower, spectacularly increased the height to which water could be raised. A typical drainage wheel surviving from Rio Tinto is 15 feet (4.6 m) in diameter, and entirely constructed of wood, the hubs and bearings of oak, the rest of pine: wooden dowels avoided problems with rust. The axle is square in section and made of bronze. Twenty-four spokes run alternately from each hub to the inside of the rim, which is hollow and rectangular in cross section. The openings through which the water was scooped up from the sump and discharged at the top of the circuit are on the side of the wheel and roughly quadrant-shaped, their straight edges being on the inner side and leading end of the compartment. Wheels were prefabricated and assembled underground. Assuming a working efficiency of 60 percent for the Archimedean screw, the output would have been about 1,320 gallons

(5,000 l) an hour. One of the most ambitious drainage schemes (Rio Tinto) involved a succession of eight pairs of wheels designed to raise the water almost 100 feet (30 m). Each wheel of a pair revolved in the opposite direction to avoid turbulence. Wear at the top of the treads shows that the wheels must have been operated like a treadmill, but the treads are so narrow—only 2 inches (5 cm) thick—that the operator must have suffered great discomfort.

Vitruvius (*On Architecture* 10.7.1) also describes Ctesibius' force pump. Although part of such a device was discovered in mine workings, it played no part in drainage.

MINING TOOLS AND EQUIPMENT. Mining tools showed little change in form throughout the Greek and Roman periods of antiquity. Hammers, picks, wedges, and iron gads continued in use. Pliny (*Natural History* 33.72) mentions also a "battering device" (*fractaria* or *malleus*) used in gold quartz mining: it carried 150 pounds (68 kg) of iron to give it more momentum. Miners wore sandals, caps of esparto grass, and, in one case at least, bronze helmets. A bas-relief unearthed near Linares shows a gang of miners complete with tools, possibly a bell, a container for oil, and a lamp. About his middle each wears what appears to be a protective apron over his tunic.

MINING TECHNIQUES. Pliny (*Natural History* 33.70–73) supplements Diodorus Siculus' account of mining techniques. He writes:

> The third method will have outdone the achievements of the Giants. By means of galleries driven for long distances the mountains are mined by the light of lamps—the spells of work are also measured by lamps, and the miners do not see daylight for many months. . . . Arches are left at frequent intervals to support the weight of the mountain above. . . . Masses of flint are encountered and are burst asunder by means of fire and vinegar

> [for quenching], although, as this method makes the tunnels suffocating through heat and smoke, they are more often broken to pieces with battering devices. . . . The men carry the stuff out on their shoulders, each man passing the ore on to the next man in the dark, while only those at the end of the line see daylight. . . . When the work is completely finished, beginning with the last they cut through, at the tops, the supports of the arched roofs. A crack gives warning of a crash and the only person who notices it is the lookout man on the top of the mountain. By shout and gesture he gives the order for the miners to be called out and at the same time flies down from his pinnacle. The fractured mountain falls asunder in a wide gap, with a crash which it is impossible for human imagination to conceive and with an incredibly violent blast of air.

Pliny's account seems to be a conflation of underground mining and a form of opencast.

HAULAGE. Underground the ore was carried in sacks or baskets, sometimes perhaps in bronze containers, as in Greek mines. The Romans also used wooden trays, reinforced with iron bands, which were dragged along the gallery floor to the base of the shaft. Drums from Rio Tinto and hubs from Ruda (Romania) show that windlasses were used to raise the ore to the surface.

ORE PROCESSING. Both Greeks and Romans used the same techniques to process the mined ore. The mining complex above ground included a processing plant (*ergasteria*) in which the metal-bearing part of the ore was separated from the accompanying waste material prior to smelting. The processes of such concentration, called collectively ore dressing, were purely physical, involving no chemical changes. The ore was broken up in mortars (*angeia lithina*) of very hard volcanic stone (Strabo, 10.5.16) and subsequently ground to the size of small grains of millet in mills (*myloi*) consisting of a cone-shaped central stone and an enclosing ring rotated by means of wooden handles. The grains were then passed through stone sieves (*salakes* or *koskinoi*) suspended by ropes to allow oscillation. The final process before smelting was the washing of the ore, which imitated the effect of rivers on alluvial material.

The separation of the metalliferous fraction from the untreated milled ore relied on the fact that grains of different density (weight) offer various degrees of resistance to a suitably regulated volume of water directed over them. The earliest application of this method was simple. The grains were shaken in sieves under water (jigging) and the lighter material remained in the sieve while the heavier passed through. As the demand for silver increased, however, a large-scale system of separation had to be devised. A typical washery (*plynterios*), "B" at Agrileza, consisted of a flat plastered floor or table, measuring 29 × 36 feet (9.45 × 11.45 m). This was surrounded by water channels that ran to two settling tanks. A long water tank at one end had a row of funnel-like holes (tuyères) in its wall facing the table, and a reservoir or cistern (*endocheion*) behind. The water in the cistern was released as needed into the intermediate tank and emerged through the funnel holes as powerful jets, falling forcefully onto the granulated ore spread out below in inclined serrated troughs. Slaves washed the ore by hand. Water was recycled from the settling tanks, and part of the washery was roofed to minimize water loss by evaporation.

Modern experiments show that at least a 63 percent concentration of the metal content was possible by this method. A further improvement was made by the introduction of helicoidal washeries, circular marble sluices with a diameter of approximately 20 feet (6 m). The rim had depressions which acted as riffles, with a difference in depth between the first and the last of 4–5 inches (10–12 cm), the whole forming an ellipsoid. The flow of water across the ore again provided an extremely effective means of gravity separation. As mentioned, these methods of ore dressing continued through Roman times. The Aljustrel Tables of the second century A.D., discussed below, record that ores were "freed" (*expedire*) in processing by pounding (*frangere*), hand sorting (*cernere*), and washing (*lavare*).

Greek and Roman Mine Administration

In Greece the state exercised considerable if not complete control of the mines, certainly from the time the third contact was reached at Laurium; this is confirmed by Aristophanes (*Wasps* 659). In the fourth century B.C. officials called *poletai* were responsible for auctioning mine contracts, and they generally supervised mining operations. Fragmentary mining lease lists are extant for the period 367–306 B.C. Mining rights were sold for twenty drachmas, but it is not certain whether this was a registration fee, rent, or one-time full payment. Leases probably ran for a seven-year period, except for mines already in production, which were limited to three years. The actual rent may have been two minas a year (100 drachmas = 1 mina). Xenophon (*Ways and Means* [*De Vectigalibus*] 4.49 f.) suggested that mines should be nationalized, and refers to the benefits that would accrue to the state from "investing" in mines—from revenues, local markets, and state-owned houses and furnaces.

In Ptolemaic Egypt mines had been de facto state property and this arrangement continued under the Romans. Under the republic mines were contracted out to tax farmers (*publicani*) to avoid the need for a large bureaucratic administration. In the newer provinces—Britain, Noricum, Dalmatia, Pannonia, and Dacia—the mines were left in charge of contractors (*conductores*), men of social standing (knights or freedmen), and occasionally were leased to private persons whose undertakings were checked and taxed by the *publicani*. Although mines like the Metalla Sallustianum and Livianum remained in private hands, the system changed under the principate and Augustus appointed procurators to administer the mines in Spain. State control culminated in a general order (*lex data*) of Vespasian that governed the exploitation of the mines. During the later empire the tendency to decentralization is evident in the *Lex Metalli Vipascensis,* an imperial ordinance covering working conditions in the mines of Vispasca (western Spain). Issued during Hadrian's reign (A.D. 117–138) and also known as the Aljustrel Tables after the name of the district, the ordinance covered all aspects of mining. Evidence relating to iron mines (*ferrariae*) throws light on general administrative arrangements. The procurator (*procurator metallorum*) was assisted by a number of subordinate officials, including an *assessor,* whose main role was the administration of justice in mining districts; a *iudex arcae ferrariarum,* who acted as an arbitrator in respect of state money; a *vilicus,* a general overseer who carried out the orders of the procurator; and an *actor ferrariarum,* who collected tolls.

LABOR FORCE. Greek miners (*metalleus* and *metalleutes* are interchangeable terms) were mainly slaves, owned by Athenian citizens and metics. The fee of one obol a day (*apophora*) that the slave earned was paid to his owner. Many Athenians had only a few slaves, but Nicias, the politician and general, and Hipponicus, a wealthy citizen, had 1,000 and 600, respectively. The Romans employed slaves, criminals, and, later, Christians as miners (*fossor* and *metallicus*). Freedmen (*mercenarii*) under labor contracts were also used, and as Tacitus (*Annals* 11.20) records, even soldiers on one occasion. That some slaves were chained is confirmed by

the evidence of a skeleton from Kamareza (Laurium) with its anklebone still fettered. At Rio Tinto there are blocks with rings attached. Miners were also forcibly transported to other regions and countries, as the Pirustae sent from southern Dalmatia (Albania) to Dacia.

WORKING CONDITIONS. Diodorus Siculus (3.12.3–13.3) describes the terrible working conditions of Nubian miners and his picture is true also for conditions prevailing in Roman mines, certainly until the second century A.D.:

> Those who are thus condemned [to work in the mines] being very numerous and all in fetters, are kept constantly at work without any repose, and are jealously guarded to prevent their escape; for they are watched by companies of foreign soldiers who speak a language different from theirs to prevent their winning over any of them by friendly intercourse, or appeals to their humanity. . . . Unkempt, untended as they are, without even a rag to hide their shame, the awful misery of these sufferers is a spectacle to move the hardest heart.

Above all the threat of a mining disaster was ever present. Statius (*Thebaid* 6.880–885) vividly likens the burial of a miner under a roof fall to the sudden crushing of a wrestler by his opponent. Skeletons of more than fifty entombed miners were discovered in ancient workings near Iconium (Konya, in Asia Minor). Poisonous fumes, hookworm infestations, mercury vapor (in the cinnabar mines), and suffocation added to the many causes of death.

By the time the Aljustrel Tables were formulated in the second century A.D., the nature of the labor force had changed. Skilled, freeborn miners, under contract, were increasingly employed in the mines to compensate for the shortfall of forced labor. The authorities were compelled by ordinance to make substantial efforts to improve the miners' lot. They now provided, for example, public baths with hot water throughout the year, and the services of cobblers, barbers, and clothes cleaners (fullers). Furthermore, education was encouraged by the exemption of schoolmasters from taxes when they taught in mining settlements.

QUARRIES

Unlike mining, quarrying was for the most part opencast. Occasionally, however, stone was obtained from galleries underground, as at Syracuse (limestone), on Paros (marble), and in Spain (selenite).

Greek Quarries: Materials and Sources

LIMESTONE. In the archaic period readily available limestone (*lithos porinos*), or local coarse-grained stone, was generally used in Greece and elsewhere, as extant sculpture and buildings confirm. The term *poros* was applied to both calcareous tufa and fossiliferous limestone and became a generic name for all soft, easily worked stone. Herodotus (5.62) observes that the front of the temple of Apollo at Delphi was of Parian marble, while the rest of the building was of tufa *poros,* which is abundant in the vicinity of Mount Parnassus. According to Pausanias (*Description of Greece* 5.10.2), the temple of Zeus at Olympia was built with the fossiliferous limestone *poros*. Soft stone was also suitable for sculptures at a time when the tools and techniques of wood carving were still being used. The most famous source of limestone in the ancient world was at Syracuse where, after the failure of the Athenian expedition in 413 B.C., 7,000 Athenians and their allies were imprisoned in the quarries, which were fully exploited under Hieron II (269–215 B.C.). There, one rock face was more than 88 feet (27 m) high and 6,560 feet (2,000 m) long, and it has been estimated that over 52 million cubic yards (40 million m³), or more than 112 million tons of stone, were extracted in antiquity.

MARBLE. The Greek term *marmaros* (Lat. *marmor*) was used to include not only types of marble but also granite, porphyry, and all stones capable of taking a high degree of polish. Marble was first used on a limited scale for Cycladic sculptures (third millennium B.C.), and before the fifth century B.C. it virtually replaced limestone. The main sources of marble were on Paros (Mount Marpessa) and Naxos, and in Attica (Mount Pentelicus [Pendelikon] with twenty-five quarries at Spilia, and Mount Hymettus). Marble was also quarried in the Peloponnesus at Doliana, near Tegea (Piali). Green marble (porphyry) is found at Croceae, near Gythium (Githion, in the Peloponnesus). To this list Theophrastus (*On Stones* [*De Lapidibus*] 6) adds Chios and Thebes (Egypt), although the latter source probably refers to granite (syenite) mixed at Aswan (ancient Syene). To some extent the different types of marble are distinguishable in appearance and petrographically. Parian marble is formed of large transparent crystals and has a glistening white surface; Naxian is gray. Pentelic is the only marble containing traces of iron, so that when its surface is exposed to the weather it gradually acquires a golden patina, as at the Parthenon. Hymettan marble is gray, or bluish gray, and of more recent geological formation. In the Hellenistic period Parian marble continued to be in demand and, after 166 B.C., Pentelic was exported from Athens. The taste for colored marble from Euboea and Thasos, and for serpentine from Tenos and Egypt, developed under the Romans.

GEOCHEMICAL IDENTIFICATION OF MARBLE AND MARBLE SOURCES. The problem of identifying marbles of Greek, Anatolian (Asia Minor), and Italian origin is extremely complex. Visual identification, based on macroscopical examination of color, brightness, grain, and other physical characteristics, can be far from conclusive. Geochemical analysis, however, provides additional, absolute evidence. Minor and trace elements (iron, manganese, and strontium) allow marbles from Ephesus, Proconnesus (Marmara island), and Luna (Luni, Carrara) to be distinguished. Sodium and manganese content separates certain Anatolian marbles from Attic. Analysis based on the isotopic ratios of carbon ($^{13}C/^{12}C$) and oxygen ($^{18}O/^{16}O$) help to identify marbles from quarries in Asia Minor, at Marmara, Aphrodisias (Geyre), and perhaps Acroinum (near modern Afyonkarahisar). It is also possible to characterize Pentelic and Proconnesian marble. The evidence of calcium/strontium ratios is limited, but Ephesian marble (or Docimean, after Docimeium [Esçekarahisar] in Phrygia) can be isolated from other types. The combination, therefore, of the evidence of petrology and geochemical data examined in the light of their historical and archaeological contexts may well be able to provide characteristic "prints" of the main types of marble and their sources.

Roman Quarries: Materials and Sources

The main sources of stone are recorded by Strabo, Vitruvius, Pliny, and Pausanias.

TRAVERTINE. Calcareous limestone (travertine) was the earliest stone employed in Rome for building. The ancient walls of the city were constructed of this stone, and travertine can be seen in situ on the Tarpeian rock, a formation nearly 500 feet (150 m) thick. Limestone continued to be quarried well into imperial times, the most extensive workings being near Tibur (Tivoli), described by Strabo (5.3.11). The white color of travertine is admirably suited for imitating Greek marble, and it acquires a brownish patina when weathered.

TUFA AND PEPERINO. Varieties of soft stone were found near Rome, especially in the neighborhoods of Fidenae and Mount Alba; these include calcareous tufa and a grayish brown tufa (*lapis Albanus*). Peperino, a light porous volcanic rock basically of sand

and cinders, was used by Roman builders and sculptors. Strabo (5.3.11) refers to *lapis Gabinus,* the stone of the Gabii (Castiglione), also of volcanic origin.

BASALT. Hard, durable basaltic rock (*silex*) was employed for paving roads as Livy (41.27.5) records. It was hewn in polygonal pieces that were fitted together with great accuracy. The sewers (*cloacae*) in Rome were also constructed of basalt. Although the main variety is black, Pliny (*Natural History* 36.168) states that a white variety was also produced in quarries round the lake to the south of Volsinii (Lake Bolsena).

MARBLE. The prohibitive cost of marble meant that Roman buildings were only faced with marble slabs. Marble was also used for decorative purposes during the empire, especially in houses. The quarries near Luna are first described by Strabo (5.2.5), who wrote: "The quarries of marble, both white and mottled and bluish gray, are so numerous and of such a quality, yielding monolithic slabs and columns, that they supply the material for most of the superior works of art in Rome and the rest of the cities likewise." The quarries were extensively worked from 100 B.C. onward, especially during the principate of Augustus. Tibullus (2.3.43–45) observes that the streets of Rome were crowded with wagons loaded with marble, and Pliny, commenting on the inordinate desire for marble shown by the Romans (*Natural History* 36.2 ff.), complains about the environmental consequences of quarrying: "Mountains were made by nature herself to serve as a kind of framework for holding firmly together the inner parts of the earth. . . . We quarry them and haul them away for a mere whim." Pliny (*Natural History* 36.125) repeats a commonly held belief in the ancient world "that marble actually grows in quarries; and the quarrymen [*extempores*] moreover assert that the scars on the mountain sides fill up of their own accord."

ROMAN SOURCES OF STONE OUTSIDE ITALY. Under the empire the provinces were ransacked in the search for rare stones, and many quarries passed into imperial control under an assessment of dues payable to the state (*ratio marmorum*). A storehouse of foreign marble has been discovered by the Tiber. Many of the quarries served local needs, but stone was exported from Athens, from the Greek islands, Egypt, and Asia Minor. Pliny (*Natural History* 36 *passim*) lists the main varieties of marble, which include: Lucullean; Hymettan (sometimes called *lapis lychnites*), quarried in underground galleries; Carrara, claimed to be whiter than Parian; Thasian; Chian; Carystan; Numidian, a yellow marble with red veins; and Augustan and Tiberian, although these may be types of granite. Quarries at Heliopolis (Baalbek, in Lebanon) were intensively worked under Antoninus Pius (A.D. 138–161). Green Lacedemonian (Spartan) marble, listed by Pliny (*Natural History* 36.55), is probably porphyry. Limestone was employed in Belgic Gaul, Egypt, and Britain. In the latter province Bath stone (oolite), tufa, and slate were common.

Pliny (*Natural History* 36.160) later discusses selenite (*lapis specularis*), which "in Hither Spain is dug at a great depth by means of shafts but is also found just beneath the surface enclosed in rock." Selenite likewise occurred in Cyprus, Cappadocia (less transparent), and Sicily. Different varieties of porphyry, a much sought-after stone, were quarried in Egypt between Asyut and the Red Sea, where there were also quarries of hornblende granite on Mons Claudianus: exploitation of these probably began under Emperor Claudius (A.D. 41–54).

Greek and Roman Quarrying Techniques

Literary references to quarrying techniques are limited, but they may be supplemented by the evidence of unfinished blocks and ancient buildings. The Greeks and the Romans quarried stone in rectangular blocks, and regular chisel marks in horizontal rows on them show that ancient quarrymen first ran a groove round each block with a chisel and then forced it out with wooden wedges, which, after insertion, were saturated with water. Iron wedges were used for basalt, and fire to split stone (calcareous tufa) from Tusculum (Latium). The roughly dressed blocks were approximately the size needed for their subsequent use. Further evidence comes from a granite quarry in the Odenwald (southwest Germany), where blocks at all stages of preparation still remain on the slopes. These show horizontal rows of holes, the distance apart determined by the type of stone being worked. An altar stone shows deep incisions accurately cut with a saw to indicate the intention to split this into smaller blocks.

The preparation of thin sections or slabs of stone was achieved in two ways. In selenite, the cleavage habit of the mineral was utilized and, as Pliny (*Natural History* 36.160) states, it was "split into plates as thin as might be wished." More often stone was cut by sawing either by a conventional saw (*dentata serra*) or, more commonly, by a wire of high tensile strength used in conjunction with sand. Pliny (*Natural History* 36.51) describes the latter: "The cutting of marble is effected apparently not by iron but by sand for the 'saw' merely presses the sand upon a very thinly traced line and then the passage of the instrument, owing to the rapid movement to and fro, is in itself enough to cut the stone." In modern practice a wire rope and sand are still used. Pliny (*Natural History* 36.52) further explains that "the Ethiopian variety of this sand is the most highly esteemed. . . . It cuts without leaving any roughness [burring]." Ausonius (*Mosella* 362–364) vividly describes saws driven shrieking through smooth blocks of marble, and by the fourth century A.D. waterpower was used to drive the saws. The idea of cutting marble into slabs is said to have originated in Caria (southwestern Asia Minor), and Pliny (*Natural History* 36.47) writes that "the earliest example that I can discover is that of the palace of Mausolus of Halicarnassus, the brick walls of which were decorated with white marble from the island of Proconnesus [Marmara]."

In Italy Carrara marble was commonly sawn into thin slabs and used as a veneer for decorative purposes. Pliny (*Natural History* 36.48) writes: "The first man in Rome to cover with marble veneer whole walls in his house, which was on the Caelian Hill, was, according to Cornelius Nepos, Mamurra, a Roman knight. . . . Gaius [Julius] Caesar's chief engineer in Gaul." Characteristically he adds (36.51), "Whoever first discovered how to cut marble and carve up luxury into many portions was a man of misplaced ingenuity."

BIBLIOGRAPHY

SOURCES

The following works, published in the Loeb Classical Library series, are of particular interest: Aristotle, *Meteorologica*, H. D. P. Lee, trans. (1952); Diodorus Siculus, *Library of History* C. H. Oldfather *et al.*, trans., 12 vols. (1933–1967); Pausanias, *Description of Greece* (*Periegesis tes Hellados*), W. H. S. Jones and R. E. Wycherley, trans., 5 vols. (1918–1935; v. 5 rev. ed. 1955); Pliny the Elder, *Natural History*, H. Rackham *et al.*, trans., 10 vols. (1938–1963); Strabo, *Geography*, Horace L. Jones, trans., 8 vols. (1917–1932); Vitruvius, *On Architecture* (*De Architectura*), Frank Granger, trans., 2 vols. (1931–1934); Xenophon, *De Vectigalibus* (*Ways and Means*), Edgar C. Marchant, trans. (1925; repr. 1956).

Editions with Commentary

C. Plinius Secundus (Pliny the Elder), *Natural History*, Hubert Zehnacker, trans. (into French) (1983); Theophrastus, *De Lapidibus* (*On Stones*), D. E. Eichholz, trans. (1965), and *On Stones*, Earle R. Caley and John F. C. Richards, trans. (1956).

STUDIES

Mining: General Works

Oliver Davies, *Roman Mines in Europe* (1935); John F. Healy, *Mining and Metallurgy in the Greek and Roman World* (1978); Jacques Ramin, *La technique minière et métallurgique des anciens*, Collection Latomus (1977); Peter Rosumek, *Technischer Fortschritt und Rationalisierung im antiken Bergbau* (1982).

Mining Sites

Edouard Ardillon, *Les Mines de Laurion dans l'antiquité* (1897); Constantin E. Conophagos, *Le Laurium antique et la technique grecque de la production de l'argent* (1980); G. Heinrich, "Ein Besuch der Silbergruben des Herodot auf Siphnos, Kykladen," in *Der Aufschluss*, **32** (1981); Hansjörg Kalcyk, *Untersuchungen zum attischen Silberbergbau: Gebietsstrucktur Geschichte und Technik* (1982), and "Bergbaugeschichtliche und geologische Notizen zur Insel Thasos/Griechenland," in *Der Aufschluss*, **34** (1983); H. Mussche, "Thorikos in Archaic and Classical Times," in *Miscellanea Graeca*, fasc. 1 (1975); Gunther A. Wagner and Gerd Weisgerber, *Silber, Blei und Gold auf Sifnos: Prähistorische und antike Metallproduktion*, Bochum, No. 31 (1985).

Roman Mining

Jose Maria Blásquez, *Explotaciones mineras en Hispania durante la república y el altro imperio romano* (1969); G. D. B. Jones, "The Roman Mines at Rio Tinto," in *Journal of Roman Studies*, **70** (1980); R. F. J. Jones and D. G. Bird, "Roman Gold-mining in Northwest Spain, II: Workings on the Rio Duerna," in *Journal of Roman Studies*, **62** (1972); P. R. Lewis and G. D. B. Jones, "Roman Gold-mining in Northwest Spain," in *Journal of Roman Studies*, **60** (1970).

Mining: Special Studies

John F. Healy, "Mining and Processing Gold Ores in the Ancient World," *Journal of Metals,* **31** (1979); Robert J. Hopper, *Trade and Industry in Classical Greece* (1979); Franz Kiechle, *Sklavenarbeit und technischer Fortschritt im römischen Reich* (1969); J. G. Landels, *Engineering in the Ancient World* (1978); Siegfried Lauffer, *Die Bergwerkssklaven von Laureion,* 2d ed. (1979); Helmut Wilsdorf, *Bergleute und Hüttenmännern im Altertum bis zum Ausgang der römischen Republik* (1952).

Quarries: General Works

Marion E. Blake, *Ancient Roman Construction in Italy from the Prehistoric Period to Augustus* (1947); Angelina Dworakowska, *Quarries in Ancient Greece,* Krystyna Kozlawska, trans. (1975); Robert J. Forbes, *Studies in Ancient Technology,* VII (1963); Roland Martin, *Manuel d'architecture grecque, 1: Matériaux et techniques* (1965).

Mineralogy

John F. Healy, "Problems in Mineralogy and Metallurgy in Pliny the Elder's *Natural History,*" in *Technologica economia e società nel mondo romano,* Atti del Convegna di Como (1980), and "Pliny the Elder and Ancient Mineralogy," in *Interdisciplinary Science Reviews,* **6** (1981).

Geochemical Analysis

The following articles deal with identification of Greek, Anatolian, and Italian marbles and their sources: M. Coleman and S. Walker, on stable isotope analysis, in *Archaeometry,* **21** (1979); L. Conforto *et al.,* on trace element analysis, including Fe, Mn, Sr, and insoluble residues, in *Archaeometry,* **17** (1975); L. Lazzarini *et al.,* on Ca/Sr ratios, in *Archaeometry,* **22** (1980); L. Manfra *et al.,* on carbon and oxygen isotope ratios, in *Archaeometery,* **17** (1975).

Greek Taxation

ROBERT J. LITTMAN

THE FORM OF GOVERNMENT and the economic structure of society determine the nature of a tax system. Aristotle wrote, "It is manifest that the state is one of the things that exist by nature, and that man is by nature a political animal." He meant by this that it is man's nature to live in a polis, an organized political community. The state, even on the most primitive levels, is a center of public finance. It needs money and services from its citizens to perform its functions. The more complex the state, the greater the size of its bureaucracy and the level of its public services, and hence the greater requirements for income. That is not to say an absolute correlation exists between complexity and public expenditures. Political philosophy can influence public spending. For example, twentieth-century Britain, a country steeped in socialist philosophy, taxes its citizens more heavily than the United States and concomitantly expends a greater percentage of its gross national product on direct social services. In general, the more sophisticated the society, the greater the public expenditures and the more complex and greater the taxation. A preindustrial state thus will have neither the degree of public expenditures nor the level of taxation of a postindustrial state.

The nature of public finance, and taxation as an integral part of it, changed rapidly in the late eighteenth and early nineteenth centuries. The wars of the French revolutionary period and the consequent need for increased revenue contributed to the introduction of a general income tax in Great Britain (in 1798, 1802, 1803, and 1806). This tax was not a departure in principle from older taxes, but only in method. For example, the tax act of 1803 in Britain had two aspects: a tax on all gross income from real estate, rents, and public salaries withheld at source, that is, before it passed into the hands of recipients; and a tax on industrial earnings and interest on capital (with the first £60 exempt). The Industrial Revolution intensified these trends and brought a great change to the nature of public finance with the rapid increase of wealth and the growth of new forms of wealth among the different classes in the community. Taxes that had been well suited to a simpler, more agricultural society became under these new conditions unjust and gave rise to dissatisfaction. Because land no longer was the chief measure of wealth, as it had been in most of human history, a system of taxation geared to land ownership would not fall equitably on all parts of the society.

Adam Smith probably best expressed the premodern philosophy of taxation in *The Wealth of Nations,* written in the eighteenth century and published in 1776. He promulgated four general maxims, on equality, certainty, convenience, and economy:

(1) The subjects of every state ought to contribute towards the support of the government, as nearly as possible, in proportion to their respective abilities; that is, in proportion to the revenue which they respectively enjoy under the protection of the state.

(2) The tax which each individual is bound to pay ought to be certain, and not arbitrary. The time of payment, the manner of payment, the quantity to be paid, ought all to be clear and plain to the contributor and every other person.

(3) Every tax ought to be levied at the time or in the manner in which it is most likely to be convenient for the contributor to pay it.

(4) Every tax ought to be so contrived as both to take out and keep out of the pockets of the people as little as possible, over and above what it brings into the public treasury of the state.

Taxation in pre-twentieth-century times had as its purpose the raising of revenue to allow the state to meet its public expenditures. While in the twentieth century this has remained a major aim of taxation, two other purposes, almost equal in importance, have arisen. Taxation is seen as a vehicle to regulate and guide the economic system of society and to shape its social structure.

EARLY GREEK WORLD

Taxation, like poverty, has always been with us, even in premonetary societies. Western history begins in the valley formed by the Tigris and Euphrates rivers, in the third millennium B.C. Taxation was an integral part of the societies that flourished there. Ancient Greek society was no different. The history of ancient Greece is divided into several main periods: the Mycenaean, the Homeric age, the archaic, the classical, and the Hellenistic. The Mycenaean world consisted of small kingdoms, centralized and bureaucratic in nature and similar to the political organizations of the Near East. Taxes in the form of tribute and forced labor existed. After the collapse of the Mycenaean world in the twelfth century B.C., a society along feudal lines developed, as reflected in the poems of Homer, the *Iliad* and the *Odyssey.* These works, the only literary documents for Greek history between the twelfth and eighth centuries, describe many events that date from the Mycenaean world. The works themselves, which in their final form belong to the eighth century ·B.C., may contain Mycenaean material, but also many elements of the ninth and eighth centuries. Homer's poems thus probably describe a world between the Mycenaean and his own eighth-century society, with details of both but being true to neither. Consequently, they provide only a glimmer of what taxation was like in the period between the twelfth and the eighth centuries.

In feudal societies such as that of Homeric Greece, governmental functions were in the hands of officials who owned land. Commerce and industry, as yet underdeveloped, required that the people make public contributions in products and services, which could be commanded without remuneration. The primary public duties involved the organization and leadership of military operations and the administration of justice. Society was organized along kinship lines, and the kinship groups constituted the political and judicial structures. Extensive public finance was not necessary. Warfare was conducted by members of kinship groups who were not paid by the state but who contributed services. The state religious worship was in the hands of clans who supplied products and services. Since Homeric society was premonetary, other media of exchange were found. One method was the exchange of gifts. The heroes in the *Odyssey* entertain guests, giving them presents (weapons made of metals and precious objects) and they expect a return either in services or goods.

ARCHAIC AND CLASSICAL GREECE

The archaic and classical periods of Greece between the eighth and fourth centuries B.C. saw the efflorescence of the polis, the Greek city-state, and the development of the state's fiscal role. The polis grew out of kinship groups descended from a common male ancestor and tied to that ancestor's home territory—a patrilineal, patrilocal grouping common to people speaking Indo-European languages. The kin groups— the tribe, phratry, clan, and family (*oikos*) required contributions from their members for corporate functions. These might consist of military labor in times of war, contributions of food or materials, or labor to maintain the group's religious shrines. Another factor, very important in the growth of taxation, was the invention and widespread adoption of coinage. Coinage originated in the late seventh century B.C. and in the sixth century spread swiftly throughout the Greek world. The increased economic sophistication of society, the development of a fiscal role by the state, the financing of mercenary armies, and the growth of trade and commerce were stimulated by and stimulated the use of coinage. When a central power developed that was required to provide public services and concomitantly to raise revenue, we have the elements of taxation as we know it.

Although some tyrants of Greek cities occasionally levied extensive taxes on the citizenry for payment of mercenaries in the sixth century, public expenditures were small before the Persian Wars at the beginning of the fifth century. At Athens, for example, public offices were unpaid, as were soldiers. Liturgies, a class of voluntary contributions (see below), supplied money for ships and other services. The state had only to supply daily expenses of administration, a few public works, rewards for the destruction of wolves (a law ascribed to Solon), gifts for poets and physicians, and offerings and sacrifices to local or Panhellenic divinities.

As Greek city-states progressed from the archaic to the classical period, from rural agricultural societies with few public institutions requiring state expenditures to a mixed economy of trade, commerce, and agriculture, their needs for revenues multiplied.

Since data are much more extensive for classical Athens than any other Greek state, this city-state may serve as a paradigm, however imperfect, for taxation in the classical period. Taxation was the primary vehicle for Greek cities to raise money. Other sources existed, but they were less regular and generally smaller in scale, and they varied from state to state. These included tribute and income from state properties. Although Athens owned the silver mines at Laurium, most states did not have mining interests. Xenophon (*On Taxation* [*Vectigalia*]) observed, "To none of the many cities that are situated nearby does even a small vein of silver reach." Beyond Athens, the islands of Siphnos and Thasos had gold and silver mines that were state-owned. The city-state might own rural and urban property, houses, colonnades, pastures, olive orchards, and slaves. These sources produced minimal revenues, and thus it was only through an extensive system of taxation that the state could meet its financial needs.

797

Public Expenditures

Before discussing Athens' system of taxation, it is useful to survey where the money went. Public expenditures were made generally in three areas: for internal security and external defense, for internal administration, and for grain distributions to the people. Fifth-century Athenian streets were patrolled by an assortment of police groups that were paid by the state—city police, rural police, forest wardens, market police, overseers of weights and measures, and grain wardens. The large number of city police was particularly conspicuous. Dressed in outlandish foreign garb, carrying odd-looking curved bows, these public slaves, mostly from Scythia (southern Russia), kept order in the law courts and assemblies. At first they numbered about 300, but by the late fifth and early fourth century 1,000 are said to have kept the peace, with a budget of approximately forty talents. The budget for internal administration covered religious sacrifices and public works such as temples, monuments, and building programs. Grain was distributed to citizens below cost.

Salaries were another major category of expense. Several thousand men were paid to participate in the senate, the law courts, and the assembly. Senators were given either five obols or a drachma a day. Pericles instituted pay for dicasts (judges or jurors), either one or two obols a day. In the fourth century assembly members were also paid. Thus, from the mid fifth to early fourth century Athens moved from unpaid public service to almost universal pay for all offices. However, by comparison to some modern states where as much as 20 to 40 percent of the work force might be employed by local, regional, or national governments, the Athenian state employed a minuscule number of workers.

Athens spent large sums on military needs, including such fortifications as the Long Walls that were built from the city to Piraeus. They were financed largely from Persian spoils and voluntary contributions. Other forts and fortifications throughout Attica, including Sunium, Eleusis, and Phyle, were built and maintained by regular revenues. Before the time of Pericles, citizens paid for their own military equipment. The state assumed the costs of land fortifications, and also certain naval expenses, including the maintenance of docks and the building of triremes. Up to 440 B.C. Athens paid for her wars from current income, which included tribute from her allies.

During Pericles' rule, and especially after his death (429 B.C.), military expenditures, as well as public programs, increased. In peacetime the city maintained 1,600 archers, 1,200 cavalry, and 500 guards of the docks, who cost the state about 300 talents per annum. In wartime expenses escalated. The siege of Samos, led by Pericles in 440/439 B.C., cost 2,000–2,400 talents. Estimates on the expenditure for the Peloponnesian War (431–404 B.C.) vary from 35,000 to 47,000 talents. Toward the end of the fifth century pay for citizen soldiers was introduced, and a proliferation of mercenaries added to the military expenditures of the city-states.

Taxation as Revenue

As public services and expenditures mushroomed in the fifth century, Athens sought more diverse and widespread means of raising revenue to meet increased expenses. Various sources were available, such as income from state property, including slaves and silver mines. Law courts were another source, providing forfeited deposits by litigants in public trials, fines, and confiscations of property for crimes. Yet another irregular source of revenue was warfare. Tribute from members of the Delian League provided Athens with enormous sums in the fifth century, financing the building of the

Parthenon and other civic works under Pericles' building program and creating urban prosperity. The city treasury stood at 6,000 talents at the outbreak of the Peloponnesian War in 431 B.C.

However, the most dependable and certain source of revenue for the city—and for Greek cities in general—was taxation. Direct taxation on citizens and regular taxes on citizens' property were regarded as degrading for a city-state, although the tyrants Pisistratus, Hippias, and Hipparchus in the sixth century levied taxes on citizens in several forms. However, direct taxation of noncitizens was a common practice. Metics (free foreign residents) were subject to a head tax called *metoikion,* which amounted to twelve drachmas for men and six for women without a working husband or son. Failure to pay resulted in enslavement. Although metics were principally responsible for the commerce of Athens, they were barred from owning land. Consequently, they had to purchase all their food and goods—on which there was a market tax—while most Athenians tended to work small farms and thus grew or manufactured for themselves most of their needs. They might purchase luxury items and certain necessities at the market and pay market taxes on these items, but these items represented only a small part of their consumption. Consequently, the market tax fell disproportionately on the metics. This, in addition to the head tax, meant that the metics contributed a larger share of the Athenian revenue than either their wealth or numbers would warrant in a society with an egalitarian tax base.

Indirect taxation was divided into two major categories, customs duties and excise taxes. In the Homeric period gifts were given to kings as the price for permission to trade—a forerunner of customs duties. Harbor fees and tolls for crossing water or land were common during all periods. At Corinth tolls were charged on goods transferred across the isthmus. Athenians levied taxes on wares that passed from the (Thracian) Bosporus to the Aegean. In the fifth century Athens imposed a tax of 1 percent on exports and imports, later raising it to 2 percent at the end of the century. These taxes were applied to slaves also. When a wealthy traveler or merchant, even a member of the Athenian empire, came to Athens, he paid an import duty on all property he brought with him, even personal slaves, and upon leaving paid an export duty. At times of financial emergencies these taxes could be raised dramatically. From 410–406 B.C., for example, during severe war years for Athens, a 10 percent duty was levied on all produce brought from the area of the Black Sea. At another time of financial and political crisis in 413 B.C. Athens abolished the tribute imposed on her allies, replacing it with a 5 percent tax on all trade in the harbors of the Athenian empire. These customs duties fell indiscriminately on Athenians, metics, and foreign tradesmen. Their purpose was to raise revenue, not to regulate the economy or to protect local industries. Protective taxation appeared only later, and in only a few instances during the Hellenistic period.

Excise duties, called *eponia,* provided another major source of tax revenue. These were equivalent to modern sales taxes but on a much smaller scale. Not every commercial transaction was taxed; the *eponia* fell primarily on sales that occurred in the agora, Athens' trading center at the foot of the Acropolis. Most goods sold there were taxed, as were those sold by foreigners and even goods belonging to and sold by the city. The amount of the *eponia* was not fixed. For example, the tax on eels differed from that on fish. The general level was fixed at around 1 percent, but many goods were taxed at a higher rate. Articles of prime necessity may have been systematically taxed less heavily; honey, for example, was taxed at a higher rate than barley. *Eponia* were also collected on the auction of contracts, offices in the assembly, and confiscations. Evidence exists of *eponia* in other states, such as Erythrae (Ildırı) in Ionia, where they varied from 2 to 5 percent. Other taxes in various Greek cities included gate tolls, taxes on foreigners to trade in the agora, and taxes on anchorage, rights of unloading, and fishing rights. Even common commercial activities such as prostitution were taxed. Brothel-keepers paid a special excise tax called *pornikos telos.* Its purpose was not to discourage prostitution, but to raise revenue. These indirect taxes fell equally on all residents of Athens engaged in commercial transactions, whether they were metics, foreigners, poor, or rich.

"Eisphora," Liturgy, and "Epidoseis"

Although direct taxation for citizens, such as income, head, and wealth taxes—as opposed to taxes on transactions—was frowned upon, it did exist in some cases, particularly as greater revenue was required for Athens in the late fifth century when public expenses increased and tribute from the Delian League no longer met Athens' financial needs. After the overthrow of the tyrants, occasional direct taxation took two forms, the *eisphora* and the liturgy. The latter was a popular tax, paid willingly with civic pride, although the *eisphora* was considered oppressive. The *eisphora* was an extraordinary direct tax, levied in times of emergencies, such as wars, when the state could find no other way to meet expenses. It was tax on wealth, which included movable wealth and real property. This system originated in the fifth century B.C. After the defeat of Persia in 480, which resulted in acquisition of booty, and the formation of the Delian League, which entailed military and economic contributions paid by its members to Athens, Athens had no need for special taxes. But in 428/427 B.C. a financial crisis resulted from

the Peloponnesian War and the revolt of Lesbos. To meet it the state resorted to an *eisphora* amounting to a total of 200 talents. To pay it, the three highest classes of citizens, the *pentakosiomedimnoi,* the *hippeis,* and the *zeugitai,* were divided into one hundred tax groups, known as *symmoriai,* and assessed 166 2/3 talents. The balance, 33 1/3 talents, was paid by the metics. The lowest class of citizens, *thetes,* were exempted. The *zeugitai,* largest in number, had to pay only 16 2/3 talents, while 50 talents were paid by the *hippeis* and 100 by the *pentakosiomedimnoi.*

The *eisphora* continued into the fourth century and was intermittently imposed, usually during wars. In 400 B.C. it was levied during peacetime to pay the public debts that had arisen from the civil war between the Thirty Tyrants and the democrats of Piraeus. In 378/377 B.C. the *eisphora* was reformed and a new regressive system was introduced with a fixed rate applied to all citizens except the lowest citizen class, who seem to have been exempted. The *eisphora* was levied again in the 370s, with a new method of collection, called the *proeisphora,* that forced the wealthy to aid in tax collection. In 373/372 B.C., 300 of the wealthiest Athenians were required to give the treasury the full amount of the *eisphora,* and were made responsible for collecting money from individual taxpayers. If they failed to collect the full amount, they had to absorb the difference themselves. The demes named the 300 on each occasion, but after about 340 B.C., the 300 became a standing college. Fifty of the 300 appear to have been metics. The last major *eisphora* of the fourth century was levied in 335 B.C. when Athens revolted against Macedon after Philip II's death. *Eisphorai* were imposed during succeeding centuries, but details of the system in later periods are unknown.

Although the *eisphora* was a direct but irregular tax, the institution known as the liturgy was a more regular direct means of raising revenue for the state. In one sense, however, it was not a tax. The essence of any tax is its compulsory nature and originally the liturgy apparently was voluntary. However, by the late fifth and early fourth centuries, it assumed a compulsory quality. The liturgy was practiced in most of Greece and is attested, among other places, in Athens, Byzantium, Siphnos, Aegina, Mitylene, and Thebes.

The liturgy made private individuals responsible for bearing the costs of certain public functions. These functions included the *choregia* (the production of a chorus at dramatic festivals), the *hestiasis* (the provision of a banquet for a tribe at festivals), the *architheoria* (the leadership of a state group to foreign festivals), and the *hippotrophia* (the maintenance of a horse for military purposes). The liturgies, often of religious origin, were taken on from a sense of honor or duty to the kin group or to the state. Aristotle (*Nicomachean Ethics* 4.2.11) writes:

> Magnificence involves expenditures which we call honorable, e.g., expenditures on the worship of the gods—votive offerings, buildings, and sacrifices—and similarly on the various forms of worshiping the lesser divinities, and on public enterprises which people ambitiously vie with one another to undertake, as, for example, when they think they should equip a chorus or a trireme or give a feast for the city in a brilliant fashion.

Rich citizens assumed these obligations and took pride in them. Political figures such as Alcibiades assumed liturgies in order to increase their favor with the populace. Individuals often spent excessive sums on these functions. Writes Aristotle (*Politics* 5.8.20): "In democracies it is necessary to spare the wealthy. . . . It is better to prevent wealthy citizens, even those who are willing, from performing expensive but useless liturgies, such as *choregiai*, *lampadarchiai* [the pro-

duction of torchlight processions], and the like."

Liturgies fell into two main classes, regular and extraordinary. The regular, which occurred at fixed times during the year, included entertainments for state guests—*choregiai* and *gymnasiarchiai* (maintenance and training costs of contestants in the torch races)—and religious embassies. The extraordinary liturgies, such as the *proeisphora* and trierarchies, were levied on an ad hoc basis and often required anticipatory payments. Liturgies were assigned in various ways. The *archon eponymos* would choose an individual for the *choregia* for tragedy and comedy at the Dionysiac festival, while the ten tribes would select the person responsible for the dithyramb.

The *choregia* was the major regular liturgy. Those chosen to undertake it were obligated to form a chorus for dramatic, musical, or orchestral contests held at various times in the year. They were compelled to meet the expense of costumes and masks, to pay members of the chorus and its leader, and to provide food and shelter for the chorus during the training period. Choruses varied in size and in expense. The *choregia* for flute players was the most costly, followed by tragedies, comedies, and dance contests. The expense varied from 300 to 5,000 drachmas. By the end of the fifth century *choregiai* had grown so expensive that no one person could afford them, and the institution of the *synchoregia*, or dividing the obligation among several individuals, arose.

The trierarchy was the most burdensome nonregular liturgy. Its origin probably dates to the fifth century. A trierarchy involved the maintenance of a ship and its rigging. The state provided the trireme and the rigging. The trierarch advanced money for the crew's salaries and for rations—expenses for which he would theoretically be repaid by the state—and supplied the *epiphora*, additional pay given annually to the crew. Trierarchs usually spent forty to sixty minia (4,000 to 6,000 drachmas). In recognition of the costs incurred, trierarchs were excused from other liturgies and were not required to undertake a second trierarchy until a fixed period of time had elapsed.

Since liturgies were theoretically levied only on the wealthiest citizens, a person who believed that he was inequitably selected could pick another individual whom he considered wealthier and challenge him through a court action called *antidosis,* either to undertake the liturgy or to exchange property with him. If the person challenged was in fact poorer, he could opt to exchange property; if he were wealthier, then the liturgy should by rights belong to him. Despite this remedy, the liturgy did not fall on all men of wealth in a systematic pattern, and there were many inequities.

Although the liturgies were imposed at irregular intervals on a very small number of people and affected only the wealthiest citizens, they were still numerous. By the fourth century over a hundred regular civil and religious liturgies existed. The civic honor attached to the institution, particularly in the fifth century, made it a relatively popular form of irregular taxation, both among those on whom the costs fell and among the general populace who enjoyed the entertainments.

The *epidoseis*, a voluntary contribution to the state, especially in wartime, was another source of revenue. *Epidoseis* usually followed a decree of the assembly appealing to the populace for funds to provide arms, ships, grain, or public sacrifices, or to repair theaters. Wealthy citizens considered it their duty to contribute. Although the voluntary nature of these public contributions prevailed in the fifth century, the institution of *epidoseis* was formalized in the fourth and became virtually compulsory. Although such contributions cannot be considered a tax, they nonetheless served to complement revenues yielded by regular taxes and to reduce somewhat the necessity for others.

Tax Collection

The ancient world lacked the large bureaucracies that typify modern states, and an efficacious way to collect taxes without the use of state employees was to farm out the job. Public auctions were held, and contracts for collecting taxes were leased to the highest bidder. The amount received for the contract represented the state's total revenues from that lease. The state set the taxes as a fixed fee or a percentage of the value of the transaction. The tax contractor or farmer could not change the tax rate. He kept whatever he collected, and everything above the cost of the contract and his expenses was profit. The various taxes were leased out separately. One tax farmer might secure the rights to the harbor-use fees, another to the "fiftieth," the tax on imports. When revenues were extremely large, as in the case of the fiftieth in Athens, syndicates were formed to buy the contract.

The advantage of tax farming for the state was that it allowed a steady return without the necessity of involving the state in collection. To prevent default on the part of tax farmers, the state required that they provide sureties, and if they failed to pay the sums contracted they were liable to loss of citizenship. Another advantage was that the hostility of the population to taxes was directed toward tax farmers rather than toward the government. In the fifth century B.C. at Athens, Andocides (*On the Mysteries* [*De Mysteriis*] 133) comments that "This Agyrrhius . . . was a farmer-in-chief of fiftieths, . . . and you know what sort of men they are!"

The powers of tax farmers were considerable. They even had the ability to bring delinquents to court. Diogenes Laertius (6.16) records that the father of the philosopher Bion (fourth century B.C.) "having fallen victim to a tax farmer, was sold with all his household." Josephus (*Jewish Antiquities* [*Antiquitates Judaicae*] 12.4) reports that the tax farmers in Ptolemaic Egypt had the power of life and death over taxpayers. Despite abuses by greedy contractors, the institution of tax farming generally worked successfully. It accomplished its tasks and minimized government bureaucracy.

TAXATION IN THE HELLENISTIC WORLD

The defeat of Greece by Philip II of Macedon and the conquest of the Persian Empire by his son Alexander the Great at the end of the fourth century B.C. greatly altered the eastern Mediterranean world. The major difference in taxation between the Hellenistic and classical worlds arose out of their different political structures, namely empire and city-state, respectively. In addition, the Seleucid and Ptolemaic empires, ruled by Alexander's successors, retained many features of the earlier political, fiscal, and economic structures of the Persian Empire.

The contrasts between empire and city-state generally are as follows:

1. Revenues from royal lands are prominent. In the Seleucid and Ptolemaic empires the land holdings of the state were much more extensive in proportion to the amount of land ruled than in the case of the city-state.

2. Empire-states owned many of the country's natural resources in addition to land. Furthermore, they created monopolies on many of these commodities, especially salt. In contrast, city-states possessed fewer resources and had fewer monopolies.

3. Tribute from cities and political entities within empire-states was a major source of state revenue. The Delian League's tribute, a contribution to Athens, was an exception to the general city-state pattern.

4. The bureaucratic structure of the Seleucid and Ptolemaic empires was more extensive than that of the old city-state. National, regional, and urban bureaucracies existed.

5. Because the empire-state's political and tax structure accumulated public revenues, the kingdoms, unlike the typical city-state, built up treasuries with large reserves.

Seleucid Taxation

The major literary evidence for economic conditions in the early Hellenistic period is the second book of *Financial Management* (*Oeconomica*). Ascribed to Aristotle, it is in reality a third-century A.D. epitome of a work by an unknown author of the late fourth or early third century B.C. now designated pseudo-Aristotle. The writer discusses four types of financial organizations: those relating to the Persian king, the satraps of the king, the polis or city-state, and the private individual. He views the Hellenistic world as balanced by two types of political and economic organizations—oriental monarchies and Greek city-states. Pseudo-Aristotle distinguishes six classes of royal revenue in the Seleucid Empire arising from land, other state property, trade and commerce, land tolls and other taxes, cattle, and persons. Revenue from land was yielded by a form of land tax and applied perhaps only to royal lands. Revenues raised from state property were considerable. Commercial taxes derived from customs dues and harbor dues and were collected by the satraps. Revenue was also provided by tolls, a sales tax, market taxes, and taxes paid upon the registration of documents. A personal tax was levied on such groups as artisans.

In the Seleucid Empire land was ordered in a manner similar to Egyptian land classifications. In addition to the king's "royal land," certain land belonged to the Greek cities, to temples, and to various tribes.

Some royal lands were assigned to specific groups, for such purposes as the founding of new cities and for settling veterans. Royal land was farmed by hereditary tenants who paid a tribute in money or kind. Taxes may also have been imposed on city land lying within the royal domain. These land taxes may in fact have been the tribute that cities are known to have paid to the king. (In Roman times cities in Asia paid as tribute a tenth of the produce of the city lands. The system may also have existed under the Seleucids.)

Various other taxes existed, the most important being the salt tax. Salt pans were regarded as royal property, and people were not only taxed for the maintenance of these areas but were also required to purchase salt from the government. The fiscal system of the Seleucids was inherited from the Persians. The exact size of the state's annual revenues is not known, but it is known that great sums were spent on the Seleucid army and navy, on colonization, and on gifts and bribes used to affect foreign policy.

Ptolemaic Egypt

After the death of Alexander and the inauguration of the Ptolemaic dynasty, Greek civilization and culture overlaid the Egyptian, including areas of taxation. The tax system that evolved resembled the Seleucid, but it had some major distinctive features. The most striking was the adoption by the Ptolemies of the highly developed native bureaucracy that predated them. In oriental monarchies king and country were identical. As owner of the land, the king was owed obedience by the people and the fruits of their work. The Ptolemies adopted these Egyptian social principles, but they patterned the economic system on the Greek model. Thus laws written with elaborate instructions regulated the state's bureaucratic offices. In the area of taxation Greek influ-

ence in terminology and organization was particularly strong. The Ptolemaic system ignored, however, the basis of Greek economy, wherein private property was recognized and protected by the state.

Among the several classes of land, there may be distinguished royal land, "released" land (land granted by the government), and possibly "political" land (land assigned to the new Greek cities such as Alexandria and Ptolemaïs). Royal land was worked by the free peasantry, who paid a yearly rent, probably 20 percent of the crop, to the king. Peasants were also required to pay many other taxes for the privilege of cultivating their land. The Ptolemies also collected taxes from cleruchic land—land acquired through military means, then divided among the soldiers and mercenaries involved in the conquering of the land. The cleruchs' taxes were similar to those paid by royal peasants and included a tax on sown land, a tax for the upkeep of embankments, and a tax for guard and medical services. In addition, cleruchs were liable for regular taxes paid by the rest of the population.

As in the Seleucid Empire, a salt tax existed and it produced a great deal of revenue. Salt was obtained from mines, lakes, and the sea. Salt pans belonged to the government; in turn the government licensed traders to sell salt. The tax was paid on top of the purchase price. Nitre, alum, leather, papyrus textiles, spices, and perfumes, many of which were government monopolies, were other items taxed by the state.

Although no head tax or income tax was levied, property, including houses and slaves, was taxed, as were legal transactions, registration of private documents, sales, auctions, and inheritances. Import and export taxes were collected, and internal commerce was taxed. In general, the number of taxes was much greater in Egypt than in the Seleucid Empire and in classical Greece. The strict pharaonic control of the land during previous millennia and the highly bureaucratized nature of Egypt's political and economic regimes were major factors in the pervasiveness of the Ptolemaic tax system.

Before the Ptolemies, taxes were collected by government officials. Following Greek custom, the Ptolemies introduced tax farming and created a hybrid Greco-Egyptian system. While in Greece tax farmers purchased the right to collect taxes, in Egypt they did not themselves deal with collection. Rather, they guaranteed that the full amount in cash or kind would be collected. Their role was to watch the producers of revenue and the collectors alike to ensure that the money came in. If the collecting fell short, they made up the difference; if a surplus occurred, they pocketed it, along with their regular salary. This system provided checks and balances on both the government tax collectors and the tax farmers and removed the need for the central government to enforce the tax system.

Greek Cities

The Hellenistic period did not introduce substantial changes to the centuries-old tax system established in Greek cities. A major modification, however, came in the area of liturgies. In the classical period liturgies had been quasi-voluntary; in Hellenistic times they gradually became regularized. Greek cities resorted to liturgies in an attempt to solve general financial difficulties. They also created special magistrates to oversee the collection of the liturgies. Although the *choregia* had been the most burdensome of the liturgies in the classical period, it was replaced in the Hellenistic period by the *sitonia*, which obliged rich citizens to buy grain for the city. They were provided funds by the state for the purchase of grain and were responsible for securing its supply. But often they incurred liabilities and were

forced to use their own funds. The *agoranomia* was the second most onerous duty; it entailed management of the market, especially in questions of supply and price.

When cities lacked the funds necessary for the magistrates in charge of liturgies to operate, money for the procurement of grain, olive oil, and fish were provided by the subscriptions called *epodoseis*. In theory these were voluntary, but in reality they were compulsory in this period. The burden fell once more on the wealthy. Other revenue-producing measures were adopted, such as donations and the sale of franchises to metics. The liturgical magistracies were a sign of the deteriorating prosperity of Greece in general, attended by population problems and increased poverty of the soil.

ANCIENT VERSUS MODERN TAXATION

The taxation systems of both classical Athens and Hellenistic Greece may seem to have been extensive. A multitude of items were taxed, but compared to the modern world the level of taxation was minimal. Today virtually every economic transaction is taxed. Throughout the industrialized world, almost every purchase of food, every bit earned or spent, all real property owned is subject to some kind of tax. The average earner in the United States, Canada, Britain, continental Europe, or Japan pays from 18 to 33 percent in direct income tax; the more extensive the social services a country provides, the higher the income tax rate. The total tax percentage is increased by at least 5 percent if sales and excise taxes, death duties, and other indirect taxes are added. By contrast, taxation in Athens and in the Hellenistic world, except in a few cases, would not have exceeded 5 percent of the average income. The benefits received by modern taxpayers are enormous. Although taxation touches every aspect of economic life today, so does government expenditure, from public education, scientific research, the arts, roads, and social services, to military and economic development. In short, the governments keep our complex societies functioning.

In contrast to the premodern systems, current taxation systems are systematic. In the United States, a federal income tax is levied to procure funds for government spending on what is considered the province of the federal government: defense, social security, regulatory agencies, research, education. Almost all the states also impose an income tax, and most levy a sales tax to raise money for state functions, local needs in health, roads, education, police, fire, and garbage collection. Many cities levy similar taxes. At federal, state, and city levels a budget is set and the income is produced to meet that budget. In the Greek world taxation was haphazard and unsystematic. Fiscal budgeting was seldom practiced and tax increases, except in extraordinary situations during war, would have been drastic measures.

The haphazardness in the tax system reflects the ancient attitudes to taxation, that is, the lack of any coherent philosophy of taxation. Government expenditures, except in war, were minimal. In general, questions such as the rights of individuals and equity of taxation were not paramount. Even the institution of the liturgy, which was a virtual tax leveled on the rich, was not applied in an equitable manner, but rather capriciously. If we look at Adam Smith's four principles of taxation, Greek taxation violated the two main principles, that of equality (that is, taxation in proportion to revenue enjoyed under the protection of the state) and the principle of certainty and freedom from arbitrariness. Smith's two other principles, convenience of payment

and economy of overhead, applied to the Greek system.

Modern Western societies have a highly developed philosophy about taxation. The government has a priority on the income and property of the individual. This is reflected in the United States by the idea that income from every conceivable source is taxed, while deductions from income tax are concessions, permitted only where specifically granted by the government. The government thus has the right to tax individuals to procure funds to benefit the society as a whole. In keeping with this philosophy, the government considers that it has the right to use taxation to formulate economic and social policy. In previous centuries taxation was employed in isolated instances for social purposes, such as the taxes on spinsters at the time of Augustus in the first century B.C. to encourage women to marry and have children. In general, however, social and economic regulation was never a main thrust of the tax laws. Modern Britain is perhaps an extreme example of the social uses of taxation. There taxation has been used as a vehicle for the redistribution of wealth, to reduce economic differences. Methods that have been employed include death duties, income tax reaching a marginal rate of 98 percent, and in some cases taxes that exceeded 100 percent. Although this tendency has been somewhat retarded in periods of conservative party government, nonetheless the tax system of Britain has succeeded in producing a vast leveling of economic status. Modern governments also use taxation to discourage activities of which they disapprove and to encourage others. Taxes on luxury goods have historically been imposed. Society, which frowns on the use of alcohol and tobacco and tries to discourage their consumption, salves its conscience and at the same time raises revenues by taxing these items.

Taxation is also used in modern societies to aid in regulating the economy. The tax treatment of oil production in the United States is a good example. Since oil exploration is an extremely high-risk endeavor, with multimillion-dollar losses not uncommon, the government stimulates oil exploration by allowing tax benefits for drilling costs. More important, the underground pool of oil that feeds a producing well can be treated as a capital asset; the decrease in value of the asset as the oil supply is depleted can be offset against each barrel of oil pumped. The net result of such a depreciation allowance is that relatively little income tax is paid on oil from producing wells. Were the government to refuse the oil companies these tax benefits, many companies, especially the smaller ones, might go out of business. Then either the government itself would have to enter the oil business, or the cost of oil would escalate significantly. Another example is tax benefits for real estate. During a depressed state of the building industry and a growing shortage of houses, the federal government encouraged the building of commercial and residential property by providing faster and larger tax write-offs of the costs involved. Through these tax incentives what before was uneconomical to build became profitable. For individuals, federal and state governments have created nonbusiness-related deductions whose sole purpose is to promote socially desired goals. Health care is encouraged by granting tax deductions for medical expenses and medical insurance. Similarly, charitable giving is stimulated through tax deductions for contributions, and tax-exempt status for qualified organizations. In short, the modern government acts as a social regulator through incentives provided by the system of tax laws.

Unlike the modern use of taxation for social and economic regulation of the society, as well as the production of income, taxation in Greece, in general, had as its sole purpose the raising of revenue by the state. As in most preindustrial societies, the services provided by the state in return for taxation were minimal; public services on the modern scale simply did not exist. Direct income tax or head taxes were not levied, except on certain classes, such as metics or artisans. Instead, sales taxes of various sorts and liturgies were the normal means for raising funds. The lack of a well-organized system of taxation with budgets and overall financial planning resulted in the multiplication of petty taxes that were of little value in producing revenue in a systematic fashion. The result was that Greek states did not have large surpluses, with a few exceptions such as Athens during the mid fifth century and the Hellenistic kingdoms. Consequently, these states were condemned to a condition of continual bankruptcy. In raising funds there was a lack of regard for the rights of individuals and the economic advantages of the community. The paramount issue was the needs of the state.

Taxation was considered by the ancient Greeks as burdensome and oppressive. A representative view is perhaps expressed in the play *The Soldier or Tychon* by Antiphanes, writing in the late fourth century (frag. 204):

Any human being who counts on having anything he owns secure for life is very much mistaken. For either an extraordinary tax snatches away all his fortunes, or he becomes involved in a lawsuit and loses all, or as a former commander he is mulcted in the surplus expense or, chosen to finance a play, he has to wear rags himself after supplying golden costumes for the chorus, or having been appointed trierarch he hangs himself, or sailing his ship somewhere he is captured, or in walking or sleeping he is murdered by his slaves. No, nothing is certain. . . .

BIBLIOGRAPHY

SOURCES

Antiphanes, *The Soldier or Tychon* in *The Fragments of Attic Comedy,* John Maxwell Edmonds, ed. and trans., vol. 2 (1959); Aristotle, *Nicomachean Ethics,* Martin Ostwald, trans. (1962).

STUDIES

Andreas M. Andreades, "The Finance of Tyrant Governments in Ancient Greece," in *Economic History,* **2** (1930), and *A History of Greek Public Finance,* Carroll N. Brown, trans. (1933); Hendrik Bolkestein, *Economic Life in Greece's Golden Age,* rev. ed. (1958); James J. Buchanan, *Theorika: A Study of Monetary Distributions to the Athenian Citizenry during the Fifth and Fourth Centuries B.C.* (1962); Moses I. Finley, *Studies in Land and Credit in Ancient Athens: 500–200 B.C.* (1951); Johannes Hasebroek, *Griechische Wirtschafts- und Gesellschaftsgeschichte bis zur Perserzeit* (1931: repr. 1966); Fritz M. Heichelheim, *An Ancient Economic History,* II (1964): Humphrey Michell, *The Economics of Ancient Greece,* 2d ed. (1957); Johann Oehler, "Leiturgie," in August F. von Pauly, Georg Wissowa, and Wilhelm Kroll, eds., *Real-Enzyclopädie der classischen Altertumswissenschaft* (1893–); W. Kendrick Pritchett, "Attic Stelai," in *Hesperia,* **22** (1953), "Fourth-Century Athenian Sales Taxes," in *Classical Philology,* **51** (1956), and "Sales Taxes in Ancient Athens," in *Archaeology,* **7** (1954); Mikhail Rostovtzeff, *The Social and Economic History of the Hellenistic World,* 3 vols. (1941); Constantin D. Stergiopoulos, *Les finances grecques au VIe siècle* (1949); Rudi Thomsen, *Eisphora: A Study of Direct Taxation in Ancient Athens* (1964).

Roman Taxation

BRENT D. SHAW

In 1879, BENJAMIN FRANKLIN wrote to his friend the French scientist Jean-Baptiste Le Roy on the peculiar nexus of taxes and governments, even new ones such as the United States of America: "Our Constitution is in actual operation; everything appears to promise that it will last; but in this world nothing can be said certain, except death and taxes."

The Roman state, too, ought to have known about these certainties, for it inflicted more of both on the inhabitants of its world than did any premodern state in the West. But the demands that the Roman state imposed on its subject peoples differed substantially from the modern experience of taxation. The modern term "taxation" is indeed ultimately derived from the Latin *taxatio,* but in Latin *taxatio* meant an estimation, a valuation, and was used as often in a moral as in a material sense to indicate someone's worth. In ancient Rome the phenomenon that is now designated by the single term "taxation" was subsumed under a vast array of compulsory duties, services, and payments made under the threat, and indeed the actual use, of force. Money payments made directly to the state in return for ser-

vices were only a small part of this broad spectrum of public obligations. The significance of the demands made by the Roman state should not be underestimated. Cicero described tax revenues as "the very sinews of the state," and in a speech before a Roman popular assembly (*On the Command of Pompey* 2.4–7; 7.17) he repeatedly portrayed an attack on Rome as an attack on its revenues.

The Roman state did not have a centralized network of taxation, integrated with a market economy and directed to meet public services, but rather a bewildering maze of specific, often regional, imposts. Since state revenues were not an integral part of a market system, they did not share the pervasive nature of modern taxation policy, in which taxes are used as a fiscal instrument to control broader economic forces. The obvious example of the absence of this fiscal element in Roman tribute are the *portoria,* or transit tolls assessed as a percentage (usually 2 to 5 percent) of the value of goods that crossed any state-defined boundary, provincial or intraprovincial. There is no evidence that these tolls, which generated considerable income for the state, were ever used as a fiscal device for trade protectionism, as monetary policy, or to control the flow of goods and services in the economy. It is therefore very misleading to refer to them as "customs duties." The critical difference between modern customs duties and Roman *portoria* illustrates the conceptual difficulties that confront anyone who attempts to explain taxation in the Roman Empire.

The papyri of Roman Egypt, which have preserved detailed records relating to tributes in the empire, indicate the existence of hundreds of different taxes. Taxes were levied on persons, grain land, olive land, vine land, land in and out of production; on vines, olives, wine, and oil; and on sheep, goats, pigs, camels, donkeys, horses, and on the produce they carried. There were taxes for irrigation ditches and their upkeep; for river levees and watchtowers; for prison guards, desert patrols, and ferry police; for the billeting of soldiers; and for the upkeep of baths. There were taxes on salt and beer; on dyers, fullers, tailors, clothiers, potters, builders, bankers, and prostitutes; on fish and fishermen, bread and bakers, flour and millers; on painters; on honey, beeswax, and dung; taxes on general sales; taxes for archives and for record keepers; for land measurement and for surveyors; even taxes on pigeons and pigeon nests (calculated by area). There were special taxes levied on tax collectors who failed to collect their quota of taxes and surtaxes on the poor who failed to make their payments. Yet this brief review hardly exhausts the list. To make sense of the types of taxes and how they were collected and expended by the state it seems best to begin with a look at the tribute, the one major tax imposed by Rome throughout its history.

TRIBUTUM

The main terms used in Latin for the major tax on wealth are *tributum* and *vectigal,* which in most usages are synonymous. Strictly speaking, *tributum* was the main imposition made directly on a person's material wealth, while *vectigal* was the revenue or income produced by this imposition. (There is no evidence to support an oft-repeated assertion that by tribute the Romans meant direct tax and by *vectigal,* indirect tax.) Since receipts were in effect the same as the tax, the two words were used interchangeably, with no significant difference in meaning. Tribute was also often referred to as *stipendium,* presumably because it was largely used to pay soldiers' wages (*stipendia*). The commonest terms for the payment of tribute were collection (*conlatio, collatio*) and offering (*inlatio, illatio*). If the terms recall the vocabulary used in churches today, that is probably because the state wished to render the image of these burdens innocuous. It liked to portray tribute as a generous and voluntary offering given by willing subjects and not prompted by force and compulsion. Throughout the history of the Roman Republic tribute was part of a nexus of power, including foreign relations and the use of armed force, that remained under the firm direction of the senate. Surplus revenues flowed into the *aerarium Saturni,* the Treasury of Saturn, which fell under senatorial control. All expenditures from it were controlled by the senate through its magistrates, including the quaestors and censors (Polybius, *Histories* 6.11–18). Later, in the period of the principate, the emperor came to control the revenues stemming from those provinces under his control through a system of provincial treasuries (*fisci*), with a central *fiscus* in Rome. Although some emperors still paraded an official respect for the senate's control of the Treasury of Saturn—for example, as described by Dio Cassius (72.33.2) on the actions of Marcus Aurelius in A.D. 178—the fact that the officers in control of the treasury were imperial appointees effectively guaranteed the emperor's de facto control of all state revenues.

Republican Rome shared with most other ancient city-states the ideal that those who enjoyed the rights of full citizenship should be exempt from tribute payments. This ideal often had to bow to the exigencies of harsh reality, for the Roman state was often compelled to levy direct imposts on its citizens in order to meet extraordinary expenditures that could not be met in any other manner, above all those incurred by heavy warfare. Direct taxation of this type is first attested as provoked by Rome's first major external war in 405–396 B.C. against the neighboring town of Veii (Livy, 4.59.11–60.8). Tribute was not imposed continuously from that date, but it had become fairly regular by the mid fourth century (Livy, 7.27.4). Such crisis financing, however, was regarded as a distasteful necessity, and Cicero believed the state should avoid it at all costs (*On Duty* 2.74). But the Romans also believed that the state should refund to its citizens surplus funds. This idea was not purely theoretical, and repayments are on record for 293 B.C. (Dionysius of Halicarnassus, *Roman Antiquities* 19.16.3) and for 186 B.C. (Livy, 39.7.4–5).

THE CENSUS

The ideal of the exemption of Roman citizens from having to pay tribute, despite the fact that they might be called upon to pay it in special circumstances, draws attention to the critical importance of personal status. Early republican society was basically divided between citizens (and near citizens) and noncitizens or foreigners, each group having different privileges and responsibilities that affected their political rights, liability to tribute, and obligation for military service. These duties and privileges were integrally linked in the institution of the census, which was conducted every five years. The censors made an evaluation of the personal wealth of each citizen, including his property holdings, in order to determine his rank in the political community. The assigned status indicated the degree to which he was responsible for military service and the relative proportion of tribute he might be called upon to pay in emergencies.

Personal status affected the levying of all types of taxes, not just tribute. When the emperor Augustus established a new military treasury (*aerarium militare*) in A.D. 6 to provide retirement bonuses for soldiers, he found that the personal funds he had allotted to it were inadequate. Soon thereafter he was compelled to institute two new taxes earmarked for the military treasury. One of these, a 5 percent charge on inheritances (*vicesima hereditatum*), applied only to Roman citizens, so it was beneficial in this instance not to have citizen status. The new taxes generated sufficient revenues to pay the soldiers' retirement bonuses, which amounted to some 100 million sesterces a year. Indeed, these taxes were important enough to be thought the principal motive behind Emperor Caracalla's decision in A.D. 212 to extend Roman citizenship to all the free inhabitants of the empire (Dio Cassius, 78.9.5; 12.2).

Status factors other than citizenship also mattered in taxation. From the first century A.D. onward, soldiers, especially veterans, were exempt from numerous demands and burdens of personal service, including tribute (*Berlin Papyrus* 628). Ethnic origins also affected tax assessments; Jews, for instance, had to pay special poll taxes. The tax status of most people was determined by such factors as sex, citizenship, and property. In Egypt, for example, a special tax was levied on unmarried women possessing property valued over 20,000 sesterces. Thus the major role of the census was to make an accurate assessment of each taxpayer's status, as required by the state.

From descriptions of census requirements, the general forms that personal declarations of status took for the collection of tribute in republican Italy can be reconstructed (Dionysius of Halicarnassus, *Roman Antiquities* 4.15.6; *Tablet from Heraclea*). Adult male heads of households made their declarations to censors, if they lived in Rome, or to municipal magistrates if they lived in Italian towns. Given the difficulty of the declaration and the low level of literacy at the time, there is little doubt that it was made orally to the staff of the magistrate, who recorded the details.

The declaration (*professio*) began with the full name of the declarant, including the name of his father or his patron. It continued with the estimated valuation of his landed property, including slaves (at some point these values were standardized on a list of tribute property issued by the censors and called the *forma censoria*); an oath sworn in good faith as to the truth of the declared valuation; the names of his wife and children and their ages; and his place of residence (town or rural district). The legal penalties for failure to make a declaration included forfeiture of property, public flogging, and enslavement. In the quasi-autonomous towns and villages of the republic far from Rome, the local chief magistrates were required to carry out a census within sixty days of receiving an order from Rome. They had to store the records in the town archives and send copies to Rome where, within five days of receipt, they were placed in the state's central archives.

While citizenship ideally exempted an individual from paying tribute, it did not remove his liability for state expenditures. Most such expenditures in the early republic were met by minor imposts designed to meet specific costs; examples are fees for pasture, water, road travel, punishment, and burial. But the cost of warfare was one major expenditure that could not usually be met by such means. Once the legions were fighting on a large scale, state expenditures rose dramatically. In the period after 330 B.C. and

particularly after 260 B.C., Rome's military machine was in almost constant operation. Consequently, tribute payment increasingly became a permanent part of citizen life. A major turning point in citizen-state relations resulted from the virtual institutionalization of the war machine and its success, by the 180s and 170s B.C., in conquering large parts of Italy and lands bordering on the Mediterranean. The latter conquests led to a massive influx of booty and other wealth that enriched the elite and, more important, led to the permanent acquisition of subject lands and peoples.

TRIBUTE AND THE PROVINCES

The payment of tribute thus underwent a fundamental transformation that was closely tied to Rome's emergence as a world power. Once conquest provided it with adequate resources, the Roman state pursued the principle of tribute-exempt status for its own citizens and shunted the expense of warfare and conquest from inhabitants of the political core of the empire to those in the conquered periphery. In effect, Rome exported the debt incurred by imperial expansion. The transfer of tribute solely to the provinces was justified on two grounds: the "traditional" exemption of citizens from paying tribute and the responsibility of conquered peoples for the costs of war (Cicero, *Against Verres* 2.3.6.12–13; 2.3.40.91, and *To His Brother Quintus* 1.1.11.33–34; Tacitus, *Histories* 4.74). For people in the provinces tribute became a mark of their servitude, a brand of captivity (*nota captivitatis:* Tertullian, *Apology* 13.6, and *To the Nations* 1.12). Since conquered provincial communities specifically bore the costs of soldiers' wages (*stipendia*), they were often referred to as stipendiary towns and cities (*civitates stipendiariae*).

The shift from temporary tax to permanent tribute was achieved in two stages. In the first phase of its conquest of the Mediterranean, Rome transferred the costs of war from its own citizens to conquered communities in the form of a time-limited tribute that a defeated state had to pay. The promise was that after a certain year tribute would no longer be due. These early time-limited payments were exacted from the 260s to the 170s B.C., the main period of conquest in the formation of the empire. The vocabulary used to describe such payments, *phoros, tributum,* and *vectigal,* was no different, however, from that later used to describe the same taxes when they became permanent. That was the second stage in this process: the removal of the time limit on these payments and the full realization of the hard fact of Roman imperialism—that they were to be a permanent obligation. This final change in the nature of Roman taxation coincided with the political shift marked by the abandonment of treaties as a way of controlling relations between Rome and its subjects and the move to various forms of direct rule. With routinized administration came routinized tribute.

After 167 B.C. revenues from provincial sources were sufficiently regular to allow the Roman state to abandon the imposition of tribute on its own citizens (Cicero, *On Duty* 2.76; Pliny the Elder, *Natural History* 33.17). Technically speaking, tribute payments were only suspended because other revenue sources were more than adequate for state needs. By shifting the imperial debt burden to the provinces, a deep contradiction arose within the empire. Conquest brought vast tracts of land outside Italy—in Africa, Sicily, Spain, Gaul, and elsewhere—into private Roman hands. After 167 B.C. these landowners claimed exemption from tribute, based on their personal status as Roman citizens. The Roman government recognized the seriousness of the situation that, if allowed to continue, would undercut the state's revenue base. The doctrine that emerged to circumvent such a development marked the transition of Rome from a city-state to a world empire: the grounds for the determination of tribute liability were shifted decisively from personal status to land and territoriality, which now took precedence. This new rule was formally enunciated by Roman surveyors as early as the first century A.D. (Sextus Julius Frontinus, Agennius Urbicus) and by the renowned jurist Gaius in the second century (*Institutes* 2.7.21), who held that "final ownership of provincial land belongs to the Roman people, or to Caesar" (*in provinciali . . . dominium populi Romani est, vel Caesaris*).

A fundamental distinction now existed between land in Italy and provincial land. If a Roman citizen held land outside Italy, he could not claim exemption from tribute. On the land he held, which was owned by "the Roman people," a fiction meaning the government, he owed ground rent (*vectigal*) regardless of his citizen status. Provincial land could be owned privately, as if full private ownership in Roman law applied to it (*ex iure Quiritium*), but it was still subject to a state ground rent or tribute. It was therefore classified as "private land that is nonetheless subject to tax" (*ager privatus vectigalisque*) because of the novel doctrine that the state retained final ownership of it. While the major tax of the state was fundamentally a tax on provincial land, the persistent modern division of Roman taxes into a *tributum solis* (land tax) and a *tributum capitis* (a head, or poll, tax) is based on no consistent historical evidence, even for later imperial times.

The export of the imperial debt revolutionized the concept and practice of tribute. With the conquest and absorption of each new territory, the Roman government extended the census in order to list all persons and properties subject to tribute; they were thus called *tributarii* or *stipendiarii.* The rationale for maintaining a separate census of

Roman citizens liable to tribute and military service disappeared. For tax purposes the important distinction now lay in whether or not one owned Italian or provincial land. Censuses of Roman citizens in Italy were taken intermittently until the end of the republic, and then occurred with decreasing frequency during the early empire; the last census was taken in the reign of Vespasian (A.D. 69–79). The important censuses now were those that recorded owners of provincial land, and their main function was less to fix the personal status of the individual than to fix the status of the land he owned. Because of the disparate absorption of different territories into the empire, each provincial census retained certain regional peculiarities. Some, such as the census taken in Sicily, were modeled on the five-year census intervals of republican Italy, whereas others had a different periodicity, such as the fourteen-year intervals occurring in Egypt. In many regions censuses were irregular and, as in Gaul, were sporadically taken whenever the emperor ordered one.

The shift in importance from personal status to land status is manifest in the provincial census declarations typical of the empire. Although retaining some of the personal elements of the earlier declarations, they emphasize details about the status of the land. The schedule (*forma censualis, censoria*), which also included official valuations of various properties subject to tribute, now required the name of the property or farm; the city in whose territory it was located and the name of the rural district; the names of two of the adjoining properties or farms; the area of the land that had been put into production within the last ten years (vines and olive trees were specifically enumerated; total area given over to the growing of vines, olives, meadowland, or left in pasturage or uncleared forest, measured in *iugera*, was also itemized); special features of the property, such as fish ponds,

gates, or saltworks; and the number of all persons, such as slaves, attached to the property, including their origins, ages, duties, and particular skills. (Attached tenants, or *coloni*, were declared certainly by the later empire, but perhaps much earlier as well.) (Ulpian, "On Censuses," *Digest* 50.15). Land was attached to the city in whose territory it was located, and owners had to declare their property in that city, not wherever they happened to reside.

LAND SURVEY

The new emphasis for tax purposes on the condition of the land involved new problems of measuring accurately the land's productivity. Here is how the Roman land surveyor Hyginus stated the problem (*On the Establishment of Boundaries* 9 f., L):

> Lands subject to tribute have many different statuses. In some provinces they owe a set portion of the harvest [in some a fifth, in others a seventh]; in still others a money payment. The amount is assessed by a valuation of the land itself. Set values are established for [different types of] land, as for example, in Pannonia [Hungary] where the categories are prime agricultural land, second-class agricultural land, prime meadowland, productive forest, common forest, and open grazing land. For all these different land types a rate is established on a *per iugerum* basis, according to the level of their fertility.

The trend was also marked by a second development, one correlated with land-status taxation policies, and one that has repeatedly been characteristic of the imposition of imperialistic administration on peripheral societies. This is the "reorganization" of the landscape by subjecting it to a system of Cartesian-rational, geometrical-pattern measurement that ignores traditional boundaries or the use of natural terrain features such as streams in defining divisions and subdivisions of land area.

The Romans developed an elaborate system of surveying cities and the lands around them called centuriation, after the *centuria* (century), a land unit containing 100 *heredia* (two *iugera* side by side constituted a square *heredium*). The *centuria* was usually square-shaped and measured about 2,400 Roman feet (776 yds. or 710 m) to a side. The checkerboard patterns that resulted from Roman surveys marking lands in northern Italy, North Africa, Spain, Gaul, Britain, and the Danubian countries are still visible, as revealed in aerial photographs. Ancient maps of a Roman survey around Arausio (Orange, in southeast France) that have been preserved on stone reflect the imposition of a regular rectangular or square pattern of survey lines over the entire landscape.

The main purpose of these extensive surveys was political control, by which every piece of land could be located and assigned a tribute status. In the Orange cadastres, or tax-liability registers, the main categories are *ex tributario,* exempt from tribute; *reliqua coloniae,* owing tribute to the municipality of Arausio; and *rei publicae,* owing tribute to the central state. Under this system the Roman government was able to achieve a minute precision of land measurement that made it possible to determine the amount of tribute due down to the hundredth, and even the thousandth, part of a pint (*sextarius*) or the equivalent dry measure. From a different perspective, these detailed registers are highly suggestive of the government's ability to exercise social control, one that is almost wholly obscured by the nature of the sources of taxation.

TAX COLLECTION

During both republican and imperial times, the state was faced with the more pragmatic problem of how it was to collect the tribute due from each area. This problem had become especially acute in the century between 250 and 150 B.C. that marked the first period of major overseas conquest. In the early republic, tribute was collected intermittently; later, when the obligation to pay tribute was exported to the colonies and had become a permanent institution, the problem became more complex because of the great variety of ways in which tribute was assessed and the highly seasonal nature of the agricultural production upon which it was based. Tribute collection therefore fell into the same category as any ad hoc task faced by the state, such as special building projects and the requisitioning of military supples. Because of its internal structure and its peculiar relationship to market forces, the ancient state rarely developed permanent institutions to deal with ad hoc demands. Rather, it tended to rely temporarily on middlemen whom it empowered to act on its behalf in such matters.

Since ancient taxation ultimately rested on an agrarian base, which by its nature was erratic from year to year, the state had to find a way to assure itself of stable and reasonably predictable sources of income. The only significant revenue source other than taxes tied to agricultural production were the mines that yielded precious metals, above all gold and silver. In the relatively stagnant economies of antiquity, this particular source of revenue was so critical that it could suddenly and dramatically alter the income of a community, and ancient states invariably appropriated mining operations within their territories. But the fluctuations in materials and labor needed to work the mines presented governments with a problem similar in nature to the instability of agricultural production.

To reconcile these problems, Rome, like other ancient states, tended to rely on persons who already had wealth. It accepted monies (or at least guarantees) from them equivalent to the taxes due, and allowed them the right to collect taxes, and to make a profit on the enterprise. The rewards were high. In the case of the North African provinces, for which some evidence exists, the tax level set by the state was between 10 and 12 percent of production, but the amount the tax "agent" could legally collect was over 33 percent, an allowance for expenses and profit of more than twice the tax itself. Because the ancient state was obliged to operate in this manner, the cost of the tax collection was not built into the tax, as in most modern systems, but was instead a substantial amount added to the tribute base. And by law it had to be paid by the tributary just as surely as the tax itself.

The collection of tribute was therefore one of those privileges that, along with construction projects and army supply and provisioning, the state sold or leased on contract to individuals who bid for the right to enjoy them. Censors were the principal magistrates charged with making the contracts, and they held bidding sessions every fifth year in Rome. Nontax elements were usually grouped together and referred to as "other than tribute" (ultro tributa), whereas the tribute itself was called "revenue" (vectigal). When the state was at war, the provisioning of armies remained the most important of the ultro tributa, and it probably continued to rival tribute collection in value. Persons who bid for and accepted these contracts were referred to as publicani—government men.

PUBLICANI AND SOCIETAS

Theoretically, any Roman citizen was eligible to enter the bidding. But senators, as part of the state itself, were forbidden from direct involvement with the contracts. Therefore, only nonsenatorial upper-class Romans were rich enough to undertake them, and tribute collection thus became a virtual monopoly of men of equestrian status. Although there were probably many thousands of wealthy individuals throughout the empire who in a broad sense had such status, the equestrians who came to be of importance were those in the political center of Rome. They became actively involved in the rising tide of government contracts and the massive profits they yielded. To speak of important equestrians was equivalent to speaking of the publicani; remarks by Cicero in On the Command of Pompey (2.4; 6.14–7.18) are typical.

Certainly by the period of the first Punic Wars (264–241 B.C.), and perhaps even earlier, contracts for government services had become so big that individuals could not take them on alone, both because of the financial resources needed to support a bid and because of the risk of serious loss. Therefore, most tribute collection contracts were bid for by groups of men acting in concert. The group or association (societas) was headed by a manceps who, in bidding on its behalf, had to provide securities to the Roman magistrate who held the auction. The securities, usually land, were registered and held by the state as collateral against final payment of the tribute or, in case of default, against services. The partners (socii) who joined the manceps in the bid were also held responsible in case of default. To ensure control over them, the magistrate kept a list of their names. Socii other than the manceps could also offer lands as collateral, in which case they were designated as guarantors (praes; pl. praedes) or coguarantors (copraedes). The magistrate issued receipts (cauta) for such collateral properties, which were then registered in the public records.

With the export of tribute-paying to the provinces, bidding associations tended to become more permanent. Both the incestuous nature of the auction and its bidding process and the immense advantage a group that was entrenched in the field collecting tribute would have militated in favor of the same *societas* holding a particular government contract from one bidding session to the next. Consequently, the groups often assumed a more formal internal structure. A large *societas* was usually structured so that the director (*magister*) resided in Rome while a deputy (*promagister*) managed the day-to-day business of tribute collection in the field. The *promagister* and his record-keeping staff, composed mostly of slaves owned by the *societas,* conducted direct negotiations with the provincial communities that were required to pay tribute.

Persons other than the *socii* of a group might also profit from a contract operation, even though not themselves formal members of the *societas.* Very little is known about these partners (*participes*) or associates (*adfines*), but doubtless the funds they contributed to the company entitled them to a prorated share of the profits. This sort of investment opportunity was one way that senators could circumvent their formal exclusion from direct participation. Not that senators were particularly disadvantaged, since nothing precluded their heavy involvement in profiting from tribute collection in other ways. The honorable Brutus, for example, lent money on a vast scale to Salamis (Cyprus) to help it meet its tribute payments, for which he earned 48 percent interest (Cicero, *Letters to Atticus* 5.21).

The profits earned by the *publicani* from tribute were immense. If the few attested instances we have are any indication, the profit was well in excess of the amount of the tribute itself, even after allowing for legitimate expenses. Indeed, there does not seem to have been any formal control on the *lucrum,* or profit, that could be made by the *publicani,* nor on the additional charges that they seem to have been free to demand from tribute payers. These matters, it seems, were

settled by direct negotiation between the provincial community and the representatives of the *societas,* although the Roman governor could mediate if he wished. But his powers were severely constrained. The correspondence of Cicero and his brother Quintus regarding their respective governorships of Cilicia (southern Asia Minor) and Asia (western Asia Minor) shows how the governor, with a small staff and military force at his disposal, was almost entirely at the mercy of local communities and the *publicani* (Cicero, *To His Brother Quintus* 1.1.8–35). On the whole, the "government men," acting in collusion with the governor and the powerful elite of each community, tended to have a decisive voice in any conflict of interest involving provincial taxpayers.

Given the unbridled power of the *publicani,* it is hardly surprising that provincials of almost every rank feared and loathed them intensely. Indeed, the mere act of paying tribute became a test of loyalty to the Roman regime (Paul; Romans 13:1–7; in Judaea, it assumed a special significance: Matthew 22:15–22). The tribute collector came to be viewed as the vilest of human beings; merely to associate with one was a mark of degradation and social shame (Luke 15:1; 18:9–14; 19:1–10; Matthew 5:43–48; 11:19; 21.31). Increasingly the language of tribute came to be used in contexts of ritual pollution in general (Tertullian, *On the Veiling of Virgins* 11). Therefore, given the source and context of Cicero's counterclaim that Sicilian taxpayers actually liked Roman *publicani,* we can only take it as confirmation of the opposite: that they were generally despised and hated. The hatred was fueled in no small part by the oppressive level of tribute once it was paid by the individual, by the grotesque levels of corruption that were institutionalized as part of the system of collection, and by the violence frequently employed by collectors in extracting taxes.

CORRUPTION, ABUSES, AND VENALITY

The means by which officials made arbitrary extra charges on the taxpayer are so well attested from early to later empire as to be regarded as a customary part of the system. They included the use of loaded weights and measures, the manipulation of prices in commuting from taxes in kind to taxes in money, the computation of delivery charges, especially to remote destinations, and so on (Cicero, *Against Verres* 2.3.82.189–190; Tacitus, *Agricola* 19.4). With regard to force and compulsion, we know that tax collectors not only had their own hired thugs, but also had access to the use of regular Roman soldiers in their brutal treatment of the unfortunate who could not meet their demands. Philo, a Jewish resident of Alexandria of the early first century A.D., has left a graphic account of one such raid (*On Special Laws* 3.30). Persons who owed taxes and could not pay because of their poverty were savagely beaten, as were their wives, parents, children, and other relatives. When the beatings elicited no payments or information on other persons who had fled to escape payments they could not make, the collector and his agents employed torture and even murder. No doubt the case of Egypt may be somewhat exceptional; but it is not without parallels in other regions of the empire, in almost every epoch one might investigate.

Some peasant taxpayers accepted this brutal and repressive system as normal in the relations they established between themselves and the collectors. They computed bribes, kickbacks, and protection payments as regular expenses, and sometimes entered them in their account books. Another peasant response was more drastic: unable to pay taxes, they abandoned the land and became fugitives. Tax outlaws, abandonment of farms, and deserted lands (*agri deserti*) were recurrent problems in the early history of the empire, whether in Egypt, Syria, Judaea, or Sicily (as reported by Cicero in his speeches against the former governor Verres); later they occurred throughout the Roman Empire as a whole.

Publicani were used by the Roman state to collect almost every tax the state assessed, not just tribute. Technically such persons were "private," in the sense that they did not hold political office. But it is quite misleading to suggest, as is often done, that the tribute-collecting associations represented "private enterprise" in the service of the state. Such a formulation only perpetuates an erroneous conception of the relationship between the ancient state and private agents in general, and the *publicani* and the Roman state in particular. In fact these companies had no objective existence in any private sphere of the economy independent of the state. Their sole purpose was to enter into state contracts in order to achieve a degree of self-enrichment on a scale and with a rapidity that was unparalleled in any sphere except that of military conquest itself. Because the government failed to construct a complex of permanent institutions to deal with the ad hoc problems created by its own existence, Rome never gained adequate control over the actions of its own agents.

The power that accrued to the *publicani* as a result of the shortfall in the state's own apparatuses is illustrated by two stories. The first relates to the earliest state contracts known in detail, awarded in 215 B.C. in the midst of the second war with Carthage. According to Livy's account (23.48 f.), the praetor put out for bid contracts for food and clothing for the Roman armies in Spain. Three groups came forward with bids. Livy was surprised at the honesty with which the contracts were performed, even though within a year two of the *publicani* were known to have been involved in a scheme to defraud the government of large sums of money by means of the special concessionary terms they secured on the Spanish contract (Livy, 25.3). When the fraud was brought to the attention of the senate in 214, the senators felt that they could not act because they depended absolutely on the *publicani*. When the popular assembly tried to take action the following year, the *publicani* and their strongmen broke it up. Although both the senate and the tribunes attempted to take further actions against the culprits (Livy, 25.4), there is no evidence that they were ever brought to heel, or that the Roman government ever gave serious consideration to changing the system under which they operated.

The second story directly involves tribute collection, and specifically the massive revenue from the gold mines of Macedonia after the conquest of the Greek kingdom in 169–167 B.C. It is interesting to note that at this time the senators could conceive of only two possibilities for operation of the mines. One was to allow the Macedonians to continue operating them, a course the senators regarded as dangerous, and the other was to allow their operation by *publicani;* no other option seemed feasible (Livy, 45.18.3–5). The problem with the second option was by then all too apparent to the senate: whenever *publicani* became involved in large-scale operations, the small element of public law and order Rome managed to establish in the provinces was jeopardized. Rather than face this prospect in Macedonia, where the stakes were high, the senate recoiled from doing anything and closed the mines. That the senate chose this alternative is an indication of the power that resided, by default, in the hands of its agents. Although it allowed the iron and copper mines to be worked—at only half their former tax return, thereby restricting the profits of the *publicani*—the senate soon found that in the matter of the gold mines it was trapped; it bowed to necessity and reopened them in 158 B.C., again using the *publicani* it could not do without. It

was precisely because of this deep-seated, and fully justified, fear that the Roman Senate moved first by means of a *lex censoria* to control the extent of mining operations for precious metals in Italy by firms of *publicani*, and then finally took the extreme step of banning all such mining in Italy, declaring the land itself sacrosanct (Pliny the Elder, *Natural History* 3.33.78; 3.37.202; 3.20.138). The conflict between the senate and its private agents was potentially so dangerous that this irrational act (irrational in purely economic terms) was still in force in the late first century A.D.

TAXATION IN THE PRINCIPATE

The system that tolerated and perpetuated the parasitic attachment of the *publicani* to the Roman economy was less than desirable, since it derogated so much power that ought to have resided with the state. Only a major crisis could have changed it. That crisis was the evolution of the principate during a long series of internal wars that culminated in the one-man rule of the emperors. The period of the principate was a notable shift away from dependence on nonstate agents in tribute collection. The extent of the shift from the bid and contract system can be exaggerated, since the historical evidence (particularly epigraphical sources) pertaining to *publicani* is missing. Many sources, such as law codes, that deal with the later empire indicate that tribute-collecting agents were still widely used, as was the system of contracting-out the right to profit from collection. Moreover, when the state began supervising the collection more directly, many parts of its operation, such as the shipping of tribute in kind (mainly cereal grains) from the provinces to Rome, remained in the hands of private contractors.

Two developments lessened the state's dependence on *publicani*. First, the great increase in the number of Roman-type provincial communities with municipal governments (*coloniae, municipia*) was matched by the central government's desire to rely more directly on them to collect tribute. Local town councils and councilors (*decuriones*)—one of whom assumed the title of *susceptor* or *exactor* and was named head collector—were held responsible for collecting the tribute and forwarding it to Rome. In times of political disintegration the local collectors were held responsible, as the *publicani* had been, for defaults, which they had to pay out of their own pockets. In better times they stood to make not inconsiderable profits from their role as government agents.

The second development relates to the growth of a widespread network of the emperor's personal agents (*procuratores*) found in all provinces. The equestrian procurators, who had their own slaves and freedmen, increasingly acted as supervisors and controllers of the flow of tribute to Rome. During the republic the chest or treasury (*fiscus,* literally, a basket) kept by the *publicani* in each provincial center was the repository for tribute monies, and it was the only mechanism the state had for storing and dispensing its funds in the provinces. But during the empire each province came to have a *fiscus* that was run by the emperor's personal agents who supervised the collection of provincial tribute. Nevertheless, private agents could bid for the right to collect tribute and to profit from that operation, and they remained an integral part of the system. However, they tended now to be known as *conductores,* since the right was leased rather than sold. Although these leaseholders worked in tandem with imperial supervisors, they were still motivated by the massive profits inherent in the system, and corruption remained the essence of its operation. If necessary, the *conductores* used what influential Roman connections they had to make sure the emperor did not inspect the books too closely (Fronto, *Letter to Marcus* 5.34–35).

Another aspect of the new constellation of political forces that evolved in the early first century A.D. relates to the usurpation by the emperors of tributary powers that the senate had monopolized earlier. These fiscal powers were jealously preserved as a source of imperial *officia,* or duties, that the emperor could impose on his subjects. Any new or additional taxes had to be approved by the emperor and carry his signature. By his fiat new taxes could be created and old ones abolished. An example, although perhaps exotic, is the taxes decreed by the emperor Gaius (Caligula) (Suetonius, *Lives of the Twelve Caesars,* "Gaius" 40):

He brought into effect new and unheard-of taxes [*vectigalia*], first through the *publicani,* and then, because the profit was overwhelming, through centurions and tribunes of his praetorian guard. There was no object or person on which some sort of tribute was not imposed. A set fixed tax was exacted from foods that were sold throughout the city. Also, a fortieth was levied on sums taken in court litigation or acquired from any sort of legal judgment whatsoever, and penalties were imposed on anyone who settled out of court or abandoned his case. An eighth was taken from the daily earnings of porters. From their daily earnings prostitutes had to pay as much as they received for one performance. In the preamble to the law it was stated that those who had once been whores and pimps were to pay this tax, even those who had subsequently become respectably married.

BENEFICIA

Emperors also jealously guarded their fiscal power because it was a source of imperial favors (*beneficia*) that they could bestow on communities and individuals. The emperor could exempt personal friends from tax payments, could grant permanent immunity to provincial communities (by making their land equivalent to Italian land in status), or could give temporary relief to communities in trouble.

A typical case of the latter type of imperial benefaction is the gift of 10 million sesterces and remission of tribute for five years granted by the emperor Tiberius to the city of Sardis (in Asia Minor) after it suffered a devastating earthquake in A.D. 17 (Tacitus, *Annals* 2.47). Tax remissions were sometimes combined with other favors as part of a package of gifts granted by the emperor to a community as a reward for its services. The emperor Claudius granted citizenship plus ten years of immunity from tribute to the people of Volubilis (in Morocco) as a reward for their loyal armed service to the Roman state in a local emergency (Maurice Euzennat *et al.*, eds, *Inscriptions antiques du Maroc* II 94 [1982]). Such grants were unusual. The duty of paying tribute was carefully preserved in the face of other honors. Thus, when Roman citizenship was awarded to an African chieftain with the concession that it would in no way infringe upon the laws and customs of his own tribe, no such flexibility was shown when it came to tax. Whatever other concessions might be made with regard to citizenship, the same decree explicitly pointed out that they were not in any way to diminish the tributes and revenues of the Roman people and the treasury (*L'Année épigraphique* 534 [1971]). Emperors could also issue an en bloc remission of tax debts for the whole empire. When this occurred, it is evidence of an administrative inadequacy of the tribute collection system. In A.D. 118 the emperor Hadrian was moved to cancel tribute payments worth 900 million sesterces; he was apparently the first emperor to do so (Dio Cassius, 69.8; *Scriptores Historiae Augustae*, "Hadrian" 7.6; Dessau, *Inscriptiones Latinae Selectae* 309). In A.D. 178 Marcus Aurelius remitted tributes that had accumulated in the intervening period, ordering the records to be burned publicly in the forum at Rome (Dio Cassius, 72.32.2).

RECEIPTS AND EXPENDITURES

How successful was Rome in collecting the tribute owed it? The evidence of tax records is meager. Rome tended to take over traditional systems of taxation, but a great difference could exist between the tenth exacted by pre-Roman regimes and the tenth extracted by a rapacious conquering power. In a reply written to governors who had requested an increase in local taxes, the emperor Tiberius is reputed to have advised, "It is the job of a good shepherd to shear the sheep, not to skin them alive" (Suetonius, *Lives*, "Tiberius" 32). The advice, if actually given, was surely related in part to the comparative efficiency of the Roman system. But in fact the existence of many taxes is known only by chance. Although levied on seemingly trivial matters, they nonetheless produced amazingly large revenues. Emperors who established new taxes certainly could not have despised the surplus they yielded. An example case is the emperor Vespasian's tax on urine (Suetonius, *Lives*, "Vespasian" 23):

> To his son Titus who complained to him that he had even put a tax [*vectigal*] on urine, Vespasian put some money from the first payment under Titus' nostrils, and asked him if the smell offended him. "No," said Titus. "That's odd," said Vespasian, "it comes from piss."

An illustration of the fortuitous knowledge of taxes of this type is the chance survival of a senatorial decree dated A.D. 177 that indicates the existence of a tax on the sale of condemned criminals and others to exhibitors of gladiatorial shows. The senate abolished the impost, despite objections from the treasury that this tax produced 20 to 30 million sesterces a year (*Fontes Iuris Romani Anteiustiniani* I 295–297). And a 1 percent sales tax (*centesima rerum venalium*) established by Augustus soon produced revenues equivalent to half those of a rich province (Tacitus, *Annals* 1.78.2; 2.42.4). Many other incidental taxes of this kind must have passed in and out of existence, leaving no trace or record.

How much revenue did taxation produce for Rome? Even in the case of tribute, perhaps the best-documented tax, it is impossible to know. Insofar as tribute rates are concerned, most seem to have been collected at about 10 percent on production. This was true of republican Sicily, where the tithe (*decumae*) was based on Greek precedents. Rates at this time for other conquered areas, like Spain and North Africa, seem to have depended on the amount of tribute demanded by the Roman state (*certum aes*). Although a fixed amount, the *certum aes* appears also to have approximated 10 percent or so in the long run, but the total revenue produced is unknown. There are in the sources only proxy measurements, including a few references to net balances in the treasury and total expenditures required. Twice, following the deaths of the emperors Tiberius and Antoninus Pius, there was a surplus in the central treasury of some 2.7 billion sesterces (Suetonius, *Lives*, "Gaius" 37.3; Dio Cassius, 74.8). But in most periods the total income merely sufficed to meet normal expenditures. If the central state was afflicted by warfare, especially internal warfare, which severely disrupted normal tribute collection, then receipts fell disastrously behind expenditures, since the fiscal system had little room to maneuver. When the emperor Marcus Aurelius was confronted with vastly increased expenditures stemming from the northern frontier wars (in the A.D. 160s), he was caught in a dilemma. Since he could not bring himself to impose higher levels of taxation on the provincials, he was left with an empty treasury and no financial resources. According to a perhaps dubious account, the desperate emperor was reduced to selling off his own household furniture, crockery, and his wife's fine dresses at

an auction in the Roman Forum to raise the cash needed for state expenditures (*Scriptores Historiae Augustae,* "Marcus Aurelius" 17.4).

How considerable the gap between receipts and expenditures could become is revealed by the internal wars of A.D. 69–70. The emperor Vespasian ascended the throne following a brief period of internecine war and found the treasury empty. He estimated that 40 billion sesterces would be required to meet immediate expenditures. That is probably as fair an estimate as we shall ever find, and we might note in passing that it is by far the largest single figure mentioned in all antiquity (and therefore suspect). Vespasian renewed old taxes and added new and heavier ones. He increased the tribute from the provinces, doubling it for many of them (Suetonius, *Lives,* "Vespasian" 16). Since normal tribute payments could not meet the increased costs of the military in times of internal warfare, whoever commanded the central government resorted to surrogate forms of taxation and seized the assets of the upper class, usually those of political opponents. This was often accompanied by large-scale political purges. During almost every period of internal conflict—whether between Marius and Sulla in the 80s B.C., Octavian (the future Augustus) and Antony in the 40s and 30s B.C., or the civil wars that ended with the ascendancy of Vespasian in A.D. 69 and of Septimius Severus in A.D. 193—the property (and sometimes the lives) of wealthy political opponents was taken. Thus the rich no less than provincials paid for Rome's internal wars.

Because of the severe constraints on the growth of its tax base, the only way in which the government could increase its revenues was to implement a series of surtaxes (usually 1 percent) over and above the 10 percent base. Even in the late republican and early principate periods, these surtaxes were simply known as "demands" (*indictiones*) and seem to have been imposed fairly regularly (Pliny the Younger, *Panegyric* 29.4). Most well-informed estimates of the receipts provided by all types of tribute to the government fall in the range of about 1.5 billion sesterces annually. These estimates are only of the value of receipts; they are not real sums, the actual amount of coin flowing into the central treasury. For one thing, much of the tribute was paid in kind, not in coin or precious metals. The provinces of Africa and Egypt, for example, provided much of their tribute in grain as part of a payment in kind called *annona* (from *annus,* year), indicating the annual agricultural production on which it was based. Only part of the *annona* could be converted into coin by the central government by selling it in the large urban imperial markets. A substantial proportion of the *annona* grain was distributed directly to feed the urban populace, especially that of Rome and, later, Constantinople. Then, too, much of the provincial tribute was never sent to Roma but was used locally to reimburse soldiers, imperial officials, and others stationed in the region.

Therefore, it is extremely difficult to present a clear picture of the "imperial budget." Only gross estimates, for example, of the cost of soldiers' services, perhaps the single largest item in state expenditures, can be offered. The wage bill of the imperial army during the principate, when the army numbered about half a million men, probably amounted to 600 to 700 million sesterces a year. The figure is entirely notional and gives no real idea of the government's actual need for coin each year. Evidence from soldiers' personal pay records shows that their wages were docked for food rations, clothing, minor equipment, and other expenses, and that after such deductions they often received only a quarter or less in cash (*Geneva Latin Papyrus* 1). So the amount of coin the state would have had to provide for the army each year might only have been about 150 to 200 million sesterces.

Two other major areas of state expenditure were administration (after the A.D. 320s this would have included the church hierarchy) and major building projects such as aqueducts, roads, and temples. Administrative expenses are difficult to estimate. Although the Roman Empire was remarkably underadministered (as compared, say, to empires in the Orient), the 150 to 200 upper-level officials (governors, procurators, and others) and their staffs must have absorbed between 150 and 200 million sesterces per annum in carrying out their official and legal duties. Government construction projects, most of them concentrated in major urban administrative centers and especially in Rome, drained staggering sums from the treasury. The bill for road construction and repairs could run to 100,000 sesterces per (Roman) mile (*Corpus Inscriptionum Latinarum* 9.6075). The cost of the port facilities constructed at Ostia under Claudius appalled his engineers (Dio Cassius, 60.11.1-5). Some idea of the monetary outlay required can be had from the cost of building one of the major aqueducts supplying water to the city of Rome: 46 miles long, it was finished in fourteen years at a cost of 300 million sesterces (Pliny the Elder, *Natural History* 36.122).

The distribution of receipts and expenditures described above is much the same as that reflected in a sycophantic piece written by the court poet Statius in honor of the imperial freedman Claudius Etruscus who, in the reign of the emperor Domitian (A.D. 81–96), was in charge of the imperial treasuries (*Silvae* 3.3):

To you alone was entrusted the administration of the imperial treasuries, the revenues accruing from every people, the income of the whole wide world. All that Spain produces from its gold-bearing mines . . . all that is harvested from Africa's grain fields and crushed on the threshing-floors of the torrid Nile . . . all these are entrusted to your administration alone, what the North Wind and the wild East Wind and the cloud-bringing South Wind carry to Rome; it would be easier to count the drops of rain in winter or the leaves on the trees! What a vigilant man! What an able mind! How quick to estimate how much is needed by the Roman armies all over the world, how much by the tribes of citizens; the cost of upkeep of temples and of aqueducts, of the forts that protect our shores and the wide network of long-distance roads; the gold needed to make his master's [i.e., the emperor's] high ceilings glitter, the amount of ore required to be melted down to make statues of the gods, the metal that has to ring as it is turned into coin in the fires of the Italian mint.

However much these words were intended for overlavish praise of an ex-slave, they do seem to reflect rather closely the picture of the Roman tax system that can be pieced together from our other sources. The words emphasize the importance of the precious metals from the mines, the produce of grain fields, and the vast inflow of a countless variety of small produce in kind from all regions of the empire. And they rank massive expenditures on the army, feeding and entertaining the populace of Rome, public construction projects, the upkeep of roads and defensive works, the luxury expenditures of the emperors, and the production of coinage as the principal outlays to be borne by the state treasury.

THE TAX BURDEN

From the facts of the Roman tribute system presented here, two points should be emphasized. First, the tribute system was not tied to any conception of the state providing and paying for public services, however nec-

essary. Where rudimentary services did exist, for example, roads or water supply, specific charges were made, over and above tribute payments, to support them. A major exception was the free or subsidized distribution of grain to citizens in the capital cities of the empire: Rome and, later, Constantinople. Out of the massive shipments of thirty million *modii* (a *modius* was about a peck: 8 quarts U.S. or 8.8 liters dry measure) in tribute grains annually from Sicily, Africa, and Egypt, probably 10 million *modii* or more was used to feed the masses of the capital. Second, the 10 percent portion of production (plus *indictiones*) that the state expected to receive from tribute hardly bore any relation to the sum the average tributary paid, which was much higher. Two factors were of paramount importance: the normal profit and the gratuity to which every tribute-collecting agent was entitled, and the ability of powerful men to unload a disproportionate amount of tribute burden onto the weak, who had no influence with the tax collector. The result was that the unprotected peasant proprietor paid taxes closer to a half than to a tenth of his total production.

The drastic debasement of currency throughout the empire after about A.D. 230 brought a significant change in the tribute system. The next half century witnessed continued devaluation, to the point that currency was largely abandoned as a means of collecting major state revenues. Increasingly, emperors turned to the collection of commodities and services rather than currency. This shifted the responsibility for collection, and thereby power at the center, from the emperor's financial agents, the treasury, and its officials, to the office of the praetorian prefect (and commissary officers), which had traditionally handled requisitions in kind. The system was standardized somewhat from the time of Diocletian (A.D. 284–305), when central tax officials tried to reduce persons and movable properties to standard units of calculation called "heads" (*capita*) and real property to units called "yokes" (*iuga*). These units allowed the praetorian prefecture to calculate its needs reasonably well in each category and then to assess taxes in kind for each region. The new system proved more complex than this brief outline might suggest, since it tended to accept preexisting regional differences in modes of computing tax liability and transmuted them into *capita* and *iuga*.

The collection of taxes in kind was also linked to a perceptible rise in the level of personal services requisitioned by the state and its agents. These services had always been an integral part of Roman taxation. The ability of the state to demand corvée (compulsory, unpaid labor) was implicit in its powers from the beginning and was passed down—even as early as 45 B.C.—to the municipalities, where town councils were empowered to demand five days or more of labor from each adult male inhabitant as well as the services of his draft animals ("Law of Urso [Osuna] or of the Colony of Julia Genetiva," *Inscriptiones Latinae Selectae* 6087, 98). Demand services might also include the use of animals to transport goods or persons (*angariae*) to any specified destination at the behest of a state official. Indeed, Roman soldiers frequently seized horses, donkeys, and other transport animals and rode them to their next destination. Other services related to the onerous support of public roads and relay posts, maintained for the use of state officials, and to the equally onerous and much resented billeting of army troops whenever commanders required lodging and and food for their men. Personal services that might be demanded covered a wide range, from providing bakers for government food distribution benefits to providing actors for imperial entertainments. Since they were provided by local individuals, abuse and extortion were

common. After the reestablishment of a solid and dependable gold currency during the reign of Constantine I (A.D. 306–337), there was a trend back to the payment of taxes in coin, and perhaps a commensurate decline in payment in kind.

From the beginning to the end of its empire, Rome was perhaps most identified in the experience of ordinary people with the forcible payment of tribute. There was no avoiding it. At first, the local wealthy had a privileged position within Rome's pervasive power; when it was in their interest, they served the state as regional tax collection agents. As the tax structure of the principate began to crumble and it was no longer profitable to play this role, they began to abandon it by flight (thereby adopting much the same strategy as peasants faced with impossible tax demands). As early as the reign of Hadrian (A.D. 117–138), the government added the task of tax collection to its list of compulsory duties. As always, the powerful used their personal power and connections to gain exemption from the new rule and to pass the burden on to the weak and the unprotected. Communities also used their resources to this same end. For those who did not possess such protection, tribute payment remained a daily experience that, like the existence of the emperor himself, was a constant reminder of their subservience (Tertullian, *To the Heathens* 1.12). They never escaped it. In Egypt, when the bodies of poor peasants were taken for burial their relatives had to pay yet another tax for the interment (see Dio Cassius, 64.3.4, for this matter in Britain). Benjamin Franklin was right. But however inevitable both taxes and death were in his world, he was to make quite certain that at least one of them did not pass without representation of his interests. Therein, I suspect, lies the critical difference between tax and tribute, between our experience and that of Roman imperialism.

BIBLIOGRAPHY

SOURCES

Hyginus: there is no standard English translation for the work of this writer; Statius, *Silvae*, J. H. Mozley, trans. (1928); Suetonius, *The Twelve Caesars*, R. Graves, trans. (1979).

STUDIES

Armées et fiscalité dans le monde antique (1977), especially the chapters by Gabba, Corbier, Van Berchem, and Nicolet; Ernst Badian, *Publicans and Sinners: Private Enterprise in the Service of the Roman Republic* (1972; rev. ed. 1983), a readable but partisan interpretation of the role of the *publicani* in the republic; Karl Bernhardt, "Immunität and Abgabenpflichtigkeit bei römischen Kolonien und Munizipien in den Provinzen," in *Historia*, **31** (1981), an up-to-date guide to the literature on tax exemptions granted to urban communities; Jochen Bleicken, *"In provinciali solo dominium populi Romani est vel Caesaris:* Zur Kolonisationspolitik der ausgehenden Republik und frühen Kaiserzeit," in *Chiron*, **4** (1974), a comprehensive review of the question of tribute and land. Lucio Bove, *Ricerche sugli "Agri Vectigales,"* (1960); Peter Brunt, "The 'Fiscus' and Its Development," in *Journal of Roman Studies*, **56** (1966), the best work on the subject, and "The Revenues of Rome," in *Journal of Roman Studies*, **71** (1981), a useful outline in English of Lutz Neesen's work (see below).

René Cagnat, *Étude historique sur les impôts indirects chez les Romains* (1882); André Cerati, *Caractère annonaire et assiette de l'impôt foncier au Bas-Empire* (1975), a detailed analysis of tax trends in the late empire; Maria Rosa Cimma, *Ricerche sulle Società di Publicani* (1981), a good outline of the operations of the *publicani;* Mireille Corbier, *L'Aerarium Saturni et l'aerarium militare: administration et prosopographie sénatoriale* (1974), collates all the evidence on the central state treasury.

André Déléage, *La capitation du Bas-Empire* (1945), a standard work on late imperial poll taxes; O. A. W. Dilke, *The Roman Land Surveyors: An Introduction to the Agrimensores* (1971), a clearly written introduction to a most difficult subject; Henri van Effenterre, ed., *Points de vue sur la fiscalité antique* (1979), an important collection of essays, especially that by Nicolet; Moses I. Finley, *The Ancient Economy,* 2d ed. (1986), an indispensable guide to the general context of tribute in the ancient world; Peter Garnsey, "Grain for Rome," in Peter Garnsey, Keith Hopkins, C. R. Whittaker, eds., *Trade in the Ancient Economy* (1983); Francesco Grelle, *Stipendium vel tributum: l'imposizione fondiaria nelle dottrine giuridiche del II e III secolo* (1963), on the juridical theories of tribute.

Focke Hinrichs, *Die Geschichte der gromatischen Institutionen* (1974), a comprehensive analysis of the land surveyors; Keith Hopkins, "Taxes and Trade in the Roman Empire (200 B.C.–A.D. 400)," in *Journal of Roman Studies,* **70** (1980), a provocative essay; Arnold Hugh Martin Jones, *The Later Roman Empire, 284–602: A Social, Economic, and Administrative Survey* (1964), especially chapters 12 and 13, an account closely reflecting the primary sources for the period, and "Taxation in Antiquity," in Peter Brunt, ed., *The Roman Economy: Studies in Ancient Economic and Administrative History* (1974), a good overview.

Siegfried de Laet, *Portorium: étude sur l'organisation douanière chez les Romains* (1949; repr. 1975), a standard work on one of the more important taxes in the empire; Naphtali Lewis, *Inventory of Compulsory Services in Ptolemaic and Roman Egypt* (1968), and "Census, Taxes, and Liturgies, or Rendering unto Caesar," in his *Life in Egypt Under Roman Rule* (1983), a readable account of the best-known tax system in the empire; Wolfgang Liebeschuetz, "Money Economy and Taxation in Kind in Syria in the 4th Century," in *Rheinisches Museum,* **101** (1961).

Lutz Neesen, *Untersuchungen zu den direkten Staatsabgaben der römischen Kaiserzeit (27 v. Chr.– 284 n. Chr.)* (1980), a comprehensive overview with exhaustive notes and bibliography, but less inspired in interpretation. Claude Nicolet, *Tributum: recherches sur la fiscalité sous la république romaine* (1976), and "Census" and "Aerarium," in his *The World of the Citizen in Republican Rome* (1980), a convenient summary of his arguments in English; for his revisionist views on tribute in the republic, see "Le stipendium des alliés Italiens avant la Guerre Sociale," in *Papers of the British School at Rome,* **46** (n.s. **33**) (1978); Georges Pieri, *L'Histoire du cens jusqu'à la fin de la république romaine* (1968), a convenient summation of views on the census; André Piganiol, *Les documents cadastraux de la colonie romaine d'Orange* (1962).

John Richardson, "The Spanish Mines and the Development of Provincial Taxation in the Second Century B.C.," in *Journal of Roman Studies*, **66** (1976). Geoffrey Rickman, *The Corn Supply of Ancient Rome* (1980), a synopsis of a major aspect of the *annona* system; Emile Schürer, "The Census of Quirinius, Luke 2:1–5," in *The History of the Jewish People in the Age of Jesus Christ (175 B.C.–A.D. 135),* vol. 1, T. A. Burkill *et al.,* trans., Geza Vermes and Fergus Millar, revs. and eds. (1973), a review of taxation and census in first-century Judaea that is much broader than its title might indicate; Emin Tengström, *Bread for the People: Studies of the Corn Supply of Rome During the Late Empire* (1974); Sherman Leroy Wallace, *Taxation in Egypt from Augustus to Diocletian* (1938; repr. 1969), an encyclopedia-style survey useful as a work of reference.

Insurance and Banking

WESLEY E. THOMPSON

BANKING

While the mechanisms of ancient banking are well known, the importance of banks in ancient society is very difficult to judge. For one historian of late Rome, Peter Brown (1972), banking is one of the "capillaries" through which the blood of the economy flowed; for others, banks are conspicuous by their absence. The evidence, as so often for ancient institutions, is uneven and defective: we have enough epigraphical material from the bank of the temple of Apollo on Delos to permit statistical analysis; for private bankers at Athens, courtroom speeches prompt the anecdotal approach; for most other places, only snippets of information exist. Thus any survey of banking and insurance depends on a variety of sources and is tentative in its conclusions.

Private bankers were normally resident aliens and could be found at tables in the marketplaces of all the great and small cities. (*Trapeza* means table in Greek; hence, *trapezites* means banker, a word that passed into Latin. Bankers at Rome were called *argentarii*, dealers in silver.) These businessmen provided their customers with such important services as currency exchange, safekeeping of money and documents, business and personal loans, and the opportunity to earn a profit from their savings.

Merchants who brought foreign currency into a town often chose, or were required by law, to exchange it for domestic coin. Some cities sold bankers the exclusive right to effect such transactions, and even determined the exchange rate. At Olbia, the important grain center on the Black Sea, for instance, a decree fixed the value of the very popular electrum stater of Cyzicus but allowed the parties to agree on the exchange rate of other coins (Pleket, no. 7). We find that in fourth-century Athens someone trying to convert the silver drachmas of Aegina had to pay five drachmas for each one hundred (or fraction thereof) offered in exchange for Athenian coins. Bankers also exchanged one domestic coin for another: at Pergamum about the time of Hadrian they took in silver coins of high value in return for bronze fractions that people needed for ordinary purchases. The bankers were supposed to pay out seventeen asses to the denarius and keep the eighteenth for themselves (Bogaert, no. 28). An integral part of exchange was the testing of coins for genuineness, with the touchstone or at times even by cutting. Greek bankers frequently put their own marks on coins with a punch to indicate their acceptability.

It is clear that most citizens preferred the safety of keeping their money hidden at home, but merchants in a foreign city would normally trust their funds to a banker for protection. A bank account also had the inestimable advantage of enabling the merchant to travel to another city, secure in the knowledge that in his absence the banker would carry out his instructions to transfer some or all of his money to a partner, agent, or creditor. The designated recipient could be known to the banker personally, identified by an intermediary nominated by the depositor, or—at least in the Hellenistic period—introduced by a letter from the merchant, guaranteed by his seal, which forms the basis of the plot of Plautus' *Weevil* (*Curculio*). Conversely, it seems likely that a debtor could settle his obligation to an absentee businessman by making a deposit in the latter's bank account.

Occasionally a man who did not regularly employ a banker would deposit money so that a purchase or other transaction could be effected through the bank. A client of Hyperides, who affected the persona of a love-smitten rustic, borrowed money from friends, which he deposited in a bank in order to buy the slave boy whom he adored (Hyperides, *Against Athenogenes* 4). And the story of Scipio Aemilianus' order to his banker to pay out dowries for his aunts (Polybius, *Histories* 31.27) is probably to be understood in the same way: he did not normally keep the enormous sum of fifty talents in the bank, he deposited it specifically to meet his obligation. The purpose of such deposits seems to be the publication or verification of the transfer of the money. In

Roman law, "the books of *argentarii* were regarded as unimpeachable legal evidence, and . . . bankers [had] to disclose their entries as evidence on behalf of anyone to whose case they were relevant" (Crook, p. 233).

Bankers generally conducted transactions at their tables and counted the coins as they passed from one party to the other, but in Roman comedy, whether based on Greek originals or reflecting specific Roman practice, we see that a banker might accompany his customer to a creditor's house (Plautus, *Comedy of Asses* [*Asinaria*] 433–439) or move funds from one account to another by a simple bookkeeping transaction without physical transfer of the coins (Terence, *Phormio* 921–922).

The prevailing view today is that ancient banks made loans for consumption rather than for productive purposes. But the evidence for Athens, meager as it is, suggests just the opposite. The sources mention loans from Athenian bankers to start a perfumery (probably to buy oil and exotic vegetable essences for compounding), to buy mining concessions, and to refinance the purchase of a merchant vessel (Lysias frag. 38; Demosthenes, 40.52; 33.4–12). In the last instance, the original lenders were foreclosing on the ship, and a go-between arranged to have a banker supply three-quarters of the price and a private lender the remainder. The intermediary then guaranteed repayment of the loans and assumed ownership, but not control, of the ship, which served as security. One speaker describes how a banker would lend on a cargo of imported timber stored in a warehouse and gradually recoup the loan as the merchandise was sold (Demosthenes, 49.35–36). Clearly, any kind of import could be financed in the same way. Athens' foremost financier, Pasion, once alleged that his bank made very extensive loans to a young man from Tauris (Crimea) who trafficked in grain

(Isocrates, 17.12), and one should infer that these advances, if genuine, went to support his business activities.

The Crimean replied that, far from owing money to the bank, he had a large deposit there, but he was hard-pressed to meet Pasion's argument that the young man acknowledged his own desperate position by allowing a friend to borrow from the bank instead of supplying the money himself. If this was true among businessmen, a fortiori it held for farmers and rentiers. Thus when Athenians needed loans to meet emergencies, such as war taxes or other civic exigencies, they looked for help to relatives, friends, or powerful neighbors. Besides, since the borrowers would have had little to offer as security other than land and houses, they could not have used the services of a banker, who, as an alien, could not have owned real property.

The only example of borrowing from a bank in such straits is instructive (Demosthenes, 53.4–13). An Athenian captured by pirates borrowed from a friend to reimburse some foreigners who paid his ransom. The friend, strapped for cash, took a loan from a banker and pledged vessels of precious metal. The singularity of this transaction is shown by the identity of the borrower: as the son of the banker Pasion, he had contacts that the ordinary Athenian did not have. (According to Demosthenes, 36.4–6, once Pasion obtained citizenship, he had something like 20 percent of his loans secured by land or apartment houses, but it is not known whether the borrowers took these loans in order to purchase these properties for investment or whether the real estate had been inherited or bought previously and was now being used as security for a loan to pay, say, a daughter's dowry.)

A final category of loans is the exception that proves the rule. Pasion regularly lent money to the general Timotheus to finance his campaigns (Demosthenes, 49 *passim*),

but these were anomalous in bearing no interest. Clearly they were not part of the bank's normal commercial activity but represented an attempt by a naturalized citizen to curry favor with the Athenians and, as Pasion's son says, to gain influence with a powerful leader. Earlier in his career he was able to "send" the popular politician Agyrrhius to reconcile a dispute between the bank and two of its clients (Isocrates, 17.31).

The private banker was an active participant in the commercial world of the Mediterranean cities. Notice, for instance, how Phoenician traders, captains, and shipping agents honored the Roman banker Marcus Minatius as a benefactor (Bogaert, no. 2). Pasion's successor had an overseas trader for a partner and engaged in shipping (Demosthenes, 49.31; 45.64). Bankers like him were well placed to make loans to merchants who were their customers, since they knew the finances and character of these men, their standing among other businessmen, and current conditions of Mediterranean trade. Bankers sometimes cooperated with other lenders in financing clients, such as the ship captain and perfumer mentioned above, and the banker in Plautus' *Weevil* (679–686) is seen scurrying around to other banks trying to raise a loan for a depositor.

Private banking was a chancy affair, since it involved using other people's money to make commercial loans. Pasion and his successor advanced from slavery to wealth, but in the 370s a run on the banks at Athens wiped out several proprietors. Pasion survived but had to accept default or deferral of payment on numerous loans. The public was angry with the bankers, and their depositors must have been badly hurt (Demosthenes, 36.36–52; 49.68).

In addition to private banks, many cities had temple banks, established to safeguard the money of the divinity and, by conservative lending, to raise money to finance festivals and other expenses of the cult. These institutions also administered legacies that pious men and women bequeathed to support the celebration of specific rites. Hundreds of inventories from the shrine of Apollo on Delos can be used to trace the functioning of the bank there and its relations with the private banks of this important center of sea trade.

When Athens controlled the sanctuary, both before 314 and after 166 B.C., its officials lent sacred funds to citizens and governments of various states for a fixed period of time and exercised diligence in exacting interest and repayment of principal. When the Delians themselves exercised authority over the treasury of the god, they appointed temple wardens who gratified the electors' wishes to use Apollo's sacred property for their own benefit. (Cities frequently misappropriated monies donated to charitable foundations.) During the period 314–166 only the state of Delos itself and individual Delians needed to apply for a loan. The city used Apollo's treasury as a reserve to be tapped whenever an unexpected expense had to be met. The assembly then passed a decree authorizing itself to borrow in order to buy grain following a crop failure or to award a silver crown to one of its royal benefactors. Once tax revenues came in, the city quickly repaid the advance.

But private citizens frequently abused the privilege of borrowing, and temple officials were very lax in enforcing the rights of Apollo. In the century and a half of Delian control private borrowers were far more numerous than in the Athenian periods, the loans were generally fairly small, the duration unlimited, and although landed security was routinely demanded, the treasurers did not press the debtors to pay interest or principal and seldom seized the security to satisfy a delinquency. The inscriptions do not specify why Delians borrowed; it may have been to pay taxes or dowries, but again the sums are often sufficient for the purchase of a productive asset, such as a slave or real estate. In sum, it is not clear whether the loans were for the purpose of consumption or investment, nor to what extent the laxness of administration encouraged people to indulge themselves at the god's expense.

Temple treasurers would normally be unacquainted with the techniques of lending to shopkeepers and merchants who sailed the Aegean, so whatever risks were inherent in these businesses would be increased by their ignorance of the trade. Moreover, for administrative convenience it was useful to find long-term borrowers rather than make loans that constantly had to be rolled over. Lending for an indefinite period on landed property was ideal for these officials. The ultimate in this type of lending can be found in a scheme promulgated on Amorgos, where an endowment was loaned in perpetuity, in tranches of up to 200 drachmas each, to those giving security worth no less than 2,000 drachmas (*Inscriptiones Graecae* 12.5. no. 515). Neither borrower nor lender was permitted to call for repayment of the loan, and whenever the security was sold or pledged, the interest on the 200 drachmas went along as a fixed charge against the property. Hands (1968) provides details on Trajan's similar plan to support his charities.

Merchants and investors seeking to arrange financing and business deals through a go-between used private banks, but temple banks did accept deposits from private individuals seeking absolute safety instead of profit. The point is neatly illustrated by the lie that the cunning slave fabricates in Plautus' *Bacchides* (277–313): his master, to escape pursuit by pirates, sailed back to Ephesus and lodged his money at the temple of Artemis. Centuries later, Dio Chrysostom (31.54–55) can cite this very shrine as a model of integrity:

You know about the Ephesians, of course, and that large sums of money are in their hands, some of it belonging to private citizens and deposited in the temple of Artemis, not alone money of the Ephesians but also of aliens and persons from all parts of the world, and in some cases belonging to states and kings, money which all deposit there in order that it may be safe, since no one has ever yet dared to violate that place, although countless wars have occurred in the past and the city has often been captured. . . . Well then, do they take any of these monies when any need arises, or at least borrow them—an act which perhaps will not seem at all shocking? No; on the contrary, they would sooner, I think, strip off the adornment of the goddess than touch this money.

Conversely, the very measures that temples took to protect funds made for cumbersome operations, for often there was a prohibition against opening the treasure chamber more than a few times a year. At Delos, for instance, it seems that the treasurers were permitted to take in receipts four times annually and to remove funds once a month. Thus, as revenues came in throughout the year, the officials had to place them temporarily in several private banks until the scheduled opening of the cella. Likewise, they had to deposit reserves there in anticipation of necessary expenditures.

It was probably to eliminate this problem and to simplify administration—so argued Bogaert in 1968—that during the Hellenistic era some Greek cities established what they called "public banks," which performed some of the functions of private banks but primarily served to receive and spend tax monies in accordance with the city's budget and the decrees of the assembly. These public institutions were generally manned by elected officials, had just one important customer, and bore only a superficial similarity to private banks.

A similar "bank royal," leased to private businessmen, operated on a gigantic scale in Ptolemaic Egypt, with branches throughout the villages of the realm, collecting taxes and rents for the king's account. More suited than civil servants to meet the needs of other businessmen, the lessees performed such services as exchanging currency, accepting deposits and making payments for private customers, and lending for both royal and private accounts. They made both consumption loans and commercial loans.

How can the banks' importance in the economy be assessed? It seems that throughout the classical period banks played only a small part in financing the production and consumption of goods and the acquisition of property. Many businessmen and farmers paid for the expansion of their activities out of profits; people in need borrowed from friends and relatives. Even the man who sought a loan from a stranger did not have to strike his bargain with a banker. Although private bankers sometimes offered interest, they had to compete for deposits against other businessmen, such as the perfumer mentioned by Hyperides (*Against Athenogenes* 6), and had to combat public misgivings about their solvency.

Numerous passages show that the typical Athenian kept his money at home, not in the bank, and the many coin hoards found around the shores of the Mediterranean suggest that this was true in most places. After all, a depositor could have no control over the way a banker invested his funds, but by making his own loans an investor could satisfy himself about the character of the borrower and the nature of the security, whether real estate or merchandise. A trader was naturally better placed than a banker to finance a colleague sailing on the same ship. (Merchants were also obliged to grant trade credit to the small shopkeepers who retailed the goods that they imported.) And many citizens sought to lend money at interest as a sideline to their regular occupation, ranging from the lowly farmer who would send his bailiff to the forum three straight days looking for someone to borrow his surplus cash (see the "likely story" in Plautus, *Comedy of Asses* 419–446) to Pompey and Brutus, who dispatched agents throughout the Mediterranean to place their enormous fortunes to the greatest advantage.

When Greek or Roman businessmen needed to raise large sums, they formed syndicates, but this was seldom necessary. Ancient manufacturing establishments could gain little from economies of scale; owners or superintendents would have been hard-pressed to manage effectively large numbers of slave craftsmen. Where there was no need for large accumulations of capital, there was no need for a large commercial bank to channel the savings of many into the hands of a few entrepreneurs. Banks greatly facilitated commerce, and thus were indeed capillaries, but were only a minor factor in financing it.

INSURANCE

The weaknesses inherent in private banking, the risk of bankruptcy, and the absence of corporate ownership that could transcend the life of a bank's founder also inhibited the development of private insurance underwriting and required people who today would purchase one form of insurance or another to fall back on their own resources. When insurance in the ancient world is considered, those stipulations of maritime commercial loans that excused repayment in the event the security for the loan (a ship or a cargo) was lost at sea come to mind. But it is doubtful whether this practice should be classified, to use modern terms, as insurance or simply as a nonrecourse loan, where the lender must bear the loss if the value of the security is severely impaired.

The normal arrangement seems to have required a merchant to use some of his own money plus the loan, in roughly equal proportions, to purchase merchandise for export. The lender was paid a fixed sum of interest, in the range of 20 to 30 percent, before the borrower recovered his investment and realized a profit (if any). The former was well protected against price fluctuations, which could be violent, and the latter stood either to make big gains or to incur big losses. In a shipwreck he would lose his whole stake, and maybe his life as well, but at least he or his heirs did not have to come up with an amount equal to his original investment in order to reimburse the lender.

The rules of this game permitted a trader, in theory at least, several options. With, say, 2,000 drachmas to invest, he could increase his exposure by borrowing an additional 2,000 drachmas in the hope that a successful venture would double his reward for the use of his time and the risk of his life. He could, however, shift some of the risk by borrowing 1,000 drachmas, putting up half of his own savings, and buying 2,000 drachmas' worth of goods. He would then deposit (or invest) the remainder of his own money on dry land or lend it to another merchant sailing in a different ship. We have insufficient evidence to show what strategy traders normally followed.

If the maritime loan involved insurance, why did the ancients not separate this aspect from the credit component? Why could the lender himself not get insurance? For answers, such scholars as Violet Barbour must turn to the history of modern marine insurance when insurers tried to avoid meeting their commitments after a wreck by delay, pleas for abatement, litigation, or outright refusal to pay. "The majority of merchants and shipowners preferred to avoid [marine insurance] except when war made the seas even more unsafe than usual" (Barbour, p. 587). Whereas the modern buyer of real estate can obtain title insurance, an Athenian buyer depended on the guarantee of the seller, whom he could prosecute in an Athenian court. But, following a shipwreck, it was very difficult to track down a merchant borrower or his heirs, and perhaps even more difficult to win a judgment in his native city. It would have been equally troublesome to collect from a writer of maritime insurance. Since a lender in the classical period faced such a problem, he added a fee to cover the risks of the sea and for indemnifying the debtor against the obligation to repay. If insurance entered into these maritime contracts, it was self-insurance by the lender.

An unquestionable example of insurance is found in a decree of Miletus passed in 205/4 B.C. in order to raise revenue for the city after a lengthy war had strained the finances of the state and a large portion of the citizen body (Pleket, no. 35). Finding it impossible to levy taxes across the board, Miletus offered its citizens, both men and women, a lifetime annuity. In return for 3,600 drachmas subscribed during the current crisis, the city guaranteed to return one-tenth of the premium each year for life, plus a death benefit of 150 drachmas for burial. Future tax revenues were earmarked to fund this annuity program, and stringent penalties were specified against any who tried to abrogate the obligation.

Here it would seem that, just as temple and public banks could offer safety and stability to depositors and donors of charitable foundations, Miletus could guarantee what no private bank could offer. Clearly the element of patriotism was very strong in this scheme, and it would be a mistake to suppose that subscribers would (or could) nicely calculate what their rate of return was going to be. The 10 percent figure is simply a traditional yield on a safe investment. The circumstances were extraordinary, and the idea of annuities did not spread. The normal provision for old age was investment in property.

In imperial Rome there existed the sort of scheme that upon its reappearance in the early modern period led to the present forms of life insurance. People gathered under the protection of a god, sometimes organized in occupational guilds or as retainers of one of the great aristocratic families, to form burial associations. One such group charged an admission fee of 100 sesterces, plus monthly dues totaling fifteen sesterces a year. Upon the death of a member, mourners received a total of fifty sesterces at his funeral, and his estate received 250. Since dues plus interest at 10 percent would have amounted to 300 sesterces in seven years, the insurance aspect was more attractive than the savings feature of the program. But this scheme too had elements other than simple insurance protection, for these clubs met frequently to banquet and commemorate the dead. As part of the good fellowship, members supplied some of the food and drink, and subsidies given by patrons paid for the rest.

The clubs, as Keith Hopkins (p. 213) feelingly observes, were

> symptomatic of an urban society, in which many people needed to rely on fellow club members, unrelated by blood or marriage, for help in performing traditional funeral rites. They helped men cope with an anxiety that they would perhaps die without kin or cash with which to provide a proper burial.

When necessary, then, private individuals could join together in societies that provided a stability and permanence missing from private banking.

BIBLIOGRAPHY

SOURCES

The speeches of Demosthenes and Isocrates can be found in the Loeb Classical Library. Especially useful are two volumes of the *Epigraphica* series: H. W. Pleket, comp., *Texts on the Economic History of the Greek World,* I, (1964) and Raymond Bogaert, comp., *Texts on Bankers, Banking and*

Credit in the Greek World, III (1976). For the work of Dio Chrysostom, see *Dio Chrysostom,* James Wilfred Cohoon and M. Lamar Crosby, trans., 5 vols. (1932–1951).

STUDIES

The standard work on Greek banking is Raymond Bogaert, *Banques et banquiers dans les cités grecques* (1968). Nothing of its scope is available in English, and nothing of its quality has been produced on banking in the Roman world. See also Violet Barbour, "Marine Risks and Insurance in the Seventeenth Century," in *Journal of Economic and Business History,* 1 (1929); Peter R. L. Brown, *Religion and Society in the Age of Saint Augustine* (1972); John A. Crook, *Law and Life of Rome* (1967); Arthur R. Hands, *Charities and Social Aid in Greece and Rome* (1968); Keith Hopkins, *Death and Renewal* (1983); Claire Préaux, *L'Économie royale des Lagides* (1939); Wesley E. Thompson, "A View of Athenian Banking," in *Museum Helveticum,* 36 (1979), and "The Athenian Entrepreneur," in *L'Antiquité classique,* 51 (1982); Timothy P. Wiseman, *New Men in the Roman Senate 139 B.C.–A.D. 14* (1971).

Piracy

LIONEL CASSON

WHEN, ACCORDING TO Homer's *Odyssey,* the Cyclops Polyphemus found Odysseus and his men in his cave he asked, "Strangers, who are you? From where do you sail the roads of the sea? Are you on business or do you wander at random as pirates do?" Piracy, in that remote age, was just another way of making a living, more dangerous than carrying cargo but no less respectable. And, although it gradually lost its respectability, its appeal never waned during antiquity. There were periods when some naval power was strong enough to police the seas effectively, but as soon as its hand weakened freebooters were back at their work.

The Mediterranean was a natural breeding ground for pirates. The land along its coasts in many places was poor, able to provide but a bare existence; the populations had to find other ways to support themselves or live a life of destitution. The many rocky indentations provided hideouts for corsairs' light craft but left the heavy merchantmen no place to take shelter. The many calms condemned sailing ships to helpless immobility as pirate galleys ran them down.

The first form of piracy seems not to have been the plundering of ships at sea but of communities along the coast. When Odysseus and his men left Troy to return home, they pounced on a town in Thrace on the very first leg of the journey and "sacked the city and killed the men and, taking the women and plenty of cattle and goods, divided them up." Likewise, when Odysseus finally returned to Ithaca, alone and disguised in beggar's rags, and was asked who he was, he gave out the story that he was from Crete—notorious for its pirates—and had led a raid on an Egyptian town, a raid that had misfired (*Odyssey* 14.245–359):

I got the urge to ready some good ships and crews and lead a raid against Egypt. I had nine ships and it did not take me long to get them manned.

The men feasted for six days; I had plenty of animals on hand to sacrifice and to eat. On the seventh we slipped our mooring and set sail from Crete. The wind was fair, a fresh northerly, and we sped along as if we were running downstream in a river. Nothing went wrong on any of the ships. We sat around the decks while the wind and the helmsman kept the course. No one even fell sick. In five days we arrived at the river of Egypt and anchored.

I left men to guard the ships and sent a scouting party to find out what they could and report. But they rashly took matters into their own hands and immediately began to plunder the countryside, killing men and carrying off women and children. The word soon reached a city: the people heard cries at dawn and came out on the run. Soon the plain was full of men and horses; bronze armor flashed everywhere. My men could not fight back: Zeus the god of thunder had sent panic upon them and destruction threatened on all sides. Many of us were killed, the rest carried off as slaves.

Odysseus was a practiced liar, and he put into this cock-and-bull story details (Crete as the home of pirates, the northerly breeze that sped them to Egypt) that his hearers would recognize as plausible. Over and above the details, it was the sort of story the Ithacans, an island people, would accept without question, for they were forever hearing reports of such pirate attacks. As Thucydides wrote (1.5.11):

> In ancient times both Greeks and non-Greeks who lived along the coasts or on islands, once they found out how to make their way across the seas, turned to piracy. They would fall upon and plunder the towns, which were either unwalled or mere groups of villages. This was a lifelong pursuit for them, one that had not as yet received any stigma but was even considered an honorable profession. . . . So, because of piracy, cities long ago, both in the islands and along the coasts of the mainland, were preferably built far in from the sea.

With the passing of the centuries, piracy came to be stigmatized as dishonorable, but that did not thin the ranks of those who practiced it. In the fourth century B.C. Athens had to set up a naval base in the Adriatic Sea to protect her commerce from the virulent Illyrian pirates of the Yugoslav coast. Loss to pirates was a risk that shippers, ship-

owners, and those who lent money to them always reckoned on when they drew up contracts or set interest rates. One of Demosthenes' cases, for example, involved funds that were left in deposit with a banker by a merchant on the eve of his departure from Athens bound for Libya. The merchant never returned to claim the money, since "soon after he sailed off, in the vicinity of the Argolic Gulf, his belongings were seized by pirates and carried off to Argos and he was shot by an arrow and died" (Demosthenes 52.5).

Obviously, there had been a fight; the victims had not tamely submitted but put up a struggle. In investigating the wrecks of ancient merchantmen, underwater archaeologists now and then come across weapons or fragments of armor. The finds can be ambiguous, for the items may have been part of the cargo, or perhaps the gear of a passenger who was a soldier. However, from the wreck of a merchantman that went down sometime in the first century B.C. in the strait between Corsica and Sardinia, divers excavated a helmet with a piece of the wearer's skull inside it. Here there can be no ambiguity: at the moment the vessel sank, the helmet had not been stowed away in the hold or in a passenger's trunk but was on its owner's head. People aboard a ship threatened by a storm do not normally wear helmets, but they certainly might do so aboard one threatened by a band of pirates.

Danger did not come only from bands of men who had turned to freebooting as a way of life. Many states considered piracy a legitimate form of maritime enterprise. In 230 B.C., at a time when Rome's commerce was falling prey to the notorious Illyrians (as Athens had earlier), she sent a deputation to Queen Teuta to complain. Her answer was that Illyrian sovereigns never interfered with what their subjects did at sea, thereby anticipating by over a millennium and a half another famous queen's defense of Sir Francis Drake, Sir John Hawkins, and their ilk. It was as hard in ancient times as later to distinguish between pirates and privateers. In an age that had no international law, governments could enforce foreign compliance only by indiscriminate reprisal, and even the most respectable Greek states did not hesitate to send ships to pounce on innocent voyagers who happened to be fellow citizens of a recalcitrant foreigner. Naval commanders, unhappy when pay was in arrears, could interpret their orders liberally and attack any likely-looking prizes that came along. As far as the victim was concerned, it made scant difference whether he was attacked by a gang of freebooters looking for profit or by the crew of an Athenian man-of-war out to avenge an alleged offense by one of his compatriots. Even worse, states would occasionally use pirates as a temporary supplement to their naval forces. Demetrius I Poliorcetes (the Besieger) enlisted bands of pirates when he laid siege to Rhodes in 306 B.C., and Philip V of Macedon quietly engaged Cretan pirates to pillage Rhodian shipping.

Although the ancient pirate freely attacked merchantmen on the high seas, his stock-in-trade was, as it had been in earliest times, loot from coastal communities. A rich town might offer a lucrative return in booty, but it also had the resources to defend itself; a miserable village would have little booty, but its people could be carried off to slave auctions and there was scant risk in attacking it. "Pirates came into our land at night," reads an inscription on a monument that the people of Amorgos—a small island in the Aegean—set up shortly after 300 B.C., "and carried off young girls and women and other souls, slaves and free, to the number of thirty or more." A monument on nearby Naxos recalls a raid in which pirates seized 280 people. All were eventually ransomed, but the price must have cut deeply into many a Naxian's savings.

Had they not been ransomed, the captives might well have ended up being put on sale at Delos, in the center of the Aegean. Delos was sacred to Apollo and was the site of a famed sanctuary to the god, but the island somehow became a wide-open commercial center for all sorts of transient commerce and the major center for the slave trade. The geographer Strabo said the market there could handle 10,000 a day. To be carried off by pirates and sold into slavery was so regular a feature of life that it is often mentioned in Greek literature. A standard scene in the romantic comedies is the reunion of parents with a long-lost child who had been carried off as an infant by pirates and sold.

Although pirates were to be found everywhere in the Mediterranean, certain areas acquired special reputations. In the east, the Cretans were notorious as early as Homer's day. To the west, the Illyrians were so well organized that they worked in packs and at their height, in the latter half of the second century B.C., could put to sea no fewer than 220 ships. Farther west, "Tyrrhenians," as they were called, infested the sea beyond Italy; the name very likely was given to various groups, whether Etruscan, Italian, or Greek from southern Italy, that operated there.

Ancient literature is full of lurid references to the successful forays of pirate bands, and documentary records add their unvarnished witness. Both kinds of sources show clearly that the odds favored the marauders. When they were caught, however, they could expect scant mercy. In the story of the aborted pirate raid that Odysseus concocted, they were killed or enslaved. Under Roman law the official punishment for pirates was beheading, crucifixion, or exposure to wild beasts, and it was stipulated that this be done as publicly as possible and that the prisoners be displayed on a cross or pillory "so that the sight will deter others from the same crimes." Pirates who fell into the hands of enraged locals very likely fared even worse. They may have been burned alive, as is known to have been the fate of pirates seized by the inhabitants of Milos at a later date.

Pirates perforce used only galleys, generally the smaller and lighter types that were swift. A particular favorite among Greek pirates was the *hemiolia* or "one and a halfer." On going into action, the crew of ancient war galleys normally unstepped mast and sail and left them ashore, since such bulky gear would be in the way, and there was no room aboard to store it; the ships from then on depended solely on their oarsmen. But pirate craft could not do this since their sails were essential for running down their prey or escaping after a raid. The *hemiolia* met their special needs. It was a galley with two superimposed banks of oarsmen, so designed that when the quarry was overtaken and the boarding action ready to begin, half the rowers in the upper bank—those between the mast and the stern—were able to secure their oars and leave the benches. This not only left ample space in the stern where mast and sail could be lowered and stowed away; it also freed a dozen or so hands to carry out the work. Another type of ship that pirates favored was the *myoparo*, a simple open galley that was extraordinarily fast yet seaworthy. Less powerful than the *hemiolia* and lacking its unique feature, the *myoparo* had the great advantage of being cheaper to build and maintain and easier to man. Illyrians developed a special type of galley called *lembos*. What distinguished it was a design and build that gave it all-important speed and maneuverability. Galleys of this type varied greatly in size and rowing arrangements. Some were large enough to carry fifty rowers, some only sixteen; some had rowers arranged in two banks, some in one. The *lembos* was so successful that Greek navies and later the Roman navy adopted it as a standard unit.

The history of piracy in the ancient world is interwoven with the history of naval power. When a state built up its maritime forces so that it could patrol the seas, the tide of piracy ebbed—only to return once the patrollers relaxed their vigilance. Fortunately, only coastal areas required attention.

Pirate craft were, in a sense, oversized racing shells; they did not have room to carry supplies that would enable them to stay at sea more than a few days. In fact, all fighting galleys, whether used by pirates or by navies defending against them, had the same limitation: it was almost always mandatory to put in to shore at night so that crews could get food, cook, and sleep on the beach. (Galley slaves who spent twenty-four hours a day chained to an oar belong to a much later age, the fifteenth and subsequent centuries of the Christian era; in ancient times pirate oarsmen were free, and naval oarsmen were either citizens doing military service or well-paid hired professionals.) Thus, once a merchantman had gained the open water, it could consider itself safe until it neared shore again at the end of its voyage. Naval powers wishing to protect their commerce did not have the impossible task of surveillance over the whole sea, but rather the quite feasible one of coastal patrol.

Shortly after 480 B.C., in the wake of the Greeks' stunning victory over the Persians, Athens built a maritime confederacy in the Aegean that maintained a fleet more powerful than any that had hitherto sailed those waters. For half a century it kept them free of the ancient scourge. When the Peloponnesian War broke out in 431 B.C., however, the fleet became occupied with military duties. The war sparked widespread privateering on the part of Athens' enemies and a recrudescence of piracy. For three decades after the end of hostilities (404 B.C.), piracy was rampant until Athens, rising from defeat, put together a second maritime confederacy, which resumed patrols. Particular care was given to the route that led to the

Black Sea as far as the Crimea, since the city was almost totally dependent on imported grain, much of which came from the fertile fields of southern Russia. To make sure the supplies arrived, the navy furnished galleys to convoy the grain ships along certain vulnerable stretches.

The appearance of Philip II of Macedon and his son Alexander brought an end to Athens' existence as an independent power; and when her fleet was defeated in 322 B.C., she no longer played a role in controlling piracy. Alexander set about creating a replacement, and in his energetic fashion made an excellent start, but his efforts stopped abruptly when he died in 323.

Rhodes next took up the cudgels, and with singular success. An island state, she maintained from early times a small but respected navy and emerged toward the end of the third century B.C. as a major naval power in the eastern Mediterranean. Her keynote was freedom of the seas, so that her sizable merchant marine might sail its routes unmolested. During the last quarter of the third century and the first half of the second, Rhodes kept the eastern waters free of pirates. Her navy did not include heavy galleys that required hundreds of rowers (unlike the fleets of the Ptolemies and the Seleucids); rather, it favored the quadrireme, heavy enough to serve as a ship of the line and yet light enough to provide maximum maneuverability. Against pirate ships, however, even the quadrireme was too slow. So Rhodes incorporated into her squadrons a large number of a special type of galley called the *triemiolia* or "trireme-hemiolia," which combined the advantages of the two-banked *hemiolia* favored by pirates and the trireme, the standard three-banked Greek war galley that could outfight any pirate ship it caught. Like all ancient men-of-war, the trireme was made to go into action without any sailing gear aboard, and a galley under oars alone could never run down a quarry under oars and sail. Rhodian shipwrights elected to fight the devil with fire: they created the *triemiolia* to chase down the *hemiolia*. It was a fast type of trireme revamped in the manner of the vessel it was intended to fight. It was so made that during a chase all banks could be manned and sail carried; when the time came to close in for the kill, it became a "two and a halfer": the top row of oarsmen abaft the mast would quit their benches, leaving a space into which mast and sail could be lowered.

A surviving inscription from Rhodes reveals with laconic vividness what life in her navy could be like. It is on a gravestone that once stood over the tomb of three brothers who, like so many of their compatriots, joined the navy when boys. All were killed in different actions, none of which was against an enemy fleet but in the grinding daily work of the Rhodian navy—encounters with pirates. Two of the actions are not detailed but the third is: it took place in the straits between Crete and Greece, near Cape Malea, a spot so favored by pirates that ancient Greek sailors had a proverb, "Round Malea and forget about getting home."

The seas did not remain clear for very long. By the beginning of the second century B.C. Rome had become the commanding power of the ancient world. She nursed a grievance against Rhodes and in 167 B.C. decided to teach the independent-minded island a lesson by making Delos a free port, a haven where no port customs dues were charged. Although Delos' harbor was far inferior to that of Rhodes, many skippers and merchants switched to the free port, with the result that harbor receipts at Rhodes soon plummeted from 1 million drachmas to 150,000. Rhodes could no longer afford to maintain the navy that had so successfully kept down piracy. Corsairs returned with such virulence that by the beginning of the next century they managed to bring chaos to every corner of the Mediterranean. In this intense wave of freebooting the leading role was played by a new troupe, pirates from Cilicia.

Cilicia, on the southeastern coast of Asia Minor, is an area of rugged inland mountains and a serrated coastline with precipitous headlands. One town, Coracesium (Alanya, Turkey), was a veritable miniature Gibraltar, perched on a rock that dropped a sheer 500 or 600 feet to the sea. Here, the most dangerous, best organized, most widespread group of pirates to roam the Mediterranean made their headquarters. And here, as their success became known, men from all over flocked to swell the ranks. By the early decades of the first century B.C., the pirates of Cilicia practically controlled the seas. They commanded over a thousand ships and had arsenals at strategic spots stocked with weapons and supplies. Their intelligence service, a corps of agents who fraternized with crews of merchantmen along waterfronts, discovered the nature of ships' cargoes and their destinations, and passed the word to headquarters. The pirates raided the coasts for slaves so ruthlessly that they depopulated certain areas. They opened a slave market thirty miles from Coracesium that became second only to the one at Delos. Numerous coastal cities willingly paid protection money to be spared attack, and some entered into formal treaties permitting the Cilicians access to their ports and markets.

Shortly before 70 B.C. the pirates' activity reached a crescendo. Their galleys ranged the coast of Italy itself and carried off members of wealthy families to hold for ransom. One pack actually broke into the harbor at Ostia and destroyed a naval flotilla stationed there. In a sense the pirates were biting the hand that fed them, since Roman buyers were the ultimate purchasers of most of the slaves they put on the block, but that did not deter them. Indeed, for Roman citizens they devised what might be called an ancient version of walking the plank. When a captive declared that he was a Roman in the hope of saving himself, the pirates would stage an elaborate charade. First, they would pretend to be frightened and humbly beg for pardon; then they would solicitously dress the victim in his toga—the mark of the Roman citizen—assuring him that it was to keep them from making the same mistake a second time; and then, when well out to sea, they would drive him onto the ship's ladder, prod him down, and wish him well on his walk home. On one famous occasion the joke went the other way. A gang seized Julius Caesar when, as a young man, he sailed from Rome to Rhodes to study law. They made the mistake of not recognizing him as no ordinary captive, although he gave them plenty of clues. They set a ransom of twenty talents—an enormous sum—on his head, and Caesar conscientiously pointed out that he was worth at least fifty. They accepted the revised figure and sent off some of those who had been taken with him to collect the cash. While they were away, Caesar treated his captors as if they were his personal retinue. He ordered them to keep quiet while he took a siesta, commandeered them as an audience while he practiced his oratory, and chastised them when they failed to appreciate the finer points of his style and delivery. The pirates were apparently amused, particularly when Caesar promised he would return after his release and kill them all. When the ransom was paid, Caesar went to nearby Miletus to raise a fleet, returned, and crucified all the pirates he could find. As a special favor for their decent treatment of him during his captivity, he allowed their throats to be slit before nailing them to the cross.

But the man who gave the coup de grace to the pirates of Cilicia was not Caesar but his political arch rival, Pompey the Great. In 69 B.C. a pirate fleet sacked Delos so thoroughly that the island's commercial career was ended once and for all. Other pirate fleets operating throughout the Mediterranean practically closed the seas to shipping. Rome was finally goaded into action, for the supplies of imported grain on which the inhabitants relied were endangered. Pompey was appointed commander in chief of emergency operations and was given virtually unlimited authority to deal with the situation. The whole of the Mediterranean and territory up to fifty miles inland were placed under his jurisdiction; he could requisition ships, men, money, and whatever supplies he needed from the governor of any Roman province or from any ruler bound by treaty to Rome. Pompey must have been certain he would receive such wide-ranging powers, for the plan he put into action, which was based on them, was too carefully thought out to have been made on the spur of the moment; it was a masterpiece of strategy and, under his able leadership, everything ran like clockwork.

First, he needed ships. He got them in Rome's usual fashion: by commandeering the forces of such allies as Rhodes, Massilia (Marseilles), the cities of Phoenicia, and others that maintained efficient navies. But the key to Pompey's success was the scale and thoroughness of his arrangements, which left nothing to chance. He divided the whole Mediterranean shoreline into thirteen sectors, each with its own commander and fleet. The essence of his plan was cooperation: each fleet was to attack the pirate nests in its sector simultaneously, while Pompey himself, at the head of a mobile force of sixty vessels, swept from Gibraltar eastward, driving the pirates into the arms of forces lying offshore, or forward into a cul-de-sac off Cilicia.

Within forty days Pompey had obliterated pirates from the western Mediterranean and was ready to deal with those who had fled to the Cilician home base. As he approached, first individual ships and then packs of them began to surrender. When he drew siege lines around Coracesium, the hard-core remnants gave up. In three months, Rome under Pompey's leadership had accomplished what no other power had been able to do for centuries. Unlike Caesar, who crucified pirates in the traditional manner of punishment, Pompey proved lenient and modern in his approach. Pirates deemed capable of reformation were resettled in inland towns in the belief that away from the temptations of their old life, they could embark upon a new one.

Having cleaned the seas, Rome now resolved to keep them that way. For over two centuries she succeeded, thanks chiefly to the splendid naval organization that Augustus created. Before his reign (31 B.C.–A.D. 14), Rome had never had a permanent navy. Augustus not only established one but so perfected it that little had to be done by subsequent emperors. Following Pompey's lead, he divided the Mediterranean into sectors and apportioned them among major and minor fleets. The two major fleets, one based on Italy's west coast at Misenum near Neapolis (Naples) and the other on the east coast at Ravenna, were made up of ships of the line, including the heaviest units. They were assigned to defend the waters against any hostile naval power; in actuality, since Rome had no rivals on the sea, this meant that they had little to do. However, they also operated certain subsidiary bases along the Italian coasts and on the islands of Sardinia and Corsica, and these carried out regular anti-pirate patrols. The minor fleets, made up of light, fast craft, were based at Seleucia on the north Syrian coast and at Alexandria in Egypt. Augustus' successors added more such squadrons wherever Rome had shipping to protect: in the Black Sea, on the Danube, near the mouth of the Rhine, on the English Channel. The standard craft used by these squadrons was the so-called Liburnian galley, Rome's adaptation of the Illyrian pirates' *lembos.*

The minor fleets were not for naval combat. During the first two centuries A.D. Rome was supreme on the seas; there was no nation that could possibly challenge her. Furthermore, had there been any, the task of meeting it belonged to the two fleets based in Italy. The other squadrons were for carrying dispatches or important persons, and for patrolling the coasts to make sure that the plague Pompey had stamped out would not return. For two centuries they did the job supremely well.

In A.D. 269 a horde of Goths ripped up and down the Aegean, spreading havoc among the islands. Goths on the warpath were nothing new: the movement of barbarian nations that was to contribute so drastically to the decline and fall of Rome was well under way. What was new was to find them on the sea. Rome's navy, like so much else in her empire, had by this time decayed; the patrols were no longer carried out with their former effectiveness, or were not carried out at all. By A.D. 230 piracy had erupted again; between 253 and 267 mobs of Goths were using the Aegean and the Black Sea to get to their maraudings. By 284, when Diocletian was crowned emperor, the minor squadrons had vanished from the Mediterranean and the two once-great Italian fleets had shrunk to mere skeletons. Piracy returned to the Mediterranean, not to be finally stamped out until the destruction of the Barbary corsairs in the nineteenth century.

BIBLIOGRAPHY

SOURCES

Homer, *Odyssey,* Robert Fitzgerald, trans. (1961); Thucydides, *The Peloponnesian War,* Rex Warner, trans., rev. ed. (1954).

STUDIES

Lionel Casson, *The Ancient Mariners* (1959); Piero Gianfrotta and Patrice Pomey, *Archeologia subacquea* (1981) (discovery of a helmet with part of a cranium inside); Henry A. Ormerod, *Piracy in the Ancient World* (1924).

RELIGION

Divinities

JOHN FERGUSON

DIVINITIES OF MINOAN CRETE

In the background to the later history of Greece stands "Minoan" Crete, a civilization emerging in the third millennium B.C. and coming to fruition in the second with the construction of the palaces at Knossos, Phaistos, Mallia, and Tylissos. There was prosperous agriculture, craftsmanship in pottery, bronze, and ivory, naval skill, and of course a highly developed technology for building in wood and stone.

From the earliest stages, surviving figurines are predominantly of the human female or of birds and animals. By the first half of the second millennium we can trace the supremacy of a great goddess, or a collection of goddesses. She rules over nature, over mountain and plain, sea and sky and moon, vegetation and its growth, sexuality, life and death. She is mistress of the animals, huntress, president of the dance. She is associated with sacred tree and sacred pillar, with animals, birds, and snakes, with lily and poppy, with cow and goat and dove and, above all, snake. We cannot give her a single Cretan name. As Demeter, she is said to have come to Greece from Crete (*Homeric Hymns* 2.123). As Europa, her marriage is associated with trees and birds and a bull. As Eileithyia, she passed to the Greeks in blessing childbirth. Britomartis, "sweet maiden," is one of her ancient Cretan names, Dictynna another, Ariadne a third. As Pasiphae (queen of Minos), she bears the name of the moon that shines on all. The Greeks might find in her Hera, or Apollo's mother, Leto.

It is only later that a male deity comes alongside the goddess; he has no place in the Neolithic period. When he first appears he is subordinate but needful, young, handsome, and armed. It is he who dies that nature may live again. She is the continuity of nature, he the discontinuity. Later, he challenges her place of dominance. The bull is associated with him. He becomes one with the Greek Zeus, who took on some of his myths of birth, and of death. One of his Minoan names was Hyacinthus, later associated with Apollo. Another was Talos, sun-god and bull-god (in one version a bronze guardian of Crete fashioned by the smith-god Hephaestus), who became Zeus Talaios.

The sacred marriage between sky and earth, sun and moon was theirs; in the Homeric *Odyssey* (5.125–128) it was between Demeter and Iasion, son of Zeus. The myth of Pasiphae, who hid in a manufactured cow to couple with a bull, also reflects the sacred marriage.

ZEUS

When the Hellenes, a people speaking an Indo-European language, swept down in successive waves from the north, they brought with them their sky-god Dyaus, or Zeus. The Swedish historian Martin Nilsson once said that this is all that we know about these people. The root meaning of the god's name is "shining"; he was originally the god of the bright sky, but this was forgotten, and he ruled in sun and storm, darkness and light. For a nomadic people, the sky-god was naturally supreme, and he remained so long after they had ceased their wanderings. In Homer's *Iliad*, a poem that shaped and perpetuated the picture of the gods, Zeus rules by strength and wisdom: if all the other gods and goddesses were to try to pull him from the sky, they would fail, whereas he could haul them all up if he had the mind (8.18–27). Ruling "among all the immortals," he is "father of gods and men." He lives in the sky, or on Olympus, the great mountain where a belt of cloud often separates earth from sky, and at his very nod all Olympus shakes (*Iliad* 1.530). The thunderbolt is his weapon, and in small bronze statuettes he is often portrayed wielding it.

This sky-god was identified with the divine infant of Crete, embodiment of youth and fertility, consort of the goddess, a god who dies and is born again, as the vegetation —and the year itself—dies and is born again. The associations in this later incarnation are with the earth and the underworld rather than with the sky.

The great temple of Zeus was at Olympia, where the festival held every fourth year in his honor was a period of truce among the Greeks. The celebrated cult statue by the Athenian sculptor Phidias resided here, accounted one of the wonders of the world. A tough Roman general said that before it, he felt in the presence of the god. The educationalist Quintilian thought it added to revealed religion (*Education of an Orator* [*Institutio Oratoria*] 12.10.9). The eloquent Dio (Cocceianus) Chrysostomos of Prusa wrote (*Orations* 12.51), "I think that if one heavy burdened in mind, having drained the cup of misfortune and sorrow in life, no longer visited by sweet sleep, were to stand before this image, he would forget all the griefs and troubles that are incident to the life of man."

In the supremacy of Zeus lay the seeds of a later monotheism, or virtual monotheism, especially among the Stoics; for example, Aratus of Soli (*Phaenomena* 1–5):

Zeus is to be our starting-point. We men never leave
his name unspoken. Every street is filled with Zeus,
every concourse of men, the sea and ports
are filled with him. We all need Zeus at all times.
We are his offspring.

In one of the hymns reflecting the religious movement of Orphism he is characterized as all-encompassing (pseudo-Aristotle, *On the Cosmos* 401a29–b5):

Zeus the first, Zeus the last, the Lord of the Lightning,
Zeus the head, Zeus the center, the source of all being,
Zeus the stay of the earth and the starry sky,
Zeus the male, Zeus the immortal maiden,
Zeus the breath of all things, Zeus the surge of unquenchable fire,
Zeus the root of the ocean, Zeus the sun and the moon,
Zeus the King, Zeus the ruler of all, the Lord of the Lightning.

THE TWELVE

Classical Greeks spoke of, and even swore by, "the Twelve," their major gods. The Altar of the Twelve at Athens was the point from which distances were measured, and a sanctuary. This implies that by this period there was a structured hierarchy of divinities. They were depicted on the Parthenon frieze in the fifth century B.C. and listed by Eudoxus in the fourth.

First, of course, is Zeus. Hera, Zeus's consort, must come next. She was surely the Earth-Mother, although some have questioned this. The Sacred Marriage (*hieros gamos*) was an ancient concept involving the impregnation of the earth by the sky to secure the fertility of the land. Various myths told of the union of Zeus with different goddesses, Demeter, Semele, Persephone, Europa. Hera, the powerful goddess of the powerful plain of Argos, became in myth his lawful wife. In Arcadia she was known by the three titles Maid, Wife, Widow (Pausanias, *Description of Greece* 8.22.2). All women worshiped her. She was especially the guardian of marriage and childbirth.

Poseidon, Zeus's brother, was in Homer's myth allotted the sea when Zeus received the sky and Hades the underworld (*Iliad* 15.190–191). Some commentators see in him a form of Zeus brought by earlier invaders, but pushed out to sea by later comers who did not recognize him as their own god. Others conjecture that he was originally the "consort of Earth." The sea is his domain and the trident or fish spear his symbol. Fresh water is his too, and he creates springs by stamping or striking with his trident. He is also Hippios, a god of horses. He is the cause of earthquakes, and one of his titles is Earth-Shaker.

Demeter is the Earth-Mother (literally) or possibly the Corn (Grain)-Mother. She is certainly the power expressed in the fertility of the crops; the rationalist Prodicus saw her as the personification of bread. She was powerful in Arcadia. A myth told of the way in which her daughter Kore (virgin; the maiden), or Persephone, was abducted by the god of the underworld but eventually allowed to return to her sorrowing mother for part of the year. This is a myth of the barrenness of the earth under Demeter's curse, the seed corn being stored underground before it is brought out and sown. Pluto, the god of the underworld, is also the god of the wealth to be found in the golden grain. The Athenian women honored the goddess and her daughter at the early summer festival of the Skira, when piglets were thrown into the earth, and in the more widely celebrated late-autumn festival of the Thesmophoria, when the remains of the piglets were recovered and offered with the seed corn. More influential was the worship of Demeter at Eleusis, where the concept of dying to new life was carried further, and initiates into the Mysteries learned "the way of living in happiness and dying with a better hope" (Cicero, *On Laws* [*De Legibus*] 2.14.36). The supreme representation of Demeter is perhaps the seated statue from Cnidos, now in the British Museum.

Apollo, in many ways the embodiment of the Hellenic spirit, was not in origin Hellenic. His name is not found in texts of the Mycenaean age. His two great cult centers, at Delphi and Delos, and his double name, Phoebus Apollo, suggest a double origin; perhaps a northern god of the assembly was fused with an eastern sun-god. He was an oracular god, consulted by individuals about "crops or children" (Euripides, *Ion* 303) and by states on matters of high policy. He was a god of destruction and of healing, a god of music and culture, a god of youth. He carries the bow in war and the lyre in peace. Ironically, the most majestic representation of him survives not in one of his own sanctuaries, but on the pediment of the temple of Zeus at Olympia. There he stands impassively, towering above the strife between Lapiths and the centaurs, who were endeavoring to rape their women.

Artemis became the sister of Apollo in myth. She was the Great Goddess of Asia Minor, mistress of the animals (*Iliad* 21.470). Her temple at Ephesus was one of the Seven Wonders of the World; a solitary column now recalls it. Her cult statue was covered with protuberances that appear to be breasts, although some scholars believe them to represent the *ova* of the sacred bee. The Greeks tamed her and turned her into the virgin huntress exquisitely portrayed in Euripides' *Hippolytus;* her motherhood was projected onto her attendants, as in the myth of Zeus and Callisto. Even in her virginity, she aided mothers in childbirth.

Ares, like Artemis, is mentioned nowhere in Mycenaean texts. He was perhaps in origin a sun-god from Thrace, and was to the Greeks a cruel and bloodthirsty deity of war. He aroused scant devotion and no affection.

Aphrodite is the fertility goddess of Asia in another form. She crossed from Asia to Cyprus, and the little isle of Cythera, and finally to the great port town of Corinth, where her sacred prostitutes were believed to contribute to the fertility of the natural world. She was "born of the foam": the foam of the sea and the foam surrounding the semen. An exquisite statuette in Rhodes shows her wringing out her hair. She is Love incarnate, Love divine, as C. T. Seltman put it, of all the Olympians "the most alarming and the most alluring."

Hermes was a friendly, popular god, perhaps in origin the god of the cairn, which guides wayfarers through the hills. He stood at the entrance to houses, an upright stone with head and sex organ for good luck; he marked boundaries too. Because he guided travelers, he became the messenger of the gods. He guided the souls of the dead to the underworld. He helped shepherds with their flocks, and traders. He also took on the myths of the trickster.

Pallas Athena seems to be a blend between the Valkyrie-like daughter of Zeus brought in by the Hellenes and the pre-Hellenic goddess of Athens, who had some totemic association with the owl. At Athens she inspired loving adoration. As invoked in Aristophanes' *The Knights* (*Equites*) 581–586:

> Pallas, our city's protector,
> ruler of a land of piety,
> a land outstanding among
> all lands in war,
> and poetry, and power,
> come.

So too at Lindos on the island of Rhodes, where a remarkable chronicle tells of some of her epiphanies in grace and protective power.

Hephaestus is in origin the power of fire, at first in its volcanic manifestations. He becomes the god of fire in general, patron-god of smiths and, like them, lame. His temple in the smiths' quarter at Athens (often wrongly known as the Theseum [Theseion]) is one of the most nearly complete classical temples. In a Beauty-and-the-Beast myth, he was married to Aphrodite, who cuckolded him with Ares. In the famous story he used technology to trap them in a wire net, and called in the other gods, only to hear Hermes say that the experience would be worth the disgrace (*Odyssey* 8.340–342).

Hestia is the hearth-goddess, the Cinderella of the Olympians.

DIONYSUS

When Dionysus arrived as a latecomer—or had a cataclysmic revival—he tended to oust Hestia from the Twelve, destroying the balance of male and female, though he himself had an effeminate streak. He was a god of the moist, of the sap in vegetation, of the vine and intoxication, of nature in the raw, of ecstatic religion, of tragedy and comedy. His power in fertility is shown in the phallus carried at his festivals, and the ithyphallic nature of his attendant satyrs and sileni, though never the god himself. In Greek myth he was child of Zeus and Semele, but when his mother was cataclysmically destroyed by Zeus's thunderbolts, he was rescued from her womb and placed in his father's thigh, from where he came to birth. In another, late myth, he was killed as an infant and eaten by the Titans. They were destroyed by Zeus, and from their ashes arose mankind, part earthly, part divine. The god's heart was rescued, and from it the god was reborn. Dionysus seems to have originated in Thrace, but he has links with Asia Minor also. In addition to satyrs and sileni, the god has women around him, bacchantes or maenads, often portrayed in ecstatic dance with flowing robes. His divine bride is Ariadne, originally a goddess from Crete; in one vase painting she is a nurse receiving the child Dionysus into her care. Later myth has Ariadne a princess abandoned by Theseus on the island of Naxos, found by the god and taken as his bride, and, according to one story, escorted to heaven in his chariot. Roman sarcophagi show her sleeping and forlorn; the god's kiss will awaken her, as he can awaken his initiate from the sleep of death. But in one wall painting from Rome she welcomes him and extends a bowl for him to fill with the miracle of wine. The memory of his reentry, and the resistance to it, is indelibly recorded by Euripides in *The Bacchants* (*Bacchae*). In the Hellenistic age Dionysus is associated with mystic rites; the Villa of the Mysteries at Pompeii is a unique monument of this.

OTHER GREEK DIVINITIES

Although the Twelve plus Dionysus were given the highest place in Greek worship, there were scores of other divine powers, who might sometimes appear closer to ordinary men and women.

There were powers of nature. Helios, the sun-god, with his all-seeing eye, was honored in oaths. It was normal to offer an act of adoration to the sun at daybreak (Plato, *Laws* 10.887e), as Socrates did after his twenty-four hours in meditative trance at Potidaea (Plato, *Symposium* 220d). Helios was the great god of Rhodes; at Cos he was worshiped with Hemera, Goddess of Day; at Athens he had an altar for wineless offerings, and a priestess. Rivers and springs were worshiped. Achelous, the great river of northwest Greece, is honored on a coin of Metapontum (Metaponto) in Italy or in an inscription from Mykonos in the Aegean (Dittenberger, *Sylloge Inscriptionum Graecarum* 373.35). Scamander, the river of Troy, had his own priest (*Iliad* 5.77); in later years we know that girls before marriage went to bathe in the river and spoke the formula "Scamander, receive my maidenhood as a gift" (pseudo-Aeschines, *Letters* [*Epistulae*] 10). As well as the river-gods there were nymphs, naiads and dryads, and oreads, coming from springs, trees, and mountains. Other spirits of fertility and blessing include the Horai (Hours or Seasons—whose names, Thallo and Karpo, imply growth and fruition); the Charites or Graces; and the Muses. Pan, a shepherds' god from Arcadia whose name derives from a root meaning "pasture," was later given a more universal function.

The underworld had its own awesome powers, honored at night with black-skinned or -furred sacrifices, whose blood drained downward into a trench. The god of the dead may be called Zeus, but he is "another Zeus" (Aeschylus, *The Suppliants* [*Supplices*] 231) and bears such titles as Chthonios (of the earth) or Katachthonios (below the earth). Or he may be the brother of Zeus, Hades, or Pluto. There are legendary judges, Minos and Rhadamanthys. Goddesses too, Persephone and the terrible Hecate, worshiped at crossroads (haunted places), and sometimes identified with Artemis. Perhaps here too we should mention the Erinyes or Furies, spirits of punishment (and the Maniai, spirits causing madness, worshiped at Megalopolis), who were hopefully identified with the Eumenides (Kindly Ones) or the August Semnai.

Some divine powers who received worship have been described as abstractions, although they are really concrete personifications. Such are Eris (Strife), Ara (Curse), Phobos (Fear), Eros (Love), Aidos (Respect), Eleos (Pity), Eirene (Peace), Homonoia (Concord), Pheme (Rumor), Mnemosyne (Memory), Moira (Fate), Tyche (Fortune). When it was proposed to introduce gladiatorial shows into Athens in the second century A.D., the Cynic philosopher Demonax said that they would first have to abolish the Altar of Pity. The Fates were prominent in cult at Sparta and Thebes. Tyche won the scorn of philosophers: "Human beings have invented an image of Fortune, a cover-up of their own folly" (Democritus frag. 119 in Eusebius, *Preparation for the Gospel* [*Praeparatio Evangelica*] 14.27). But she was a great protector of cities in the Hellenistic age, and the statue of the Fortune of Antioch by Eutychides became world-famous.

HEROES AND OTHERS

The Greek term *hero* covers a variety of disparate beings, from minor gods to glorified humans, all gifted with power and all the recipients of cult. Sometimes they are mythologically identified as the offspring of a deity and a mortal—Heracles, or the Dioscuri Castor and Polydeuces (Pollux) being examples—but that alone does not make a hero in the technical sense. There are oddities about the cult. The Pythagoreans laid down that heroes should be worshiped from midday only (Diogenes Laertius, *Lives and Opinions of the Famous Philosophers* [*Vitae Philosophorum*] 8.33). Some sacred laws suggest that offerings made to heroes bear the unclean taint of death upon them; others direct that portions of the sacrifice be freely distributed. There is a curious passage in which Herodotus (2.44) applauds those states that have two cults of Heracles, one as an Olympian immortal and one as a hero subject to death.

Among the most influential of these demigods is Heracles, a possibly historical character of massive prowess from Tiryns. The twelve labors divinely imposed on him were later seen as heroic exploits in the service of mankind, and he was venerated as the averter of evils. He is typically portrayed with lionskin, club, and bow.

Asclepius was probably a skilled physician from Thessaly, in myth struck down for daring to raise the dead. His great healing sanctuaries were at Epidaurus, Cos, and Pergamum (Bergama); he was introduced to Athens in 420 B.C., and to Rome in the early third century. He inspired deep personal affection, as can be seen in the writings of the hypochondriac Aelius Aristides, a Sophist of the second century. He is portrayed as a kindly, bearded figure, accompanied by staff and healing snake.

Orpheus appears as a kind of counterpart of Dionysus. He too came from Thrace, but he espoused Apollo rather than Dionysus. He was a legendary musician, whose music brought his wife back from the dead, and who was torn to pieces by maenads, worshipers of Dionysus. Somehow, somewhere, in the seventh or sixth century he became the founding figure in a new cult of salvation. However obscure its origins, the cult was persistent; witness the Orphic Hymns from some brotherhood of Roman imperial times. Witness too the fact that Severus Alexander, emperor in A.D. 222–235, had the image of Orpheus in his private chapel, and the influence of the Orpheus figure in art on Christian iconography.

The list of heroes is practically endless. They include legendary ancestors, Theseus at Athens, Pelops, for whom the Peloponnese is named, and city founders such as Hagnon at Amphipolis, whose honors were transferred to the Spartan "liberator" Brasidas (Thucydides, 5.11; Aristotle, *Nicomachean Ethics* 5.1134b23). This last is an example of honors paid to a clearly historical individual on his death: so, too, with the Athenian Cimon (Plutarch, *Cimon* 19.4). One of the oddest of these stories relates to a boxer named Cleomedes, who was disqualified for killing his opponent. He returned to his home in fury and pulled the school down over the children. He then took refuge in a temple and vanished. The Delphic oracle told the people to honor him with sacrifices as the last of the heroes.

Hero-worship offered some kind of precedent for ruler-worship, though the precedent was extended to worship of a person still living. Alexander the Great, extensively heroized before his death, had certainly been a founder of cities: witness the countless Alexandrias. So were the Hellenistic monarchs great city founders. To the populace they were gods manifest (Epiphanes), or benefactors (Euergetes), like Heracles. A remarkable episode took place when Demetrius I Poliorcetes (the Besieger) visited Athens in 307 B.C. The Athenians sang him a hymn and give him the Parthenon as his palace; other gods were far away, deaf, indifferent, lifeless, but he was present, real, and endowed with the power to give them peace.

ROMAN DIVINE POWERS: THE *NUMINA*

It seems that the oldest strand of religion at Rome incorporated a belief not in anthropomorphic deities, but in *numina,* divine powers of a limited function, with no original existence except in relation to the function over which they presided. They had mostly to do with farming and family life. The evidence is largely, but not entirely, late and antiquarian, but there is good reason to think that these beliefs existed very early. For example, Fabius Pictor, a historian of the third century B.C., records that the priest of Ceres, goddess of the crops, invoked Vervactor (Turner of fallow land), Reparator (Preparer of fallow land), Imporcitor (Plower with furrows), Insitor (Grafter), Obarator (Plower-up), Occator (Harrower), Sarritor (Hoer), Subruncinator (Weeder), Messor (Reaper), Convector (Binder), Conditor (Garnerer), and Promitor (Producer from store) (Servius, *Commentary on Vergil's Georgics* 1.21). To this list we can add Spiniensis (thorny), Sterculius (Manurer), Puta (Pruner), Nodutus (of the grain stalks), and Mellonia (of honey).

Numina presided at the birth of a child. Alemona looked after the fetus, Nona and Decima (Ninth and Tenth) watched over the final months before birth, Partula took care of parturition, Licina, Candelifera, and the Carmentes helped to bring the child into the light. A magical ceremony then drove away evil spirits with axe, stake, and broom, invoking Intercidona (Cleaver), Pilumnus (Staker), and Deverra (Sweeper). Cunina guarded the cradle, Vagitanus induced the first cry, Rumina was responsible for breastfeeding, Edusa and Potina for eating and drinking, Fabulinus for speech, Statulinus for standing up, and Abeona and Adeona preserved the child's going-out and coming-in.

This way of thought persisted. When Hannibal approached the gates of Rome and retired again, the Romans invoked Rediculus Tutanus (Returner Savior), although it is hard to see what existence he might have had except on that one occasion. Similar, though capable of wider extension, was Catulus' vow at Vercellae (Vercelli) to erect a temple to the Fortune of This Day (Plutarch, *Parallel Lives,* "Marius Caius" 26.2; Cicero, *On Laws* 2.11.28).

The conferring of gender upon such powers is almost an irrelevancy. Pales, or Pares, a shepherd's divinity, is ambiguously masculine or feminine, and Venus, later the great goddess of love, has a name neuter in form.

Some of the later and more familiar deities seem originally to have been powers with a limited function. Names like Saturnus, Neptunus, and Vertumnus are adjectival in form. Some are inherent in an object rather than a process: Janus in the door, Vesta in the hearth (compare the Greek Hestia), the Penates in the store, Ceres in the grain, Flora in the flowers, Pomona in fruit, Terminus in the boundary stone, Robigus in the rust that attacks grain. We may also note the Lares, ostensibly powers of the farmland, sometimes identified with the ancestors. Buried in the soil, they may bless it; some have particular functions in that regard, such as guarding the point where farm tracks meet, or (in the household god [*Lar familiaris*]) protecting the whole work force and coming with them into the villa. Within the family, we find the Genius, power of fertility in the male, an honored numen of precise function. It has been argued that Juno was in origin the corresponding power of the female.

THE THREE GREAT ROMAN DEITIES

There are clear indications of a triad of deities honored by the archaic Romans. Jupiter, like Zeus, is the Indo-European sky-god, Dyaus (Sanskrit, "sky") or *Diespiter* (day-father). He was always supreme. Mars, in classical times always the god of war, had in early times a strong agricultural function. Whether this was the war-god fending off the enemies of the crops, or whether he was perhaps originally a storm-god fulfilling both functions is controversial. He was later identified with Ares. Quirinus was the god of the Roman people in peaceable assembly: *Quirites* are the citizens, and the etymologically related *curia,* the senate house. He was later identified with the legendary founding father Romulus.

The Jupiter-Mars-Quirinus triad was replaced under Etruscan influence by the dominant Capitoline triad, whose temple was on the Capitol, and who in imperial times dominated cities throughout the world. Jupiter remained supreme, but he was now accompanied by two goddesses: Juno, the Etruscan Uni, the power of fertility in woman, who became his consort and was identified with Hera; and Minerva, a patroness of crafts, who found her parallel in the Greek Athena.

GROWTH OF THE PANTHEON

We know of other gods worshiped from early times: Vesta of the hearth, whose fire was tended by the Vestal Virgins, and who always came last in prayers; Janus of the door, who came first in prayers, and was portrayed looking both ways; powers of the year, such as Mater Matuta, the morning-mother, or Anna Perenna, usually regarded as a year-goddess; and powers of the wild, such as Silvanus and Faunus.

As the Romans came into contact with surrounding peoples, including the Greeks of Campania, their pantheon grew. There was Diana, goddess of the wildwood on the hilltop at Aricia, whose priest, "the king of the grove," slew his predecessor and was slain in turn; she became one with Artemis. There was the mysterious woodland goddess Feronia, worshiped widely in Italy. There was Venus, a *numen* of the garden. There was Fortuna, an oracular deity in Praeneste and Antium, and a bringer of blessings. There was Apollo, the Etruscan

Aplu, honored in Veii, Rome's great enemy. There was Hercules, the Greek Heracles, revered as a god by merchants, and Mercury, the very spirit of merchandise, who was identified with Hermes.

The Romans came to have a somewhat ambivalent admiration of all things Greek. It is the highest claim of their poets to have introduced into Latin some form of Greek literature. They came to identify members of their own pantheon with the Greek Olympians, and to adopt the Greek myths. For the most part the indigenous Roman gods have no myths; their stories are borrowed from the Greeks. Some of the equivalences we have noted. The water-spirit Neptunus became Poseidon. The grain-spirit Ceres (from the same root as *creare*, "create") was Demeter. An ancient volcano-god, Volcanus, was identified with Hephaestus. Dionysus was found in the vegetation-god Liber Pater, whose partner, Libera, was unified with Ceres. So the Greek Twelve became dominant at Rome.

THE ABSTRACT AS PERSONAL

It was a natural development from the early cult of the *numina* that in a more sophisticated Roman age the principles that govern human behavior should find their expression in the divine, especially as the same thing had occurred among the Greeks.

The cult of Victoria (Victory) went back to time immemorial (Dionysius Halicarnassus, *Roman Antiquities* [*Antiquitates Romanae*] 1.33); a shrine was dedicated to her in the Samnite Wars in 294 B.C. (Livy, *History of Rome* [*Ab Urbe Condita*] 10.33). It was her temple on the Palatine that first received the black stone of Cybele in the symbolic bringing of the Great Mother to Rome in 205 B.C., in response to the requirement set by the Sibylline books and the Delphic oracle for victory in the Second Punic War. Victoria

was an enduring goddess. A key debate in the conflict between Christian and pagan in the later fourth century A.D. involved the Altar of Victory in the senate house at Rome.

Fides (trustworthiness) was another whose introduction was lost in the mists of prehistory (*Roman Antiquities* 2.75); her classical representation was as a matron bearing corn ears or fruit. Concordia (concord—the Greek Homonoia) had a shrine from 367 B.C., when peace was established between nobles and commoners (Plutarch, *Parallel Lives*, "Camillus" 42; Ovid, *The Roman Calendar* [*Fasti*] 1.639). A temple was dedicated to Salus (well-being; later and more narrowly, health) in 302 B.C., though the cult may well have flourished appreciably earlier. The third century B.C. saw a considerable accession of these new deities to the Roman pantheon, including Spes (Hope), Honos (Honor), Virtus (Manliness, Courage; later, Virtue), Mens (Intelligence: perhaps a counterblast to the "Fortune" of Hannibal after his victory at Lake Trasimene).

These and others, such as Pax (peace), are to be taken as gods, not as literary conceits. Horace, and his hearers, were thinking of real powers when he wrote for the secular games, or *Ludi Saeculares* (Secular Song [*Carmen Saeculare*] 57–60):

Already Trust, Peace, Honor and Chastity
(come from our past) and Virtue (long
  neglected)
have confidence to return, and Plenty,
  endowed with
a full horn, can be seen.

Juvenal put it cynically (*Satires* 1.112–116):

Though pernicious Pelf has no temple—
yet—though we've built no altars to Cash,
as we honor Peace, Trustworthiness, Victory,
  Virtue
and Concord (with roosting storks answering
  our greeting),

it is Wealth who receives our most sincere worship.

Yet behind the cynicism lies the sense of divine powers neglected.

THE *INTERPRETATIO ROMANA*

As the Romans spread over the world they never destroyed the deities and practices they found, except those of the druids, who were a focal point of political opposition and whose human sacrifices were a convenient pretext for their suppression. Instead, the Romans adopted, adapted, and assimilated. One significant aspect of this was the use of Roman divine names for local deities, the *interpretatio Romana*. Thus Zeus, and after him Jupiter, was identified in the East quite naturally with the local supreme god: at Heliopolis (Baalbek, Lebanon) with Hadad, the consort of Atargatis; at Doliche (Duluk) in Commagene (southeastern Turkey) with the old supreme god of the Hittites of that same name. These fusions spread over the Roman world. Jupiter Heliopolitanus is found in Athens, Pannonia, Venetia, Puteoli (Pozzuoli), Rome, Gaul, and Britain. Jupiter Dolichenus traveled with the soldiers even more extensively. Melkart of Tyre was assimilated with Heracles/Hercules, Eshmun of Sidon with Asclepius/Aesculapius. In North Africa, Ba'al—the Lord—was usually identified with Saturn, although Jupiter acquired some of his former devotion.

In the Celtic West a relatively few Roman gods acquired a large number of cult titles by identification with local deities. At Bath, Sulis, originally a sun goddess, then the power of the healing springs, became equated with Minerva. We find Apollo Maponus (a god of youth) at Corbridge and Ribchester, Apollo Cunomaglus (a god of the hunt) at Nettleton. Mars acquired an incredible number of aliases: Thincsus at Housesteads, Lenus (a god of healing) at Trier, Ocelus in Carlisle, Cocidius (perhaps the river Coquet) at Bewcastle, Alator and Toutates at Barkway, Medocius at Colchester, Corotiacus at Mattlesham, Condates at Bowes, Braciacae (perhaps a god of beer) at Bakewell, Belucairus at Carvoran, Nodens (Nuada of the Silver Hand) at Lydney and Lancaster, Olludius at Custom Scrubs, Rigisamus at West Coker. Others from Britain include Jupiter Taranus (a thunder-god) from Chester, Mercurius Andescociuoncus from Colchester, Hercules Saegon from Silchester, Silvanus Callirius (otherwise unparalleled) from Colchester, and Silvanus Vinotonus from Bowes. This assimilation was not one-sided, for just as there was an *interpretatio Romana* there was also an *interpretatio Celtica*: as the Celtic gods were romanized, the Roman gods were celticized. Thus Hercules sits cross-legged, rather like the Buddha, a totally un-Roman representation. In a fourfold representation of Mercury, now in Paris, two of the heads are Roman and beardless, two bearded and Celtic.

CULT TITLES OF DIVINITIES

In both Greece and Rome individual gods appear under a multiplicity of cult titles. Sometimes the titles represent different functions of the deity concerned, just as may occur today if the same person happens to be an elected official and a practicing physician; there is a different approach to him both in place and manner depending on the kind of consultation sought. Sometimes they represent the fusion of a Greek or Roman god with a foreign divinity.

The range of cult titles is bewildering. In the first volume alone of his monumental study *Zeus*, A. B. Cook lists some 250 cult titles or epithets applied to Zeus, as well as some fifty applied to Jupiter. Lewis Farnell

(*The Cults of the Greek States*) finds about a hundred cult titles of Athena. Even a particular function may be diversified by different epithets. As a war-goddess she may be Promachorma, or Areia, or Stratia, or Alkidemos, or Nikephoros (Bringer of victory) or simply Nike (Victory, as in the charming little temple on the Acropolis at Athens).

The Romans present a similarly bewildering variety, and not only in late or provincial combinations. Take Juno, a very early divinity. As June Quiritis she was worshiped in all the ancient divisions (*curiae*) of the state; she and she alone. As June Populina she was the power of the infantry, the people (*populus*) under arms. As Juno Caprotina she came from Fidenae (Castel Giubileo) and was associated with fertility rites. As Rumina she blessed Rome, though the title was later associated with breast-feeding. Juno Februa (and similar epithets) associated her with ritual cleansing. Juno Lucina perhaps belonged to the grove (*lucus*), although later Romans identified her with light (*lux*). Juno Regina was herself queen, but perhaps in origin the goddess who blessed one of the kings. Juno Moneta was the warner or recorder; she protected money and the mint. Juno Sispes or Sospita was a protector from Lanuvium. Juno Sororia had to do with the swelling breasts of young girls; her altar was very old. Juno Opigena presumably brought material prosperity, although this later was regarded as consisting in children. Juno Pomona similarly brought the blessing of fruit. Juno Cinxia, Iterduca, and Domiduca were regarded as powers of marriage, ungirdling the bride, leading her out and bringing her home, personifications of *numina;* so with Pronuba, matron of honor. Juno Ossipagina set bones, whether broken or immature. Thus the many titles of the goddess relate either to differences of origin or to differences of function. But there is some indication of a changing function, an originally military function being reinterpreted in relation to the life of women.

The evidence is conflicting about the attitude of worshipers to the same god under different cult titles. From Greece one of the clearest examples of such a distinction is that of Xenophon, who was under the wrath of Zeus Meilichios and under the protection of Zeus Basileus (Xenophon, *The March Up Country* [*Anabasis*] 7.6.44; 7.8.4). At Rome we find Cicero taking the point of view that was politically and forensically advantageous. He defends the decision of the Romans in 133 B.C. to consult Ceres at Henna (Enna) in Sicily rather than at Rome because Ceres of Henna was prior, although the real reason was an assertion of Rome's political authority in the disturbed state of Henna. But he equally holds that sacrilegious acts committed by Verres against the temples of Juno in Melita (Malta) and Samos are an offense to the Roman goddess Juno Regina (Cicero, *Against Verres* [*In Verrem*] 2.4.32.71; 2.4.46.103–104; 2.5.72.184). There is not much doubt that Jupiter Heliopolitanus or Jupiter Dolichenus was regarded in some ways as distinct from Jupiter Optimus Maximus. But how did the average Roman worshiper respond to the temples of Jupiter Feretrius and Jupiter Optimus Maximus, hard by one another on the Capitol?

FURTHER DEVELOPMENTS

Even in the republican period the Roman Senate occasionally made deliberate moves to import new gods. Early in the third century B.C. they brought in Asclepius/Aesculapius to the island in the Tiber where the sick have ever since been treated. At a key point in the war with Hannibal they introduced the Great Mother (Cybele) from Asia Minor in the form of a black baetyl (sacred stone); then, horrified by the orgiastic cult and the self-castration of the priests, they clamped down on Roman participation. The cult came to new prominence in the reign of Claudius.

In the Hellenistic age, some of the Egyptian cults had begun to spread, and spread further under the Romans. Sarapis (Serapis), an invention of the Ptolemies to provide a new universal god, became much loved; he was found in Londinium (London) in the Mithraeum. Isis, whose temple in Rome was a place for assignations, acquired a deep personal devotion. The racy, bawdy *The Golden Ass* (*Metamorphoses*) of Apuleius has its climax in devout initiation into her salvific mysteries; the sculptural image-convention of her with the infant Horus was taken over by Christian artists to show Mary and Jesus. Isis made universal claims. She is described in inscriptions as "having ten thousand names"; in a Latin inscription she is "Thou one who art all things." She reveals herself to Apuleius as the first of the heavenly beings, the single appearance of the gods and goddesses, the Mother of the Gods, Minerva, Venus, Diana, Proserpina, Ceres, Juno, Bellona, Hecate, Nemesis; her true name, known in Ethiopia and Egypt, is Queen Isis. In a hymn written by one Isidorus, it is she who is Discoverer of all life; she grants ordered society, introduces laws, reveals sciences, finds out the nature of flowers and fruits, brings the Nile to brim over the land of Egypt. Thracians, Greeks, Syrians, Lycians honor her under the name of their own gods. She is all-saving (*Hymn* 1.29–34, Vanderlip [1972]):

All who are held in the destiny of death, all in
  bondage,
all who are racked with pain which will not let
  them sleep,
all men journeying in a foreign country,
all who sail on the great sea in stormy
  weather,
when ships are wrecked and men lose their
  lives—

all these find salvation if they pray for your present help.

Yet careful study of the inscriptions suggests that if this was a missionary religion it was not especially successful and, in Africa and Gaul, for example, remained exotic.

The same was even more true of the Jewish god, who would brook no rivals. Jewish practices left them something of a people apart. They did make proselytes "god-fearers," but they were seemingly not many, although Josephus makes extravagant claims of influence and initiation (*Against Apion* [*Contra Apionem*] 2.59 ff.). The Jewish Yahweh was sometimes identified with a god derived from Philadelphia (Amman, Jordan) called Hypsistos—Most High. He too was identified with Zeus. The very exclusiveness of the Jews led to a fascination with their god, and his name in variously garbled forms is prominent in magical papyri.

Under the Roman Empire, Mithraism spread among soldiers, traders, and civil servants. It came from Persia, and worshiped both the great god of order and light, Ahura Mazda, and Mithras, a savior and an intermediary in the battle against the forces of chaos and darkness. Mithras was an attractive figure, but the French historian and philosopher Ernest Renan was wrong in thinking that he might have conquered the world. The spread of Mithraism was limited, and the chapels small.

The Roman emperors took over the Hellenistic practice of ruler-worship, but in general followed the practice by which a good ruler (being himself the son of a divine predecessor) might be coopted to the heavenly senate on his death. Only megalomaniacs were worshiped in their lifetime. Mark Antony appeared as Dionysus incarnate, Gaius (Caligula) took up position between his brother gods Castor and Pollux, Commodus donned the guise of Hercules. Augustus set the proper precedent. His very name had a sacred aura. Apart from Egypt, where he virtually had to be the divine monarch, he did not permit himself to be worshiped unassociated with other deities, although honor might be paid to *numen Augusti, genius Augusti,* or Augustus together with Rome (the city goddess). But he expected and was awarded deification at death, which Julius Caesar had received before him. The better emperors remained self-deprecating. Tiberius rebuked a flattering courtier who spoke of his sacred duties: "You mean my laborious duties." He was a Hercules who might expect divinity as a reward for his labors, not a god incarnate. Claudius tried to stop being called a god in Egypt, himself, although the prefect in promulgating the decree called him a god. There is a delightful story of the blunt soldier-emperor Vespasian, feeling his death coming on, saying, "Oh dear! I think I'm becoming a god!"

In the third century A.D. the Roman armies were being battered by the forces of Persia, who honored the Sun. Syria, where the Sun was supreme, was playing an increasing part in Roman affairs. In A.D. 274 Aurelian formally installed the Unconquered Sun as the supreme god of the Romans. Macrobius made comprehensive claims for the Sun. If he rules the other luminaries he must be responsible for all that goes on. The other gods are potencies of the Sun. Apollo is the name we give to the Sun's healing power, Mercury to his gift of speech, Ceres to the gift of grain, and so on. Even Jupiter is only a name for his supereminence (Macrobius, *Saturnalia* 1.17–23). This espousal of the Sun had a curious aftermath. Constantine's family were worshipers of the Unconquered Sun. He had a vision of a cross superimposed on the sun, a Christian symbol with his ancestral god. When he established Sunday as a day of rest in the Roman Empire, it was as "the day of the worshipful Sun." Constantine created the Christian Empire, with a new god. But the god he worshiped was syncretistically conceived, a god of power, not a god of love.

BIBLIOGRAPHY

SOURCES

Aeschylus, *Septem quae supersunt tragoediae* (*Seven Extant Tragedies*), Denys L. Page, ed. (1972); Apuleius, *Apology,* Harold E. Butler and Arthur S. Owen, eds. (1914), and *The Golden Ass* (*Metamorphoses*), William Adlington, trans. (1920, 1962); Aratus of Soli, *Arati Phaenomena,* Jean Martin, ed. (1956); Aristophanes, *The Knights* (*Equites*), Robert A. Neil, ed. (1901); Aristotle, *Nicomachean Ethics,* Harris Rackham, trans. (1945), and *On Sophistical Refutations, On Coming-to-be and Passing-away, On the Cosmos,* Edward S. Forster and David J. Furley, trans. (1955); Cicero, *The Verrine Orations,* Leonard H. Greenwood, trans., 2 vols (1960); Dio Chrysostom (os), *Discourses* (*Orations*), J. W. Cohoon and H. Lamar Crosby, 5 vols. (1932–1951); Diogenes Laertius, *Vitae Philosophorum* (*Lives and Opinions of the Famous Philosophers*), Herbert S. Long, ed. (1964); Wilhelm Dittenberger, ed., *Sylloge Inscriptionum Graecarum,* 4 vols. (1915–1924).

Euripides, *Bacchae* (*The Bacchants*), Eric R. Dodds, ed., (1960), *Hippolytus,* John Ferguson, ed. (1984), and *Ion,* Arthur S. Owen, ed. (1939); Eusebius, *Praeparatio Evangelica* (*Preparation for the Gospel*), Edwin H. Gifford, ed. (1903); Rudolf Hercher, ed., *Epistolographi Graeci* (1871); Hesiod, *The Homeric Hymns and Homerica,* H. G. Evelyn-White, trans. (1940, rev. ed. 1959); Homer (*Works*), David B. Monro and Thomas W. Allen, eds., 5 vols. (1912–1920); Josephus, *The Life: Against Apion,* Henry St. John Thackeray, trans. (1956); Juvenal, *Sixteen Satires,* Peter Green, trans. (1967); Macrobius (*Works*), Jacob A. Willis, ed., 2 vols. (1963); Pausanias, *Description of Greece,* James G. Frazer, ed., 6 vols. (1898); Plato, *Laws,* Robert G. Bury, ed., 2 vols. (1926; repr. 1968), and *Lysis, Symposium, Gorgias,* Walter R. M. Lumb, trans. (1939); Plutarch, *The Parallel Lives,* Bernadotte Perrin, trans., 11 vols. (1967).

Quintilian, *The Education of an Orator* (*Institutio Oratoria*), Harold E. Butler, trans., 4 vols. (1970);

Servius, *In Vergili carmina commentarii* (*Commentaries on Vergil's Poetry*), Georgius Thilo and Hermann Hagen, eds. (1881–1902; repr. 1961); Xenophon, *Anabasis* (*The March Up Country*), Carleton L. Brownson, trans., 2 vols. (1921–1922).

STUDIES

Norman H. Baynes, *Constantine the Great and the Christian Church* (1929); Arthur B. Cook, *Zeus*, 3 vols. (1914–1940); Georges Dumézil, *Archaic Roman Religion*, Philip Krapp, trans., 2 vols. (1970); Lewis R. Farnell, *The Cults of the Greek States*, 5 vols. (1896–1909); John Ferguson, *The Religions of the Roman Empire* (1970), and *Greek and Roman Religion: A Source Book* (1980); William W. Fowler, *The Religious Experience of the Roman People* (1911); Jean Gagé, *Apollon romain* (1955); William K. C. Guthrie, *The Greeks and Their Gods* (1950); Kurt Latte, *Römische Religionsgeschichte*, 2d ed. (1967).

Martin P. Nilsson, *Geschichte der griechischen Religion*, I (1967), II (1961), and *A History of Greek Religion*, F. J. Fielden, trans., 2d ed. (1949); Arthur D. Nock, *Essays on Religion and the Ancient World*, Zeph Stewart, ed., 2 vols. (1972); Robert M. Ogilvie, *The Romans and Their Gods in the Age of Augustus* (1969); Walter F. Otto, *The Homeric Gods*, Moses Hadas, trans. (1954); Robert E. A. Palmer, *Roman Religion and Roman Empire* (1974); Lily R. Taylor, *The Divinity of the Roman Emperor* (1931); Jules Toutain, *Les cultes païens dans l'empire romain* (1907–1920); Vera F. Vanderlip, *The Four Greek Hymns of Isidorus and the Cult of Isis* (1972); Georg Wissowa, *Religion und Kultus der Römer*, 2d ed. (1912).

Myths and Cosmologies

MICHAEL SIMPSON

MYTHS WERE FOR THE GREEKS the equivalent of the Bible for the ancient Hebrews. The Hebrews have been called "the people of the Book." The Greeks, as Bernard Knox says, "are the people not of the Book but of the myth" (1979, pp. 17, 18).

Attempts have been made to divide Greek thinking into an earlier, "mythical" phase and a later, "rational" one, but so clear-cut a distinction cannot be maintained. Myths never ceased to be important to the Greeks and to play a role in their thinking. As rational thinking developed, particularly in the latter half of the fifth century B.C., an awareness of myth, as such, also developed. But myths retained their value to the Greeks as a source of understanding. As Plato says at the end of the *Republic* (in the person of Socrates), "And so, Glaucon, the *muthos* was saved and did not perish, and, if we heed it, it may save us" (621b8–c1).

DEFINITIONS

Muthos, the Greek source of the word "myth," has the general meaning of "word," "speech," and "story." Aristotle in the *Poetics* gives *muthos* the special technical meaning of "plot," at one point defining plot (*muthos*) as the imitation of an action (1450a3–5) and adding: "For by plot [*muthos*] I mean structure." "Structure," here, is D. W. Lucas' correct rendition of the literal Greek, "the putting-together of the events." As Lucas says, "The story is a preliminary selection from the stream of events; in the plot the story is organized" (1968, p. 100).

The Greek word and Aristotle's special use of it provide two starting points for defining myth: (1) language is its province and (2) myth is a structure, a "plot," a putting-together of events. To this we may add that myths are the product of oral societies, not literate ones; it is spoken, not written, language that is the original province of myth. According to Eric Havelock, people in oral cultures think differently from people in literate ones, for whom writing makes possible a new kind of discourse, characterized by the term "conceptual": "Nonliterate speech had favored discourse describing action; the postliterate altered the balance in favor of

861

reflection" (1982, pp. 7–8). Myths are preeminently a discourse of action.

We know Greek myths primarily through Greek literature, which includes oral poetry. Greek literature was composed in and for a society that at first was oral (on its way to becoming literate), and then literate (by the end of the fifth century B.C.), while retaining features of its earlier, oral stage. Greek literature thus reflects the tension "between the modes of oral and documented speech" (Havelock, 1982, p. 187). The myths are in fact oral society's legacy to Greek literate culture, a legacy that never ceased to influence the thought of these "people of the myth."

Oral societies are traditional societies. They strive to maintain connection with their past, which means that the older generation must create and maintain connection with the younger generation. Telling stories is one way of doing this, stories which the older generation heard when it was young from a still older generation, and which the present younger generation, when it grows older, will tell to its successor generation. These stories, which link the generations, will be related to all those aspects of the society that it must take into account for its preservation and well-being.

We may now give a definition of myth as a "traditional narrative structure" or, in G. S. Kirk's words, as a "traditional tale" (1974, pp. 22 ff.). There are many other definitions of myth, based on different theories, each of which emphasizes a particular aspect of a society, or of human beings, or of the human mind, to the exclusion of other aspects. Percy Cohen (1969) identifies seven theories of myth. Following and amplifying Cohen, Kirk (1974) discusses the limitations of five "monolithic theories" that define myths variously as portraying nature, as explaining place names and customs, as evoking a past creative era, as accompanying rituals, and as establishing a charter for the

existence of a people. Additionally, he delineates five theories that view myths as "products of the psyche": myths express something repressed, fulfill a wish, or create an emotional condition (Aristotle); myths are analogous to dreams or daydreams (Freud and others); myths reveal the collective unconscious and contain "archetypes" (Jung); myths are symbolic (Cassirer); myths reflect the workings of the human mind (Lévi-Strauss)(pp. 38–91).

A "traditional tale" may contain elements of folktales, which are, as Kirk says, "simple tales of adventure, intrigue and ingenuity, sometimes with giants or other supernatural components" (1974, p. 24). As the term "traditional" indicates, the origin of a myth is not important, while its transmission and preservation are all-important. In the words of Walter Burkert, "A tale becomes traditional not by virtue of being created, but by being retold and accepted." In the process of transmission, a tale can suffer omissions and misinterpretations, yet still retain its identity. This process implies that a tale is independent from a particular text or a particular reality. Its identity must come, therefore, from "a *structure of sense* within the tale itself." Such structures would be elements of plot or various themes. A tale as a structure of sense is derived from "basic biological or cultural 'programs of actions.' " Myths of quest, for example, can be derived from the program of action ordered by the biological imperative "get": " 'go out, ask, find out, fight for it, take and run.' " (Burkert, 1979, pp. 2–18). Burkert goes on to say that a myth thus applies to something of collective importance, and that includes almost all aspects of human existence: institutions of family and society, gods and rituals, disease, the seasons, the availability of food, laws governing marriage and incest, and the order of nature and the universe—all of these can become the subjects of myths.

The relation between myth and ritual remains controversial after almost a century of discussion. Burkert's view of this relation seems the most balanced: While "myth does not grow directly out of ritual," the two are, nevertheless, "closely allied." The function of ritual is "to dramatize the order of life," while myth "clarifies the order of life." Moreover, myth "frequently explains and justifies social orders and establishments, and in so doing it is related to ritual, which occurs by means of social interaction" (1983, pp. 31, 33).

THE CHARACTER OF GREEK MYTHS

Myths served as history for the Greeks who, as a "traditional" people, used the past to give meaning to the present. Myths were, in a sense, the past preserved, interpreted, and applied to the present. They told the Greeks who they were as a people, providing, as M. I. Finley says, a "mythical charter" for "Hellenic self-consciousness" (1975, p. 26).

Greek poets, beginning with nameless oral bards, shaped and developed the myths as they retold them, functioning as seers of the past, and it was Homer and Hesiod, Herodotus says (2.53), who created a theogony for the Greeks, gave the gods their epithets, assigned them their prerogatives and functions, and described their forms. For the Greeks, then, myth and literature are inextricably bound together.

Kirk (1974) divides myths into those (1) describing the origin of the universe, (2) describing the birth and development of the gods, (3) narrating the early history of human beings, and (4) relating the exploits of heroes. The corpus of traditional tales (particularly tales belonging to the first and second type) can be thought of as a "system of classification, a particular way of ordering and conceptualising the universe," according to Jean-Pierre Vernant (1980, p. 94).

The system classifies powers, for the Greeks conceived of the universe as an elaborate interconnected organization of multiple powers which operate in several areas: in nature, in human society, in individual human beings, and in the other world. These powers—the gods especially, but also other divine and semi-divine powers—do not stand outside the universe and the world. They are immanent, not transcendent (Lloyd-Jones, 1971, p. 160).

The myths of the origin of the universe (cosmogony) and of the birth and development of the gods (theogony), as related in Hesiod's *Theogony* and in Apollodorus' *Library* and discussed below, use the genealogical catalog as their basic ordering device for classifying the powers of the universe. That is, Earth, who comes into being on her own and produces Sky, mates with Sky and gives birth to divine powers. These mate in turn to produce the gods, whose various unions give rise to yet other divine beings. Norman O. Brown sees in the genealogical series "a pattern of progressive differentiation" represented as a "process of evolutionary proliferation" (1953, pp. 15–16).

Several points should be stressed. First, in Hesiod's view, all life in its particular aspects is charged with divinity. Second, the genealogical catalog conveys the essential relatedness, the connections, among all the phenomena of life. Third, this system of divine powers is conceived, by means of genealogy, as a vast humanlike family, and these powers are modeled on human beings. Finally, their "family relation" instructs us to consider them as a system, rather than singly, in isolation from each other, and, indeed, according to Vernant, they cannot otherwise be understood (1980, p. 99).

Kirk notes two distinctive characteristics of Greek myths, particularly heroic myths: (1) "Fantastic elements—elements not only remote from real life and the actually possible, but also genuinely imaginative in conception—are few"; and (2) Greek myths are concise and formally neat, they "do not sprawl or indulge in irrelevant detail or complication" (1970, pp. 182, 190). Moreover, the very number of heroic myths in comparison to myths of gods or other supernatural beings makes Greece unique. "No other ancient culture is similar" (Kirk, 1974, pp. 215).

Kirk (1970) constructs a "motif-index" of twenty-four "commonest themes" and of eight "special, unusual or bizarre themes" in Greek myths. The "commonest themes" exhibit four preoccupations: (1) "contests and quests, particularly involving monsters"; (2) "the relations between men and gods"; (3) "the presence in the background of the gods themselves"; and (4) "stresses within the family" (pp. 187 ff., 202). Kirk views the repeated references to family stress in Greek myths as "a broad response to a continuing human characteristic" (p. 194); Philip E. Slater (1968, 1974), however, thinks Greek myths exhibit a pathology specific to ancient Greek society and the Greek family.

Carrying the structuralist thinking of Kirk and others to its furthest extent, Charles Segal (1983) uses the term "megatext" to describe the corpus of Greek myths. By megatext he means not only the themes and tales available to oral poets, but also "subconscious patterns or 'deep structures' . . . which tales of a given type share with one another." Within the megatext, "specific literary narrations of particular myths . . . operate as sub-texts, exploiting particular aspects of the megatext, commenting on it, or sometimes making explicit certain networks of interconnection implied but not openly stated in the megatext" (p. 176).

GREEK MYTHS

Hesiod's *Theogony* is the major primary source for the Greek mythic account of the origin of the universe, the birth and development of the gods, and the early history of human culture. The existence of human beings is taken for granted; there are no myths of their creation. Hesiod's *Works and Days* supplements the early history of men narrated in the *Theogony*. Apollodorus' *Library* is an additional source for these myths. Other works, in addition to these, narrate myths of the development or the lives of the gods: the *Homeric Hymns*, the *Iliad* and the *Odyssey* of Homer, Pindar's *Odes*, and the tragedies of Aeschylus, Sophocles, and Euripides. Since such narrative is not the purpose of these works (except for the *Homeric Hymns*), the myths are presented in fragmented and allusive ways.

The Origin of the Universe

According to Hesiod, Void, Earth, and Desire came into being first (and uncaused). Void produced Darkness and Night, and Night, with Darkness, gave birth to Light and Day. (*Chaos,* the Greek word here rendered "Void," means a "yawning" or a "gaping.") At the very beginning, then, we have that which exists (Earth), that in which it exists (Void), and the means to further creation (Desire). Furthermore, Void is the natural parent of Darkness and Night and grandparent of Light and Day since it is the medium they fill.

Earth gave birth to Sky and, next, to bodies of water. With Sky, Earth produced the twelve Titans; the three Cyclopes, who fashioned the thunder and the lightning bolt and gave them to Zeus; and the three monsters known as the "Hundred-Handed." Because Sky did not allow his children to be born, but hid them, rather, in their mother, Earth, she fashioned a sickle and urged her children to attack their father with it. Her son Cronus volunteered to do so and, while Sky and Earth lay together making love, Cronus cut off his father's genitals with the sickle. When he cast them over his shoulder drops of blood fell on Earth, as a result of which she gave birth to the Furies and the Giants. Sky's genitals landed in the sea, in which, floating, they emitted a white foam from which Aphrodite was born. (Her name means "born from foam.") She is the goddess of love.

Next, Hesiod tells of the births of a host of beings such as Destruction, Death, Sleep, Blame, Grief, Retribution, Deceit, Love, Old Age, and Strife, all the offspring of Night, and, as offspring of Strife, Distress, Distraction, Famine, Sorrow, Wars, Battles, Murder, Slaughters, Lawlessness and Madness, and Oath. For us, most of these are abstractions. For Hesiod, in the words of M. L. West, "they are invisible, imperishable, and have great influence over human affairs; they must be gods" (1966, p. 33).

The Birth and Development of the Gods

After narrating the births of the offspring of Sea and Earth and of their multiplying children, Hesiod returns to the Titans, offspring of Earth and Sky. Among them, Rhea and Cronus produced the gods Hestia, Demeter, Hera, Hades, Poseidon, and Zeus, the last destined to be king of the gods. Like his father Sky before him, Cronus was opposed to his children and swallowed them as they were born—all but Zeus, whom Rhea secretly gave birth to on the island of Crete and hid in a cave there. She deceived Cronus by offering him, in place of Zeus, a stone wrapped in baby blankets, which he accepted and swallowed. Later Cronus was again deceived, this time by Earth, and vomited up his children, beginning with the stone, the last thing he had swallowed.

The gods, offspring of Cronus and Rhea, fought the Titans for supreme power for ten years until Zeus released the Hundred-Handed from the chains in which Sky had earlier bound them and enlisted them on the side of the gods. With their help, the gods won a bloody battle. They imprisoned the Titans below earth in Tartarus, where they are guarded by the Hundred-Handed. Following the gods' victory over the Titans, Earth advised the gods to invite Zeus to be their king. He, in return, gave them their rights and privileges.

Metis (Intelligence) conceived Athena with Zeus, but he swallowed Metis while she was pregnant and gave birth himself to Athena from his head. With various consorts, Zeus produced the Hours, the Fates, and the Graces. Zeus and Demeter together produced Persephone, whom Hades stole from her mother to be his bride. Next, Zeus fathered with Memory the Muses, and, with Leto, Artemis and Apollo. Hera became Zeus's wife and gave birth by him to Hebe (Youth), Ares, and Eileithyia (the goddess of childbirth). Resentful of the birth of Athena (from Zeus's head), Hera by herself gave birth to Hephaestus, the smith of the gods. Finally, Zeus had Hermes (by Maia), Dionysus (by Semele), and the hero Heracles (by Alcmene).

According to W. K. C. Guthrie (1950), twelve of these gods composed a canon in the classical period known as the pantheon: Zeus, Hera, Poseidon, Demeter, Apollo, Artemis, Ares, Aphrodite, Hermes, Athena, Hephaestus, and Hestia. Dionysus replaces Hestia in the panathenaic festival carved on the east frieze of the Parthenon at Athens.

Brown notes that the human cosmos is founded upon "polar tension," which is created by the juxtaposition of contrasting catalogs of divine powers. For example, the descendants of Night, grouped around Death, Vengeance, Deceit, and Strife, are juxtaposed with the catalog of Nereids, the fifty daughters of Nereus, the son of Sea, who "form a group of gracious influences in the human cosmos" (1953, pp. 27 ff.).

The polarity in the human cosmos between Night and Nereus runs back to Void and Earth, from whom they are respectively descended and who form the basic polarity in the physical cosmos. As Brown says, "The polarity in the human cosmos is derived from the polarity in the physical cosmos" (1953, p. 28). The descendants of Void and Earth never intermarry. The polarity is continued in the children of Earth and Sky, who produce not only the Titans, "the parents of order in the physical, divine, and human cosmos," but also the Cyclopes and Hundred-Handed, "who are symbols of disorder and violence" (Brown, 1953, p. 28).

In three areas of human culture Zeus develops the "seeds of progress" contained in the Nereids (and in the Oceanids, daughters of Ocean, a kind of doubling of the Nereids). First, Zeus actualizes "the potentialities of Law" in his union with Themis (Divine Law) who gives birth to the Hours and the Fates. Next, Zeus actualizes "the potentialities of art" in his union with Eurynome, who produces the Graces, associated with "festive occasions which promote art," and in his union with Mnemosyne (Memory), who becomes the mother of the Muses, associated with the various arts. Third, Zeus "brings to final perfection the religion of beauty" by fathering, with Leto, Apollo and Artemis (Brown, 1953, pp. 30–31).

Hesiod's universe, from its origin to human culture, is composed of powers ordered by genealogical catalogs into a "family system," but also divided into "good" and "bad." Zeus and the other gods, while early born in the universe, did not create it and were, in fact, created by it. Zeus is the dominant power in this system of powers, but he presides rather than rules over it.

The manifestations of Zeus's power warrant a closer look. In nature, the sky is the arena for that power, which controls the weather (rain, lightning, and thunder), the cycle of day and night, and the seasons. In human society, Zeus's power is present in the king, extending, through him, into the areas of battle, council, and the meting out of justice. The power of Zeus resides in the home, supporting the (male) head of the family and extending to marriage, which creates the family unit and legitimates its hierarchical order of father, wife, and children. Zeus's power protects strangers and suppliants who enter the house. According to Vernant's analysis (1980), the range of that power illustrates the function of divine powers in general: "They make it possible to integrate the human individual into various social groups, each with its own ordered way of functioning and its own hierarchy; and to integrate these social groups, in their turn, into the order of nature which is then made a part of the divine order" (p. 97).

We noted above that the gods, who make a system of interacting powers, do not stand outside the world but are an integral part of it. We may also note that they did not create the universe, the world of nature, nor mankind, but were themselves created by earlier powers. So the gods, while immortal, are not eternal. Nor are they all-powerful and omniscient. Rather, they have specific knowledge and specific powers and so come into conflict with each other, conflict which Zeus adjudicates. Each god, in fact, as Vernant says, "represents an authentic aspect of being, expresses one part of reality, stands for a particular type of value without which the universe would, as it were, be mutilated" (1980, p. 103).

Although the gods may at times influence destiny, they do not rule it. Zeus in the *Iliad* (16.433 ff.) would like to save his son Sarpedon, who is destined to die in battle. Hera warns him that the gods will not support him if he intervenes, for if he defies Sarpedon's fate and saves him, some other god may do the same for his son, chaos could then ensue, and Zeus would lose his supremacy.

The gods manifest themselves in the lives and affairs of a human being in "sudden impulses, in the plans and ideas that come into his head, in the panic or frenzy that grips the warrior, or in a surge of love or a feeling of shame" (Vernant, 1980, p. 104). Events in the world, however, can have multiple causes. Patroclus, mortally wounded by Hector, interrupts his conqueror as he vaunts over him to say that destiny and Apollo killed him (and of men, the Trojan Euphorbus who had struck him with a javelin). Hector, he says, is but the third to slay him (*Iliad* 16.849 ff.). These multiple causes refer to separate levels of reality and so do not exclude each other.

As gods of major importance to Greek myths, Demeter, Athena, Apollo, and Dionysus merit further consideration here. As noted above, Demeter is the offspring of Cronus and Rhea. The myth of Demeter formed the basis of the Eleusinian Mysteries, the most widespread rites of ancient Greece, performed at Eleusis, near Athens. The rites were secret, and there were heavy penalties for revealing them. The Eleusinian Mysteries originally celebrated fertility, but their focus was broadened to include an afterlife for humans. As Kirk (1974) says, "The renewal of crops became a pledge of renewal for the initiates themselves, of life after death" (pp. 249–250).

According to the Homeric *Hymn to Demeter*, Hades, the brother of Zeus (and of Demeter) to whom the underworld was given, seized Demeter's daughter, Persephone, while she was picking flowers in a meadow with the daughters of Oceanus and took her to the underworld to be his queen. Demeter heard Persephone's cry but could not reach her and did not know who had carried her off. Distraught with grief and refusing to eat, she searched for her everywhere. When she learned from Helios (the Sun) that Hades, with Zeus's connivance, had kidnapped Persephone, Demeter, her grief mixed with rage, abandoned the company of the gods and wandered the earth, stopping finally at Eleusis, where the royal family took her in. She eventually revealed her identity and a temple was built for her. Still grieving for her daughter, Demeter withheld the earth's

crops for a year. Alarmed at the threatened destruction of human life, Zeus and the other gods tried to persuade her to relent, but she refused. Zeus then demanded that Hades release Persephone. He agreed, but secretly gave her a pomegranate seed to eat that required her to return to him for a third of every year. Demeter rejoiced at the return of her daughter and allowed fields to bear crops again. After revealing her rites and mysteries to the king and princes of Eleusis, she returned to the gods on Mount Olympus, the home of the gods.

Athena was born from the head of Zeus after he swallowed Metis, with whom he had conceived the goddess, to forestall a prophecy that Metis was destined to bear a daughter equal to Zeus in strength and intelligence. Athena became the patron goddess and namesake of Athens by defeating Poseidon in a contest for dominion over Attica, the region in which Athens is located. In the contest, Poseidon produced the sea, but Athena created the olive, and the gods judging the contest awarded Attica to her for having made the more valuable contribution (Apollodorus, *The Library* 3.14.1). Aeschylus in the *Eumenides,* the third play of his trilogy, the *Oresteia,* makes Athena the founder of the court of the Areopagus, Athens' highest court. In the latter half of the fifth century, the Athenians built the magnificent temple to Athena known as the Parthenon (from *parthenos,* meaning maiden; Athena was a virgin goddess) and erected a huge gold and ivory image of the goddess in it.

Athena is the patron of Odysseus in the *Odyssey* of Homer where we see her at the beginning of the poem pleading with Zeus to bring her protégé home to Ithaca from Ogygia, the island paradise that is the home of Calypso, a minor goddess who detains him there. She works on Odysseus' behalf on Ithaca before he arrives, and upon his return helps him to rid his palace of the suitors who have invaded it in his absence and threatened his family. The connection between goddess and mortal is intelligence deployed in tricks, disguises, and deceit, and they are, as Athena herself says, "Two of a kind, . . . /contrivers, both. Of all men now alive/you are the best in plots and story telling./My own fame is for wisdom among the gods—/deceptions, too" (*Odyssey* 13.296–99, Robert Fitzgerald, trans., [1961], p. 225).

Sophocles' tragedy the *Ajax* portrays Athena as a cruel goddess, for to protect Odysseus and the other chieftains at Troy from a murderous assault by Ajax she attacks the hero in a most vicious way: she destroys his sanity. But Athena operates here simply by exercising power in her province, the mind, just as Poseidon in the *Odyssey* operates in his, the sea, when he shipwrecks Odysseus, and as Aphrodite exercises power in her province, human passion, when she destroys Hippolytus by inciting sexual passion for him in his stepmother (in Euripides' play *Hippolytus*).

The Homeric *Hymn to Apollo* names the small, unattractive island of Delos as the place where Leto came to give birth to Apollo after all other lands had refused her out of fear. She bore the god under a date palm, to which she clung during her labor, the spot becoming, as T. W. Allen *et al.* say, "one of the most famous sights in antiquity" (1936, p. 202).

While Delos was revered as Apollo's birthplace, the god made Delphi the seat of his worship, where he himself laid the foundation of his temple. At a nearby spring he killed a great she-dragon and from the rotting of the carcass (Greek *putho,* "make to rot"), the place was given the name Pytho, and Apollo took the epithet Pythian. He established his oracle (seat of prophecy) at Delphi by miraculously bringing there a Cretan ship, the crew of which served as his priests (*Hymn to Apollo* 277 ff.). The temple of Apollo at Delphi was the most important religious center in ancient Greece.

Apollo's attributes are the lyre and the bow, and he is god of healing, poetry, and prophecy. Pindar describes his functions thus: "He is the god who sends/mortal men and women/relief from grievous disease, Apollo,/who has given us the lyre,/who brings the Muse/to whom he chooses, filling the heart/with peace and harmony. He holds the dark/chamber of prophecy." (*Pythian* 5.63 ff., Frank Nisetich [1980], p. 192). In the *Iliad,* Apollo answers his priest Chryses' prayer by shooting his arrows among the Greek host—animals and men— to create plague: the god of healing is also god of disease (1.43–53).

Apollo also had great importance for the Greeks as a source of order in the community. In Aeschylus' trilogy the *Oresteia* Apollo commands Orestes to avenge his father's death by killing his mother and then defends him in a trial for murder at Athens that Aeschylus makes the mythical origin of Athens' highest court, the Court of the Areopagus. In Sophocles' *Oedipus the King,* Oedipus names Apollo as his destroyer (1329–1330), who through his oracle prophesied Oedipus' fate to him, thus paradoxically bringing it about. Here he is prophetic knowledge, the counterpart on the level of the divine, as it were, of the terrible self-knowledge that is Oedipus' true fate.

Like all gods—all powers in the universe— Apollo is savage and ruthless when offended: when Marsyas challenged him to a contest in music and, predictably, lost, Apollo killed him by skinning him alive (Apollodorus, *The Library* 1.4.2). When Niobe boasted that she had many more children than Leto (*Iliad* 24.605–608); or that her children were more attractive than Leto's (Apollodorus, *The Library* 3.5.6), Apollo and his sister Artemis killed them all (*Iliad* 24.602–617).

For Pindar, who mentions Apollo frequently in his *Odes,* the god is preeminently god of poetry, poetry of the lyre, that is, poetry of order and peace:

Golden lyre, rightful possession of Apollo/ and the bright-haired Muses,/to you the dancers listen/as they begin the celebration,/and the singers/follow the rhythm/plucked on your trembling strings/in prelude to the chorus;/it is you that quench the lancing bolt/of ever-flowing fire and lull Zeus' eagle/perched on his scepter/with folded wings—/the king of birds. . . . /Your shafts cast enchantment/on the mood of the gods/through the skill of Apollo/and the deep-breasted Muses (*Pythian* 1.1–12, Nisetich, trans. [1980], p. 155).

This aspect of Apollo led Nietzsche to oppose Apollo and his spirit—the spirit of control and order—to that of Dionysus, the god associated with the liquid, exciting music of the flute and rites of ecstasy and self-abandonment, although, according to Nietzsche, Greek tragedy depended upon a fusion of the Apolline and the Dionysiac.

Hesiod's *Theogony* (940–942) records Dionysus' birth as the offspring of Zeus and Semele, and Apollodorus' *The Library* (3.4.3) tells the story of Semele, pregnant with Dionysus, who was frightened to death by Zeus's thunderbolt when, at her request, he appeared to her in the form in which he appeared to his wife Hera. Zeus rescued the unborn fetus from the dead Semele's womb and sewed the baby into his thigh, where it remained until it was due to be born.

Eric R. Dodds calls Dionysus the god of all liquid nature, "the liquid fire in the grape, . . . the sap thrusting in a young tree, the blood pounding in the veins of a young animal, all the mysterious and uncontrollable tides that ebb and flow in the life of nature" (1960, p. xii). As Kirk (1974) notes, the god was imported into Greece from Phrygia in Asia Minor after the year 1000 B.C. He was

not one of the pantheon of twelve Olympian gods. The myths about Dionysus narrate the opposition in Greece to the disruptive, orgiastic—but ecstatic—rites he introduced and the terrible vengeance he took upon those who opposed him: Lycurgus, the king of Thrace (Apollodorus, *The Library* 3.5.1; compare also *Iliad* 6.132–140); the daughters of Proetus, king of Argos (Apollodorus, *The Library* 2.2.2); and Pentheus, king of Thebes (Euripides, *The Bacchants* [*Bacchae*]; Apollodorus, *The Library* 3.5.2).

In Euripides' late tragedy *The Bacchants,* Dionysus makes Pentheus insane and contrives his ghastly death at the hands of his mother and other women who, in a state of madness induced by Dionysus' rites, tear Pentheus apart. *The Bacchants* gives a sharp and clear sense of the god's immense power, and of his subtle, effortless, and deadly use of it.

While Euripides portrays Dionysus as a terrifying figure, Aristophanes, in his comedy the *Frogs* (produced in 405 B.C., and so written about the same time as *The Bacchants*), presents the god in a comic role in which he is, by turns, "haughty master, yearning poet-lover, adventuresome traveler, clownish oarsman, disquieting coward, timorous visitor, feckless opportunist, squealing whipping-boy, impressionable judge, vulgar buffoon, unscrupulous umpire" (Stanford, 1962, p. xxx). By juxtaposing the portrayals of Dionysus in these two plays one sees just how complex the Greeks' thinking about their gods could be. The modern view of Dionysus is ably discussed by Henrichs (1984), who traces its formation "before and after 1872."

The Early History of Human Beings

The myths of the early history of mankind are told primarily in Hesiod's *Theogony* and *Works and Days,* although there are myths or fragments of myths in other authors that supplement the accounts given in Hesiod. These myths center around a golden age, Prometheus, and the fall of men.

In *Works and Days* (109 ff.), the myth of the five ages of men begins with the race of gold. This was "in the time of Cronus, when he ruled in heaven" (111). Men lived like gods, carefree, unaging, and feasting. Instead of dying, they simply fell asleep. The earth bore food without being tilled.

In the Golden Age, humans and gods dined together, particularly at marriages, such as those of Peleus and Thetis, the parents of Achilles, or of Cadmus and Harmonia (Pindar, *Pythian* 3.86 ff.), but on other occasions as well: Tantalus was said to have cooked and served his son Pelops at a dinner he prepared for the gods (Pindar, *Olympian* 1.35 ff.; he refutes the tale).

The Golden Age was followed by a silver age in which humans lived short and sorrowful lives because of their misdeeds. Zeus ended this age and it was followed by an age of bronze, filled with war and violence, the members of which destroyed each other. Next came the fourth or heroic age, in which heroes (or "demi-gods") died in military expeditions such as the Trojan War. The fifth age was one of iron and coincided with Hesiod's own time (*Works and Days* 127–201).

A separate tradition records the destruction of the earth by a flood sent upon human beings by Zeus because of their evils, as exemplified by the sons of Lycaon who offered Zeus human flesh to eat when he came to dine with them (Apollodorus, *The Library* 3.8.1–2). This myth is perhaps to be joined to those mentioned above that describe mankind's feasting with the gods (feasts that often ended in disaster). Deucalion and Pyrrha alone survived the flood by building an ark and entering it when the flood-causing rains came. After the flood, they recreated the human race by throwing stones over their shoulders (Apollodorus, *The Library* 1.7.2).

Since Deucalion was the son of Prometheus, and Pyrrha was the daughter of Prometheus' brother Epimetheus, the myth of the flood and the myth of Prometheus can be loosely connected. Hesiod narrates the latter myth in *Theogony* (507–616) and *Works and Days* (42–105).

Prometheus (Forethought) and his brother Epimetheus (Afterthought), Hesiod tells us, were the sons of the Titan Iapetus and Ocean's daughter Clymene. Epimetheus harmed mankind by accepting Zeus's gift of woman. Prometheus was tied up by Zeus, who drove a spear through his middle and set an eagle upon him to eat his liver daily, although it grew back at night.

Prometheus was punished because he earlier deceived Zeus at Mecone (when men and gods were in conflict) by dividing an ox and covering the edible portions with the unappetizing belly, while over the inedible bones he placed shining fat to make them more appealing. Zeus saw through the ruse but nevertheless chose the bones and fat. He punished men for Prometheus' deception by withholding fire from them, but Prometheus stole fire for men, hiding it in a hollow fennel stalk. Zeus then "fashioned at once an evil thing for men in return for fire" (*Theogony* 570), for he commissioned Hephaestus, the smith-god, to create woman. The new creature was brilliantly and beautifully fitted out by Athena and Hephaestus (who made her a crown of gold). From her came the race of women, who are an evil for men, for a man must marry a woman or die childless, while if he does marry, continual evil is his lot.

This tale is supplemented in *Works and Days:* The gods hid from men the means of life, by which one day's work could supply them for a year, because Zeus was angry at Prometheus for the theft of fire. As the price for fire Zeus gave men an evil, woman, created by Hephaestus, taught household skills by Athena, given the charm that creates desire by Aphrodite, and having received from Hermes a shameless mind and deceiving nature. The woman was named Pandora (Gift-of-all), because each god gave to her a plague for mankind as a gift, and Hermes brought her to Epimetheus. Forgetting Prometheus' instructions never to accept a gift from Zeus, Epimetheus received Pandora.

Before Pandora, men lived free from woes, toil, and disease, but she removed the lid from the jar she carried, which contained the gods' "gifts," and scattered all of them except for Hope among men. And so endless troubles afflict mankind, earth and sea are full of evils, and diseases silently range among men night and day.

For Vernant (1980), the major motif of these "interlocking" myths is "hiding": all the means to life once freely available to men without effort by them are now hidden, that is, man must labor in order to have them. The earth must be tilled to produce its fruits, fire must be carefully preserved (hidden in ashes) and continuously fed, the female must be labored over and she must herself labor to produce human offspring. Moreover, apparent blessings are deceptive: every "gift" from the gods is a trick or deception, in contrast to its pleasing appearance. Truly good things are "hidden" by being placed in evils, which humans must contend with to have the benefit of the good things. "The logic of the story reflects the ambiguous character of the human condition," that is, "human existence is governed through the gods' 'hiding' operations, by a mixture of goods and evils, by ambiguity and duplicity" (Vernant, 1980, pp. 168, 176–181). In summary, the myth of Prometheus defines the status of man. Pandora symbolizes the ambiguity of human existence, in which Hope alone, a kind of "blind foresight," makes it possible for men

to live out their lives (Vernant, 1980, pp. 183–185).

The myth of Prometheus was important to the Greeks, as one judges from Aeschylus' use of it to create his Prometheus trilogy, of which only one play, *Prometheus Bound,* is preserved. According to Dodds (1973), the Sophists in fifth-century Athens (or Protagoras, at least, if we can accept Plato's account in *Protagoras* 320c2–322d5) found the myth a congenial vehicle for expressing their belief in progress.

Kirk (1974) notes that Greece is "almost unique in its proliferation of heroic myths as distinct from divine or heavily supernatural ones" (p. 215). Myths of the heroes contain elements of quite different kinds: folktale motifs, history, material from cults and rituals, speculative material (e.g., "infringement of heaven and hell"), and etiology ("explanations of place-names and specific customs"). The organizing process, particularly in the literate era, played an important role since it led to the introduction of some material, the rationalizing of other material, and the suppression of details. Finally, wish-fulfillment played a part in the development of heroic myths (pp. 213–214).

The major motifs of myths of the heroes, used repeatedly with different mythical characters and in different locales, as Kirk notes, are

tricks to surmount difficulties; transformations of physical shape; fulfillment of a task or quest, often involving a giant or monster; accidentally killing a friend or relative; attempting to dispose of an enemy by setting him an apparently impossible task; winning a contest for a bride; being punished in various dramatic ways for impiety; killing one's own child for various reasons; displacing a parent or an old king; taking revenge by seducing a wife or killing children; defending one's mother against an oppressor; circumventing the wiles of a lecherous or an ambitious woman; founding a city or an institution; making use of special weapons to overcome seemingly impossible odds; journeying to the underworld or trying to overcome death; falling in love with a god or goddess (1974, pp. 214–215).

To these "the basic narrative motifs of prophecy or cursing" are to be added (1974, pp. 213–214).

Greek myths were told in Greek literature, oral and written, and visual art—vase painting and sculpture—drew its mythical themes from literature. Most of that literature—the estimate is 95 percent—has perished, although from fragments and references in other authors we know the subject matter of a great deal of that which has been lost. To gain a sense of the body of myths of heroes, although not necessarily of the importance of individual myths in that corpus, the reader can survey the heroic myths presented by Apollodorus, who presumably had most of Greek literature before him when he put together his compendium of Greek myths.

The major surviving literary sources of our knowledge of the heroic myths are the epic poems, the *Iliad* and the *Odyssey* of Homer; the odes of Pindar (and Bacchylides); and the tragedies of Aeschylus, Sophocles, and Euripides. The story of the *Iliad,* whose hero is Achilles, takes place in the tenth and last year of the Trojan War, while the *Odyssey* narrates the return home of Odysseus from that war. There are references in these poems to other heroes of myths, for example, to Bellerophon in the *Iliad* (6.155 ff.) and to Oedipus in the *Odyssey* (11.271 ff.).

Greek antiquity knew a collection of poems called the Epic Cycle. The Epic Cycle drew upon the entire body of heroic myths, except for those narrated in the *Iliad* and the *Odyssey,* which preceded it. Of these epics, only fragments and very short accounts (abridgments by Photius of synopses by Proclus) survive. Poems in this group narrated the beginning of the world and wars in heaven (the battle of the Titans, told also by Hesiod); the story of Thebes, including the myth of Oedipus (*Oedipodea*), a poem entitled *Thebais,* and one entitled *Epigoni* ("Sons of the Seven," i.e., the Seven Against Thebes); and the complete Trojan story—the *Cypria,* the *Aethiopis,* the *Little Iliad,* the *Sack of Troy,* the *Returns,* and the *Telegony.* These last-named poems, comprising the Trojan Cycle, told the story of the Trojan War from the Apple of Discord to the death of Odysseus at the hands of Telegonus, his son by Circe, leaving spaces, as it were, for those parts of the story told in the *Iliad* and the *Odyssey.*

The *Iliad* and the *Odyssey* had achieved canonical status even by the archaic period, for they alone of the various epics were recited in their entirety at the quadrennial panathenaic festival in Athens, instituted by Peisistratus, tyrant of Athens, in 566 B.C. Moreover, the Homeric poems were the basis of ancient Greek education. As means to the acculturation of youth, "encyclopedias" of Greek culture, as Havelock (1963) says, they were the source of that culture's sense of itself. Thus, the importance of these works and the importance of the myths from which they were articulated cannot be overestimated. The myths in Homer helped the Greeks to learn who they were.

Almost all of Pindar's epinician odes, written to celebrate victors in athletic contests at the four great athletic festivals in Greece (the Olympian, Pythian, Nemean, and Isthmian games) use myths to illustrate aspects of the truth the poet wishes to present to his hearers. Since these odes were commissioned for specific occasions, the circumstances of composition—for whom, where, upon what occasion—must have played an important role in determining the poet's choice of myths. For example, Pindar composed eleven of his forty-five surviving poems for victorious athletes from the small island of Aegina, the home of the hero Aeacus, father of Peleus and Telamon, who were, respectively, the fathers of Achilles and Ajax. Ten of the Aeginetan poems use myths of Aeacus, his sons Peleus and Telamon, and grandsons Ajax and Achilles.

Heracles founded the Olympian games, and Pindar uses this myth of Heracles in two *Olympian* odes. Embodying human achievement, Heracles frequently appears in other odes, which generally celebrate achievement. A lesser contemporary of Pindar, Bacchylides, draws from the myths of Heracles, Proteus king of Argos, the Trojan war, and Theseus, among others in his nineteen surviving odes (many of which are fragmentary or incomplete).

Although only thirty-one complete tragedies survive antiquity—seven by Aeschylus, seven by Sophocles, and seventeen by Euripides—Knox (1979) notes that from fragments, titles, or both, we know the subjects of 262 additional tragedies. The total of 293 tragic dramas for which we know the myths comprises almost one-third of the original corpus of slightly more than one thousand tragedies produced in the Attic festivals of tragedy in the fifth century. The largest number of these by far (sixty-eight) have the Trojan War and its aftermath as their subject. Myths of the house of Cadmus and of Thebes occupy the next largest group (thirty-three), with the myths of the house of Tantalus (from Pelops through Atreus to Iphigenia) the subject of thirty-one. The myth of the quest for the Golden Fleece occurs in twenty-one plays, while Athenian myth (including Theseus) is found in nineteen. Heracles or his children are the subject of fourteen, Crete and the line of Europa, the myth of Perseus, and Odysseus and his adventures are each the subject of ten tragedies. Eight plays use the myth of the Calydonian boar hunt, seven draw from the myth of Bellerophon and his family, and

Ixion and his descendants are the subject of six. The remaining titles include two plays each involving Prometheus, Melanippe, Phaethon, and Tyro.

Although it is not possible in this short space to narrate myths of individual heroes, the importance of one hero, Heracles, should be noted. As G. Karl Galinsky says, "Mythological tradition and the ancient literary tradition endowed Herakles . . . more richly than any other ancient hero" (1972, p. 297). He was "the one true Panhellenic hero, . . . the national hero of Greece," in that "all over Greece Herakles was worshipped as . . . the averter of evil, which was understood in its broadest sense—war, death, ghosts, sickness, and the trials and tribulations of life in general. Against all these the common man called upon him as a trusty and invincible divine helper" (pp. 3–4).

Even so, he is "the most difficult [hero] to reconstruct," as Kirk (1974) points out: "In some ways he was a source of mystery to the Greeks themselves, particularly because of his ambivalent status as both hero and god: he alone started as a hero and was raised up to be a god on Olympus" (p. 176).

Ancient mythographers, as Nilsson (1972) notes, divided the myths of Heracles into three cycles: (1) the Twelve Labors, performed at the command of Eurystheus; (2) incidentals, actions performed while he executed his labors; and (3) deeds, warlike expeditions undertaken on his own or with others. These are framed by myths of his birth and of his death and apotheosis (see Apollodorus, *The Library* 2.4.8–2.7.8).

Heracles' madness, as a result of which he killed his and his brother's children and undertook the Twelve Labors in expiation of the murders; the labors themselves; his enslavement to Omphale, the Lydian queen, as punishment for murdering Iphitus in another fit of madness; and his trip to and return from the underworld, from which he brought Cerberus, its doglike guardian; his painful death and ultimate translation to the heaven of the gods provide a model for human salvation, Greek-style: man is his own Messiah. Through suffering and toil he saves himself.

In *Nemean* (1.33–72) Pindar presents the most reverential account of the hero. He narrates the life of Heracles from birth to apotheosis, concluding, "[Teiresias] prophesied [that] he would enjoy unbroken peace/for all time, repose in the gods' blissful hall,/a perfect reward for his vast labors, /with lovely Hebe for his bride;/and that . . . /he would praise the sacred law" (Nisetich, trans. [1980], p. 236). In these last lines, Rose says, "the poet as well as the hero looks with magnificent inclusiveness over the whole heroic career from birth through seemingly endless and omnipresent trials to blissful attainment, and finds it all good" (1974, p. 162).

To the modern reader, the myths told in the surviving tragedies have a greater hold upon the imagination than the myth of Heracles, who plays a role in only four extant dramas—Sophocles' *Women of Trachis* and *Philoctetes,* and Euripides' *Alcestis* and *Heracles* —in the last named of which he of course plays a major role. The persecution of Heracles' children by Eurystheus, who compelled the hero to perform the Twelve Labors, is the subject of a fifth play, Euripides' *Heraclidae.*

The myths of the family of Agamemnon are found in eight dramas: Aeschylus' *Oresteia* trilogy; Sophocles' *Electra;* and Euripides' *Electra, Iphigenia in Aulis, Iphigenia in Tauris,* and *Orestes.* Six tragedies use myths of the Trojan War: Sophocles' *Ajax* and *Philoctetes,* and Euripides' *Helen, Hecuba, Andromache,* and *Trojan Women.* The myth of Oedipus is the basis for six tragedies: Aeschylus' *Seven Against Thebes;* Sophocles' *Antigone, Oedipus the King,* and *Oedipus at Colonus;* and Euripides' *Suppliant Women* and *Phoenician Women.* Aeschylus uses the myth of the daughters of Danaus (descendants of Io) in his *The Suppliants.* Euripides' *Medea* has the myth of Jason and the Argonauts as its source, while the *Hippolytus* of Euripides draws upon the myth of Theseus. All but one of the remaining extant dramas use myths of the gods: Aeschylus' *Prometheus Bound* and Euripides' *Ion* and *The Bacchants.* Aeschylus' *Persians* is the only surviving drama using historical, not mythical, material.

As for myth's role in tragedy, Vernant notes that tragedy was a "social institution which the city, by establishing competitions in tragedies, set up alongside its political and legal institutions." The drama enacted the conflict between the city's roots in the "ancient heroic legend," which was its past, and its "new forms of legal and political thought." "Tragedy is born," Vernant says (quoting Nestle), "when myth starts to be considered from the point of view of a citizen" (Vernant and Vidal-Naquet, 1981, p. 9).

NEAR EASTERN INFLUENCE ON GREEK MYTHS

Greek myths, while distinctive, show considerable influence from the Near East. This influence is perhaps to be expected because of Greece's geographical proximity to the Near East, which promoted association, and because of Greece's expanded contacts with the Near East in the Mycenaean period (*ca.* 1600–1100 B.C), contacts that were resumed in the eighth and seventh centuries as Greece emerged from the turmoil accompanying the breakup of the Mycenean palace-kingdoms. Crete and Cyprus also offered points of contact, as did the Greek settlements in Asia Minor, particularly for the latter period.

Jameson (in Kramer, 1961) rightly cautions against assuming oriental influence in themes that are common both to Greek and Near Eastern myths. We can nevertheless observe clear parallels to Near Eastern myths both in Greek myths of the gods and myths of the heroes. For example, the story of the succession of Cronus, who castrates his father Sky and is in turn displaced by Zeus, has a clear parallel in the Hittite-Hurrian myth of the god Kumarbi, who castrates his father, Anu, with his teeth, thus removing him from rule, and is himself displaced by the storm god. Another parallel to the succession of Cronus, although not so distinctive as that of the Hittite-Hurrian one, can be seen in the Babylonian Creation Epic (known as the Enuma Elish), in which the god Apsu is replaced by Ea, and Tiamat by Marduk. West (1966) sees a third parallel in the *Phoenician History* of Sanchuniathon.

The myth of Demeter, whose daughter Persephone is carried off to the underworld by the god Hades and who then withdraws from the world in anger, causing crops to cease growing, has a close and often-noted parallel with the Hittite myth of Telepinus, the disappearance of whom (in anger) stops the growth of crops and births of animals and so threatens to end life on earth. Burkert (1979) also observes a parallel between the myth of Demeter and Persephone and the Mesopotamian myths of Inanna-Ishtar.

Several major Greek gods are thought to have been imported from the Near East. Kirk (1974) sees origins in Asia Minor for, among others, Apollo, Artemis, Aphrodite ("the Greek version of Sumerian Inanna, Akkadian Ishtar, Canaanite Anath," p. 258), and Dionysus (who retains "something of the role of a fertility consort to the Asiatic Great Mother known to the Greeks as Cybele," p. 258).

Both Greek and Mesopotamian myths share the concept of an underworld to which human beings pass after death. The myth of Deucalion, Pyrrha, and the flood (discussed above) is parallel to the Near Eastern flood story, which "was firmly established in Mesopotamia as early as the third millennium B.C. and spread from there all over western Asia during the next two millennia" (Kirk, 1974, p. 262). The Hebrew version of the flood myth is found in Genesis 6–9:17.

The myth of Hippolytus, the pattern of which occurs in several Greek myths, has an Egyptian parallel in "The Story of Two Brothers" as well as the familiar Hebrew parallel of Genesis 39, the story of Joseph and Potiphar's wife.

We have observed that one of the distinctive characteristics of Greek myths, setting them apart from myths of other cultures, is the large number of heroic myths (and of heroes) in contrast to myths of gods. Even so, parallels between heroic myths of Greece and Near Eastern myths have been noted. Above we referred to the myth of Hippolytus and parallels in Egyptian and Hebrew myths. Kirk (1974) points out an additional parallel in the similarity between Achilles and Patroclus, two fast friends, the lesser of whom loses his life while acting on behalf of the greater, and the Babylonian hero Gilgamesh and his friend, the lesser hero Enkidu.

A more striking example of Near Eastern influence, because it involves the most popular Greek hero, is that of Heracles, Near Eastern parallels to whom, as Burkert (1979) notes, occur in Sumeria as early as about 2500. Various pieces of evidence have suggested that Heracles may be "a wholesale import from the eighth-century orient" (pp. 80–83).

We began with Knox's observation that the ancient Greeks were "the people of the myth" in contrast to the ancient Hebrews, "the people of the Book." Through the poems of Homer, those cultural "encyclopedias" and the basis of education for the young; through the poems of Hesiod; through tragedies, performed yearly at Athens in the fifth century in a state-supported festival; through lyric poetry such as Pindar's; in their temples and on vases used daily, the tales provided, in Finley's words, a "mythical charter" for their sense of themselves as a people (1975, p. 26).

Roland Barthes has suggested that myth "transforms history into nature." That is, the particular, the historical, is made by myth to seem natural, universal, "the way things are" (1972, pp. 129, 141). So, too, for the Greeks, for, as Finley says, "Pan-Hellenic or regional consciousness and pride, aristocratic rule, and especially their right to rule, their pre-eminent qualifications and virtues, . . . these and other, comparable, ends were served by the continual repetition of the old tales. . . . The objective was . . . the enhancement of prestige or the warranty of power or the justification of an institution" (1975, pp. 25, 28).

The Greek myths—the particulars of a history transformed into nature—have helped to shape the literature (and the mind) of the West for more than 2500 years. Whether or not this has been a good thing—Auden in his poem "The Shield of Achilles," for example, thought not—the durability of their myths testifies to the imagination and artistry of these people.

ROMAN MYTH

The Romans lacked a rich corpus of myths such as the Greeks had, for, as Grant (1962) says, "the Romans themselves, unlike the Greeks, were not a myth-making people" (p. 305). The absence of a mythical tradition at Rome has been attributed to the fact that the early Romans did not conceive their gods, primarily agricultural deities associated with cult, in human form. It was Greek influence that eventually overcame "this anti-mythological reluctance to see the gods as human . . ." (Grant, 1962, p. 305).

Greek influence, in fact, led to the Hellenizing of the Roman gods. In the second century B.C. the poet Ennius adapted the principal Roman gods to the Greek pantheon, making a parallel Roman pantheon (Greek counterparts given in parentheses): Juno (Hera), Vesta (Hestia), Minerva (Athena), Ceres (Demeter), Diana (Artemis), Venus (Aphrodite), Mars (Ares), Mercurius (Hermes), Jovis (Zeus), Neptunus (Poseidon), Vulcanus (Hephaestus), and Apollo (frags. 60–61, Warmington [1955], p. 22). The order is Ennius', and he added the Greek Apollo to the Roman pantheon.

The absence of myths does not mean that the Romans did not care about their past. They cared passionately, particularly after Rome established its dominion over Italy and became a national entity. A series of writers, beginning with Naevius in the third century, continuing with Ennius in the second, and culminating in Vergil and the historian Livy in the first, created a past for the evolving Roman nation, consciously mixing borrowed Greek myths with Roman history and legend to produce what might be called a national literature for national purposes.

Literacy facilitated the task of these writers. They were literate themselves, and they drew upon Greek literature, which was available to them because it was written, in addition to their own. Literacy, in short, made it possible for Roman authors to borrow and to adapt in a way that an oral tradition does not allow. Moreover, their own literacy and the availability of written literature for their use enabled these writers to fashion highly wrought, complex works that consciously employ and develop myths, interwoven with history and legend, to carry out specific artistic (and political) programs. Literacy thus created a major difference between Roman and Greek traditional tales.

A striking example of such borrowing (and of the difference between Greek and Roman myths) is that of Aeneas, the hero of

Vergil's *Aeneid,* written in the latter part of the first century B.C. He is a prominent Trojan prince and warrior in the *Iliad* (e.g., 5.166 ff.; 20.79 ff.), where it is said that he and his line will survive the Trojan War (20.302–304), and his birth is mentioned in Hesiod's *Theogony* (1008–1010) and the Homeric *Hymn to Aphrodite* (196 ff.; 254 ff.). According to Hellanicus, a fifth-century Greek historian, Aeneas came to Italy after the Trojan defeat. Naevius, Rome's first epic poet, drew upon this tradition in his epic, the *Punic War,* which included an account of Rome's origins. Borrowing from Naevius, Ennius, and many other authors, both Greek and Roman, Vergil makes Aeneas the hero of the *Aeneid,* his national epic of the founding of Rome. The epic narrates the destruction of Troy, Aeneas' escape from the city with a small band of Trojans, their wanderings, and their arrival and wars in Italy. Vergil ends the *Aeneid* with Aeneas successfully (if not happily) established in Italy and soon to marry Lavinia, daughter of Latinus, king of Latium, in whose territory Aeneas and his followers had arrived. Iulus, also known as Ascanius, Aeneas' son by the Trojan Creusa, who died at the sack of Troy, will succeed him. The poem presents Aeneas as the emblem of the Roman, toiling to bring his band to Italy and establish it there, and struggling, with limited success, to carry the burden of his high destiny. Through the story of Aeneas, moreover, Vergil gives Rome a manifest destiny (world-rule), making it present from the origin of the nation. In the *Aeneid,* then, we see a conscious "mythologizing" of Rome's origins.

The Trojan War, the outcome of which brought Aeneas to Italy, was fought toward the end of the thirteenth century B.C., while Rome, according to Roman tradition, was founded by Romulus in 753. The last king of Rome was expelled and the republic was established in 510. The first-century B.C. historian Livy fills in the story in Book One of his history of Rome. He briefly narrates Aeneas' arrival in Italy and his successful attempt to make a new home for himself and the Trojans. Aeneas died in a battle not long afterward, and his son, Iulus-Ascanius became king. (Livy, referring to him only as Ascanius, says he may have been the son of Aeneas and Lavinia.) Livy names Ascanius' successors some thirteen kings, down to Numitor, whose brother Aemulius drove him from the throne, killed his male children, and made Rhea Silvia, Numitor's daughter, a Vestal Virgin, thus preventing her from bearing offspring (Livy, 1.3).

When Rhea bore twin sons (claiming the god Mars as their father), Aemulius imprisoned her and ordered the twins to be cast into the Tiber River. Since the Tiber had overflowed its banks, the servants charged with the task were unable to approach the river, so they instead left the infants (in a floating basket) in a shallow pool of flood water. When the flood waters receded, a she-wolf, making for the river to slake her thirst, was drawn by the babies' crying. A shepherd discovered the wolf, who had offered her teats to the twins, gently licking them with her tongue. He took the boys home to be reared by his wife, naming them Romulus and Remus (Livy, 1.4).

Their identity was revealed when they were grown, and they killed their greatuncle Amulius, who had usurped the throne, and restored it to their grandfather. They founded a settlement in the region where they had been exposed as infants but quarreled over who should be king, and Romulus killed Remus. Now the unchallenged ruler of the new city, Romulus gave it his name and Rome was born (Livy, 1.5–7). Livy goes on to narrate the actions of Romulus, who instituted the Roman Senate, and of his people, including their seizing the women of the Sabines, a neighboring tribe, to provide wives for themselves (Livy, 1.8–9).

After a long and successful career, Romulus was translated into heaven, and the king-ship was offered by the senate to Numa Pompilius. There followed a series of kings, chosen by the people and ratified by the senate, until the kingship was seized by Tarquinius Superbus (Tarquin the Proud), Rome's last king.

A war-making tyrant, Tarquinius Superbus was deposed after his son, Sextus, an officer in the army, raped Lucretia, the wife of a fellow officer, who submitted to him when he threatened to kill her and place beside her corpse the naked body of a slave whom he would also kill. After Sextus left her bed, Lucretia summoned her husband and father and two of their friends, told them of Sextus' rape and the circumstances under which it occurred, demanded that they avenge her shame, and stabbed herself. One of the friends who heard her story was Lucius Junius, a nephew of the king, who had long feigned stupidity to avoid the king's eye and so was named Brutus (Dullard). He abandoned his guise, showed his true mind, and incited the army to remove the king. Livy says that the period of kingship from the founding of Rome in 753 to its liberation was 244 years. Thereafter, in place of a king the Romans elected two consuls annually to govern (Livy, 1.10–60).

Such was the tradition accepted by the Romans as the history of the origin of Rome and the development of the republic. "Legend" is perhaps the more accurate term, a mixture of myth and history.

An account of Roman myth, however brief, cannot fail to mention the Roman poet Ovid, a younger contemporary of Vergil and Livy, who made brilliant use of Greek myths in his *Metamorphoses,* fifteen books of dactylic hexameters in which he narrates 250 tales of "forms changed into new bodies" (1.1–2). Ovid does not simply retell the myths. Rather, he uses stories of metamorphosis to show that

all things change, nothing dies; our spirit wanders here and there, entering bodies at will, shifting from beasts to men and back to beasts, and never dies. . . . All things flow, all forms are shaped in wandering. Time itself glides in constant movement, like a river, for neither stream nor light hour stands still, but as wave pushes wave, is rushed and, as it rolls, rushes the one before, so moments pursue and are pursued, and are always new (15.165–184).

Only the Word can fix this constant flux, uttered out of pain if uttered at all, by poet, or victim, or artist-victim. (See, for examples, the story of Jupiter and Io, 1.568–746; the story of Actaeon, 3.138–252; and the story of Tereus, Procne, and Philomela, 6.424–674).

Ovid is the best source of many Greek myths: Apollo and Daphne, Phaethon, Echo and Narcissus, Daedalus and Icarus, Orpheus and Eurydice (also told by Vergil), and Pygmalion, among others. He gave Greek myths their most original literary expression in the post-Greek age and made us see their strange and distant life.

BIBLIOGRAPHY

SOURCES

Aeschylus, in *The Complete Greek Tragedies,* vol. 1. David Grene and Richmond Lattimore, eds., (1959); Apollodorus, *The Library,* in *Gods and Heroes of the Greeks,* Michael Simpson, trans. (1976); Aristotle, *Poetics,* Donald W. Lucas, ed. (1968); Bacchylides, *The Poems and Fragments,* Richard C. Jebb, ed. and trans. (1967); Ennius, in *Remains of Old Latin,* Eric H. Warmington, ed. and trans., vol. 1 (1935); Euripides, in *The Complete Greek Tragedies,* vols. 3, 4, David Grene and Richmond Lattimore, eds. (1959); Hesiod, *Theogony* and *Works and Days,* in *Hesiod: The Homeric Hymns and Homerica,* Hugh G. Evelyn-White, ed. and trans., rev. ed. (1959); Homer, *The Iliad of Homer,* Richmond Lattimore, trans. (1951),

The Odyssey, Robert Fitzgerald, trans. (1961); *Homeric Hymns* (see under Hesiod); Livy, *History of Rome* (*Ab Urbe Condita*), in *Livy: The Early History of Rome*, Aubrey De Sélincourt, trans. (1960); Pindar, *Odes*, in *Pindar's Victory Songs*, Frank J. Nisetich, trans. (1980); Ovid, *Metamorphoses*, Rolfe Humphries, trans. (1955); Sophocles, in *The Complete Greek Tragedies*, vol. 2, David Grene and Richmond Lattimore, eds. (1959); Vergil, *The Aeneid of Virgil*, Cecil Day Lewis, trans. (1953).

STUDIES

Thomas W. Allen, W. R. Halliday, and E. E. Sikes, eds., *The Homeric Hymns*, 2d ed. (1936); Roland Barthes, "Myth Today," in *Mythologies*, Annette Lavers, trans. (1972); Norman O. Brown, trans., *Hesiod: Theogony* (1953); Walter Burkert, *Structure and History in Greek Mythology and Ritual* (1979), and *Homo Necans* (1983); Percy Cohen, "Theories of Myth," in *Man*, **4** (1969); Eric R. Dodds, ed., *Euripides: Bacchae* (1960), "The Ancient Concept of Progress," in *The Ancient Concept of Progress and Other Essays on Greek Literature and Belief* (1973); Moses I. Finley, "Myth, Memory and History," in *The Use and Abuse of History* (1975); G. Karl Galinsky, *The Herakles Theme* (1972); Michael Grant, *Myths of the Greeks and Romans* (1962); William K. C. Guthrie, *The Greeks and Their Gods* (1950).

Eric A. Havelock, *Preface to Plato* (1963), and *The Literate Revolution in Greece and Its Cultural Consequences* (1982); Jane Henle, *Greek Myths: A Vase Painter's Notebook* (1973); Albert Henricks, "Loss of Self, Suffering, Violence: The Modern View of Dionysus from Nietzsche to Girard," in *Harvard Studies in Classical Philology*, **88** (1984); Geoffrey S. Kirk, *Myth: Its Meaning and Function in Greek and Other Cultures* (1970), and *The Nature of Greek Myths* (1974); Bernard Knox, "Myth and Attic Tragedy," in *Word and Action: Essays on the Ancient Theatre* (1979); Samuel N. Kramer, ed., *Mythologies of the Ancient World* (1961); Hugh Lloyd-Jones, *The Justice of Zeus* (1971); Henri I. Marrou, *A History of Education in Antiquity*, George Lamb, trans. (1956); Martin P. Nilsson, *The Mycenaean Origin of Greek Mythology*, 2d. ed. (1972); James B. Pritchard, ed., *Ancient Near Eastern Texts Relating to the Old Testament*, 3d ed. (1969); Peter W. Rose, "The Myth of Pindar's First *Nemean*: Sportsmen, Poetry, and Paideia," in *Harvard Studies in Classical Philology*, **78** (1974).

Karl Schefold, *Myth and Legend in Early Greek Art* (n.d.); Charles Segal, "Greek Myth as a Semiotic and Structural System and the Problem of Tragedy," in *Arethusa*, **16** (1983); Philip E. Slater, *The Glory of Hera* (1968), and "The Greek Family in History and Myth," in *Arethusa*, **7** (1974); William B. Stanford, *Aristophanes: The Frogs*, 2d ed. (1962); Jean-Pierre Vernant, *Myth and Society in Ancient Greece* (1980); Jean-Pierre Vernant and Pierre Vidal-Naquet, *Tragedy and Myth in Ancient Greece* (1981); Martin L. West, *Hesiod: Theogony* (1966).

For bibliography through 1973 see John Peradotto, *Classical Mythology: An Annotated Bibliographical Survey* (1973).

Magic

JOHN FERGUSON

INTRODUCTION

The article "Magic" in the *Oxford Classical Dictionary* begins: "Magic is a complex of practices through which man exercises power on the world around him by irrational means." This is in fact highly misleading. Magic is the control of the environment by means that are deemed rational and even scientific by its practitioners; Lynn Thorndike actually wrote a *History of Magic and Experimental Science.*

Magic is distinguished from religion in that magic is compulsive. That is to say, in magic the result is bound to follow provided that the ritual has been meticulously carried through and is not countered by a more powerful magic; the spirits or forces summoned are compelled to respond—and, presumably, to obey. In religion the answer to petition depends on the independent will of supernatural beings: they may respond or not, as they choose; the ritual or prayer has no power to compel them to do so. A more elaborate table of antitheses might run:

Magic	Religion
Undifferentiated	Differentiated
Impersonal or collective	Personal or individual
External	Internal
Taboo	Ethics
Relations of fear	Relations of reverence

But magic and religion are not totally distinct from one another. Precise formulaic accuracy may be requisite in religious petitions; invocation of divine beings is frequent in magical spells. Sir James Frazer was too tidy when he postulated an age of magic before the age of religion; the two walk side by side.

Two of the commonest forms of magic are sympathetic and contagious. In sympathetic magic an act in one field will have parallel results in another. Melt a wax image and your enemy will waste away; leap high and your crops will grow tall. In contagious magic an act toward something that has been in contact with the person or thing to be magicked acts as a channel of magical power. So the Pythagoreans were told to smooth the impress of their bodies from their beds on rising, no doubt for fear that the impress would become such a channel. So too the cut hair and nail clippings of the priest of Jupiter at Rome had to be buried with the utmost precautions against being stolen for magic.

Another useful analysis of distinctions within magic differentiates between productive, protective, and destructive magic. Productive magic would include fertility magic and rainmaking. At Crannon in Thessaly the citizens had a bronze car that they produced in time of drought, loaded with an amphora full of water; the rattling of the car and the spilling of the water were rain magic. Protective magic is involved in healing and precautions against the evil eye; the bulla, a phallic amulet hung around the neck of a Roman child, is a good example. Destructive magic is aimed at producing disease or death or destruction to property. Curses inscribed on tablets of lead—a dark, heavy metal—and buried in the ground are a common form of such magic in ancient times (Dessau, *Inscriptiones Latinae Selectae* 8753):

> I invoke you, Spirit, whoever you are, and lay it upon you from this hour, this day, this moment that you torment and destroy the horses of the Green and White, kill and crush the charioteers Clarus Felix Primulus Romanus, leave no breath in their bodies. I lay it upon you in the name of one who set you free in season, the god of sea and air IAO IASDAO OORIO . . . AEIA.

This curse is the desperate effort of a betting man. Combinations of vowels such as those at the end were supposed to have peculiar magical power and are associated with demonic beings.

Magic permeated all classes of society of Greece and Rome throughout the entire period. Tacitus (*Annals* 2.69) tells how the ill-

ness of Germanicus (A.D. 19), nephew and adopted son of the emperor Tiberius, was worsened by his conviction that he was being magicked, and that under the floor and within the walls were found the disinterred remains of human bodies, magic formulas, curses, Germanicus' name scratched on lead tablets, human ashes charred and soaked in blood, and other magical devices designed to consign souls to the powers below.

Magical power resides in the colors red and black; in odd numbers, in which the god delights (Vergil, *Eclogue* 8.75); and in palindromes such as ΑΒΛΑΝΑΘΑΝΑΛΒΑ or the word square, with its mirror image:

RO**T**AS	SA**T**OR
OPERA	AREPO
TENE**T**	**T**ENE**T**
AREPO	OPERA
SA**T**OR	RO**T**AS

The mirror images also read the same from top down or bottom up. The righthand arrangement may be translated, "The sower, Arepo, guides the wheels with care," but the square, written with a tau cross (the shape of the cross in Christ's crucifixion) at the letter **T** positions, is seemingly a Christian acrostic. The word TENET (from *tenere,* to hold, as a belief; to hold fast to, again as to a belief) forms a cross through the center; the remaining corner letters can be added to the ends of the cross to form

```
          P
          A
          T
          E
          R
PATERNOSTER
          O
          S
          T
          E
          R
```

with two A–O pairs (= alpha, omega: the beginning and the end) left over.

Magic and religion are thus not to be totally dissociated from one another. The lustration or cleansing of officiants before a sacrifice, or the ritual bathing in the sea by initiates to Eleusis, is part of a religious ceremony, but with strong overtones of magic. Various "scapegoat" ceremonies are known from the Greco-Roman world, and offer similar features. The Greek word for the individual chosen as a scapegoat is *pharmakos*. We find an instance of this ceremony in the festival of the Thargelia at Athens, when, according to Harpocration, two men were "led out" of the city to be purifications, one for the men, one for the women. From other sources it seems that they were beaten out with branches, and perhaps originally burnt alive, although in classical times the ritual was symbolic. At Massalia (Massilia, Marseilles) a criminal, condemned to death, was maintained at public expense for a year, then killed as a *pharmakos* for purification of the city.

MAGIC IN GREECE

From Greece we may take one or two examples of magical practices from different periods.

Hesiod's *Works and Days* is a practical treatise on farming that has been described as a didactic and admonitory medley. Throughout the text there is a strong emphasis on doing the right thing at the right time. Farming is a religious activity; its success depends on the favor of the gods; thus, the poem starts with the praise of Zeus. Later the poet goes on to offer miscellaneous precepts to his reader. "Do not be disagreeable at a large dinner party" seems simple enough. Immediately following are: "Wash your hands before offering a libation," "Do not stand upright facing the sun to make water,"

and "Do not expose your sex organ to your domestic hearth when you are defiled by sexual intercourse." Here we are on the borderline between magic and religion. When we reach the precepts "Never set the ladle on the mixing bowl at a drinking party; deadly ill luck is attached to that," and "A male should not wash in water used by a female; that is followed for a period by bitter penalty," we are in the field of magic. To lay one object across another is dangerous, and to lay an empty ladle over a full wine bowl is to threaten the wine; and by sympathetic magic, contact with water used by the "weaker sex" might be expected to weaken the male.

A second example is from the Pythagorean precepts. These include the admonitions to abstain from beans, not to pick up things that fall to the floor, not to touch a white cock, not to stir the fire with a knife, to rub out the mark of a pot in the ashes, not to sit on a bushel measure, not to wear a ring, not to have swallows in the house, to spit on one's nail parings and hair trimmings, not to make water on or stand on one's nail parings and hair trimmings, to roll up one's bedclothes on rising and smooth out the imprint of the body, and to touch the earth when it thunders. All of these injunctions are attributed to Pythagoras, with moralistic interpretations; for example, to stir a fire with a knife is to rouse passions with intemperate language, swallows are gossips, and to roll up the bedding is to be always ready for the next stage of life's journey. Clearly these are not the original intentions, which are magical, although it is possible that Pythagoras was taking popular sayings and giving them a philosophical purport.

The Superstitious Man in the *Characters* of Theophrastus (*ca.* 370–288/285 B.C.) engages in typical magical practices. He asperses himself with holy water and puts a sacred laurel leaf in his mouth before going out for the day. If a cat crosses his path, he stands stock still until someone else has passed or continues only after throwing three pebbles across the road. He is always purifying his house on the grounds that it has been "visited" by Hecate. If an owl hoots while he is out, he is disturbed and cries "Athene is queen." He avoids treading on graves or coming into contact with a dead body or a woman in childbirth. On the fourth and seventh of each month he engages in special rituals. He takes dreams very seriously. And so on.

One of the finest fictional examples of magic is in the second *Idyll* of the Greek poet Theocritus (*ca.* 270 B.C.). An injured girl is casting a love spell:

> Wryneck, draw my lover home.
> Delphis caused my pain. Against Delphis I
> set fire to
> this laurel, and as it crackles loudly, and
> suddenly
> catches and burns away to invisible ash,
> so may Delphis' flesh waste in the fire of love.
> Wryneck, draw my lover home.
> As I melt this image with divine favor,
> so may Delphis of Myndos be melted with
> love.
> As this bronze wheel turns by Aphrodite's
> grace,
> so may he turn and turn before my door.
> Wryneck, draw my lover home.

The wryneck is a bird whose curious neck movements may have seemed supernatural; it is fastened to a wheel and then spun around to bind the charm fast.

MAGIC IN ROME

Healing and Protection

Magic and medicine may be closely interwoven. So today in West Africa a *babalawo,* a native doctor, may have an acute knowledge of herbal medicine, but he is likely to hedge his treatment with spells and formulas.

In Cato the Elder's *On Agriculture* (160), the following passage appears between two sections devoted to sensible and scientific methods, the first for avoiding soreness on a journey, the second for planting asparagus:

> Any kind of dislocation will be cured by the following charm. Get hold of a green reed four to five feet long, split it down the middle, and have two people hold it against your ribs. Begin the chant "Motas vaeta daries dardares astataries dissunapiter," and keep it up till they meet. Wave a knife over them, and when they meet, so that both halves of the reed are touching at both sides, seize them in one hand, and cut right and left. If you now bind the pieces round the dislocation or fracture, it will heal. Even so, chant every day, and with a dislocation use this formula: "Huat haut haut istasis tarsis ardannabou dannaustra."

Pliny the Elder, omnivorous and credulous, preserves some curious lore. Thus an herb growing on a statue's head, wrapped in a piece of clothing and tied with red string round the neck, will cure a headache immediately (*Natural History* 24.106.170). An herb called reseda (Linnaeus' *reseda alba*) will cure inflammations, but for the cure to take effect the sufferer must spit three times saying, "Reseda, alleviate [Lat. *reseda*] these diseases. Do you know, do you know what chick it is that has torn up these roots? Let them have no head or feet" (27.106.131). Similarly, Marcellus Empiricus (12.24) says that you may ease toothache by standing with your shoes on under an open sky on the living earth, seizing a frog, opening his mouth, spitting into it, and asking him to take away the toothache with him, and letting him free; but the day and hour must be well-omened.

Magical amulets were a protection against disease. A medical scientist of Galen's caliber can recommend an engraved stone as a protection against dyspepsia. Campbell Bonner in a classic study (1950) identifies the main diseases that amulets were designed to ward off—digestive complaints, eye disorders, gynecological complaints, sciatica, hydrophobia ("Flee, demon hydrophobia, from the wearer of this amulet"), and consumption ("Rescue me from the wasting and the disease").

The Romans were especially fearful of the power of the evil eye. Protective measures included the phallic amulet called *fascinum,* colored threads, an unidentified plant, and apotropaic (evil-averting) gestures.

Magic in Literature

Something of the hold that magical thought had on the Roman mind may be seen from its persistent occurrence in literature. Horace had a feud with Canidia, whom he characterized as a witch (*Epodes* 5, 17; *Satires* 1.8). The picture of her includes authentic black magic. She wears black; there are no fastenings on hair, clothes, or feet that might bind her by her own magic. She makes mysterious howling sounds. She tears a black animal victim so that the blood gathers in a ditch, thus invoking the dead and the underworld powers. She makes two effigies, one of wool for herself, and one of wax for her lover, and melts the wax image. She buries a wolf's beard and the tooth of a spotted snake.

Vergil (*Eclogue* 8) has a love spell borrowed from Theocritus. More notable is Dido's magic. The priestess calls on three hundred gods and powers of the underworld, scatters pretended waters of Avernus, takes herbs slivered by a bronze knife in the light of the moon, mixed with black poison, and a charm from a newborn foal (Vergil, *Aeneid* 4).

Ovid is fascinated by witchcraft. A madam named Dipsas wants to draw Corinna away to more lucrative customers. She is a witch, says Ovid. She can reverse the flow of water, knows herbal lore, spins the magic wheel, deals in love philters, controls the weather, alters the face of the moon and stars, changes herself to an owl by night, traffics with the dead (*Loves* 1.8). The passage is revealing precisely because it takes the form of a trivial, witty poem, not a mythological excursus; it is a description of a current practice. In Ovid's *The Roman Calendar* (*Fasti* 2.571 ff.) we meet a witch invoking Tacita, the "silent goddess," and see how with three fingers she puts three cloves of frankincense under a mousehole in the door, binds enchanted threads with a dark spindle, turns seven black beans over in her mouth, roasts the head of a small fish (pilchard) sealed with pitch and pierced with a bronze needle, pours a few drops of wine on it (drinking the rest herself), and goes off muttering, "We have set a curb on evil tongues, and inauspicious lips." (Ovid's *Metamorphoses* is also full of magic.)

Tibullus, Lucan, and Seneca might also be cited, as well as the prose writers Petronius and Apuleius.

Three Historical Examples

The Age of Augustus was a credulous age. Anaxilaus, a magician, a Pythagorean, and an alchemist, produced curious effects at dinner parties, making guests appear pale as corpses or black as Ethiopians, or with the appearance of donkeys' heads. Thessalus of Tralles, a medical scholar, wrote to the emperor about the way the Egyptian priests summoned up the god of healing Asclepius (Aesculapius). It was no doubt done with mirrors. These are illusionists' effects, but there was a credulous public to embrace them.

Pliny the Elder has a delectable story about a freedman named Gaius Furius Chresimus, who got better farming results than his neighbors and was charged by them with magical practices. He was acquitted when he appeared in court with excellent tools, well cared for, and said, "These, citizens, are my magic spells." The point is that the charge was brought (Pliny the Elder, *Natural History* 18.8.41–43).

Apuleius himself, who could tell a good witch story when he chose, was charged with acquiring a rich wife by sorcery. He had no difficulty in laughing the charges out of court, but in the course of his plea actually did offer a cautious defense of magic (*Apology* 26).

BIBLIOGRAPHY

SOURCES

Apuleius, *Apology,* Harold E. Butler and Arthur S. Owen, eds. (1914); Cato the Elder and Varro, *On Agriculture,* William D. Hooper, trans., rev. by Harrison B. Ash (1967); Hermann Dessau, *Inscriptiones Latinae Selectae,* 3 vols. in 5 (1892–1916); Diogenes Laertius, *Vitae Philosophorum* (*Lives and Opinions of the Famous Philosophers*), Herbert S. Long, ed. (1964); Hesiod, *The Homeric Hymns and Homerica,* Hugh G. Evelyn-White, trans. (1914; rev. ed. 1959); *Horace,* Edward C. Wickham, ed., 2 vols. (1874); Ovid, *Loves* (*Amores*), Edward J. Kenney, ed. (1961), *Fasti* (*The Roman Calendar*), Sir James G. Frazer, trans. (1929), and *Metamorphoses,* Frank J. Miller, trans., 2 vols. (1956); Petronius and Seneca, *Apocolocyntosis,* Michael Heseltine and W. H. D. Rouse, trans. (1916); Pliny, *Natural History,* Harris Rackham *et al.,* trans., 10 vols. (1938–1967); Tacitus, *Annals,* Henry Furneaux, ed. (1897); *Theocritus,* Andrew S. F. Gow, 2 vols., 2d. ed., (1965); Theophrastus, *Characters,* Hermann Diels, ed. (1909); *Vergil,* Roger Mynors, ed. (1969).

STUDIES

Adam Abt, *Die Apologie des Apuleius* (1907); Auguste Audollent, *Defixionum Tabellae* (1904); Alphons A. Barb, "The Survival of Magic Arts," in *The Conflict between Paganism and Christianity in the Fourth Century,* Arnaldo Momigliano, ed. (1963); Campbell Bonner, *Studies in Magical Amulets, Chiefly Graeco-Egyptian* (1950); John Ferguson, *The Religions of the Roman Empire* (1970), and *Greek and Roman Religion: A Source Book* (1980); Andrew Lang, *Magic and Religion* (1901); Joyce E. Lowe, *Magic in Greek and Latin Literature* (1929); Joseph J. Mooney, *Old Roman Magic* (1919); Eugene Tavenner, *Studies in Magic from Latin Literature* (1916); Lynn Thorndike, *A History of Magic and Experimental Science,* I (1923).

Greek Cults

SUSAN GUETTEL COLE

INTRODUCTION

The Greeks had no word for religion because Greek religious activity was not divorced from human experience and the ordinary activities of everyday life. The gods were thought to be everywhere, able to see all human activities (Euripides, *The Bacchants* [*Bacchae*] 393–394). Organized according to function, they were believed to provide for all human needs and to protect all human endeavors (Lycurgus, *Against Leocrates* 13.2; 15.4). In return, people offered prayers, sacrifices, and votive offerings, and tended the sanctuaries of the gods. Religious activities accompanied all important transactions, both public and private, because the gods were believed to oversee the production of food, to offer protection in times of danger, to send healing in times of sickness, and to provide for success in times of war. During the classical period, in both personal and in public life, no significant undertaking began without consulting a god and no success went without a vow of thanks, a votive offering, or a public dedication. Further, in Athens during the classical period most significant religious activity was organized according to participation in a group, whether the family, the phratry (male kinship group), deme (residential district), professional organization, or the city.

SACRED PLACES

The Greeks divided their land, both urban and rural, into that which was sacred to the gods (*hieron*), and therefore subject to restrictions, and that which could be freely used. A place considered sacred could be a marked-off area or enclosure (*temenos,* literally an area "cut off"), a sanctuary with or without a building (*to hieron*), or simply a grove, spring, or cave. A sacred area could exist out in the country, at the top of a mountain, or in the middle of the city. Athenians worshiped Zeus Ombrios, a god of rain, on nearby Mount Hymettos, where they left inscribed dedications (Pausanias, 1.32.2; Langdon, *A Sanctuary of Zeus* 5–7). They worshiped Pan in caves on Mount Parnes (Menander, *Dyskolos* 1–4) and on Mount Hymettos, and the Eumenides in a grove at Kolonos (Sophocles, *Oedipus at Colonus* 39–43). The Athenian agora (marketplace)—the area of the city where most important political activities and business transactions took place—was full of altars, small shrines, and temples. All Greeks were supposed to be able to recognize what was *hieron* or sacred and to abide by whatever local rules existed. At Athens part of the agora was marked off by *perirrhanteria* (lustral basins) so that people could symbolically purify themselves before stepping into the sacred area. People touched by special forms of pollution were not allowed in the marked-off area (Aeschines, 3.176). Inability to enter the agora because of pollution could restrict a citizen from participating in the political life of the community.

Local rules about the use of sacred areas were sometimes recorded on inscriptions controlling access to sanctuaries. There was considerable variety in the restrictions. The activities of birth, sexual intercourse, and death were not allowed in sanctuaries (Herodotus, 2.64; *Inscriptiones Graecae* II [1035.10–11]). Further, people could be restricted from access to a sanctuary because of contact with a corpse, contact with or experience of childbirth, miscarriage or abortion, recent sexual intercourse, the wearing of certain clothing, the eating of certain foods, or the carrying of certain weapons or types of metal. Of such activities the only ones recognized as polluting in all areas of Greece and in all periods of Greek history were contact with a dead person and contact with or the experience of childbirth.

Some sacred areas were considered more sacred than others. Describing the migration of Attic farmers and villagers into Athens at the time of the Peloponnesian War (431–404 B.C.) and the resulting shortage of housing, Thucydides distinguishes between those sacred places that could be inhabited and places like the Acropolis and the Eleusinion (temple of the Eleusinian goddesses Demeter and Kore, located in the agora), which because of their great sanctity were completely restricted from habitation.

Greek temples, called *naoi*, were built in sacred areas and because they were considered to be places where divinities resided, were not themselves usually places of worship. Most forms of worship took place outdoors at altars near the temples. Temples usually faced east, and commonly the main altar was aligned with the entrance to the temple. The main room of the temple, the cella, contained a statue of the god and often was open to the public only during regularly scheduled festivals. Large sanctuaries had other buildings associated with the temple, some for the display of votive offerings, others (porticos [stoas]) where visitors could relax in the shade from the sun, observe ceremonies conducted in open areas, or stay overnight. Greek sanctuaries were full of objects dedicated by grateful worshipers: large stone statues, small ceramic figurines, painted ceramic plaques, pottery, inscriptions on stone, articles of clothing, and weapons or armor. Because ritual eating played a part in Greek worship, special buildings with permanent fixtures for dining were often located within sanctuaries. Because dramatic and athletic contests were organized around special divinities, the larger sanctuaries might have a theater as well as a stadium. Theaters were associated with Dionysus and were found in cities throughout the Greek world, but there were also theaters in major sanctuaries of Apollo at Delphi, of the great gods (*Theoi Megaloi*) at Samothrace, of Asclepius at Epidaurus, and at the Amphiareion at Oropos and at other sanctuaries elsewhere. There were major stadiums at the sanctuary of Zeus at Olympia, the sanctuary of Apollo at Delphi, the sanctuary of Poseidon at Isthmia, and the sanctuary of Zeus at Nemea, all places where Panhellenic athletic events were regularly scheduled.

FORMS OF WORSHIP AND TYPES OF RITUAL

The Relation with the Divine

Greek devotion to the gods was defined by the regular performance of traditional forms of religious ritual. It was felt that there was a distinction between the divine realm and the human realm, but that the gods could make their power felt in the human realm, and that people, by performing certain prescribed ceremonies, could communicate with the divine. Important aspects of the relation between the human and divine are evident from the words used to mark this relationship. The word *hieron* means "filled with divine power" and is used to refer to something, a place, a thing, or an activity, found in the human realm. *Hieron* marks off an area or a thing where a god makes divine power felt and can be used of a sacred place, a sacred object, a sacred rite, or a sacrificial victim. A person must be in a certain state (*katharos,* purified) to approach that which is *hieron* in order to perform the sacred rites, *ta hiera.* Reverence toward the gods is defined by the performance of these rites, whether through words—prayers, hymns, oaths, curses, or questions to an oracle—or through actions—sacrifice, libation, making an offering, or giving a votive gift. *Eusebes,* which can be translated as "reverent," refers to the inner feelings of the person who observes the rules of cult and ritual; *hosios,* usually translated as "pious," refers to the external behavior of the person who performs the established rituals.

In conventional terms, piety was usually defined by ceremonial actions and ritual activities, not by moral behavior. There are indications, however, that some people thought otherwise. For instance, *to hosion,* "that which is pious," is usually used to define human activities directed toward the gods. *To dikaion,* "that which is just," is usu-ally used to characterize human behavior directed toward other people. In one of Plato's dialogues Socrates induces Euthyphro to define piety (*to hosion*) as a system of sacrifice and prayer (*Euthyphro* 14c), but elsewhere (12d) in the same dialogue he suggests to Euthyphro that piety might have some relationship to justice. Euthyphro, who seems to represent the traditional Greek view, is at a loss to characterize the relationship between piety and justice, but some Athenians must have been aware of the connection because it is occasionally implied that piety toward the gods is related to or even dependent upon just actions toward other human beings. A fragment from New Comedy sums up the issue: "Anyone who believes that he secures the god's favor by sacrifice . . . is in error. For a man must be useful by not seducing virgins or committing adultery or stealing or killing for money" (Menander frag. 683 Körte trans. Dover p. 254).

Prayers

We know of Greek prayers from two major sources: literature (especially Homeric epic and Attic drama) and inscriptions. Prayers in literature tend to be highly structured and formulaic, divided into three parts: an invocation to the god, with reference to the god's function; reasons for the god's positive support, usually the record of the past service of the person making the prayer; and the request. A famous Homeric example comes from the *Iliad* (1.37–42) where Chryses, who has lost his daughter to Agamemnon, prays to Apollo for the destruction of the Greeks:

Hear me, god of the silver bow, you who protect Chryse and sacred Killa and rule Tenedos with your power; if ever I built up a temple pleasing to you, if ever I burned for you fat thighs of bulls or goats, fulfill this wish for me:

may the Danaans pay for my tears with your arrows.

The prayer of Chryses is of great consequence for the fortunes of the Greeks at Troy; it also serves as a device by which the poet generates the plot of the *Iliad.*

In ordinary life prayers do not always have such tremendous consequences, but serve simply to provide a means of asking for a god's attention. People were most likely to pray at the beginning of a new project (Plato, *Timaeus* 27c). On the personal level prayers marked the beginning of a new day (Plato, *Symposium* 220d), or the beginning of the farming season (Hesiod, *Works and Days* 465–469). On the public level, prayers were offered at Athens at the beginnings of meetings of the ecclesia or assembly (Aeschines, 1.2.3; Thucydides, 8.70), and to Zeus Boulaios and Athena Boulaia on entering the bouleuterion, meeting place of the boule, the Athenian council (Antiphon, 6.45). Prayers were offered at the beginning of dramatic or athletic contests, at the beginning of military campaigns (Thucydides, 2.74; 6.32) and to mark the beginning of a political alliance (Tod, *Greek Historical Inscriptions* II, 144.6–12). People prayed for success in love and success in war, for health and safety, for good crops, for children, and for wealth and good fortune. Prayers were often accompanied by sacrifice, and the gods were expected to listen to people's requests. The gods were expected to offer protection and success in this life; what happened after death was not so much a concern.

Hymns

Hymns were prayers set to music and sung to the gods. Plato calls hymns the original type of song (*Laws* 700b), and Pollux distinguishes paeans (to Apollo), dithyrambs (to Dionysus), and prosodia (a general type of processional hymn), among others, in his compendium of Greek terms (*Onomasticon* 1.38). We have few texts preserved from the archaic and classical periods, but from later accounts it seems that hymn-singing by trained choruses was a regular feature of communal worship. Each sanctuary probably had its own songs (Julian, *Letters* 89.25), and although daily ritual with regular singing of hymns may have been rare, hymns were sung as a special part of certain festivals and at certain critical events. Choruses of local residents, divided according to sex and age group, performed traditional and new hymns at annual festivals of local gods. We know of dithyrambic contests, where hymns were sung by choruses of men and boys as a regular part of the Athenian Dionysia. Young girls sang hymns to Artemis at many sanctuaries throughout Greece. Greek armies marching into battle sang a paean, not only to call on the god for support, but also to preserve order while approaching the enemy (Thucydides, 5.69–70).

Votive Offerings

The Greek worshiper expected not salvation after death, but rewards in this life for piety and service to the gods. In order to acknowledge divine protection and to secure continuing attention from the gods, Greeks made token gifts to the gods for favors received. The votive offering is the logical extension of sacrifice and prayer. Theophrastus said that people sacrificed to the gods for three reasons: to honor them, to thank them, or to ask for something they needed (*On Piety* frag. 12 Pötscher, 42–44). As a concrete example of thanks for favors received, Greeks often felt obliged to give back a portion of the gift or a symbol of the gift. The parts of the sacrificial victim burned for the gods was a token gift for the sustenance animal food provided for humans. Farmers donated part of the first fruits of their crops. Victors in battle donated part of the spoils taken from the enemy. An apprentice craftsman might dedicate his first successful project. Often these offerings were the fulfillment of an obligation previously promised in a prayer and were made in a spirit of thanks when the solicited object or service had been granted. Thousands of objects were stored in sanctuaries and special buildings were often built to house and protect them. Warriors dedicated their arms and armor, craftsmen dedicated their tools, athletes dedicated their athletic equipment, women dedicated pieces of their weaving and the spindles and loom weights used to make the fabric. Poets dedicated copies of their poems, and contest victors dedicated their prizes. Sometimes a painted plaque or a stone relief with inscription and picture was dedicated instead of the object itself. Votive inscriptions not only give thanks for gifts received, but also sometimes contain a prayer for other similar gifts in the future. Gifts were made to the gods to mark important transitions during the course of life: birth of children, entry to adolescence, and marriage. People made dedications after delivery from disaster: shipwreck, earthquake, or illness. In a time of uncertain medical treatment, health was a valuable commodity, and the gods of health and healing were especially popular.

Oaths

In early Greek society, where written contracts did not exist, oaths played an important function in sanctioning and preserving agreements between private individuals, between the individual and the city, and between cities. Oaths were important in private life, in commerce and trade, and in public political relationships. The swearing of an oath always involved the gods as witnesses, and made the parties to an oath liable to punishment by the gods if the oath were broken. Athenians swore oaths to mark important stages in their lives: young men swore the ephebic oath when taking on the

duties of adult citizenship; fathers swore an oath when introducing a son to the phratry. Oaths marked the transition from private to public status: jurors swore an oath before undertaking jury duty; magistrates swore an oath on taking public office. Oaths were protected by the gods and at Athens were considered to be an important element in holding the democracy together (Lycurgus, *Against Leocrates* 79). Piety involved not only respect for the gods, but respect for oaths (Isocrates, 1.12–13). The swearing of an oath bound the parties to a curse, should that oath be broken. It would have been up to the gods to send the specified punishment if either party failed to live up to the oath. The worst punishment a man could face was considered to be the loss of family, children, and descendants. For this reason children were often made the object of a parent's curse when a parent swore an oath. Herodotus reports (6.86) an oracle that describes the punishment for those who do not remain true to oaths sworn; they would be pursued by the unnamed child of Oath, a monster with no hands and no feet, who would destroy the family and the whole family line. A man who died without children would not be remembered in family cult; his family and his ancestral gods would die with him. Further, he would have failed in his duty as a citizen because in the city's eyes the purpose of having children was to preserve and to protect the fatherland (*patris*) and the altars of the gods (Euripides, *Erechtheus* frag. 50 Austin, 14–15).

THE FAMILY AND CULTS OF THE LIFE CYCLE

House and Home

Theopompus, a historian of the fourth century B.C., tells a story that illustrates popular belief about correct religious behavior. He says that Apollo, asked to name the best worshiper of the gods, named Clearchus, an unknown citizen of Methydrion in far-off Arcadia. When the enquirer searched him out and asked how he worshiped, Clearchus himself explained that he participated modestly in public festivals, decorated his statues of Hermes and Hecate with garlands at each new moon, and cared for the sacred objects inherited from his ancestors, offering to them incense and two kinds of cakes (F. Jacoby, *Fragmente der griechischen Historiker* 115 F 344). Clearchus is simple and unpretentious, but he is regular in the performance of his religious duties, both recognizing the festivals of the gods of his city and remaining loyal to the gods of his family.

Because the family was considered to be the basic unit of social interaction and the basic unit of the city, the city itself had a stake in maintaining the cults of the family. Devotion to and care of ancestral images handed down in the family (*ta patroa hiera*) were the duties of every citizen, and the person who neglected these traditional family symbols wronged the city (Lycurgus, *Against Leocrates* 25–26). At Athens candidates for important magistracies were asked to demonstrate that they maintained statues of Apollo Patroos (a god who protected the phratry and the paternal side of the family), Zeus Herkeios (Zeus who protected the courtyard of the family home), and their family tombs (Aristotle, *Constitution of Athens* 55.3). Athenians kept statues of Zeus Herkeios in their houses (scholion to Plato, *Euthydemus* 302d), and every family maintained small altars in and around the house itself for rites in honor of other divinities who protected the life of the family. Numerous Athenian vase paintings show pictures of men and women offering sacrifices or making ritual gestures to hermae, stone pillars topped by a human head with erect phallus in front. Domestic hermae protected the house; public hermae protected the public space of the city. The depth of feeling inspired by these images and their rites is indicated by the public indignation and outrage aroused in Athens when in one night in 415 B.C. almost all the hermae in Athens were mutilated by political agitators (Thucydides, 6.27; Andocides, 1.37–38).

In addition to household hermae and statues of Hecate, as Clearchus mentions, there were other divinities who were important to the family. The hearth itself was considered sacred and, personified as the goddess Hestia, received sacrifices and tendance (Diodorus Siculus, 5.68.1). Small images of household divinities were kept in small cupboards, sometimes shaped like little temples (scholion to Aeschines, 1.10). Each family selected those divinities of special importance, but common household divinities were Zeus Ktesios, Zeus who protects property, represented by a two-handled jar wreathed with wool and filled with water, oil, and grain or fruit (Athenaeus, 473b–c), and Apollo Agyieus, protector of the street, represented by a pointed pillar set up at the street door (Aristophanes, *Wasps* 875). Only the family and their close friends could worship their individual Zeus Ktesios (Isaeus, 8.15–16). Small household altars have been found in residential areas excavated by archaeologists, and some idea of the possible variety of household divinities is indicated by a group of altars from Hellenistic Thera with inscriptions not only to Hestia and Zeus Ktesios, but also to Zeus Kataibates (who protects from lightning), Zeus Soter (who saves), Hygieia (a goddess whose name means health), Stropheus (personification of the socket in which the house door pivots), Tyche (goddess of fortune), and Agathos Daimon (the god who brings good luck), among others.

Birth

Births were announced by hanging on the door an olive wreath for a boy, a ribbon of wool for a girl. The distinction is important because rituals marking the maturation process for boys differed from those marking the maturation process for girls. The olive wreath symbolized the awards for men in Greek competitive life: athletic, political, and military. The woolen ribbon symbolized the domestic life anticipated for a girl.

A few days after a birth, family members and birth attendants gathered to perform a celebration designed to rid the family and baby of pollution incurred by the process of birth itself and to recognize the infant as a member of the family. Aristotle says that the child was not named immediately at birth because families waited to ascertain the infant's chances for survival (*History of Animals* 588a9–10). The number of days is variously recorded as five, seven, or ten, possibly because of differences in local practice, or possibly because in some families purification ceremonies were conducted separately from naming ceremonies. The key ritual was the Amphidromia (literally a "running around"), in which an adult ran around the hearth carrying the infant. The hearth symbolized the center of the family and the ceremony marked the acceptance of the child as a human being and its introduction into the family circle.

Rites for Boys

The rites performed for and by young boys marked the stages in their physical growth and development and their gradual introduction into the male organizations of the city and the activities of public life. Sometime during the first year of a son's life, his father presented a sacrifice (the *meion*) at the Apatouria, a festival of Apollo held annually in the phratries. Phratries were organizations of male kin groups who controlled inheritance and the distribution of property in the family line. Their sacrifices and banquets were restricted to males. In a society where births were otherwise not publicly recorded, this initial sacrifice at the Apatouria provided the means for a public announcement of a son's birth and prepared the way for his formal acceptance into the phratry later when he reached adolescence.

Another important ritual marking the introduction of young boys into the male community was the Choes, named for the tiny pitchers given to each child during the celebration. The Choes took place during the Anthesteria, a festival of Dionysus in early spring on the first day of which the wine from the previous vintage was tasted for the first time. On the second day a special celebration seems to have been devoted to young male children about three years old. They were wreathed with flowers and given tiny pitchers of wine by their fathers. Drinking the token amount of wine symbolized their joining of male society. The celebration of the Choes marked an important stage in the life of a young male child; in an Athenian inscription of the second century it is listed together with birth, the *ephebeia* (period of military training for young men, see below), and marriage, three other significant stages in the male life cycle (*Inscriptiones Graecae* II 1368.130). Many of the miniature pitchers from the festival, decorated with scenes of young male children at play, have been found by archaeologists.

The next important ritual for young boys occurred when they passed from childhood into adolescence, and like the *meion*, was celebrated in the father's phratry during the Apatouria. On the day called Koureotis, the third day of the Apatouria, a father whose son had reached adolescence presented a sacrifice called the *koureion* at the time of the formal entry and enrollment of his adolescent son into his phratry. The sacrifice seems to have accompanied the ceremonial cutting of the boy's hair, an act that symbolized the transition from childhood to adolescence. The ceremony was witnessed by adult phratry members and younger boys. Adult phratry members voted on the introduction of sons to the organization, and the father had to swear an oath that his son was legitimate and born from a mother to whom he was legally married (*Inscriptiones Graecae* II 1237.109–111). If the father's phratry members did not accept a boy as the legitimate son of his father, they removed the victim from the altar (Isaeus, 6.22). If, however, the adult members accepted the offering of the *koureion,* the boy was recognized as an official member of the phratry. The boys for whom the sacrifice was performed participated in the event and served meat to the phratry members (Demosthenes, 43.82).

At the age of eighteen an Athenian male was registered in his father's deme or voting district and thereby crossed the boundary into the *ephebeia,* the next stage of the maturation process. The *ephebeia* was a two-year period of military training and preparation for the adult responsibilities of the male citizen. The examination of the young man at the beginning of the *ephebeia* was entirely a civil affair, but during the period of training the Athenian ephebes were associated with the cult of Apollo Lykeios and also sacrificed to Artemis Agrotera. When they finished their training, they swore an oath to defend their city and to obey its laws. The oath is preserved on an inscription of the fourth century B.C. (Tod, *Greek Historical Inscriptions* II, 240). The swearing of the ephebic oath marked the assumption of lifelong military obligations and the assumption of the responsibilities of adult male citizens; nevertheless the swearing of the ephebic oath was far more than a simple civil event. The ephebes swore their oath in the sanctuary of Aglaurus on the Athenian Acropolis (Demosthenes, 19.303). In the oath itself civil and sacred responsibilities were closely associated. The young Athenian swore to defend both the sacred and the secular and to honor the ancestral sanctuaries. The oath

calls as witnesses the goddess Aglaurus (daughter of Cecrops, the first Athenian king), Hestia (who symbolizes the sacred hearth of the city as well as the sacred hearth of the home), Enyo, Enyalios, Ares, Athena Areia (divinities associated with war), Zeus, Thallo (a goddess of growth and increase), Hegemone (personification of leadership), and Heracles (associated with male strength and courage). Because the cults of the city were closely associated with the success of the city in peace and war, the young citizen, by swearing allegiance to the city and its laws, also swore to protect the rites and institutions associated with the city's gods.

Rites for Girls

There is no certain evidence that girls were ever presented to their fathers' phratries at Athens, but there were rituals associated with the maturation process of girls and young women. These rituals prepared girls not for public life, but for marriage, motherhood, and domestic duties. One festival associated with young girls was the Arrhephoria, an annual festival of Athena in which two young girls who had lived on the Acropolis for a year helping to weave a new robe for the goddess carried secret symbols down into a sanctuary of Aphrodite of the Gardens, deposited them there, and brought up something else (Pausanias, 1.27.3). The meaning of the rite is never explained by any ancient writer, but a myth told about the three daughters of Cecrops— Aglaurus, Herse, and Pandrosus—seems to offer a clue to the rite. After the virgin goddess Athena resisted rape by Hephaestus, his semen fell upon the ground. When the child Erichthonius was miraculously born from the earth, the virgin goddess Athena put the baby into a chest, gave it to Pandrosus, and told her not to look inside. Her two sisters, however, overcome with curiosity, peeked inside. They were frightened by a snake entwined around the baby and threw themselves from the Acropolis to their deaths (Apollodorus, 3.14.6). The conjunction of the snake, simultaneously a symbol of death and regeneration, with an infant born from an attempted forbidden union suggests that the symbols in the basket carried by the Arrhephoroi had to do with death and fertility. A scholiast tells us that the secret symbols carried by the Arrhephoroi were models of snakes and male genitalia (scholion to Lucian, p. 276 Rabe). Further it is likely that the special pastries given to the girls to eat (anastatoi, leavened cakes, Athenaeus, 114a) were formed in shapes of snakes or phalli. The goal of the girls' underground journey was the sanctuary of Aphrodite, who was the goddess of sexuality. The young Athenian girls who participated in the Arrhephoria were not allowed to see what they carried because they were too young to know the secrets of Aphrodite, and because they were still in service to Athena, a virgin goddess.

Some have interpreted the ceremonies of the Arrhephoria as initiation ceremonies, but because the festival involved only two girls per year, it is difficult to see how it could have been thought of as an initiatory rite for all Athenian girls in the classical period. Other ceremonies, especially those associated with Artemis, had a wider clientele and seem to have served a broader social function. Among these rites were the *arkteia*, ceremonies that prepared girls for sexual maturity and for their adult roles as wives and mothers. The *arkteia* were celebrated every four years at the festival known as the Brauronia. At Brauron, a village in eastern Attica, Artemis was worshiped as goddess of childbirth and infancy and as protector of young unmarried girls. People walked to Brauron from Athens to take part in the festival during which young girls called *arktoi* (bears) performed the *arkteia*, rituals in which they shed their clothes and danced in honor of Artemis (Aristophanes, *Lysistrata* 645). Schematic scenes of their dance have been preserved on small vases found in the sanctuary and in more detail on vases found elsewhere. The girls are identified with the bear and, as with the Arrhephoria, the rituals are in part explained by a myth. In this particular story a little girl's carelessness led to the death of Artemis' sacred bear (scholion to Aristophanes, *Lysistrata* 645). By imitating the bear, the girls participated ritually in the wildness of the animal. The ritual therefore condoned a type of activity antithetical to that of well-behaved Athenian girls and married women, but in the context of the cult at Brauron, where Artemis was worshiped as protector of women in childbirth and as Kourotrophos (nourisher of young children), the *arkteia* should be seen as rites preparing girls for marriage and childbirth. By experiencing temporarily, in a controlled ritual setting, what was ordinarily forbidden, the girls learned from its opposite their future acceptable role.

The *arkteia*, like the *koureion* for boys, marked the end of childhood for girls and the beginning of a transitional period eventually culminating in adult status: citizenship for the male and marriage for the female. The young girls, by participating in the dance, put themselves under Artemis' protection during that dangerous period of transition when their virginity had to be especially protected, the period between menarche and marriage. In recognition of this they performed rituals for Artemis on the eve of marriage when they dedicated their toys to her.

The Greek Wedding

The divinities associated with marriage were Zeus and Hera, Apollo and Artemis, and Peitho, goddess of persuasion. The major activities associated with the wedding ceremony were directed at the bride, for whom the ceremony signaled not only a change in sexual status, but also a change in residence. Before the wedding the bride was purified by a ritual bath with water brought from a special spring in a special pitcher (*loutrophoros*) made especially for this purpose. On the day of the wedding, after a wedding feast in the home of the bride's father, the major event was a procession to the home of the new husband. The bride was dressed in special clothing and her head was veiled. She was attended in the procession by friends who carried torches and sang the wedding hymn to Hymen, a god of marriage. When the bride arrived at her new home she was received by her husband's family with the same ceremony used to incorporate a new slave into the family. The groom's family seated her at the hearth and poured over her dried fruit and nuts as a sign of prosperity and fertility of the family (scholion to Aristophanes, *Wealth* 768). She was given a quince to eat, a fruit that symbolized her potential fertility as wife and mother. The important event of the wedding ceremony was not an exchange of words between the bride and groom, but their first act of sexual intercourse together. Friends stood outside the door of the marriage chamber, singing the wedding hymn to the wedding god Hymen; they also tried to make noise to confuse evil spirits. On the day after the wedding night the parents of the bride brought gifts, and her mother made a dedication to Hera, the goddess of marriage.

Artemis' protection of the young bride did not end at marriage. The biological and social goal of a woman was the production of a healthy child. Artemis, in her role as Lochia, continued to protect women until the birth of the first child. The Greek word for bride, *nymphe,* continued to be used of a married woman until after she had borne a child (*Palatine Anthology* 7.528). In recognition of this function of the goddess, families made sacrifices to Artemis at Brauron and parents dedicated many statues of children there in thanks for the birth of healthy babies. Numerous reliefs showing families sacrificing together and many statues of young children, both boys and girls, have been found in the sanctuary there.

CIVIC CULTS

Festivals

Each city had its patron deity, whose sanctuary adorned the city center and whose image often adorned the city's coins. Each city also had temples, shrines, and altars of a multitude of different gods and heroes. The entire year was organized around the regularly scheduled festivals in honor of these gods and although there were many similarities between different areas of Greece and Greek-occupied territories, every city had its own calendar, in which each month was named for a different significant local festival. Because of the way in which literary and epigraphical sources have been preserved and discovered, we know more about the Athenian calendar of festivals than that of any other city. At Athens seven days out of each of the twelve months were regularly devoted to monthly festivals of divinities important to the city. On these days the ecclesia (assembly) did not meet, although the boule (council) did. The deities concerned were the new moon (for which sacrifices were performed on the first day of each month), Agathos Daimon, Athena, Heracles, Hera, Aphrodite, Artemis, Apollo, Poseidon, and Theseus. In addition to the monthly festival days there were annual days devoted to major festivals. During these, neither the ecclesia nor the boule normally met. This means that on major festival days the entire male citizen body would have been free to participate.

During festivals restricted to women, such as the Thesmophoria or Theogamia, the ecclesia could meet. An Athenian inscription records the unusual meeting of the ecclesia in the theater during the Thesmophoria because the Pnyx, the normal meeting place for the ecclesia, was being used for the women's festival (*Inscriptiones Graecae* II 1006.50–51, 122 B.C.). When the total number of known monthly and annual festival days is added together, it can be seen that at least 150 days per year were devoted to festivals. Festivals were an important part of the religious and social life of the city. In antiquity the week was not divided into working days and days for relaxation. Festivals therefore provided the only interruption of civil and business affairs. This was noticed by Pericles in his funeral oration when he said that regularly scheduled festivals and sacrifice provided recreation for the people when their work was done (Thucydides, 2.38). Further, for most people, whose diets were normally restricted to bread, vegetables, dairy products, fish, and fruit, festivals, with their accompanying public sacrifices, provided feasts of meat relished by participants (Aristophanes, *Clouds* 386–387).

Although some festivals were restricted to women (the Thesmophoria, parts of the Skira, the Haloa, and the Theogamia), and some were restricted to men (the Apatouria, and perhaps the Dionysia and the Anthesteria), many festivals were open to men and women alike, citizen and noncitizen. Slave women were excluded from the Thesmophoria, but slave men dined with their owners at the Anthesteria. One annual celebration, a sacrifice to Heracles at Kynosarges (a gymnasium in the deme Diomeia) was especially for those who, although sons of Athenian fathers, would not have been eligible for Athenian citizenship after 451 B.C. because their mothers were foreigners (Aristotle, *Constitution of Athens* 26.3). Children attended festivals with their parents (Aristophanes, *Clouds* 861–864). For women of citizen class, whose activities were normally restricted to the home, festivals (and funerals) provided an opportunity for seeing people outside the home. Festivals also provided an opportunity for young men to meet young women (a frequent motif in the plays of Menander; see also Euripides, *Hippolytus* 24–28; and Lysias, 1.8). Although most festivals were open to everyone, it should be noted that working people might not always have been free to attend. An inscription recording a contract for a group of workers at Eleusis indicates that they worked for forty consecutive days straight through the festivals of the Kronia, the Synoikia, and the politically important Panathenaia (329/328 B.C.), (*Inscriptiones Graecae* II 1672.32–33).

The Athenian year began with the month Hekatombaion, corresponding roughly to the month of July. The most important festival during that month was the Panathenaia, devoted to Athena, the major Athenian goddess. The activities of the festival may have taken up as many as eight days during the classical period, but the main day was always the twenty-eighth day of the month, considered to have been the birthday of the goddess. The central activity was the presentation to the goddess of a new peplos (robe) woven during the preceding year by a group of females that included the young *arrhephoroi*, the little girls who lived on the Acropolis and served Athena. The frieze of the Parthenon, Athena's temple on the Acropolis, shows the procession of the representatives of the entire citizen body and metics (resident aliens) as they proceeded along the Panathenaic Way through the streets of the city and the agora up to the Acropolis, bringing the new robe and animals for sacrifice to the goddess. The procession included basket-carriers, the women who wove the peplos for the goddess (*ergastinai*), male citizens, women carrying implements for sacrifice, water-carriers, charioteers, and cavalry riders carrying olive branches. A focal celebration was the sacrifice on the Acropolis after the sacrificial fire had been lit by torches carried from the altar of Eros in the Academy. The cattle for the sacrifice were supplied by city funds, which in 335 B.C. amounted to 4,100 drachmas, enough for more than one hundred sacrificial victims (*Inscriptiones Graecae* II 334). The meat for the sacrifice, except for the thighs burned for Athena, was distributed by the deme to the people. Every four years the Great Panathenaia were held, celebrations that included athletic contests, poetry contests where rhapsodes gave recitations from the *Iliad* and the *Odyssey,* musical performances, dances performed by men in military armor, horse races, and a ship contest in the Piraeus. In the classical period the Panathenaia were much more than a simple procedure for reclothing the goddess; they had become a demonstration of Athenian excellence in mental and physical prowess.

There were at least thirty-five other major civic festivals scattered throughout the year and celebrated for various divinities. Some were agricultural festivals: the Stenia, Thesmophoria, Skira, Haloa, and Proerosia, celebrated in honor of Demeter for the purpose of guaranteeing the growth of grain and other plant foods; the Oschophoria and the Anthesteria, wine festivals associated with Dionysus. The Thargelia and Pyanepsia, both having to do with the growing of edible plants, were associated in the classical period with Apollo, a deity whose functions were not agricultural. Apparently the rituals of the festival associated with plant foods predated the introduction of the worship of Apollo at Athens and may have originally been associated with a fertility deity, perhaps Demeter, who as Demeter Chloe is worshiped on the first day of the Thargelia. Some festivals had rituals performed to effect purification: during the Thargelia two men called *pharmakoi,* one representing the men of Athens, the other the women, were beaten and driven out of the city as scapegoats in order to drive away the impurities associated with the residents. Purification of the temple of Athena was the purpose of the Kallynteria, and purification of the goddess herself was the function of the Plynteria, when the statue of Athena was taken down and bathed in the sea. All three of these festivals took place in the same month, roughly corresponding to May.

Some festivals had a single specific purpose. The Genesia were ceremonies in honor of the dead, and the Synoikia commemorated an important event attributed by the Athenians to Theseus, the confederation of the villages of Attica under the political jurisdiction of Athens. Many festivals, however, were so old or so obscured by ritual secrecy that already in antiquity their origins and original purposes were not recorded or explained. The Bouphonia, a sacrifice to Zeus at the Dipolieia, seems to belong to this category. The Arrhephoria, perhaps because of the secrecy associated with the carrying of the sacred objects, was another festival never explained. The original functions of the Lenaia and the Dionysia are not clearly understood, but both were clearly associated with Dionysus. Originally vintage festivals, by the classical period they had become associated with Dionysus' function as god of the theater and were the occasion for the great dramatic contests in which the major works of the Greek tragedians and comic dramatists were annually performed.

Athletic contests were a part of many festivals. The major Athenian athletic contests were staged at the Great Panathenaia, but similar events played a part in other festivals throughout the year. During the Mounichia in honor of Artemis, the ephebes conducted ship races in the harbor at Piraeus. The Olympieia in honor of Zeus included cavalry exercises and military drill contests, and the Bendideia in honor of the Thracian goddess Bendis had a torch race.

Although the origins of some festivals remained obscure even in antiquity, changes were often made in old, established festivals to accommodate changes in political policy, and new festivals could be introduced as the cults of new and foreign gods became part of the established ritual of the city. The original festival of the Panathenaia was probably centered around the presentation of the new peplos to Athena. It was only in the sixth century under the impetus of the political reorganization of the Peisistratid administration that the athletic contests were added to the traditional festival. As Athens increased in wealth and political importance, this festival became a vehicle for the expression of political strength of the democracy, both internally and externally. The political significance of this festival is demonstrated by the involvement of the cities allied to Athens in the middle years of the fifth century B.C. In recognition of Athenian superiority, during the period of the Athenian empire, each of the allies was required to send to the festival of the Great Panathenaia a cow for sacrifice and a suit of armor. Inscriptions record some of the donations (Meiggs and Lewis, *Selection of Greek Historical Inscriptions* 46.41–43; 49.11–12; 69.56–57). Another festival that seems to have adapted itself to changes in political climate is the Synoikia. Already closely associated with the political history of the city, when a truce was concluded with Sparta in 374 B.C. this festival was expanded to include sacrifices to Eirene, goddess of peace. The sacrifices were offered at an altar of Eirene in the agora. Even though the truce itself was short-lived, the institution of these particular sacrifices at this time seems to indicate the people's dissatisfaction with the series of wars that had plagued their recent history.

Festivals for women emphasize women's role in fertility and usually derive their significance from an analogy between female fecundity and the fertility of the earth. Several Athenian festivals were restricted in whole or in part to women: the Stenia, Skira, Thesmophoria, and the Haloa. In addition the Gamelia, a marriage festival in honor of Hera, seem to have been reserved exclusively for women. Because the ecclesia could meet on the day of the festival, men would not have attended. The Skira, Stenia, Thesmophoria, and Haloa were in origin agricultural festivals, and even for city residents never lost their agricultural meaning or significance. The Stenia and Thesmophoria were devoted to Demeter, the Skira to Demeter, Athena, and Poseidon, and the Haloa to Demeter and Dionysus. In all of these festivals the rites in honor of Demeter excluded men. In addition women had to refrain from sexual intercourse for the Skira and Thesmophoria; to ensure abstinence they ate garlic.

The Thesmophoria were celebrated in the fall at the time of the planting of the winter wheat. The first day of the festival was devoted to the sacrifice of piglets, animals especially associated with Demeter. The piglets were thrown into underground chambers called *megara*. The rite is associated with the myth of the disappearance of the swineherd Eubouleus and his pigs into a chasm in the earth when Hades ravished Kore. As part of the festival specially chosen women brought decayed matter up from the underground chambers. The decayed matter was mixed with the seed grain and placed on altars. This ceremony was intended to encourage the fertility of the soil and to promote the successful growth of grain, Demeter's gift, but the festival had another dimension as well. Arguing that the earth is the mother of all, Plato says that in conception and reproduction earth does not imitate woman, but woman imitates earth (*Menexenus* 238a). The rituals of the Thesmophoria originally promoted the fertility of the earth, but the significance of the ceremony as an official festival of the organized polis was its role in promoting the fecundity of the women of Athens in order to provide future citizens for the city. In the classical period, only married women were allowed to attend (Isaeus, 6.49–50). Slaves and resident foreigners were excluded. During the period of the festival the women camped out on the Pnyx, the hill where the male assembly normally met. The women's festival actually mirrored the male assembly. The women were organized according to deme, they elected two leaders (Isaeus, 8. 19), followed certain well-established procedures, and at the end celebrated with banquets paid for as a liturgy (*leitourgia*) by a husband from each deme (Isaeus, 3.80). On the second day of the festival the women fasted, sat on the ground, and engaged in ritual verbal obscenity designed to increase not only the fertility of the earth, but also to encourage their own. The third day, named Kalligeneia (Day of Beautiful Offspring), celebrated Demeter's role as bringer of the fruits of the earth, and also celebrated the women's own reproductive role. The role of the women as producers of citizens is emphasized by Aristophanes when he has one of his female characters say that women should honor at their festivals those who have produced sons, valuable citizens of the state (*Women at the Thesmophoria* 832–835).

Rituals for War

War was the ultimate contest for the Greek city-state, and just as the gods presided over contests in music, poetry, and athletics, so too were they believed to preside over the contests of war. The gods could make their intentions known through oracle, prodigy, epiphany, or sacrifice. Polit-

ical leaders consulted oracles before deciding to make war and planned their strategy according to the answers given. Those about to engage in battle paid special attention to prodigies or omens, unusual natural events such as earthquakes, comets, thunder and lightning, or the strange behavior of animals. Sacrifices were made when an army departed from its city, when it left its own territory and crossed the border into the territory of the enemy, and when it engaged in battle. The inner organs of the sacrificial victim were examined by a professional prophet or seer (*mantis*) and an engagement could be postponed if the omens were not favorable. Military commanders traveled with seers and consulted professional prophets, but it was considered important for soldiers and officers to be able to interpret the sacrifices themselves (Onasander, *Duties of a Commander* 10.25–27). Soldiers marching into battle sang the paean to Ares and Enyalios. The eventual outcome of battle was believed to be determined by the gods, and fighters vowed before fighting to offer sacrifices and votive gifts should their attempts be successful (Aeschylus, *Seven Against Thebes* 271–279). When the battle was over the leaders of both sides ceremonialized the truce by pouring libations. Sacrifices of thanks were offered on the occasion of victory, and victors erected trophies of wood, bronze, or stone on the battlefield and later made dedications of booty and armor in sanctuaries.

LIFE AND DEATH

Introduction

Although most Greek religious activity involved group participation, some cults had a special appeal for the individual. Among these were the Eleusinian Mysteries, celebrated at Athens and Eleusis and incorporated into the Athenian calendar as a regular festival. Mysteries were secret ceremonies that offered special benefits after death to participants. The rites were group ceremonies, but the ultimate benefit was directed toward the individual. Other mysteries were celebrated elsewhere; the most famous were those at Samothrace. Already known at Athens in the late fifth century (Aristophanes, *Peace* 277–278), the Samothracian rites found their greatest popularity in the Hellenistic period, when the Samothracian sanctuary became one of the great international cult centers of the eastern Mediterranean. The mysteries at Samothrace offered to initiates protection at sea, especially important to the Greeks, who traveled so much by sea. Because proper burial rites were so important, death at sea was greatly to be feared.

In the late fifth century B.C., at the time of the Peloponnesian War, many ceremonies with a special appeal to the individual were introduced at Athens. Some, like the healing rites of Asclepius from Epidaurus or the rites of Bendis, a Thracian goddess similar to Artemis, were at first limited to private groups and only later incorporated into the official civic calendar (Ferguson, *Greek and Roman Religion* 95–104). Others, however, seem to have always remained the province of small, private religious groups or associations. The ecstatic rites of the Corybantes and Sabazius belong to this type, as do the private initiation ceremonies so harshly criticized by Demosthenes (18.259; 19.199) and the sacrifices and incantations so depreciated by Plato (*Republic* 364b–c).

Dionysus is a god who has both a public and a private side. As the god of wine and the god of the theater, he was an official god of the city and his festivals were incorporated into the public calendar well before the classical period. His major festivals were the Anthesteria, Lenaia, Dionysia, and Oschophoria. Dionysus, however, was also worshiped by small groups, and for these groups other functions were often stressed. Some private men's groups worshiped Dionysus as god of wine, holding regular banquets in his honor (*Inscriptiones Graecae* II 1368). Small groups of women celebrated rites from which men were excluded (Aristophanes, *Lysistrata* 1), but whether these were the same as the wild exuberant maenadic celebrations known from myth and described so convincingly by poets like Euripides is unlikely.

Dionysus is also associated with myths of death and regeneration. Associated with the figure of Orpheus, these stories have been the object of scholarly speculation and dispute. Recent archaeological finds—inscribed bone tablets together with an inscribed bronze mirror from Olbia, a Greek colony on the north coast of the Black Sea, and an inscribed gold tablet from Hipponium (modern Vibo Valentia)—provide evidence for widespread activity of small, secret groups who called themselves *mystai* (initiates) and believed that Dionysus could provide protection after death. These small groups present almost a countercurrent to the conventional and traditional Greek cults, and the very secrecy of their activities makes it almost impossible to reconstruct how they functioned and what they believed. Some consistency in practice and belief can be assumed, however, because it is known that written texts about myths associated with Orpheus circulated widely and could have been used as the basis for private ceremonies (Demosthenes, 18.259; 19.199).

Healing Cults

Conventional Greek religion seems to have paid little attention to the health of the soul after death; a far more pressing need was the health of the body during life. Several Greek gods presided over health and cures from sickness. Asclepius was the major

Greek healing god; originally considered a hero, he was the son of Apollo, the god who both sent disease and released victims from disease. In myth Asclepius challenged Zeus and Hades by preserving too many people from death (Diodorus Siculus, 4.71.1–4), but in cult he was considered to have achieved divine status and was revered for saving people from illness. His major center was Epidaurus, where he seems to have been associated with the earlier god Apollo Maleatus. The earliest altar and small building associated with Asclepius at Epidaurus date from the late sixth century B.C. The first major temple with cult statue was not built until the fourth century, but by that time the Epidaurians had established the worship of Asclepius at Aegina (Aristophanes, *Wasps* 122–123, performed in 422 B.C.). Asclepius himself was taken to Athens during the Peloponnesian War after a serious plague had ravaged the Athenian population. The poet Sophocles is said to have received the god into his own home (Plutarch, *Numa* 4), but a more accurate account of his arrival is described in an Athenian inscription. The inscription says that the god was led to the Eleusinians and was provided with a sanctuary of his own in the archonship of Astyphilos (420/419 B.C.). The god sent to Epidaurus for his sacred snake, symbol of his regenerative powers (*Inscriptiones Graecae* II 4960). The sanctuary of Asclepius was located on the south slope of the Acropolis, close to a natural spring. A pit lined with cut stone located nearby may have been the place where the sacred snake was kept.

The cult of Asclepius spread steadily after the fifth century, an indication of the growing popularity in that period of divinities who responded to personal needs. The festivals and rituals of the city continued to be important and continued to be recognized, but people also began to look beyond the communal rites to rituals that provided relief from personal anxieties. At Athens the cult was officially recognized by the city, but

in all periods and in all places it was private worshipers who provided steady interest in the god and his power. Eventually there were shrines of Asclepius throughout Greece, the Aegean islands, Asia Minor, North Africa, and Italy. In the Hellenistic period the diffusion of this cult becomes a measure of the penetration of Hellenism into the Mediterranean world. Important sanctuaries have been excavated at Epidaurus, Corinth, Athens, Cos, and Pergamum. Inscriptions and dedications testify to a steady interest throughout the Greek and Roman world.

People visited sanctuaries of Asclepius to preserve their good health and to be cured of diseases if they were not healthy. The established procedure required purification, sacrifice, and incubation. Sanctuaries of Asclepius always incorporated a natural spring, the water of which seems to have provided the means for preliminary purification. It is said that an inscription at the sanctuary at Epidaurus required that those who entered the temple be pure not only in body, but also in thought (Porphyry, *On Abstinence* 2.19). Those who were wicked were not supposed to enter a sanctuary of Asclepius (Philostratus, *Life of Apollonius* 1.11). Aristophanes describes a bath in the sea before entry to the Asclepieium (*Wealth* 656–657). An inscription from the Asclepieium at Pergamum specifies that those consulting the god enter the temple only after purification and that they enter barefoot, wearing white, without rings or belts (Sokolowski, *Lois sacrées de l'Asie mineure* 14). After entering the sanctuary, the worshiper made a preliminary sacrifice. Typical preliminary offerings were cakes and fruit (Aristophanes, *Wealth* 660–661, 677).

The high point of the visit took place while the worshiper slept. It was thought that the god himself appeared either in a dream (*Inscriptiones Graecae* IV 121–122 *passim*) or in the state between sleeping and waking (Marinus, *Life of Proclus* 30). The god appeared to worshipers as he is depicted in temple sculpture, a mature, bearded man, calm and reassuring. Sometimes he administered the cure immediately, sometimes he gave instructions for therapy to be followed later. Occasionally worshipers thought that the sacred snake licked them in sleep and affected an immediate cure. The god is supposed to have used surgical procedures, to have administered drugs and medications, and to have advised physical therapy. Some of the recorded procedures are well within the range of ordinary ancient medical practice. Miracle cures attributed to the god may have been exaggerated because people desperately ill may have irrationally attributed any improvement to a dream about the god's visit. Most of the ancient testimony describing miracle cures in temples of Asclepius survive from inscriptions set up by the administrators of the sanctuaries. Personal experiences are usually described in the third person, as if the temple administrators kept notes on successful cases and inscribed summaries of these in order to inspire future visits to the sanctuary. One such example (*Inscriptiones Graecae* IV [1] 122, no. 27) describes a surgical procedure:

A man came who had an abscess in his belly. He went to sleep in the temple and saw a dream. The god seemed to him to order his accompanying attendants to grab him and hold him, so that the god might cut open his belly. The man ran away, but they caught him and tied him to the table. After this the god cut open the man's stomach, cut out the abscess, stitched him up again, and untied him from his bonds. And after this he went out healthy, and the floor in the *abaton* was full of blood.

Another (*Inscriptiones Graecae* IV [1] 122, no. 42) describes a miraculous cure:

Nikasiboula of Messenia went to sleep in the temple because she wanted to have children, and she saw a dream. It seemed to her that the god approached her with a snake creeping after him; she had intercourse with this snake and from this were born to her in a year's time two male children.

The illnesses and conditions are not extraordinary: blindness, paralysis, lameness, tapeworm, lice, tuberculosis, hepatitis, infection, pleurisy, birthmarks, headache, arthritis, dyspepsia, and gout. Women were prone to problems associated with reproduction: prolonged pregnancy or sterility. In both types of situations the women were always said to have been rewarded with the birth of a healthy child.

After a successful cure, people were required to offer a sacrifice and sometimes to make a votive offering. There was no special animal specified for sacrifice; oxen, pigs, and goats are sometimes mentioned. A common sacrifice to Asclepius, however, especially from ordinary people without extensive financial means, was a cock or rooster. Socrates' reminder to Crito to sacrifice a cock to Asclepius is in keeping with the typical sacrifice to that god (Plato, *Phaedo* 118a; *Inscriptiones Graecae* IV [1] 41.6; Herondas, 4.16). The rooster was identified with dawn, and was an appropriate animal for sacrifice by a person who woke up cured in the morning, having dreamed of the god.

Hundreds of votive offerings have been found in sanctuaries of Asclepius. We know from literary sources that people dedicated money, pictures, plants, poetry, or a piece of their personal possessions. Among surviving examples, however, the most common are ceramic models of the part of the body cured. More examples survive at Corinth than anywhere else. Archaeologists there have found and reconstructed many heads, legs, feet, arms, hands, female breasts, and male genitalia. Eyes and ears are also dedicated, either singly or in pairs; cures for blindness figure among the testimonials and ear infection is also mentioned. Frequent representations of male genitalia may be evidence of functional problems. Sterility does not seem to be a concern of males in the testimonials, where sterility seems to be considered strictly a female problem. Among the votive offerings women's problems in reproduction and lactation are indicated not only by the high number of representations of breasts, but also by small models of uteruses and even an ovary.

Some people were skeptical about the cures attested. One inscribed testimony concerns a woman from Athens, named Ambrosia. She laughed when she saw the reports of miraculous cures at Epidaurus, believing that it was impossible for a person to be cured by a dream. Nevertheless she submitted to the procedure herself. In her dream the god promised to cure her eye, but because of her scorn, he required that she dedicate a silver pig. He cured her eye with surgery and drugs, and the next day, her sight in that eye was restored (*Inscriptiones Graecae* IV [1] 121, no. 4). Other people were eager to secure the god's protection, but it is clear that Asclepius was thought to advocate moderation. In one case he refused to offer treatment and care to a rich man who had given too ostentatious a sacrifice. The god argued that the wealthy man must have been trying to conceal wrongdoing (Philostratus, *Life of Apollonius* 1.10). On another occasion a person tried to ask for too much from the god. Artemidorus reports that a man prayed to Asclepius that he would sacrifice a rooster to him if he stayed healthy for a year. He came back the next day and prayed that he would sacrifice another rooster if he did not go blind. The god appeared to him at night and said, "One rooster is enough." The man remained healthy, but suffered from a serious eye problem. Artemidorus comments, "The god was satisfied with one prayer and declined the other" (*Interpretation of Dreams* 5.9).

There is no evidence that incubation in temples of Asclepius was limited to a certain date or to a certain time of year. People could seek the god at any time. In addition to incubation and cures, temple services were a regular feature at sanctuaries of Asclepius. Priests and assistants offered regular sacrifices on altars of Asclepius. The sacrifices were accompanied by prayers and hymns. Because of his relationship to Apollo, Asclepius was honored with the paean, Apollo's song. Inscribed paeans have been found in sanctuaries of Asclepius: a second-century copy of a paean written by Sophocles in Athens (*Inscriptiones Graecae* II 4510), a paean of the fourth century B.C. at Erythrai, and the paean of Isyllus at Epidaurus (*Inscriptiones Graecae* IV [1] 128, III.32–IV.56, *ca.* 300 B.C.), among others. Aelian implies that it was customary in sanctuaries of Asclepius for the paean to be sung in the morning (frag. 98 Hercher) and Aristides says that hymns were sung at the daily opening of the Asclepieium at Pergamum (47.30 Keil). Sometimes these daily services were attended by large groups of people; Herondas describes the crowd rushing into the temple at dawn (4.54).

Larger groups of people attended the major festivals of Asclepius. These were held regularly at many of the important temple sites. The festivals at Athens were called Epidauria, an indication of their origin. Elsewhere these festivals were called Asclepieia. These festivals included grand processions: at Eretria even young boys and girls under seven years old took part (*Inscriptiones Graecae* XII [9] 194, late fourth or early third century B.C.). At Lampsacus children were let out of school and slaves were let off from work (Sokolowski, *Lois sacrées de l'Asie mineure* 8, second century B.C.).

The Mysteries

The Eleusinian Mysteries had their home at Eleusis, a small town northwest of Athens. The site was inhabited in the Mycenaean period, and there are Mycenaean and Geometric period foundations beneath the remains of the archaic temple, but the date of origin for the mysteries themselves is clouded in some obscurity. The most important early evidence for the mysteries is the Homeric *Hymn to Demeter,* a narrative poem in dactylic hexameter dated before the middle of the sixth century B.C. The hymn describes the grief of Demeter after her daughter Kore is abducted by Hades, god of the underworld, and Demeter's subsequent punishment of the gods and humankind when she takes away her gift of grain and causes a devastating year of famine. In the myth the situation is resolved by the mediation of Hermes, who engineers a bargain between Demeter and Zeus whereby Kore will spend one third of the year with Hades (the winter) and return in spring to spend the rest of the year with her mother. This part of the myth explains Demeter's control over grain (the food of civilized people), the change of the seasons, and the association of death (the underworld) with life, all themes prominent in earlier Near Eastern myths.

What makes this story different from other versions is the prominent role of the mother-daughter relationship and a new section of the story grafted on to the older myth in order to anchor the myth to Eleusis itself. This section occurs before Demeter withholds grain and takes place at Eleusis, where Demeter has taken refuge. According to the story, she meets the king and queen of Eleusis, Keleos and Metaneira, and becomes the nurse of their infant son, Demophoön. Trying to make the child a substitute for her lost daughter, she seeks to make him immortal by feeding him ambrosia (the food of the gods) and by laying him every night in the fire to burn off his mortality. Enraged when she is discovered by Metaneira, Demeter reveals herself as a goddess and demands that in recompense the Eleusinians build a temple for her where she

can establish for them her rites or mysteries (*orgia*). This section of the story provides the explanation for the origin of the mysteries and confirmed for the Eleusinians themselves the participation of the goddess herself in their history. The last lines of the poem show that those who had seen the rites of Demeter at Eleusis had a share in special blessings, even in the underworld after death. It is this offer, clearly a part of Eleusinian belief, that made the rites at Eleusis different from most rites to other divinities elsewhere; the mysteries were concerned not only with benefits for the present life, but also with benefits after death.

The difference in goals required a difference in the structure and content of the rites. The rites at Eleusis were secret and initiates were never to divulge to the uninitiated what they had learned or seen. Unlike other Greek rituals, the mysteries were conducted inside a building and took place not by day but by night. The temple at Eleusis was not a conventional rectangular Greek temple with cult statue of the divinity, but in its final form a large square building with stepped ramps on three sides from which participants viewed the ceremonies performed by priests in the central area. Further, there was a small, closed room (*anaktoron*) in the center of the hall where special sacred images were kept, to be displayed by the hierophant (head priest, literally "the one who shows the sacred things") at a certain critical moment in the ceremony.

Sometime during the late sixth century B.C. the temple at Eleusis (called the Telesterion) was rebuilt and the main gate to the sanctuary was moved from its earlier position facing the sea to the side of the sanctuary facing the road to Athens. The physical changes in the structure of the sanctuary and the new orientation toward Athens were results of political domination of Eleusis by Athens. By this time the organization of the mysteries had come under the control of the *basileus* at Athens, the archon or magistrate in charge of religious affairs for the city. The Athenians moved part of the preliminary ceremonies to Athens, built (in the early fifth century) the Eleusinion, a sanctuary of the Eleusinian goddesses in the central agora at Athens, and eventually required for participation at the Eleusinian rites in the fall (the Greater Mysteries) a preliminary initiation in the spring (the Lesser Mysteries) at Agrai, just outside the city wall.

The Lesser Mysteries required fasting, sacrifice, and purification in preparation for the major ceremonies later. The Greater Mysteries were divided into two stages: *myesis* and *epopteia*. *Myesis* was the first stage, prerequisite to *epopteia*, the higher stage, for which initiates had to wait one year. The Greater Mysteries began on the fourteenth day of Boedromion (early October), when the images sacred to Demeter were brought from the *anaktoron* at Eleusis to the Eleusinion at Athens. By the classical period the formal requirements for the mysteries had become well established. Anyone could participate; the only people excluded were murderers and those who could not speak Greek. A fee was charged; in the fourth century B.C. it amounted to fifteen drachmas for *myesis*. Slaves were not excluded if someone paid their fee (Demosthenes, 59.21).

On the first day all participants gathered at the Stoa Poikile in the agora where the sacred herald (*hierokeryx*) recited a proclamation giving the requirements for initiation. On the next day the initiates (*mystai*) paraded to the sea, a distance of about three miles, where they waded in the water to purify themselves and a piglet for sacrifice. The sacrifice was followed by feasting after which the initiates may have fasted until they reached Eleusis. The transition from Athens to Eleusis, a distance of about fourteen miles, involved a daylong procession of all participants. The Athenian ephebes, crowned with myrtle, accompanied the initi-

ates. During the course of the journey a hymn was sung to Iacchos, god of the procession, identified after the fifth century with Dionysus. Toward evening, just before arriving at Eleusis, the initiates had to cross a bridge over the river Kephisos. Men disguised as women stood on the bridge to shout insults and obscenities at the initiates, perhaps to mark the transition from the merriment of the journey to the solemnity of the rites, perhaps to banish evil spirits who might disturb those rites. After arriving at Eleusis initiates observed a dance by women bearing the *kernos*, a special pottery vessel sacred to Demeter. They also drank the *kykeon*, a mixture of water, barley, and mint.

What actually happened later in the Telesterion during *myesis* and *epopteia* is not known, but we do know that special things were said, special things were shown, and special things were done. Proclus says that initiates shouted to the sky "Rain!" and to the earth "Conceive!" (commentary to Plato's *Timaeus* 293c). Hippolytus tells us that one of the things revealed at the *epopteia* was a piece of wheat (*Refutation of All Heresies* 5.8.39). The symbolism of grain and reproduction seems to have played an important part in the ceremony. Tertullian, the early Christian critic of the mysteries, claims that the great secret revealed was nothing but an image of the male genitalia (*Against the Valentinians* 1). What for Tertullian was an object of disgust was for the Eleusinian participant a symbol of regeneration. Sophocles indicates that initiates would be three times blessed or happy after death because they would have a special existence in the underworld (frag. 837 Radt). There were no special lessons to learn at Eleusis (Aristotle frag. 15 Rose), there was no special moral instruction, but as Pindar puts it, the initiate who has seen the secrets at Eleusis is happy after death because of understanding the beginning and the end of life (frag. 137 Snell). Demeter's initiates worshiped her for her gift of grain, the food which made human society possible, but they also worshiped her because the grain itself, which flourishes, dies away, and grows again, was a metaphor for their own expectations and hopes.

BIBLIOGRAPHY

SOURCES

Artemidorus, *Interpretation of Dreams*, Robert J. White, trans. (1975); John Ferguson, *Greek and Roman Religion: A Source Book* (1980); Frederick C. Grant, *Hellenistic Religions* (1953); Margherita Guarducci, *Epigrafia Greca IV. Epigrafi sacre pagane e cristiane* (1978); Homer, *The Iliad of Homer*, Richmond Lattimore, trans. (1951); *Inscriptiones Graecae*, 2d ed. (1873–; *editio minor* 1924–1940); F. Jacoby, *Fragmente der Griechischen Historiker* (1923–); Russell Meiggs and David Lewis, *A Selection of Greek Historical Inscriptions to the End of the Fifth Century B.C.* (1969); David G. Rice and John E. Stambaugh, *Sources for the Study of Greek Religion* (1979); F. Sokolowski, *Lois sacrées de l'Asie mineure* (1955), *Lois sacrées des cités grecques* (1969), and *Supplement* (1962); Marcus N. Tod, *A Selection of Greek Historical Inscriptions* II (1940).

STUDIES

Allaire Chandor Brumfield, *The Attic Festivals of Demeter and Their Relation to the Agricultural Year* (1981); Walter Burkert, *Homo Necans: The Anthropology of Ancient Greek Sacrificial Ritual and Myth*, Peter Bing, trans. (1983), originally published as *Homo Necans* in German (1972), *Greek Religion Archaic and Classical* (1985), originally published in German as *Griechische Religion der archaischen und klassischen Epoche* (1977), and *Structure and History in Greek Mythology and Ritual* (1979); John Camp, *Gods and Heroes in the Athenian Agora* (1980); Susan Guettel Cole, "New Evidence for the Mysteries of Dionysos," in *Greek, Roman, and Byzantine Studies*, **21** (1980), and *Theoi Megaloi: The Cult of the Great Gods at Samothrace* (1984).

Marcel Detienne, *The Gardens of Adonis: Spices in Greek Mythology* (1977); Ludwig Deubner, *Attische Feste* (1932; repr. 1966). E. R. Dodds, *The Greeks and the Irrational* (1951), and "The Religion of the Ordinary Man in Classical Greece," in *The Ancient Concept of Progress and Other Essays on Greek Literature and Belief* (1973); K. J. Dover, *Greek Popular Morality in the Time of Plato and Aristotle* (1974); Emma J. Edelstein and Ludwig Edelstein, *Asclepius, A Collection and Interpretation of the Testimonies*, 2 vols. (1945); Arthur Fairbanks, *Handbook of Greek Religion* (1910); Lewis Farnell, *The Cults of the Greek States* I–V (1896–1909); W. S. Ferguson and A. D. Nock, "The Attic Orgeones," in *Harvard Theological Review*, **37** (1944), and "Orgeonika," in *Hesperia*, Supplement 8 (1949); Louis Gernet, *The Anthropology of Ancient Greece* (1981); R. L. Gordon, ed., *Myth, Religion and Society* (1981); W. K. C. Guthrie, *Orpheus and Greek Religion* (1932), and *The Greeks and Their Gods* (1950).

Jane Harrison, *Prolegomena to the Study of Greek Religion*, 3d ed. (1922), and *Themis*, 2d ed. (1927); Albert Henrichs, "Changing Dionysiac Identities," in Ben F. Meyer and E. P. Sanders, eds., *Jewish and Christian Self-Definition* (1982), and "Greek Maenadism from Olympias to Messalina," in *Harvard Studies in Classical Philology*, **82** (1978); Mary Brooks Berg Hollinshead, *Legend, Cult and Architecture at Three Sanctuaries of Artemis* (Diss., Bryn Mawr 1979); Mabel Lang, *Cure and Cult in Ancient Corinth*, Corinth Notes 1 (1977); Merle Langdon, "A Sanctuary of Zeus on Mount Hymettos," in *Hesperia*, Supplement 16 (1976); Ivan Linforth, *The Arts of Orpheus* (1941; repr. 1973); Raoul Lonis, *Guerre et religion en Grèce à l'époque classique* (1979); Nicole Loraux, "Le lit, la guerre," in *L'Homme*, **21** (1981); Jon D. Mikalson, *The Sacred and Civil Calendar of the Athenian Year* (1975), and *Athenian Popular Religion* (1983); George E. Mylonas, *Eleusis and the Eleusinian Mysteries* (1961).

Martin Nilsson, *Geschichte der griechischen Religion* (I, 1950; II, 1961), "Roman and Greek Domestic Cult," in *Opuscula Romana* n.s. 1 (1954), *Greek Piety* (1969), and *Greek Folk Religion* (1971); Arthur Darby Nock, *Essays on Religion and the Ancient World*, Z. Stewart, ed. (1972), and "Religious Attitudes of the Greeks," in *Proceedings of the American Philological Society*, **85** (1942); H. W.

Parke, *Festivals of the Athenians* (1977); Robert Parker, *Miasma: Pollution and Purification in Early Greek Religion* (1983); A. W. Pickard-Cambridge, *The Dramatic Festivals of Athens,* 2d. ed. (1968); W. Kendrick Pritchett, *The Greek State at War,* III: *Religion* (1980); Noel Robertson, "The Riddle of the Arrhephoria at Athens," in *Harvard Studies in Classical Philology,* **87** (1983); Carl Roebuck, *Corinth,* XIV: *The Asklepieion and Lerna* (1951); E. Rohde, *Psyche,* W. B. Hillis, trans. (1925), originally published in German (1910); H. J. Rose, "The Religion of a Greek Household," in *Euphrosyne,* **1** (1957); W. H. D. Rouse, *Greek Votive Offerings* (1902); J. Rudhardt, *Notions fondamentales de la pensée religieuse et actes constitutifs du culte dans la Grèce classique* (1958).

Erika Simon, *Die Götter der Griechen* (1969), and *Festivals of Attica: An Archaeological Commentary* (1983); Richard Stillwell, ed., *The Princeton Encyclopedia of Classical Sites* (1976); R. A. Tomlinson, *Greek Sanctuaries* (1976); John Travlos, *Pictorial Dictionary of Ancient Athens* (1971); Jean-Pierre Vernant, *Myth and Society in Ancient Greece* (1980); H. Versnel, ed., *Faith, Hope and Worship* (1981); C. H. Weller *et al.,* "The Cave at Vari," in *American Journal of Archaeology,* **7** (1903); Martin L. West, *The Orphic Poems* (1983); U. von Wilamowitz-Moellendorff, *Der Glaube der Hellenen* (1931); R. E. Wycherley, *The Stones of Athens* (1978); Froma I. Zeitlin, "Cultic Models of the Female: Rites of Dionysos and Demeter," in *Arethusa,* **15** (1982); G. Zuntz, *Persephone* (1971).

Roman Cults

JOHN FERGUSON

ANCIENT RELIGION WAS PRIMARILY a matter not of belief but of cult, not of creed but of ritual action. The Latin for religion is not *religio*, but *cultus deorum*, the worship of the gods. William Warde Fowler, in his book *The Religious Experience of the Roman People* (1911), defined religion as "effective desire to be in right relation with the Power manifesting itself in the Universe." The Romans were seeking the *pax deorum*, the favor of the gods.

Relations between deities and humans were governed by the divine law (*ius divinum*), as relations between the citizens were governed by the civil law (*ius civile*). In early days, the distinction was doubtless not absolute. The Twelve Tables placed civil law under the sanction of divine law. Cicero distinguishes between the two while linking them (*On Behalf of Sestius* 42.91). Later jurists accentuated the division (Gaius, *Institutes* 2.2). A special word, *fas,* of uncertain derivation, was employed for that which is permissible by divine law; it is used in the early calendars to indicate when civil business may be transacted without incurring divine displeasure.

The *ius divinum* had to be maintained precisely. In this sense, the legalism of the Pharisees was freedom itself compared with the legalism of the Romans. The ritual of an offering had to be exact: the formulaic prayers word-perfect, the accompanying gestures without variance. Any mistake meant the repetition of the whole ceremony from the beginning, or at the very least, an expiatory offering. At Iguvium (Gubbio) in Umbria, a complex ritual of sacrifice involving formulaic prayer and sacred dance was carried out at the several gates of the city by priests called Fratres Atiedii. If there was any error or faltering they had to go back to the first gate and start all over again. The formulas in Roman prayers (as at Iguvium) were repetitive and replete with synonyms: "prevent, avert, and ward off"; "my farm, lands, and fields." The words might be repeated three times over. Care had to be taken to mention every divinity who might be involved, although this was sometimes covered by such phrases as "all the other gods and goddesses."

FORMS OF CULT

The Latin *sacer,* the root of our "sacred," means "consecrated to a divinity," and so touched by superhuman power. To sacrifice is to make something over to a god. It is the commonest Roman ritual and constitutes offering and prayer. No doubt in its simplest form there is always an element of *do ut des* (I give to induce you to give). But sacrifice is never a crude bribe. In many societies a gift is a means to establish a relationship; it does not guarantee the granting of a petition. So, too, sacrifice is often a communion, a sharing between god and worshiper. And the element of prayer, however formulaic, is always personally addressed. Sacrifices may involve animal victims, or they may be bloodless, and consist in cereals, or saltcake, which sputters with good omen when cast on a fire, or beans, honey, cheese and milk, or wine poured out in libation. Animal victims must be spotless. If offered to the gods above, they must be white and placed on a high altar, by day; if to the gods below, they must be black, and their throats cut by night with an incision made from underneath so that the blood will flow into an unlit trench.

Lustration, or purification, is a second form of ceremony. One of the most celebrated examples is the lustration of the fields by the rite of Ambarvalia, a ceremonial procession of pig, sheep, and ox, the *su-ove-taurilia,* accompanied by a prayer to Mars to ward off evils and bring prosperity to the farm. Purification was frequently a part of a larger festival. The shepherd at the Parilia, a shepherds' festival, began the day by purifying his flock. To do this he sprinkled them with fresh water, swept out the folds and decorated them with leafy boughs, burned sulfur and touched the sheep with it so that they bleated, and made a bonfire of well-omened crackling wood (Ovid, *The Roman Calendar* [*Fasti*] 4.735–792). An act of atonement or reparation (*piaculum*) was made in restitution for an offense, in order to restore the *pax deorum.* It nearly always consisted in animal sacrifice.

Finally there was the vow (*votum*), private or public. The worshiper, or the state, made a promise of an offering to the god if he received certain blessings. Many inscriptions contain the formula VSLM (*votum solvit libens merito,* he gladly paid his vow duly). A notable historical, or perhaps legendary, example is the *devotio*—self-sacrifice in battle—by Publius Decius Mus in 340 B.C. In a long, complex, and repetitive formula he invoked the blessing of all the gods and goddesses of Rome and her enemies, and vowed to Earth and the Dead the forces of the enemy together with himself; he then rode to his death (Livy, 8.9.9). Another was the *ver sacrum* or vow of spring 217 B.C. in the dark days of the war with Hannibal. The Romans promised to dedicate to Jupiter all the spring-born animals five years later if the state should be preserved so long (Livy, 22.10).

PRIESTS AND OTHER RELIGIOUS OFFICIALS

During the rule of the kings, the king was also priest, the intermediary between the human and the divine. With the establishment of the republic, the religious duties formerly exercised by the king were largely divided between the *pontifex maximus* and the *rex sacrorum.* The word *pontifex* literally means "bridge-builder," and the title perhaps reflects the religious aspect of this dangerous and important task. The *rex sacrorum* kept the name of "king" as King of the Ceremonies. These officials were not specially trained experts, nor marked out by special sanctity of life. Cicero (*On His Home* 1.1), addressing (and flattering) the College of Priests on the subject of his own house, began:

Gentlemen, our ancestors were divinely inspired in many of the institutions they devised, nowhere more brilliantly than in their determination that the same people should preside over religious observances and political decisions, purposing that our leading citizens should protect the state by the right observance of religion, and preserve religion by the wise administration of the state.

The College of Priests expanded from three to sixteen. They held office for life and were charged with controlling the observances of the religious calendar.

There were fifteen priests known as *flamines;* the word is thought to be cognate with an ancient word for sacrifice, and nothing to do with a root meaning "a gust of wind." The major *flamines* were attached to Jupiter, Mars, and Quirinus. The priest of Jupiter was hedged round with taboos. He might not ride a horse, see the army drawn up for war, take an oath, wear a ring of full circle, have any knot in his clothing, touch or name a she-goat, raw flesh, ivy, or beans, be in the open air without a hat, touch bread fermented with yeast, pass under an arbor of vines, take off his inner tunic except indoors, or touch a dead body. His hair must be cut by a freeman, not a slave, and the clippings of hair or nails buried under a fruitful tree. The feet of his bed must be smeared with clay; no one else must sleep in it, and he must not spend more than three nights away from it. And so on (Aulus Gellius, *Attic Nights* 10.15). These taboos suggest great antiquity. So do the other deities with *flamines,* ten of whom are known. They are an ancient and obscure group: Volturnus, Pales, Furrina, Flora, Falacer, Pomona, Volcanus, Ceres, Portunus.

The Vestal Virgins, dedicated in service to the hearth goddess Vesta, formed an important group. They were six in number, of upper-class family, enrolled well before reaching their teens, and served for thirty years,

after which they might retire and marry if they chose. While serving, they had to remain strictly chaste; the punishment for unchastity was to be buried alive and the scourging to death of the man concerned. The Vestals had to tend and keep alight the fire on the sacred hearth, make the sacred salt, guard the contents of Vesta's store, take part in various rituals, and fetch water from the sacred spring.

The augurs were a college of three, later extended to sixteen. They were diviners charged with observing signs to tell whether the gods did or did not approve a proposed course of public action. A group originally of two augurs (*duoviri*), then ten (*decemviri*), then fifteen (*quindecimviri*) were appointed *sacris faciundis,* for the conduct of special rites. They were in charge of the Sibylline Books, which were consulted at times of public emergency, and more widely of the foreign cults introduced through the agency of the books. They were regarded as one of the major colleges, or bodies of priests. Another group of augurs, introduced only in 196 B.C., was the *epulones,* at first three in number, then seven, then ten. They had charge of sacred banquets, a popular aspect of religious ritual.

The fetials were a college of twenty priests charged with international relations. They operated in pairs: one called the *verbenarius* (herb-man) carried sacred herbs; the other, the *pater patratus* (roughly, fulfilling or achieving father), pronounced a conditional curse on Rome if it were the first to break the treaty that he was ratifying, and was also responsible for demanding satisfaction from another state if its representatives gave offense. The fetials were called not a *collegium* or college, but *sodales,* associates. Other minor priesthoods were also constituted of *sodales:* the Salii, the leaping priests of Mars; the Luperci, who were responsible for the strange fertility rite of Lupercalia; the mysterious Sodales Titii, who also were perhaps engaged in fertility ritual; and the Arval Brethren, whose labors blessed the fields and who in a very ancient hymn invoked the Lares or Lases and Mars or Marmar. To these were added in imperial times the priests of the imperial cult.

THE CALENDAR

The calendar that controlled the festivals of the Roman year survives in fragmentary inscriptions, which can be fleshed out by literary references. It was a compilation of the priesthood to control religious observances. The original ten-month year, beginning in March, a suitable start of the year for a farming and fighting people, is still commemorated by the names September, October, November, December (seven, eight, nine, ten). The change to a twelve-month year came, however, as early as the sixth century. Janus, the god of openings, presided over January; and it seems certain that the start of the civic year was transferred to January centuries before 153 B.C., the date traditionally given.

Each month had three fixed points. The Kalends, a new moon festival, fell on the first day of the month. The Ides fell in midmonth, traditionally on the full moon of a lunar month, actually on the thirteenth day of a short month and the fifteenth of a long one. The Nones fell, counting inclusively, nine days before the Ides. Hence the mnemonic:

> In March, July, October, May
> The Nones fall on the seventh day.

In other months they fell on the fifth. The Kalends were sacred to Juno, the Ides to Jupiter. Every month saw a regular routine. On the Kalends one of the priests watched for the new moon, and he and the *rex sacrorum,* the priest in charge of ritual, offered joint sacrifice. The chief priest then announced to the people, "Juno Covella, I proclaim you on the fifth/seventh day." Juno Covella was the deity of the hollow or crescent. No festival, except the Poplifugia —the mysterious "flight of the people"— was held before the Nones, although there was a further sacrifice to Juno in the interim. At the Nones the festivals for the month were proclaimed publicly. At the Ides, the priest of Jupiter led a sheep called "the Ides sheep" along the Sacred Way to the Capitol for sacrifice.

The calendar of Roman festivals has a number of standard markings that are affixed to particular days. F is attached to *dies fasti,* days on which civil action was lawful. These number forty-two, although there were some others available. N is attached to *dies nefasti,* days on which such legal transactions and political assemblies were religiously forbidden; they number forty-eight. C is a *dies comitialis,* propitious for a political assembly, and there are 195 such days. EN stands for *endotercisus,* an archaic form of *intercisus* or "severed." On such a day the morning and evening was *nefastus,* the rest of the day was *fastus.* The mysterious NP defies certainty; a reasonable conjecture has it refer to *dies nefasti publici,* certain official holidays on which normal business was banned; there were forty-nine of these. We may also note that two days (24 March, 24 May) are marked QRCF (*quando rex comitiavit fas*—legitimate for business when the king has dismissed the assembly—after a special meeting to ratify wills), and one (15 June) QStDF (*quando stercus delatum fas*—legitimate for business once the rubbish has been disposed of—since the temple of Vesta had its annual cleaning on that day).

Most festivals fell on odd days of the months, for "the god loves odd numbers" (Vergil, *Eclogue* 8, 75). One important feast, the Latin festival, was movable; the date was announced by the incoming consuls. It was a spring festival in honor of Jupiter Latiaris, held on the Alban Mount, originally by the League of the Cities of Latium. After a libation of milk and offerings of agricultural produce, a pure white heifer was sacrificed and its flesh distributed in token of unity. Puppets called *oscilla* were hung from trees. These may have been surrogates for human sacrifices, substitutes in the hope that Jupiter would spare the living, or they may have been apotropaic (evil-averting) charms.

THE FESTIVALS

To get a picture of the religious year we must look at some of the main festivals.

March was sacred to Mars, protector of the crops and god of war.

1 March. Festival to Mars, including the dance of the Salii or leaping priests, clashing sword and shield. This has been given three interpretations: preparation for the campaigning season, apotropaic ritual driving out evil spirits from the new year by thunder-magic, and leaping to invite tall crops. The Salii sang an ancient and obscure hymn.

Matronalia. A festival of Juno, when husbands gave presents to wives, and ladies entertained their servants.

7 March. Festival to Vediovis, perhaps a double of Jupiter, or perhaps a kind of anti-Jupiter.

9 March. A processional dance by the Salii with shields.

14 March. Equirria. A horse-racing festival, perhaps preparation for campaigning, agricultural, or both, unusual in falling on an even date.

Mamuralia. Apparently a "scapeman" festival in which a man dressed in skins was beaten out of the city, bearing the wreckage of the past so that the new year might start afresh. Mamurius is perhaps a form of Mars, and represents the Mars of the old year.

15 March. Festival of Anna Perenna, clearly a year-goddess. There was considerable sexual license (Ovid, *The Roman Calendar* 3.523 ff.; Martial, 4.64) vaguely linked to fertility ritual.

17 March. Liberalia. Liber Pater was a god of fertility and wine, later identified with Dionysus/Bacchus. This was a country festival of spring fertility rites, involving the adoration of the phallus (Augustine, *City of God* 4.11; 6.9; 7.21). It was also the festival of a boy's coming of age.

Agonalia. This recurs on 21 May, 11 December, 9 January. Beyond the fact that a ram was sacrificed (to whom is unknown), little is certain about it.

19 March. Quinquatrus, a festival to Mars, five days (inclusively) after the Ides. An accident of history associated Minerva with it.

23 March. Tubilustrium. The purification of the trumpets.

April is said to have been the month "when fruits and flowers and animals and seas and lands open" (*aperire*). It was under the protection of Venus, originally a power of the garden, later identified with the Greek Aphrodite, who presided over spring fertility, and the opening of the seas to shipping.

1 April. Veneralia. Festival of Venus. Apparently two festivals merged: an aristocratic rite to Venus and a popular one to Fortuna Virilis (Fortune), charged with blessing the male.

4–10 April. Megalesia. Games in honor of the Great Mother Cybele, brought from Pessinus in Galatia (central Asia Minor) in 204 B.C. in the form of a black baetyl (sacred stone). The even date was probably a historical accident of the date of her arrival. There were theatrical performances. The games went on for a week, until 10 April, the date of the dedication of the temple. But Roman citizens were banned from participation in the Mother's more orgiastic rites conducted by eunuch priests.

15 April. Fordicidia. Sacrifice of a pregnant cow to the Earth Mother. The Vestal Virgins were associated with the festival, which was designed to ensure the fertility of the land.

19 April. Cerialia. Festival of Ceres, preceded by a week's games in the Circus Maximus, where white robes were worn. A curious practice, not properly understood, involved the release of foxes with torches attached to their tails. In the countryside, milk, honey, and wine were offered to the goddess of growth (*creare*), and the sacrificial victim was carried three times round the growing crops.

21 April. Parilia. Festival of Pares or Pales, a shepherds' spirit of indeterminate sex. We have a full description of the country festival from Ovid (*The Roman Calendar* 4.735 ff.). At daybreak the fold and sheep were cleaned out and purified. A bonfire was kindled of wood that would crackle with good omen. Offerings were made of grain and milk, and prayer offered four times to the deity by the shepherd facing east. He washed his hand in dew, drank milk and mulled wine, and leaped through the bonfire; this last was a common ritual all over Europe for centuries. At Rome the ashes of the unborn calves from the Fordicidia mixed with the blood of the October horse (see 15 October below) were thrown on the fire before the ritual leap, whose fertility power becomes even clearer.

23 April. Vinalia. The spring wine festival, a libation of the previous year's vintage to Jupiter before anyone else sampled it. But somehow Venus, the garden-power, also became involved. So the calendars and Ovid (*The Roman Calendar* 4.863 ff.) indicate, and Plutarch (*Roman Questions* 45) says that great quantities of wine flowed from the temple of Venus.

25 April. Robigalia. Festival to satisfy Robigus or Robigo, the spirit of rust or mildew on corn, and prevent him or her from assailing the crops. Ovid (*The Roman Calendar* 4.905 ff.) has an eyewitness account of a procession leading apparently to the old limit of Roman territory. The priest, napkin in hand, offered on a sacrificial fire wine, incense, and the entrails of a sheep and a puppy (a brown animal for the brown spirit—or to protect the golden corn).

27 April. Floralia. Spring festival of the ancient Italian flower goddess Flora. Hares and goats, both embodiments of sexual fertility, were released. Beans and pulse, fertility emblems, were scattered among the crowds. Bright clothing was worn; honor to the flower goddess was the occasion for an Easter parade of new clothes. By night there were brilliant illuminations.

May was a month of ambiguous promise. The name was perhaps derived from the goddess Maia, a goddess of increase (*mag-*), later identified with the similarly named mother of Hermes/Mercury. But there were also sinister spirits that might affect the growth of crops.

1 May. Sacrifice of a pregnant sow to Maia by the priest of Vulcan; why by a priest so affiliated is not clear.

Sacrifice of a sow to Bona Dea, the Good Goddess, whose cult was confined to women.

Offering to the Lares Praestites, the Guardian Spirits.

9, 11, 13 May. Lemuria. Festival of the Dead, when ghosts walked. Ovid (*The Roman Calendar* 5.421 ff.) describes a domestic ritual. The paterfamilias rises at midnight. He has no sandals on his feet or fastening on his clothes, for any knot might bind the evil power to him. He makes an apotropaic gesture, washes his hands in clean water, and moves through the house, spitting out black beans with his head turned to one side, saying, "With these beans I redeem me and mine." This he does nine times. The ghosts are believed to collect the beans and so to leave the family in peace. He then cleanses himself again, clashes bronze vessels together (an apotropaic ritual; bronze, unlike iron, belongs to the older world of the spirits), and repeats nine times, "Shades of my fathers, away."

21 May. Agonalia. As on 17 March.

23 May. Tubilustrium. Purification of the trumpets, as on 23 March. It is not clear why it should be repeated two months later.

29 May (?). Ambarvalia. The Beating of the Bounds was a movable feast (not in the calendar) that may finally have settled onto 29 May. We have several accounts of it (Cato the Elder, *On Agriculture* 141; Tibullus, 2.1; Vergil, *Georgics* 1.345; Strabo, *Geography* 5.3.2). It was a purification of the land. A sacrificial procession of pig, sheep, and ox (*su-ove-taurilia*) moved around the outskirts of the farms and around the frontiers of archaic Rome. The public ceremony seems to have involved the College of the Arval Brethren. The festival was in honor of Mars, protector of the crops; he was associated with Ceres and Bacchus, and there were prayers to Janus and Jupiter. We have the text (Cato the Elder, *On Agriculture* 141.2–3) of the main prayer to Mars:

> Father Mars, I pray and implore you that you will be propitious and kindly to me, our household and home. For this reason I have enjoined the sacrificial offering of pig, sheep, and ox to process round my field, land, and farm, so that you may prevent, ward off, and avert diseases, visible and invisible, barrenness and destruction, accident and bad water and that you will permit the crops and fruits of the earth, the vines and plants to grow and prosper, and that you will preserve the shepherds and their flocks in safety and give health and prosperity to me, our household and home.

There were offerings of cake, and the sacrificial victims were killed, but if the omens were unfavorable, further offerings had to be made. It was a holy day and a holiday, when the people, ritually cleansed and wearing spotless white, with olive or oak leaves in their hair, sang and danced and uttered no words of ill omen. The whole is charmingly depicted by Tibullus.

The word June is no doubt derived in some way from the Latin word for youth (*iuvenis*), but Juno did not have much to do with it, and in the countryside Mercury, Hercules, and Fors Fortuna were thought to preside over it. Nevertheless, it was a dangerous month, and the first half was unpropitious for marriage.

1 June. Carneria. Festival of an obscure and ancient goddess Carna, to whom bean meal and lard were offered for good digestion and the health of the internal organs. A somewhat garbled account in Ovid (*The Roman Calendar* 6.159–162) seems to refer to this, and links it with the protection of the inner organs of young children against evil spirits; this involves apotropaic ritual, the offering of the raw intestines of a two-month-old sow, and the prayer:

> Night-birds, spare the boy's guts.
>   A small victim falls for a small boy.
> Take heart for heart, I pray, entrails for
>   entrails,
>   This life we give you, to spare a better.

9 June. Vestalia. Festival of Vesta, power of the hearth. The offering was of salt cake (*mola salsa*), made with ears of spelt (a form of mountain wheat) gathered on 7, 9, and 11 May and salt prepared from brine, baked, and cut with a saw (curiously of iron rather than the bronze usual in ancient rituals), and water fetched from a sacred spring in special vessels that might not be set down on the journey.

11 June. Matralia. Festival of an old Italian goddess, Mater Matuta, a mother goddess who was regarded as a power of light. The decoration of the statue was entrusted to a married woman of one husband only. Slave women were excluded, except for one who was ritually beaten; it is hard to know whether the beating was a fertility rite or a warning. Sacred cakes were baked in earthenware molds and offered to the goddess. Strangest of all, women made supplication primarily for their nephews and nieces, not for their own children. It is possible that this arose from a misunderstanding: *Puella sororia* is a girl with swelling breasts, an adolescent, but might be taken to mean a sister's daughter. If it was a misunderstanding, in classical times the misunderstanding prevailed.

15 June. Cleansing and subsequent closure of Vesta's temple, marked, as we have seen, QStDF.

July was Quinctilis, the fifth month, before it was renamed in honor of Julius Caesar. It was a season of harvest, under the protection of Jupiter, Apollo, and Neptune.

5 July. Poplifugia, meaning "the flight of the people." As the only major festival (written in large letters on the calendars) before the Nones, it almost certainly therefore commemorates a historical event on that date. The Roman antiquarians told a myth of the people running away when Romulus vanished during a storm, or referred to a historical attack by the people of Fidenae (Castel Giubileo) just outside Rome. These appear to be rationalizations. The origins of the cult are lost in antiquity.

7 July. Nonae Caprotinae. We have too many differing accounts and explanations of this festival. According to one version it commemorated a historical event when slave women, dressed as noble ladies, succeeded in disarming an attacking force and making them vulnerable to the Roman soldiers. Booths of fig-tree boughs (*caprificus*) were put up, and slave women had a mock battle. The fig was a fertility emblem, and striking with boughs of a fertile tree in mock battle

is a familiar practice to enhance fertility; the historical event and the commemorative practice do not seem reasonably matched. Another tradition links the festival with the disappearance of Romulus at Goat's Marsh (Caprae Palus); here there is blurring with the Poplifugia. Varro tells us that women, free and slave, made offering to Juno Caprotina under a wild fig tree, using fig sap in place of milk. Fig-tree boughs were used for some purpose, perhaps as suggested above. Finally, some people think that the whole thing is in origin a simple agricultural practice of bringing the wild fig and the cultivated fig together to encourage pollination.

13 July. Ludi Apollinares. Climax of an (eventually) eight-day festival in honor of Apollo, instituted as a one-day festival during the war with Hannibal. In 212 B.C. the *praetor urbanus* was in charge and the *decemviri* were responsible for the sacrifices: an ox to Apollo, a cow to Latona, and two she-goats, almost certainly to Diana. All the victims had their horns gilded. The congregation wore garlands, and there were private entertainments throughout the city. Later the festival became more and more elaborate, with horse racing, wild animal hunts, and dramatic performances; it was immensely popular.

15 July. Cavalry parade, for the formal recognition of those entitled to serve, in honor of the Dioscuri (Castor and Pollux, the Greek Polydeuces), who helped the Romans to victory against the Latins at Lake Regillus in *ca.* 499 B.C.

19, 21 July. Lucaria. Festival of the grove. Perhaps originally a propitiation of the spirits of the woodlands on whose terrain the farmers were encroaching. In *On Agriculture,* Cato the Elder gives a formulaic prayer to be spoken with the offering of a pig by a farmer proposing to clear a grove.

23 July. Neptunalia. Neptune was a water

god identified with Poseidon. We know little of the festival, but a summer ritual against drought would seem appropriate. We know that shady coverings of boughs were made, a practical precaution in summer.

25 July. Furrinalia. Varro says of Furrina: "Honor was paid to her among those of old, who established an annual sacrifice and assigned her a special priest, but her name is scarcely known, and only to a few at that" (*On the Latin Language* 6.19). Even less is known of her festival.

August was Sextilis, the sixth month, before it was renamed for Augustus. It was a month of harvesting and storing. The presiding goddess was Ceres, and sacrifices were made also to Spes (Hope), Salus (Health), and Diana.

13 August. Festival of Diana, involving a holiday for slaves (after the harvest?). Some of the complexities of the calendar are seen in that several other divinities (apart from Jupiter, this being the Ides) were also honored on this day: Vertumnus; Fortuna Equestris; Hercules, either under the title Conqueror or Unconquered; Castor and Pollux; the Camenae, water spirits identified with the Muses; and Flora. These cults commemorate the dedication or restoration of temples in their honor.

17 August. Portunalia. Festival of Portunus, the god of harbors and ferries, perhaps also of barn doors and warehouse doors. Curiously, the only recorded function of his priest was to oil the armor of Quirinus.

19 August. Vinalia. A second festival of wine (see 23 April above), no doubt to bless the new vintage.

21 August. Consualia. Festival of Consus, the deity of grain storage, celebrating the close of harvesting (harvest home).

23 August. Volcanalia. Vulcan (Volcanus) was an ancient fire god, whose temple (because of the fear of urban fire) was outside the city, but who had an altar in the Forum Romanum. At the festival the people drove animals into a fire as surrogates for themselves (Varro, *On the Latin Language* 6.20).

25 August. Opiconsivia. Ops was a goddess of plenty: another harvest festival.

27 August. Volturnalia. Festival of Volturnus, an ancient god with an Etruscan name, about whose origin and function we can only guess, and of whose cult we know virtually nothing.

September was under the official authority of Vulcan, but the main religious activity of the month was the Ludi Romani (Roman games) in honor of Jupiter. The calendars mark none of the festivals in capital letters.

5–19 September. Ludi Romani in honor of Jupiter Optimus Maximus whose temple on the Capitol was, according to tradition, dedicated on 13 September 509 B.C.; the games expanded on either side of that date. The festival began with a procession described by Dionysius of Halicarnassus as an eyewitness (7.72 ff.). It passed from the Capitol through the forum to the Circus Maximus. The magistrates came first, then young men, mounted and on foot, four-horse and two-horse chariots, athletes, dancers dressed for a war dance, and musicians, actors dressed as satyrs, more musicians, and bearers of censers and sacred vessels. Then came the gods in the form of images carried on the shoulders. It was a comprehensive assembly of the immortals; the *di indigetes* and *di novensiles* (indigenous gods and borrowed or imported gods); the Olympians; Saturn (the Greek Kronos), god of the old order; Ops, the power of plenty; Themis, the Greek power of justice; Mnemosyne, the Greek power of memory; the Parcae (Fates), Muses, and Graces; and the deified heroes, among them Hercules, Aesculapius (Asklepios), and Castor and Pollux. Behind the gods followed the ani-

917

mals destined for sacrifice. Upon arriving in the Circus, the priests cleansed themselves and the animals with water and saltcake under the direction of the consuls. The attendants then performed the sacrifice, striking the victim with a club in such a way that it fell on the sacrificial knives. The animals were dissected, and a small portion of each further purified and offered up on the altar with a libation of wine. The games included chariot racing, running, boxing, wrestling, and the *lusus Troiae* or Troy game, a war dance on horseback the complexity of which has occasioned much speculation. There were also dramatic performances.

October had festivals to Mars and Liber, to mark the end of the campaigning season and the completion of the vintage.

11 October. Meditrinalia. Festival to Jupiter (the goddess Meditrina is a late invention; the name is perhaps derived from an old word for winepress). It seems to have been a ceremonial libation, perhaps with formal tasting, of the new wine.

13 October. Fontinalia. Festival in honor of the spirit of wells and springs; garlands were offered at both.

15 October. The "October Horse," a two-horse chariot race held in the Campus Martius. The righthand horse of the winner (i.e., the strongest, as races were run counterclockwise) was sacrificed to Mars by the priest of Mars on an altar in the Campus Martius. The horse's head was cut off and was the object of battle between the inhabitants of two regions of the city. The horse's tail was carried to the Regia—traditionally the home of Numa Pompilius, Rome's second king, and seat of the *pontifex maximus* during the republic—where its blood was dripped onto the sacred hearth. Some of the blood apparently was kept for the Parilia in April. It is hard to know whether to interpret this as an agricultural ritual (the horse being

a familiar corn spirit), a military ritual, or both.

19 October. Armilustrium. Festival in honor of Mars for the purification of the army and its weapons at the end of the campaigning season.

November was under Diana's protection. No festivals are marked with capital letters in the calendars.

4–17 November. Ludi Plebeii. The Plebeian games probably date from 220 B.C. and rank in importance with the Ludi Romani.

December was under Vesta's protection. It contains six festivals that the calendars record in capital letters, as well as others of some importance.

3 December. Festival to Bona Dea. A women's festival, private except for the presence of the Vestals. It was sacrilegiously desecrated by Publius Clodius Pulcher in woman's dress in 62 B.C. The Good Goddess was a power of fertility in women. The meeting place, a large room in a private house, was adorned with vine leaves, wine was offered to the goddess, although it was called milk in the ritual, and a pig was sacrificed. There was sacred music and dancing and the revelation of holy mysteries.

5 December. Festival to Faunus, an offering of wine, kid, and incense on a simple earth altar to the dangerous spirit of the wildwood, followed by a dance on the farmland (Horace, *Odes* 3.18). This was a country festival not observed in the city.

11 December. Agonalia, as on 17 March, 21 May, 9 January. This was seemingly in honor of Indiges (the Native?) or Sol Indiges (the Native Sun).

Septimontium. Apparently a very early festival that was still flourishing around A.D. 200 and is mentioned only in late calendars. Sacrifices were offered on some or all of the early Seven Hills: Palatium, Velia, Fagutal,

Cermalus, Caelius, Oppius, Cispius. It will be noticed that the festival thus antedates the incorporation of the Quirinal and Viminal and does not mention the Capitol. On the Palatine, the offering was to Palatua, goddess of the hill.

15 December. Consualia. Consus, the power of the storehouse, had a festival on 21 August. It is hard to see why he had another at this date. We can deduce horse racing and mule racing, and the ceremonious garlanding of the animals.

17 December. Saturnalia. One of the most famous and popular festivals, it expanded to fill the next seven days. Saturn was a god of the old order, perhaps, although not certainly, a power of sowing. The festival fell around the time of the winter solstice. It began with a major sacrifice and banquet. It inaugurated a time of jollification and role reversal during which masters waited on servants. A king of the feast was appointed in each family. Presents were exchanged, terra-cotta dolls were given to children and wax candles to friends.

19 December. Opalia. Festival to Ops, spirit of plenty, following four days after the festival to Consus, as in August.

21 December. Divalia Angeronae. The calendar found at Praeneste (Palestrina) has a damaged note that can be confidently restored:

> The festival of the goddess Angerona who was named from the disease angina because she had once prescribed remedies for it. They set up a statue of her, with mouth bound, on the altar of Volupia in order to warn that no one should communicate the secret name of the city.

Angerona is a mysterious minor power. Other possible derivations include that from *angor* (pain or anxiety) or *angere* (raising up the sun after the solstice). Volupia is a spirit of pleasure. The statue had either mouth bandaged, or finger to lip, like the Egyptian-Greek Harpocrates. The secret name of Rome is a fascinating concept. To possess a person's name is to possess power over him (cf. *Genesis* 32:25–30). T. S. Eliot's archetypal cat has its own secret name, ineffable, deep, and inscrutable, which the cat alone knows; hence its singular independence. So with Rome.

23 December. Larentalia. Acca Larentia is cast for various roles in the mythic history of early Rome. The name Acca suggests a mother goddess (Sanskrit *akka*). As for the second part of the name, she may be the mother of the Lares, ancestral spirits of the home and farmland; or she may be one with the old Sabine goddess Larunda. The festival consisted of funeral rites at her tomb.

25 December. Brumalia. Not in the republican calendars, but, from the time of Julius Caesar, the day of the winter solstice.

January was under Juno's protection. It contained two movable feasts. One, early in the month, was the Ludi Compitales, honoring the Lares of the Crossroads. Woolen dolls were hung up as surrogates or substitutes for all the members of the household. Fattened pigs and honeycakes were offered, and there was sport, jollification, and dancing. The other, late in the month, was the Paganalia or Sementivae (if they are indeed the same), a country sowing festival in honor of the Earth-Mother and Ceres; offerings were made of a coarse-wheat cake and a pregnant sow, and prayers offered for the protection of the crops.

1 January. Inauguration of the consuls, at least from the mid second century B.C. The auspices were taken and the consuls donned their robes and made a procession to the Capitol. There, each offered a white bull before the temple of Jupiter Optimus Maximus and renewed the vows of the Roman state.

9 January. Agonalia. The fourth celebration, following 17 March, 21 May, and 11 December.

11, 15 January. Carmentalia. Festival of Carmenta or Carmentis, a power of prophecy and a woman's spirit blessing childbirth. April was propitious for marriages, May and early June were not, so April marriages and January births were not uncommon. It is not clear why 13 January was omitted.

February was protected by Neptune; the name is derived from *Februa,* purificatory offerings, but the exact reference is uncertain. It included two movable feasts, Fornicalia, or the Feast of Ovens, and Amburbium, the beating of the city boundaries.

13 February. Parentalia. Festival of the Dead, surprisingly not recorded in capital letters. By contrast with the Lemuria, the dead were here conceived as gentle, not terrible. The festival was directed especially to parents and family. The offerings were simple, as reported by Ovid (*The Roman Calendar* 2.535–540):

> The dead ask little; love is as good as a rich
> gift,
>   No greedy gods below!
> Enough a tile wreathed with votive garlands,
>   A sprinkling of corn, a few salt grains,
> Bread soaked in wine, some loose violets
>   Set on a potsherd in the middle of the
> road.

The public ceremony was inaugurated by the senior Vestal.

15 February. Lupercalia. The Luperci were an association of priests. They met in the Lupercal, where the she-wolf had suckled Romulus and Remus, to sacrifice goats and a dog and to offer sacred cakes made by the Vestals from the first fruits of the harvest in the previous year. They smeared the head of two leaders with the sacrificial knife and wiped off the blood with wool soaked in milk. Then the celebrants wrapped themselves with the skins of sacrificial goats and ran through the city striking with thongs of goatskin all whom they met, especially women, who were believed to become fertile as a result.

17 February. Quirinalia. Festival of Quirinus, god of the assembly later identified with Romulus.

21 February. Feralia. The culmination of the Festival of the Dead, with sacrifice of sheep.

22 February. Caristia. Festival of the Dear Ones, a patching up of quarrels within the family on the day after the ceremonies with the Dead were completed.

23 February. Terminalia. Festival of Terminus, god of boundaries. Neighboring landowners met at their common boundary, each garlanding his side of the marker stone. They built an altar and lit a fire, offering corn, honeycombs, wine, and the blood of a lamb or sucking pig (Ovid, *The Roman Calendar* 2.639 ff.).

24 February. Regifugium. The Expulsion of the Kings, held on an even date for historical reasons. But there may have been a deeper ritual significance, since the *rex sacrorum* (the priest presiding over the sacrifice, bearing the name of king) after sacrificing had to flee as if he had performed a sacrilegious act.

27 February. Equirria. Horse racing in honor of Mars, as on 14 March.

MILITARY CALENDAR

We have a very different calendar of military festivals, dating from the first half of the third century A.D., from the Mesopotamian frontier fortress of Dura-Europos. The first full entry (Frye *et al.* [1955]), for 3 January, runs:

> In view of the public proclamation and fulfillment of vows, for the safety of our Lord Marcus Aurelius Severus Alexander Augustus

[A.D. 222–235] and for the eternal duration of the empire of the Roman people, an ox to Jupiter Greatest and Best, a cow to Juno, a cow to Minerva, an ox to Jupiter the Victor . . . a bull to Mars the Father, a bull to Mars the Victor, a cow to Victory.

Similarly on 9 January:

In view of the honorable discharge of those returning in full enjoyment of privileges and of the calculation of military pay, an ox to Jupiter Greatest and Best, a cow to Juno, a cow to Minerva, a cow to well-being, a bull to Mars the Father (Frye *et al.* [1953]).

On two dates in May the standards are crowned with roses, with an act of prayer. But although the old gods are there—Jupiter and Mars of course, and Minerva and Neptune with noticeable popularity—the military calendar is dominated by the imperial cult. It stretches back to Julius, Augustus, and Claudius, and includes Trajan's niece and Hadrian's mother-in-law, Matidia, although there is a natural stress on more recent members of the imperial family. In April there are five festivals. Three are imperial birthdays. One honors the imperial rule of the Divine (deified) Septimius Severus (A.D. 193–211). One is for the birthday of Rome the Eternal City. Military religion consisted not of pious pep talks, but of observances.

PRIVATE CULT

The religion of the state and the religion of the family were closely interconnected, as we can see in the position held by Vesta, or in the fact that Juno, prominent in the state cult, is originally correlative to the Genius found in private cult. Private cult was defined by the second-century A.D. antiquarian and grammarian Festus as pertaining to individuals, households, and ancestral families. Correspondingly, the state, ultimately through the *pontifex maximus* and his colleagues, exercised a controlling authority over private cult; it was their responsibility to see that the traditional rituals were duly carried out, without unacceptable innovations.

Private cult centered on the home, and the principal recipients of worship were Vesta, the Penates, the Lares, and the Genius. Vesta was the spirit of the hearth, and at the daily meal an offering of saltcake and other food was placed on a clean plate and thrown onto the fire. When the hearth was divorced from the dining area, it is not clear whether the offering was made in the kitchen or in an alcove set aside as a private shrine (*lararium*), or whether a portable brazier was brought in.

The Penates were spirits of the pantry or larder; no impure person was allowed to enter there. Libations were offered to them at mealtimes. The Lares seem to have been powers of the farmland and of the ancestors buried therein. The *lar familiaris* came into the house with the *familia,* or members of the household, and was honored by the alcove-shrine *lararium,* which sometimes incorporated an altar. The Lares and Penates were honored at all family festivals. Any member of the household going on a journey would pray to them for a safe return, and on his return hang up his traveling kit near the *lararium.* The Genius was the power of fertility in the male and was believed to reside in the head of the paterfamilias. It was naturally associated with the marriage bed, or *lectus genialis.* It is sometimes represented in art by a sacred snake. The Genius was worshiped with libations of wine, incense, and offerings of flowers on the birthday of the paterfamilias and on other family festivals.

The *lararium* would contain not only the symbol of the Lares, but also those of other deities to whom the household was especially beholden. In *lararia* at Pompeii, twenty-seven deities were found represented in paintings, most frequently Fortuna (twelve), Vesta (ten), Bacchus (eight), Amor (seven), Jupiter (seven), Mercury (seven), Hercules (six), Venus Pompeiana (five). Statuettes found in or near *lararia,* omitting the Lares themselves, include fourteen of Mercury, eleven of Minerva, ten of Venus, eight of Jupiter, seven of Hercules, five of Harpocrates (Harpichruti, an Egyptian god of silence), three each of Aesculapius, Diana, Fortuna, and Isis (who is also identified with Fortuna), two each of Apollo and Neptune, and one each of Bacchus, Hygieia, Juno, Persephone, Priapus, Sol, and the Egyptian gods Anubis and Horus. It is interesting that at Herculaneum, where people had more time to escape, few statuettes were found; the people must have taken their household goods with them. The emphasis might vary in different regions, but the picture may be taken as typical. That urbane and cultured emperor, Severus Alexander, was said to have a large *lararium* where he also kept statues of the deified emperors, Alexander the Great, ancestors, and holy souls including Orpheus, Abraham, Christ, and the first-century Neopythagorean sage Apollonius of Tyana. He would repair there in the early morning on nights when he had not slept with his wife (*Scriptores Historiae Augustae*, "Severus Alexander" 29).

The home was also the scene of some of the key rites of passage, ceremonies designed to ensure a person's successful transition from one social status to another. At the time of birth, for example, sacred rites were carried out with an ax, stake, and broom to drive away the dangerous spirits of the wild in the name of the curious godlings Intercidona (cleaver), Pilumnus (staker), and Deverra (sweeper). The child was laid on the lap of Mother Earth to give it a soul, if we may trust parallels from elsewhere, and

lifted up by the father in acknowledgment of paternity. Then, on the *dies lustricus* (the ninth day for boys and eighth for girls) the child was purified and formally brought into the religious life of the family, and given its name and protective amulet.

Marriage was a religious ritual. A well-omened day was found. The bride, barely in her teens, put off her girlish clothes and dedicated them to Fortuna Virginalis, the goddess who blessed girls. She donned a special costume, invoking the girdling power of Cinxia, with an orange headdress to protect her on the dangerous passage from her father's gods to her husband's; her hair was parted with an iron spearpoint, and arranged in six curls, three and three, secured with a wreath. She carried spindle and distaff and was escorted by two boys whose parents were alive, and a third bearing a torch of whitethorn. The matron of honor had to be married to her first husband as his first wife. She anointed her husband's door with wolf's fat or a substitute, invoking another godling, Unxia. She was lifted over the dangerous threshold. She then entered her husband's religious circle with the words, "Where you are Gaius, I am Gaia," and touched water. In one pattern of marriage called *confarreatio,* there was a ritual common meal uniting the couple. On the morning after the bridal night the woman made offering to her husband's household gods.

At death, the nearest relative tried to catch the dying man's last breath; he closed the eyes of the dead and called his name. The body was washed and anointed, dressed in honorific garments, and laid out with feet toward the door. A branch of cypress was set over the door. The period between death and burial was a week. An aristocratic funeral was a thing of pomp and circumstance, with a procession accompanied by the masks of the ancestors. It culminated in a sacramental meal in which living and dead shared. The house was ceremonially purified.

The dead were considered imbued with power. They were honored collectively as *Di Manes,* the divine spirits of the dead. Rites at the tomb were renewed annually and at the Feralia. The Parentalia, of which this formed the last day, was a period of honoring privately the family dead. The Lemuria was a more sinister occasion when ghosts were thought to move about the house. We have already noted the rites used by the paterfamilias to dispel their malign power.

BIBLIOGRAPHY

SOURCES

Aulus Gellius, *The Attic Nights,* John C. Rolfe, trans., 3 vols. (1954–1961); Cato the Elder and Varro, *On Agriculture,* William D. Hooper, trans., rev. by Harrison B. Ash (1960); Cicero, *Orations,* William Peterson, ed., vol. 5 (1952), and *On Divination,* Arthur S. Pease, ed. (1963); Gaius, *Institutes,* Francis M. de Zulueta, ed. (1946–1955); Livy, *History of Rome,* Benjamin O. Foster *et al.,* trans., 14 vols. (1919–1959); Ovid, *Fasti (The Roman Calendar),* James G. Frazer, trans. (1929); *Scriptores Historiae Augustae,* David Magie, trans., 3 vols. (1921–1932); Strabo, *Geography,* Horace L. Jones, trans., 8 vols. (1917); Albius Tibullus, commentary by Michael C. J. Putnam (1973); Varro, *On the Latin Language,* Roland G. Kent, trans., 2 vols. (1938); *Vergil,* Roger Mynors, ed. (1969).

STUDIES

Cyril Bailey, *Phases in the Religion of Ancient Rome* (1932); Jennifer M. Cobb, "The Cult of Vesta in the Roman World," M. Phil. diss., Open University, Milton Keynes (1983); Georges Dumézil, *Fêtes romaines d'été et d'automne* (1971); John Ferguson, *The Religions of the Roman Empire* (1970), and *Greek and Roman Religion: A Source Book* (1980); Robert O. Fink, Allan S. Hoey, Walter F. Snyder, "The Feriale Duranum," in *Yale Classical Studies,* **7** (1940); William W. Fowler, *The Roman Festivals* (1899), and *The Religious Experience of the Roman People* (1911); R. N. Frye *et al.,* "Inscriptions from Dura-Europos," in *Yale Classical Studies,* **14,** edited by Harry M. Hubbell (1955); Gordon J. Laing, "The Origin of the Cult of Lares," in *Classical Philology,* **16** (1921); James W. Poultney, *The Bronze Tablets of Iguvium* (1959); Herbert J. Rose, *Primitive Culture in Italy* (1926); Howard H. Scullard, *Festivals and Ceremonies of the Roman Republic* (1981); Jules Toutain, *Les cultes païens dans l'empire romain* (1907–1920); Georg Wissowa, *Religion und Kultus der Römer,* 2d ed. (1912).

Greek Priesthoods

JUDY ANN TURNER

CROWNED PRIESTESSES AND PRIESTS majestically headed the panathenaic procession as it wound snakelike along the Sacred Way. The destination was the Athenian Acropolis. The purpose was to keep an ancient appointment, to perform traditional rites for the protection and nurture of the people and the state. In classical Athens such religious celebrations were perhaps the grandest of that age, but throughout Greece priestly officials bore the same grave responsibilities as intermediaries between often whimsical gods and helpless men, and carried on traditions that would endure for nearly another millennium.

The priestly attendants of state cults served in roles as ancient as Greek religious practice itself. The rituals for the city (polis) were rooted in similar rites that parents performed around the family hearth for the welfare or purification of the household (Odysseus' actions in the *Odyssey* 22.459 ff.). State religion was family religion grown large and patriotic. But alongside state religion was popular folk religion, ranging from sheer superstition to countless cults that addressed a person's daily concerns. The Athenian religious calendar of the classical period was typical. Every month was host to at least one festival, often more. All cults—public, private, large, small, widespread or local—had priestly officials. Rituals required flawless priestly performances in accord with ancestral customs. Even Spartans delayed battle if sacrifices were improper or unfavorable (Thucydides, 5.54 f.). Religion's importance is shown by Socrates' death sentence for atheism and impiety (Plato, *Apology* 22, 26).

The origins of Greek priesthoods remain obscure, prehistoric. The earliest extant documents (Linear B tablets, *ca.* 1200 B.C.) depict female and male priests in fully developed, specialized capacities: guardians of temple keys, workers of sacred bronze, and performers of duties bearing other cult or temple servant titles. Some of these titles, as well as some of the specific deities, continued and reappear in the seventh century B.C. when Greeks resumed writing and emerged from the four or so twilight centuries of their dark age. The earliest authors still present priestly officials as highly respected. Priests' duties on behalf of the community remained crucial, their power indisputable. For example, Agamemnon must return Chryseis because her father is a priest of Apollo (*Iliad* 1.6 ff.). In the late sixth century the Athenian priestess of Athena personally forbade the Spartan king's entrance into her temple on the Acropolis. He disregarded her words and later suffered a terrible death (Herodotus, 5.72 f.). Priests retained great authority and respect until the Christian Roman emperor Theodosius I banned pagan faiths in A.D. 391.

By custom, priestesses served goddesses; gods were attended by priests. Greeks extended this principle of like gender to animal sacrifices: male animals were normally sacrificed to gods; goddesses received female animals as their sacrifices. The necessity for female priestly officials afforded some women a chance to better their circumstances in a society geared toward male dominance. By service in the cult of a goddess, some ambitious, capable, fortunate women rose to prestigious offices and held administrative posts of great power. Women might serve alongside men as priests in certain cults, particularly those honoring both male and female deities. Records show husbands and wives as collegial priests and priestesses in various cults.

There were some exceptions to the custom of using priests of the same gender as the deity. Certain cults of Athena, such as that of Athena Lindia at Rhodes, used boy-priests, and some cults of Apollo or Zeus, as at Delphi and Dodona, had female oracles. In cults where both types of anomaly occurred, adult males had charge of administrative affairs. At Delphi a college of priests could interpret the words of the prophetess.

ACQUISITION OF A PRIESTHOOD

The oldest method of obtaining a priesthood was probably inheritance. Hereditary priesthoods routinely belonged to a family (*oikos*) or to a clan (*genos*). The major Athenian priesthoods of Athena Polias and of Poseidon Erechtheus were hereditary in two separate branches of the Eteoboutad clan. In hereditary priesthoods bloodlines counted. The patrilineal priority allowed for matrilineal inheritance, if needed, to continue a family line. Such inheritance through a female was common enough that Greeks had a special term (*epikleros*) for a female carrier of the line. When an *epikleros* inherited and functioned in the place of her deceased or nonexistent brother, she passed on various family properties, including priesthoods. Yet Greek preference for patrilineal principles explains some complicated patterns in the descent of feminine priesthoods. Notable is the priesthood of Athena Polias, which seems to have passed to the eldest surviving daughter of the eldest male of a particular branch of the Eteoboutad clan. But methods of inheritance varied. At Halikarnassos (Bodrum) in Caria (southwestern Asia Minor) the priesthood of Poseidon passed serially to all males of one generation (from oldest brother through the youngest) before it was available to the next generation.

The concept of hereditary priesthoods was embedded in the Greek mind. Even Plato (*Laws* 6.759a–c) says that they should not be disturbed. Eteoboutad priesthoods of Athena Polias and Poseidon Erechtheus, Eumolpid sacred expounders (*exegetai*), and other posts remained hereditary in their respective clans even after those cults became state cults (*ca.* seventh century B.C.). Such priesthoods remained hereditary for almost a thousand years. Several clans possessed hereditary priesthoods in the Eleusinian Mysteries (for example, the priestess of Demeter from the Philleidai; the herald from the Kerykes clan; the *hierophant* and *hierophantid* from the Eumolpidai). Hereditary priesthoods were prominent both on the mainland and throughout Greece.

Priestly families zealously guarded their hereditary offices by a policy of intermarriage. This policy, combined with the Greeks' fear of impiety if ancestral customs were changed, assured the preservation of hereditary priesthoods.

Wills and testaments were used to pass on some priesthoods. Women as well as men could inherit and bequeath such priestly offices. In a third century B.C. inscription from the island of Thera (Santorini), Epikteta willed her family priesthood and one of the Muses to the oldest male descendant of her daughter, Andragora. Another inscription of that time states that a widow from Erythrae (Ildırı) in Ionia (western Asia Minor) inherited a priesthood from her deceased husband and she, in turn, bequeathed it to her younger son. In the third century B.C., at Halikarnassos, Poseidonios, founder of a cult of Apollo and other gods, stipulated that his eldest male descendant should inherit the priesthoods of these cults.

Other means by which Greeks acquired priesthoods included appointment, election, allotment, and purchase. Appointment to major priesthoods was rare, but was common for lesser sacerdotal posts. At Athens the king-archon, a type of priest, appointed sacerdotal officials, especially those concerned with specific festivals: *kanephoroi* (basket bearers), *ergastinai* (weavers of Athena's robe), *arrephoroi* (girls serving Athena), *gerarai* (a priestly college of elderly women), and hearth initiates for the Eleusinian Mysteries. An inscription from Kos (in the Dodecanese Islands, north of Rhodes) records a priest's right to appoint his assistant priest (*neokoros*). In a cult of Dionysos Thyllophoros on Kos the chief priestess appointed priestesses for the cult's many local deme priesthoods.

Election to a priesthood is rarely attested. Evidence for elected priesthoods coincides with the rise of the democracy at Athens. But prior restrictions on priestly candidates diminished the democratic aspects of most elected posts. For example, two of the four *epimeletai* (cult administrators) of the Eleusinian Mysteries—who were elected by a show of hands—had to belong to existing priestly clans, the Eumolpidai and the Kerykes. At Amorgos, in an unusual case, an elected priestess of a cult of the Mother in the first century B.C. was required to pay a substantial fee after her election. Her ability to pay seems a type of prerequisite, and her payment close to purchase of the office.

The lot—selection by chance, such as blind drawing—was another democratic means of assigning a priesthood. The method of lots, according to a Greek's thinking, allowed the "deity to make the choice" (Plato, *Laws* 759c), but it also suited democratic trends in classical Athenian politics. The earliest known case of lot choice appears in the state priesthood of Athena Nike (last half of the fifth century B.C.). Allotment gained popularity, causing the quip that priesthoods so assigned were posts that anyone could fill. The priesthood of Asklepios in Piraeus seems to have been allotted, despite priestly duties that required much expertise. Allotted priesthoods are attested widely, but most often on the mainland, suggesting Athenian influence.

In contrast, the purchase of priesthoods is most commonly attested in the islands of the Greek East, and not once on the mainland. Most records of purchased priesthoods come from Asia Minor in the third and second centuries B.C., perhaps a result of increased wealth in that region following Alexander's successful capture of eastern treasure. The fourth and later centuries saw frequent political and economic changes, which coincided with a decline in traditional religion. Mystery cults and groups such as *orgeones* (worshiper associations), which tended more to personal religious needs, filled the vacuum. In this context, purchase of priesthoods—even as financial investments—becomes more understandable. Greeks seemingly saw no sacrilege in buying a priestly office. A long Erythraean inscription (third century B.C.) records the mass-purchasing of priesthoods, particularly by a large and extended family who seemed to speculate in priesthoods, for they bought and sold some offices on the same day. Owners could resell, divide, or bequeath their purchased priesthoods. By the close of the second century B.C., purchases of priestly posts sharply declined, perhaps due to economic downturns.

QUALIFICATIONS FOR A PRIESTHOOD

Criteria for priestly office varied from cult to cult, but generally required a "good" family background. Plato (*Laws* 759c) stipulates "good birth" for priests and priestesses. A third century B.C. inscription attests that this was required, for example, in the Halikarnassos priesthood of Artemis Pergaia: the priestess' patrilineal and matrilineal ancestors had to have been recorded in the citizen rolls of the city for three generations. This was in fact a significant restriction, for only an elite group would probably be able to document such enrollment in any Greek city. Study of several centuries' inscriptions containing names of sacerdotal persons at Athens reveals their frequent kinship with other priestly or political figures. Being of a prominent family was an important or even tacit qualification for holding many priestly offices. Even the hearth initiate—a symbolic representative of the whole Athenian polis —regularly came from an elite family background.

Other regulations pertained to age; sexual experience or lack of it (married, widowed, virginal); and at times, family wealth or prominence. Rules about appropriate age for certain priesthoods were strictly enforced. Boy-priests of Athena (as at Lindos in Rhodes) were indeed boys, not men. Mature age was required of the *gerarai,* elderly women who examined the king-archon's wife for fitness to be the ceremonial bride of the god Dionysos in the Anthesteria festival. Prepubescent girls, aged seven to eleven years, served as *arrephoroi* in Athena Polias' cult. Young males (*epheboi*) and female basket bearers (*kanephoroi*), as lesser sacerdotal festival participants, were required to be teen-aged virgins. Diodorus Siculus (16.26) says that originally Apollo's oracle at Delphi was a young virgin girl, but later a change required her to be an elderly woman.

Virginity was normally required of priestly attendants in cults of virgin deities such as Artemis. The priestess and priest of Artemis Hymnia had to remain virgins for their entire lives. Some cults did not require virgin priests, but did insist upon celibacy during tenure in office. Married priestesses served in cults of married deities, as in cults of Hera. And marriage was not only allowed, but also necessary in some hereditary priesthoods in order to provide legitimate heirs for the priestly offices.

Similarities in gender, age, sexual experience, or other characteristics between priestly servant and deity may result from ancient belief that the priest or priestess during performance of rituals actually embodied the spirit of the deity. Scholars who accept this theory rely mainly upon vestiges of prehistoric rites, such as the wearing of animalskin robes. For example, priests of Herakles wore lionskin robes; the "bear-girls" of Artemis at Brauron in Attica wore bearskins while performing ritual dances.

After an aspiring officeholder met requirements of age, gender, proper family ties, virgin or married status, then a cult's specific regulations had to be met. Some cults had very restrictive rules. An inscription (183/182 B.C.) from the cult of the Mother in the Piraeus prescribes that the assistant to the chief priestess be chosen from a group of former priestesses. But cult rules could change, and this same cult modified its rules a decade later to allow a short-term priestess (a *zakoros,* whose office usually carried a one-year tenure) to serve for life.

TENURE IN PRIESTLY OFFICES

Cults might alter the length of their priesthoods' tenures, but generally there was a correlation between the tenure and method by which a priesthood was filled. Normal custom was that priesthoods assigned by lot carried annual or brief tenure of two to four years, or from festival to festival. Lifelong tenure regularly accompanied offices that were hereditary or purchased. One inscription states that a priestess of the Mother in Amorgos (first century B.C.) can retain her office for ten years if she wishes. Lower-echelon sacerdotal offices might be held only briefly or just on one occasion.

DUTIES AND FUNCTIONS

The size and type of a cult determined the range of its priestly officials' duties. A few cults opened their doors only once a year and required little of their priests. Most cults were much busier, and large cults had many specialized priestly posts. Duties might concern administration, regulation of cult affairs, assessing fines for prohibited behavior, keeping the cult's treasury, making loans (in deme priesthoods), keeping up the buildings, preparing for festivals, and overseeing housing for priests and visitors. This last duty could be major: at the sanctuary of Asklepios on Kos there were numerous rooms for patients seeking the god's cure for their illnesses.

Many cults tended to routine needs of in-dividuals: purification of homes after a birth or death, officiating at weddings and funerals, administering oaths. At Kyrene the priestesses of the cult of Artemis performed rites for new brides. At Athens the priestess of Athena visited homes of newlyweds, besides performing her many state rituals. Priestly officials' acts bound the social fabric together. All priestly duties were taken seriously. Herodotus' account (8.51.2) that only some priestly officials and a few residents who were too poor to flee remained on the Acropolis as the Athenians abandoned their city during the Persian invasion illustrates how seriously priestly officials regarded the obligation to fulfill their duties.

SOCIAL STATUS OF PRIESTLY OFFICIALS

Indications of the high social status of priests appear in the numerous inscriptions erected by the state or by private persons to praise individual priests and priestesses or subsacerdotal persons. Wealthy nonsacerdotal families sought marriage ties with priestly families, ostensibly for the added prestige that only priesthoods carried. Similar motivation surely underlay many cases of wealthy families who purchased priesthoods.

LEGAL STATUS OF PRIESTS AND PRIESTESSES

The enhanced legal status inherent in a priestly office benefited priestesses more than priests. No longer needing the legal guardianship of her *kyrios* (father, husband, brother), a priestess acted in her own behalf, signing documents, administering cult affairs, suing in court if necessary. She could be sued as well. In one famous case the priestess of Demeter sued the *hierophant* for performing on an illegal day sacrifices that were her exclusive right to perform. There were legal limits to priestly authority, and priests were subject to annual audit. The fourth century B.C. witnessed so many lawsuits involving priestly officials that some scholars believe it was a time of religious instability. The concurrent rise in cults outside traditional religion substantiates this view.

ECONOMIC STATUS, BENEFITS, AND REWARDS

Standard rewards for priestly service were parts of sacrificial victims, their hides, and perhaps housing and a salary. Rich cults such as the Eleusinian Mysteries afforded a private house to the priestess of Demeter. She also received *apometra* (emoluments) of 100 drachmas, and an obol (one-sixth drachma) from each person initiated into the mysteries. This was at a time when a workman's daily wage was one-and-a-half drachmas. In contrast, the priestess of Athena Nike received only fifty drachmas annual salary, her share of sacrifices, and perhaps housing. Lesser priests might receive the minimum. Lower-level priests at Eleusis received only half an obol per initiate. The Salaminioi decree (366 B.C.) details disproportionate shares to the priests and priestesses—the state pays for the priests' performances, priestesses get only part of the sacrifice and a loaf.

Beginning in the third century B.C. certain priests receive awards of gold crowns, some worth as much as 1,000 drachmas. Other benefits included free meals for life at public expense, freedom from the public-service obligations called liturgies, the right to erect one's statue, honorific decrees from the people or from one's family, and the right of *proedria*—front-row seats at the theater. Such special rewards were doubtless recom-

pense for special service that might have been expensive for the priest.

Some cults gave priests the sole right to enter the temple, as was the case for cults of Eileithyia at Olympia and Aphrodite at Sikyon on the Corinthian Gulf. The priestess of Demeter Chamyne at Olympia had a special seat at the Games. In certain cults priests or priestesses had rights of eponymy —the use of their names to identify the years of their priesthoods.

Special privileges and lucrative benefits were appropriate for priests in a culture that counted religion as necessary in every aspect of life and in the proper functioning and well-being of society. Greek religion had no body of writings or unifying dogma, but endured largely through its priesthoods. The Delphic oracle and the Eleusinian Mysteries lasted a thousand years. By blending tradition and flexibility, Greek priesthoods survived when political systems did not. Foreign conquerors respected and embraced elements of Greek culture, religion, and some priesthoods. These priestly offices continued to meet the needs of local worshipers, while the ever-widening umbrella of Greek religion protected foreign cults, mixing them with its own. Toleration and adaptability were keys to the Greek priesthoods' success. When Roman rule had become a permanent fact of life in Greece, it is not surprising to find old religious customs of Greek priesthoods adapted to cults of Roma and Augustus and other cults of the Roman conquerors.

BIBLIOGRAPHY

SOURCES

Johannes Kirchner, ed., *Inscriptiones Graecae II*, especially 1034–1317b, 3789–4350, 2d ed. (Pars I, 1916; Pars III, 1935), and *Prosopographia Attica*, 2 vols. (1901–1903; repr. 1966); *Pausanias, Guide* to Greece (*Perigesis tes Hellados*), Peter Levi, trans., 2 vols. (1971); Franciszek Sokolowski, comp., *Lois sacrées de l'Asie Mineure* (1955), *Lois sacrées des cités grecques* (1962), and *Supplément* (1969).

STUDIES

F. R. Adrados, "Sobre las Arreforias o Erreforias," in *Emerita,* **19** (1951); P. J. Bicknell, *Studies in Athenian Politics and Genealogy* (1972); John-Christian Billigmeier and Judy Ann Turner, "The Socioeconomic Roles of Women in Mycenaean Greece: A Brief Survey from Evidence of the Linear B Tablets," in Helene P. Foley, ed., *Reflections of Women in Antiquity* (1981; repr. from *Women's Studies,* **8** [1981]); Molly Broadbent, *Studies in Greek Genealogy* (1968). Walter Burkert, *Griechische Religion: der archäischen und klassischen Epoche* (1977); Kevin Clinton, *The Sacred Officials of the Eleusinian Mysteries* (1974); L. Deubner, *Attische Feste* (rpt. 1969); G. S. Dontas, "The True Aglaurion," in *Hesperia,* **52,** 1 (1983).

G. W. Elderkin, "Studies in Early Athenian Cult," in *Classical Studies in Honor of Edward Capps* (1936); L. R. Farnell, *Cults of the Greek States,* 5 vols. (1896–1909; repr. 1977); Douglas D. Feaver, "Historical Development in the Priesthoods at Athens," in *Yale Classical Studies,* **15** (1957); Eugen Fehrle, *Die kultische Keuschheit im Altertum* (1910); William S. Ferguson, *Priests of Asklepios, University of California Publications in Classical Philology,* **1** (1907); Elizabeth S. Holderman, *A Study of the Greek Priestess* (1913); Boromir Jordan, *Servants of the Gods* (1979); Ph.-E. Legrand, "Sacerdos," in Daremberg-Saglio, *Dictionnaire des antiquités grecques et romaines,* **4,** pt. 2 (1911); David M. Lewis, "Notes on Attic Inscriptions (II)," in *Annual of the British School at Athens,* **50** (1955).

Jules Martha, *Les sacerdoces athéniens* (1882); Ronald Mellor, Θέα Ῥώμη (1975); Jon D. Mikalson, "Religion in the Attic Demes," in *American Journal of Philology,* **98** (1977); Martin P. Nilsson, *Geschichte der griechischen Religion,* 2 vols., 2d ed. (1955); James Oliver, *The Athenian Expounders of the Sacred and Ancestral Law* (1950); Herbert W. Parke, *Festivals of the Athenians* (1977); Noel Robertson, "The Riddle of the Arrhephoria at Athens," in *Harvard Studies in Classical Philology,* **87** (1983); Robert Schlaifer, "Notes on Athenian Public Cults," in *Harvard Studies in Classical Philology,* **51** (1940); Paul Stengel, *Die griechischen Kultusaltertümer* (1920); Johannes Töpffer, *Attische Genealogie* (1889); Steven V. Tracy, "Athens in 100 B.C.," in *Harvard Studies in Classical Philology,* **83** (1979); Judy Ann Turner, *Hiereiai: Acquisition of Feminine Priesthoods in Ancient Greece,* Ph.D. diss., Univ. of California, Santa Barbara (1983); Sam Wide, *Lakonische Kulte* (1893, repr. 1973); L. Ziehen, "Ἱερεῖς," in Pauly-Wissowa, *Real-Encyclopädie,* **8** (1913).

Roman Priesthoods

MARY BEARD

THE MAJOR PRIESTS of the Roman state were normally drawn from among the political elite at Rome, from the city's magistrates and generals. They were quite unlike the priests with whom we are familiar in modern world religions: they did not undergo any special training; they were not normally professionals, with full-time paid employment in their priesthood; they did not act as moral advisers or seek to influence the behavior of people at large; they were drawn to their priesthood by no particular spiritual "calling"; they were in most cases indistinguishable in dress or day-to-day activities from those outside the priesthood. As we might predict from the close connection that always existed between Roman religion and Roman politics, the category of Roman priest largely overlapped with that of Roman politician; there was no separate priestly caste.

Roman priests were many and varied. We cannot now document their full range, since evidence for most of the small or local cults of Rome is almost entirely lacking. Yet it is clear that the Roman priesthood was not a unitary body but comprised a wide variety of different priestly groups, with different titles, different functions, different qualifications, and different methods of selection. Most priests, for example, were male, but a few, notably the Vestal Virgins, were female. Although many had limited ritual obligations, not extending beyond participation in one or two festivals a year, others had wide-ranging, possibly time-consuming ritual, ceremonial, and administrative duties. Most held office for life once they had entered the priesthood, but some, notably the Vestal Virgins, served a fixed term or had the option of resigning their office after a certain number of years. Some were selected for priestly office by a process of cooption, that is, simply chosen by the existing priests to fill a vacancy left by the death of a colleague; others came to be chosen by popular election. The differences are endless and generalization impossible. Indeed, it is sometimes

933

hard to see what common features linked that group of Roman citizens whom we conventionally know as "priests."

A further difficulty for the modern inquirer lies in the nature of priestly functions, for many of the religious functions that we tend to associate with a specialist priesthood were at Rome carried out by other types of institutions or personnel. The performance of sacrifice, for example, is in many religions the prerogative of the priests alone. In Rome, by contrast, the priests had no necessary role in the ritual of sacrifice: each head of a household (paterfamilias) could and did sacrifice on behalf of his own family; the major magistrates sacrificed on behalf of the Roman state. Likewise, the power of decision-making in matters of religion rarely rested with the priestly groups. It was the senate (and later the emperor) that possessed authoritative power here: the senate decided on the introduction of new cults and rituals (for example, the cult of Cybele in 205 B.C.) and the senate outlawed unacceptable religious practices (for example, cults of Bacchus in Italy in 186 B.C.). Priestly functions in Rome were not solely in the hands of the so-called priests.

The seemingly confusing array of priestly groups can best be understood by dividing the subject into three sections: first, a review of the range of traditional priesthoods in republican Rome; second, a discussion of the changes that occurred under the principate within that traditional structure, and of the eventual demise of Roman priesthood under the influence of Christianity; third, a consideration of the new forms of priesthood that came with Rome's expanding empire, as the horizons of Roman religion extended far beyond the city of Rome to include the whole of the Mediterranean world. This division is broadly chronological, but it does not provide a detailed narrative history of Roman priesthood. Such a history is impossible, given how little we know of the origins of the individual priestly groups and of any changes in their organization and function before the second century B.C.

TRADITIONAL PRIESTHOODS OF THE ROMAN REPUBLIC

The traditional priesthoods of the republic may themselves be considered under three headings: the so-called four major or eminent colleges (quattuor amplissima collegia) of priests; the apparently primitive priesthoods that, at least by the late republic, were together administered under the aegis of one of those colleges, the college of pontiffs; and the various groups of priests, now conventionally called sodalities, whose obligations were centered on the performance of a single ritual or on a very limited series of rituals.

The Four Major Colleges

The most prominent priestly groups in the republic, at least by the second century B.C., were the colleges of pontiffs (pontifices), augurs (augures), the priesthood of fifteen (quindecimviri sacris faciundis), and the seven feasters (septemviri epulones). Whatever their original form, these colleges came to be so similar in organization that they were spoken of (and legislated for) as a group, separate from other priesthoods. They shared, in particular, a method of recruitment by popular election distinct from the other priestly groups, for they alone came under the provisions of the Domitian law (Lex Domitia) of 104 B.C., which removed from the priests the right to coopt new members into their college and transferred the power of selection to a specially constituted assembly of the people.

In function, however, the colleges were quite distinct one from another. On the one hand, the pontiffs (a group that, like the augurs, grew to comprise fifteen members in the late republic) had a wide administrative and ritual competence: their participation was required in numerous state festivals; they administered various areas of religious law (concerning, for example, adoptions, and tombs and burials); they advised the senate on the handling of matters of religious importance.

The augurs, by contrast, were mainly concerned with signs from the gods (as observed, for example, in the flight patterns of birds or in claps of thunder) and with determining, on the basis of these signs, whether the gods approved the actions planned by the state and its magistrates, such as the holding of an assembly, the passing of legislation, or the start of a battle. On occasion the augurs observed and announced these signs themselves; they had, for example, the right to interrupt an assembly at any moment if they saw an ill omen. But more often they acted as specialist advisers while magistrates watched for omens, or they symbolically marked out areas of the sky within which signs might be observed.

The fields of the two remaining colleges were yet narrower. The main task of the priesthood of fifteen was the care of the Sibylline Books, a collection of written oracles that the priests consulted on the instruction of the senate at times of crisis. Since a common result of such consultation was the introduction of a new foreign cult into the city, by association the fifteen came to oversee all the official religious imports into the city. The feasters (founded in 196 B.C. as an offshoot of the pontifical college) were simply concerned with arranging the ritual meals (*epula*) regularly offered to the gods.

The four colleges were also differentiated in relative prestige. Membership in the two oldest colleges, the *pontifices* and *augures* (whose history stretched back into the regal period of Rome), was always considered more distinguished than the office of either *quindecimvir* or *septemvir*. And within the pontifical college the post of chairman (*pontifex maximus*) was particularly prized. Indeed, a form of popular election was already instituted for this post by the third century B.C. and the competition for it was keen.

Three "Primitive" Priesthoods

Under the general supervision of the college of pontiffs came three types of priests very different from any of the four major colleges. These were the Vestal Virgins, the *flamines* (a title related etymologically to the Hindu Brahman) and the *rex sacrorum* (king of religious rites). All are believed to have originated in the earliest strata of Roman religion. All were subject to more or less severe restrictions on their behavior. All were selected for their priesthood by the *pontifex maximus* himself, with no element of popular election.

The six Vestal Virgins were the only important female priests in republican Rome. Their main task was the guarding of the sacred hearth of the city in the temple of Vesta in the Forum, whose flame should it be extinguished portended danger for the state. Girls were chosen for this priesthood between the ages of six and ten and were thereby bound to chastity for thirty years. For those who infringed this rule the penalty was notorious—death by burial alive. It was a strict regime, which some did not sustain, but there were compensations. Living together in a house in the Forum outside the ties of their families, the six Vestals gained from their priesthood power and prestige beyond that attainable by other women in Roman society. And indeed, despite the right to resign their office after thirty years, most chose to remain in the priesthood for life.

The fifteen *flamines* were, individually, the priests of fifteen gods and goddesses in the

Roman pantheon, and their duties were primarily concerned with the cult of their particular deity. The most important of these (and the only ones about which we have a reasonable amount of evidence) were the three so-called major *flamines:* the priests of Jupiter (*flamen Dialis*), Mars (*flamen Martialis*), and Quirinus (*flamen Quirinalis*). These had been priests of the principal triad of divinities in the earliest period of Rome's history, and throughout the republic they retained more strikingly primitive features than any other priests. Not only were they always drawn from the patrician class, but their day-to-day behavior was restricted by a wide range of taboos. This was particularly the case with the *flamen Dialis,* whose many taboos, recorded with care and curiosity by later Roman antiquarians, such as Aulus Gellius in *Attic Nights* (10.15), included prohibitions on the wearing of a ring, being away from one's bed more than three nights, taking an oath, touching leavened bread, and much more.

The priestesses of Vesta and the major *flamines* (especially the *flamen Dialis*) had several distinctive features in common. Unlike other priests, they had traditional costumes as a permanent mark of priestly status: the Vestals wore the dress of a married woman (despite their imposed virginity) and a special hairstyle normally restricted to girls on the day of their wedding; the *flamines* wore a close-fitting skullcap with a spike of olive wood attached, known as an *apex.* Both also, more than any other Roman religious officials, found in their priesthoods a full-time activity: the Vestals lived permanently in the house next to the temple; the *flamen Dialis* was said to treat every day as if it were a holy day. In fact the taboos surrounding him made it very difficult for the holder of this office to engage also in an active political career, although such a career was not explicitly forbidden. The resulting unpopularity of this priesthood among the Roman aristocracy was no doubt one of the factors that caused the office to be left unfilled in the last years of the republic.

The *rex sacrorum* also fell under the aegis of the pontifical college. Less well-documented than either the *flamines* or the Vestals, this office seems to have originated at the expulsion of the Roman kings (traditionally 510 B.C.), when a special priesthood was instituted to take over the religious duties that had previously fallen to the king (*rex*). No chance was taken that these once royal, priestly duties should ever again be associated with political power: the *rex sacrorum* was explicitly barred from undertaking any form of public political office.

The Priestly Sodalities

Finally, some Roman republican priests owed their status entirely to the role they played in one or two rituals and had no religious obligations or authority outside the performance of those ceremonies. Modern writers have tended to call these groups sodalities or associations (*sodalitates*) to distinguish them from the four major colleges —a useful distinction, but not one that was consistently made by ancient authors.

A clear example of this type of priest is the *Salii,* who twice a year (at the beginning and end of the military campaigning season) danced a ritual leaping dance through the streets of Rome and sang a traditional hymn, no longer comprehensible to the Romans of the late republic. Another example is the *fetiales,* who were concerned with rituals associated with the declaration of war and the making of treaties. The evidence for these groups is, however, patchy. Some republican sodalities are known to us by little more than their names: the Arval Brethren (*fratres Arvales*), for example, whose rites are known to have concerned the agricultural prosperity of the state, and the entirely obscure *sodales Titii.* In all cases, even where the ritual obligations are well documented, we are largely ignorant about the methods of organization of this kind of priestly group.

PAGAN PRIESTS IN THE PRINCIPATE AND LATER

The formal structure of republican priesthood continued in the principate and was even actively encouraged by Augustus and his successors. Throughout pagan antiquity senators displayed their priesthoods alongside their political offices in public records advertising their careers. Right up to the fourth century A.D. traditional priestly rules were still applied. We have, for example, a vivid description of the burial alive of an offending Vestal in the reign of Domitian (Pliny the Younger, *Letters* 4.11); three hundred years later, more than fifty years after the reign of Constantine (the first Roman emperor to be converted to Christianity), the same punishment for the same offense could still be contemplated (Symmachus, *Epistles* 9.147–148, with reference to the offense of one of the Vestals of Alba, a group similar to those at Rome).

Yet in other respects the change in political structure that came with the principate substantially affected the priestly groups of Rome. The widely diffused character of the Roman priesthood, appropriate to the republican aristocracy of (at least notional) equals, gave way to a system effectively dominated by the emperor. The emperor, for example, always took the office of *pontifex maximus* as an element of his imperial powers and, contrary to republican custom, he was regularly granted supernumerary membership of all the priestly colleges.

The ritual obligations of the traditional priests also came to center on the emperor and his family. The inscribed records of the Arval Brethren, which survive in large quantity from the imperial period, demonstrate this clearly. Not only did they undertake various rituals of the mysterious goddess Dea Dia (as they presumably had done during the republic), but also a large part of their priestly activity came to be concerned with sacrifices and ceremonies on behalf of the emperor and his family. Such a refocusing of the traditional priesthoods was in addition to the foundation of a range of new priesthoods exclusively devoted to the cult of deified emperors. These were modeled, in form and title, on the traditional priesthoods of the republic: the cult of Julius Caesar, for example, was in the hands of a *flamen* and that of the deified Flavian emperors in the hands of *sodales Flaviales*. In function, however, such priests were entirely untraditional, entirely imperial.

There was no sharply defined end to the pagan priesthoods of Rome with the rise of Christianity. Between the reign of Constantine I (A.D. 306–337) and the last quarter of the fourth century, there was little attempt at the legal suppression of paganism and many prominent senators remained pagan and held pagan priesthoods. In the 380s, however, direct action was taken against paganism and its priests. Flavius Gratianus (Gratian), became in A.D. 381 the first emperor to reject the office of *pontifex maximus,* and he likewise deprived the traditional priesthoods of their funds and property. Of course, the removal of official funds from pagan priesthoods did not necessarily signify the immediate end of such offices. Private subsidy was probably still available from rich pagan aristocrats and the series of legal prohibitions on pagan activity that still seemed necessary well into the fifth century A.D. should probably make us think rather of a gradual disappearance of pagan priestly offices over that period.

ROMAN PRIESTS AND THE ROMAN EMPIRE

Roman priesthood comprised more than the priests of the city of Rome, who have so far formed the subject of this survey. Rome's political control of her empire took Roman priesthoods into the provinces. From the first century A.D., priesthoods of the deified and living emperors were established in many parts of the Roman world, either on the initiative of the Roman government or with its tacit approval. They were held as honors by members of the elite in the provinces, and no doubt contributed to binding the provincial aristocracy more closely to the central Roman power. In the western part of the empire the form of these offices was often closely modeled on the traditional priests of Rome itself; the title *flamen,* for example, is common in this context and in at least one case (the flaminate of Narbonese Gaul—see *Inscriptiones Latinae Selectae* 6964) the provincial priest was bound by a set of taboos reminiscent of those imposed on the *flamen Dialis* at Rome.

Conversely, and even more strikingly, Rome herself was subject to influence from the outside. As the Roman Empire expanded to embrace first Italy and later the whole of the Mediterranean world, Roman religion came into contact with a wide variety of other types of cult and religious officials. Some of these remained localized—on the Danube, for example, or in Asia Minor —and may be called "Roman" only insofar as they existed in a geographical area that was included within the territorial boundaries of the Roman Empire. Others, however, spread to the center of the Roman world, or were even actively imported. These originally foreign cults extended yet further the range of Roman priesthood as a whole. Consider, for example, the priests of Isis, a prominent Egyptian goddess, whose cult was popular in Rome and Italy at least by the early principate. These were full-time religious professionals, resident at their temple and clearly marked out from the laity of the cult in dress and manner of life. Rigorously trained for their duties, they not only often performed arduous ritual duties, but also engaged in periods of contemplation and asceticism. Likewise the priests of Cybele, whose cult was imported into Rome in 205 B.C. These oriental devotees startled the Romans by their exotic costume, their long bleached hair, and their practice of self-castration on initiation into their priesthood. Such priests were not Roman in the strictest, ethnic sense of the word, but were very much part of the cosmopolitan religious life of Rome and Italy for most of the historical period. They should not be neglected alongside the more traditional *flamines,* pontiffs, and augurs.

BIBLIOGRAPHY

SOURCES

Arval Brethren, *Acta fratrum Arvalium, quae supersunt,* W. Henzen, ed. (1874); Aulus Gellius, *The Attic Nights,* E. Capps, T. E. Page, W. H. D. Rouse, eds., John C. Rolfe, trans., 3 vols. (1926–1928); H. Dessau, ed., *Inscriptiones Latinae Selectae,* 3 vols. (1892–1916); Pliny the Younger, *Letters and Panegyricus,* E. H. Warmington, Betty Radice, trans., 2 vols. (1969); Quintus Aurelius Symmachus, *Quae supersunt, Monumenta Germaniae Historica Epistles*, O. Seeck, ed. (1883).

STUDIES

Mary Beard, "The Sexual Status of Vestal Virgins," in *Journal of Roman Studies,* **70** (1980); Mary Beard and J. A. North, *Pagan Priests* (1987); Auguste Bouché-Leclerq, *Les pontifes de l'ancienne Rome* (1871; repr. 1976); Georges Dumézil, *Archaic Roman Religion,* Philip Knopp, trans., 2 vols. (1970); D. Fishwick, "Flamen Augustorum," in *Harvard Studies in Classical Philology,* **74** (1970); M. W. Hoffman Lewis, *The Official Priests of Rome under the Julio-Claudians: A Study of the Nobility from 44 B.C. to 68 A.D.,* Papers and Monographs of the American Academy in Rome, **16** (1955); J. Scheid, *Les Frères Arvales: recrutement et origine so-*

ciale sous les empereurs julio-claudiens, Bibliothèque de l'École des Hautes Études, Sciences religieuses, **77**, (1975).

G. J. Szemler, *The Priests of the Republic: A Study of Interactions between Priesthoods and Magistracies,* Collection Latomus, 127 (1972); Maarten J. Vermaseren, *Cybele and Attis: The Myth and the Cult,* M. H. Lemmers, trans. (1977); G. Wissowa, *Religion and Kultus der Römer* 2d ed. (1912); Reginald E. Witt, *Isis in the Graeco-Roman World* (1971).

Divination and Oracles: Greece

JOHN POLLARD

ONE OF THE MOST STRIKING differences between the ancient and modern worlds was the former's all but pathological concern with the future and naive belief that future events could be divined. The Greeks, despite their vaunted rationalism, were no exception. Divination of all types was widely practiced from the earliest times; prophets were honored as the mouthpieces of gods and their advice was keenly sought by kings and chieftains. The Delphic oracle enjoyed universal esteem and the pronouncements of the Pythia were regarded as divinely inspired. It is true that we still believe that some future events, such as the weather and economic cycles, can be forecast with reasonable accuracy, but our judgment is based on scientific observation or the construction of mathematical models. We no longer accept the view, as did the Greeks, that men's fate or future conduct can be revealed or determined by such mundane activities as the drawing of lots, the interpretation of dreams, sneezing, or the heeding of chance remarks or the way birds fly. True, astrology, palmistry, and fortune-telling by other means still flourish, as does water divining,

but there is nothing in modern times remotely resembling the degree of importance attached to prophecies or oracles by the Greeks not only as individuals but also collectively as city-states. Belief in divination is partly psychological and partly religious: "To the psychology of anxious moments and solemn occasions may be traced the growth of the sub-rite of divination and the observance of omens" (Halliday, *Greek Divination*, p. 8).

METHODS OF DIVINATION

The most ancient branch of divination was the pseudoscience of augury, that is, divining the future by observing the direction of flight, the activities, or the cries of birds. In Homer, bird omens are always sent by the gods, and the Greeks regarded certain species of birds as the emissaries of individual deities. The eagle was the bird of Zeus, the falcon of Apollo, and the owl of Athena. Such identification was not exclusive; Athena, for instance, sent a heron to encourage Odysseus and Diomedes (*Iliad* 10.273), and once appeared disguised as a swallow (*Odyssey* 22.236–240).

Cicero, the Roman statesman and philosopher, distinguished between two kinds of divination, one a science based on observation, the other an art owing more to intuition, although perhaps the latter was more prominent in the Homeric era. Calchas, the augur who so enraged Agamemnon by announcing that the only way to appease Apollo and so rid the Greeks of the plague that beset them at Troy was to restore the captured Chryseis to her father, Apollo's priest, himself operated by the favor of Apollo. Calchas is described by Homer as "the most excellent by far of augurs, who knew both things that were now and due to come and had been before and guided the ships of the Achaeans to Ilios through his powers of divination" (*Iliad* 1.68 ff.). In other words, in Homer's day an augur and a prophet were one and the same.

In addition to famous augurs like Calchas and Tiresias, the renowned Theban seer, less professional practitioners are mentioned by Homer: Helenus, Priam's son; Ennomus, the Mysian leader; Theoclymenus, the mysterious prophet of the *Odyssey* who is gifted with second sight; as well as Helen, Circe, and Calypso. Several of the more famous seers were associated with snakes, which, dwelling as they do in holes in the earth, were regarded as connected with chthonian (underworld) powers and as, in some sense, their epiphanies. Helenus, his sister Cassandra, and Melampus, whose ears were licked by snakes, were able to understand the language of birds. Tiresias, on the other hand, sustained a change of sex after witnessing two snakes coupling and was blinded by Hera for revealing the secret that women derived more pleasure from intercourse than men.

In the Homeric *Hymn to Hermes* (542–548) Apollo promises that

Whosoever cometh relying on
The cries and flight of birds of good omen
Shall benefit from my voice. I will not
Deceive him. But whoever trusteth in
Idly twittering birds and seeks to search out
My mantic art against my will; to learn
More than the gods that live forever, shall,
I promise, set out on a vain journey.

In other words, authentic augurs were every bit as jealous of their craft as modern doctors; quacks (who, according to the comic poet Aristophanes, abounded in Athens) were unwelcome. As the suitor Eurymachus observes in the *Odyssey* (2.181–182), "Many birds go to and fro under the rays of the sun, but not all are ominous," and Hector, the Trojan leader, actually scoffs at the art when an eagle appears before the Trojan army carrying a snake, which bites the eagle and forces the great bird to release it. Polydamas pronounces it an omen of disaster, but the angry hero thunders in rebuke (*Iliad* 12.237–240):

You bid me to pay heed to long-winged birds,
For which I show no regard or concern,
Whether they fly to the right (the lucky
　　　　　　　　direction) and the east,
Or to the left they go to murky dark.

But it is rather his companion's spirit of defeatism that rouses Hector's ire, and there is no reason to suppose that the art was not taken more seriously in cooler moments.

For Hesiod, in *Works and Days*, augury is basically a practical art devoid, for the most part, of religious overtones. He is concerned with augury only insofar as the observation of the flight and cries of birds is a sound guide to a change of season or weather (448–450):

Pay heed when you hear the voice of the crane,
Crying every year from the clouds on high:
For she brings the sign to plow and shows
　　　　　　　　　　　　　　　forth
The season of rainy winter.

Likewise (566–568):

> Then the shrill-voiced daughter of Pandion,
> The swallow, comes into the sight of men
> At the time when spring is just beginning.

On the other hand, it is an ill omen if a crow settles on a half-built house.

A work on augury was attributed to Hesiod in later times, but was certainly not genuine. Our knowledge of Greek augury, apart from Homer, is based on references in the poets and prose writers of the classical period, an important epigraphical fragment, a late treatise, and the titles of some works that have not survived. The Homeric augur divined the nature of an omen by applying the primitive maxim that a bird that appeared from the right was good, whereas one that appeared from the left was bad—a view that, curiously, was the precise opposite of the Roman belief. This maxim was not confined to the Greeks; it is of almost universal application and may be due, as H. J. Rose suggests in *Primitive Culture in Ancient Greece,* to the physiological fact that "the right lobe of most human brains is a trifle the better developed" (p. 42). However this may be, the mere fact that the majority of mankind is dextral and that the right hand is the stronger of the two must undoubtedly have impressed the primitive mind. Such a consideration probably underlies many of the superstitions connected with the danger of moving "widdershins"—counterclockwise, against the sun—and the ancient convention in art that figures facing toward the right are lucky. Wine is still passed from right to left, and lots were so passed in Homer. But right and left are arbitrary terms and the question arises as to whether the augur oriented himself in relation to some fixed object or direction before taking an omen. Omens do not always appear from the same direction in Homer; hence we must assume that for the Greeks at least, it was often purely a matter of chance in what direction the augur faced.

Prometheus, in Aeschylus' play, claims to have invented the science of augury in a passage remarkable for the technical terms employed (*Prometheus Bound* 484–488):

> The flight of birds with crooked talons clearly
> I divined, both which were propitious
> And by nature lucky, the habitat
> Each possessed and their mutual hatreds,
> Affections, and associations too.

"Birds with crooked talons"—raptorial birds like eagles, vultures, and hawks—played a major part in augury, as symbolic of power in all its forms. In *Agamemnon,* Aeschylus distinguishes between the king and his brother, Menelaus, in terms of eagles (111–114):

> One black, the other white of tail,
> Appearing hard by the palace, on the
>   spearhand [i.e., from the right]
> Their alighting watched by all.

In *Seven Against Thebes,* Aeschylus actually draws a distinction between the authentic augural art and that of extispicy (divining by examining entrails). On the other hand, Sophocles' *Oedipus the King* represents the hero as having solved the riddle of the Sphinx without recourse to augury, although Thebes possessed a lookout (as did Sciron in Attica) from which to observe birds. Also, augury played an important part in the ritual at Thebes of the Spodian Apollo.

Xenophon, the Athenian general, recalled that when he was leaving Ephesus to meet Cyrus the Younger, whose claim to the Persian throne he was supporting, an eagle had screamed from its perch on the right. The omen was interpreted as portending suffering rather than royalty or glory, since small birds mob seated eagles. From this he concluded that he should decline the offer of the

943

position of commander-in-chief, even if he were pressed to accept it.

Curiously enough, a unique attempt was made at Ephesus as early as the sixth century B.C. to codify the laws of augury, of which the following fragment survives (*Sylloge Inscriptionum Graecarum* 1167):

> Line of flight from right to left. If the bird disappears from sight the omen is favorable; but if it raises its left wing and then soars and disappears the omen is ill. Line of flight from left to right. If it disappears on a straight course, it is an ill omen; but if it raises its right wing and then soars and disappears the omen is good.

In later Roman times Aelian (*On the Characteristics of Animals* 1.48) divided the science into four sections—birds' cries, flight, perching, and activity—and their divine significance was recognized by the philosopher Porphyry (*On Abstinence* 3.5). The latest treatise was written in the eleventh century by Michael Psellus, who referred to a work, otherwise unknown, by a certain Apollonius of Lacedaemon (Sparta). The science, however, had become so complicated by Byzantine times that whereas a raven croaking on the right was a good omen, a crow was only so when it cawed on the left.

Augury was only one branch of divination, although a major one. Virtually any occurrence of an involuntary or arbitrary nature was regarded as ominous. Indeed, Aristophanes pokes fun at Athenian credulity in his comedy *Birds* (719–721, Benjamin B. Rogers, trans. [1930]):

> A Rumor's a bird, and a sneeze is a bird,
>   and so is a word or a meeting,
> A servant's a bird, and an ass is a bird.
>   It must therefore assuredly follow
> That the birds are to you (I protest it is true)
>   your prophetic divining Apollo.

A sneeze was quite involuntary and therefore an omen. It was regarded by the Greeks as a sign of good luck, and when a sneeze interrupted Xenophon's address to his troops everyone assumed that the gods were on their side.

Dreams, too, played an important part in divination, for it is through dreams, as Agamemnon claims (*Iliad* 2.63–64 ff.), that Zeus reveals his will. During the second century A.D. Artemidorus of Daldis wrote a work, still extant, on the significance of dreams, every type of which is described in the most minute detail. But it was in connection with chthonian powers such as heroes and in particular with the rite of incubation—that is, sleeping in a sacred spot and receiving guidance from a god or hero—that dreams were most in vogue. The oracle of the hero Trophonius at Lebadeia (Livadia) is a well-known example, for Pausanias, the ancient guidebook writer, has given an account of the elaborate ritual in his *Description of Greece* (9.39.5); the subterranean chamber he mentions has recently been discovered:

> Within the enclosure is not a natural chasm in the earth, but an artificial opening fashioned with the most accurate eye to detail. The shape of the structure is like an oven. The width across would be about six feet and one would not suppose the depth to exceed twelve. They have made no staircase leading to the bottom, so when a man comes to visit Trophonius they bring a narrow, light ladder. On descending, he finds an opening between the floor and the masonry. Its width appears to be two feet and its height one. The visitor lies prone on the floor, holding cakes kneaded with honey, and pushes his feet through the hole. He then follows himself, trying to force his knees through the opening. After the knees the rest of the body is drawn through, just as the largest and swiftest rivers will catch a man in a whirlpool and draw him under. Once those who have thus entered the shrine are within, they learn the future in various ways, some through visions and others from what they hear. . . . Next, the inquirer is led by the priests not immediately to the oracle, but to certain springs of water, which lie close to-

gether [these too have been identified and most oracles were associated with springs]. There he must drink of the water called Forgetfulness in order that he may forget everything that he formerly thought of. After, he drinks another water, that of Memory. Thereby he recalls what he sees below.

At the oracles of the hero Amphiaraus at Oropos in Attica and of the goddess Ino at Thalamae in Laconia, cures were also effected through dreams. At the former of these sites, gold and silver coins were dropped in the sacred spring by those who had been cured, a practice still common at holy wells. Most famous of healing shrines was that of Asclepius at Epidaurus in the Argolid, where invalids slept in a dormitory attached to the temple and records of miraculous cures have survived. A unique firsthand account of revelations received at the shrine of Asclepius at Pergamum survives in the *Sacred Teachings* of Aelius Aristides, who, like Artemidorus and Pausanias, flourished during the second century A.D.

Lecanomancy, divination by peering into water, usually in a basin (*lekane*)—the ancient equivalent of gazing into a crystal ball —took various forms. Typical was the oracle of Demeter, the corn goddess, at Patras, where a mirror suspended above a spring was employed by invalids to find out whether they were destined to live or die. At the oracle of Apollo at Patara in Lycia the wishes of consultants were reflected in the surface of a spring.

Drawing lots (chance selection achieved by any means) has been popular in all ages. Today state lottery tickets are on sale in most cities, while gamblers flock to try their luck at games of chance in Monte Carlo, Las Vegas, and other centers. The difference, of course, is that the moderns seek short-term gains, while the ancients, who also gambled, employed lottery to divine the future. Cleromancy, divination by lots (*kleros*), was widely practiced from Homer's time onward. In the *Iliad* (7.180 ff.) the heroes drew lots to decide who should face Hector, but they first prayed to Zeus in order to ensure the choice of either Ajax or Diomedes, the two most redoubtable Greek champions after Achilles had withdrawn from the war. In fact, the lot fell to Ajax, as the god controlled the outcome. According to Pindar (*Pythian Odes* 4.190–191), the seer Mopsus dispatched the Argonauts propitiously, "divining by birds and holy lots." An ancient note on this passage states that dice were available in temples and their use was a traditional practice. Lot drawing took place both at Delphi and Dodona, the two best-known oracles in Greece, but was regarded as an inferior form of divination. "Many throw the dice, but few are genuine seers," as one proverb had it.

It was said that at Delphi a cup filled with pebbles was set above the tripod on which Apollo's priestess, the Pythia, sat. The pebbles were used to draw lots. The art was said to have been invented by the Thriae, nymphs of Mount Parnassus, who were inspired by eating honey. According to another tradition the priestess drew beans, and Plutarch (*Moralia* 492) tells us that Aleuas the Red became king of Thessaly when the Pythia drew his name inscribed on a bean. Probably the lot-oracle was used for casual visitors who could not afford a full Delphic seance. As for Dodona, Cicero records a tradition that because a monkey scattered the lots once when the Spartans were consulting the oracle, their visit was in vain.

The gods' statues were believed to react in various ways during religious ceremonies. Supposed sweatings by the images of Christ or the Virgin Mary are regularly reported from southern Europe. Such phenomena had their counterpart in ancient times. The statue of Heracles was said to have sweated before the Spartan defeat by the Thebans at Leuctra, and the Palladium, Athena's protective image at Troy, broke out in a salt sweat of displeasure when the statue was removed. A different reaction was noted on

945

the part of the miniature statue of Artemis Orthia at Sparta. It was believed to become unbearably heavy when held by her priestess if the beaters, who scourged the backs of Spartan boys until they bled on the altar, relented when moved by compassion or personal beauty. Again, the statue of Hera at her famous temple near Argos once flashed fire from her breast, instead of from her head, and so dissuaded Cleomenes, the Spartan king, from attempting to capture the city.

Extispicy or haruspicy (divination from entrails) was apparently unknown to Homer, but was later practiced at Livadia in connection with Trophonius' oracle. Pausanias describes the numerous sacrifices to various gods a visitor was obliged to make before descending into the underground chamber. A soothsayer was present to observe the entrails and report from their various peculiarities whether Trophonius would be well disposed or not. Later a ram was sacrificed, and if the entrails were unfavorable the others did not count. Extispicy was also practiced in connection with Apollo Ismenus at Thebes, as well as on the altar of Zeus at Olympia, but never in Greece on the scale customary among the Romans—although Euripides in his *Electra* presents a picture of Aegisthus reading the entrails.

Necromancy—divination by communication with the dead—was not much practiced in ancient Greece, despite the famous example of Odysseus' visit to the Cimmerians, whose land was adjacent to the place of the dead, in order to consult the ghosts. In fact, Artemidorus, the writer on dreams, was of the opinion that sleeping in tombs was a waste of time.

Cledomancy (*kledon,* meaning an omen in a chance saying) in some sense survives. "Out of the mouths of babes and sucklings," we say when an innocent remark becomes loaded with meaning, or "Odd you should say that: we were only just talking of . . ." So

when the suitors spy Odysseus, successfully disguised as a beggar, the dramatic irony is heightened by their praying that the gods may grant him his dearest wish, whereupon the hero "rejoiced at the omen" (*Odyssey* 18.117). Such sayings, as we shall see, were utilized by oracles.

ORACLES

Most prestigious of all methods of divination was the consulting of the famous oracles—centers scattered throughout the Greek world at which pronouncements from specific deities could be obtained. The deity, usually—but by no means exclusively—Apollo, was approached through the medium of a priest or priestess, who delivered a piece of inspired advice (also known, somewhat confusingly, as an oracle). The advice came in response to some question put by the consultant, and might be political, religious, or personal in nature. In addition to the pronouncements of the official oracular centers, many oracles supposedly delivered by such semimythological prophets or prophetesses as Musaeus, Bacis, or the Sibyl were in common circulation. Aristophanes refers to Sibylline oracles, while Plato maintained in the *Phaedrus* (244b) that "the Sibyl and other prophets, who employ divine inspiration, have correctly predicted the future."

Of the prophets, or rather prophetesses, who were divinely inspired, most famous of all was the Pythia at Delphi. The old name for Delphi was Pytho, where Apollo was reputed to have slain the dragon Python, and it was from this ancient title that the Pythia, an elected and elderly priestess, derived her name. The *omphalos* (literally, navel) at Delphi marked the spot where, according to myth, two eagles dispatched by Zeus in different directions finally met and so determined the center of the world. In fact, despite its apparent remoteness on the slopes of Mount Parnassus, Delphi was eminently accessible by sea, and its convenient central location was doubtless largely responsible for its remarkable popularity. Here advice was eagerly sought when plagues occurred, catastrophes that were as often as not attributed to the perpetration of some ancestral outrage in the far distant past. The offended deity had to be propitiated and the oracle would explain why.

Not only individuals but also whole delegations came to consult the oracle on any number of topics, ranging from the religious to the political. Solon, the Athenian statesman, actually appointed two officials to conduct a liaison with Delphi. The oracle's fame became so widespread that it was consulted by the rulers of Lydia in western Asia Minor, and both Alyattes and his successor Croesus sent offerings to Delphi of an unparalleled magnificence. Croesus claimed to have tested the powers of all the other notable oracles, but found them all wanting, save Delphi and the Amphiareum at Oropos. So he sent to both inquiring whether he should make war on the Persians and seek an ally, only to receive the reply that if he attacked Persia he would destroy a great empire. Unfortunately the empire proved to be his own. When Croesus complained that he had been misled by the oracle, the Pythia replied that she was not to blame, that the monarch should have sent again to inquire which empire was meant. According to Heraclitus (frag. 244), "The Delphic oracle neither speaks out nor disguises its meaning, but gives a broad hint." It was left to the inquirer to interpret for himself. If he misunderstood that was his affair.

Most of the oracles quoted by Herodotus are plainly literary fabrications, at least in the form presented. How far ambiguity was a part of Delphic stock-in-trade is now impossible to say, although the Greeks, like Herodotus, clearly accepted it as dogma.

Certainly, the nonliterary oracles recorded in inscriptions are, for the most part, simple and direct. Would-be emigrants were reputed to have sought Apolline sanction before setting out abroad to found new colonies. Delphic influence may have been exaggerated in this connection, but its propaganda was certainly active in this and other fields. As the supreme arbiter on questions of religion, pollution, politics, law, or ethics (above all, the oracle preached moderation), Delphi's authority was rarely questioned. Even Thucydides forbears to criticize, although the oracle was said to have "Medized"—that is, acted as a kind of fifth column during the Persian invasion—and apparently was not above taking bribes. That Delphi survived so very long as the accredited religious center of the whole of the Greek world is a remarkable tribute to its powers of organization; how it obtained and stored information remains a mystery.

The precise details of a Delphic seance may only be surmised. After sprinkling a goat with water to see how it would react before it was sacrificed, the priests escorted the Pythia to the temple of Apollo. But first she was required to wash in either the Castalian spring or the one named Cassotis. Consultants were also required to wash, which was not the same as undergoing purification. In the temple, seated on the tripod that apparently was regarded as a seat of mantic power, the Pythia replied to the questions put by the consultants after the manner of a medium in a state of real or affected trance. The priests presumably fulfilled the roles of interpreters and recorders (although some modern scholars have denied this), and doubtless they tampered with the wording on occasion. Whether the Pythia chewed bay leaves as an aid to inspiration or, since the consultants were said to "descend," held court in a subterranean chamber must remain undecided. What we do know is that consultants were required to offer a costly cake in addition to providing sacrifices of sheep and goats, the skins of which were sold by the Delphians to help eke out their meager living.

Delphi was only the most famous and influential of the Apolline oracles. Others included Abae in Phocis; Tegyra, Mount Ptoon, and Thebes in Boeotia; Delos; Corope in Thessaly; as well as Claros, Grynium, Patara, and Branchidae (Didyma) in Asia Minor. Both Abae and Branchidae were sufficiently famous to have been included in the list which Croesus tested, while Mys, the Persian envoy, visited Abae, Thebes, and Ptoon. At Ptoon, he received an oracle in the dialect of Caria (southwestern Asia Minor), or perhaps it sounded like Carian, since the prophet gabbled in an unintelligible way. At Branchidae the birds that nested in the temple were sacred and regarded as the god's suppliants. When a certain Aristodicus took a nest he was rebuked by a voice from within. Both lecanomancy and omens played a central part at Patara, and the priestess, as an aid to inspiration, was imprisoned for a time in the temple.

Although Zeus, as his son Apollo was the first to acknowledge (*Homeric Hymn to Hermes* 532), was the ultimate source of inspiration, his oracles were not as highly regarded as those of Apollo. This was doubtless largely due to the remoteness of the best known of the centers: Dodona in the northwest of Greece, and Ammon in North Africa. The oracle at Dodona in Epirus is mentioned by Homer, who refers in the *Iliad* (16.234) to the Selli, a band of earth-squatting priests unique in Greek religion. In the *Odyssey* (14.327 ff.) the hero is said to have gone to Dodona to hear the counsel of Zeus "from the high-tressed oak." Interpreting from the rustlings of leaves was also unique to Dodona, but later the oracle was operated by priestesses. Consultants recorded their inquiries, most of them of a simple and personal nature, on strips of lead, which were then rolled up and handed in. Dodona also possessed a lot-oracle.

Next in importance was the oracle of Zeus-Ammon situated in the oasis of Siwa, near the Greek colony of Cyrene in Libya. It was said to have been consulted by Cimon and Lysander, but its most distinguished visitor was Alexander the Great. The god's image was said to nod in assent like Zeus in the *Iliad*. The oracle of Zeus at Olympia was associated with the god's great altar. Herodotus refers to it in passing (8.134) as resembling that of the Ismenian Apollo in Thebes, inasmuch as inquiry was made through the medium of victims: in other words, by extispicy. Pausanias says that the prophets at this oracle plastered the altar with mud from the Alpheus River.

Other gods possessed oracles too, including Gaia (Earth), the original incumbent at Delphi, Dionysus, and Hermes. Gaia's oracles were situated at Aegae, near Corinth, and at Olympia and operated, like all chthonian powers, through dreams. Dionysus, the wine god, possessed oracles both in Thrace and at Amphikleia in Phocis. Like that of Asclepius at Epidaurus, they provided cures for sickness and the cures were given in dreams; the priest acted as interpreter and was divinely inspired. Dionysus possessed underworld association and so his rites were analogous to those of heroes.

Of the oracle of Hermes at Pharae in Achaea (near Patrae, the modern Patras), Pausanias has this to say (*Description of Greece* 7.1.22):

> You consult the god in the evening, burn incense on the altar and fill the lamps with oil. Light them and place a coin on the altar to the right of the god's image. Then stop your ears, leave the market place, take your hands from your ears and the first words you hear are the answer to your query.

This was an organized case of cledomancy and closely allied to cleromancy. It is perhaps significant that Hermes was consulted at night, for among his other functions was conducting the dead. The river Acheron, which flows through a rugged gorge in Thesprotia, actually boasted an oracle of the dead. According to Herodotus (5.92), Periander, tyrant of Corinth, consulted this oracle after his wife's death. When her ghost complained that she was cold he stripped all the women and had their clothes burned.

This brief survey has attempted to trace Greek methods of divination from augury to oracles, methods in which the basic assumptions were always the same. Gods or heroes did not deal with men directly, but through omens of every conceivable description: the sudden appearance of birds, the fall of lots, the content of dreams, the occurrence of sneezes and chance remarks. Divination was even possible, although the method was not revealed, by means of a humble sieve (Theocritus, *Idylls* 3.31). At a higher level, the gods could be approached through priests or priestesses, who were believed to be inspired and able to reveal the divine will. Apollo was regarded as the chief oracular god and his center at Delphi enjoyed supremacy throughout the Greek world. Nevertheless, local oracles continued to flourish and survive into late Roman times. The simpler methods of divination also remained popular and have their counterparts today. Man alone of earthly creatures is prey to worries about the future, and the Greeks were no exception to the general rule. On the contrary, their concern with the future and the firm belief that the gods could divulge it, if they were so minded, colored the whole of Greek life.

BIBLIOGRAPHY

SOURCES

Aelian (Claudius Aelianus), *On the Characteristics of Animals*, A. F. Scholfield, trans. (1958–1959); Aeschylus, *Agamemnon, Seven Against Thebes, Prometheus Bound*, Richmond Lattimore and David Grene, trans. (1953–1956); Aelius Aristides, *Aelius Aristides and the Sacred Tales*, C. A. Behr, trans. (1968); Aristophanes, *Birds*, Benjamin B. Rogers, trans. (1930); Artemidorus of Daldis, *The Interpretation of Dreams (Oneirocritica)*, Robert J. White, trans. (1975); W. Dittenberger, *Sylloge Inscriptionum Graecarum* (1915–1924); Heraclitus, fragments found in *The Presocratic Philosophers*, Geoffrey S. Kirk, John E. Raven, and Malcolm Schofield, eds., 2d. ed. (1983); Herodotus, *The History*, A. D. Godley, trans., 4 vols. (1920–1924); Hesiod, *Works and Days*, M. L. West, ed. (1978); Homer, *Iliad*, Richmond Lattimore, trans. (1951), *Odyssey*, Richmond Lattimore, trans. (1965–1967), and *Hymn to Hermes*, in Apostolos N. Athanassakis, trans., *The Homeric Hymns* (1967); Pausanias, *Description of Greece*, W. H. S. Jones, trans., 5 vols. (1918–1935); Pindar, *Odes*, Sir John Sandys, trans. (1915); Plato, *Phaedrus*, H. N. Fowler, trans. (1914); Plutarch, *On Pythia's Oracles, On the Decline of Orades*, in *Moralia*, Frank C. Babbitt, trans., 16 vols. (1927–76); Porphyry, *On Abstinence*, in Thomas Taylor, trans., *Select Works of Porphyry* (1823); Michael Psellus, *On Divination from Shoulder Blades and Birds*, R. Hercher, ed., *Philologus*, **8** (1853); Sophocles, *Oedipus the King*, Stephen Berg and Diskin Clay, trans. (1978); Thucydides, *History of the Peloponnesian War*, Charles F. Smith, trans., 4 vols. (1919–1923); Xenophon, *The March Up Country (Anabasis)*, W. H. D. Rouse, trans. (1958).

STUDIES

Pierre Amandry, *La mantique apollienne à Delphes* (1950); Auguste Bouché-Leclercq, *Histoire de la divination dans l'antiquité*, 4 vols. (1879–1882; rev. ed. 1963); Eric R. Dodds, *The Greeks and the Irrational* (1951), and *Christian and Pagan in an Age of Anxiety* (1965); R. R. Dyer, "The Evidence for Apolline Purification Rituals at Delphi and Athens," in *Journal of Hellenic Studies*, **89** (1969); A. J. Festugière, *Personal Religion Among the Greeks* (1954); Robert Flacelière, *Devins et oracles grecs* (1961); Joseph Fontenrose, *The Delphic Oracle: Its Responses and Operations with a Catalogue of Responses* (1978); Sir William Halliday, *Greek Divination* (1913); Leicester B. Holland, "The Mantic

Mechanism at Delphi," in *American Journal of Archaeology,* **37** (1933).

K. Latte, "The Coming of the Pythia," in *Harvard Theological Review,* **33** (1940); R. G. A. van Lieshout, *Greeks on Dreams* (1980); N. Marinatos, "Thucydides and Oracles," in *Journal of Hellenic Studies,* **101** (1981); Martin P. Nilsson, *Geschichte der griechischen Religion,* 2 vols. (1955); Herbert W. Parke, *The Oracles of Zeus* (1967), *Greek Oracles* (1967), "Three New Inquiries from Dodona," in *Journal of Hellenic Studies,* **88** (1967), and *The Oracles of Apollo in Asia Minor* (1985); Herbert W. Parke and Donald E. W. Wormell, *The Delphic Oracle* (1956); John R. Pollard, *Seers, Shrines and Sirens* (1965), "Greek Religion," in *Encyclopaedia Britannica,* vol. 8, 15th ed. (1974), and *Birds in Greek Life and Myth* (1977); Herbert J. Rose, *Primitive Culture in Ancient Greece* (1925).

Divination and Oracles: Rome

JOHN FERGUSON

ORIGINS: ETRUSCAN DIVINATION

It was vital to the Romans to enjoy the *pax deorum* (favor of the gods). There were two main ways of ascertaining the will of the gods. One was divination, the interpretation of signs believed to be supernaturally provided. The other was the oracular response, a direct answer provided by the god through his minister to a direct question. "Etruscan religion," wrote Raymond Bloch (1958)—to which the Romans owed so much—"was a revealed religion." Cicero, with a Roman scholar's awareness of the cultural debt owed the older civilization, tells the story of the origin of Etruscan divination (*On Divination* 2.23): A farmer of Tarquinii (Tarquinia) cut a deep furrow while plowing. From this emerged a being called Tages, with the face of a child and the wisdom of age. The plowman raised a shout, the people came rushing, and Tages dictated the laws governing the practice of divination. According to other versions Tages was the son of a genius (a male fertility god), and grandson of Jupiter. Other accounts attribute the revelation to a nymph named Begoe or Vegoia (for example, Servius, *Commentaries on Vergil's Aeneid* 6.72).

The *disciplina Etrusca* (learning of the Etruscans) was contained in three works: the *libri haruspicini* (books of divination), on foretelling the future through examination of the entrails of sacrificial victims; the *libri fulgurales* (books of lightning), dealing with the interpretation of lightning flashes; and the *libri rituales* (books of rites), treating a comprehensive variety of topics, including prodigies.

Fundamental to all techniques of divination is what has been called the doctrine of orientation. It implies a consistent pattern through the universe: macrocosm and microcosm, respectively objectified by the overarching sky and the liver of a sacrificial victim. Pliny the Elder in his encyclopedic *Natural History* (2.55.143) notes that the Etruscans divided the sky into sixteen sections, four major quarters each subdivided into four. For divination, an observer faced south; thunder and lightning to the east or left were favorable, to the west or right unfavorable. A *templum* (from a root meaning "to cut") was originally a divinatory section of the sky, and in early Latin the phrase *caeli templa* (holy areas of the sky) is not uncommon. *Templum* then came to mean the section of ground designated for divination, as marked off by an augur with his rod. The sky section was the greater *templum*, the designated ground section was the smaller *templum*. The scheme of division was pervasive. A century ago an ancient bronze model of a sacrificial victim's liver was discovered at Piacenza. On it were described the names of a large number of Etruscan deities, and the positioning of the names parallels the divisions of the sky described by Martianus Capella in the fifth century A.D. The microcosm reflects the macrocosm.

The haruspices, or diviners by entrails, varied in their historical prominence in Rome. They were naturally prominent under the Etruscan kings. With the coming of the republic (509 B.C., traditionally) the Romans were less overtly interested in such divination. They sought knowledge not of the future but of the favor of the gods (*pax deorum*). But in times of crisis they turned to the haruspices. Under the early empire (from 31 B.C.) the practice of haruspicy lapsed. Claudius revived it in an antiquarian spirit, and it proved remarkably persistent. The Christian emperor Theodosius I (A.D. 379–395) ruled that if the palace were struck by lightning the haruspices must be consulted. In A.D. 408 Etruscan diviners offered their services to save Rome from the Goths; the Christian bishop said that he would not object, provided the consultations were kept secret. In the sixth century, Laurentius Lydus was still discussing the claims of haruspicy.

Another aspect of Etruscan divination was the interpretation of prodigies, that is, extraordinary occurrences. Books known as *ostentaria* preserved the lore and principles. Writes Macrobius, "If a sheep or ram is tinged with purple or gold, it promises fortune and the height of prosperity for the leader of the group and his family; his house extends future generations in glory and increased blessing" (*Saturnalia* 3.7.2). Cicero's speech *On the Reply of the Diviners* is important in this context. There were rumblings under the ground in Latium. The haruspices were called in to interpret, and Cicero quotes their actual words. The gods showing their anger were Jupiter, Saturn, Neptune, the goddess of earth, Tellus, and the Heavenly Powers. The reasons for their anger were the neglect of religious rites, the sacrilegious assassination of politicians, and disregard for oaths. The portended dangers included strife between nobles and commoners, plots against the state, and the subversion of the existing order. Curiously, Cicero does not mention the expiatory ceremonies prescribed.

DIVINATION: NATURAL AND ARTIFICIAL

"There are two kinds of divination," wrote Cicero, a cool rationalist even though a practicing augur at the time. "The first depends on scientific skill, the second on nature" (*On Divination* 1.6.11).

Although the distinction between the natural and the scientific is somewhat blurred in Cicero, natural divination is immediate in its application. It falls into two categories, dreams and prophetic inspiration. We know that the Romans inherited and adapted a number of Greek books on the practical interpretation of dreams; theoretical discussions survive in such late authors as Synesius and Macrobius (fourth through fifth centuries A.D.). Prophecy, however, was less important at Rome than in Greece. On the whole, the Romans wanted to know not what was going to happen but whether the gods approved.

Artificial divination requires human skill,

Cicero's "scientific skill," for interpretation. It is of many kinds; for the Romans the most important was augury, divination by observing the actions of birds. Cicero (*On Divination* 1.41.92) attributes it to Phrygians, Pisidians, Cilicians, Arabs, and Umbrians. It was common in Greece. Signs detected from birds were of two kinds. *Impetrativa* were those deliberately sought. For example, the sacred chickens were given food; if they so ate it that some dropped from their beaks, that was a good sign. One of the great blasphemies was that perpetrated by Publius Claudius Pulcher, consul in 249 B.C. during the First Punic War. Told that the sacred chickens would not eat, he said, "Then let them drink!" and had them flung into the water, where they drowned (Cicero, *On the Nature of the Gods* 2.3.7 ff.). *Oblativa* were signs observed but unsought. A person possessing the *auspicia* (authority to observe birds), at first the king, later the augur, marked out a *templum* or holy space in a rectangle. A formula freed it from its past associations. Then the Etruscan practice of observation was followed. Livy gives a good account of one form of procedure in his description of the accession of the legendary king Numa Pompilius (1.18.6):

> An augur (appointed for that purpose in perpetuity for the future) escorted him to the citadel, and sat him on a stone facing south. The augur covered his head and took a seat on Numa's left, holding in his right hand a twisted staff unmarred by knots, called a *lituus*. From there he looked out over the city and the countryside, prayed to the gods, and marked off the extent of the sky from east to west, designating the southern area as right and the northern as left. He fixed in his mind a landmark opposite him as far away as the eye could reach. Then he transferred his staff to his left hand, laid his right on Numa's head, and prayed, "Father Jupiter, if it is the divine will that this man, Numa Pompilius, whose head I am touching, be king of Rome, send us sure sign within the bounds I have set." He then outlined verbally the auspices he desired to be sent, and on their appearance Numa was proclaimed king and came down from the sacred place.

Augurs were public figures, and the office might be used politically with a right of veto. Writes Cicero: "What an augur ceremoniously bans as unjust, irreligious, immoral, and dangerous, must in no circumstances be performed on pain of death" (*On Laws* 2.21). An ironic episode in the career of Julius Caesar occurred in 59 B.C. Although consul and *pontifex maximus,* for purely political reasons he defied the vetoes of his consular colleague Marcus Calpurnius Bibulus, who withdrew to his house "to observe the heavens."

Other forms of artificial divination included: observation of animals, on which the credulous Pliny the Elder has a good deal to say; observation of human actions (sneezes and the like); haruspicy, covering the observation of lightning, the inspection of entrails, and the interpretation of portents and prodigies; observation of lifeless objects; the reading of weather signs; and astrology. This last pseudoscience came from Chaldea, in Babylonia, and was fostered by the Stoic philosophers, whose deterministic theories gave it intellectual justification. The astrologers were called Chaldeans or mathematicians (because of their calculations); they were notoriously influential in the reign of Tiberius, who retired to Capreae (Capri) "with his Chaldean flock" (Juvenal, 10.94).

THE SIBYLLINE BOOKS

The story of the Sibylline Books is one of the stranger episodes in Roman religious history. The books purportedly contained the revelations of the Sibyls, legendary prophetesses at some ten locations throughout the ancient world. According to legend an old woman, one of the Sibyls, offered nine volumes at an exorbitant price to Tarquinius Priscus (traditionally, the fifth king of Rome, 616–579 B.C.). When he refused, she destroyed three, and then three more. He succumbed, taking the last three at the price originally demanded for the nine (Dionysius of Halicarnassus, 4.62.1–6; Pliny the Elder, *Natural History* 13.88). The books were placed in the custody of a special priestly college and consulted only by decision of the senate at times of national crisis. It is clear that the association of the books was Greek; their proximate source the Greek colony of Cumae (Cuma) in Campania, and their more distant source perhaps Erythrae (Ildırı) in Ionia; and their prescriptions Greek. It has been questioned whether a collection of this kind could have been in circulation in the sixth century, and some have argued that the formal collection dated from 367 B.C.

A reported consultation of the Sibylline Books during a time of famine in 496 B.C. resulted in the founding of a temple to Ceres, Liber, and Libera—that is, Demeter, Dionysus, and Persephone, the deities of agricultural fertility. In 399 at the time of the siege of Veii, a winter of unusual severity was followed by a summer of heat and plague. A *lectisternium* was prescribed, a ceremonial banquet attended by pairs of deities in the form of images reclining on couches; there was a period of forgiveness, reconciliation, goodwill, and holiday. In 349 a pestilence called out the prescription of dramatic entertainments. In 293 in a terrible epidemic the books prescribed the introduction of the healing god Aesculapius (Asclepius) in the form of a snake on the island in the Tiber where the hospital of San Bartolomeo still stands. In 249 during the First Punic War, the *Ludi Saeculares* (games of the century)—to be repeated every century—were instituted on the prescription of the books.

The disasters of the war with Hannibal led to repeated consultations. Among the many special provisions were a *ver sacrum* (holy springtime) in which all the valuable products of the spring, including the children, were dedicated to Jupiter; after the defeat at Cannae (219 B.C.), a Greek man and woman and a Gallic man and woman were buried alive; in 205 it was declared that Hannibal would leave Italy if the Great Mother of Pessinus were brought to Rome (in the form of a black baetyl [sacred stone]); once she had come, the senators found her worship too orgiastic and decreed that no Roman should participate.

The consultations continued from time to time. The original collection of the Sibylline Books was destroyed in the Capitol fire of 83 B.C. and was replaced by material garnered from several sources. The last recorded consultation was in A.D. 363 (Ammianus Marcellinus, *History* 23.1.7). The collection was finally destroyed at the time of Stilicho's reign, A.D. 395–408 (Rutilius Namatianus, *On His Return* 2.52).

THE ORACLES OF ITALY

In general, the widespread use of various techniques of divination in the Italian world left less room or less need for consultation with oracles than was the case in the Greek world. Some of the oracles in Italy were Greek in origin. Such was the oracle of Calchas in Daunia (Apulia), where the consultant sacrificed a black ram, slept on the victim's fleece, and received the answer to his inquiry in a dream (Strabo, *Geography* 6.3.9). So, too, with the oracular cavern of the Sibyl at Cumae. The oracle of Faunus was an indigenous Italian oracle of considerable antiquity. It operated in two groves, one by the well of Albunea at Tibur (Tivoli), the other on the Aventine Hill. At Tibur, the consultant had to abstain from eating meat and from sexual intercourse for some days.

Thereafter the ritual was not unlike that in Daunia. The priest sacrificed a sheep. The consultant, wearing plain clothes and no ring, was lustrated (purified) three times with water from the well, and touched with the bough of a sacred beech tree; he then slept on the fleece and received his answer in dreams. We know also of answers given in the ancient Saturnian verse. People flocked to this oracle from all over the peninsula (Vergil, *Aeneid* 7.81 ff.; Dionysius of Halicarnassus, *Roman Antiquities* 5.16.2–3). An early oracle of Mars is recorded at Tiora Matiene in the Sabine country of central Italy; here the oracle was delivered by a woodpecker (Dionysius of Halicarnassus, *Roman Antiquities* 1.14.5).

At Antium (Anzio) there was an oracle of Fortuna where two sister goddesses were worshiped. The oracular answer was given by some mechanical device whereby the statues leaned forward; this implies that the request was simply for the goddess's favor (Macrobius, *Saturnalia* 1.23.13; Suetonius, *Domitian* 15). A story of Gaius (Caligula), however, records the oracle as telling him, "Beware of Cassius!" This must have involved a different type of response (Suetonius, *Caligula* 17). At Praeneste (Palestrina) the oracles were given by lots, billets of oakwood inscribed with archaic letters, said to have been discovered by a certain Numerius Suffustius. The lots were placed in a *sitella*, a narrow-necked urn that was filled with water and then shaken up by a boy. The narrow neck allowed only one lot to emerge, which the consultant extracted (Cicero, *On Divination* 2.41.85). Another lot-oracle was at Caere (Livy, 21.62.8).

Less organized and formal was the practice of oracular consultation of works of literature—Homer, Vergil, and later the Christian scriptures. This might consist of writing texts on billets of wood and using the *sitella,* or it might consist of simply opening the text of the author at random. Exam-

ples of the *sortes Vergilianae* (oracles of Vergil) recur throughout the lives of the emperors (for example, *Scriptores Historiae Augustae,* "Hadrian" 2). Augustine records (*Confessions* 4.3) that in his day people would turn at random to the pages of some poet whose intentions were totally different and find his lines miraculously pertinent. Augustine himself on a celebrated occasion (*Confessions* 8.12.29) heard the voices of children playing, "Take; read. Take; read," and opened his Bible to be confronted with St. Paul's injunction to abandon the way of the flesh (*Epistle to the Romans* 13.13). Such practices—the *sortes sanctorum* (oracles of the holy ones)—were discouraged repeatedly by church councils, which is evidence enough that they were widely practiced.

ORACLES OF THE EASTERN EMPIRE

It should not be forgotten that from a comparatively early stage the Romans were in touch with the Greek world, and after the Hannibalic wars (218–201 B.C.) they spread over the eastern Mediterranean. The very limitation of the Italian oracles made the Romans more interested in the Greek oracles, and as Romans settled in the East for longer or shorter periods, and as the inhabitants of the eastern provinces became Roman citizens, so the oracles of the East became a part of the religion of Rome. Four examples may be given.

The first is Delphi. Here the traditions are limited but real. A legend associating Romulus with the Pythian oracle is late and not Roman. The earliest legend from Rome goes back to its traditional last king, Tarquinius Superbus, who had seen a sinister omen. He sent his sons Titus and Arrius to the oracle at Delphi accompanied by Lucius Junius Brutus, who was pretending imbecility. The two sons asked which would become king. The oracle replied, "Young men, he among you who shall be the first to kiss his mother will hold the highest power in Rome." Brutus discerned the reference to Mother Earth, kissed the ground, ousted the Tarquins, and became consul. The story is no doubt apocryphal; it is significant that a century or two later the Romans wished to believe it (Cicero, *On the Republic* 2.24.44; *Brutus* 14.53; Livy, 1.56).

Other stories of contact with Delphi during the Roman Republic date from the siege of Veii (405–396 B.C.) and the draining of the Alban Lake, leading to the dedication of a golden bowl to the oracle; from the Samnite Wars in the fourth century; and from the third-century struggle with the Gauls, again with a dedication. With the Second Punic War we are on firmer historical ground. Quintus Fabius Pictor was sent in 216 B.C. to Delphi to inquire how to secure victory. The account derives ultimately from the historian-delegate himself (Livy, 23.11.1 ff.; Plutarch, *Parallel Lives*, "Fabius Maximus" 18). The promised victory was long delayed, but after the battle of the Metaurus in 207 a gold crown was dedicated at Delphi. Delphi was also consulted over the bringing of the Great Mother as prescribed by the Sibylline Books.

After the Second Punic War the Romans did not again corporately consult Delphi, although individuals might. By the imperial period the shrine was in some decay (Strabo, *Geography* 9.3.8). Nero's reign, however, began a period of imperial patronage. The intellectually inquisitive Hadrian asked where Homer was born and received a rather gushing reply that somewhat oddly associated the poet with Ithaca. We have a few records of political oracles toward the end of the second century A.D. and beginning of the third, such as the scarcely ambiguous punning response in A.D. 193–196 when Pescennius Niger, Septimius Severus,

and Clodius Albinus were jockeying for power:

The dark one [*niger*] best, the African [Septimius Severus] good, the white one [*albus*] worst.

But that is all. When Julian the Apostate (A.D. 361–363) was seeking to revive paganism he sent the doctor and quaestor Oribasius to Delphi, only to receive the response (Cedrenus, 304a):

Tell the king, the monumental hall has
        fallen to the ground.
Phoebus no more has a hut, has no
        prophetic bay,
No speaking stream. Even the voice of the
        water is quenched.

The oracles of Apollo in Asia Minor are a second example of eastern oracles that exercised an effect upon Rome. The oracle at Branchidae (Didyma) in Ionia, enshrined in a temple with remarkable features, retained its early prominence, but under Roman rule it was surpassed by the oracle at Claros, which belonged to the Ionian city Colophon. By A.D. 200 this oracle was commanding a large staff, including a formal choir to sing special anthems, and its reputation had spread to Dalmatia, Numidia, Sardinia, and even Britain. The answers were sometimes obscure:

A man shoots stones from a whirling sling
And kills with his casts gigantic grass-fed
        geese.

The Cynic philosopher Oenomaus poured scorn on these enigmatic utterances, but stock formulas could sometimes be ingeniously used.

The extraordinary story of Alexander of Abonutichus in Paphlagonia (northwestern Asia Minor) in the second century A.D. offers a third example of eastern oracles. Lucian tells the story hostilely. Alexander was something of a fraud, and in an assumed state of ecstasy discovered an already planted newborn snake in a goose egg; this he declared to be the incarnation of the god Asclepius. He had a tame full-grown snake, which he fitted with a cloth mask and held on his lap to give oracles in a darkened room. The human-headed snake appears on coins, a fact that is testimony to the immense reputation the oracle attained. Publius Mummius Sisenna Rutilianus, proconsul of Asia who became Alexander's son-in-law, Marcus Sedatius Severianus, governor of Cappadocia, and even the emperor Marcus Aurelius himself were among Alexander's dupes, and the oracles survived for three-quarters of a century after his death.

Finally, the Egyptian oracles remained prominent. From Oxyrhynchus we have a set of questions to an oracle from the late third century A.D. They reflect the anxieties of the times: "Shall I become bankrupt?" "Shall I become a refugee?" "Have I been bewitched?" "Is my property to be put up for sale?" Such questions as "Shall I become a senator?" and "Shall I become an ambassador?" reflect similar anxieties; they arise not from ambition but from the expense of high office. Some of the questions are domestic. "Am I to be reconciled to my son?" "Am I to be divorced from my wife?" (*Oxyrhynchus Papyri* 1477). Human anxieties do not deeply change.

OMENS AND PRODIGIES

Concern over omens and prodigies remained strong. The *Scriptores Historiae Augustus* is full of them: in the reign of Antoninus a Tiber flood, a comet, a two-headed child, quintuplets, a crested serpent that ate itself, barley growing from the treetops, a pride of

naturally tame lions; under Commodus (A.D. 180–192) footprints of the gods leaving the forum, a blaze in the sky, a sudden darkness on the first of January, firebirds. The brief glory of Maximinus I (A.D. 235–238) and his son Maximus was foreshadowed by a snake coiling round his head as he slept, a vine with clusters of purple grapes, a shield blazing in the sun, a lance split in two by lightning. Severus Alexander's death was presaged by a victim escaping from sacrifice and splashing him with blood, by falling trees, by the words of a druid, and by some words of his own.

Omens were not necessarily world-shaking portents. They could relate to ordinary people. Pliny the Elder has a great deal of material on ancient omens. There must have been many who (like Augustus) put their right shoe on first, or thought it a good omen to set out on a long journey in a light drizzle, few who did not think it good to have incense, saltcake, or the sort of wood and leaves that would make a fire crackle and spurt with good omen.

BIBLIOGRAPHY

SOURCES

Ammianus Marcellinus, *History*, John C. Rolfe, trans., 3 vols. (1935); Appian, *Roman History*, Horace White, trans., 4 vols. (1964); Augustine, *Confessions*, John Gibb and William Montgomery, eds. (1927); Sextus Aurelius Victor, *Origo Gentis Romanae* (*The Origin of the Roman People*), Giulio Puccioni, ed. (1958); Cedrenus, *Chronicle*, Immanuel Bekker, ed., 2 vols. (1838–1839); Cicero, *On Divination*, Arthur S. Pease, ed. (1963), *De Republica, De Legibus* (*On the Republic, On Laws*), Clinton W. Keyes, trans. (1951), *On the Nature of the Gods* (*De Natura Deorum*), Joseph B. Major, ed., 3 vols. (1891), and *Brutus*, Alan E. Douglas, ed. (1966); Dio Cassius (Cassius Dio Cocceianus), *Roman History*, Earnest Cary, trans., 9 vols.

(1961); Dionysius of Halicarnassus, *Roman Antiquities,* Earnest Cary, trans., 7 vols. (1947–1961).

Isidore (Isidorus Hispalensis), *Etymologiae (Origins)*, Wallace M. Lindsay, ed., 2 vols. (1911); Juvenal, *The Satires*, John Ferguson, ed. (1979); *Lactantius*, Samuel Brandt and Georg Laubmann, eds., 2 vols. (1890–1897); Livy, *History of Rome*, Benjamin O. Foster *et al.*, trans., 14 vols. (1919–1959); Macrobius, *Saturnalia,* James A. Willis, ed. (1963); *Oxyrhynchus Papyri*, Bernard P. Grenfell and Arthur S. Hunt, eds. (1898–1984); Pliny the Elder, *Natural History,* Harris Rackham *et al.*, trans., 10 vols. (1938–1962); Plutarch, *Parallel Lives,* Bernadotte Perrin, trans., 11 vols. (1957); Rutilius Namatianus, *On His Return* (*De Reditu Suo*), Charles H. Keene, ed. (1907).

Scriptores Historiae Augustae, David Magie, trans., 3 vols. (1921–1932); *Select Papyri* III, Denys L. Page, ed. (1950); Servius, *Commentaries on Vergil's Aeneid,* Georgius Thilo and Hermann Hagen, eds. (1887–1923); Silius Italicus, *Punica,* James D. Duff, trans., 2 vols (1927–1934); Strabo, *Geography,* Horace L. Jones, trans., 8 vols. (1928–1961); Suetonius, *Lives of the Caesars,* John C. Rolfe, trans., 2 vols. (1914–1930); Valerius Maximus, *Factorum et Dictorum Memorabilium Libri IX,* Karl Kempf, ed. (1888); *Johannes Zonaras*, Ludwig Dindorf, ed., 6 vols. (1868–1875).

STUDIES

Raymond Bloch, *The Etruscans,* Stuart Hood, trans. (1958); Auguste Bouché-Leclerq, *Histoire de la divination dans l'antiquité,* 4 vols. (1879–1882); William W. Fowler, *The Religious Experience of the Roman People* (1911); Herbert W. Parke and Donald C. W. Wormell, *History of the Delphic Oracle,* 2 vols. (1956); Herbert W. Parke, *Greek Oracles* (1967).

Sacrifice and Ritual: Greece

MICHAEL H. JAMESON

SOURCES

In a civilization such as that of the classical Greeks, which had no bible or collection of central sacred texts and no priestly caste to interpret theology and define orthodox practice, religion was manifested primarily by the performance of traditional rites. Belief in a god, recognition of his or her reality and power, was shown by the performance of ritual in the divinity's honor, and, most conspicuously, by the sacrifice of animals. Greek literature and documentary texts abound with references to rites but have little to say by way of explanation of them. Explicit comment comes mostly from the small minority who were critical of traditional religion; more rarely, comment comes from learned defenders, who were probably not much closer to the mainstream of belief. We find ourselves in the position of alien observers of a variety of ceremonies whose meanings we must often infer from the contexts and the incidental remarks of the participants. The ethnographic analogy is fitting; although cultural descendants, we are alien to ancient modes of belief. In many ways, the religious life of the Greeks is closer to that of a complex, nonliterate traditional culture than it is to the text-based, revealed religions such as Judaism, Christianity, and Islam.

In literature the poets and the historians are valuable sources. Some of our most detailed descriptions come from the Homeric poems. Ritual permeates every play of Aeschylus' trilogy, the *Oresteia*. Euripides' *Electra* contains a vivid account (774–858) of the killing of Aigisthos while sacrificing to the Nymphs. Herodotus, curious about the religious practices of other peoples, writes about them in Greek terms. Xenophon was conscientious in the practice of ritual and in recording its performance in his writing. For particular local cults the traveler Pausanias of the second century A.D. is especially valuable. The lexicographers and scholiasts contain explanations and incidental, learned information, often excerpts from lost treatises on the rituals of different cities or regions of Greece. There is discussion of ritual and criticism of animal sacrifice in the works of the Peripatetic philosopher Theophrastus, writing in the late fourth century B.C., who was excerpted and supplemented by the Neoplatonist Porphyry in his *On Abstinence from Animal Food* (third century A.D.) and satirical but sharp criticism comes also from Lucian's *On Sacrifices,* written in the second century A.D. but drawing on Cynic philosophers of the Hellenistic period. Theoretical support for animal sacrifice comes only in Sallustius' *On the Gods* of the fourth century A.D. when paganism was in retreat before Christianity.

To literary and learned sources must be added the numerous inscriptions dealing with matters of cult, conventionally but misleadingly referred to as sacred laws (*leges sacrae*). They are for the most part the resolutions of public bodies or private organizations, containing instructions for the conducting of sacrifices and festivals. An important group is in the form of calendars arranged by the days for specific cult observances. For the organizations involved, the financial consequences of making the sacrifices may often have been a more important reason for setting up the inscription than a concern for correctness in procedure and timing. (See the three collections of Sokolowski and for a translated example, see Sokolowski, 1969, n. 20; Rice and Stambaugh, 113–115). The inscriptions take for granted the regular procedures, which everyone knew, and concentrate instead on such details as what victims were to be offered to which god and, among men, who got how much of the meat. This practical information complements and corrects the picture we derive from literature.

Lastly there is the contribution of archaeology and art. Excavation and chance survival show us the plan of shrines, items of cult equipment (altars, water basins, incense burners, libation vessels, iron spits), the less perishable of dedicated objects and, much more rarely, the burned bones of sacrifices. Representations of ritual in art may themselves be votive objects in the form of reliefs that represent and make permanent acts of ritual such as a family's offering an animal to a god. From secular art the vast repertoire of scenes from life and literature provided by Attic vase-painting of the later sixth and the fifth century B.C. adds many details and shows what types and what phases of ritual the vase-painters liked to paint and their customers liked to see. Both their emphases and avoidances can be revealing.

SACRIFICE

The Greeks, for all their divisive tendencies, everywhere shared the same basic set of religious practices, which they elaborated in distinctive ways for local cults and particular festivals. This essay concentrates on the basic and universal forms of religious practice. At the heart of virtually every cult was animal sacrifice, and the most common word for sacrifice (*thusia*) came to be used for "festival" and "cult" in general. (The occasional explicit avoidance of animal sacrifice was itself an expression of the character of that particular cult.)

Animal sacrifice has been found in one form or another throughout the world. In antiquity it was practiced by other Indo-European peoples (Indic, Iranian, Hittite, Italic, Celtic, and Germanic, to list only the best-known examples) and by the neighbors of the Greeks in the Near East. Each culture had its own forms, and, when language gives us access to them, various conceptions and motivations become apparent. Within each culture a range of practices corresponds to an equally wide range of concerns. The Greeks of the historical period were heirs not only to the peoples who brought an Indo-European language to the Aegean but also to the pre-Greek Aegean cultures of the Bronze Age. The Greek-speaking but Cretan-influenced Mycenaeans would have already possessed the basic system of rituals used later in the historical period, since its uniform spread in the subsequent Dark Age seems improbable. No doubt some of their practices, just as some of their divinities and myths, were of Aegean and, in particular, of Cretan origin—perhaps the deposition, without burning, of grains and fruit, and perhaps the exceptional reverence for the bull in certain cults. But we are largely limited to guesswork. The differences may have been no less significant than the connections.

Some scholars have gone back beyond the Bronze Age to Neolithic and Paleolithic sources for Greek practice, on the assumption that the survival of human behavioral patterns from primitive farming, hunter-gatherer, or even primate stages of society is significant for understanding the practices of the classical Greeks. More secure and informative results for the student of classical civilization may come from placing the religious practices in their own cultural context. Within the span of Greek history certain changes of practice and attitude can be observed, perhaps mostly among the educated and reflective minority. More striking than change, however, is the persistence of animal sacrifice as the major rite in essentially the same form from Homer (ca. 700 B.C.) until its suppression, not always effective, by the first Christian emperors in the fourth century A.D.

A description from Homer's *Iliad* (1.447–474) shows the main features of the principal rite:

Quickly they set the sacred hecatomb [the oxen] in order around the well-built altar, and then washed their hands and took up the barley for scattering. For them Chryses prayed loudly, lifting up his hands: "Hear me, god of the silver bow [Apollo], you who stand over Chryse and holy Killa and who rule in might over Tenedos. Truly, if you ever listened to my prayer before and gave me honor, and

greatly smote the army of the Achaians, do you now also accomplish my wish, do you now at last defend the Danaans against the horrible plague.' So he spoke in his prayer, and Phoibos Apollo heard him.

When they [too] had prayed and tossed the barley forward, first they drew back the heads [of the oxen] and cut their throats and skinned them, and cut out the thighbones and wrapped them in fat, folding it in two, and placed on them raw [bits of meat]. The old man [Chryses] set them to burning on the split wood and poured bright wine over them. The young men alongside him held five-pointed sticks [for roasting the innards] in their hands. When the thighbones were burned and they had tasted the innards, they cut up the rest [of the meat], pierced it on spits and roasted it carefully, and drew it all off the fire. When they had ceased from their toil and had prepared the feast, they feasted, nor did any man's spirit lack [a share] of the evenly divided feast. When they had put aside the desire for drink and food, the young men crowned the mixing bowls with wine, and after making a libation with the cups they passed [the wine] to everyone. All day the young men of the Achaians appeased the god with song, chanting a fine *paian*, singing of the far-working god [Apollo], and he was delighted to hear the song.

While animal sacrifice was the major rite, it needs to be seen in the spectrum of ritual acts available to the Greek worshiper. The simplest form of address to the gods, prayer accompanied only by gesture, can be put at one end. In the description of a sacrifice quoted from the *Iliad* a specific request is contained in the prayer that Apollo cancel Chryses' previous prayer for vengeance on the Achaians, which, although made as he walked alone by the sea and so unaccompanied by other ritual, had reminded the god of Chryses' past sacrifices to him (*Iliad* 1.34–42). At the other end of the spectrum we may set the complex festival lasting many days, involving many gods, a variety of offerings and ceremonies, and numerous religious and civic officials and members of the community. Well-documented examples of the last are the Panathenaia and the City Dionysia of Athens, and the Mysteries at Eleusis nearby.

In between these come simple rites such as libation—the pouring of liquids (most commonly wine), mentioned in the middle of the sacrifice described above and at the end of the subsequent feasting; the offering or manipulation of foodstuffs—grain (such as the barley scattered by Chryses) and fruits, dishes of food, and complete meals; and the offering of other gifts, such as statues or objects of value made of precious metals, or, on a more modest level, clothing or even the simplest items of pottery, sometimes mere tokens such as tiny clay cups. All these may be independent acts or may accompany sacrifice; the first two, libation and food offerings, are essential elements in the full rite. All may express the same general sentiments: desire for the gods' attention and good will. Associated with the rites, but not themselves ritual acts, are the feasting that often follows animal sacrifice (which may be the scene of further ritual) and the athletic, musical, and dramatic competitions that come to dominate major festivals such as that of Zeus at Olympia or the Panathenaia at Athens.

Many rites that used these elements, including the slaughter of animals, were not primarily concerned with addressing gods and reaffirming the relations between them and their worshipers. Thus, the supernatural was introduced into critical relations between men, as in witnessing an oath, a treaty, or a grant of suppliancy. Ritual was required at significant transitions in life—birth, admission into a group, marriage, and death—but the immortal gods could not have contact with the entry into or the departure from life. Birth, death, disease, and sex incurred pollution in various degrees, and pollution required rites of purification

and aversion. Divination was probably part of every sacrifice, if only to observe whether the sacrifice was acceptable, and so many sacrifices were made primarily for divination that the term "to look for good sacrificial signs" (*kalliereisthai*) was used simply to mean "to sacrifice." Signs were especially important before deciding to engage the enemy in battle. But before actual combat began a separate, distinctive sacrifice was made. We see that the purposes for which the elements of Greek ritual were deployed went well beyond the explicit establishment or renewal of relations between the honored divine and the dependent human. For many rites the naming of the gods involved was relatively unimportant or even omitted. The action itself, engaging the supernatural in human concerns, was paramount.

The forms of ritual and the terminology the Greeks used do not always correspond precisely. What we may call normal sacrifice, which is what the verb *thuein* and the noun *thusia* most commonly refer to, was used for most of the purposes just mentioned, but it could be modified depending on the occasion and context, and, in certain respects, its form could approach types of rite that contrasted sharply with it, such as those in which none of the victim's flesh was eaten. Examples are oath sacrifices and the killing of an animal before battle. In antiquity a major distinction was made between the verbs *thuein* and *enagizein* (e.g., Herodotus, 2.44.5). Modern scholars have seen here a general rule that for Olympian gods sacrifice was made on raised altars and the participants partook of the flesh of the victim and of the other food offered, whereas the dead, heroes, and gods of the underworld (socalled chthonic figures) received sacrifice placed on a low altar or in a hole in the ground or a tomb, without the performers eating any of the food offered. These distinctions do not fit neatly with the subtly varied range of actual practice, but roughly they mark the two extremes between normal *thusia* and what we may for convenience call "powerful actions."

THE ELEMENTS OF RITUAL

Prayer

Access to the supernatural, either simply by prayer or elaborately by sacrifice, was not restricted to individual specialists or priestly groups. This seems natural for simple, personal prayer, but such accessibility is found all the way up the scale. No priest is needed if the householder wishes to approach a household form of Zeus, such as Zeus Ktesios (of property) by means of sacrifice in his own courtyard. If he wishes to address a god of a particular shrine, he may find that a priest or a commission controls access; a Greek priest was essentially the functionary charged with the ritual for a particular god at a particular shrine. But even there the priest does not necessarily monopolize the performance of ritual. At the Amphiareion at Oropos the individual worshiper prays over the *hiera,* the parts to be burned, and then deposits them on the altar if the priest is not present or is engaged in public sacrifices (Sokolowski, 1969; n. 69; Rice and Stambaugh, 127–128). Animal sacrifice, while often serving as the centerpiece of a complex, specialized ritual, may also be no more than the conspicuous reinforcement of an individual's prayer. The pouring out of wine in libation, the burning of incense, the deposition of cakes or fruits before a statue or on a fireless altar all serve, more economically and therefore more frequently than sacrifice, to reinforce the prayer. Normally no sacrifice will be without a prayer even if of the most general character, as for "all good things." The Spartans are cited for a characteristically laconic prayer for "the fair in addition to the good" (Plutarch, *Moralia* 239a).

The Greek word for praying, *eukhesthai,* has also the sense of vaunting. It has been observed that the Homeric prayer at least has an element of self-assertion, declaration of worth. Indeed, the Greek in his addresses to the supernatural stood upon his dignity. Kneeling was not unknown but seems to have required special circumstances, and was more frequent among women than men. More commonly men and women stood upright and raised a hand to signal their desire for the god's attention, or held the hand in the direction of the altar if a sacrifice was underway. A general pattern has been observed in literary versions of prayers (we lack examples actually used in ritual): invocation, identifying the god; argument, giving the grounds for the god's heeding the prayer; and the petition itself. The Greeks, however, did not feel constrained to use an unvarying and prescribed format without which the prayer would fail.

Although prayers asked for or expressed gratitude for benefits, they might also be directed against misfortune, present or impending, or they might direct misfortune against others. A curse is a hostile prayer. Private curses could be scratched on lead tablets (the so-called *defixiones*) addressed to underworld gods and deposited in the ground, especially in wells or graves, as a form of magic. A famous instance of public cursing was exercised against Alcibiades and the others accused of desecrating the Eleusinian Mysteries in 415 B.C. (Plutarch, *Alcibiades* 33). An oath was a particular, conditional prayer. The oath-taker requested that benefits be bestowed upon him if he kept his oath, but that he receive the opposite if he failed to do so. Oaths too could be strengthened by combination with sacrifice.

Prayers could be embodied in poetry sung by an individual or by a chorus. Hymns, in essence, are sung prayers, and song in

Greece was often accompanied by dance. The song and dance performed at a festival in a sanctuary were pleasing things for men and gods alike. Although many of the poems that survive were more in the nature of independent works of art than ritual acts, the message the words conveyed was only part of their function. A specialized form of prayer was the *paian,* associated with the god Apollo (a god Paian was also known as an independent divinity and, unlike Apollo, his name has been read on a Mycenaean tablet). In origin it seems to have been a call for protection against dangerous forces and thus had a purificatory and healing function. But it was also sung as soldiers moved forward into battle where, too, dangers threatened.

Washing

Cleansing with water to remove specific impurities or simply the dirt of daily, profane life before engaging in a ritual act was universal: "Never pour a libation of bright wine after dawn with unwashed hands to Zeus, nor to the other immortals. For they do not heed you so but spit back your prayers" (Hesiod, *Works and Days* 724–726). In animal sacrifice the handwashing (*chernibes*) was indispensable and in the classical period a distinctive metal vessel (*chernibeion*) is seen in representations of sacrifice. Raised water basins of stone were placed in sanctuaries. The action of washing or of sprinkling with water should, of course, be seen as symbolic, not hygienic: Hesiod enjoined the washing of hands and prayer before fording a stream with one's feet (*Works and Days* 737–741). Understandably, the metaphor of washing underlay many rites of purification.

Incense, Flowers, Branches, Fillets

Ritual action could be set off from ordinary behavior in various other ways as well—by the clothing and adornment of the partic-

ipants, and by avoidance in preparation from contact with death and sometimes sex and certain foods. Among the most frequent marks of festal, special behavior was the burning of incense, either valuable scents imported from the Near East or native herbs. An incense burner is often to be seen in depictions of processions or shrines, but incense was also burned on an altar with or without other offerings, and was regarded as a pleasing, modest offering. The Eleans burned incense along with wheat mixed with honey every month on all the altars at Olympia, and placed olive branches on them and poured libations of wine (Pausanias, 5.15.10). Libations and incense were used in domestic rites for Zeus Ktesios made by private persons "on behalf of themselves" (Antiphon, 1.18). But it might also be prohibited in certain chthonic cults (for Hekate, see Sokolowski, 1962, n. 133).

Flowers are mentioned as offerings or as adornments of participants in ritual. Crowns were worn and branches of laurel and olive carried, sometimes wrapped in strands of wool. They might be deposited on altars or before the god's statue. Victims were draped with fillets—decorative bands—of wool. The display and manipulation of these materials served both as elements in more complex rituals and as independent acts, especially in the devotions of the poor and of those who were regularly and frequently pious. The laurel-bearing (*Daphnephoria*) is an example of those ceremonies that involved the carrying of branches, flowers, and fruits. The Attic *eiresione* was an olive branch wrapped in wool and hung with various fruits (Proclus in Photius 321B Bekker; Pausanias in Eustathius' *Commentary on the Iliad* 22.495; Rice and Stambaugh, 136–137).

Libations

Even more common was the use of liquids: they might be poured into a vessel that was then deposited in a significant spot, or poured on an altar, a rock, or the ground, or into a grave or a hole. A distinction was generally made between *spondai,* in which a small quantity of the liquid was poured out from a drinking vessel and the rest drunk by the worshiper, and *choai,* in which all was poured out; the latter was used especially to procure the powers of the earth and to honor the dead. Oil or scented oil, that is, perfumes or ointments, could be smeared on a sacred object. In the Greek world the favored liquid, of course, was wine, either straight or mixed with water, as the Greeks themselves usually drank it. But since wine was normal, avoidance of wine expressed a divergence from the norm, either for entire rites or at significant stages of a complex ritual. Water, milk, oil, or honey might be required instead of wine; when termed *nephalia* such alternates were associated with avoidance of the blood resulting from animal sacrifice (see Pausanias, 1.26.5, for Zeus Hypatos).

The pouring of liquids was quick and simple, the equipment and the ingredients being close at hand. In art it stands for ritual and reverence in general. A distinctive vessel, the *phiale,* usually of metal, is often shown, and was a common dedication in sanctuaries. Achilles reserved a special vessel for libations to Zeus, which he purified with sulfur and water before praying for the success and safe return of Patroclus from battle (*Iliad* 16.225–232). Libation is used at critical moments such as when a warrior leaves for war. In art, the man holds a cup and a woman (a wife, daughter, or sister) pours from a pitcher into the cup, whereupon the man tips the cup to pour the contents onto the ground or an altar. In complex ceremonies, especially animal sacrifices, libations occur at various points, punctuating and accenting the procedure. Most prominent is the pouring of wine on the flaming altar when bones, fat, and parts significant for divination are deposited in the

fire accompanied by a prayer. We hear at times of the avoidance of libation for all or part of the sacrifice, presumably for the same reasons that wine is avoided in some independent rites.

Some specialized forms deserve mention. Libations were used to mark a treaty, so the term *spondai* came to be used for such agreements. Elaborate and specialized libations were developed for banquets and especially for the separate symposium that followed the meal. On the other hand, *choai,* in which all the liquid was poured out, were especially associated with the dead. Thus the libation-bearers (*choephoroi*) who give the title to the second play in Aeschylus' *Oresteia* are bringing libations to the grave of Agamemnon. Oil for the dead was also treated distinctively in fifth-century Athens, deposited at and in the grave in the decorated flasks we call white-ground lecythi (*lekythoi*).

To the modern mind the most extraordinary development was the conception of gods themselves participating in ceremonies of libation, attested almost exclusively in art (see also Sappho, 2.13–16). At the simplest, gods are shown seated in votive reliefs and on vase paintings holding a cup, usually a *phiale.* At other times they are actually pouring a libation. A winged Nike (Victory) flutters above an altar, a supernatural figure in the female role, pouring from a jug into a sacrificer's cup which he tips over the flames on the altar. Even Apollo may be shown actively pouring as well as passively holding out his cup. The meaning of these scenes remains disputed, but the total effect is clear enough: the gods share in a reciprocal ceremony, between mankind and themselves and between themselves and greater divine figures.

Food

The sustenance that preserves human life was naturally a focus of much attention in ritual, conceived of both as a gift and, like wine, as material to be displayed and manipulated. All food was used, from raw fruits and unground grains to complete, cooked meals. Barleycorns were tossed on the victim and on the altar in normal animal sacrifice. Dried fruits and nuts were showered on a bride and a new slave when introduced into the household (see scholiast on Aristophanes, *Plutus* 768; Rice and Stambaugh, 144). A collection of different grains formed the offering known as "all-seeds" (*panspermia*), a variegated symbol of fertility. Clay vessels with many little compartments (*kernoi*) were used for such collections of grains (Polemon, in Athenaeus 11.478c). Pots of cooked grains or beans (*chutrai* in Athens) were deposited at the establishment of an altar, as well as being presented to a god (Aristophanes, *Plutus* 1197). Flour was mixed with liquids to form the offering known as a *pelanos*, or formed into cakes or in the shapes of animals; secret shapes, probably of the sexual organs, were used in mystery cults and women's cults. A list of materials to be supplied for the exclusively female festival Thesmophoria of the Attic deme of Cholargos includes about 3 1/2 dry quarts (4 l) each of barley, wheat, barley groats, flour, and dried figs; about 3 quarts (3 l) of wine; about 1 1/2 quarts (1.5 l) of olive oil; about 1/2 quart (.5 l) of honey; about 1 dry quart (1 l) each of white and black sesame seeds and poppy seed; two rounds of cheese weighing not less than 2 1/4 pounds (1 kg) each; and 4 1/2 pounds (2 kg) of garlic (Sokolowski, 1962, n.124). A variety of cakes and breads are depicted on reliefs or in clay models found in sanctuaries. But the offering of a pinch of plain flour by the man from Hermion was an example of modest piety such as Greek moralists were fond of citing (Porphyry, *On Abstinence* 2.15).

The concept of "first fruits" (*aparchai*) had wide application, not least to the harvests of fields and orchards, although the Greek term, unlike the English, does not have an explicit agricultural reference. Ancient theorists who disapproved of animal sacrifice saw in such vegetarian offerings pure, primeval piety. But the idea of first fruits was also applied to meals, with an offering being made to the gods of a part of the meal, whether daily fare or an elaborate banquet, before men themselves began to eat. It was also sometimes used to describe elements in a full-scale sacrifice.

Gods—especially the lesser, more familiar figures—heroes (dead persons with continuing power to affect the living), and even the lesser dead were treated as guests at full meals of cooked food. Our earliest example is from the *Odyssey* (14.434–436) where Eumaeus sacrifices a boar to entertain his disguised guest, Odysseus, and sets aside one portion out of seven of the cooked meat for Hermes and the Nymphs. Tables were prepared regularly for the Dioskouroi (e.g., Herodotus, 6.127). A distinctive type of ritual that carried this approach further may be referred to as "hosting the gods" (*theoxenia*) although the practice was more widespread than this particular term. Couches as well as tables were prepared and sometimes the images of the gods were brought to the feast (Sokolowski, 1955, n.32). The Cretans reserved a table for Zeus Xenios in the mess houses where citizen men took their meals (Pyrgion, in Athenaeus, 4.143 f).

In one way or another the gods were assumed to take pleasure in the cooked food presented on these occasions. But as a rite *theoxenia* was not confused with sacrifice. At a normal sacrifice, the gods did not come to feast as guests; what was burned on the altar was not their food (although comic poets might have the gods complain as if it were), places were not set for them, and cooked portions were not normally reserved. But it does seem that in the course of time some blending of the two rites occurred when part of the flesh of the sacrificed animal was placed on sacred tables, ostensibly for the gods, in practice—and often quite explicitly—for eventual use by priests of the sanctuary. Nonetheless, the rationale was the same as that for placing fruits and cakes upon tables or fireless altars: to consecrate them and leave them available for the use of men.

Objects of Value and Significance

In the employment of valuable objects in ritual, the dominant concept was that of gift-giving, so far-reaching in traditional societies. But these objects also lent themselves to a range of expressive functions, as when a craftsman dedicated his tools, a warrior his arms, an athlete his discus or jumping weights. Part of the rewards of success in war or even in a profession such as fishing or herding, once converted into objects of lasting value, could be dedicated in part as first fruits or a tithe (dekate). The Greeks normally distinguished between enduring objects "put up" to the gods (anatithemi) and perishable material such as food and animals. It is revealing that occasionally a conflation of terms occurred, as in the Arcadian "sacrifice up" (anathuo) used in reference to votive objects. An inscribed Greek hexameter from Bulgaria shows the close connection between prayer, sacrifice, and gift: "Having prayed my prayer with sacrifices I dedicated my gift" (Van Straten, "Gifts for the Gods", p. 65).

In early Greece domestic animals were one of the chief measures of wealth, used in exchange and gift along with metal and metal objects, cloth, and clothing. For most people in a largely agrarian society, animals were the most easily available objects of value after fruits and grain, and it should be remembered that once they were killed, however much the sacrificer and his friends enjoyed the meat, his store of wealth was depleted. As time went on, with the growth of towns, industries, and trade, fewer persons of modest means had access to animals for sacrifice. However, the set patterns prevailed, not only because of the conservatism of ritual but also because of the other functions of animal sacrifice—the exceptional, festal food and conviviality they offered men and, at the other pole, their utility for rites that drew on the expressive functions of blood and killing.

MODES OF CONSECRATION

A distinction was made between normal types of communication between men and gods and those forms that were more limited, directed, and impersonal—powerful actions, discussed later. The distinction comes out especially in the ways in which the materials used in ritual were consecrated. The general Greek term for the result of consecration, when something has been made sacred, is hieros (to do hiera is to sacrifice, a victim is a hiereion, a priest a hiereus, and a sanctuary a hieron). Rites directed toward heroes and the dead may use a different terminology, enagizein, meaning "to put in agos (under a curse)," or "to make something awful," and enages, meaning "subject to a perilous consecration," so that the object is shunned or completely destroyed, which is also usually the result in the case of powerful actions.

Normal procedure made use of the process of moving from the ordinary, profane world to the special, supernatural world. There was passage in space, for the private person going with one's offerings from one's home to a sanctuary, or publicly and most conspicuously the grand processions (pompai) representing a whole community with officials, guests, soldiery, gifts, and victims, moving through the physical space occupied by the community to the sanctuary and demonstrating to men and gods the identity of those who were acting and the materials they were using. There was marking by means of crowns, garlands, branches, special clothing for men and women, fillets or gilding of the horns for animals, and music. There were even cases of the animal having the name of the group making the offering written on its side (Sokolowski, 1955, n. 9). The time chosen might be special: a particular day or series of days in the year or in a cycle of years, or, more rarely, a specific day every month.

The place of ritual, if a sanctuary, was already separated from the profane world outside; or it would be marked off by preliminary rites to create a symbolic circle into which the participants entered. At its center was an altar, with or without an image of the god, and there might or might not be a building to shelter the image and nonperishable offerings. (This was the primary function of a temple; in classical Greece interior altars for ritual use were rare.) The indispensable instrument for communication with the supernatural was the altar, simple (sometimes in the form of a hearth) or elaborate, low or high (the theoretical distinction between low and high as corresponding to chthonic and Olympian figures may not have been rigid). For heroes and the dead an actual or supposed grave or a pit served the same function. The participants might also have separated themselves notionally, as well as by means of display, from the ordinary human world, through abstention for a period from contact with the life processes—birth, death, and sometimes sex. More important was the closed, separate nature of the group performing the rite, which defined itself in various ways: by the inclusion of only members of a family, a larger kinship group, a club, a local community, or only the women or men of that community, or by the exclusion of foreigners or members of other Greek ethnic divisions, such as Dorians or Ionians.

The making over of an offering, conse-crating it to the gods, drew on several modes of thought. As a gift the entire object, or a part regarded as first fruits or as a token of the whole, could be brought into the divine sphere by deposition in a sacred place; or consecration could be achieved by conspicuous destruction of token or significant parts; or finally, and most rarely, there was total destruction, associated primarily with powerful actions. In the more complex rituals there were combinations of all these methods.

Gifts of value, other than food and animals, were normally made over simply by deposition in the appropriate sacred context. The ultimate fate of the gifts varied. To make space they were sometimes buried in deposits, but at other times they were recycled, especially if they consisted of precious metal. The humblest offerings, such as miniature clay pots or lead wreaths, may simply have been dumped. Stealing a precious object from a temple, and so depriving the gods of something of value, was universally condemned but not infrequently practiced. What was sacred (*hieron*) was not necessarily dangerous or unavailable for human use, unlike what was awful (*enages*).

Many food offerings were also consecrated by deposition, accompanied by prayer, gesture and, often, libation. For incense, burning was necessary, but not for flowers and cakes. Liquids, we have seen, were subject to every kind of treatment—smeared, deposited in vessels, poured over sacred objects or on burning parts of a victim on the altar or into the ground, or consumed mostly or entirely by worshipers. Burning, which is at the root of the most common Greek word for sacrifice, *thuein,* "to make smoke," was standard when an animal was the object, but usually only when some parts of the animal were sacrificed. To destroy all the victim by fire, that is, holocaust, was an exceptional and vivid expression of deviation from the norm. What is unique to sacrifice, of course, was the preceding step—the killing of the victim, the most dramatic change in the status of what was offered. Burning some parts and eating the rest (except for the valuable skin) was characteristic of normal sacrifice; burning all or disposing of the dead animal in some other way characterized types of powerful actions. A boar used in a sacrifice supporting an oath taken by Agamemnon was tossed into the sea after being killed (*Iliad* 19.250–268) and Poseidon and the river gods might receive whole victims in this way. Deposition, burning some, burning all, or throwing the object away constituted the range of possibilities; their use and combination helped to express the range of purposes in ritual.

NORMAL SACRIFICE: THE PROCEDURE

To examine a normal, full-scale sacrifice in detail, we take another description from Homer. It is exceptionally detailed but, as is the nature of the epic style, contracts as well as expands the standard formulas of description. We are not told, for instance, where the sacrifice takes place, and there is no mention of a well-built altar as in the *Iliad* 1.447 ff. The account referred to in the following paragraphs is from the *Odyssey* (3.430–463):

> So the cow came in from the field and Telemachos' companions from their swift, balanced ship. . . . And Athena came to be present at the rites. The aged horseman Nestor gave the gold [to the smith]. He skillfully poured it over the horns of the cow that the goddess might be pleased with the delightful sight. Stratios and noble Echephron led the cow by the horns. Aretos came from the chamber carrying the handwater [for ritual washing] in a bowl decorated with flowers, and in her other hand she had the barley grains in a basket.

The victim is a herd animal, not used for work, and here a female, as was usual but not invariable for a goddess. The gilding of the horns is an extravagant form of the decking-out of the victim. A young woman carrying a basket is often seen leading the procession in representations in art. In later periods the knife used to cut the victim's throat was also carried in the basket (Euripides, *Iphigenia at Aulis* 1565–1567), and this has been thought to be deliberate concealment, as if to deceive the victim. But in the *Odyssey* account no such pretense is suggested, as the next sentences show: "Thrasymedes the steadfast stood by with the sharp ax in his hand, to strike down the cow. Perseus held the bowl for the blood."

The altar was spattered with the victim's blood, either directly from the victim's cut throat or, as here, from the bowl held below the throat of a larger victim. In normal sacrifice the blood was used and the altar might already show the stains of previous sacrifices, but bloodshed was not the primary focus of the procedure.

> The aged horseman Nestor made the ritual beginning [*katarcheto*] with the handwater and the barley for scattering, and he prayed much to Athena as he gave first fruits [*aparchomenos*] by tossing hairs cut from the head [of the cow] into the fire.

The officiant, who is the leader of the sacrifice, and usually the other participants as well dip their hands in the water and sprinkle water on the victim. The victim's nodding its head when sprinkled was taken as a sign of assent to the approaching slaughter (but it may not always have obliged). It should be noted, however, that the bellowing or bleating of the struggling animal as it was led to sacrifice was regarded as pleasing to the god (*Iliad* 20.403–405). After a declaration of holy silence and a prayer by the officiant, the unground barleycorns are tossed on the victim, the altar, and perhaps the bystanders, making a link between the sacrificers, the animal, and the point of contact with the supernatural. The barleycorns have been seen by both ancient and modern theorists as representative of man's earliest cultivated food; their ritual use was seen by the ancients as having a purificatory function, and by some moderns as offerings to the earth, local spirits, or the dead. The hair cut from the victim's head represents the whole animal, and just as men and women commit a part of themselves to the gods or to their dead by dedicating a lock of hair, so the hairs continue the dedication of the animal to the god. The Greek terminology combines notions of a ritual beginning (*katarchesthai*) with those of an offering of first fruits (*aparchesthai*). The right to perform this critical step in the procedure was valued and its withdrawal from the Corinthians by their own colonists, the Corcyraeans, contributed to the outbreak of warfare between the two cities. (Thucydides, 1.25.4, uses the term *prokatarchesthai*, literally, "to take the lead in making the ritual beginning.") The failure of the barbarian Scythians to observe this stage in sacrifice was remarked upon by Herodotus (4.60.2). Nestor's sacrifice in the *Odyssey* proceeds:

Now when they had prayed and tossed the barley forward, straightway Nestor's son, proud Thrasymedes, standing close, drove the ax [down on the cow], and it cut through the tendons of the neck and removed her strength. The cry was raised by the daughters and daughters-in-law of Nestor and by his revered wife.... Then [the men] raised and held up the cow from earth of the broad ways. Peisistratos [Nestor's son], leader of men, cut her throat. When the black blood poured from her, the spirit left her bones.

The act of killing in normal sacrifice (as opposed to the powerful actions described below) is never represented in art and was never imitated on stage. It has been the focus of much modern discussion of the history and significance of Greek sacrifice. But although it was the final and most violent step in consecrating the victim and converting it into food for men, the Greeks of the classical period evidently did not wish to dwell on it. This may be seen either as a deliberate minimizing of its importance or an acknowledgment of its dangerous power. The cry raised by the women at this point has been interpreted as an attempt to drown out the victim's death rattle, but Euripides once referred to it as designed to summon the god (frag. 351 Nauck), which is consistent with the other demonstrative acts in the procedure, including the lifting up of the animal, a feat occasionally mentioned in later sources as well.

The *Odyssey* account continues:

They quickly divided her up. They cut out the thighbones, all in due order, and covered them in the fat, folding it in two, and on them they laid raw [bits of meat]. The old man set [all this] to burning on the split wood and poured bright wine over it.

What was set in the altar fire, accompanied by a prayer as well as the libation mentioned here, was primarily the bare thighbones wrapped in fat and was worthless as food, as the story of Prometheus' deception of Zeus makes clear (Hesiod, *Theogony* 535–557). Hesiod describes the division of an ox that took place at a time before the separation of men and gods. Prometheus gave Zeus the choice of a pile of bones covered with the folded roll of fat or of the oxhide covering the good meat. Zeus was aware of the trick, Hesiod assures us, but chose the fat and bones, which therefore is what men burn on altars.

Nestor in this *Odyssey* account and other sacrificers in Homer put raw bits of meat, perhaps taken from all parts of the victim and serving altogether as a symbol of the whole animal, on the bones and fat. This practice (*omothetein*) is not certainly found after Homer. It is possible that at one time the marrow of the bones was thought to contain the essence of the animal's life. But in fact the predominant Greek view did not, despite Hesiod's story, see the parts burned as a gift to the gods in isolation from the rest of the victim. Although there were modifications of the Homeric rite, which entailed setting aside edible parts for special treatment, the fact that the comic poets of classical Athens continued to present the gods complaining about the worthlessness of what men did not themselves use shows that, if sacrifice was seen as a division between gods and men, the gods lost out. That was one way of looking at the rite, one that Hesiod and the comic poets knew how to exploit for their own purposes; but as we shall see, it was not the one that made this form of sacrifice synonymous with generous piety throughout the history of Greek paganism. Taken as part of the whole procedure, the conspicuous destruction of part of the animal and the creation of savory smoke from the fat constitute the final step in the sequence of acts that makes over the animal to the god. The proper burning of these parts marked the successful completion of the sacrifice. To cancel an unwanted sacrifice, local officials at Aulis in Boeotia (whence Agamemnon set sail for Troy) swept the altar clean of the *hiera* deposited by the intruding Spartan king Agesilaus (Xenophon, *History of Greece* [*Hellenica*] 3.4.4).

In post-Homeric sacrifice a major interest in the butchery, which was sometimes assigned to specialists, was the inspection of the condition of the innards of the victim for purposes of divination. So important was it to obtain good omens (*kala hiera;* literally, fair consecrated things) that the verb "to get good omens" (*kalliereisthai*) came to be the equivalent of "to sacrifice." Although seers (*manteis*), highly skilled interpreters, were employed, responsible officials such as generals also needed to understand the signs.

Prometheus in Aeschylus' play claims to have taught man the art of interpretation (*Prometheus Bound* 493–499):

> . . . the smoothness of the innards and what color of the bile would be pleasing to the gods, and the variegated shapeliness of the liver's lobe. The leg-bones covered with fat and the long chine I burned and set men on the path to the difficult art of interpretation, and I made them see the flaming signs to which they had been blind before.

Two stages in the sacrifice are required for the exercise of this art, the first at the time of butchery when the innards, including the liver, would be inspected and their character, especially any abnormality, noted; the second when certain parts of the animal were set on the fire, accompanied by libation, gesture, and prayer. Aeschylus' Prometheus speaks of "the long chine," and we know from other sources and from many Attic vase-paintings that this, the ox-tail with the base of the spine, was burned and signs taken from its behavior, which, as experiment has shown, was to curl up in a striking fashion. Teiresias' description of a failed sacrifice in Sophocles' *Antigone* (1005–1014) as well as Prometheus' mention of the bile shows that the gall bladder was also observed for signs, as was the behavior of the thigh bones and the fat.

To conclude Nestor's sacrifice:

> The young men beside him held five pronged sticks [with the innards to be roasted on the fire]. When the thighbones had been burned and they had tasted the innards, they cut up the rest [of the meat] and skewered it on spits and roasted [the meat] holding the sharpened spits in their hands.

The first meat to be eaten was the *splanchna* (certain of the innards—usually lungs, heart, liver, kidneys, and spleen) skewered and roasted over the altar at the same time that the bones and fat were being burned. By contrast the rest of the flesh in Homer was roasted later, also on spits, but after Homer it was often boiled (Herodotus, 1.59.1), if not taken home for cooking, given to friends, or sold. A strong bond was created by jointly taking the innards in the hands and eating them. The act expressed the sense of community, and being excluded from the community could be described as being deprived of sharing in the *splanchna.* (This is depicted comically in Aristophanes, *Wasps* 654.) The innards were also used in other rites. They were held in the hands and placed on and off altars or sacred stones in oath-taking and in rites of admission of young men to the adult community (Herodotus, 6.67–68; Sokolowski, 1969, n. 151d). In the classical period the gods are also brought into this circle when portions of the innards are placed on the hands or knees of statues, on a table or on the altar (Aristophanes, *Birds* 518–519; Sokolowski, 1969, n. 151d). The importance of the innards for divination and the store set upon their being held and tasted jointly indicate that they were felt to have special significance, as in sacrifices in other parts of the world.

The meal that follows in many Homeric descriptions of sacrifice (see *Iliad* 1.467–474, quoted earlier) was enjoyable and socially important but not an essential part of the sacrifice and not usually shown in art. Occasional requirements in inscriptions that there be "no carrying away" (*ouk ekphora* or *apophora*) of the meat, or that dining take place in the sanctuary, show that it often did not. Sacrifices were probably the only source of meat. The priests who were in charge of sanctuaries and were the chief beneficiaries of regulations specifying their shares often must have sold the quantities they received. It was difficult for Christians in Greece at the time of Paul to obtain meat that was not the result of pagan sacrifice (1 Corinthians 8:10). Thus, when formal eating

together, beyond the tasting of innards, did take place, it was a distinct ritual action.

Joint, festal meals are often mentioned (Athenaeus, 4.148f–149c) and dining rooms have been found in many sanctuaries (Sokolowski, 1969, n. 47; Rice and Stambaugh, 125–126). Eating together involved human fellowship in the first instance. But in a larger sense the gods were the hosts in their sanctuary and the meat came from the animal given to the gods. They were recognized with libations, songs, and prayers, and sometimes, with the laying of couches and setting a share of cooked food on tables, they became participants (*theoxenia*). Such table fellowship among men, and to a degree with the gods, was especially characteristic of the smaller cult organizations, hereditary or private. The requirements for dining on the spot seem to be an attempt to underline the unity and identity of worshipers joined together in honoring gods or heroes.

The assignment of portions to the participants was one of the major social functions of sacrifice. Although most participants received a fair share in the "equal feast," as it is often called in Homer, distribution of special parts or extra portions permitted the recognition of social distinctions and honors for guests and for local officials or benefactors. Odysseus, as honored guest in the hut of Eumaeus, received the chine of the butchered hog (*Odyssey* 14.437), as did the kings of Sparta (Herodotus, 6.56), who also received a double portion (Xenophon, *Constitution of the Spartans* 15.4). A dominant concern of the *leges sacrae* is the proper assignment of parts and portions, beginning with those of the priests who saw to the setting up of these texts in their sanctuaries (see the collections of Sokolowski). The most valuable single item derived from an ox was the hide and this, as well as skins from goats and sheep (the latter of which could be used in other rituals), was usually reserved for the priest in public sacrifices, except where, as in Athens, the state financed a large program of public sacrifices throughout the year and recouped some of its expenses with the sale of hides. (There is a partial record of the income from the sales for the year 334–333 B.C. in *Inscriptiones Graecae* II, 2d ed., 1496; Grant 32.) An interesting development was the practice of placing some of these priestly perquisites on the sacred tables where gods and especially heroes received food offerings by deposition, discussed above. As the cult officials had rights to what was placed on the tables, the placing of cooked portions and, even more, raw flesh honored the god without diminishing the privileges of the priests. We may detect here a gesture toward increasing what was explicitly assigned to the god.

The variety and complexity of ritual in an actual festival of the classical or Hellenistic periods are hard to recapture in a brief summary. Aside from assorted offerings of foods, liquids, branches, flowers, and incense, several different types of victims, varying in species, age, and sex might be offered to a bevy of gods, goddesses, heroes, and heroines, at different times in the festival and by means of different rites. Thus in a group of normal sacrifices by the Athenian clan (*genos*) of the Salaminioi to seven gods and heroes, consisting of a goat, sheep, pigs, and an ox (to Herakles), there appears the holocaust offering of a ram to Herakles' companion in myth, Iolaos (Sokolowski, 1962, n. 19; Rice and Stambaugh, 83). The calendar of this clan and that of the country deme of Erchia (Sokolowski, 1969, n. 18) are especially revealing of the structure of festivals composed of multiple sacrifices. Whereas some of the principles may have been very old, such as the sacrifice of three victims of different species (for example, an ox, a sheep, and a pig), other combinations are likely to reflect the ideas of contemporary religious experts. A rule that was interpreted more strictly in the course of time was that of offering male victims to gods,

females to goddesses. But the principle of appropriateness (*ta preponta;* see Sallustius, 16; Grant, p. 192) was more far-reaching and lent itself to the expression of various concerns, such as ensuring the fertility of the earth through the offering of a pregnant victim to Demeter, or potency through the offering of an uncastrated victim on Mykonos to Poseidon, with no women present at the sacrifice (Sokolowski, 1969. n. 96; Grant, p. 8). Much of the time we are able to observe the distinctions that were made but do not understand the full implications of what were distinct idioms in the ritual language of the Greeks.

POWERFUL ACTIONS

Deviations from normal procedure were used to express different religious concerns. The dead and heroes (conceived of as the great dead) might be recognized with food and liquid offerings, which would not be tasted by the living, or by animal sacrifice in which the animal was completely destroyed and stress was laid on the blood. (Such rites corresponded to the Greek term *enagizein.*) The most famous example is the ritual Kirke instructs Odysseus to carry out when he reaches the edge of the underworld (*Odyssey* 10.517–537; he proceeds to do so in the following book, 11.23–50):

Dig a pit a cubit's length in either direction, and around it pour a libation [*choe*] to all the dead, the first [of water] mixed with honey, the next with sweet wine and the third again with water. Over them sprinkle white barley meal. Pray at length to the strengthless dead [promising that] when you come to Ithaca you will make a pyre in your halls, heaping it up with fine things [presumably all would be burned up] and that to Teiresias alone you will sacrifice an all-black sheep which is the best in your flock. When you have prayed to the famous peoples of the dead, sacrifice a ram and a black ewe, turning them toward Erebus but bending away from its streams yourself. There will come many spirits of the dead. Then do you instruct your men to skin and burn up the sheep which you have slaughtered with the pitiless bronze, and pray to the gods, powerful Hades and dread Persephone. Do you yourself draw your sharp sword from your thigh and sit there, and do not allow any of the strengthless dead to come near the blood [to drink] until you have made your inquiries of Teiresias.

No doubt this is not a description of any actual rite, but it incorporates several elements that stand in contrast to normal sacrifice—the pit, the completely poured libations, the black color of one victim, the collection of the blood in the pit while burning entirely the flesh and bones, and the bonfire holocaust and black victim promised once Odysseus reaches Ithaca. In practice, it is not so much the figures to whom the rites are directed as the purpose of the rite that determines its character. The dead were given meals and the living might eat with them. Heroes often received normal victims in normal sacrifice, after which the sacrificers made use of the flesh of the victims. But if the aim was to emphasize the separation, to put distance between men and the dead or the gods associated with them, then deviant rites such as these were performed. Gradations could be expressed. The Sikyonians in sacrificing to Herakles, a man who became a god, "after burning the thighbones of a lamb on an altar eat part of the flesh as from a normal sacrificial victim and burn part as though to a hero" (Pausanias, 2.10.1).

Purification rites were either routine, as before the opening of an Athenian assembly, or marked important transitions for a group, such as death and childbirth, or were used in an emergency, so as to permit social contact with a murderer or to restore a community after the bloody incursion of enemies (Polybius, 4.21.8–9). The materials used were primarily water and the blood of slaughtered animals, whose bodies were carried around the persons or the space to be purified. Small pigs were regularly used for such purposes, but we hear also of dogs (associated with Hekate) and doves (associated with Aphrodite). As a whole, these are rites of separation in which the water, blood, and animals were thought of as taking on the pollution so that when disposed of these off-scourings (*katharmata*) carried the danger away with them. In a wider sense purification has been seen as a science of division, demarcating significant aspects of life. We have noted its use in marking the separation of the place and participants of sacrifice from the ordinary, profane world. Purification was also the rationale behind seasonal expulsions from the community of human scapegoats (*pharmakoi*) of the annual washing of gods' statues, as in the Attic Plynteria for the old wooden statue of Athena, and in complex rituals for the renewal of the community's fire.

The term *sphagia*, literally "slaughterings," or more precisely "throat-cuttings" or "blood-lettings," is applied to a number of these powerful but, when compared to normal sacrifice, relatively simple and single-minded actions. The emphasis on the flow of blood is so strong that for them alone the moment of actually killing the victim is depicted in art. The Spartans before crossing frontiers and rivers would sacrifice and observe the omens. On the battlefield they sacrificed a she-goat to Artemis Agrotera. We do not hear of specific gods in the battlefield rites of other Greeks and in all cases the victims were probably disposed of completely, without burning parts on a fire. In an oath sacrifice Agamemnon makes the preliminary consecration of a boar by cutting some hairs from its head, calls Zeus, Earth, Sun, and the Furies to witness his oath, and cuts the boar's throat; the herald then throws it in the sea (*Iliad* 19.252–268). In this case we may suppose that the action is expressive of the fate awaiting the perjurer. An oath-taker might, however, be required to come into potentially dangerous contact with the divine by taking the victim's innards in the hands as he swore (Herodotus, 6.67–68).

Generally, the purposes expressed in these powerful actions overshadowed the notion of communication with a particular deity. The killing before battle (to be distinguished from the frequently mentioned divination by means of normal sacrifice before deciding to engage the enemy) mimes the bloodletting for which the combatant needs supernatural support. Seen as a group, all these *sphagia* are best taken as powerful, accompanying gestures, giving weight and seriousness to a critical action, be it an oath, a boundary crossing, a prayer to the winds, or a battle. (On the *sphagia* before battle, aptly described as "unusual ritual remedies . . . to cope with extraordinary psychological strain," see Henrichs, "Human Sacrifice in Greek Religion," p. 216.)

Human sacrifice, prominent in myth, was conceived of as *sphagia,* or as *enagismata* to the dead. According to myth, Iphigenia was killed, or about to be killed, at Aulis to appease Artemis' anger and gain favorable winds for her father's fleet. Polyxena was killed on Achilles' grave. There is no unambiguous evidence for human sacrifice in classical Greece, and the account of Themistocles' sacrifice of three Persian captives before the battle of Salamis (Plutarch, *Themistocles* 13.2–5) can be shown to be unhistorical. Its persistence in Greek thought can be seen as the haunting memory of a past reality or, more probably, as the imaginative, symbolic, and extreme form of rituals actually practiced. If killing an animal was a powerful action, killing a human being was the most powerful action possible. The possibilities for imaginative use by the poets were richly exploited, not simply for melo-

dramatic purposes, it has been argued, but also to bring into play the more complex overtones of the meaning of sacrifice in Greek society.

ANCIENT VIEWS ON SACRIFICE

A sense of how Greeks understood their rites can be derived from various incidental comments and the few explicit discussions that have survived. But it is also legitimate to consider the symbolism and inner logic of their performance of ritual, which may not be articulated fully in their texts. At this point the modern scholar's interpretation is bound to intrude.

The Greeks commonly spoke of their sacrifices as honors (*timai*) shown to the gods who, as a result, became favorably disposed (*hileoi*) to men. Philosophers might point out that the gods did not need material things, much less food (see Plato, *Euthyphro* 14), but all took it for granted that sacrifice was a form of gift-giving to the gods. Even critics of animal sacrifice like Theophrastus saw the honoring of the gods as the motive (Porphyry, *On Abstinence* 2.24):

There are altogether three reasons why we sacrifice to the gods: to show them honor, to give them thanks, or to express our need for some benefit. It is as though we were treating with good men when we give first fruits to the gods. We honor the gods while trying to turn aside misfortune or obtain benefits [looking to the future] or when we have already been well treated by them or simply through appreciation of their favorable disposition toward us.

On the popular level many myths taught the dangerous consequences of failing to pay the gods honor and give them due recognition. Gift-giving in socially traditional and economically premodern societies is a complex matter that establishes a reciprocal relationship. The analogy between human relations and those between men and gods was generally accepted, and Aristotle's practical formulation could be applied to both men and gods: "A gift is not only a bestowal of property but also a token of honor; which explains why the honor-loving as well as the money-loving desire it" (*Rhetoric* 1. 5.1361a). And there were social benefits in sacrificial generosity. It was the first advantage of being wealthy that one could honor the gods on a grand scale, according to Xenophon; helping one's friends and adorning one's city were the other two (*Household Management* [*Oeconomicus*] 11.9).

Valuable objects dedicated in temples, even though not manifestly accepted by the gods, were obviously gifts. So too were the fruits and cakes deposited on an altar or table, but available for men to consume when not burned up. How did normal animal sacrifice, after which the good meat was consumed by men, constitute a gift? Consistent with these other offerings, the unstated but implicit assumption was that the gods were presented with the whole animal; how precisely they received and enjoyed this gift, or other gifts, was a matter into which the Greeks, like most peoples who are accustomed to symbolic and expressive acts, did not much inquire.

The Homeric formula was that libation and savory smoke on the altar were the gods' honorific share (*geras*) in the equal feast (*Iliad* 24.69–70), and Hesiod used the notion of the division of a victim at the feast of men to tell how Prometheus arranged for all the flesh, hidden in the skin, to go to man when Zeus chose the bones covered with fat (*Theogony* 535–557). The poet used the unfair division as a key element in his elaborate depiction of the ambiguous relations of gods and men and of man's place in the cosmos.

Hesiod's story had little if any effect on normal practice and views through the centuries, nor was it intended to. Athenian comic poets also played on the joke and had

gods complaining about the wretched parts burned on the altars (see the examples gleefully cited by the Christian Clement of Alexandria in his *Miscellanies* [*Stromateis*] 7.6, 850 Potter). Aristophanes exploited the Homeric phrase and had the gods discomfited when the savor of sacrificial smoke was intercepted (Aristophanes, *Birds* 1515–1524). But another poet contrasted the stinginess of a ten-drachma sheep with extravagant expenditure on wine, cheese, honey, eels, and flute-girls for the feast that followed—the god got the sheep, not the rest (Menander frag. 319 Kock in Athenaeus, 8.364d). Here we are back to the way the Greeks customarily saw themselves, as consecrating whole animals to the gods. More numerous and finer animals were pleasing to the gods, not a larger share of the same animal. Statues of sacrificial animals were of whole animals, not portions. This view of sacrifice, embedded in a tradition of ritual and symbolic behavior, did not lend itself to rational analysis and, while implicit in ancient criticism, has not left us any serious justification. But the overall effect of elaborately and demonstratively moving an animal into the god's sphere, killing it in the god's presence, creating conspicuous smoke, and observing the god's reaction through various signs, all according to ancestral custom, satisfied and endured.

Ancient critics, concerned with violence and some at least with the notion of the transmigration of spirit between men and animals, approved vegetarian offerings, seen as "first fruits," which they regarded as original and pure (Theophrastus, in Porphyry, *On Abstinence* 2.20). The Neoplatonic pagan philosopher Sallustius, however, included animal sacrifice in a broad interpretation of offerings as first fruits (16, in Grant 192):

Since everything we have comes from the gods, and it is just to offer to the givers first fruits of what is given, we offer first fruits of our possessions in the form of votive offerings, of our bodies in the form of hair, of our life in the form of sacrifices.

In simpler terms the concept of first fruits had wide currency in Greek religious thought, being manifested in the process of preliminary consecration and being applied at times to the parts burned on the altar. The notion of giving a part of a whole very likely gained ground. In addition to rare cases of additional parts of the victim being burned, we have noted the post-Homeric practice of putting a share of the innards on the god's statue or table and the placing of raw parts and cooked portions on sacred tables (the latter, to be sure, for use by cult personnel).

Ancient moralists, unlike Xenophon, insisted on the greater piety of the modest worshiper over the extravagant sacrificer (see Theopompus in Porphyry, *On Abstinence* 2.16; Rice and Stambaugh, 101–102). For Theophrastus a pure mind constituted the best first-fruits offering (Porphyry, *On Abstinence* 2.61). The idea that unjust behavior could be canceled by indulgence in sacrifices was rejected (Plato, *Republic* 364b). These are the dangers inherent in any system of offering and were not peculiar to Greek practice. In the structure of normal sacrifice there was no sense of a necessary, predictable outcome of the prayer and offering. Even the signs, it was recognized, might be misread. The incongruity between a man's pious offerings and the fate he might meet was spelled out in the case of the conscientious sacrificer, Hector, in our earliest text (*Iliad* 24.66–70). The process of communication by means of gift-giving was subject to the same uncertainties and errors of judgment as any other. By contrast, the powerful actions—purifications, oath sacrifices, battlefield sacrifices—as limited expressions of human concerns and as self-contained acts

were less ambiguous and conditional, and less the subject of discussion.

MODERN THEORIES

Modern interpretations of ancient ritual have naturally tended to reflect the intellectual concerns of the scholar's own time. The notions of sacrament and communion, prominent when the scholarship of religion was much concerned with Christian sacrifice, are now rarely invoked, but recent emphasis on the scapegoat is surely not unrelated to the fate of Jesus Christ. Modern interest in the origins of human behavior has looked to the practices of hunting cultures to explain the particular treatment of the sacrificial animal by the Greeks. It has been argued that guilt at killing the prey on which man depended for his sustenance and a wish to make symbolic restitution are behind the masking of the act of killing in sacrifice and the burning of the fat and bones and (in Homer) representative parts from the whole animal (*omothetein*). Survival of these attitudes are claimed for the Athenian *bouphonia* (literally, ox-murder) ritual, especially as described by that advocate of vegetarian offerings, Theophrastus (Porphyry, *On Abstinence* 2.9–10). There the ox selects itself by eating grain on the altar, and there is an elaborate passing on of the guilt for killing the ox, which is restored in the form of the hide stuffed with straw. In normal sacrifice the sprinkling of water on the victim's head, sometimes described as aimed to produce its nodding assent to being killed, the concealment of the knife in the basket of barleycorns, and the drowning out of the animal's death rattle by the women's ritual screaming are all seen as preserving "the comedy of innocence." For historical Greece, sacrifice is thought to embody and control human aggressive violence through reenactment of a ritual created by Paleolithic hunters. (The approach just outlined is best known in Burkert, 1983.)

While the question of origins must remain speculative, it is likely that attention is more profitably directed to pastoral and agricultural societies than to those of hunter-gatherers. There is room for disagreement as to how relevant the issues of human violence and its containment are to the practice of normal sacrifice and its connotations in classical Greek society, in contrast to the explicit violence of the throat-cutting *sphagia*. The *bouphonia* is a distinctive rite that by its very divergence from the norm expresses different concerns. Significantly, the victim is a plow ox, normally a prohibited victim. Explicit awareness that a norm is violated by killing a work animal rather than a food animal is certainly an ingredient in a rite that was a byword for the incomprehensibly archaic in Aristophanes' time (*Clouds* 984).

Another influential school of thought also stresses the control of violence in the act of killing and the legitimizing of the eating of meat of domestic animals. Through its associated myths sacrifice is seen to rank with marriage and agriculture as distinguishing civilized man from both beasts and gods. Careful attention to distinctions in the manner of cooking and consuming foods has thrown light on a range of categories of thought. (The approach is associated with a group of French scholars influenced by structuralism: see Detienne and Vernant; Vernant, "The Myth of Prometheus"; Vidal-Naquet). The level at which some of these conceptions operate may, however, be somewhat removed from the historical circumstances in which most Greek ritual was practiced. For that, the work of scholars who have been at pains to delineate the distinctions to be found in the performance, conception, and vocabulary of Greek ritual in general is especially valuable. (See Nock, 1972; Rudhardt, 1958; Casabona, 1966; Van Straten, 1974; 1981; Versnel, 1981.)

This essay has concentrated on sacrifice and related rituals to the neglect of the varied contexts in which they are embedded and the diverse functions the particular ceremonies and festivals as a whole could serve. (For a sense of the rich possibilities, especially on the connections between myth and ritual, see Burkert, 1970.) Finally, another fruitful dimension is that of the complex relationship between ritual and poetry. There, indeed, modern sacrificial theories, which have to some degree derived their inspiration from Greek poetry, can prove more rewarding than at the level of social history.

BIBLIOGRAPHY

SOURCES

Aeschylus, *Prometheus Bound,* David Grene, trans., in David Grene and Richmond Lattimore, eds., *The Complete Greek Tragedies,* I (1960); Frederick C. Grant, ed., *Hellenistic Religions: The Age of Syncretism* (1953); Hesiod, *The Works and Days,* Richmond Lattimore, trans. (1959); Homer, *The Iliad of Homer,* Richmond Lattimore, trans. (1977), and *The Odyssey of Homer: A Modern Translation,* Richmond Lattimore, trans. (1977); Augustus Nauck, ed., *Tragicorum Graecorum Fragmenta* (1964); Pausanias, *Description of Greece,* James G. Frazer, translation with commentary (1897; repr.1965); Porphyry, *On Abstinence from Animal Food,* Thomas Taylor, trans., Esme Wynne-Tyson, ed. (1965); David G. Rice and John E. Stambaugh, eds., *Sources for the Study of Greek Religion* (1979); Franciszek Sokolowski, *Lois sacrées de l'Asie Mineure* (1955), *Lois sacrées des cités grecques: Supplément* (1962), and *Lois sacrées des cités grecques* (1969).

STUDIES

Jan M. Bremer, "Greek Hymns," in H. S. Versnel, ed., *Faith, Hope and Worship* (1981); Walter Burkert, "Jason, Hypsipyle, and New Fire at Lemnos," in *Classical Quarterly,* **20** (1970), *Struc-*

ture and History in Greek Mythology and Ritual (1979), *Homo Necans: The Anthropology of Ancient Greek Sacrificial Ritual and Myth* (1983, orig. pub. in German, *Homo Necans* [1972]), and *Greek Religion*, John Raffan, trans. (1985; orig. pub. in German, *Griechische Religion der archaischen und klassischen Epoche*, 1977); Jean Casabona, *Recherches sur le vocabulaire des sacrifices en Grèce, des origines à la fin de l'époque classique* (1966); Marcel Detienne and Jean-Pierre Vernant, eds., *La cuisine du sacrifice en pays grec* (1979); Arthur Fairbanks, *A Handbook of Greek Religion* (1910); Helene P. Foley, *Ritual Irony: Poetry and Sacrifice in Euripides* (1985).

David Gill, S. J., "*Trapezomata:* A Neglected Aspect of Greek Sacrifice," in *Harvard Theological Review,* **67** (1974); Albert Henrichs, "Human Sacrifice in Greek Religion: Three Case Studies," in Jean Rudhardt and Olivier Reverdin, eds., *Le sacrifice dans l'antiquité* (1981), and "The 'Sobriety' of Oedipus: Sophocles *OC* 100 Misunderstood," in *Harvard Studies in Classical Philology,* **87** (1983); Michael H. Jameson, "Sophocles' *Antigone* 1005–1022: An Illustration," in Martin J. Cropp, Elaine Fantham, and S. E. Scully, eds., *Greek Tragedy and Its Legacy: Essays Presented to D. J. Conacher* (1986); Geoffrey S. Kirk, "Some Methodological Pitfalls in the Study of Ancient Greek Sacrifice (in particular)," in Jean Rudhardt and Olivier Reverdin, eds., *Le sacrifice dans l'antiquité* (1980).

Arthur Darby Nock, "The Cult of Heroes," in *Harvard Theological Review,* **37** (1944), and *Essays on Religion and the Ancient World,* II (1972); Robert Parker, *Miasma: Pollution and Purification in Early Greek Religion* (1983); W. Kendrick Pritchett, "The Military Mantike," in Pritchett, *The Greek State at War,* pt. III (1979); Jean Rudhardt, *Notions fondamentales de la pensée religieuse et actes constitutifs du culte dans la Grèce classique* (1958); Erika Simon, *Opfernde Götter* (1953); Folkert T. Van Straten, "Did the Greeks Kneel Before Their Gods?," in *Bulletin antieke Beschaving,* **49** (1974), and "Gifts for the Gods," in H. S. Versnel, ed., *Faith, Hope and Worship* (1981); Jean-Pierre Vernant, "The Myth of Prometheus in Hesiod," and "Sacrificial and Alimentary Codes in Hesiod's Myth of Prometheus," in R. L. Gordon, ed., *Myth, Religion and Society* (1981). H. S. Versnel, "Religious Mentality in Ancient Prayer," in Versnel, ed., *Faith, Hope and Worship* (1981); Pierre Vidal-Naquet, "Land and Sacrifice in the *Odyssey:* A Study of Religious and Mythical Meanings," in R. L. Gordon, ed., *Myth, Religion and Society* (1981); Ludwig Ziehen, "Opfer," in Pauly-Wissowa, *Real-encyclopädie der classischen Altertumswissenschaft,* XXXV (1939).

Sacrifice and Ritual: Rome

JOHN A. NORTH

OUR UNDERSTANDING OF ANCIENT ROMAN paganism is based very largely on accounts of ritual activities and ritual actors; only in Cicero's time do we have the beginnings of theological discussion and of debate about the existence and significance of the gods (Cicero, *On the Nature of the Gods* [*De Natura Deorum*]). There is much descriptive and visual material in the form of reliefs, coins, mosaics, and other representations, but we lack interpretations of the significance of these rituals; indeed, it is probable that such discussions never existed. There is also no substantial body of mythology associated with ritual to help the problem of interpretation; where festivals and myths are brought together, as in Ovid's *The Roman Calendar* (*Fasti*), the strong admixture of Greek literary traditions and the playfulness of Ovid's own treatment of them combine to make any interpretation problematic. Unlike the corresponding Greek rituals, Roman rituals have not recently received any profound reinterpretation; this is, no doubt, a direct consequence of having little mythology and no early literary sources to compare with Hesiod and Homer. At least in its basic

structure, Roman sacrifice is very similar to Greek, as the ancients themselves noticed (Dionysius of Halicarnassus, 7.72.15 ff.), but the similarity can justify only a cautious transferring of interpretation, since similar ritual actions may be understood quite differently in different social situations.

Responsibility for maintaining the many complicated rituals and taking decisions about ritual proprieties lay with the colleges of priests. From an early date, the different colleges seem to have had defined areas of responsibility: the augurs, for the auspices—ritual consultations of the gods before taking action; the *fetiales* for rituals of declaring war and making peace; and the *pontifices* for sacrifices, burial rites, and a wide range of other rituals. This does not mean that the priests necessarily carried out the ritual actions themselves. Normally, important rituals on the city's behalf would have been performed by the city's elected magistrates, especially the most senior of these, the consuls and praetors. However, the priests did also have ritual programs of their own; in fact, some of the fullest evidence we have concerns a set of priestly rituals, because the inscribed rec-

981

ords of one group—the Arval Brethren—survive for a long period from the beginning of the principate. The Brethren's descriptions of cult acts show a good deal of change over the years, which must mean that error, forgetfulness, or conscious amendment played their part, even when such consistent recording was going on. This is surprising because we know from other evidence that Roman tradition showed an obsessive concern that ritual should be carried out with the greatest possible accuracy. The smallest mistake in the execution of the prescribed form was understood to be fatal to the success of the whole ritual sequence; so, if the wording of a prayer went wrong, not just the prayer but the whole ceremony might have to be repeated. The repetition was technically called an *instauratio*. Again, if the consul made a minor ritual error on his way to hold the elections, the validity of the election might be challenged. It is not, of course, impossible that scrupulousness about the particular celebration should have been combined with tolerance of long-term changes in procedure, whether deliberate or accidental.

In early Rome, ritual action preceded and accompanied all everyday public and private events. In the later Rome, which we know better, there were still many different kinds of ritual performance. Some were annual festivals, governed by the ancient calendar and related to the agricultural, political, and military year; some preceded major events, such as assemblies to pass laws, meetings of the senate, campaigns and battles, the making of treaties, or the declaration of war; some happened in fulfillment of a vow taken on behalf of the city or by private persons. Family ceremonies marked the occasions of an individual's private life—birth, coming of age, marriage, death, and burial. In the republican period, though not later, an extremely important source of ritual action and ritual innovation was the regular annual

routine of dealing with prodigies (*prodigia*): the senate received reports each year from Roman Italy about events such as the birth of monsters, "blood," "milk," or "stones" raining from the sky, strange noises or lights in the heavens, and so on. These were held to show that there was some serious disruption in the right relationship between Rome and the gods. The priests advised the senate and the senate decreed appropriate ceremonial means for averting the bad effects. Not surprisingly, the most terrifying prodigies tended to be reported at times of crisis for the city, after great defeats or failures; dealing with the prodigies provided opportunities for organizing rituals of renewal and of social reconsolidation. The celebration of victory included the triumph, the famous procession through the streets of Rome, in which the general, dressed as the god Iuppiter (Jupiter), rode in a chariot through the streets of Rome to the Capitoline Hill, where he held a great sacrifice to the god.

Constant reference to the gods and goddesses by means of vows, prayers, consultations, and sacrifices should be seen as an integral part of the life of Rome; in a real sense, the Romans felt that the gods, through these rituals and consultations, participated in all the activities of the Roman state. The underlying belief was not that the gods guaranteed success, but that their help and approval were an essential precondition for any successful action. In the Roman understanding, the gods had both a claim to priority, since they were actively involved in the foundation of the city, and the power of determining whether to support an enterprise or not; but the way their interchange with men is described reveals an assumption on the part of the Romans that the gods were rational—even legalistic—in their mentality. They demanded piety, constant care and attention, and the scrupulous fulfillment of any obligations accepted. But in negotiations and ritual dealings, they accepted a role in which men—priests or magistrates—could to a great extent determine and define the terms of the deal. This assumption did not involve impiety or cynicism, but simply reflected the belief that the gods were not remote and beyond human comprehension; they were part of the rational community of which the city consisted, and for which senate and people, magistrates and priests were together responsible.

THE CALENDAR AND THE LUPERCALIA

The richest of all our sources of knowledge about these rituals is the Roman religious calendar, of which copies survive from various parts of Roman Italy, put up mostly in the time of Augustus. One of these copies, coming from Praeneste (Palestrina) in Latium, contains notes on the festivals, derived from the work of the Augustan antiquarian Verrius Flaccus. From this religious calendar, together with Ovid's *The Roman Calendar* (providing a commentary on the festivals of the first six months of the year), ancient dictionaries, and commentaries on such texts as Vergil's *Aeneid,* as well as the vituperative comments of Christians such as Arnobius, it is possible to put together a great deal of information deriving from the learned antiquarians of the first century B.C., on whose work all these sources ultimately depended. A striking feature of this tradition is the degree of variation to be found in the interpretation and even the reporting of the rituals of annual festivals. This has sometimes been thought to suggest that, by the time of these antiquarian writers, the true meaning of the ritual actions had been forgotten; and it is true that, in a few cases at least, the Romans had forgotten all but the actions to be performed or the words to be recited. But forgetfulness is not necessarily the key. To assess the question it will be

helpful to consider in some detail one of the festivals whose ritual program is relatively well known, although highly controversial—the Lupercalia festival of 15 February.

The festival was led by the Luperci, special priests divided into two groups; they met at a sacred cave at the foot of the Palatine, called the Lupercal; there they held a sacrifice of goats and (unusually) a dog. The blood from these sacrifices was wiped from the knife onto the foreheads of two of the Luperci and then cleaned off again with some wool dipped in milk, and the two at this point gave a laugh. There was a great feast and afterward the Luperci, dressed only in loincloths that they made from the skins of the sacrificial goats, ran through the streets in a circuit beginning and ending at the Lupercal. As they ran, they struck at the spectators with leather strips, also made from the skins of the slain goats. The name of the priests suggests *lupus* (wolf) and a possible interpretation is that the purpose was to guard the flocks of the early community from wolves; but our sources seem rather to suggest that this is either a purification ritual or one promoting the fertility of the women. Both these views can be supported by elements of the ritual, because women struck by the running Luperci were supposed to be made fertile, while the blood ritual and the running of the circuit both suggest the warding off of dangers or of polluting influences. February was a month of purification, and the leather strips themselves were called *februae*, instruments of purification. Part at least of the route ran through the valley between the early hill settlements, originally used as a cemetery, so perhaps protection from the power of the dead was at least one of the objectives.

There is, however, still another side to be considered. Our reports and explanations of the rituals offer many connections with the story of the Roman founders, the twins Romulus and Remus (Livy, 1.3 ff.). Each of the two groups of Luperci was connected with one of the founders; the Lupercal was said to be the very place where the she-wolf nursed the abandoned twins; and the ritual laughter was explained by a story of a competition between the twins and their followers, of which the running through the streets would have been a survival. Since Romulus, Remus, and their followers were herdsmen, it would not be surprising if the ritual were concerned both with the goats and with the protection of the flocks—and the whole community—from wolves. Yet another layer of meaning seems to be evoked by the most famous historical celebration of the Lupercalia on 15 February 44 B.C.—a scene familiar from Shakespeare's version of it. Julius Caesar had had a new group of Luperci added to the traditional two, to be called after his own family, the Luperci Julii; the leader of this group was Marcus Antonius and, while running the circuit, he broke away to offer the crown of Rome to Caesar—who refused it. There can be no doubt that the connection with the foundation myth and with Romulus as the first king of Rome must have been in the minds of those who arranged this incident; Caesar was, after all, joining with the founders, and only the founders, in having Luperci set up in his honor. But Antonius, and presumably Caesar, must have felt that this was the right context for devising the coronation ritual that Rome so obviously lacked.

In many ways, the Lupercalia festival is characteristic of Roman rituals. First, it is strongly connected with a specific place in Rome and with a specific historical—or pseudohistorical—tradition. The ritual has the function of marking out the place and recalling the tradition, thus annually reaffirming the importance of the link; the Romans themselves were in fact well aware of the importance of Rome the city in their religious life (Livy, 5.51 ff.—the speech of Camillus). It does not matter for this purpose whether the story of Romulus and the Lupercal is one of the most ancient parts of the ritual; it quite probably is not, for the second important characteristic of Roman ritual is its capacity to take on new levels of meaning as new situations arise. There is no need in the case of the Lupercalia to seek out the "original" or "true" meaning—just as there is no hope of finding it. It is precisely because of the shortage of fixed theology or doctrines that ritual programs can adjust themselves—through omitting, adding, misunderstanding, and reinterpreting—to new conditions of life.

THE RITUAL OF SACRIFICE

In almost all these festivals and ceremonies, the central ritual was the sacrifice of an animal. The act of sacrifice was also the most familiar representation of religious life on reliefs and in mosaics, so that even the ritual instruments—the axes, knives, bowls, and sprinklers—were used as decorative elements in relief sculpture. The sacrifice itself involved a ritual program of some complexity; modern interpretations have tended to be determined by the degree of emphasis placed on the various stages. The ceremony opened with a procession in which the victim or victims, decorated for death, had to come willingly to the altar, placed generally outside a temple. The victim was then sanctified by a sprinkling of meal and wine (the ritual was called *immolatio*), and a prayer (*precatio*) was offered to the god or goddess to whom the sacrifice was to be made, always naming the divine recipient. At some point in the sequence, incense was sprinkled onto a fire—this is the most familiar scene in the reliefs. The actual killing was not done by a priest or magistrate, but by special assistants; death had to be cleanly and swiftly achieved by an ax or knife at the neck, or both together. The death of the victim was not the end of the matter, although it is the last scene commonly represented. The carcass was butchered into specified cuts. The entrails received special attention. They were examined for signs by specialist priests called "haruspices," who might report that the god or goddess had not found the victim acceptable. If the victim did pass this examination, the meat was cooked, certain cuts were offered to the god, and the rest of the meat was made available for a feast for worshipers and priests.

From beginning to end, the sacrificial rite was bound by rules and traditions that fixed every step of the procedure. The choice of victim, its preparation, and the slaughtering, butchering, and cooking were all traditional activities calling for knowledge and skills without which no successful offering could be made. The victims had to be of high quality; they had to be of a particular color for the type of deity; they had to be of the same sex as the receiving deity; sometimes their age was specified; and some deities required a particular species of victim. There were special instruments with special names used in the ceremonial; and there was a special vocabulary for the cuts of meat, not used otherwise. We know a good deal about all these from Arnobius of Sicca, who was apparently writing not long after his conversion from paganism and who makes great fun of these obscure and, to him, revolting details (Arnobius, *Against the Gentiles* [*Adversus Gentes*] 7).

The success of the sacrifice could not be guaranteed in advance. Indeed, the procedure might go wrong at every stage. If the victim resisted, let alone escaped, before being brought to the altar, that would be a disastrous omen. The same applied to other mistakes in the course of the ritual. At the stage of the extispicy, it was not unusual for the victim to be rejected on the inspection of the entrails by the haruspices; we are told of various defects of the internal organs that could lead to rejection—the liver sometimes dissolved in a loathsome flux, or no heart could be found at all. If the first victim failed

to reach the completion of the ritual (called *litatio*), then more victims had to be sacrificed until the deity had found one acceptable. If this state of acceptance (*perlitatio*) could not be reached, then it would be dangerous to proceed to action. After defeat, it was sometimes rumored or conjectured that *perlitatio* had never been attained by the commanding magistrate (Livy, 41.15).

At one level of interpretation, it is not too difficult to analyze what was happening in this sequence of ritual actions. Routes of communication between humans and deities were evidently opened up by the ritual sequence itself: humans were using prayer to send specific messages to specific deities; the deities replied through the vital organs examined in the extispicy or through the failure or success of the whole ritual process, including the presentation of the victim, the recitation of the prayers, the act of killing, the handing over of the divine share, and so on. The basic material of the ritual consisted of elements of human diet: the victims were almost, but not quite, always domestic animals (sheep, cattle, pigs, goats); the ritual of sanctification—the *immolatio*—used cereal and wine; the later stages consisted of cooking the raw meat and feasting. A sharp division is made between the portions humans can eat and the portions presented to the deity. So it can be said, as in the parallel Greek case, that the ritual (at a deep level, not necessarily that of the awareness of the participants) identified what it was to be human in terms of human diet and created boundaries between man and beast on the one hand, and man and god on the other. It is significant that the arrival of a ruler cult, challenging precisely this boundary between men and gods, posed problems in terms of ritual expression, which had to be negotiated in one way or another by worshipers in the different parts of the empire.

The evidence of relief sculpture from the great monuments of Rome and of provincial cities gives us another view of the meaning of the sacrificial ritual. Various different moments are selected—the procession to the altar, the moment before the fatal blow was struck, the moment at which the sacrificer sprinkled incense on the altar, and (though only very occasionally) the moment of the reading of the entrails. Frequently, the scene is a composite, with elements from the different stages forming a timeless mosaic of the action. The ceremonial is often represented in loving detail, including the knives and axes, the priestly vestments, and the decoration of the victim. The different classes of participant are strongly differentiated. The slave assistants (who do the actual work of killing, butchering, and cooking) are naked from the waist up, while the nobles, whether sacrificer or onlookers, wear togas or priestly dress. Above all, attention is focused on the figure of the sacrificer—most frequently, from Augustus onward, the emperor himself. In other words, the representation of sacrifice is used to display social differentiation and to create an image of the power of the main symbolic actor. It is deeply significant that the practice of sacrifice and hence the power of this image existed almost throughout the empire. Even the Jews accepted sacrifice in principle; only the Christians completely rejected it.

BIBLIOGRAPHY

SOURCES

Arnobius, *Against the Gentiles* (*Adversus Gentes*), Archibald Hamilton Bryce and Hugh Campbell, trans. (1871); Attilio Degrassi, *Fasti Anni Numani* (*Calendar of the Year of King Numa*)—*Inscriptiones Italiae* XIII, Fasti et Elogia, fasc. 2 (1963), the basic publication of the calendars; Dionysius of Halicarnassus, *The Roman Antiquities of Dionysius of Halicarnassus*, Earnest Cary, trans. (1943); Frederick Clifton Grant, *Ancient Roman Religion* (1957), a collection of translated sources; Wilhelm Henzen, *Acta Fratrum Arvalium* (*Minutes of the Arvalian Brothers*) (1874), part trans. Grant, *op. cit.* 233–238; Livy, *History of Rome*, Books I–V, Aubrey De Selincourt, trans. (1965; 2d ed. 1971), informative commentary by R. Ogilvie; Ovid, *Fasti* (*The Roman Calendar*), Sir James George Frazer, trans. (1929).

STUDIES

Raymond Bloch, *Les prodiges dans l'antiquité classique* (1963); Georges Dumézil, *Archaic Roman Religion*, Philip Krapp, trans. (1970); William Warde Fowler, *The Roman Festivals of the Period of the Republic* (1899); Marcel Detienne, *Myth, Religion, and Society*, Richard L. Gordon, ed. (1981); Michael Grant, *Roman Myths* (1971; rev. ed. 1973); Kurt Latte, *Römische Religionsgeschichte* (1960); Bruce MacBain, *Prodigy and Expiation* (1982); John A. North, "Conservatism and Change in Roman Religion," in *Papers of the British School at Rome*, **44** (1976); Simon R. F. Price, "Between Man and God: Sacrifice in the Roman Imperial Cult," in *Journal of Roman Studies*, **70** (1980); Jean Rudhardt, Olivier Reverdin, eds., *Le sacrifice dans l'antiquité* (1981); Inez Scott Rybert, *Rites of the State Religion in Roman Art* (1955); John Scheid, *Religion et piété à Rome* (1985); Howard Hayes Scullard, *Festivals and Ceremonies of the Roman Republic* (1981); Christoph Ulf, *Das römische Lupercalienfest* (1982); H. S. Versnel, *Triumphus* (1970); Stefan Weinstock, *Divus Julius* (1971); Georg Wissowa, *Religion und Kultus der Römer* (1902; 2d ed. 1912; repr. 1971).

The Afterlife: Greece

EMILY VERMEULE

INTRODUCTION

Greek ideas about what happens to the human self after death were based on myths, as in all cultures. Myths about the afterlife were not primarily religious, in the strict sense, in the earliest phases of Greek belief as recounted in literature. Religion and ethical and social principles guarded the dead body rather than the soul, which were usually distinguished as *soma* and *psyche.* The soul was on its own, after death, far away and difficult to recall by grief or prayer. A remembered image of it, or of the animated body, the *eidolon,* might visit a sleeping mourner in dreams, usually to announce that it would never come again. The main cause for repeated appearances from the world of the dead into the sleeping consciousness of the living was some religious failure in the matter of burial. An improper or incomplete burial did not release the soul from the living community completely enough to allow it to join fully with the community of the dead. There was a barrier between the two worlds, usually thought of as dark water: a river, sometimes Acheron, or a reed-surrounded lake. The barrier was almost impossible for the soul of the dead one to cross under its own powers, which were severely diminished in death; it needed a soul guide (*psychopompos*) toward the unknown world of the dead, usually Hermes, and an aid, who was in later Greek thought to be the ferryman Charon, for the physical crossing.

These common ideas about what the Greeks believed in matters of life and death are distilled from many kinds of unequal evidence. It is most unlikely that any two Greeks actually had exactly the same ideas about an afterlife. There were sets of conventional ideas, expressed for many by the best poets. The poetry of the Homeric epic songs was particularly influential, but the Homeric picture of the afterlife was modified many times by later poets, and eventually by prose writers, priests concerned with the "mystery" religions, oracular centers and powers, and some influence from adopted foreign cults. The early epic idea of equal, grim death for everyone was modified, especially in the sixth to fourth centuries B.C., in favor of the possibility of

987

personal immortality for those few selected for virtue or for participation in a closed sect. The threads of all these ideas and hopes are difficult to follow because they received unequal expressions in surviving writings; they seldom match the more mute but undeniable evidence from graves and tombs.

THE EPIC

Ideas of the afterlife are clear and consistent in the early epic songs. However, it should be stressed that the Homeric poems evolved over a great number of centuries before they were fixed in writing, and the older *Iliad* does not in all respects match the younger *Odyssey*. The older poem seems, from our limited perspective, to be less given to individual creative and decorative flourishes, and to express more accurately a general set of early beliefs. Still, since there is in the region of about one thousand years of poetic development within the *Iliad* itself, full consistency should not be expected. The *Odyssey* contributes the two unusual but influential visits to the underworld, the *nekyiai*, of books eleven and twenty-four, which are so picturesque as to be unforgettable once heard or read, but which may not match normal ideas.

The Epic Cycle, the set of poems about the prelude to the Trojan Wars, the fates of Troy, and the returns of the heroes from Troy, are less concerned with metaphysical speculation about the forms of the afterlife than they are with the poignant or romantic deaths of individuals, and the mourning surrounding their passing; they provide less insight into Greek beliefs in general.

At the start of the *Iliad*, the poet celebrates the many Achaean heroes whose "powerful souls" were sent to Hades by the anger of Achilles, while their "selves" (*autoi*) became a "snatching" for dogs and birds of all kinds (1.3–4). These verses, peculiar as they are, set the dichotomy between body and soul with deliberate grandeur at the head of the greatest of all Greek poems. The *Iliad* is far more a poem about death, dying, mourning, and loss than it is about the afterlife, but a vision of the afterlife must stand in severe understanding behind all the manipulations of wounded, broken, and abandoned bodies. The distinction between the soul (*psyche*) and the self (*autos*) is odd enough by later religious standards, but it is indeed the way most Greeks incline, toward the fastidious and respectful treatment of the corpse rather than toward fancies of the released and now happier animating breath or life principle. The condition of the soul after separation from the body was weak and fatigued, and its surroundings in Hades generally dark and unattractive. If one tries to create consistent belief from the various formulas of the *Iliad* one must suppose that the adjective "powerful" applied to souls is an epithet transferred from the moment of full warrior power in the last fight, before accident of spear or sword broke the power and created the soul as a separate entity. Souls in collective groups in the underworld are normally thought of as "strengthless heads" (*amenena karena*) in which even the powers of individual recollection were gone. Neither *psyche* nor *eidolon* has wits (*phrenes*), although it can wail and even shed tears (*muretai*), from some mysterious nonphysical source.

The appearance of a dead soul to the living is classically presented in *Iliad* (23.65 ff.) when, as Achilles falls in exhausted sleep on the shore at Troy, grieving for his dead companion Patroklos, the *psyche* of Patroklos visits him, "like himself in every way, in size and fine eyes and voice and with similar clothing about his flesh." This strange passage, much imitated in later literature, illustrates the difficulty in using human language to describe those incompletely dead. In most other Homeric passages the escape of the *psyche* from the body is a parallel phenomenon to the mist of darkness, or death, shed over the eyes, the extinction of the power of sight and insight, the light from within the eye that illumines the outer world. But in this visitation during sleep by a remembered and beloved image, there is still some lingering power, to speak and see, to accuse ("You forget me, Achilles"), and to want—a touch of the hand (23.75), and even a sense that the bones of the dead will be lonely if not buried in one urn with the bones of the friend.

This kind of endowment of the soul with a temporary body for the purposes of poetic vision is repeated at various intervals in Greek writing; it is not logical, but poetically and imaginatively necessary for the successful creation of an illusory scene. So the dead Elpenor appears to Odysseus without his body, his *soma*, which was left unburied back at Circe's house (*Odyssey* 11.51–78). The bodiless *psyche* certainly has the power to speak, although the body itself had broken its neck in a drunken fall from the rooftop; it has the necessary and now perhaps traditional errand to warn the living to take proper care of the body, still in an incomplete transition. Both Patroklos and Elpenor allude to the closed society of the dead, and complain how the *psychai* of the dead whose transitions have been completed keep them at a distance, and do not permit them to cross the river or enter the gates of Hades while they are still sensed to have an aura of life, or at least of unburial, about them. A purist might wonder about the aspect of clothing, left presumably upon the body but also appearing on the dead vision; this must be only a poetic extension of the universal and deeply held compulsion to cover the dead, not to expose them to humiliation or ridicule in their helpless nakedness. Throughout the history of such fictions, most ghosts are clothed. The poet of the *Odyssey* also imagines the shades of the dead

as appearing as they were at the moment of death: "Marriageable maidens and much-enduring old men . . . and many wounded with bronze spears, and war-killed men holding their bloodied armor" (11.38–41), a morbid fancy later elaborated in Bacchylides' vision (5.71–84) of the dead Meleager in the underworld, shining in bronze armor among the dead, still able to recognize the living intruder Herakles come to fetch Cerberus, the hound of death.

TOPOGRAPHY OF THE UNDERWORLD

Many children have been brought up on Bulfinch's *Mythology*, where, in the chapter called "The Infernal Regions," a clear account is given of Vergil's vision of the Other World. There is the mysterious cave of the Sibyl in a gloomy forest, where the Lake Avernus lies, its surface covered with mephitic vapors, and, on the threshold of Hell, an intrepid hero like Aeneas might meet the abstract evils and terrors of the world: Grief, Age, Disease, Fear, Hunger, Poverty, Death. Monsters—hydras and chimeras—guard the entrance, while the boatman Charon plies a brisk trade upon the black waters of the river Kokytos. Beyond, the three-headed, snake-haired hound Cerberus guards the landing, but succumbs easily to a sweet medicated cake. Farther still, Minos, king of Crete, now a judge in the underworld, waits to examine the deeds of the dead. Beyond, again, lie the fields where the heroes of the Trojan War wander and reminisce. There is a division between the regions of the condemned and Elysium, and walls of a mighty city where Phlegethon rolls its fiery waters, a gate of adamant, and an iron tower where an avenging fury keeps guard with a scorpion whip. From the city rise groans and the sound of the scourge, the creaking of iron and clanking of chains, where the judge Rhadamanthys holds examination of the wicked, and assigns punishments. The gulfs of Tartaros stretch deep beneath the brazen gates, as far beneath earth as heaven is above, and there the immortal sinners lie—Tityos and Ixion and Tantalos and Sisyphos, all in peculiarly fitting torments. But, in the Elysian Fields, a balancing group of happy souls plays games, dances and sings and exercises—exercises what, one wonders?—while Orpheus plucks chords from his lyre, and heroes fallen for their country, or poets and priests and artists rejoice. There is also the river Lethe, Forgetfulness, where souls can be returned to earth to make lives of increasing purity, as animals or insects.

This lurid and overblown Roman account probably could not have been given in those particular morbid tones by any Greek but Plato, and it is only partly a scene of Greek imagination. It is, of course, the basis for many of the later conventions, and follows the *nekyiai* of the *Odyssey* in many particulars: the crossing of water, the infant and wounded shades, the meadow of heroes, the embodied souls that can bleed and sweat and groan, feast and game and sing. The concern for judgment and punishment is rather late in taking a firm hold on general Greek consciousness, and it is not, perhaps, until means of obtaining justice above ground are too often despaired of that rewards in another life are promised as the ultimate hope.

Minos is already a sceptered judge in the *Odyssey* (11.568), seated among the dead; the old Egyptian and Near Eastern image of the enthroned ruler may be part of this conception, like the Egyptian judgment of the soul. Aiakos and Rhadamanthys join him to form a triad of judges—perhaps because of other triads, such as the Hours (Seasons), Graces, or because of the supreme Olympian triad, Zeus/Sky–Poseidon/Ocean–Hades/Underworld. This group, two princes of Crete and one from the island world of Aigina, ought to have old Bronze Age associations, although the literary testimonies for their review of the deeds of souls are not common before the fifth century B.C., nor is the whole concept of the guilty but purifiable soul common before the spread of Pythagorean beliefs in the sixth century. The most familiar passages are in Plato but Pindar, earlier, had praised the upright judgments of Aiakos and Rhadamanthys (*Olympian* 2.75; 8.31; *Pythian* 2.73; *Isthmian* 8.25).

Cerberus was a highly popular jagged-toothed guardian hound of the gates of Hades, or the porch of his hall, from the sixth century on in Greek painting, and was celebrated earlier by Hesiod (*Theogony* 311, 769). Underworlds are always gated and guarded, in Egypt, Sumer, and Babylon as in Greece, and the fanged swallower is a proper warden considering the close association with dogs and dead bodies from the start of the *Iliad,* and in early Greek art as well. His popularity stems partly from the pleasure painters took in designing his two or three heads, sprouting snakes.

THE KING AND QUEEN OF THE DEAD

Hades is pervasive in the *Iliad.* A dead hero enters his "house" or his "gates," but beyond this sense of place, like a royal palace in a walled town of the Bronze Age, there is little picturesque description, since the older Homeric poets do not think of the afterlife in lingering or positive terms.

Hades is one of the three great gods, with Zeus and Poseidon; in the triple division of immortals in the upper air, mortals on earth, and the dead below, he has the most subjects. He is cast in the form of a Bronze Age king or warrior, a man famed for horses and horsemanship, a charioteer, yet without family or descendants apart from the queen he stole from earth, Persephone. The kingdom of Hades is distinct from the prison of Tartaros, windy and deep, where rebellious immortals are locked away behind a triple bronze door so they can no longer threaten the orderliness of Olympian rule (Hesiod, *Theogony* 807 ff.). Hades is not a killer, never emerging from his misty kingdom except to win a wife or, once, wounded by Herakles, to travel to Olympus to seek healing (for the dead do not heal any more than they generate or grow crops, in the older Greek view). Persephone is released (as most of the dead are not) to her mother, or to the earth and sunlight, only on partial terms, and must always return to the dark. The actual agent of death is Thanatos, a darkness.

THE ARCHAIC PERIOD

The lyric poets of the sixth century B.C. often used death as a decorative device to reflect on the fleeting quality of life and on its miseries, whether from lack of love or of other sustenance. Because the word *thnetoi* (mortals)—derived from *thanatos,* referring to death-and-darkness—is commonly used for all human beings, the presence of mortality is close behind all the archaic texts, but the destination of the dead is not often considered. The didactic elegiac poets stress how good it is to die defending one's polis, wounded in front, as a brave fighter, not behind as a fleeing coward, and how such a man may be immortal even when he is "under earth" (Tyrtaios, 9.32); this immortality is conferred by fame, reputation among friends, in the city, and among poets. This *kleos* (undying fame) is the verbal and memorial intellectual equivalent to the *tumbos* (grave mound) erected by mourning family and friends. Sappho speaks derisively to a rival poet about her future—invisible, fluttering among the dark dead in Hades, with no memory of or longing for her on the earth above (58d).

Even the great Homeric *Hymn to Demeter,* the model poem for the founding of the mystery cult at Eleusis, does not express a real belief in a better afterlife for initiates in the cult. There are unfulfilled routes toward immortality in the poem, as when Demeter annoints the baby Demophoön with ambrosia, like a god's child, and holds him in the fire by night; she would have made him "deathless and unaging" had not his mother with mortal foolishness interfered (236–247). This is an old common wish and fantasy, as heroes at Troy can say "if we could be unaging and deathless forever" (*Iliad* 12.323), as an expression of hopelessness. Belief in the actual attainment of immortality came later. There is only a veiled promise, at the end of the *Hymn,* that initiates in the mysteries become *olbioi* (blessed ones), while the uninitiated do not have the lot of "like things" under the misty darkness (479–482). The release of Persephone for two-thirds of the year from that darkness into the sunlight on earth is, however, a pervading gleam of generalized hope for devotees of the fertility cult.

In the late sixth century two important but obscure intellectual movements, called, respectively, after the naturalist and astronomer Pythagoras of Samos and the mythic poet Orpheus, began to create among small groups of followers a belief that one's soul might not entirely die when separated from one's body. Early writings are not attested for either of these sects. Pythagoras seems to have thought that the soul is somehow divine, and so immortal, but has been condemned for faults in purity to be locked into a body, as in a prison, of man, animal, or plant. The early poetic anecdote that attests to his belief in metempsychosis has the philosopher stop a man from beating a dog, because he recognized the voice of a friend in the howling (Xenophanes frag. 6 Diels). The soul could eventually be released from its cycle of imprisonment by a discipline of purity and self-criticism.

Orphic literature, of which little that is accurate is known, discussed the probable origin of the world and the gods, a cosmogony, and the nature of man. Its view of the latter, like that of Pythagoreanism, seemed to regard the body as a prison (*soma, sema*) and the soul as a divine spark derived, mythically, when the ancient Titans ate the royal god-child Dionysos and were struck by lightning from Zeus; man was modeled out of those ashes. Man thus contained evil titanic flesh encasing a morsel of dionysiac divinity, and consequently immortality. By discipline and abstinence, especially from eating murdered animals, the evil elements might be purged and the divine soul eventually released from the cycles of metempsychosis. (What happens to it on release, whether it joins the air, or is protected in a favored part of the underworld, is uncertain.) From the fourth century onward a series of thin hammered gold tablets was buried with members of the sect, instructing them in the protocol of approaching the underworld. The instructions usually included a topographic guide mentioning a spring with a white cypress by it, where the soul must not drink (the spring would be Lethe, causing forgetfulness of everything learned in the long course of existence); they should pass on to the river of Memory, Mnemosyne, and explain to the "guards" that they are children of earth and starry night, an ancient divine ancestry.

Both Pythagoras and Orpheus valued a system of judges and judgments in the underworld, in the belief that justice would be done at least for those who had tried to be pure and disciplined on earth, once or often. Punishment for the wicked is either corporeal (whips, starvation, labor, torture) or condemnation to life for another cycle.

Plato in the fourth century offers the most elaborated beliefs about the immortality of the soul (*Apology* 40–41; *Phaedrus* 245–250; *Gorgias* 493, 523–527; *Phaedo* 66–70, 79–80, 107–114; *Republic* 10.614 ff.). His myths and images perhaps seem innovative to us but were in fact absolutely traditional, since even the dimmest and grimmest Homeric *psyche* was immortal in its stay in Hades, that immortality conferred particularly on fictitious characters (Agamemnon, Ajax, Achilles) by the poet. Those heroic models for dead souls must have affected beliefs about the *psychai* of ordinary people; the *psyche* could never be lost from Hades, even though the names of individuals might be forgotten with the passage of time unless written firmly on an enduring tombstone. Plato's imaginative accounts of the judgment of deeds in the underworld is not different in kind from the statements in *Odyssey* 11, only enlarged with extra judges like "Triptolemos [the fertility deity of grain] and other sons of god" (*Apology* 41a). Plato shares the *Odyssey* poet's inconsistencies about the inability of the soul to remember anything or speak unless "enlivened" with sacrificial blood or libations; yet it is freely able to converse and answer questions of any inquiring soul like Socrates who might have newly joined the community of the dead (*Apology* 40). In the myth of Er the Pamphylian, left for dead ten days on the battlefield and only recalled to the land of the living on his funeral pyre on the twelfth day, there is a typical *nekyia* or account of a visit to the underworld. It offers imaginative detail (*Republic* 10.614 ff.), including wild men of fiery aspect who keep sinners from escaping the jagged, mysteriously roaring mouth of hell, and who inflict bodily punishment: binding, flaying, dragging, carding. These are the first servant-devils for the Greeks, figures who had long been acknowledged in Egypt and the East. The idea of inflicting bodily punishment on a naked, that is, bodiless soul, starting in the *Odyssey*, is elaborated in Plato and will continue in most imaginative versions of the afterlife.

In later times visits to the underworld could be arranged routinely for the living, either through consulting the shades of the dead in a dramatic setting like the Nekyomanteion in Epirus or the physical descent into a chasm connected to the underworld as in the oracle of Trophonios at Lebadeia (Livadia) in Boeotia. Such visits are vividly mimicked in the *Frogs* of the Athenian comic dramatist Aristophanes.

PARADISE

From at least the time of the *Odyssey* and the poet Hesiod, in the late eighth or early seventh centuries B.C., there was a sporadic belief that certain favored heroes—and later, ordinary people—would not wander in the desolate dark of Hades but could be mysteriously translated to the Isles of the Blessed somewhere off in Ocean. In the *Odyssey* (4.561–569), this special fate is promised to Menelaos because he has married Helen, the daughter of Zeus, and is son-in-law to the sky god and chief Olympian. The poet does not specify that Helen shall join him there, for the afterlives of women and children were never of much concern to Greek storytellers. The magical place is called Elysion (*Elusion pedion*) at the ends of earth, where blond Rhadamanthys already is, and where "means of life" are easy to procure in a place where there is no snow, "not much winter," and never any rain. The odd title Elysium is not used again until the third-century B.C. poet Apollonius of Rhodes revived it; his verses are throughout much influenced by the *Odyssey*. The more normal expression "Isles of the Blessed" (*Nesoi Makaron*) appears first in Hesiod's account of the generations of man (*Works and Days* 170 ff.); the heroes are translated there, "and they live with no sorrow on their spirit in the islands of the blessed beside the deeply swirling ocean, prosperous heroes for whom the grain-giving field bears honey-hearted harvest ripening three times a year." The emphasis on plentiful food and lack of labor in getting it seems strongly affected by Egyptian ideas of the Ialu Fields, or Field of Reeds, where the dead thrive in eternal sunshine and pleasant breezes, eating, drinking, making love, sleeping and waking, the latter so important when death is viewed as a form of sleep from which there is no waking. In the fifth century B.C. the poet Pindar elaborated the scene, in a weatherless world of equal nights and days, with water and trees and gold blossoms (*Olympian* 2.61–74, for a prince of Sicily, where such eschatological ideas were old and strong). In his *Songs of Mourning* (*Threnoi*) Pindar paints a meadow red with roses under sunshine, fruit trees, where the blessed dead achieve happy prosperity with sports (wrestling, horses) and music, enjoying the fragrance of sacrifice to the gods. For wicked souls, by contrast, there are rivers of darkness and a pit of death (frag. 129–130 Snell).

The belief in a happy aftermath to death, originally restricted to divine relatives and heroes, eventually expanded to include other virtuous and religious persons who escaped eternal darkness by membership in a mystery cult, by "living the good life" through philosophy or by purgation of wicked deeds in the cycles of metempsychosis.

FUNERALS AND TOMBS

The most elaborate funeral in Greek literature (until Alexander the Great's imitative funeral for his friend Hephaistion) was the funeral of Patroklos in *Iliad* 23. The battlefield circumstances and poetic desires both made it unusual, but the underlying routine is not markedly different from ordinary practice, since every funeral requires certain technical observances and ritual behavior. Patroklos was cremated; cremation and inhumation alternate at various periods in Greek history, and eventually family members could choose the mode; the rest of the ceremonial procedure seemed not to change much from one rite to the other.

Achilles and his followers the Myrmidons drive their chariots three times around the corpse (which has been washed and anointed and clothed in shroud and mantle), mourning and weeping in the formal funeral lament (*goos*). In the evening large numbers of cattle, sheep, and goats are slaughtered and burned, in a funeral banquet, and the blood runs freely about the body. At dawn wood is collected from every quarter of the hills and brought to the camp by mules. The soldiers dress themselves in bronze and yoke the chariots, which lead a large funeral procession, followed by foot soldiers carrying the corpse, with Achilles holding the head. (In many classical funerals there was a special horse-drawn carriage with the bier.) The mourners cut off locks of their hair and cast them on the body. The huge pyre is built in an open space, cattle are slaughtered and skinned, the corpse is covered by their fat and the animal bodies are laid close by. The chief mourner sets jars of honey and unguent tilted against the bed of the corpse at the top of the pyre. Unusually, four horses, two pet dogs, and twelve young Trojans of good family are added to the sacrifice. Achilles makes a libation to the winds to light the pyre, which burns all night while he makes libations of wine to the psyche of Patroklos from a gold mixing bowl. At dawn, when the pyre has blackened and the flame died away, it is drenched with wine; the bones are carefully collected separately from the bones of the sacrifices, set in a gold jar, and covered with fat; and an earth tumulus is heaped up over all.

A normal classical funeral followed similar though less extravagant steps. The body was washed and anointed in olive oil, wrapped from head to foot in a cloth and covered with another cloth. It lay on a couch with pillows, the eyes closed, the chin tightened with a band, and the feet often pointed toward the door, facing the journey to the cemetery. The house itself was cleaned and hung with wreaths and sprays of leaves: marjoram, celery, laurel, and myrtle were favored. The family and clan held the vigil wake (*prothesis*) over the body, and sang the mourning song, the *goos,* declaring love and loss. The burial took place at night, with a chariot procession and foot mourners in early days, the bier on a cart or a coffin carried on the shoulders for the carrying-forth (*ekphora*). Before dawn the grave was closed and a mound heaped up. There was usually a grave marker, sometimes a large vase, from the sixth century onward often a stone stela or even a statue in the round. The body was felt to dwell in the grave or the gravestone, which often spoke in the first person to passersby, announcing the name of the dead and his father, and inviting contemplation or pity. In many cemeteries, usually outside the walls of towns, there were family plots and burials over several generations. The tomb would be visited on anniversaries and other occasions of grief and hung with wreaths and fillets; offerings of cakes or oil were brought and left at the stone. Fifth- and fourth-century stones were often carved to suggest the immanent indwelling nature of the dead, who greeted the visitor with handclasp or serious glance and unperturbed face.

HERO CULT

In early Greek history, especially in the ninth and eighth centuries B.C., in a number of places grave gifts were brought to tombs of the Bronze Age dead, and a small hero cult established. The recipients of such cult might be nameless, the Hero; or mythological, Aktaion; or obscure, Akademos. The choice of a tomb as a place to link the present to the past was a natural one. Occasionally cults of the dead were established not at tombs but at the places they were thought to have died, like the cult of Menelaos' helmsman Phrontis at Sounion. The spirit of the dead might be perceived as angry and needing to be placated, or as beneficial, approving new owners of the land, or defending the state boundaries in time of war, like Oedipus at Colonus. Some cult tombs were thought to be oracular, like the chasm of the seer Amphiaraos.

On the whole, the Greeks were serious and witty, picturesque and thoughtful, about the processes of death, the separation of the dead from the social context, the passage to another world, and the possibility of communication between the living and the dead. Their ideas perhaps owed something to older cultures; ours owe much to them, for the ideas they encoded in myths, visions, and practice stand ancestrally to our own, and their landscapes of the underworld and thoughts about body and soul have never been more grandly expressed.

BIBLIOGRAPHY

STUDIES

Herbert Abramson, "A Hero Shrine for Phrontis at Sounion?" in *California Studies in Classical Antiquity*, **12** (1979); G. Ahlberg, *Prothesis and Ekphora* (1973); Margaret Alexiou, *The Ritual Lament in Greek Tradition* (1974); Manolis Andronikos, *Totenkult, Archaeologica Homerica* Band. III, Kapitel W (1968); E. Bickel, *Homerischer Seelenglaube* (1925); E. Bruck, "Totenteil und Seelgerät im griechischen Recht," in *Münchener Beiträge zur Papyrusforschung*, **9** (1926); Walter Burkert, "Elysion," in *Glotta*, **39** (1960), *Lore and Science in Ancient Pythagoreanism* (1972), "Le laminette auree," in *Orfismo in Magna Grecia* (1975), "Tote, Heroen, und Chthonische Götter," and "Mysterien und Askese," in *Griechische Religion der archäischen und klassischen Epoche* (1977), and *Homo Necans: The Anthropology of Ancient Greek Sacrificial Ritual and Myth*, Peter Bing, trans. (1983).

J. Nicholas Coldstream, "Hero-cults in the Age of Homer," in *Journal of Hellenic Studies*, **96** (1976); Susan G. Cole, "New Evidence for the Mysteries of Dionysos," in *Greek, Roman, and Byzantine Studies*, **21** (1980); A. Dietrich, *Nekyia*, 2d ed. (1913); B. C. Dietrich, *Death, Fate and the Gods* (1965); Eric R. Dodds, *The Greeks and the Irrational*, Sather Classical Lectures, XV (1951); Lewis R. Farnell, *Greek Hero Cults and Ideas of Immortality* (1921), and *The Cults of the Greek States* (1869–1909); William S. Ferguson, "The Attic Orgeones," in *Harvard Theological Review*, **37** (1944); James G. Frazer, *The Fear of the Dead in Primitive Religion* (1933).

Robert Garland, *The Greek Way of Death* (1985); Gherardo Gnoli and Jean-Pierre Vernant, eds., *La mort, les morts dans les sociétés anciennes* (1982); H. Gundolf, *Totenkult und Jenseitsglaube* (1967); William K. C. Guthrie, "The Chthonioi," "Hopes and Fears of the Ordinary Man," and "The Orphics," in *The Greeks and Their Gods* (1950), and *Orpheus and Greek Religion*, 2d ed. (1952); K. Heinemann, *Thanatos in Poesie und Kult der Griechen* (1913); Sally C. Humphreys and Helen King, eds., *Mortality and Immortality: The Anthropology and Archeology of Death* (1982); F. Jacoby, "ΓΕΝΕΣΙΑ [GENESIA]: A Forgotten Festival of the Dead," in *Classical Quarterly*, **38** (1944), and "Patrios Nomos: State Burials in Athens and the Public Cemetery and the Kerameikos," in *Journal of Hellenic Studies*, **64** (1944); Richard Janko, "Forgetfulness in the Golden Tablets of Memory," in *Classical Quarterly*, **34** (1984).

Georg Karo, *An Attic Cemetery* (1943); Donna Kurtz and John Boardman, *Greek Burial Customs* (1971); Richmond A. Lattimore, "Themes in Greek and Latin Epitaphs," in *Illinois Studies in Language and Literature*, **28** (1942); Walter Leaf, "Homeric Burial Rites," in *Commentary on the Iliad*, app. L (1902); H. Lorimer, "Pulvis et Umbra," in *Journal of Hellenic Studies*, **53** (1933); Ludolf Malten, "Elysion und Rhadamanthys," in *Archäologisches Institut des deutschen Reichs, Jahrbuch*, **28** (1913), and "Leichenspiel und Totenkult," in *Römische Mitteilungen*, **38–39** (1923–1924); Martin Per Nilsson, *Greek Popular Religion* (1940), *Geschichte der Griechischen Religion*, 2d ed. (1955), and "Immortality of the Soul in Greek Religion," in

Opuscula Selecta, **3** (1960); Arthur D. Nock, "Cremation and Burial in the Roman Empire," in *Harvard Theological Review,* **25** (1932), and "The Cult of Heroes," in *Harvard Theological Review,* **37** (1949).

H. W. Parke, "Anthesterion," in *Festivals of the Athenians* (1977); J. Pieper, *Tod und Unsterblichkeit* (1968); M. Popham, E. Touloupa, and L. Hugh Sackett, "The Hero of Lefkandi," *Antiquity,* **56** (1982); Theodora H. Price, "Herocult and Homer," in *Historia,* **22** (1973); Ludwig Radermacher, *Das Jenseits im Mythos der Hellenen* (1903); P. Raingeard, *Hermès Psychagogue* (1935); E. Reiner, *Die rituelle Totenklage der Griechen* (1938); Robert Renehan, "The Meaning of σωμα [soma] in Homer," in *California Studies in Classical Antiquity,* **12** (1979); Nicholas J. Richardson, *The Homeric Hymn to Demeter* (1974); Erwin Rohde, *Psyche,* W. B. Hillis, trans. (1925); Ursula Schlenther, *Brandbestattung und Seelenglauben* (1960); Albrecht Schnaufer, *Frühgriechischer Totenglaube,* Spudasmata, **20** (1970); Charles Segal, "The Theme of the Mutilation of the Corpse", *Mnemosyne,* Supplement **17** (1971); Anthony Snodgrass, "Les origines du culte des héros dans la Grèce antique," in Gherardo Gnoli and Jean-Pierre Vernant, eds., *La mort, les morts dans les sociétés anciennes* (1982); Christiane Sourvinou-Inwood, "The Boston Relief and the Religion of Locri Epizephyrii," in *Journal of Hellenic Studies,* **94** (1974); G. Soury, "La vie de l'au-delà," in *Revue des études anciennes,* **46** (1944); Emily Vermeule, *Aspects of Death in Early Greek Art and Poetry* (1979); Joseph Wiesner, *Grab und Jenseits* (1938); Ulrich von Wilamowitz-Moellendorff, *Der Glaube der Hellenen* (1926; rev. ed. 1932); Gunter Zuntz, *Persephone* (1971).

The Afterlife: Rome

JOHN A. NORTH

INTRODUCTION

For the early days of Rome—before the rapid expansion of power that began in the second half of the fourth century B.C.—we have no way of knowing the beliefs of the Romans about any religious question, apart from what can be inferred from their ritual practices and from the archaeological record. Our knowledge of and direct access to the thoughts of individual Romans improves in exactly the period when their power was expanding and their community was broadening to include all the free inhabitants of Italy as well as many immigrants from the East. After the period of Cicero, Livy, and Vergil, that is, from the first century A.D. onward, it becomes harder still to be sure who should be included in the "Roman world"; the range of this article corresponds roughly to those who spoke Latin and lived in Italy and the western provinces, but these people are far from ever having formed a coherent community. However, as Christianity and the other major religious groups competed on an empire-wide basis, it makes no sense to analyze religious history on the basis of a single city; the religion of the "Romans" can no longer be written in terms of their original home. It is possible that pagan beliefs and practices remained stable throughout this long period, that the radically different attitudes toward death and the dead which we find in the late antique period were entirely an alien growth, brought in by Christianity and strongly resisted by pagans. If so, it is precisely these questions that are at issue in any discussion of the afterlife in the Roman world.

EARLY ROME

The early Romans, like their later successors, maintained ritual relations with their dead. There were two festivals in the ancient calendar, the Parentalia (13–21 February) and the Lemuria (9, 11, 13 May). Both were public festivals, which is why they were marked in the calendars, but their recorded rituals took place in distinctly different family contexts. At some point during the period of the Parentalia, the family went out to the tombs of their dead forebears, that is,

997

outside the city, for the dead were not allowed within the walls. There offerings were made, which, according to Ovid (*The Roman Calendar* [*Fasti*] 2:533–545), might be very humble: "The spirits ask for little." The May festival involved the dead in a different guise —as Lemures, threatening ghosts—and this time invading the house itself: the father had to get up at midnight, make a sign to avert the spirits, wash his hands in spring water, and cast black beans over his shoulder, saying, "With these beans I redeem me and mine." It is often said that these festivals represent different attitudes to the dead, the Lemuria being the more primitive, but this is based on nothing but a faith that the more frightening must be the more primitive. In both cases, there are minimum offerings which must be made if the dead are to remain content; this in turn implies that they have the power to harm, that they are still a force to be respected. The spirits may ask little, but they do ask.

It is a long way from the belief that the family dead as a group retain some power to the belief that the individual members achieve survival, even in a restricted sense of the word. To prove the latter belief was held, one might argue from the evidence of grave goods and burial practices. In this respect, Roman customs are much like those of many other societies and of their neighbors, including that of their most influential neighbors, the Etruscans. A wide range of objects was buried or placed in the tomb together with the ashes of the dead—these might be arms and armor, or everyday objects such as lamps and eating or cooking equipment. We know that quite early in Roman history there was legislation to prevent elaborate and expensive burials of this kind, that the rich were prevented from putting goods of very high value in with their dead. Thus at least the custom of placing goods in the grave must go back to an early date; using evidence from later periods, we can add that it was very common to hold a meal for the living at the tombside and to offer a share to the dead in the tomb. In some cases, there are even pipes or holes leading directly to the remains through which the meal or drink could be passed. These practices were so persistent that they were even at times adopted by Christians until the bishops eventually prevented them from taking part in what they saw as pagan rites.

What does all this mean? At first sight, the gifts of cooking equipment, food, and weapons to the dead suggests that Romans believed they would need to cook, eat, and fight in the next world as they had in this. After all, these are valuable resources that the survivors could well use themselves. It might seem to follow from these economic considerations that there must have been an underpinning belief in some kind of afterlife from an early date. This perhaps all too simple explanation ignores the complex symbolism that usually characterizes religious action and religious speech. Religious action, even in simple societies, tends to consist of everyday actions that are charged with special meanings when performed in a given context of hope or expectation. In this case, if the dead are to be given valuable presents, that can only mean "valuable to the living"; there are no values specific to the dead. In any case, the ability to alienate valuable possessions is a demonstration to the living as well as to the dead of the continuing power of the family. We should conclude, not that the early Romans had no conception of an afterlife, but that this evidence can never prove that they did or allow us to assess what the conception was. It is quite clear that they believed in the continuing power of the dead and that they attached high importance to upholding the rules that determined how the dead should be treated and placated; further than that we cannot be specific.

There is an important distinction to be made, one that will affect the interpretation of later developments. Our tradition about the religion of early Rome is a thoroughly formal and priestly tradition. It is likely that there were ideas and practices, especially popular ideas and practices, that were entirely omitted from the selective picture the priests chose to hand on. Indeed archaeological evidence of other religious practices reveals that this is in fact so. In this sense, early Romans may perfectly well have had their own views and arguments about life beyond the tomb. What is not so likely is that such ideas played any established role in the organization and working of the public religion of Rome, about which our information is more reliable than for the private thoughts of individuals.

Contemporary literature, or at least literature bearing contemporary thought, might yield a deeper knowledge of religious ideas, but there is no substantial extant literary evidence for Rome earlier than the late third or early second century B.C., by which time the Romans had already been in contact with Greek culture for some time. By the third century B.C. the Greeks had developed a range of religious and philosophical views of life and death that eventually filtered through to the knowledge of educated Romans. One source of these was the philosophic tradition deriving from Plato, whose belief in the immortality of the *psyche* was to underpin much later speculation throughout antiquity. But another, and perhaps earlier, source for the Romans would have been the beliefs and rituals developed in the Greek cities of southern Italy supported by quasi-religious groups, which looked back to Orpheus and Pythagoras as their inspirers; these groups held that the souls of the dead survived the body and would later return to earth to live new lives, perhaps in other forms. When there is at last Roman literary evidence, the picture we find is a rather suggestive, if very partial one: Plautus, the first Roman playwright whose plays have come down to us, can refer to the idea of immortality and to the idea of hell as though these are familiar to his audiences (Plautus, *The Merchant* [*Mercator*] 602 ff.; *The Haunted House* [*Mostellaria*] 499 f.; *Captives* [*Captivi*] 998 f.), though he will have found these in the Greek plays on which he modeled his work; the first writer of Roman epic, Ennius (*d.* 169 B.C.), can similarly make use of the idea of reincarnation, again as if it was familiar to his readers (*Annals* frags. 1–14). All this can be seen as the effect of the first wave of Greek influence. About the middle of the second century we have the much harder evidence of a contemporary observer: the Greek historian Polybius (*d.* 118 B.C.) lived for many years as an exile in Rome; in the course of his analysis of why the Romans had defeated the Greeks so easily (*Histories* 6.56) he points to a difference in religious attitudes:

This is why the ancients did not, in my view, act rashly or randomly when they put about among the masses ideas about the gods and about the terrors of Hades; on the contrary, I think it is the men of today who are acting rashly and stupidly when they expel such notions. Not the least of the results is that officials in Greece are unable to keep good faith—even if they only have one talent in trust, even if they are equipped with ten checking clerks, ten seals, and twenty witnesses. The Romans on the other hand have magistrates and legates handling huge sums of money, but maintaining their honesty just through the faith to which they have given their oath.

It seems to be a Greek idea, not a Roman one, that ideas about Hades (hell) were invented by the elite as a means of social control; but there is no reason to doubt that Polybius would have known whether his Roman contemporaries believed in some form of divine punishment for an oath breaker or not. We certainly know that oaths were a very important element in the public life of Rome. It remains possible that the ideas were Greek ideas, recently imported; it would, admittedly, be paradoxical to find Polybius attributing Roman good faith to Greek beliefs, which the Greeks had in the meantime abandoned; but Polybius may be right in ascribing this belief to the Romans, and wrong about its significance in determining the character of their public life.

LITERARY TEXTS

By Cicero's time (first century B.C.), many different Greek ideas were known in Rome, at least among the educated; but it is difficult to be certain how many Romans and which Romans actually believed in them. The most famous evidence comes from Cicero and Vergil; it is sophisticated, literary, and eclectic, and seems most unlikely to reflect anybody's real religious beliefs. In Cicero's own "Dream of Scipio," which forms a tailpiece to his *On the Republic,* he makes some of the great men of Rome's past return to inspire and advise the hero of the dialogue (Scipio Aemilianus); they tell him that the mortal life of great men and especially of great statesmen is only a preparation in which the soul is temporarily imprisoned in an earthly body. After death, which is a release from the body, the selected souls return in glory to the celestial sphere from which they originally came. So, life on this earth is no more than a duty to be fulfilled from which the dutiful man will not shrink. But "those who have protected, helped, or expanded their fatherland have a special place in heaven allotted to them where they will enjoy eternal happiness." On the other hand, those who fail to free their souls from the grip of sensual pleasures, who remain its slaves and who break the laws of men and of gods, take

centuries of torture before they finally return to the heavens.

An even more elaborate construction is offered by Vergil in Book Six of the *Aeneid* (426–893). The hero Aeneas is taken into the realm of the dead in order to speak to his deceased father Anchises; on the way, he visits areas devoted to different categories of the dead. He goes first to an area (like the later "limbo"), where live the dead who are neither to be punished nor rewarded for their earthly lives—there he sees those who died as infants, or in battle, or had committed suicide. Then the way divides: the left-hand path leads to Tartarus, the realm of eternal punishment, which Aeneas cannot visit, the right-hand path to Elysium, where he goes to find his father. Anchises explains the situation of the blessed dead. He draws on ideas from various sources: for instance, the idea of the Stoics that there was a soul or guiding principle implicit in the universe or the idea (which probably derives from the Orphic and Pythagorean groups) that souls are periodically reborn in human bodies. In essence, the situation (not the location) is very similar to that of the "Dream of Scipio": the supreme souls come from Elysium, spend a temporary period on earth in the service of humanity, and then return to the realm of happiness from which they had come. This enables Aeneas to meet the great heroes of the future history of Rome, living in Elysium but as yet unborn. But here, unlike in the "Dream," heaven is not reserved for the elite alone; innumerable other souls, though they may have been infected with bodily evils before leaving the earth, go through a long process of purification through suffering and so eventually recover their lost purity.

The third text that sheds some light on the problem is Lucretius' *On the Nature of Things (De Rerum Natura),* which, although written only a few years earlier, is very different from *On the Republic* and the *Aeneid*. Lucretius, a contemporary of Cicero, wrote his long didactic poem to expound in Latin the ideas of the Epicureans. Once again we have Greek ideas being brought to Rome, but this time ideas hostile to religion, not sympathetic to it. Epicurus' system was an uncompromising materialism; it implied that all the components of the universe, including both souls and bodies, are formed of combinations of atoms, which come together for a time, but eventually must be dissolved into their elements. In such a system, there is obviously no room for an afterlife, or even for gods with any effective power of intervention in human affairs. The importance of Lucretius' evidence lies in the fact that his whole poem was written deliberately with the objective of freeing his contemporaries from the terrors of punishment after death; this was, he implies, the fear that could be exploited by priests and religious fanatics to keep human beings from peace of mind and contentment. So happiness can be restored only when men are brought to understand the real workings of nature and their own lives, and thus be liberated from irrational fear of the afterlife. Lucretius' missionary endeavor becomes a nonsense unless many of his readers had some real fear of hell after death. His evidence suggests that the sophisticated constructions of Vergil and Cicero were intellectual versions of commonly held notions.

THE LATER PERIOD

Up to this point the evidence has offered only very oblique ways of assessing the beliefs of Romans other than a privileged few who still speak to us direct. Disproportionate attention has perhaps been given to the views of Cicero; rationalist though he sometimes sounds, grief at the death of his beloved daughter drove him to great lengths in his attempt to provide her with a shrine, not just a memorial (as is reflected in his *Letters to Atticus*). Beginning in the imperial period a mass of new evidence about the death of individuals becomes available in the form of funerary inscriptions and carved stone sarcophagi, many having elaborate and individual decoration. The sentiments in the inscriptions and the iconography of the sarcophagi ought to provide a rich source for the publicly stated attitudes of the better-off classes; both epitaph and tomb were expensive commemorations, and were beyond the means of the Roman poor.

Does this new funerary evidence indicate any detectable trend toward a far more widespread belief in the afterlife? At least one major change in burial practice took place in the course of the early centuries A.D. and needs to be noted. In the first century, it was still normal for the dead to be cremated, as they had been in Rome for centuries; the characteristic archaeological features are *columbaria,* underground tomb systems providing hundreds of niches for urns containing ashes. From the second century, A.D., however, burial of bodies became increasingly common; the elaborately carved sarcophagus became the standard form of burial container, and cremation gradually became less frequent throughout the empire. This development has suggested that there was a profound change in the attitudes to and conception of the dead at the time. It may be so, but there is no agreement among scholars as to its significance. To go from burning to burying might suggest a growth in the expectation of bodily resurrection, yet the pagan expectation of immortality involved the survival of the soul, not the body, whereas the Christian belief in afterlife was linked to the resurrection of the earthly body. Thus, in pre-Christian times it is not at all obvious that burying is more appropriate than burning; perhaps the reverse, if the spirit is conceived as being released from the pyre. There is no shortage of possible explanations for the change—among them fashion, the need for more ostentatious display, shortage of firewood—but none is secure enough to help prove any underlying change of beliefs.

The decorative themes on the sarcophagi seem to offer hope in solving this problem. An elaborate study of them by the Belgian scholar Franz Cumont (1942) comes to the conclusion that the sarcophagi often evoked myths and themes implying that their owners believed in the possibility of a happy future life (in the Elysian Fields or some such equivalent of "heaven") after death, and that they wanted their belief represented on their last human resting place. Cumont's argument depends on a consideration of the particular selection of myths depicted on the sarcophogi with evidence from contemporary literature showing how these myths were understood at the time. He thus tries to establish a vocabulary of meanings from which the beliefs of the dead can be established. Significant mythical figures were the Dioscuri, the sons of Zeus, who symbolized the two hemispheres, which sometimes became the worlds of the living and of the dead; and the Muses, who came to symbolize the aspiration of the man of art and philosophy to attain the immortality reserved for the cultivated. Various kinds of lunar symbolism were very common, and may be connected with the idea that the souls of the dead go to or near the moon. There is no doubt that all these myths did receive allegorical treatment; much of it can be connected, as Cumont believes, with a revival of Pythagorean ideas, a revival that began in the late republican period and was an important source of thoughts about immortality and about the disciplined life that would secure it.

Cumont's critics have suggested that he is too bold in arguing from mythical representation to belief. Many of the myths have interpretations other than those he emphasizes; in fact, many myths represented on tombs seem to bear no special meaning at all. Cumont's arguments draw on discussions in high literary and philosophical circles, and beyond them there is no evidence of a widespread Pythagorean movement. In particular, it seems likely that sarcophagus decoration was chosen from available models, not necessarily with great purpose. Thus, it becomes difficult to speculate on the beliefs of the occupant of the sarcophagus on the basis of its decoration.

Inscriptions provide more direct access to the ideas of the dead, at least of the deceased's immediate family. The great majority of gravestones give no indication of belief; they are simply memorials offered by the survivors. But it is common enough to find some reference to the hope of meeting again, or to some form of future life. Other gravestones express an uncompromising skepticism: "We are nothing and we were nothing. See, reader, how quickly we mortals pass from nothing into nothing again." This is a common enough thought for a formula of this kind to have a standard abbreviation, "NF F NS NC," meaning, "I was not; I was; I am not; I care not." It is not necessary to see this as very profound philosophy, although it implies a polemical context of some kind. No one would want an aggressive denial of the afterlife on his tomb unless belief in it was strongly felt by some of the living. The message conveyed by the inscriptions therefore fits together with that derived from the decoration of the sarcophagi: the possibility of a life after death had become an issue, with some of those whose ideas have reached us showing strong belief, some strong disbelief. But there is no sign that the belief was integrated into any particular religious system, and most of what evidence exists reflects a world of cultured speculation rather than passionate religious belief. Too much skepticism should be avoided. Cumont may have proved a great deal less than he claims, but the frequency of reference to afterlife myths in the decoration of sarcophagi at least shows that these notions formed part of the language of death with which everyone must have been familiar.

NEW CULTS FROM THE "EAST"

It may then be accepted that there is some truth in the theory that the idea of personal immortality was becoming more popular in pagan circles in the course of the imperial period. But the theory remains a weak one, unless it is possible to relate this change of belief in some way to the social and religious reality of the period. If in other societies the belief in rewards and punishments in an afterlife is often seen to be supportive of the dominant moral order, it would not be surprising if the Roman elite also was propagating or supporting the idea. But we are far from being able to prove this: what is lacking is the means not only of showing what individuals believed, but also of judging how important an element the belief in an afterlife was in the lives of individuals. We know only about the symbols that appeared on their sarcophagi, but that might have been a matter to which only an hour's or only a moment's consideration was ever given. To prove that a really important change of ideas was going on, far more would have to be proved about people's religious lives at the time. One issue that has to be faced is the relationship between pagan ideas and the development of the Christian alternative to them.

The most fundamental change in the structure of religious life in the course of this period is the development of new kinds of religious groupings based on individuals who have committed themselves by an act of choice. In the traditional civic religions of the Greco-Roman world, no important religious choices were made: birth and situation automatically determined one's participation in worship, more or less irrespective of personal opinion or feeling. By the time of the early empire, various groups within the Roman world offered distinct religious experiences, each with its own organization, priests, and funds. Although widely differing, these groups were in a sense part of a competitive system; they were part of what might be called a "market economy," in which the individual could explore different religious commitments and experiences. The Christians offered by far the most radical option: they asked adherents to reject the gods and the traditional ritual of animal sacrifice; they asked believers to isolate themselves from civic life. Pagan cults did not ask their adherents to adopt such radical commitments. Joining the cult of Isis or Mithras entailed nothing basically incompatible with the normal religious life of a Greco-Roman city, even though the Roman authorities did at times act against some of these cults.

Up to a point, the new pagan cults did resemble Christianity and diverged from the older city cults. They offered their members—those who had been ritually initiated—a new vision and a new wisdom, claiming authentication from the alien wisdom of the East. Although the oriental origin of the cults has always been doubtful, and all were deeply changed in the Greek world before they reached the West, what matters is that the initiates believed they were receiving an ancient, different, transforming truth. So a competitive relationship existed between the cults: each propagated its own version of reality, derived from a different culture, using different myths and speculations, but claiming to reveal a truth that would bring a better and richer existence to the initiate; that is why these cults are often called "mystery cults" in modern accounts, although the

Greek word *mysterion,* unlike its modern equivalent, does not necessarily imply secrecy.

It is within the competitive world of the new cults that there might be a specific role for the conception of an afterlife. If it can be shown that one or more of these groups was putting about the belief that those initiated into the rites would be rewarded with access to heaven, this might well provide the dynamic behind the whole set of changes. This view is one that has been widely held in modern times; it is, in fact, perfectly true that certainly in an earlier period at least some mystery cults did develop doctrines implying that their believers could survive death in some way. In the cities of southern Italy, which were Greek before being conquered by the Romans, Orphics and Pythagoreans believed in a cycle of birth-death-reincarnation and in the possibility that rituals and atonement could offer the chance of escape from the cycle and a peaceful, undisturbed afterlife. These views may well also have influenced the Dionysian/Bacchic cults found in parts of the Mediterranean world from the fifth century B.C. onward; this is the movement that was, in its Italian form, brutally put down by the Roman authorities in 187–186 B.C. However, it is not these particular groups that are prominent as powerful influences in the period of the Roman Empire.

For this later time the best evidence we have about the underlying notions of the mystery cults in the Roman imperial period comes to us, curiously enough, from the novel of the second-century A.D. North African writer Lucius Apuleius, *The Golden Ass* (*Metamorphoses*). His hero, Lucius, experimenting with magic, is turned into an ass; the greater part of the novel is then taken up with his adventures in this unfortunate state. He obtains release from it, thanks to the goddess Isis who responds to his prayer and instructs him how he can obtain release from the spell and how he should behave thereafter. One might expect that this would be the end of the novel, when Lucius is duly restored to his proper form again. There is in fact a long final section that is mostly devoted to explaining Lucius' experience of the cult of Isis and Osiris. He takes advice from the priests, has more visions of the goddess, and undergoes three distinct initiations: the first to Isis in Corinth, the second to Osiris when he goes to Rome, the third to Isis again, to obtain full recognition from the Roman worshipers of Isis. The text is oddly detailed and specific, with great emphasis placed on Lucius' utter devotion and gratitude; in return, the two great gods give him complete support. The striking thing is that the rewards are entirely worldly benefits: "Osiris, as god of Good Fortune, helped me make a good living as a barrister, despite having to plead in Latin not in Greek" (11.28); and "I had no reason to repent of the trouble and the expense because by the gods' favor I was soon fully compensated out of the fees that I earned" (11.30).

There is very little sign here that the prospect of a future life is in any sense what is really at issue. It could be suspected that there is a distance between the author and the narrator, who is the hero Lucius; Lucius himself suspects at one point that he is being cheated by the priests, for he has had to pay fees for the initiation each time it happened; after all, if he had experienced the mystery, why does he need to experience it again, unless the priests have been holding back some of the secrets? There could be some element of satire here, in the suggestion that both priests and initiates have far from otherworldly motives; but it is hard to think that this is more than a hint. In one passage in *The Golden Ass* (11.6) where the goddess is herself speaking, there is an explicit reference to a future life:

Your life will be happy and famous under my guardianship; then, when you have completed the measure of your time above and descended to the world of the dead, you will see me there as well in the hemisphere of the underworld, when you will be living in the Elysian Fields. You will adore me for my favor to you time and again, as a light in the shadows of Acheron and as the queen of the Stygian depths. Indeed, if you deserve my divine power through careful obedience, through religious duty and through perfect chastity, you will find out that it is I alone who have the power to prolong your life beyond the limits set by your fate.

This seems to be a quite serious and important passage whose implication is unmistakable. The climax, the final and emphatic claim made by the goddess, is not specifically connected with the afterlife at all, but with her power to extend the individual's life on this earth beyond the point fixed by fate.

It is not satisfactory to place so much emphasis on the evidence of one source, especially a novel which in no sense was intended to provide methodical information. But the picture given in *The Golden Ass* in fact matches the evidence we have from other cults. In none of them do we find a body of evidence placing concern about a life after death at the center of its religious practice. In some cults there is clear evidence that a particular deity went through a process of death and rebirth, and the deity's experience might be ritually re-created in the experience of the devotee. There is no doubt, for instance, that the Attis cult, at least in the later imperial period, was of this type. The fourth-century A.D. writer Sallustius (*On the Gods and the World* [*De Deis et Mundo*]) makes the point quite explicitly: the man who partakes in the mysteries of Attis shares the fate he suffered, but also shares in Attis' resurrection through the life-giving power of the goddess Cybele. But does this mean that he became a god, as Attis had? Or that he was just reborn into a better, richer, more beautiful state of earthly life, as Lucius seems to have been in *The Golden Ass?* Or did he attain

some more subtle, less explicitly defined intermediate state? The available evidence suggests that mystery cults offered benefits in this life, not the next.

One ritual connected with the Attis/Cybele cult was the *taurobolium,* in which an ox was sacrificed and the blood allowed to pour over the worshiper—a perversion of baptism, according to Christian sources. In general, the many inscriptions recording that this ritual had taken place do not give any indication of what it meant; in only one case is the worshiper described as "reborn into eternity." At least this single worshiper was evidently making the connection between rebirth and eternal life; the problem is that the evidence is inadequate to prove that this was the accepted meaning within the cult, and the question must be left open. Mithraism, which became the dominant cult of this kind in the third to fourth centuries A.D., presents a similar problem and invites the same treatment. The initiate passes through a succession of grades, of which the highest is "father" (*pater*); the soul of the Mithraist also goes through a corresponding succession of states. Despite arguments to the contrary, there is no evidence that its ultimate destination was a state of individual immortality.

CONCLUSION

In our present state of knowledge, the mystery cults do not provide the necessary link between religious practice and the changing climate of opinion, which the decoration of the sarcophagi indicates. If they had played this role, we should have expected to find imagery derived from the most powerful of these cults—Attis, Isis, and later Mithras—appearing prominently among the decoration of the sarcophagi. Further research might still establish such a link but it would have to be different cults from these three that would play the linking role. One possibility is the cult of Dionysus/Bacchus, which certainly existed throughout the period and whose iconography is among the most densely represented in funerary art. However, the evidence for belief in an afterlife among Bacchic groups is no stronger than that for any of the other cults; and in fact this cult's influence seems to have been at its height at an earlier period than that under discussion. Sarcophagi do indeed provide rich imagery derived from Dionysiac myth but little, if any, indication of living cult practice. It is very likely that they represent no more than a vocabulary of decorative images, evoking the journey of life, or even triumph and ecstasy, but having no specific religious reference.

The second possible hope of progress is supplied by the Underground Basilica in Rome, near the Porta Maggiore. The plan of this unique building strikingly resembles that of a Christian chapel, but it is firmly dated to the first century A.D. and has an entirely pagan decorative scheme. It is, in fact, this scheme that gives us the only indication of its significance. The central myths represented seem to refer to youth and age, life and death, the now and the hereafter. The range of mythical reference—the Dioscuri, Ganymede the gods' cupbearer, possibly Attis, certainly Sappho's leap from the rocks of Leucas—has some overlap with that of later funerary art. If this strange building can be shown to have been a cult center under Orphic or Pythagorean influence, it may then be argued that these were the powerful forces propagating belief in the afterlife and determining the mythical language used on sarcophagi.

Neither of these two possibilities can be established at the moment, for lack of hard information. Even if these suggested links could be proved, it is not likely that they would change the basic picture. That picture is that belief in immortality in some form or other was very widely disseminated in the pagan world and found varied means of expression. At times this was perceived and perhaps propagated by the elite as a means of social control, as reinforcing general moral principles. There is reason to think that in the period of the empire this attitude became more popular, or at least it became an issue, for debate as well as for erudite speculation. It would make good historical sense to suggest that this attitude was being fostered by competing religious cults, for which the offer of immortality would be the supreme reward for the initiate. In practice, there is virtually no evidence of this, except in the case of Christianity. The pagan cults seem to have focused their members' attention on this world, not on the next.

It is not altogether surprising that there has sometimes been misinterpretation of this difficult evidence. Information about the meaning of the mysteries is far from complete, one of the many reasons being that devotees took an oath not to reveal the truth. Interpretations can be based only on assumptions made by the interpreter and the explanations he can devise. To those brought up in a tradition influenced by Christianity it has seemed an unquestionable truth that the idea of immortality, once formulated, must have become an issue of supreme importance. The Christian doctrine of the mass physical resurrection of the faithful remained alien and unacceptable to pagans. Meanwhile, pagan cults continued to show vigor and innovativeness, in some cases developing conceptions critical of the conventional assumptions of ancient life. But they do not seem to have adopted as a central religious value the rejection of this world in favor of the next.

BIBLIOGRAPHY

SOURCES

Apuleius, *The Transformations of Lucius; Otherwise Known as The Golden Ass* (*Metamorphoses*), Robert Graves, trans. (1951); Cicero, *Letters to Atticus,* D. R. Shackleton Bailey, ed. and trans., 7 vols. (1965–1970), and "Dream of Scipio" in *De Republica (On the Republic),* Clinton W. Keyes, trans. (1928); Lucretius, *On the Nature of the Universe,* Martin F. Smith, ed. and trans., rev. ed. (1975); Ovid, *The Roman Calendar (Fasti),* James G. Frazer, trans. (1931); Vergil, *The Aeneid,* William F. Jackson Knight, trans. (1956).

For a collection of sources, see Frederick C. Grant, *Ancient Roman Religion* (1957).

STUDIES

Peter Brown, *The Cult of the Saints* (1981); Pierre Boyancé, *Études sur le songe de Scipion* (1936); Jérôme Carcopino, *La basilique pythagoricienne de la Porte Majeure* (1926); Franz V. M. Cumont, *After Life in Roman Paganism* (1922; repr. 1956), and *Recherches sur le symbolisme funéraire des Romains* (1942); Robert Duthoy, *The Taurobolium: Its Evolution and Terminology* (1969); Richard Gordon, "Franz Cumont and the Doctrines of Mithraism," in John R. Hinnells, ed., *Mithraic Studies,* 2 vols. (1975), and "Reality, Evocation and Boundary in the Mysteries of Mithras," in *Journal of Mithraic Studies,* **3** (1980); Keith Hopkins, "Death in Rome," in his *Death and Renewal* (1983); Richmond A. Lattimore, *Themes in Greek and Latin Epitaphs* (1942).

Ramsey MacMullen, *Paganism in the Roman Empire* (1981); Arthur D. Nock, "Cremation and Burial in the Roman Empire," and "Sarcophagi and Symbolism," in his *Essays on Religion and the Ancient World,* Zeph Stewart, ed., 2 vols. (1972); J. A. North, "Religious Toleration in Republican Rome," in *Proceedings of the Cambridge Philological Society,* **25** (1979), "Novelty and Choice in Roman Religion," in *Journal of Roman Studies,* **70** (1980), and "These He Cannot Take," *ibid.,* **73** (1983); Howard H. Scullard, *Festivals and Ceremonies of the Roman Republic* (1981); Jocelyn M. C. Toynbee, *Death and Burial in the Roman World* (1971); Robert Turcan, *Les sarcophages romains à représentations dionysiaques* (1966), and *Les sarcophages romains et le problème du symbolisme funéraire* in *Aufstieg und Niedergang der römischen Welt,* **16**.2 (1978).

M. J. Vermaseren, *Cybele and Attis: The Myth and the Cult* (1977); Henrik Wagenvoort, " 'Rebirth' in Profane Antique Literature," in his *Studies in Roman Literature, Culture and Religion* (1956; repr. 1978); Susan Walker, *Memorials to the Roman Dead* (1985).

Ruler Worship

J. RUFUS FEARS

HISTORY

Sharply defined, ruler worship is the practice of offering sacrifice and other forms of cult homage to a mortal ruler, living or deceased. As such, it represents one of the most characteristic and seminal developments in Greco-Roman polytheism of the postclassical period.

In neither inception nor formulation was ruler cult in the Greco-Roman world influenced by the quite distinct traditions of Egypt and Mesopotamia. In point of fact, ruler worship assumed a prominence in Greece and Rome that it had never enjoyed in the earlier civilizations of the ancient Near East and Egypt. Throughout the long history of the Near East, from the earliest dynasties at Sumer (*ca.* 3000 B.C.) to the Achaemenid period (*ca.* 550–330 B.C.), the political order was justified by a concept of the ruler as a mortal who served the gods as their divinely chosen vicegerent on earth. The quite distinct notion of the ruler as a god never assumed major importance in the political ideology of Mesopotamia; cult worship of rulers was a sporadic and ephemeral phenomenon, limited almost entirely to the period from Naram-Sin of Akkad through the Neo-Sumerian and early Babylonian periods (*ca.* 2230–1900 B.C.). In contrast to Mesopotamia, the concept of the ruler as godhead was fundamental to the political mythology of pharaonic Egypt. However, only a very few pharaohs were the object of actual cult worship, either in their own lifetimes or after their deaths. Such cults tended to be local phenomena, the products of specific acts of royal beneficence. Toward the end of the New Kingdom, especially under Rameses II (*ca.* 1290–1224 B.C.), cults of the living ruler did come into prominence for a period of time. Such cult activity lay particular stress upon the worship of statues of the pharaoh, which were apparently regarded as independent divine entities in themselves and capable, like the royal person, of enjoying worship in their own right.

Greece

No evidence exists to link these distant, transitory, and alien phenomena to the rise of ruler worship in Greece. Nor need we postulate any such "oriental" influence. Ruler cult arose naturally within the context of Greek ideas of cult and divinity, reflecting concepts fundamental to the religious mentality of Greek polytheism. For the Greek, the very notion of divinity assumed a power capable of rendering supernatural benefits to the community of worshipers. As a polytheist, the Greek was ready at all times to recognize a new manifestation of divine power. He was no less ready to formalize this recognition by conceptualizing, naming, and establishing a cult to the godhead that had revealed itself by such manifestation of supernatural power. The pantheon of a Greek city was thus capable of unlimited expansion and could embrace a wide range of divine entities, from great Panhellenic gods, such as Zeus and Apollo, to narrowly localized cults of spirits residing in groves and springs.

Cults of heroes provide a most significant example of such narrowly localized divine forms. A *heros* represented a very particular form of divine patron and might be invoked in circumstances or for a function felt to be inadequately fulfilled by one of the great, traditional gods. Such worship frequently drew upon popular piety and patriotism, and cults of heroes were often unique to a single city, resting upon a popular perception of a miraculous intercession of divine power by the *heros* through an act defined in time and place. Furthermore and most important, such cult worship could be bestowed upon historical persons. By the mid fifth century B.C., founders of cities were routinely awarded heroic cult honors after death. Cults of heroes were established to those whose deeds had benefited their fellow citizens, like the Greeks who died at Plataea or the two Spartans who fell at Thermopylae. A figure like the athlete Cleomedes, who became a homicidal lunatic, could equally become the object of cult by displaying awesomely terrifying and harmful power. As in the case of Cleomedes on the island of Astypalaea in the southeastern Aegean, such cults were frequently sanctioned by Delphi. A *heros* so honored was regarded as a divine being of lesser rank than the gods of Olympus and was worshiped with rites distinct from those paid to the Olympian divinities.

Precedents thus existed in archaic and early classical Greece for the posthumous worship of mortals who had distinguished themselves in a striking fashion. This heroizing of historical figures in the sixth and fifth centuries B.C. provided the immediate background to the rise of the ruler cult at the end of the Peloponnesian War. The transition from the posthumous honoring of a *heros* to the worship of a living mortal as *theos* was fostered by intellectual developments as well as by currents of popular thought in the fifth century. In concept and cult, a distinction tended to be drawn between *heros* and *theos*, between hero and god. However, Heracles provided a notable example of a hero who had been elevated to the rank of god, both in popular perception and in cult activity. Pericles, speaking in 434/433 B.C., could compare those Athenians who fell in battle at Samos with gods, not heroes (Plutarch, *Parallel Lives*, "Pericles" 8): "They had become immortal like the gods. For we do not see the gods themselves; we attribute immortality to them only through the honors we pay them and the benefits which they bestow on us. Like attributes belong to those who die for their country." These words of Pericles suggest a popular belief that mortals could achieve divinity by a beneficent act of surpassing excellence, and that by recognizing this act with divine honors, mortal men could bestow divinity upon a fellow man. The next step was to award such honors during the lifetime of the benefactor. It was a step taken during the intellectual and political crisis of the last years of the fifth century. It occurred within the atmosphere of cultural and religious transformation marked by the *The Bacchants* (*Bac-*

chae) of Euripides, with its dramatic warning of the punishment meted out to those who refused to believe that gods could appear among men in mortal forms.

The gradual development of traditional ideas, sharpened by the immediacy of political upheaval, thus laid the foundation for a seminal innovation in Greek cult life: the worship of a living mortal as a god. It was an innovation that the Greeks recognized as specifically fixed in time and place. Duris of Samos stated quite unreservedly that the Spartan general Lysander was "the first Greek to whom the cities erected altars, offered cult sacrifice, and honored with the singing of hymns appropriate to a god" (Plutarch, *Parallel Lives,* "Lysander" 18). The very words used by Duris to describe the cult sacrifice (*thysia*) and the hymn (*paian*) explicitly indicate that Lysander was worshiped as a god, not as some lesser form of divinity, such as a *heros.* Further evidence that Lysander was regarded as a full-fledged god is found in Duris' testimony that the Samians renamed the festival of Hera (*Heraia*) in honor of Lysander, celebrating it thereafter as the Lysandreia. Plutarch, our source for this quote from the now lost *Histories* of Duris, had no doubts about the validity of this testimony. Modern reservations should have been laid to rest by the discovery in 1964 of an inscription in the precinct of Hera on Samos. Referring explicitly to the Lysandreia, it provides independent confirmation of an essential detail in Duris' account.

The deification of Lysander is a fact. The event occurred within the general context of the outpouring of gratitude that followed upon the decisive defeat of the Athenians in the Peloponnesian War at Aegospotami (405 B.C.) and the restoration of freedom to those cities that had been under Athenian domination. As a specific instance, Lysander was responsible for the return of exiled members of the oligarchic faction to Samos;

and it may have been they who instituted the divine honors to the Spartan. This, the first instance of ruler cult in the Greek world, encapsulates the characteristic features of the phenomenon. In the first place, the cult, ritual, and intellectual framework are totally Greek. There is no evidence whatsoever of influence from Egyptian or Near Eastern concepts of kingship or forms of worship. Second, cult and ritual give no indication that the figure so worshiped was regarded as in any way distinct from what a modern commentator might deign to consider "real gods." Third, Lysander was deified not because of the office he held but because of the benefits that he bestowed. Cult worship was an act of homage granted in recognition of Lysander's power to render concrete and specific benefits to his friends and to harm his enemies on a grand scale by returning exiles to their home and delivering up for mass execution the leaders of those factions that had opposed Lysander and Sparta. Finally, there is no evidence that Lysander compelled worship of himself. The honor of cult worship was freely given by the cities. But the very fact of permitting and accepting such honor was viewed as an act of *hybris* on the part of Lysander. Plutarch relates the story of Lysander's deification within the framework of other acts of tyrannical excess committed by the Spartan, establishing a pattern of arrogance and unlawful violence that led to his fall from power.

The ignominious conclusion to Lysander's career could only lend support to the view that the acceptance of cult honors was an act of excess and arrogance quite likely to provoke divine punishment. That may explain why the cult of Lysander remained without immediate progeny. Two generations pass before we meet with another well-attested instance of cult honors awarded to a political leader during his lifetime. In the year 356 B.C. the citizens of Syracuse (Siracusa, in Sicily) worshiped Dion as a *heros* who had saved and benefited his fatherland. This too remained an isolated instance until, in the aftermath of the career of Alexander the Great, ruler worship emerged as a central element in the cultural and political forms of the early Hellenistic age.

Intellectually, the fourth century was prepared to accept ideas fundamental to the conceptual framework of ruler worship. Thus Plato in the *Republic* described an ideal commonwealth in which beneficent rulers would keep their eyes fixed upon heaven and govern the state on the pattern set down by the gods. For these services, the rulers, after their departure from men, would be honored as gods. Aristotle referred to the view, common among his contemporaries, that through an excess of *arete* (excellence, virtue, remarkable achievement) men became gods (*Nicomachean Ethics* 1145A). It was an idea familiar to Aristotle's pupil, Alexander. Medallic coins struck late in Alexander's life portray the victory over Porus as an act of surpassing *arete* and Alexander as the divinely blessed earthly vicegerent of Zeus, governing the world on the pattern laid down by the gods. The symbolism of these medallions does not proclaim Alexander as god; but like the painting of Apelles, representing Alexander with a thunderbolt, it does suggest that immortality achieved through *arete* awaits him after his departure from men. Sculptural portraits by Lysippus portrayed Alexander gazing toward heaven, consciously recalling the image of the ruler in Plato's *Republic* and its promise of divine honors.

The adoption of such imagery, together with the actual achievements of Alexander, created the expectation of divinity. However, despite much that has been written by modern scholars, there is nothing that permits us to assume that Alexander demanded or was accorded cult honors during his lifetime. It is certainly true that Alexander was honored in ways that later critics deemed inappropriate for ordinary mortals. However, the ruler cult presupposes the offering of actual sacrifice to the ruler. And by this strict and proper definition, we can point to no incontrovertible evidence which establishes that cults of Alexander were instituted in his own lifetime. It was after his death that his Macedonian generals realized a potent source of political legitimacy in the cult of Alexander. As such he was regarded as a patron divinity by Eumenes, Lysimachus, Seleucus I Nicator, and Ptolemy I Soter. Properly invoked, he bestowed the charismatic gift of victory and the resultant powers of kingship. Ptolemy brought his body to Egypt. Ultimately housed in Alexandria, Alexander possessed his own temple and was prayed to as one prayed to Apollo or Dionysus. By doing such homage to Alexander, men believed, Ptolemy was blessed by the gods; and the cult of Alexander played a major role in sanctioning a kingship that lacked all national and legal claims to legitimacy.

The cult of Alexander among his successors, the Diadochi, served as a prototype for one major form assumed by ruler worship in the ancient world: posthumous cults of charismatic rulers. Endowed with supernatural gifts, such a ruler, while on earth, had performed great deeds and bestowed remarkable benefits. These deeds and benefits assured him immortality. Assumed by the gods into heaven, he continued to render benefits to the community of worshipers, who bestowed upon him the divine honors associated with such immortality.

Shortly after the death of Ptolemy I in 283 B.C., Ptolemy II Philadelphus deified his father, beginning a dynastic cult that continued as long as the Ptolemies ruled Egypt. A similar dynastic cult was a central feature of the official state religion in the Seleucid kingdom as well as at Pergamum. As early as the reign of Ptolemy II (285–246 B.C.) the dynastic cult in Egypt also regularly included the living ruler. A document of 194/193 B.C. attests that, in the same way, the current Seleucid king was part of a dynastic cult that included his royal ancestors. Other living members of the royal family were also accorded worship within the framework of the dynastic cult. Among the Attalids only deceased rulers were the object of worship in the dynastic cult, while no such cult existed in the kingdom of Macedonia.

The period of the Diadochi was no less seminal for the formalization of another central feature of ruler worship in the ancient world: municipal cults of the living ruler. These are to be distinguished from the dynastic cults. Unlike these last, they were not instigated by the ruler. Instead, as autonomous entities with their own individual and distinct municipal cults and religious calendars, specific cities granted the ruler the honor of being worshiped along with the other gods of their cities. Such honor was accorded a specific ruler in response to a specific act of beneficence on his part. By creating a cult of this new god the city, as a community of worshipers, not only commemorated the beneficial act but also took steps to assure that a continuing relationship would exist between the city and the god who had rendered this benefit. Thus our earliest documentary reference to such a cult, an inscription of 311 B.C., records the establishment of the worship of Antigonus I Monophthalmos by the citizens of Scepsis in recognition of benefits bestowed by him. Such cult honors became a standard feature in the relationship between kings and cities in the Hellenistic period. Each of the Diadochi, Antigonus and his son Demetrius Poliorcetes as well as Ptolemy I, Lysimachus, and Seleucus I, were the recipients of cult honors by cities. The practice was continued under their successors; epigraphical evidence attests to a long list of Ptolemaic, Seleucid, Attalid, and Macedonian rulers so honored. By granting cult honors to a king,

the citizens admitted him to a place among the gods of their city. This in no way implied recognition of the king's sovereignty over the city. So when Rhodes established a cult to Ptolemy I, it was to thank him for his aid at the time of Demetrius' siege. The religious implications of admitting Ptolemy into the divine pantheon of Rhodes were sufficient to require the sanction of the oracle of Zeus Ammon. However, the political implication was no more than a statement of reciprocal friendship and goodwill from an independent city to a beneficent individual.

The Hellenistic ruler cult was a dynamic religious phenomenon. It marked a major innovation in the religious life of Greek cities, introducing new divine forms into their state cults and provoking innovative responses such as the cult of the Demos at Athens and Rhodes. In fifth-century art and literature, it had been common to personify the Citizen Body—the Demos. However, the institution of actual cult worship of the Demos occurs only in the Hellenistic period. The rise of cults of the personified Demos, like the worship of the personified Tyche (Fortune) of individual cities, was a byproduct of the ruler cult. Both phenomena developed out of a need to create alongside the cult of the ruler, with its expression of the political concept of monarchy, an equivalent statement for the autonomous city-state. Ruler cult also became part of the broader phenomenon of Hellenism, leaving its mark among such Hellenized monarchs as Nicomedes II of Bithynia and Antiochus I of Commagene and upon a Rome which, since the early republic, had been open to religious influences from Greece.

Ruler worship was thus an established, accepted, and significant institution in the religion and politics of the Hellenistic world by the time the Romans began to impinge upon that world. The power to perform acts of beneficence was what inspired ruler worship, and it was only natural for the Greeks to respond to the manifestation of Roman power and its conferral of specific benefits by establishing new cults. Both individual Romans, such as Titus Quinctius Flamininus at Chalcis in Euboea and Manius Aquilius at Pergamum, and collective personifications, such as the Demos of the Roman People and Dea Roma, became the objects of cult worship by Greek cities in the second century B.C. By the first century B.C. it had become quite natural for Greek cities to honor Roman governors with cults. Such action was always a response to a concrete act of beneficence on the part of the governor. The individual proconsul was free to accept such worship, as in the case of Quintus Mucius Scaevola and Publius Servilius Isauricus in Asia, or tactfully to reject these honors, as did Cicero in Cilicia. This same well-established tradition provided the framework for honoring the great charismatic generals of the late republic, Sulla, Pompey, and Caesar himself.

Rome

Cult worship of Roman governors and generals was of consequence only for the individual Greek cities that deified them. It had no meaning whatever for the Roman state cult. Ruler worship was alien to traditional Roman religion; it was imported from the Greek world. Rome's engagement with the intellectual framework of ruler worship began earlier than has generally been assumed. The cult of the Genius Publicus/ Genius Populi Romani, introduced into the state religion in 218/217 B.C., was a conscious parallel to the cult of the Demos at Athens and Rhodes. Like the worship of the Demos at Athens and Rhodes, Genius Publicus/Genius Populi Romani was a cultic statement of popular sovereignty. It provided a traditional medium through which the Roman absorbed, modified, and propagated the essential concept of the dynastic

cult of the ruler in the Hellenistic world. In precisely these terms Greek cities recognized the beneficent power of the Roman commonwealth with votive dedications of statues of the Demos of the Roman People. As long as Rome remained a free republic, the deification of the community of the Roman people was the only element of ruler worship in the state cult. There could be no place for the worship of individuals until Augustus had destroyed the substance of self-government at Rome.

It is with Augustus, not with Caesar, that we properly begin the history of ruler worship at Rome. Like Sulla and Pompey before him, Caesar had been honored in extraordinary ways, all of which tended to emphasize his special charismatic standing as one chosen by the gods and endowed with supernatural gifts, power, and virtues. None of these honors, however, included his actual worship in cults at Rome. It was only after his death that Caesar was deified and Divus Iulius assumed his place among the gods of the Roman state.

The careful use the young adventurer Octavian made of his status as son of a god (*Divi filius*) foreshadowed the keen appreciation that the statesman Augustus showed for the essential role of ruler worship in a monarchy. By a cautious and well-conceived process of innovation, absorption, and adaptation the ruler cult was integrated into the very fabric of the principate. All those forms that would characterize ruler worship under the empire were already clearly delineated under Augustus.

From the standpoint of the Roman state religion, the most important form of ruler worship was the establishment of posthumous cults of specific emperors. The apotheosis of an emperor was recognized by an official act of state. At the funeral, the emperor's soul was believed to ascend to heaven as his body was being burned. This ascension had to be witnessed and attested;

on the basis of that attestation, a decree of the senate recognized the deceased emperor's new status as *divus* and his place among the gods of the Roman state. In other words, the emperor's divinity was certified by a miracle and approved by the institution responsible for permitting any additions to be made to the official pantheon. By these actions, the senate did not make an emperor a god, rather it recognized the fact of his divinity and took appropriate steps to ensure a continuing relationship between the Roman people and this newly recognized godhead. To this end, each newly consecrated emperor was granted the necessary apparatus of cult, including his own temple and priests. Benefits rendered during his lifetime constituted the justification for divinity. In other words, the emperor was deified not as emperor, but as benefactor. This explains the fact that numerous emperors failed to achieve deification. The list of *divi* began with Julius Caesar and, of the emperors of the first two centuries, included Augustus, Claudius, Vespasian, Titus, Nerva, Trajan, Hadrian, Antoninus Pius, and Marcus Aurelius. As the list indicates, divinity tended to be recognized in those emperors who successfully completed their principate and left an heir. Of those who failed to enter the ranks of gods of the Roman state, all except the hated Tiberius were violently removed from office.

Augustus established the pattern by which Roman cult recognized only the posthumous worship of the emperor. However, he did not neglect to ensure that the living princeps was endowed with a definite aura of divine power. At Rome the cult of the Genius Augusti served this function. The Genius signified the creative force in man, that which was eternal and divine. Private individuals had a Genius, sacrificed to on their birthday. But the Genius of Augustus was elevated into the realm of official worship. In a carefully organized and extremely popular cult, worship of the Genius Augusti was linked with the *Lares compitales* (the tutelar deities of the crossroads) to celebrate the divine power that resided in Augustus and enabled him to guide and protect the Roman people as a father does his children. The divine quality conferred by the worship of the imperial genius is shown by its role in official oaths, in which one swore by Jupiter Optimus Maximus, Genius Augusti, and the Di Penates. Later, the *divi* were also included in such oaths.

The popularity of the cult of the Genius Augusti is one of many indications of the sincere gratitude and enthusiasm for the person of Augustus and for those policies that restored peace, prosperity, and security to the Roman world. The cult of the Genius Augusti provided one means of channeling that enthusiasm into forms that were productive and yet not likely to offend those Romans who equated ruler worship with tyranny. Another and equally seminal vehicle was provided by the cult of Pax Augusta. As in the case of the temple to Clementia Caesaris, decreed by the senate in 44 B.C. to honor Julius Caesar, the erection of the monument Ara Pacis Augustae celebrated in cult action the operation of a divine beneficent force in the person and deeds of Augustus. It became the forerunner of numerous cults of imperial virtues, such as Providentia Augusta and Concordia Augusta, which form a most characteristic statement of ruler worship under the empire.

Far more than in the Greek world, ruler cult at Rome put specific emphasis on forms that recognized divinity as a force dwelling in but distinct from the person of the emperor. Such was the significance of the cults of Genius Augusti and of the imperial virtues. Even more specific was the cult of Numen Augusti. Introduced by Tiberius in the lifetime of Augustus, the worship of Numen Augusti was an official part of the Roman state cult, carried out by the members of all four priestly colleges. Whatever its various shades of meaning, the word *numen* meant godhead, divinity, or divine power to the contemporaries of Augustus. *Numen* was the quality possessed by a god. In permitting the establishment of an official cult of the Numen Augusti, the first princeps came as close as any Roman emperor ever did to direct worship of himself in the state religion.

These innovations in the Roman state religion had immediate consequence only for Roman citizens. However, no less care was taken by Augustus in directing the sincere expressions of gratitude among provincials into suitable channels of cult activity. In the East, Augustus could build upon a long-established tradition of ruler worship. In the West, it fell upon him to begin the process of institutionalizing such cults among a population without prior experience of the forms and ideas of ruler worship. In both parts of the empire, Augustus encouraged cult association of himself with the deification of Rome. The basic idea that provincials, but not Roman citizens, could worship the person of the living ruler is shown by Augustus' actions in Asia and Bithynia. He permitted the Roman citizens in these provinces to build temples at Ephesus and Nicaea for the worship of Roma and Divus Julius. Those who were not Roman citizens requested and received permission to build temples at Pergamum and Nicomedia (Izmit) for the worship of Roma and Augustus. An official provincial cult of Roma and Augustus was instituted in the West at Lugdunum (Lyons) in Gaul in 12 B.C. Similar provincial cults may have been established at the instigation of Augustus in Germania, Noricum, and elsewhere in the West. The celebration of these cults was a primary function of the provincial assemblies, attesting to the role of the imperial cult as a vehicle of romanization and a public expression of loyalty to the person of Augustus and to Rome.

Moderation has been seen in this association of himself in worship with the personification of Rome. Suetonius cited as an example of Augustan moderation the fact that "he would not accept the honor of a temple, even in the provinces, unless his name was coupled with Roma" (*Lives of the Caesars,* "Augustus" 52). However, the iconography of the engraved gem known as the Gemma Augustea suggests that undue emphasis should not be laid on the self-effacing quality of such actions. There Augustus appears in divine guise as the heaven-sent savior of the human race. That he is seated alongside an adoring Roma hardly diminishes the image of Augustus' own unqualified divinity. Moreover, Augustus' contemporaries will not have overlooked the monarchical implications of cult action that equated the princeps with Rome itself. Finally, it should be emphasized that cults of Roma and Augustus represented only the officially sanctioned policy. Municipalities, private groups, and individuals could and did exercise their right to establish cults of the living Augustus, and sent embassies to inform him of their actions.

This same mixture of tradition and innovation, of ambiguity and directness, marked Augustus' attitude toward literary invocations of his divinity. Augustan writers continued and developed Hellenistic panegyrical traditions. The literature of the age is replete with references to the divinity of Augustus and with elaborate literary comparisons of the emperor to the gods of Olympus. But the princeps himself was extremely cautious about such displays of literary hyperbole. In this field as well, his moderation set the tone that distinguished a so-called constitutional emperor from the tyrant who eagerly encouraged outrageous literary paeans to imperial divinity.

In short, within the limits of admirable prudence Augustus made full use of the religious and political potential inherent in the concept of ruler worship. For two centuries after his death the history of the ruler cult in the Roman world is one of gradual development rather than of major innovations and sudden shifts in policy. The western provinces saw the extension of the ruler cult into senatorial provinces—Gallia Narbonensis, Baetica, and Africa Proconsularis—as well as into areas newly won for the empire, such as Britannia and Dacia. In the east, municipal cults remained a primary means for honoring specific acts of imperial beneficence. The second century A.D., the age of the Antonines, represented the culmination of ruler worship in the Greco-Roman world. At all levels, in Roman state cult, in municipal and provincial cults, and on a private basis, the worship of emperors, living and dead, was cultivated with an intensity never again equaled.

None of Augustus' successors went substantially beyond the limits he defined for the ruler cult and its role in the religious and political fabric of the imperial system. This holds as true for tyrants like Gaius, Nero, and Domitian as it does for constitutional emperors like Vespasian, Trajan, and Marcus Aurelius. Modern scholarship has all too frequently overemphasized the importance of the principates of Gaius, Nero, Domitian, and Commodus in the history of the ruler cult. Each of these rulers has been charged with attempting to introduce oriental divine kingship at Rome. It is a charge fabricated out of the scandalmongering accounts of authors like Suetonius and Dio Cassius, who readily availed themselves of the stock portrait of the tyrant usurping divine honors. It is a charge built upon the uncritical acceptance of literary panegyrics by authors like Calpurnius Siculus and Martial. It is a charge that utterly lacks confirmation in official sources, on the coins, or in inscriptions or papyri. The scrupulous historian will instead point out the considerable body of evidence which suggests that the ruler cult was actively fostered by the most constitutional emperors, by Vespasian as well as by the Antonines. Thus of Augustus' successors, it was Vespasian and Trajan who played the major role in institutionalizing the imperial cult in the provinces. Trajan might declare his reluctance to accept divine honors, but he nonetheless was awarded such honors in numbers surpassed by few if any of his predecessors or successors to the imperial purple. Divine honors came to Trajan from private individuals as well as from municipalities: those who most won his favor, such as Pliny the Younger, are included among those who made and had accepted offers of divine homage to him. Trajan showed no more reluctance in continuing the innovations of his supposedly tyrannical predecessors. Thus Nero was the first living emperor to appear on the coinage wearing the divine attribute of a *divus,* the radiate crown. It was a practice that Trajan continued. Gaius had been the first to secure the posthumous deification of a member of his family, his sister Drusilla. It was a precedent followed by Trajan, who saw to it that both his sister and his father, Marcus Ulpius Traianus, were deified. The deification of members of the imperial family in fact reached a peak of sorts under the Antonines, with Hadrian's deification of his mother-in-law, Matidia.

Both relative to the preceding century and in absolute terms, the third century A.D. was marked by a distinct decline in the importance of the ruler cult in the religious life of the empire. Evidence for such cult activity at the provincial and municipal levels becomes increasingly more scanty until it virtually ceases with the political crisis of the mid third century. In Roman cult, specific emperors and members of the imperial family were consecrated in the third century, but the practice of appointing new priests for each newly deified emperor seems to have been discontinued early in the century. New currents in the religious policies of emperors like Commodus, Septimius Severus, Elagabalus, Aurelian, and Diocletian stressed the emperor's role as the divinely chosen vicegerent of the gods. As early as the principates of Trajan and Hadrian, the concept of the emperor as the vicegerent of Jupiter emerged as a central element in imperial ideology; it in no sense excluded the image of the emperor as a god in his own right. The third century continued the tradition of imperial panegyric, celebrating the emperor's divinity in literature and visual representation. Thus under Aurelian and Probus, coins bear dedicatory inscriptions honoring the emperor as *Deus et Dominus.* However, as an actual cult form ruler worship became increasingly fossilized until, with the triumph of Christianity, it died a natural death.

Themes borrowed from the language and forms of ruler worship were continued and even elaborated under the Christian empire. Christian emperors like Theodosius I and Theodosius II spoke of their own *divinitas* and *numen.* The term *god* (*theos*) was used of the emperor in Byzantine protocol until as late as the ninth century. However, such expressions of imperial majesty lacked any foundation in cult activity. From the reign of Constantine onward, the actual worship of the emperor was relegated to the same category as any other form of pagan and hence false religion. Thus in 324 A.D. Constantine readily assented to the request of the citizens of Hispellum (Spello) that they be permitted to build a temple to his family, to the Gens Flavia. But he cautioned lest any temple dedicated to his name be "defiled by the evils of any contagious superstition." Constantine thus separated the titles and honors of divinity from the cult act of sacrifice. With this separation, the history of the ruler cult in the Greco-Roman world comes to an end.

CHARACTER AND SIGNIFICANCE

For half a millennium, from the dynasty of the Ptolemies to the dynasty of the Severi, ruler worship played a major role in achieving that integration of religion and politics which lay at the very heart of the ancient state. This integration has been ignored by the majority of modern students of the ruler cult, who insist upon viewing it as a political measure having "nothing to do with religious feeling" (Tarn, 1952, p. 52). In fact, the ancients did not recognize a distinction between religion and politics. Religion permeated every aspect of the state's life, providing the very basis of the sociopolitical order. Of necessity, political ideology was formulated in theological terms and expressed through cult and ritual. Religious imagery defined the ancient's conception of sociopolitical structures, and the cult life of the state mirrored each transformation in those structures.

Ruler worship reflected the most fundamental of these transformations: the decline of the city-state and the rise of monarchy as the dominant political form in the Greek world. The classical polis rested upon a concept of collective political authority. The collective identity of the citizens of an individual polis, such as the Athenians, was expressed in the communal worship of a complex of divine patrons, gods, and heroes. Social and political values inherent in a sense of collective equality precluded rather than encouraged the idea of honoring a living mortal by such worship. In the late fifth century B.C. Socrates and Lysander, to take two examples, heralded an individualism that was both symptom and cause of the demise of a sense of collective purpose in the polis. The individual who chose to obey a god rather than his fellow citizens paralleled the Spartan who permitted himself to be raised above mortals by accepting divine honors. The execution of Socrates and the downfall of Lysander represented attempts by the polis to reestablish internally the supremacy of the collective ideal. However, by the late fourth century the individual Greek city-state had largely ceased to be master of its own political destiny. It had to deal on a permanent basis with individuals like Ptolemy, Seleucus, Lysimachus, and Antigonus, who possessed the power, the opportunity, and the will to intervene in the most decisive fashion in the domestic and foreign affairs of the polis. For their part, Ptolemy and the other successors lacked any standing in law or tradition. Their royal status rested on the naked exercise of power. For both polis and king, the ruler cult offered accommodation within a traditional framework. Through cult honors the polis could express its gratitude for royal beneficence, enroll the king among its divine patrons, and yet not necessarily admit any political dependency upon him. For the king, municipal cult honors conferred status and recognition, while the dynastic cults of the Seleucids, Ptolemies, and Attalids were one form of giving legitimacy to royal power that lacked the claims of nationality or law.

The decline of the political power of the polis coincided with and fostered a transformation in men's attitudes toward the divine order. Anthropomorphism was a fundamental aspect of Greek religion. The attribution of human qualities to the gods carried along with it a willingness to concede limitations to divine power. But the early Hellenistic age witnessed a more profound feeling of the inadequacy of traditional gods to affect important areas of human life in a meaningful way. This is precisely the point made in our earliest and most explicit justification for ruler worship: the hymns sung to Deme-

trius Poliorcetes by the Athenians in 291/290 B.C. (Athenaeus, *The Learned Banquet* [*Deipnosophistae*] 6.253):

> Other gods either keep themselves far away from us or do not listen to us or do not exist or pay absolutely no attention to us. But we see you present among us, not as a statue of stone or wood but as something real. Therefore we pray to you. First of all, we pray, give us peace. For you have the power.

The hymn goes on to state specifically how Demetrius can give peace to Athens and to all Greece: by breaking the power of the Aetolians. The divinity of the ruler lay in the immediate presence of his power to benefit and even to save the community by concrete political and social actions. Such a perception was conveyed by the conferral of cult titles such as Savior (Soter), Benefactor (Euergetes), and The Manifest One (Epiphanes). In each instance, these titles implied a conception of royal beneficence and salvation that was worldly rather than spiritual.

The words of the hymn and the other marks of deification awarded to Demetrius by the Athenians became notorious in later antiquity as an example of the lengths to which flattery could be carried. However, the worship assumed this dimension only in the aftermath of Demetrius' failure. Its origin spoke to that sense of doubt in traditional religion that was reflected in the philosophy of Epicurus. It equally reflected an age blatantly willing to invest political success with the attributes of divinity. Euhemerus as well as Epicurus was alive during the first great age of ruler worship in the Greek world. His theory of the origin of the gods is rightly seen as a justification of the propriety of offering cults to mortals. He argued that Uranus, Cronus, and Zeus were all originally mortals and kings. By acts of beneficence and by conquests they came to be considered gods. Thus on the basis of his military victories and while still living among mortals, Zeus had been publicly proclaimed to be a god.

While the philosophy of Epicurus and the *Sacred History* of Euhemerus worked to lessen the divinity of traditional gods, another philosophic current, Stoicism, elevated mortals into the divine sphere. Stoic theology recognized an entire category of divinities that consisted of mortal benefactors. Through the possession and exercise of such divine qualities as wisdom, piety, virtue, good faith, and justice men had become immortal, rising to heaven to join the gods. This was little more than a development and refinement of the popular notion, recorded in Aristotle, that by an excess of virtue (*arete*) mortals become gods. But it provided the Greco-Roman with a potent philosophical and religious paradigm to justify ruler worship. In Stoic theology, these deified benefactors, like Heracles and Asclepius, were closely associated with the worship of the actual qualities or virtues, such as the personifications Good Faith (Pistis/Fides) or Harmony (Homonoia/Concordia) or Victory (Nike/Victoria). The possession of virtues by a statesman was regarded as the result of a divine gift. The beneficent statesman thus became the instrument by which the divine will was effected; immortality was his reward for such service on behalf of gods and men.

This concept of the ruler as the divinely endowed vicegerent of the gods was present at the very inception of ruler worship in Greece. Thus on a portico at Delphi Lysander was portrayed crowned with victory by Poseidon. Medallic coins represented Alexander wielding the thunderbolt of Zeus. The Rhodians described Ptolemy, whom they deified, as the instrument of Athena, who used him to bring help to her beleaguered city. In the Roman imperial period, this concept was fundamental to the charismatic image of the emperor. Cults of Genius Augusti, Numen Augusti, and of imperial virtues like Providentia Augusta, Pax Augusta, and Concordia Augusta, were official statements of a belief that divine powers worked in the person and deeds of the emperor. In this view, the emperor functions as an intercessor. Standing between the gods of Olympus and ordinary mortals, he occupies an intermediate position. He possesses divine power. His person is not profane like that of a mortal. He is sacrosanct. The title *Augustus (Sebastos)* makes it quite clear that the emperor is a sacred being, worthy of the same reverence bestowed on all things consecrated to the gods. But at the same time, men can distinguish between the godhead of the ruler and the divinity of Zeus. The cult honors paid a ruler can be called *isotheoi;* they are equal to those paid a god, but the very employment of the term suggests a distinction between ruler and gods. Similarly, a deified Roman emperor became *divus* rather than *deus.* This same distinction appears in the fact that both Greeks and Romans felt no contradiction in praying to the gods on behalf of the divine ruler. By contrast, it would have been absurd to pray to Zeus on behalf of Apollo. In these terms, it was understood that the ruler honored as god had his closest parallel with Heracles. He lived among mortals, he performed deeds of great beneficence at the behest of the gods, and his ultimate reward would be immortality and elevation to Olympus. Thus it was that the imagery of panegyric so frequently invoked Heracles as the paradigm for the imperial achievement; significantly, frescoes of the life of Heracles decorate the meeting house of the priests of the imperial cult, the *Augustales,* in Herculaneum.

The association of the emperor with Heracles spoke to the most profound aspirations of the Greco-Roman world in the imperial age: the achievement of immortality through the exercise of *arete/virtus.* The perception of the emperor as a vehicle of divine power tapped a wellspring of popular piety in the West. Ex-votos have been properly called touchstones of popular piety in antiquity. And numerous such ex-votos attest to a popular belief in the efficacious supernatural power of Numen Augusti, Victoria Augusti, Fortuna Augusti, Virtus Augusti, and Concordia Augusti. In the Greek East, the celebration of imperial mysteries at Pergamum is a notable instance of the ability of ruler worship to inspire a deep religious piety. Such expressions of personal piety are the exception. The function of the ruler as god was not of the sort to evoke private ex-votos. The benefits he bestowed were of a communal variety; statements, of gratitude accordingly took the form of communal expression. Such ritual recognition of imperial beneficence was a major force in achieving social and political integration within the vast, supranational empire of Rome. Provincial cults of the ruler, in the East and West, were a means of inculcating loyalty and a common sense of *Romanitas* among national and local groups of disparate and often conflicting backgrounds and aims. Patriotism and true religious feeling are by no means contradictory emotions. The practical purpose served by provincial cults of the emperor merely attests to widespread popular sentiment sanctioning ruler worship. Nowhere is this fusion of patriotism and religious feeling seen to better effect than in the decree of the League of Asian Cities (9 B.C.) ratifying a suggestion by the Roman governor that the birthday of Augustus mark the beginning of the calendar year. The decree hails Augustus as god, sent by Divine Providence to be the savior of mankind. Divine Providence filled him with virtue for the benefit of the human race. The birthday of the god Augustus marked the beginning of good tidings for the entire world, and he surpasses all saviors who have been or who might come.

Despite its ability to evoke such statements of profound religious significance, cult worship of living mortals never lacked for critics in the ancient world. Pagan criticism of ruler worship took two avenues of reproach. In the first place, cult worship of a living mortal violated standards of propriety between men. To offer such adulation was an act of flattery worthy only of a slave. To demand or even accept such worship was only becoming to a tyrant. It was abhorrent to free men and to a monarch who sought to rule within the confines of just laws and acceptable traditions. In the second place, to worship a living man was to violate standards of propriety about the relationship between divine and human orders. Such cults bestowed upon a mortal honors reserved for the gods. It was an act of *hybris,* which suggested that men had the power to make gods.

Both objections were voiced by the first generation to witness the institutionalization of ruler worship in the Hellenistic world. Speaking in 322 B.C., the Athenian orator Hyperides decried the offering of sacrifices (*thysia*) to mortals as an act of reckless abandon. To worship mortals was a violation of divine law and an abolition of the rites of worship owed to the gods. It was the violation of human standards of propriety that concerned commentators on the extravagant honors that the Athenians paid to Demetrius Poliorcetes. Demetrius himself was said to be offended by the deification of his mistresses and parasites. To him, these were acts of unlicensed flattery that degraded and humiliated recipient and perpetrator alike.

These themes coalesced, and the debate on the ruler cults became a standard theme (*topos*) in the rhetorical tradition of the imperial age. No history of Alexander was complete without the insertion of a fictitious debate on the propriety of worshiping him as a god while he was still alive. Those who urged such worship were represented as flatterers. Their argument rested on the parallel instances of Dionysus and Heracles, whose deeds had raised them to the rank of immortals. Alexander had achieved even more than they. Since he was certain to be worshiped after his departure from this earth, why not go ahead and pay him divine honors now while he was still among men? The opposition to these ideas was put into the mouth of Callisthenes, who in real life had counted among the chief flatterers of Alexander. But in the rhetorical tradition, Callisthenes appears among the champions of public liberty. According to Callisthenes, to worship a living mortal is to violate the well-marked boundaries between those honors suitable for men and those intended for the gods. Heracles and Dionysus had not violated these boundaries. They received divine homage only after their departure from the world of mortals. The very idea of offering divine honors to a mortal is absurd, for it suggests that men can make a god. It as an idea that is entirely alien to the Greeks and their tradition of political liberty. It is a barbarian custom suitable for the effeminate slaves of a despot. It is an act that humiliates those who conduct the worship and degrades and debases the monarch who encourages and permits such flattery. To accept such worship is an act of arrogance that will bring about divine retribution.

A proper perspective on ruler worship was fundamental to the rhetorical image of the "good emperor." Thus in Pliny's *Panegyric* and in the *History* of Dio Cassius, the good emperor is encouraged to avoid accepting divine honors. Men cannot make him a god, and the acceptance of such false honors can only tarnish the luster of a good ruler. The tyrant makes himself ridiculous by accepting such honors, and by demanding divine homage he underscores the baseness of his rule. The true king has no need for such flattery. The very qualities of excellence and virtue exemplified by his just rule

will win him true immortality in the hearts and minds of his fellow citizens and in heaven. On occasion, emperors themselves invoked this tradition of opposition to ruler worship. Tacitus attributes such sentiments to Tiberius. Claudius made his views clear in a letter to the citizens of Alexandria. "I decline my high priest and temple establishments," he wrote. "I do not wish to seem vulgar and commonplace to men by accepting such honors. And furthermore I believe that sacrifices and other divine honors have for all eternity been set apart as belonging to the gods alone" (Smallwood, *Documents Illustrating the Principates of Gaius, Claudius, and Nero* [1967], no. 370, 47–51).

The opposition was directed against the idea of worshiping living rulers. Among pagans there was little questioning of the appropriateness of posthumous deification. Indeed, Pliny praised Trajan for consecrating Nerva, "because you believed that he was a god" (*Panegyric* 89). To deify a deceased emperor was wrong only if such consecration were felt to be undeserved. The whole point of Seneca's biting satire in the *Apocolocyntosis* is that Claudius has demonstrated none of the virtues through which immortality is gained. In this same piece, Seneca is quite content to accept the divinity of Augustus, who brought peace to the entire world, put an end to civil war, established law and order, and beautified Rome with magnificent buildings.

In terms of the Roman religious mentality, opposition to the deification of living men rested on the belief that men could not make gods. Mortals could only recognize divinity, and since divinity presupposed immortality, such recognition must be withheld until the ruler had demonstrated his immortality by ascending into heaven. Along with this went a very strong sense of sacral caution. The ancient did not distinguish between religion and politics. He did, however, distinguish very carefully between the sacred and the profane. The gods, like the dead, belong to a world carefully set apart by the magic of ritual. Only at extreme peril did the living attempt to enter that world. Therein lay the sense of the warning that "divinity sometimes overtakes a man; it never accompanies him" (Curtius Rufus, *History of Alexander the Great* 8.5.16).

Thus ruler worship, including its opposition, was a natural extension of basic religious conceptions of Greco-Roman paganism. By contrast, the very idea of deifying a mortal violated the most sacred canon of Judaism. It was the greatest blasphemy to believe that the created, destructible nature of man could be transformed into the uncreated, indestructible nature of God. Judaism could admit no compromise with ruler worship. This was recognized by the wisest of Roman statesmen, Augustus. Jews were specifically exempted from any obligation to offer sacrifices to the emperor. They sacrificed instead to their God on behalf of the emperor, praying for his health and prosperity. It was an arrangement that was respected through all the trials and tribulations of Roman-Jewish relations. Even Gaius, viewed through the critical eyes of Philo, exempted the Jews from the necessity of worshiping him. It was an exemption that remained in force as late as the fourth century; a passage in the Talmud indicates that the Jews alone escaped Diocletian's edict requiring universal sacrifice.

Christianity inherited the Jewish abhorrence of ruler worship but not its status as a *religio licita,* as a foreign religion tolerated by the Roman state. Christian apologists like Tertullian might insist on their loyalty. They could point out that Christians honored the emperor in all ways becoming a mortal, viewing him as the divinely chosen vicegerent of God and as one who stood second only to God himself. However, they could no more sacrifice to the emperor or swear an oath by his Genius than they could honor the other false gods of Rome. It was this general refusal to worship the gods, who protected and guarded the commonwealth, that provoked the persecution of Christians by the Roman state. Ruler worship was involved only in the sense that the *divi* were of course included among the gods of Rome. Furthermore, a magistrate like Pliny might include the statue of the reigning emperor among the gods to whom sacrifice must be made. So too the necessity to swear an oath by the emperor's Genius presented a moral dilemma to the conscientious Christian. It was a conflict and a dilemma that ended only with Constantine and the ultimate triumph of Christianity.

The triumph of Christianity occurred in a world long accustomed to the worship of mortal men. The fundamental themes of ruler worship drew upon the wellsprings of popular piety in an age of profound religiosity, and it must be recognized that Christianity did more than borrow isolated images and titles from the developed panoply of ruler cult. The popular cult of saints was a direct continuation of the ideas and even forms of hero worship and related expressions, including cults of deified emperors. Even more significant was the importance of the ruler cult in fixing a paradigm of the emperor as universal savior. Coins proclaiming Trajan as Savior of the Human Race (*Salus Generis Humani*) evoked an image of a ruler sent by God and born of mortal parentage, a ruler who lived among men and performed acts of supernatural beneficence on their behalf, a ruler whom God had filled with virtue and who would ultimately triumph over death and ascend to heaven. There was a profound association of the message of imperial soteriology with the fundamental belief of Christianity. Ruler worship taught men to accept a savior who partook of the elements of both godhead and humanity. In that teaching lay the most enduring legacy of ruler worship to the ancient Mediterranean world and to Europe.

BIBLIOGRAPHY

The scattered ancient sources are most conveniently collected in L. Cerfaux and J. Tondriau, *Un concurrent du Christianisme: Le culte des souverains dans la civilisation gréco-romaine* (1957). This work contains full bibliographies on all aspects of the ruler cult.

STUDIES

Ernst Badian, "The Deification of Alexander the Great," in *Ancient Macedonian Studies in Honor of Charles F. Edson* (1981); J. Béranger, "L'Expression de la divinité dans les panégyriques latins," in *Museum Helveticum,* **27** (1970; repr. in *Principatus* [1975]); J. Beaujeu, "Les apologètes et le culte du souverain," in Willem den Boer, ed., *Le culte des souverains dans l'empire romain,* Fondation Hardt, Entretiens, **19** (1973), and *La religion romaine à l'apogée de l'empire* (1955); Elias Bickerman, "Consecratio," in Willem den Boer, ed., *Le culte des souverains dans l'empire romain,* Fondation Hardt, Entretiens, **19** (1973); Willem den Boer, *Heerserscultus en ex-voto's in het Romeinse keizerrijk,* in *Mededelingen der Koninklijke Nederlandse Akademie van Wetenschappen, Afd. Letterkunde,* n.s., **36** (1973); F. Bömer, "Der Eid beim Genius des Kaisers," in *Athenaeum,* **44** (1966); Glen W. Bowersock, *Augustus and the Greek World* (1965), and "Greek Intellectuals and the Imperial Cult in the Second Century A.D.," in Willem den Boer, ed., *Le culte des souverains dans l'empire romain,* Fondation Hardt, Entretiens, **19** (1973).

Martin P. Charlesworth, "Some Observations on Ruler Cult, Especially in Rome," in *Harvard Theological Review,* **28** (1935); Carl J. Classen, "Gottmenschentum in der römischen Republik," in *Gymnasium,* **70** (1963); R. Duthoy, "Les *Augustales," in Wolfgang Haase, ed., *Aufstieg und Niedergang der römischen Welt* II, 16, 2 (1978); R. Étienne, *Le culte impérial dans la péninsule ibérique d'Auguste à Dioclétien* (1958); L. R. Farnell, *Greek Hero Cults and Ideas of Immortality* (1921); J. Rufus Fears, "Response," in *Protocol of the Twenty-First*

Colloquy of the Center for Hermeneutical Studies in Hellenistic and Modern Culture (1976), *Princeps a Diis Electus: The Divine Election of the Emperor as a Political Concept at Rome,* papers and monographs of the American Academy in Rome, **26** (1977), "Ho Demos ho Romaion—Genius Populi Romani: A Note on the Origins of Dea Roma," in *Mnemosyne,* **31** (1978), review of *Thea Rome: The Worship of the Goddess Roma in the Greek World* by Ronald Mellor, *Gnomon,* **50** (1978), "The Cult of Jupiter and Roman Imperial Ideology," in Wolfgang Haase, ed., *Aufstieg und Niedergang der römischen Welt* II, 17, 1 (1981), "The Cult of Virtues and Roman Imperial Ideology," in Wolfgang Haase, ed. *Aufstieg und Niedergang der römischen Welt* II, 17, 2 (1981), "Gottesgnadentum (Gottkönigtum)" in *Reallexikon für Antike und Christentum* XI (1981), and "The Theology of Victory at Rome," in Wolfgang Haase, ed., *Aufstieg und Niedergang der römischen Welt* II, 17, 2 (1981); Duncan Fishwick, "Genius and Numen," in *Harvard Theological Review,* **62** (1969), *Studies in Roman Imperial History* (1977), "The Development of Provincial Ruler Worship in the Western Roman Empire," in Wolfgang Haase, ed. *Aufstieg und Niedergang der römischen Welt* II, 16, 2 (1978), and "The Imperial Cult in the Latin West" (in press); P. Fraser, *Ptolemaic Alexandria* (1972); E. A. Fredricksmeyer, "On the Background of the Ruler Cult," in *Ancient Macedonian Studies in Honor of Charles F. Edson* (1981).

Christian Habicht, "Die augustische Zeit und das erste Jahrhundert nach Christi Geburt," in Willem den Boer, ed., *Le culte des souverains dans l'empire romain,* Fondation Hardt, Entretiens, **19** (1973), and *Gottmenschentum und griechische Städte,* 2d.ed. (1970); Peter Herz, "Bibliographie zum römischen Kaiserkult," in Wolfgang Haase, ed., *Aufstieg und Niedergang der römischen Welt* II, 16, 2 (1978); H. von Hesberg, "Archäologische Denkmäler zum römischen Kaiserkult," in Wolfgang Haase, ed., *Aufstieg und Niedergang der römischen Welt* II 16, 2 (1978); K. Hopkins, *Conquerors and Slaves* (1978); Ronald Mellor, *Thea Rome: The Worship of the Goddess Roma in the Greek World* (1975); Fergus Millar, "The Imperial Cult and the Persecutions," in Willem den Boer, ed., *Le culte des souverains dans l'empire romain,* Fondation Hardt, Entretiens, **19** (1973); G. Niebling, "Laribus Augustis magistri primi: Der Beginn des Compitalkultes der Lares und des Genius Augusti," in *Historia,* **5** (1956); M. P. Nilsson, *Geschichte der griechischen Religion* (1955, 1974); Arthur D. Nock, *Essays on Religion and the Ancient World* (1972); H. W. Pleket, "An Aspect of the Emperor Cult: Imperial Mysteries," in *Harvard Theological Review,* **58** (1965); S. R. F. Price, *Rituals and Power: The Roman Imperial Cult in Asia Minor* (1984).

Gerhardt Radke, "Augustus und das Göttliche," in *Antike und Universalgeschichte: Festschrift H. E. Stier* (1972); Kenneth Scott, "Plutarch and the Ruler Cult," in *Transactions and Proceedings of the American Philological Association,* **60** (1929); F.

Taeger, *Charisma: Studien zur Geschichte des antiken Herrscherkultus* (1957–1960); William W. Tarn, *Hellenistic Civilization,* 3d ed. (1952); K. Thraede, "Die Poesie und der Kaiserkult," in Willem den Boer, ed., *Le culte des souverains dans l'empire romain,* Fondation Hardt, Entretiens, **19** (1973); R. Turcan, "Le culte impérial au III siècle," in Wolfgang Haase, ed., *Aufstieg und Niedergang der römischen Welt* II, 16, 2 (1978); H. Waldmann, *Die kommagenischen Kultreformen unter König Mithradates I Kallinikos und seinem Sohn Antiochus I* (1973); Otto Weinreich, "Antikes Gottmenschentum," in *Neue Jahrbücher für Wissenschaft und Jugendbildung,* **2** (1926; repr. in A. Wlosok, ed., *Römischer Kaiserkult* [1978]); S. Weinstock, *Divus Julius* (1971).

Judaism

SETH SCHWARTZ

INTRODUCTION

Most scholars agree that Judaism, practiced in Judaea, Babylonia, and elsewhere following the fall of Babylon and the Persian conquest of the Near East, is an offshoot of a singular variety of the Israelite religion. Judaism as it was practiced after about 530 B.C. differed in several essential ways from the Israelite religion before that time.

First, Judaism is characterized by an insistence on the worship of Yahweh alone. Even before 587 B.C., when the Judahite kingdom was destroyed by the Babylonians under Nebuchadnezzar, a group of Israelites—aptly named by Morton Smith (1971) the "Yahweh-alone" faction—made this revolutionary demand, and influenced a few Judahite kings, especially Hezekiah (ca. 727–698 B.C.) and Josiah (639–609 B.C.). Nevertheless, the official religion of Judah and Israel, as practiced in the temples of Jerusalem, Dan, and elsewhere, and sanctioned by the priesthood and almost all the kings, was polytheistic: Yahweh was recognized as chief god, but various Baals, Astarte, Kemosh, and others were worshiped, too.

A second difference is that Judaism tended to insist on the centrality of the Jerusalem temple: "One temple for the one God," as Josephus put it (*Against Apion* 2.193). But this insistence was not absolute; other temples and shrines continued to exist—for example, the temples of Mount Gerizim (built around 300 B.C. and destroyed in 129 B.C.) and Leontopolis (built about 160 B.C., and closed A.D. 73) and the shrines of Lachish, Mamre, and Bethel. The centrality of the Jerusalem temple had been proclaimed by a part of the Yahweh-alone faction before 587 B.C. but was widely accepted only from 622 to 609, the latter part of Josiah's reign. At all other times before 587 Israelites worshiped their gods where they pleased, although the main temple in Jerusalem was especially prestigious.

Third, no document composed prior to 587 suggests that intermarriage between Israelites and non-Israelites was controversial. Israelite men frequently married non-Israelite women (we do not know if the converse was true) without the prophets of the Yahweh-alone faction denouncing them for this. In Judaism, though, some, like Ezra and Nehemiah (mid fifth century B.C.), absolutely forbade marriages between Jews and Gentiles, either for reasons of ritual purity or because foreign spouses were expected to continue to worship foreign gods. Others permitted such marriages; for example, the high-priestly dynasty that served until 170 B.C. was connected by marriage to the aristocratic Tobiad family from Ammon in the Transjordan, and to the family of the governors of Samaria. This controversy seems to have continued at least until the Maccabean revolt (167–152 B.C.), although gradually there developed a compromise position: marriage to a Gentile was permitted provided the Gentile adopted Judaism.

Finally, Judaism was characterized by ritual observances not widespread before 587. Among these were the Sabbath, Passover (observed before 587 only, according to 2 Kings 23:21, under Josiah), Tabernacles (not observed until the mid fifth century B.C.), and various purity laws.

Although the above are unique characteristics of Judaism, in fact the very terms "Judaism" and "Jew" (*Ioudaios*, or *Yehudi*) are ambiguous. Since this ambiguity is important throughout the period dealt with by this essay, it must be briefly explored. *Ioudaios* (pl. *Ioudaioi*) or *Yehudi* (pl. *Yehudim*) primarily refers to someone who lives in, or whose ancestors lived in, the small hill-country district (*Ioudaia*, or *Yehudah*) around Jerusalem. But in the Persian period (539–332 B.C.), *Yehudi* came also to refer to anyone who worshiped only the God of Israel. This second meaning may exclude ethnic or geographic *Yehudim*, as when the author of Ezra excludes the polytheistic Judaean peasantry from this class; but it may also, especially later, include foreigners. These two meanings of *Yehudi* continued side by side throughout antiquity, contributing to our confusion. Hence, although the meaning of each individual use of the term "Jew(s)" in this account will usually be clear from the context, the reader must always remember that not every ethnic Jew (*Yehudi*) was a religious Jew, and not every religious Jew was an ethnic Jew.

THE PERSIAN PERIOD

History

A survey of the history of Judaea and Judaean settlements in Mesopotamia and Egypt in this period will necessarily be brief; the sources tell us little, and what little they tell us is notoriously difficult to interpret. Nevertheless, it is possible to deduce the outline of major events.

The fall of Babylon to the Persian king Cyrus II in 539 B.C. was welcomed by many Jews, especially descendants of those deported to Mesopotamia in 598 and 587 by Nebuchadnezzar (Isaiah 45). This goodwill was reciprocated: Cyrus himself permitted a group of deportees, led by a certain Sheshbazzar, to return to Judah and rebuild the temple of the "God of Heaven." The reconstruction failed. Then, around 522, Darius I permitted Zerubbabel, a grandson of Jehoiachin, who had been king of Judah (598–597 B.C.), Joshua the priest, and a group of followers to try again. After some delay, the building was completed in 515.

The next known event in Judah is the governorship of the Babylonian-Jewish priest and scribe Ezra, in 458 B.C. Ezra was committed to the Yahweh-alone faction, but was an ineffective politician: he rushed to push through a program that probably included the imposition of the Deuteronomic law code (roughly Deuteronomy 12–28) and certainly included a demand that the Judahites divorce their foreign wives. This demand annoyed both the well-to-do—especially the priests—and the gentry of the surrounding lands, at a time when the Persian king he served, Artaxerxes I, could not afford to annoy either. So Ezra was removed, having failed to implement his program.

In 444 B.C., when Nehemiah was appointed governor of Judah, the area had not yet recovered from the effects of an Egyptian revolt (crushed in 455) and the subsequent revolt of the satrap Megabyzus (448). Nehemiah, an enthusiastic member of the Yahweh-alone faction, was an official in Artaxerxes' court and, unlike Ezra, a talented politician; the king probably thought he could help bring about Judah's recovery. On his arrival, he first won the support of the masses by various economic measures, most prominently cancellation of debts. He could then proceed with the unpopular part of his program: enforced divorce of foreign wives, closing of markets on the Sabbath, and imposition on the priesthood of his notions of ritual purity. He further interfered in temple affairs by expelling from the building Tobiah, a wealthy Ammonite perhaps related by marriage to the high priest, along with a son of the high priest who refused to divorce his wealthy Samarian wife.

Nehemiah's administration was a turning point. The practices and policies he succeeded in imposing on Judah and the temple defined Judaism, and from 432 B.C. on, Judaism, although initially a less separatist variety than Nehemiah's, would be the religion of Judah and would also become the religion of Judahites living abroad.

The Judaization of the overseas Judahite colonies can be traced in the remote south Egyptian military settlement at Elephantine, known to us from a collection of papyri. From this Judahite colony's beginnings under the Saite kings of Egypt (664–525 B.C.) down to the late fifth century B.C., its members had their own temple where they worshiped the Israelite god, Yahu (Yahweh), and also a variety of Syrian deities, such as Eshembethel, Anathbethel, and Anathyahu. They freely intermarried with native Egyptians and non-Judahite colonists, and seem to have been unaware of the Jewish festivals. In short, they practiced the Israelite religion very much as it had been practiced in Judah

before 587. But in 419 the colonists received a letter from a Jewish official informing them that by command of King Darius II they must henceforth observe the Passover and the Feast of Unleavened Bread; the letter also provides instructions for the observance. Eight years later, when some fanatical Egyptian priests destroyed their temple, they appealed to the high priest of Jerusalem for help in rebuilding, but received no response. These two incidents show how, soon after Nehemiah, Judaism began to be, with royal consent, the official, or nearly official, religion of the Jews.

Literature

The greatest work produced during the Persian period was the final edition of the Pentateuch, about 400 B.C. This work is a compromise between the extreme separatism of Nehemiah and the assimilationism of the Jerusalem priesthood. The former is reflected in the inclusion of the Deuteronomic code (Deuteronomy 12–28), which, among many other things, frowns on marriages with foreigners (23:4 ff.; in a similar vein 7:3) and by implication ordains the centrality of the Jerusalem temple (16:6 *passim*). Assimilationism is reflected in, for example, the universalist priestly narratives in Genesis, especially chapters 1 through 11. The books of Chronicles, Ezra, and Nehemiah (which may, however, be early Hellenistic) reflect the views of Nehemiah's followers. Chronicles is striking for its Levitical bias, as are most of the Psalms dated to this period; Nehemiah favored the Levites, the hereditary class of nonpriestly auxiliary staff in the Jerusalem temple. All these large works are, in effect, the products of committees; they use the professional jargon and reflect the concerns of entire classes: the Pentateuch of the priesthood, and the Chronicles and Psalms of the Levites. But many other works composed in the period reflect the interests of individual assimilationist aristocrats. These works show that the Judahite aristocracy, or part of it, was gradually reconciled to Judaism, as well as demonstrating that the aristocrats were in touch with the literary fashions of the day.

The earliest of these assimilationist works (from the sixth century B.C.) is Proverbs 22:17–31:31, a collection of worldly sayings with little religious and no Jewish content. The passage of Proverbs 22:17–24:22 is known to depend on a collection of Egyptian sayings. Somewhat later comes Job 3–31 (early fifth century), a great dramatic dialogue about the nature of God and the problem of evil. This work, too, is unconcerned with the observances of Judaism, the Jerusalem temple, and the historical traditions of Israel, and the God it discusses is not identified with Yahweh. In the later fifth and fourth centuries, the aristocratic literature begins to move closer to Judaism. Although the author of Ecclesiastes was a cultured skeptic, he resigned himself to conformity with Judaism, just as many Athenian philosophers conformed to the public cult of their city. The authors of various short stories (Ruth, Jonah, Judith, Tobit, and Esther, some of which are from the fourth century, although others may be Hellenistic) have moved still closer to Judaism: they look with favor upon Jewish observances and the Jerusalem temple and are monotheists; yet they all promote intermarriage and other relations with the surrounding peoples. These include Ammonites and Moabites, who, according to Deuteronomy 23:4, are forbidden to join the Jewish community.

From the literary point of view, we may observe in these works an evolution in genres paralleled at every step in Greek literature. Epics and wise sayings of the archaic period (Homer, Hesiod, and Theognis, and the early narratives of the Pentateuch and Proverbs, from the eighth to the mid sixth centuries) give way to grand dramatic works about relations between the human and the divine (Aeschylus and Job in the early fifth century), which in turn give way to more personal, small-scale ruminations on metaphysical and ethical problems (the philosophers, such as Plato and Theophrastus, and Ecclesiastes, in the fourth century and later) and elegant erotic and idyllic poems and stories (Theocritus and Callimachus, and Ruth, the Song of Songs, and Tobit, from the late fourth century on).

Parallel to this adoption of international literary fashion is the gradual adoption of Greek style in day-to-day life, as in pottery and coins. In lower Galilee and along the Palestinian coast, Greek pottery and local imitations dominate archaeological finds. This sort of material gradually penetrated inland to Judah and Samaria, and by about 400 B.C. came to replace both native Israelite wares and Egyptian and Mesopotamian imports. Athenian and other Greek coins from throughout the period have been found in the interior of Palestine. More significantly, local coinage, including the provincial coinage of Judah itself from the fourth century B.C., tends to follow Attic style; one type even shows a Zeus-like figure seated in a chariot. Hence, the coinage not only illustrates the penetration of Greek culture into Judah well before Alexander, but also proves that the assimilationist leadership of the province found a loophole in the biblical prohibition against making images, especially of gods (Exodus 20:4; Deuteronomy 5:8).

THE HELLENISTIC PERIOD: 332–37 B.C.

History

Judaea (as the land was now called) went over to Alexander without a struggle in 332 B.C. In the years of fighting in Syria and Palestine that followed Alexander's death, from 323 to 301 B.C., the Jews seem to have resisted, and then slightly, only Ptolemy I Soter's conquest in 302. Probably because of this submissiveness, Alexander, and after him Ptolemy and Antigonus I Monophthalmus, seems to have permitted the Jews to retain their traditional constitution (Ptolemy held the land from 320 to 315, in 312 and 302, and after 301, and Antigonus held it in the intervening years). This means that the Jews—in Greek terms the nation (*ethnos*) dwelling around the temple of Jerusalem— were to be ruled by an aristocracy consisting of senior priests (later formed into a council called the *gerousia*) and presided over by the high priest. This aristocracy was to govern the Jews "according to their ancestral laws" (Josephus, *Jewish Antiquities* 12.142, reporting a document dating from about 200 B.C.)—that is, according to the aristocrats' interpretation of the Pentateuch.

There were two main differences between this arrangement and that prevalent in the last century of Persian rule. First, under the Successors and the Ptolemies (323–198 B.C.) Judaea did not have a satrap; in principle, the high priest was responsible for the collection of taxes and keeping the peace (he was called *prostates tou ethnous,* "ruler of the nation"). This new arrangement may have been the consequence of the second new factor: the rise of the priesthood to unchallenged prominence in Judaea, at the expense of the Levites and lay aristocrats (see, for example, Hecataeus of Abdera, *Aegyptiaca,* composed about 300 and quoted in Diodorus Siculus, *Library of History* 40.3.1–8).

But the period of unchallenged high-priestly control did not last long. Around 240 B.C., the Judaized Ammonite Joseph, whose father was Tobias (a wealthy landowner related by marriage to the high priest of Jerusalem) and who was descended from Nehemiah's Ammonite foe Tobiah, and had been commander of a Ptolemaic military

colony near Philadelphia (Amman), took advantage of a political blunder of the high priest Onias II to become the *prostates tou ethnous* of Judaea, Samaria, Transjordan, and the Palestine coast. He held this office until he made the mistake of supporting Antiochus III in the Fourth Syrian War (221–218 B.C.).

The high priests did not resume their sole leadership until the Seleucid conquest of Palestine (*ca.* 200 B.C.), in which Antiochus III was helped by the high priest Simeon, son of Onias. This resumption of control had bloody consequences, for the priesthood was now torn by factions.

The members of the upper class had long been assimilationist; although by the third century they were more or less reconciled to Judaism and in some cases strongly nationalistic, they approved of various sorts of relations with non-Jews. It is no surprise to find that Greek culture, which had made inroads into Judaea even in the Persian period, was well received by all elements of the aristocracy. But by the period of Seleucid domination, the assimilationist faction began to split. A conservative group, centered around the high priest Simeon II and his son Onias III, strongly supported the traditional Judaean political and cultic institutions and promoted observance of Jewish law. Others, poorly disposed to Judaism, rejected and would later hinder observance of Jewish law and practice of the cult, at least as prescribed in Leviticus. Lower on the social ladder, among poorer priests and perhaps Levites, separatism, which continued to reject most relations with Gentiles (1 Maccabees 1:11 ff.), and which no doubt had its own legal traditions, continued to flourish. Purely political hostility between pro-Seleucids and pro-Ptolemaics cut across other lines of division.

As long as Antiochus III and his protégé Simeon were firmly in control, all these divisions remained under the surface. But the

Roman victory at Magnesia (189 B.C.) weakened and impoverished the Seleucid kingdom, and by 176 the priests were at each other's throats; Onias III, who may have had Ptolemaic sympathies, was deposed. His brother Jason succeeded him and, around 174, received from Antiochus IV, in return for a large bribe, the right to establish Greek institutions at Jerusalem. The pious may have been displeased, but did not react openly: Jason, a moderate, had no intention of harming Judaism.

Around 171 B.C. the extreme assimilationists, led by the priest Menelaus and perhaps supported by a pro-Seleucid faction of the Tobiads, bribed their way into the high priesthood. During Antiochus' two Egyptian campaigns (in 169 and 168 B.C.), Jerusalem rebelled against him and Menelaus. As punishment, Jerusalem was deconstituted and a military colony was established in the former city. Probably with Menelaus' encouragement, the king then outlawed the observance of Judaism on pain of death, and Menelaus rededicated the temple to Zeus Olympios.

Many Jews were happy with these reforms; others conformed with distaste. But the pious, including pious assimilationists, found the new regime intolerable. The various groups that fled to the wilderness amalgamated and took to arms under the leadership of a priest, Judah (Judas), son of Mattathias, and his brothers, called collectively the Maccabees or the Hasmoneans. Late in 164 B.C., Judah invaded Jerusalem and seized the temple, and a year later Lysias (regent of the infant Antiochus V), his own kingdom torn by internal strife, ended the reforms and restored the Jewish constitution. Paradoxically, this, along with the appointment of a conservative, pro-Seleucid high priest (Alcimus), deprived Judah of popular support.

That Judah continued to fight suggests that he was now attempting to secure Judaea's independence under his own leadership. This is the first definite appearance in Jewish history of the notion that the Jews in Judaea ought to be independent of foreign rule, but Judah's fate shows that the idea was not yet popular.

In March 161 Judah managed to win one last victory over a Seleucid army. He followed this feat by concluding an alliance with the Roman Senate, marking the first appearance of Rome as a factor in Jewish history. But the senate failed to keep its promises: in early spring 160 Judah's faction was crushed, Judah was killed, and his brothers with their few surviving partisans were forced to flee to the wilderness, where they resorted to brigandage.

However, in circumstances we do not fully understand, in 152 B.C. Demetrius I, over Jewish opposition, appointed Jonathan, brother of Judah, to be high priest and commander of Judaea. After his death in 143, his brother Simeon succeeded him and secured from Demetrius II what amounted to independence. After some two and a half centuries, assimilationist rule thus came decisively to an end—another important turning point in the history of Judaism.

Under Simeon, Judaea began its transformation into a small Hellenistic kingdom. After overcoming continuing Jewish opposition, Simeon set himself up as high priest and ethnarch (dynast) and began to conquer territory, including the Seleucid military colonies in Jerusalem and Beth-Zur, Gezer, and, most important, the port city of Joppa (Jaffa). After Simeon's assassination by his son-in-law (134 B.C.), Simeon's son, John Hyrcanus I, heir to the ethnarchy and high priesthood, at once submitted to the relatively vigorous Antiochus VII Sidetes. When Sidetes died in 129 and chaos again reigned in Syria, John resumed an expansionist policy with the help of Greek mercenaries, conquering most of Samaria and parts of Transjordan and Idumaea ca. 129–125, and later the rest of Samaria and the important Greek city of Scythopolis (Beth-Shean), between 110 and 107. It is of utmost importance for the future course of Jewish history that John, followed by his successors, encouraged—and when necessary, forced—his new subjects to adopt Judaism. Also important was John's increasingly close relationship with Rome, whose policies he admired and may have imitated.

Expansion and hellenization, if not romanization, continued under John's sons Aristobulus ("Philhellene," 103 B.C.) and Alexander Jannaeus (Yannai, 103–76). These men, both high priests, officially transformed Judaea into a kingdom; they extended its boundaries to include all of Palestine (except Ascalon [Ashkelon], a Ptolemaic protectorate), the Golan, and western Transjordan. Alexander came into conflict with both Ptolemy IX Lathyrus and the Nabataeans (who claimed all Transjordan as their own), and extricated himself from his difficulties with the ancestral combination of military skill and diplomatic cunning. He overcame opposition at home, perhaps incited by the Pharisees, by brute force. The policy of Judaization, which worked well with Semitic farmers in the hinterland, was rather less successful in the many Greek cities conquered by Alexander, including Dor, Anthedon, Gaza, and Raphia (Rafa) on the coast and Panion (Panias), Seleucia, Hippos, Dium, Gadara, Pella, and Gerasa in the Transjordan: the inhabitants of some of these towns are said to have fled. As to foreign policy, Alexander apparently failed to renew the traditional alliance with Rome, possibly out of deference to Mithridates VI of Pontus and Tigranes of Armenia.

Under Alexander's widow and successor Salome Alexandra (76–67 B.C.), territorial expansion was prevented by Tigranes' presence at the very border of the Hasmonean kingdom. Alexandra emphasized good administration—a pressing need with territory

and population greatly expanded and hitherto unheard-of wealth flowing into Jerusalem. In her relations with the aristocracy, Alexandra favored the Pharisees, but had to placate the Sadducees, who controlled the temple and the army.

The compromise the queen had arranged between the aristocratic factions began to collapse even before her death, and by 67, a combination of civil war and war of succession erupted; it lasted thirty years. John Hyrcanus II, the oldest son of Alexander and Alexandra, high priest from 76 B.C. and designated heir, inherited his mother's partisans, but also had the support of an Idumaean family that had come to prominence under Alexander. The younger son, Aristobulus II, inherited his father's partisans, mostly Sadducees. The war was intensified by Pompey's conquest of Palestine in 63 B.C. and the subsequent Roman civil war, which allowed each Jewish faction to have the support of a Roman faction. Hyrcanus' weakness allowed the rise of his exceptionally shrewd and aggressive Idumaean partisans, Antipater and his son Herod. By the early 40s B.C. these men, because they had a knack for making themselves serviceable to each Roman warlord in turn, from Pompey to Octavian, came to overshadow John. The Aristobulans had trouble competing, despite their own aggressiveness, senatorial connections, and popularity in Palestine.

When the Parthians occupied Syria-Palestine in 40 B.C., they installed Antigonus, son of Aristobulus II, on the Judaean throne and took the aged Hyrcanus captive after having severed his ears, thus rendering him unfit for the high priesthood. Herod (Antipater was killed in 43 B.C.) fled to Rome and presented himself to the senate, which named him king of Judaea, without, however, giving him an army to dislodge Antigonus. Nevertheless, by 37 Herod and Gaius Sosius, governor of Syria, deposed Antigonus, who was then executed, and conquered Palestine.

Literature and Religion: 332–37 B.C.

In the Hellenistic period, Judaea was surrounded by many hellenized cities, some of whose territories—for example, those of Ascalon and Joppa—must have extended far enough inland to contain a Jewish population. Furthermore, during the Wars of the Successors and the Syrian Wars, Palestine was a battlefield on which huge armies of Macedonians, Greeks, and hellenized barbarians clashed, through which they marched, and in which some of them settled, exerting influence on the Palestinian countryside. At a higher social level, knowledge of Greek language and culture was necessary for politics and trade. For all these reasons the pace of adoption of Greek language and culture accelerated on all social levels; hence the appearance of literature written by Palestinian Jews in Greek and in typically Greek genres. A wide variety of religious viewpoints was expressed in these works, which were produced even by partisans of the Hasmoneans. Nevertheless, literary Hebrew and the old genres remained remarkably vital, especially, but probably not exclusively, in Palestine.

Before the Maccabean revolt, the points of controversy in Judaism were mostly what they had been in the Persian period: the permissibility of relations with the surrounding peoples, observance of Jewish law, and, to some extent, the exclusivity of the Jerusalem temple. However, no books advocating an extreme assimilationist position survived in Palestine, and only fragments of such works survived in Egypt.

The branch of the assimilationist group that fully accepted Judaism produced such works as Tobit and Judith, which promote Jewish law but also accept relations with some non-Judaeans. These works have been discussed above. The fullest expression of the pious assimilationist ethos is "The Wisdom of Jesus ben Sira" (Ecclesiasticus, composed in Hebrew, *ca.* 185 B.C.). Ben Sira, who is thought to have spent his young manhood as a courtier in Alexandria, lectured the well-to-do youth in Jerusalem about "wisdom," meaning fear of God, respect for Jewish law, the glories of nature, and etiquette. In his book, he vigorously advocates observance of the law. He was also well versed in the historical traditions of Israel (44–50; note the adoration of the high priest Simeon in chapter 50) and accepted uncritically the notion of the authors of these traditions that God will not permit sinners to prosper. Yet Ben Sira included in his book much "secular" wisdom, including advice on how to raise a family and how to behave at dinner parties, town meetings, and lawsuits, attacks on misspent wealth, and so on. These sections show that Ben Sira was familiar with some popular Greek philosophical ideas and may have read some late Egyptian and Greek wisdom books.

Somewhat similar to Ben Sira in outlook was his younger contemporary Eupolemus, an upper-class Jerusalem priest, who published a history called *Concerning the Kings of Judaea* in Greek in 158 B.C. In the surviving fragments of this work, Eupolemus shows detailed knowledge of Samuel and Kings, as well as reverence for the Jerusalem temple. But he also follows the canons of Greek historiography and knows some Greek mythology. Although Eupolemus implies his approval of the activities of the moderate assimilationist high priest Jason (2 Maccabees 4:18 ff.), he was probably a partisan of Judah Maccabee—illustrating how some assimilationist aristocrats made their peace with the arriviste, separatist Hasmoneans.

Pervaded by a "nationalistic" but more libertine attitude are the Book of Esther and the "Tobiad Romance" (mid second century), preserved in Josephus (*Antiquities* 12.154–236). The "Romance" (or Josephus) glories in Joseph the Tobiad's harsh treatment of the Greek inhabitants of Ascalon; Joseph himself, however, attempts to have an affair with an Egyptian dancing-girl, and, as in Esther, both Joseph and his son Hyrcanus eat at the pagan king's table without the author's disapproval. We know that the historical third- and second-century Tobiads were ambivalent toward Judaism.

Reflecting a more separatist attitude are Jubilees, Daniel, and perhaps the earlier parts of 1 Enoch (1–36; 72–82). Jubilees, probably composed in Hebrew around 160 B.C., is a highly expanded retelling of Genesis. It emphasizes, anachronistically, the patriarchs' strict observance of Mosaic law, attacks those who reject circumcision (15:33–34), warns against any sort of mixing with Gentiles (22:16–23; 30:11–26), and glorifies the priesthood (31:13–20). The concerns of the early parts of Enoch are less clear, although literarily Enoch and Jubilees have much in common. Enoch saves its harshest language for a now obscure polemic about the calendar. Best-known of this group is Daniel, published in Hebrew and Aramaic around 165. The first part (chapters 1–6) contains stories about the steadfast adherence of Daniel, a young Jewish courtier in Babylon, to Jewish law, and his ensuing problems. Chapters 7–12 contain "prophecies" of the course of world history, accurate down to 165 and apocalyptic fantasy thereafter, culminating in the complete vindication of "those who turn many to righteousness" and "the wise." Although Daniel sharply attacks Antiochus IV and his Judaean partisans, he is indifferent to the Maccabees (Daniel 11:34).

As indicated, the success of the Hasmoneans caused a drastic change in Judaism and the social and political structure of Judaea. Most assimilationists, even moderate ones, were now discredited by their association with Antiochus' reforms. Of the conservative priestly assimilationists, one group refused to accept Hasmonean rule, and so fled to Egypt, where they joined Onias, son of Onias III, whom they considered the legitimate high priest. Another, perhaps separatist, priestly group also rejected the Hasmoneans and their temple, retired to the Judaean desert, and founded the Dead Sea sect or the Essenes (the identity of the Dead Sea sect with the Essenes is far from certain). However, some—perhaps even most—of the priestly conservatives remained, were reconciled to the Hasmoneans, and retained a strong influence over public affairs. This last group may be those called Sadducees in later literature, while the Pharisees, possibly connected with earlier separatists, are said by Josephus to have emerged around the time of Jonathan.

It must be admitted, however, that almost nothing is known about the beliefs and literary activities of these groups (except the Dead Sea sect) in this period; the surviving descriptions were written much later, at a time when the groups had probably ceased to exist (from the late first century A.D. on). No known literary work can be identified with certainty as Sadducean, and only one small collection of works—the Epistles of Paul (*ca.* A.D. 55)—was definitely written by a Pharisee, albeit a lapsed one. Consequently, in the following discussion of literature, sectarian labels will be avoided.

The chief point of disagreement in the period is the legitimacy of the Hasmonean priest-kings. First Maccabees, a history covering in detail the period from 167 to 134 B.C. (composed *ca.* 110, in archaizing Hebrew), claims that the Hasmoneans are "the seed [that is, family] in whose hands is entrusted the salvation of Israel" (5:62). As historiography, the work closely imitates the Deuteronomic histories of the Bible (Samuel and Kings). The attitude of the work is separatist; throughout, the wicked are those who have made a "covenant" (in a sexual, social, or religious, not political, sense) with the surrounding Gentiles (1 Maccabees 1:11 ff.). The tremendous admiration for, if not the ignorance of, Rome expressed in chapter 8 presumably reflects the philoromanism of John Hyrcanus I.

Complementing 1 Maccabees is "Greek Esther," a reworking of the Hebrew Book of Esther, composed in Jerusalem by one Lysimachus, son of Ptolemy, shortly before 78 B.C. This book shares 1 Maccabees' separatism and aversion to Gentiles. While in the Hebrew Esther Haman's plot against the Jews is merely a by-product of his hatred of a Jewish courtier, and later the Jews take revenge only against Haman's followers, in the Greek Haman is, like all Gentiles, a born Jew-hater; the Jews consequently take their revenge on all the Gentiles. Yet the book is written in excellent Greek, showing that even under Jannaeus, the conqueror of Greek cities, Greek letters thrived in the very heart of Judaea.

Like Greek Esther, the abridgement of the five-book-long Maccabean history of Jason of Cyrene, called 2 Maccabees (*ca.* 110 B.C.) is thoroughly Greek in style. It is a rare example of a wretched, hyperdramatic, hypertheological type of history writing, containing many instances of divine intervention, gory descriptions of torture and execution, and excessive use of elaborate rhetorical devices. The book is especially concerned with the temple, and extravagantly praises Judah, who freed the temple from the Greeks. It is, by contrast, unconcerned with—some scholars claim even antipathetic to—the dynastic pretensions of the Hasmoneans. Although naturally opposed to the extreme assimilationists, the book, unlike 1 Maccabees and Greek Esther, is by no means anti-Gentile.

More explicitly anti-Hasmonean (and hostile to Pompey) is a collection of hymns, made probably in the 40s B.C., called the Psalms of Solomon (originally Hebrew). Some of the psalms denounce the (Hasmonean) family that usurped the throne of David, led all Israel into sin, and appointed wicked judges. Eventually, though, God punishes the family through the agency of a general from the far west (Pompey), who overthrows them. But the foreigner enters the temple with his troops, a terrible act of hubris, and so is murdered in Egypt and his body left unburied (Psalms 2; 8; 17).

From this period dates some or most of the material found at Qumrân, near the Dead Sea. As suggested above, the Dead Sea sect probably came into being early in the Hasmonean period; it survived until about A.D. 70. It seems to have been largely priestly at first (the first leader was a priest called "Teacher of Righteousness"). The sect rejected the Hasmonean temple, opposed the government, like the authors of Enoch and Jubilees used a solar calendar, spent much time in study and contemplation, held all property in common, strongly emphasized ritual purity, were experts at prophecy, and may have been celibate (scholars differ). We know all this because they also wrote profusely.

Two works, the Damascus Covenant and the Rule of the Community, set forth in detail the complex rules governing admission to the sect and the life of the initiates. The former also describes the history of the origin of the sect. Another important group of texts is the *pesharim* (sing. *pesher*), running commentaries on Psalms and the prophetic books of the Bible. Their chief aim is to interpret ancient prophecies as applicable to contemporary history and/or the End of Days. Concern with eschatology has its fullest expression in two works. The first, the War Scroll, is a description of the final battle between the "sons of light" (members of the sect) and the "sons of darkness" (everyone else), in which God naturally grants victory to the sons of light. The second, the Temple Scroll, is a set of laws governing the conduct of the temple service and the behavior of the king, obviously anticipating a time when the sectarians would control both temple and kingship, perhaps after the victory of the sons of light. The sect also composed many liturgical texts.

Also produced at this time were a number of Greek works, some from Alexandria, most of uncertain provenance, known only from excerpts quoted by the Church Fathers and Josephus. The earliest Greco-Jewish work survives in full; this is the translation of the Pentateuch called the Septuagint, prepared either at Alexandria or Jerusalem, allegedly in the reign of Ptolemy II. The vocabulary used is idiomatic Hellenistic Greek, but the translation is excessively literal. Nevertheless, it attained wide circulation, even a sort of canonical status, among Jews and, later, Christians. The chronographer Demetrius who wrote, about 220 B.C., a history of the Jews from the Creation to (probably) the first destruction of Jerusalem used the Septuagint as a source. He reduced the Bible stories to a straightforward chronicle (as Berosus reduced the Babylonian and Manetho the Egyptian stories) and took special care to establish a rational chronological framework for his history. It is plausibly supposed that Demetrius was influenced by Eratosthenes and the much earlier writers Hellanicus and Hecataeus of Miletus.

The work of Artapanus (*ca.* 200 B.C.) provides important evidence for Judaism as practiced in the Egyptian countryside, where it was apparently evolving as a Greco-Egyptian-Jewish syncretism. In his stories about Abraham, Joseph, and Moses, Artapanus deviates greatly from the Bible: Abraham was an inventor of astrology; Joseph established the Egyptian system of land tenure; and Moses established the Egyptian animal cults and conducted a successful campaign against Ethiopia. (Artapanus accepts the traditional Egyptian belief that the earth is Isis, but nevertheless considers Yahweh to be the supreme god.)

A purely Greco-Jewish philosophical syncretism is presented in the "Letter of Aristeas" (Alexandria, *ca.* 130 B.C.), which uses a traditional story about the translation of the Bible as a literary framework for an encomium of Judaism. But the Jewish God is identified with Zeus and the Mosaic law is considered to be in agreement with the loftiest principles of Greek philosophy, and the "Letter" distinguishes not between Jews and Gentiles but between men of God (including Jews and enlightened pagans) and those concerned only with the physical. In a somewhat similar way, the nearly contemporaneous Alexandrian Jewish philosopher Aristobulus interprets the Bible allegorically in order to harmonize it with Greek philosophy. Aristobulus too identifies Zeus with the Jewish God and considers Judaism a philosophical school.

For some Jews, Judaism was a mystery cult. This point of view seems implicit in the *Exagoge* of Ezekiel (possibly Alexandrian, second century B.C.)—a work of particular literary interest as the only Hellenistic tragedy of which large parts survive.

Jews in the Diaspora and the Greek cities of Palestine faced the constant need to defend Judaism. In the works just surveyed, the apologetic is mostly implicit: the authors semiconsciously assimilate Judaism to Greek models, not so much to impress Gentiles as to convince themselves and other Jews of the continuing value of Judaism. In a small body of works, however, the attempt to impress Gentiles is more apparent (although the desire to impress Jews as well is likely). These are works written by Jews but attributed to classical Greek authors. Books "On Abraham" and "On the Jews" were attributed to Hecataeus of Abdera, a late classical, early Hellenistic writer known to have been sympathetic to Judaism. Verses proclaiming monotheism and the sanctity of the Sabbath were attributed to Homer and the classical tragedians, among others. A large corpus of poems in the Homeric dialect and dactylic hexameter, some of which resemble in content apocalyptic books like Daniel, was attributed to the Sibyl. Finally, a collection of wise sayings with affinities to Ben Sira, but written in the Ionic dialect and dactylic hexameter, was attributed to the archaic gnomic poet Phocylides.

THE ROMAN PERIOD:
37 B.C.–A.D. 135

History

Herod's first task upon assuming the throne was to subdue the pro-Hasmonean nobility. This he did by executions and by marrying the Hasmonean princess Mariamme. Eventually, though, he also executed her and her brother, mother, and aged grandfather Hyrcanus II. In order to ensure the loyalty and impotence of the high priesthood, Herod elevated some minor Judaean and Alexandrian priests to high-priestly dignity. Appointed by the king, they now served for brief terms of variable length. By 25 B.C., Herod largely succeeded in altering the Judaean aristocracy to his own specifications.

He then had to guarantee the loyalty of Judaea, where pro-Hasmonean sentiment remained strong. He therefore built (from 25 to 13 B.C.) a string of fortified settlements extending from the coast through Samaria to the Jordan (Caesarea, Antipatris, Samaria-Sebaste, Alexandreion) and south toward the desert (Hyrcania, Herodion, Masada). Judaea was thus hemmed in. The last period of Herod's reign, until his death in 4 B.C., was occupied with palace intrigues and the execution of relatives, most notably his sons by Mariamme, Alexander and Aristobulus (7 B.C.).

Herod, as a client king subject to Rome, with highly varied and mutually hostile groups of subjects, walked a tightrope. In addition to the groups mentioned above, he had also to pacify non-Judaean Jews and Samaritans in Palestine (Herod had begun building bases of support in Idumaea, Samaria, and Galilee even before 40); pagan subjects—although Herod ruled a large pagan population, he had no Judaizing policy and, on the contrary, founded or refounded many Palestinian Greek cities and subsidized their temples; and, most important, the emperor of Rome. In addition, Herod set himself up as protector of Jewish rights throughout the Roman Empire, and cultivated the sympathy of the large Jewish population of the Parthian Empire. He also belonged to a class of Greco-Oriental dynasts and client kings who vied with one another for prestige by displaying their love of Greek culture, donating funds to famous Greek cities, temples, and festivals, and courting prominent Romans. Herod did all these things. Of particular importance is that he turned Jerusalem into a minor center of Greek culture, employing large numbers of orators and writers.

None of Herod's successors was as successful as he at balancing so many conflicting interests. At his death the situation rapidly deteriorated. Uprisings were harshly crushed by the governor of Syria, Publius Quinctilius Varus. Augustus then split Palestine, giving Idumaea, Judaea, and Samaria to Archelaus, son of Herod, and Galilee and Peraea to his brother Antipas. Archelaus was unpopular and incompetent. In A.D. 6, Augustus yielded to the demands of an embassy of Judaean and Samaritan aristocrats (in a rare display of unity) and deposed him. His territory was placed under the supervision of a Roman prefect technically subordinate to the governor of Syria; this arrangement lasted until A.D. 41.

Many Jews were dissatisfied with direct Roman rule. There was still pro-Hasmonean sentiment and an unrealizable desire for independence. Hence, speculation about the End of Days and the final deliverance of Israel flourished in some circles, and a number of messianic figures appeared. We know of five: the Golanite brigand Judas (who, however, may not have had messianic pretensions); Jesus of Nazareth; an unnamed Samaritan; Theudas; and an unnamed Egyptian Jew. Nevertheless, until the year 41 the prefects generally were competent functionaries who allowed Judaea a large measure of autonomy. The high-priestly families elevated by Herod acquired great wealth and prestige; descendants of Herod, especially Antipas, remained powerful in Judaea. The upper priests controlled the boule or city council of Jerusalem, an aristocratic body that governed the cultic and to some extent the legal and political life of Judaea. However, the period was marred by the incompetence and greed of the prefect Pontius Pilate (A.D. 26–36) and the demand of the emperor Gaius (Caligula; A.D. 37–41) that his own image be erected in the temple, which nearly caused a revolt.

The reign of King Agrippa I, son of Aristobulus (from A.D. 37 in northern Palestine, from 41 in Judaea; he died in 44) was a brief respite. Although his policies closely resembled those of his grandfather, Herod, he seems to have been more popular than Herod in Judaea. After his death, Idumaea, Judaea, and Samaria were restored to direct Roman rule; northern Palestine was soon given to Agrippa's son, Agrippa II, who also appointed the Jewish high priests.

The second set of Roman administrators (A.D. 44–66), now called "procurators," were as a group far less competent and far more rapacious than their predecessors. They consistently favored Palestinian Greeks, contributing to the desperation of the Jews. Conflicts between Jews, Greeks, and Samaritans and within the Jewish population intensified. Gangs led by members of high-priestly families fought each other and lower priests.

In May A.D. 66, the Jews of Judaea revolted following the procurator Florus' plundering of the temple and some violence between Jews and Greeks at Caesarea. The revolt, led by several upper-class priests, at first went well for the Jews. But soon it spread through all Jewish Palestine and showed signs of spreading to the Diaspora as well; there was some fear at Rome of Parthian involvement. So Nero dispatched an army, reportedly numbering 60,000, commanded by Vespasian and his son Titus. By the end of the 67 season, the Galilean revolt collapsed; its surviving leaders, and other rural rebel leaders (most important, John of Gischala and Simeon bar Giora) fled to Jerusalem and wrested control from the priests. By the summer of 69 the revolt was confined to Jerusalem and a few desert fortresses. Vespasian having now seized the imperial throne, the siege of Jerusalem was conducted by his son. On 9–10 Loos (9 Ab in the Hebrew Calendar) (that is, July/August), 70, the city fell, and the temple, which had been the center of the revolt, was destroyed. There was general slaughter and tens of thousands were sold into slavery. The remaining rebel strongholds were taken with little difficulty; the last, Masada, fell in A.D. 73.

In the immediate aftermath of the revolt, Judaea was transformed into a province with a praetorian governor and a legion. The two-drachma tax the Jews had paid annually to the temple was now paid to the temple of Jupiter Capitolinus at Rome; land belonging to known revolutionaries was confiscated. The Judaean aristocracy was in a shambles. Many upper-class priests had been implicated in the revolt and could not be considered trustworthy by Vespasian; others had deserted to Titus during the siege of Jerusalem and so were in a slightly better position. But only Agrippa II and his sister Berenice had proved their loyalty to Rome, and so presumably were allowed to retain a strong influence over Jewish affairs. Yet the first to seize the reins of power, probably with at least tacit Roman approval, was a nonpriestly Jerusalemite deserter of obscure background named Johanan ben Zakkai. He established a council at Jamnia (Jabneh), an imperial estate on the coast, for which he claimed the authority that had once belonged to the temple and the Jerusalem boule. This program is certain to have displeased the surviving upper-class priesthood, and probably Agrippa II as well. At any rate, Johanan was removed as head of the council around A.D. 80 and replaced by Gamaliel ben Simeon, descendant of an aristocratic, Pharisaic Jerusalem family. He was perhaps a protégé of Agrippa. Although more conservative and better disposed to the priesthood than Johanan, he was an aggressive leader and eventually freed himself from Agrippa's influence, if he had ever been under it (the king died about 96).

Gamaliel's precise activities can scarcely be reconstructed: he apparently traveled widely inside and outside Palestine, no doubt in part for public relations purposes, and associated himself with a group of men who formed the core of Rabbinic Judaism. Among these were Eliezer ben Hyrcanus, the Levite Joshua ben Hananiah, Akiva ben Joseph, and the priest Eleazar ben Azariah. At some point, perhaps about A.D. 110–120, his associates deposed Gamaliel and appointed Eleazar ben Azariah. The reasons for the deposition are uncertain. Perhaps it was a priestly bid to recover power, or a result of a conflict over the revolutionary movement then reasserting itself in Palestine (in the second case, Gamaliel was leader of the pro-Roman party), or both. Perhaps also the deposition was somehow connected with the great Diaspora revolt of 115–117.

At any rate, rebellion did erupt again in Judaea in A.D. 132, after Hadrian's reestablishment of Jerusalem as Aelia Capitolina. This in effect ruled out any future reconstruction of the Jewish temple. The new revolt was led by a certain Simeon ben Kosiba (called by his supporters Bar Kokhba, "son of the star"; Numbers 24:17), and apparently had the support of many rabbis. Indeed, the Wadi Murabaat and Naḥal Ḥever papyri, written or dictated by Simeon, reveal him to have been a careful observer of laws later codified in the Mishnah, the earliest document of Rabbinic Judaism. The extent and course of the revolt are unknown. It was serious enough to require the transfer east of Julius Severus, governor of Britannia. After three years the revolt was crushed. Hadrian outlawed the practice of Judaism (or he may have done so earlier); the district of Judaea ceased to be the center of Palestinian Jewry.

Literature and Religion

The best-known intellectual at Herod's court was Nicolaus of Damascus, an orator, Aristotelian philosopher, and historian, probably of pagan origin. In addition to his activities as statesman and royal tutor, he wrote a world history in 144 books, a biography of Augustus, an autobiography, and some philosophical and dramatic works. There is some evidence that Herod's successors also surrounded themselves with Greek litterateurs, many of them Jewish; but none was of the same caliber as Nicolaus.

While the Herodian court entered the mainstream of early imperial Greek culture, Herod's enemies continued in the tradition of the books of Daniel and Enoch. However, in no case can these apocalyptic works, many of which survive only in fragments, be dated or located with precision. (The interested reader may consult the work of James H. Charlesworth [1983–1985], which contains the fullest collection of this material.) Josephus and pagan authors also report a number of apocalyptic and messianic prophecies that circulated in first-century Judaea. The destruction of the temple evoked lamentation and questions about divine justice, but also the expectation that following a brief period of suffering the Messiah, the Final Judgment, and Israel's vindication would come. This view is expressed in 4 Ezra and 2 Baruch, both written about A.D. 100.

In sharp opposition to postdestruction messianism stands Flavius Josephus (Joseph ben Matthias), who was born to a well-to-do Jerusalem priestly family in A.D. 38. During the revolt, Josephus was a revolutionary general in Lower Galilee. He capped an undistinguished military career by surrendering to Vespasian (April 67) and predicting the latter's rise to the imperial throne. After the fulfillment of this prophecy in July 69, Josephus joined Titus' staff of native guides, propagandists, and interrogators. In 71 he settled in Rome, receiving citizenship and an imperial pension. In his first surviving work, *The Jewish War* (published *ca.* 80), a seven-book history of the revolt strongly influenced by Thucydides, Josephus argues that the Jewish leadership before A.D. 66—the high priesthood and Agrippa II—and the Jewish people as a whole were not the instigators but rather the innocent victims of the revolt. He also lavishes tremendous praise on Titus, defending him from charges of cruelty and incompetence, and, indeed, attributing to him practically divine powers. Josephus, like the apocalyptists, hoped for a restoration of the temple and Jewish autonomy—although, of course, 4 Ezra and 2 Baruch wanted more than autonomy. Unlike them, he thought this could be achieved, with imperial backing, through conventional political means.

His next work, *Jewish Antiquities,* published in A.D. 93, is a twenty-book history of the Jews from the Creation to A.D. 66 (books 1–11 paraphrase biblical books; modern scholars compare the work to Dionysius of Halicarnassus' *Roman Antiquities*). Josephus here abandons imperial propaganda; the tone of the book is more Jewishly "nationalistic," and its Greek style far worse, than that of *The Jewish War.* Josephus implicitly defends the antiquity and respectability of the Jews and their way of life against their detractors, apparently both Jewish and pagan. He is somewhat more pro-Hasmonean and pro-Pharisaic in this work and constantly promotes observance of Jewish law; also, he attacks both the Herodian family and the Herodian high priests, both praised in *The Jewish War.* In general, though, the work, written over the course of a decade or more, is quite incoherent, and it is often difficult to tell what Josephus is driving at.

Far more coherent—indeed, the best written of Josephus' works—is *Against Apion,* in two books (published *ca.* A.D. 98). This is an explicitly apologetic work, probably adapted from one or two Alexandrian-Jewish pamphlets. The first part contains a detailed and often intelligent refutation of the anti-Jewish comments of Greek and Greco-Egyptian writers such as Manetho, Lysimachus, Apollonius Molon, and Apion; the second part contains an encomiastic description of the Jewish "constitution," that is, the temple cult and Jewish law. At about the same time Josephus published a hastily written, literarily wretched "autobiography"; in fact, it is a defense of his military career in Galilee thirty years earlier. He attempts to defame a certain Justus, a wealthy Jew from Tiberias formerly in the service of Agrippa II who had apparently attacked Josephus in his own book about the war, if he ever wrote one, or in his "History of the Jewish Kings" (published *ca.* A.D. 96/97). Justus wrote several books that even Josephus admits were of high literary quality; unfortunately, however, Justus' works have not survived.

There were presumably other types of Palestinian Jewish response to the destruction of the temple than those of Josephus and the apocalyptists, but aside from the Christian, we know little of these. As noted above, it may be that some tendencies in Rabbinic (or proto-Rabbinic) Judaism, notably that developed by Johanan ben Zakkai, already resigned themselves to the loss of the temple; but large-scale transference of the rituals, standards, and symbols of the temple to the synagogue and the home is not likely to have been characteristic of Rabbinic Judaism as a whole until after A.D. 135.

Egypt

In the early years of Roman rule, the Jews of Alexandria struggled to be released from their inferior legal status (like native Egyptians, they had to pay the poll tax), and for Alexandrian citizenship, which individual Jews had already attained; this was a prerequisite for Roman citizenship. Many Alexandrian Greeks vigorously opposed these efforts. In A.D. 38 the Greeks succeeded in winning the support of the emperor Gaius (Caligula). The Egyptian Jews' traditional freedom of worship was consequently restricted, and they were forced to live in separate quarters in the cities. Rioting ensued. In 41, the issue came up before the new emperor, Claudius. He restored the status quo ante: the Jews were again permitted to live according to their ancestral laws, but their struggle for citizenship ended in failure. With the procitizenship (and pro-Roman) Jewish leadership thereby weakened, it was only a matter of time before the anti-Greek and anti-Roman element gained the upper hand. Indeed, in A.D. 66, they initiated an uprising that was crushed by the Roman prefect of Egypt, Tiberius Julius Alexander, himself a member of a wealthy Alexandrian Jewish family (his uncle was Philo of Alexandria). The pro-Roman faction was still strong enough five years later to prevent a new uprising, allegedly instigated by radical Judaean refugees; but within a few decades, the faction collapsed. A huge Jewish revolt erupted in Egypt, Cyrene, and Cyprus in 115 (suggesting that the Jews in the latter two places had been involved in a similar political struggle) and ended, in 117, in the near-annihilation of the Jewish population in these places.

The relatively plentiful Alexandrian-Jewish literature of the period reflects these struggles. The procitizenship faction endeavored to stress common interests and beliefs of Jews and Greeks (it could draw on Alexandrian-Jewish tradition for this), and the Jews' dissimilarity to native Egyptians: Artapanus' Judaeo-Egyptian syncretism had no followers in this group. This attitude is most coherently expressed in *Against Apion,* a work closely based on Alexandrian sources; it is implicit in the Wisdom of Solomon, 4 Maccabees, and most notably in the many homiletic works of Philo, who composed a series of commentaries on the Pentateuch in which he attempted to reconcile it with Platonic and Stoic philosophy. Biblical stories and laws were interpreted allegorically although, unlike other Jewish allegorists, Philo believed that the laws actually have to be observed. He considered Abraham, Joseph, and Moses prototypes of different Platonic cardinal virtues.

The events of A.D. 38–41, in which Philo played a leading role as Jewish spokesman, led him temporarily to abandon philosophy and write two political pamphlets, the "Embassy to Gaius" (the Roman emperor Caligula) and "Against Flaccus." In these, he blamed the disturbances on the mad emperor, his faithless prefect Aulus Avillius Flaccus, a few Alexandrian Greek demagogues, and the riffraff who supported them.

The views of the anti-Greek, anti-Roman Jewish party are presented in the earlier sections of the fifth Sibylline Oracle (probably after A.D. 70). The poem, in dactylic hexameters, denounces Egypt and prophesies its destruction. Rome is compared to Babylon, and Nero is nearly an antichrist. A messianic figure will destroy Rome and the rest of the world, after which he will build a heavenly Jerusalem on earth, in which no Greeks will be allowed.

CONCLUSION: A.D. 135–324

Only the following more or less datable facts are known about the history of this period. After Hadrian's death, Antoninus Pius abolished the persecution of the Jews, at some point after which the patriarchate was reestablished under Simeon, son of Gamaliel. (The center of Jewish population had meanwhile shifted to Galilee, although many Jews remained in Judaea.) Little is known about the extent of Simeon's authority, or his activities; he is, however, known to have been an important rabbinic authority. Under his son Judah ha-Nasi (ca. 175–220), the patriarchate was transformed into an important office, with strong similarities to the earlier office of *prostates tou ethnous;* this rise was probably a consequence of Jewish support for Septimius Severus in the civil war of A.D. 193. Judah collected taxes, appointed judges, enjoyed the support of many rabbis and perhaps the friendship of some Severan emperors. He may even have had, unofficially, the right of life and death over his subjects. He is also believed to have supervised the compilation of the Mishnah. His successors enjoyed the same rights as he, and great prestige among Palestinian Jews (the character of the patriarchs' relations with the Diaspora is unclear), but relations with the rabbis deteriorated. By the fourth century, when the patriarchate enjoyed a resurgence of authority (they had the honorary praetorian prefecture; on a fourth-century Tiberian inscription, the patriarchs are called *lamprotatoi,* an epithet that implies senatorial status), patriarchs and rabbis seem to have had no connection.

One might expect, following the great upheavals of the first and early second centuries, which were both anti-Roman and anti-Greek, that coexistence among Jews of Greek and Jewish culture would have come to an end. Indeed, the surviving literature of the period after A.D. 135 is evidence for a very different variety of Judaism than had existed previously—Rabbinic Judaism. The writings are all in Hebrew or Aramaic rather than Greek. The self-consciousness, the interest in defending Judaism, is absent. Also, the literature is thoroughly dissimilar to contemporary pagan literature: its authors were either unaware of or unconcerned with the literary styles of the day, although they did not escape the influence of popular Greek thought. What we have instead is the Mishnah (compiled *ca.* A.D. 200), a six-part compendium of laws on agriculture; holy days; family law and personal status; business, torts, and crime; the cult; and ritual purity. The Tosefta (compiled *ca.* 250) has the same topical arrangement as the Mishnah and in part presupposes and comments upon it, but often disagrees with its legal decisions and contains more narrative material (neither the Mishnah nor the Tosefta is a pure law code in the Roman sense). The legal midrashim (sing. midrash) may also date to the third century. These are the *Mekhilta of Rabbi Ishmael* and the *Mekhilta of Rabbi Simeon ben Yohai* on Exodus; the *Sifra* on Leviticus; and the *Sifrei* on Numbers and Deuteronomy. These attempt to derive rabbinic laws from the Bible through close exegesis of the relevant verses.

Although the hundreds or thousands of rabbis active in the period under discussion naturally had very diverse legal opinions, certain broad tendencies can be discerned. One of these is a tendency toward separatism. Wine, oil, and other foods prepared by Gentiles were prohibited even if in other respects they met the requirements of Jewish food laws. Any hint of involvement in pagan cults, even of the most indirect sort, was forbidden; for example, trade with Gentiles was forbidden for three days before certain major pagan festivals, presumably because the Gentile might be moved to thank his gods during the festival if the trading was successful. Another tendency is to adapt rituals and standards formerly connected with the temple for general use. Hence, the

Paschal sacrifice evolved into the Passover seder, performed at home; standards of ritual purity formerly applicable to temple functionaries were given wider application; taxes in kind once paid to the temple were to be donated to local priests and Levites. These developments constituted an attempt, in the long run successful, to keep Judaism alive after the destruction of the temple and the de-Judaization of Jerusalem.

Yet rabbinic literature by no means tells the whole story. The large Jewish settlements in Asia Minor and Italy and the smaller one in Greece, which were unaffected by the revolt of A.D. 115, were also little affected, if at all, by Rabbinic Judaism. The scanty remains of these settlements do not allow a reconstruction of the history of Judaism there; we know, however, that their liturgical language was Greek and that some Asian Jews at least were not separatist. Even in Palestine, rabbinic influence was limited. A fourth-century synagogue in Hammath (Tiberias), near the very center of Rabbinic Judaism, has a mosaic floor depicting the god Helios, as do several other Palestinian synagogues. Further evidence of similar syncretism survives in such magical books as "Sefer HaRazim" ("The Book of Mysteries") and the Hekhalot literature, as well as in the fragments of Jewish material in Greek and Coptic magical papyri from Egypt. At a higher social level, the patriarchal court was a small-scale center of Greek culture (not nearly on the same level as the courts of the Herodian kings). One or more of the fourth-century patriarchs was a friend of the great Antiochene rhetorician Libanius, and young members of the patriarchal family may have gone to Antioch for their rhetorical education.

The Christianization of the Roman Empire, accompanied by the cooptation of classical culture by the church and the gradual decline in the legal, social, and economic status of the Jews, hastened the breakdown of contact between Judaism and Hellenism; the Moslem conquest of the Mediterranean world and the decisive victory of Rabbinic Judaism seemed to complete the process, although Rabbinic Judaism itself had meanwhile absorbed a great deal of Hellenic culture. Hence, Jewish Hellenism did not disappear; it went underground only to reemerge in unprecedented splendor (though in Arabic translation) in the eleventh century.

BIBLIOGRAPHY

SOURCES

For the Old Testament, the Revised Standard Version of the Bible is adequate; for classical texts, including Philo and Josephus, the Loeb Classical Library texts are suggested. In addition, the following sources were used: Robert Henry Charles, ed., *The Apocrypha and Pseudepigrapha of the Old Testament* (1913; repr. 1964–1965); James H. Charlesworth, ed., *The Old Testament Pseudepigrapha*, 2 vols. (1983–1985); Arthur Ernest Cowley, *Aramaic Papyri of the Fifth Century B.C.* (1923); Herbert Danby, trans., *The Mishnah* (1933); Jonathan A. Goldstein, *I and II Maccabees: Anchor Bible* (1976–1984); Josephus, H. St. J. Thackeray *et al.*, trans., 10 vols. (1926–1965); József Tadeusz Milik *et al.*, eds., *Discoveries in the Judaean Desert*, 7 vols. (1955–1982); Philo, F. H. Colson *et al.*, trans., 12 vols. (1927–1953); Menahem Stern, *Greek and Latin Authors on Jews and Judaism*, 3 vols. (1974–1984); Avigdor Tcherikover and Alexander Fuks, *Corpus Papyrorum Judaicarum*, I, II (1957–1960); Yigael Yadin, ed., *The Temple Scroll*, 3 vols. (1983).

STUDIES

Gedalia Alon, *Jews, Judaism, and the Classical World* (1977); Michael Avi-Yonah, *The Jews under Roman and Byzantine Rule* (1984); Elias Joseph Bickerman, *From Ezra to the Last of the Maccabees* (1962), *The God of the Maccabees* (1979), and *Studies in Jewish and Christian History* (1976–

1980); John Joseph Collins, *Between Athens and Jerusalem: Jewish Identity in the Hellenistic Diaspora* (1983), and *The Apocalyptic Imagination* (1984); W. D. Davies and Louis Finkelstein, eds., *Cambridge History of Judaism*, 1 (1984); Louis H. Feldman, *Josephus and Modern Scholarship, 1937–1980* (1984); Jacob Freudenthal, *Hellenistische Studien* (1874–1875); Erwin Ramsdell Goodenough, *Jewish Symbols in the Greco-Roman Period* (1953–1968); Wolfgang Haase, ed., *Aufstieg und Niedergang der römischen Welt* 2.21.1 (1984); Martin Hengel, *Judaism and Hellenism: Studies in their Encounter in Palestine in the Early Hellenistic Period,* 2 vols. (1974).

Lee I. Levine, "The Jewish Patriarch (Nasi) in Third-Century Palestine," in *Aufstieg und Niedergang der römischen Welt* 2.19.2 (1979); Saul Lieberman, *Greek in Jewish Palestine* (1942), and *Hellenism in Jewish Palestine* (1950); George Foot Moore, *Judaism in the First Centuries of the Christian Era,* 3 vols. (1927–1930); Jacob Neusner, *Development of a Legend: Studies on the Traditions Concerning Yohanan ben Zakkai* (1970), and *Judaism: The Evidence of the Mishnah* (1981); Robert Henry Pfeiffer, *History of New Testament Times, with an Introduction to the Apocrypha* (1949); David M. Rhoads, *Israel in Revolution: 6–74 C.E.* (1976); Abraham Schalit, *König Herodes; der Mann und sein Werk* (1969); Emil Schürer, *The History of the Jewish People in the Age of Jesus Christ (175 B.C.–A.D. 135)*, T. A. Burkill *et al.*, trans., Geza Vermes and Fergus Millar, eds., 1–3a (rev. ed. 1973–1986); E. Mary Smallwood, *The Jews under Roman Rule from Pompey to Diocletian* (1981); Morton Smith, *Palestinian Parties and Politics That Shaped the Old Testament* (1971); Avigdor Tcherikover, *Hellenistic Civilization and the Jews,* S. Applebaum, trans. (1959); Yigael Yadin, *Bar-Kokhba* (1971).

Christianity

HELMUT KOESTER AND VASILIKI LIMBERIS

CHRISTIAN BEGINNINGS

Jesus of Nazareth was born to Jewish parents in Galilee under Herod the Great (38–34 B.C.) or Herod Antipas (4 B.C.–A.D. 39). Nothing is known about his early years. At the age of about thirty, Jesus became a follower of the Jewish prophet John the Baptist, who proclaimed a last repentance before the coming of God's final judgment. Baptized by John, Jesus began—after the Baptist's imprisonment by Herod Antipas (A.D. 27)—to preach his own message of the coming rule of God. All accounts of Jesus' ministry are contained in writings (the Gospels) produced by Christians one to three generations after his death and are dominated by the interests of these believers. Critical study of these documents has led to the conclusion that Jesus never referred to himself by any messianic title (Messiah, Son of man, Son of God, Lord), and that his message is most authentically preserved in his parables (Mark 4) and in a number of prophetic sayings that speak of the presence of God's rule among those who are willing to accept his word, love their enemies, and fol-low after him (Matthew 5–7). Jesus was reported to have performed miracles, especially exorcisms, underlining the urgency of his proclamation. Everyone was invited to the new fellowship, women as well as men, pious Jews as well as tax collectors. With all these, Jesus celebrated fellowship meals with bread and wine. The last of these meals (not a Passover meal) became the basis of the Christian sacrament of the Eucharist (Mark 14:22–25). To the Jewish establishment and to the Roman authorities Jesus was no more than one of several messianic pretenders. After a mass demonstration, remembered as the Entry into Jerusalem (Mark 11:1–10), shortly before the Passover festival of the year A.D. 30, Jesus was apprehended by the Roman governor Pontius Pilate and executed by crucifixion (John 18–19).

The Church in Jerusalem

After Jesus' death, several of his followers (Peter, James, Mary Magdalene, and entire groups of disciples) had visions that proved to them that Jesus was alive (1 Corinthians

15:5–8; Luke 24; John 20–21). They gathered in Jerusalem and formed a special religious group under the leadership of Peter and James, the "brother" of Jesus. The members of this group were soon overwhelmed by an ecstatic experience of inspiration known as Pentecost, which was understood as the coming of the spirit of the last days (Acts 2) and prompted these followers to stay in Jerusalem and to organize themselves under the Twelve Disciples as the representatives of the new Israel. Here they awaited Jesus' return in glory as the Messiah (Gk. *Christos*) or the Son of man who is predicted by the book of Daniel. Baptism was introduced as the seal of eschatological (pertaining to the end of the world) protection and for the giving of the Holy Spirit.

Soon other Jews coming to Jerusalem were persuaded to join this eschatological sect. Many of these were from the Greek-speaking Jewish diaspora. Conflicts arose very early because for some of these Jews (Hellenists) the message of the new age through Jesus' Resurrection implied that the Law of Moses (including circumcision, dietary and purity laws, and temple cult) was no longer valid. In a resulting violent confrontation one of the Hellenists, Stephen, became the first martyr of the new movement; the others were forced to leave Jerusalem (Acts 7:53–59; 8:1).

Earliest Missions

The departure from Jerusalem, to be dated as early as one or two years after the death of Jesus, marks the beginning of the Christian mission, not only to Jews in Palestine and elsewhere but also to Gentiles. Those who had fled from Jerusalem first founded circles of believers in Jesus within Jewish synagogues. As more Gentiles joined these circles, and as the leaders of the synagogues and other members reacted with open hostility, the Jesus-believers withdrew

and created independent associations that were called ecclesiae (assemblies). There is evidence that such churches came into existence within two to five years of Jesus' death in several cities of Samaria, Galilee, and western Syria. The church of the Syrian capital Antioch, under the leadership of Barnabas, a Hellenist from Cyprus (Acts 11:19–26), became the center for the subsequent expansion of Christianity.

One of the Greek-speaking Jews who had persecuted the Jesus-believers in Syria was a Pharisee named Paul. A vision of Jesus that he experienced near Damascus (A.D. 32 or 35) was understood by him as a call to proclaim to the Gentiles Jesus' Crucifixion and Resurrection as God's eschatological saving event (Acts 9). The first period of his missionary work in Arabia, Syria, and Cilicia led to conflicts with the followers of Jesus in Jerusalem who still insisted that the Law of Moses must be kept by all converts to the new religious movement. The conflict was resolved by a conference in Jerusalem (Apostles' Council, A.D. 49) in which Jesus' brother James, along with Peter and John agreed with Barnabas, Paul, and Titus (a Gentile) that the Gentile converts should not be obligated to observe the Law and that the mission to the Gentiles should be an independent organization in its own right and with its own leadership (Galatians 2:1–10).

Shortly after this conference, as further conflicts arose in Antioch over dietary laws—Antioch was still a church of both Jews and Gentiles (Galatians 2:11–14)—Paul decided to leave and to establish new missionary centers in Asia Minor, Macedonia, and Greece (Acts 16–19). Paul's organizational abilities and his continuing care for the churches he had founded in Galatia, Philippi, Thessalonike, Corinth, and Ephesus led to the establishment of a Christian presence in the heartlands of Greco-Roman culture and economy, which led to the creation of the first Christian literature: the letters of Paul that are preserved in the New Testament (Romans, 1 and 2 Corinthians, Galatians, Philippians, 1 Thessalonians, and Philemon). Paul was arrested in Jerusalem when he tried to deliver a collection of money from the Gentile churches for the Christians in Jerusalem (A.D. 56; Acts 20–22). After imprisonment in Caesarea, he was brought to Rome for trial and execution (probably A.D. 60).

THE EMERGENCE OF DIVERSITY

Paul's message about the beginning of a new age and a new creation through the death of Jesus and his Resurrection was only one of several forms in which the proclamation of Jesus was spread throughout the eastern regions of the Roman Empire and at an early date reached the capital city of Rome. Other missionaries and their converts developed different beliefs, based on independent continuations and interpretations of Jesus' ministry. They soon were drawn into controversies with the churches founded by the missionaries from Antioch who preached Jesus' death and Resurrection as an eschatological event that terminated the validity of the Law of Moses.

Jewish Christianity

The Jewish Christians in Jerusalem continued observation of the Law of Moses. Missionaries claiming authorization by Jerusalem, called Judaizers, made several attempts to convince believers in the free Gentile churches that they had to accept circumcision, dietary laws, and Jewish festivals in order to be saved. Paul's letter to the Galatians was written in reaction to their propaganda. Subsequent Jewish-Christian groups usually insisted upon the keeping of the ritual laws of Judaism, and they often rejected Paul and his letters.

After the assassination of their leader, Jesus' brother James (A.D. 62), the Jerusalem Christians left the city just before the outbreak of the Judaic War (A.D. 66–73) and moved to Pella (Amman) in the Decapolis (Jordan). Whatever little information is preserved indicates that members of Jesus' family continued for some time in positions of leadership. Some of these Jewish Christians also maintained Aramaic as their religious language, using an Aramaic translation of Matthew as their gospel (*Gospel of the Nazoreans*). Greek-speaking Jewish Christians composed a harmony of Matthew and Luke (*Gospel of the Ebionites*) that demonstrates their rejection of the virgin birth: they considered Jesus to be a human being upon whom the Spirit had descended during baptism. A Jewish-Christian prophet in Syria named Elkasai predicted that the final eschatological battle would occur three years after Trajan's Persian campaign (A.D. 117–118) and combined the observance of Old Testament purity rites (repeated ablutions) with the belief in the religious significance of cosmic powers, planets, and stars.

Like the Elkasaites, the group that produced the *Kerygmata Petrou* (later incorporated into pseudo-Clementine literature) observed the ritual law, rejected the apostle Paul, and appealed to Peter and to Jesus' brother James as the true authorities. Moses and Jesus are both seen as revelations of the "true prophet," and the Law is seen as the key to the understanding of the cosmos and of a history that is a procession of yoked pairs (syzygies) in which the weaker always precedes the stronger (Cain before Abel, Paul before Peter).

In all Jewish-Christian groups of Syria one finds a clear emphasis upon the words of Jesus. That these words were collected early as a treasure of prophecy and wisdom is evident from gospels composed of sayings, such as the *Synoptic Sayings Source*, later used by the authors of Matthew and Luke. In this writing, Jesus not only appeared as the voice of heavenly wisdom (for example, Matthew 11:25–30), but also as the one who proclaimed his return as the heavenly Son of man (Luke 17:22–37). In one instance, the tradition of these sayings is closely connected with the fulfillment of the Law of Moses (Matthew 5:17–19). In another Syrian tradition of the sayings there is no orientation toward the future, and the Law is rejected altogether. The *Gospel of Thomas* presents Jesus' words, spoken to Judas Thomas the Twin, as the words that give freedom from death to those who find their interpretation. Those were the people who could discover in themselves their divine origin, withdraw from the world, and exist as the "single one" (*monachos,* monk).

Such teaching of Jesus' wisdom can be encountered as early as the time of Paul's activity in Corinth (A.D. 51–55; 1 Corinthians 1:18–3:23), and it is closely related to the beginnings of Christian Gnosticism. Other newly discovered documents from the Library of Nag Hammadi in Egypt provide more evidence for a Gnostic interpretation of Jesus' sayings. The *Dialogue of the Savior* and the *Apocryphon of James* are in fact commentaries on these sayings that try to explore the saving wisdom of Jesus' words and thus communicate knowledge (*gnosis*) that leads to the recognition of one's divine identity and to the overcoming of death.

Johannine Christianity is closely related to this tradition, but for a long time maintained its independent identity (probably somewhere in Syria). The discourses and dialogues of the Gospel of John are largely based upon sayings of Jesus and interpret them as "words of eternal life" (John 6:63, 68). Jesus is the revealer who was the creative Word (*Logos*) in the beginning of the world, coming from the Father to bring saving knowledge. In John, however, the gnosticizing tendencies are tempered through a combination of this message with traditions about the human Jesus of Nazareth who suffered and died. The history of the Johannine community, reflected in the addition of chapter 21 (asserting the authority of Peter) to the Gospel and in the production of the Johannine Epistles (1–3 John), reveals a further accommodation to the churches that are based on the creed of Christ's death and Resurrection. 1 John rejects the Gnostic assumption that the revealer did not come in the flesh but only appeared to be human (docetism). In this revised form, the Johannine writings were finally accepted by the Catholic churches as the product of the legendary apostle John of Ephesus.

At the same time, the Gnostic interpretation of Johannine materials continued in the second century in the *Acts of John,* especially in its Gospel Preaching of John (*Acts of John* 87–105), with its famous Hymn of the Dance: "If you follow my dance, you will see yourself in me who is dancing" (*Acts of John* 96:28 f.). Pre-Christian Gnostic speculations about the creation were assigned to John in a document from the Nag Hammadi Library called the *Apocryphon of John.* John's Gospel remained popular among later Egyptian Gnostic theologians, who wrote several commentaries on this Gospel.

It is no accident that Gnostic thought is most congenially expressed in hymns. They have their origin in Jewish wisdom theology and speak of the precosmic divine generation of Wisdom, her role in the creation of the world, her descent to earth, calling those who belong to her, and finally Wisdom's return to her heavenly abode with God. Such hymns have been used for the composition of the prologue of the Gospel of John (1 John) and in the Christ hymns of Philippians 2:5–11 and Colossians 1:15–18. They are also quoted in the *First* and *Second Apocalypse of James* (Nag Hammadi Codex 5; 28.7-27; 55.15-56; 58.2-24) and in the *Acts of Thomas'* Bridal Song (5–7) and Hymn of the Pearl

(108–113). All these hymns speak in mythical language about the appearance of the preexistent Christ, creator and Logos, his bringing of gnosis, and his return to his divine origin, which signifies the heavenly journey of the human soul. These religious concepts are frequently echoed in the oldest extant Christian hymn book, the *Odes of Solomon,* which was composed in Syria in the first or second century. Gnostic motifs are especially prominent in *Odes of Solomon* 11, 15, 26, 34, 38, and 39. The same motifs reoccur in later Christian hymnology, both Catholic and heterodox.

Gnostic Sects and Schools

Gnosticism had a great appetite for the incorporation of various religious traditions and mythological speculations, and quickly developed a number of esoteric sects and schools. The most prominent, probably of Jewish origin, is Sethian Gnosticism. It is now well known through the many Sethian documents from the Nag Hammadi Library; for example, *Apocalypse of Adam, Hypostasis of the Archons, The Three Steles of Seth,* and *Gospel of the Egyptians.* Characteristic is the understanding of Genesis 1–6 as the record of an evil creation. Adam's son Seth and sometimes his sister Norea appear as the revealers and illumine those who are children of the transcendent God. Most of these documents are only superficially Christianized. Another sect is that of the Carpocratians (perhaps named after the Egyptian Horus/Harpocrates), which used a *Secret Gospel of Mark.* Carpocrates' "son" Epiphanes wrote a book, *On Righteousness,* that advocates common possession of women and goods.

Basilides, founder of a sect that was prominent in Lower Egypt, devised a system of the spiritual cosmos in 365 stages; the code word for its numerical value was *Abrasax* (which as abraxas became a prominent formula in medieval magic). The Basilidians

celebrated 6 January as the day of Jesus' baptism, on which the *Nous* (Divine Reason) came upon Jesus. This celebration is the origin of the Christian festival of the Epiphany. The most prominent Gnostic teacher was Valentinus (born *ca.* A.D. 100 in Egypt; appeared in Rome *ca.* 140). He combined elements of oriental mythology and Platonic philosophy with biblical exegesis to form a tripartite cosmological system, corresponding to his tripartite anthropology: spirit, soul, and body. The system was further refined by his students Theodotus and Marcus in the East, and Ptolemy and Heracleon in the West. Many of their works are at least partially preserved: *Excerpts from Theodotus* by Clement of Alexandria; a commentary on the prologue of the Gospel of John; Heracleon's commentary on that Gospel; a letter of Ptolemy to Flora, as well as excerpts from his major systematic work; there is also a didactic Valentinian letter. Some works from the Nag Hammadi Library, such as the *Gospel of Truth,* the *Gospel of Philip,* and the *Treatise on the Resurrection,* also belong to the Valentinian school.

Throughout the second century, Gnosticism was dominant in many areas of the Roman Empire, particularly in the East and in Egypt. A writing called the *Gospel of the Egyptians,* composed of tendentious sayings of Jesus, advocated asceticism and advised against marriage and childbirth. Jewish Christians in Alexandria also accepted Gnostic teachings, as is revealed by their *Gospel According to the Hebrews,* in which Jesus appears to his brother James after the Resurrection. Striking in this widespread Gnostic movement are its fragmentation, lack of organization, and tendency to form exclusive mystery associations that catered to the spiritual interests of the religious individual. Sacraments like baptism, and probably also a sacrament of the holy marriage (*hieros gamos*) or bridal chamber, were designed for the religious edification of the initiate, not for the building of community. It is true that Gnostic groups often abolished social distinctions and favored the emancipation of women. But the fundamental insight upon which Gnosticism is founded assigns no value to physical existence in the material realm and to social and political structures. There is, therefore, no attempt to translate the belief in equality into viable social structures. Typically, Gnosticism uses only mythical, philosophical, and pseudoscientific language, and avoids political and social metaphors and images.

THE DEVELOPMENT OF ECCLESIASTICAL ORGANIZATIONS AND NORMS

Congregations

Jesus did not leave any instructions for the organization of the church. The passage of Matthew in which Peter is designated as the "rock of the church" (16:17–20) is a later product of the Christian community, and it does not establish an ecclesiastical office, but rather a tradition of materials and writings under the authority of Peter that became dominant in Syria (*Gospel of Peter, Apocalypse of Peter*) and later in Rome (1 Peter). The earliest known church organization was democratic and resembled that of Greek associations. Special officers were chosen by election (*Didache* 15), respected because of merit (first-converted, patron of a house church), or accepted on the basis of demonstrated religious gifts (*charismata*), that is, gifts of the spirit shared by the entire community (1 Corinthians 12). Prominent among the latter offices were those of apostle, teacher, and prophet. The first known president of a congregation (*prostasis*) was a woman (Romans 16:1–2), and women occur frequently among church officers mentioned in Paul's letters (Romans 16; Philip-pians 4:2; and so on). The final disciplinary authority is vested in the whole congregation (1 Corinthians 5; Matthew 18:15–17).

The missionary endeavors of the early churches favored the ascendancy to authority of traveling preachers (apostles), prophets, and teachers who excelled in their display of spiritual power. Early church orders tried to regulate their activities (Matthew 9:35–10:42) and to protect congregations from being abused (*Didache* 11–13). Conflicts enforced the establishment of regular resident officers. In some instances the Jewish model of a board of elders (presbyters) was used; in other cases bishops and deacons were elected to take over the tasks of preaching and teaching for their local congregations (Philippians 1:2; 1 *Clement* 42). But the further growth of the churches, especially in the large cities of the East (Antioch, Ephesus) and in Rome, their fragmentation into house churches, and conflicts among Christian groups over questions of praxis and theology demanded the establishment of a single local authority.

Such a program was first developed by Ignatius of Antioch (died as a martyr *ca.* A.D. 110) and was propagated in his letters written to several congregations in Asia Minor. He recommended that there should be only one bishop in each city who presided over the board of elders, was assisted by the deacons, controlled the celebration of the Eucharist, and was responsible for the care of widows and orphans. Disciplinary, liturgical, and social tasks were thus united under one person of authority. Also promoted by the pastoral Epistles (1, 2 Timothy; Titus), the monarchical episcopate was established in several important cities by the middle of the second century. Significant leaders of Christianity are known to have held such office: Polycarp of Smyrna, Dionysius of Corinth, Anicetus of Rome. At the end of the century the office was also brought to Alexandria, where the first bishop was Demetrius (A.D.

189–231). At that time, the Christian scholar and historian Hegesippus constructed lists of bishops for the major sees in order to establish a (fictional) apostolic authority for this office.

Prophets and Teachers

The establishment of episcopal authority did not terminate the older offices of prophet and teacher. Christian prophets repeatedly renewed the eschatological proclamation of the coming of God's rule. A prophet from Ephesus, in exile on the island of Patmos, who was fighting against the emperor worship demanded by Domitian (A.D. 81–96) proclaimed the fall of Rome and the coming of the victorious Christ. His message is preserved in the Book of Revelation. After the middle of the second century, the prophet Montanus from Phrygia proclaimed himself to be the Paraclete of John 14:16 and announced the imminent coming of the New Jerusalem. Montanist churches, organized under boards of elders, where women were admitted to the prophetic office, continued into the fifth century. Many Catholic theologians did not consider the Montanists as heretics (for example, Irenaeus), and their rigorous morality persuaded Tertullian to leave the Catholic church and to become a Montanist.

The old office of the teacher found its continuation in Christian schools, which were not only concerned with the instruction of catechumens, but also devoted to the interpretation of the sacred scriptures and the editing of Christian literature. The gospels of Matthew and John owe their final form to such school activity. The leaders of Christian-Gnostic sects (Basilides, Valentinus) were primarily teachers, and Gnostic schools produced numerous biblical commentaries as well as speculative theological writings, sometimes in several editions (four different editions of the *Apocryphon of John*

are extant). That traditions under the authority of particular apostles were cultivated by these schools is evident in the production of literature under apostolic names (*Apocryphon of James, Gospel of Philip*), but also in the editing of the Pauline correspondence and the further growth of the Pauline corpus (addition of Colossians, Ephesians, Hebrews). The intellectual and literary endeavors devoted to the refutation of Gnosticism were also based on the activity of Christian schools that, at the same time, opened Christianity for the appropriation of Greek philosophy (see below on Justin, Clement of Alexandria, and Origen).

Marcion and the Canon of the New Testament

Throughout the early Christian period, the holy Scripture of the Christians was the Old Testament, interpreted typologically and allegorically. Apostolic Christian writings were abundant and still increasing in number. Thus, their authenticity and authority were problematic, nor were they universally accepted. A solution was attempted by Marcion, a wealthy shipowner from a Christian family in Sinope in Pontus (northern Asia Minor), who came to Rome *ca.* A.D. 135. Marcion's apostolic authority was Paul— not the miracle-working missionary of the Acts of the Apostles, nor the exemplary martyr admired by 1 *Clement* and by the *Acts of Paul*, but the genuine Paul who wrote the letter to the Galatians and who had taught that Law and Gospel were irreconcilable opposites. Marcion became convinced that Paul's letters had been contaminated by a Judaizing theology related to the inferior creator God of the Old Testament, a God who demanded obedience to his Law and punished transgressors mercilessly. Thus, Marcion set out to produce a purified edition of the Pauline letters and of the Gospel of Luke, which he took to be the Gospel referred to by Paul as "my Gospel." In this new edition he sought to reestablish the original message of Jesus, the Son of the foreign God, who had come to redeem humanity from the slavery of the Law and to lead people into freedom through mercy and love. When Marcion was forced to leave the Roman church (A.D. 144), he founded his own ecclesiastical organization, which spread over the entire Mediterranean world in less than a decade and continued to flourish for several centuries. The Marcionite church surpassed other Christian groups in several respects: it had its own canon of Christian scriptures (Paul's Letters and Luke's Gospel); it was hierarchically structured with bishops and boards of elders (women were also admitted to these offices); and it demanded a strict morality from all its members (abstention from sexual intercourse, meat, and wine).

The reaction of the other churches to Marcion was slow. Justin Martyr in Rome wrote against Marcion, but simply avoided using Paul's letters and refined the typological method of Christian interpretation of the Old Testament in his proof for the Gospel (using Matthew and Luke). An unknown theologian in Ephesus composed the letters to Timothy and Titus in the name of Paul, defending a Christian morality that is based upon popular ethics and the Jewish traditions, and reinforcing the exclusion of women from ecclesiastical office.

It remained for Irenaeus, a Greek theologian from Smyrna who had become bishop of Lugdunum (Lyons) in Gaul ca. A.D. 180, to answer Marcion's challenge. He combined the four gospels of Matthew, Mark, Luke, and John with Paul's letters to form a Christian scripture to be used alongside the Old Testament as the New Testament. He thus established what was to become the Christian Bible. The writings chosen for the new sacred book were those that were thought to have been used in the churches from the very beginning and that corresponded to the creed of the Catholic churches, now known as the Apostles' Creed. Divine inspiration did not play any role as a criterion in the formation of the canon. Irenaeus' work was only the first step. Lists of canonical books do not appear before the fourth century, and even then the question of the inclusion of the Book of Revelation, of some of the Catholic Epistles (2 Peter, Jude, 2 and 3 John), and of the *Apocalypse of Peter* was still debated.

THE CHURCH AND THE WORLD

Persecutions

From the beginning of its mission to the Greco-Roman world, Christianity was a religion of the urban middle class. Like other social and religious constituencies, including the Jewish synagogues, Christian churches were organized as associations. Although the Roman authorities eyed the associations with a certain degree of suspicion, always wary of their potential to create unrest, they would not take specific measures against any particular association without cause. Thus Christians were normally not molested. There is no reason to assume that Christians shared in the privileges of Judaism, because these privileges were local arrangements, not universally decreed, and they would not protect anyone in cases of unrest and turmoil. Paul, who was a Jew, was punished and expelled by Roman authorities on several occasions.

Early martyrdoms were at the hands of the Jews, and they were restricted to Palestine: Stephen (Acts 7:54–59), the Zebedee James (Acts 12:2), and Jesus' brother James (Eusebius, *Ecclesiastical History* 2.23). Persecution of Christians by Roman authorities was rare. That Nero cruelly executed Christians because he needed scapegoats after the great fire of Rome (A.D. 64) is reported by Roman historians (Tacitus, *Annals* 15.44.2–8). The martyrdoms of Peter and Paul may be related to this persecution. But this and persecutions in Rome and Ephesus under Domitian (the Revelation of John) were limited local occurrences. The concerns of Roman administrators with respect to the Christians are most evident in a letter that Pliny the Younger, during his tenure as governor of Bithynia (A.D. 111–113), wrote to the emperor Trajan (*Letters* 10.96). In this province of northwestern Asia Minor Christians had become numerous, and Pliny was concerned about the spread of the contagious disease of "false religion" (*superstitio*). But he had taken measures against them only after several people had been denounced as Christians. Brought to trial, those who insisted that they were Christians were sentenced to death, although the governor could not find any specific crimes these people had committed. Clearly, being a Christian was itself a punishable crime and Christians were simply punished for their beliefs. On the other hand, Trajan responded advising that Christians should not be sought out and that anonymous accusations should not be admitted into court. This policy remained in effect under the emperors Hadrian and Antoninus Pius.

The situation changed during the reign of Marcus Aurelius (A.D. 161–180). Roman authorities were more frequently forced to take measures against the Christians because public opinion blamed them for the misfortunes that then befell the empire. As early as the writing of the Book of Revelation in the time of Domitian, the emperor cult had been used as a test case of Christian loyalty (Revelation 13:11–17). Pliny employed the same device. Reports of Christian martyrdoms confirm this (for example,

the *Martyrdom of Polycarp,* who was executed under Marcus Aurelius). Initially, this was a test of political loyalty; its refusal was not a religious crime but a crime against the majesty of the emperor. But increasingly, especially in adverse political and economic situations, worship of "the gods of the Roman people" became a religious necessity, because the favors of the gods who were the protectors of Rome had to be secured. Nobody could detest these gods with impunity. Because the Christians refused to participate in this cult, they appeared to be a group of politically subversive atheists.

The first general persecution of the Christians must be understood against this background. It occurred under Decius (A.D. 250). In an effort to unite all people of his realm in order to meet the threat of the Gothic invasion in the Balkans and the advance of the Sassanian Persians in the East, and in an attempt to restore the old virtues of Rome, the emperor ordered all Roman citizens to sacrifice (all free inhabitants of the empire had been made Roman citizens through the Antonine Constitution of A.D. 212). The persecution was well organized—tax rolls were used for control—and very successful. Some bishops fled, others even apostatized; most members of the Christian churches either sacrificed or bought certificates (*libelli*) that affirmed that they had sacrificed. Those who refused were imprisoned. But Decius was killed in battle a year later, and a devastating plague followed upon his defeat. When many people—fearing they would die as apostates—demanded readmission, the churches were reorganized quickly (for a discussion of disciplinary problems that arose, see below on Cyprian). In A.D. 257 the emperor Valerian renewed the persecution. This time the church was prepared to meet the challenge courageously. Many suffered martyrdom (including the famous bishop Cyprian of Carthage), but the churches emerged strengthened. Almost half a century of peace followed, although Christianity still had to face the persecution under Diocletian that led to the ascendancy of Constantine.

Apologetic Literature

Christian apologetic literature began to appear in the first half of the second century, that is, in a period of Christianity's most significant expansion and consolidation. Although the declared purpose of this literature is the defense of the new faith, its real aim is the invitation to the true philosophy as a rule for life and conduct. Like the pagan protreptic literature that served as a model for these Christian writings, the apologies assert that true philosophy is a doctrine for correct living that can be taught and that will build up the moral individual as well as the community and the state. The truth of Christianity is demonstrated in two ways: it is documented on the basis of venerable old traditions (the Old Testament), and it is shown to be superior to all philosophies and to the superstitions of pagan religions.

Fragments and translations of apologies from the time of Trajan and Hadrian are extant (*Kerygma of Peter*, Quadratus, Aristides). The most influential apologist was Justin Martyr, whose two apologies are directed to Antoninus Pius and to the Roman Senate. In addition, his defense of Christianity against Judaism is preserved (*Dialogue with Trypho*). Justin's arguments are rooted in the belief that God's work in history is a consistent effort to save humankind for a future in which people live according to God's will. The history of Israel and the tradition of Greek philosophy are prefigurations of that salvation. This opened the way for Christian theology to claim the Greco-Roman tradition as its own inheritance, thus accelerating the process of hellenization.

Jesus' sayings become a part of the invitation to the true philosophical life; they recommend temperance and prudence, love of all people, caring for others, and serving everyone. The protreptic no longer provides only rules for the perfection of the individual; it also becomes an invitation to a life that is responsible for the common welfare.

Christianity as Philosophy

Justin Martyr, following in the footsteps of Jewish apologetics, had made an important differentiation: pagan religion is an abominable creation of evil demons, but pagan philosophy is a partial recognition of truth and thus a legitimate instrument of Christian theology. In agreement with the prevailing philosophy of his time, Justin accepts Platonic metaphysics and Stoic ethics. The Platonic criticism of myth and of polytheistic religion became a weapon in the hands of Christian writers, which made it difficult for pagan challengers (such as the Platonist Celsus, *ca.* A.D. 170) to find relevant arguments against the monotheism of Christian apologists. On the other hand, the Gnostics, who accepted any and every myth as a concealed statement of truth, could be refuted on the basis of the same critical philosophical arguments.

The reconciliation of Hellenic tradition and Christianity is fully achieved in the writings of Clement of Alexandria (where he taught in A.D. 180–200). He uses Plato's *Timaeus* alongside the book of Genesis in order to show that the cosmos was created by God and is not eternal. But he denies—against the Gnostics—that either the cosmos or the human body is evil. Divine Providence governs the course of the world in order to achieve God's purpose: education and salvation. The incarnation of the Logos into a human body is a particular instance of this Providence. Against the philosophers who detest faith as something that is contrary to rational thought, Clement shows that faith is the condition for all knowledge. Against the Gnostics who see faith as an inferior form of religious experience, Clement insists upon the full sufficiency for salvation of a simple faith that trusts in God's love and care. Yet the "true Gnostic" desires to advance in knowledge. He will move from material to spiritual concerns and through prayer and moral discipline reach for the union with God that will be obtained after death. Moral education is the conduct of life in which all Christians are equally challenged. Its criteria are drawn from Stoic philosophers of the Roman imperial period. Prudent judgment warns against the strict asceticism practiced by some Gnostics and by the Neopythagoreans, but also shuns the excesses of overindulgence, sexuality, and wealth. Clement is addressing the upper classes of the city with their love of luxury, elegance, and sensual pleasures. Far from recommending abstinence, he sternly insists on simplicity and moderation, commends giving to the poor, and upholds the Christian sanctions against eating sacrificial meat, military service, and the taking of oaths. Pastoral concern prompted Clement to use Stoic ethics in order to point the way to a Christian morality that could become the standard for a Christian life in the world.

Origen followed Clement as a teacher in Alexandria and continued his work. But as a religious person, he was very different. Not a convert like Clement, but raised in a Christian home, he began at the age of eighteen (A.D. 202) to instruct catechumens in Alexandria during a persecution in that city. To his father—who suffered martyrdom—he had written a letter admonishing him to stand firm in the hour of trial. Origen taught in Alexandria until A.D. 230, when conflicts over doctrine and over his ordination by Palestinian bishops forced him to move to

Caesarea Maritima in Judaea (Palestine). There he continued to teach and write until his death in A.D. 253, probably a consequence of the imprisonment and torture he suffered during the Decian persecution. As a teacher he educated an entire generation of theologians and bishops in the East, but also attracted many non-Christian students. His advice was sought in many doctrinal disputes, and he was once invited to the court of the emperor. Origen was the most prolific and influential writer of the ancient church. His literary work primarily consists of homilies and commentaries, some very voluminous and filled with an immense amount of erudite detail. Among other works, his *On First Principles* deals with fundamentals of theology, and his *Against Celsus* is a refutation of this Platonist's attack upon Christianity. Origen also composed a comparison of several Greek translations of the Old Testament in six columns (called the *Hexapla*).

Although most of Origen's work is that of a biblical theologian, his allegorical interpretation—closely modeled on that of Philo of Alexandria—is thoroughly Platonist. God is strictly transcendent, and the creation does not derive from a tragic fall but from divine goodness. However, the hierarchy of rational beings is not the result of a series of emanations (as in Platonism and Gnosticism). Rather, the free will of those beings allows them to turn away from God, and the material world has been created through Divine Providence in order to serve as a realm in which education (*paideia*) can bring them back to their divine origin. The Bible and the sending of Christ serve the purpose of educating human beings, so that they learn to move from the material to the spiritual world. This process is not mystical but moral; however, since salvation implies a movement away from the material world, Origen's ethics are more ascetic than Clement's. Origen's thought, in many ways, parallel to the Neoplatonism of his younger contemporary Plotinus, was controversial from the very beginning. But it remained the basis of Christian theology, especially in the doctrinal battles of the fourth century.

WESTERN CHRISTIANITY

The Roman Church

The beginnings of Roman Christianity are not known. When Paul wrote his letter to the Romans (A.D. 56), a Christian community must have existed there for some time. The first direct evidence comes from a letter written A.D. 96 to Corinth by the Roman scribe Clement (1 *Clement*). The *Shepherd of Hermas,* a prophetic writing offering a second repentance, mentions the same Clement. This book and 1 Peter were composed in Rome shortly after A.D. 100. All these writings reveal the presence of a Greek-speaking church whose faith is based upon the kerygma of Jesus' cross and Resurrection.

In the middle of the second century, the major theological movements from the Greek world were trying to establish themselves in Rome, the capital of the empire. Marcion from Pontus organized his separate church in this city. The Alexandrian Gnostic Valentinus is reported to have been a candidate for the office of bishop. Justin Martyr, originally from Samaria in Judaea, founded his school in Rome, where one of his students was Tatian from Assyria. The diversity of the Roman church is also visible in the Quartodeciman controversy. A strong group of Christians from Asia Minor who had settled in Rome followed the praxis of their home church in the celebration of the Easter festival. On the morning of the Jewish Passover, having fasted during the preceding night when the Jews were eating the Passover meal (that is, on the fourteenth day of Nisan), they greeted with joy their risen Lord. However, the other Roman Christians had fixed the Easter date as the Sunday following the Jewish Passover. Bishop Anicetus (A.D. 155–166) threatened to excommunicate these Asian Christians, but Bishop Polycarp of Smyrna traveled to Rome in order to intercede on their behalf. As a result, the two bishops agreed that each group should be allowed to follow its own tradition; Anicetus permitted Polycarp to celebrate the Eucharist in Rome.

A few decades later, Bishop Victor (A.D. 189–198), the first Latin leader of the Roman church, renewed the controversy and prevailed, in spite of the support given to the Quartodecimans by the bishops Polycrates of Ephesus and Irenaeus of Lyons. The indigenous Latin element of the Roman church asserted itself for the first time, although controversies with Greek theologians in Rome continued. They came to a head over the question of Modalism, a widespread and popular belief that assumes that the Father and the Son are the same person, or two different "modes" of the same being. This Modalism was opposed by those apologists who distinguished Father and Son, or God and Logos, as two different persons (Lat. *persona;* Gk. *hypostasis*). At the time of Bishop Zephyrinus (A.D. 198–217) several Modalists were teaching in Rome (Praxeas, Sabellius). When Callistus became bishop (A.D. 217–223), he excommunicated the Greek presbyter Hippolytus, an apologist who had been the most outspoken opponent of Modalism. Hippolytus became the bishop of a separate Roman church for which he wrote his own church order, the *Apostolic Tradition*—a most valuable document for the development of the liturgy. Social and cultural factors also played a role in this schism. Callistus, whom Hippolytus had accused of laxity in church discipline, was a former slave, then freedman and banker; he had been sentenced to the mines for disrupting a Jewish synagogue service, and favored the lower classes. Hippolytus was an educated Greek and a Platonist who was influential through his literary work (books against the heresies and biblical commentaries) and was sometimes called the Origen of the West. His church dedicated a statue of their bishop with a list of his works inscribed on the back. The split in the Roman church continued until both bishops, Hippolytus and Callistus' second successor, were exiled to Sardinia.

The African Church: Tertullian

Rome could claim that it was the first Christian church in the West of the empire. Soon there were other congregations in Gaul, Spain, and Germany. But the cradle of Western Christianity and of its theology was the Roman province Africa with its capital Carthage. The oldest Christian document written in Latin is a description of the martyrdom of Christians from Scillium (Numidia) who were sentenced to death by the Roman proconsul at Carthage on 1 August 180. One learns from this document that the letters of Paul were used by them in Latin translation. It is certain that the entire New Testament was translated into Latin in North Africa well before the year A.D. 200.

At that time, Tertullian, the son of a centurion in the Roman army, was converted. He had studied rhetoric and law and had a successful career in Rome, but returned to his native Carthage as a teacher and writer for the cause of the new religion. From his writings (all in the period from 195 to 220) one can learn what attracted him to Christianity: a God who was not just a philosophical idea but a God who acts in history and who calls human beings to a disciplined moral life; a Bible that is a direct and unambiguous record of God's word; and a church whose members are serious in their commitment and willing to die for their faith. Tertullian was not a philosopher, and Platonism played no role in his theology. But he was able to use all his rhetorical skills for the defense and exploration of his new faith. Tertullian is a master of Latin prose, but he uses the language as a slave he mercilessly forces into service. The result is a Latin language that did not exist before: vernacular expressions abound; hundreds of new words are coined as well as new Latin phrases for Greek expressions; alliterations, word plays, bombastic statements, antitheses, and elegant rejoinders all reveal not only his control over rhetoric, but also his passionate concern.

Among Tertullian's apologetical writings, the *Apology* is the most accomplished. It shows no philosophical interests; rather it is driven by a conviction of the possession of truth that enables Tertullian to hurl all the accusations against the Christians back into the face of the accuser with sarcastic wit, angry indictments, and legal finesse. Its novel element is a radical demythologizing of Roman political ideology: the Christians have the task of a new obedience that makes all justifications and glorifications of the state superfluous. Tertullian's antiheretical works set faithful obedience to the biblical word against meaningless speculations. Important is his contribution to the formulation of Trinitarian doctrine for the western church, which he developed in the writings *Against Praxeas*, the Roman Modalist. God is One in Three only insofar as he is acting in revelation, creating and ordering the world as the Father, prophesying and redeeming as the Son, directing the church and the believers as the Holy Spirit. This "economic" doctrine of the Trinity assumes a subordination of the Son under the Father, and of the Holy Spirit under the Son. But they are still One Being (*una substantia*) in three personae (*tres persones*). This became the standard trinitarian language in the Latin church. In his numerous other writings, Tertullian deals with questions of Christian life and church discipline. He insists upon uncompromising morality and willingness to sacrifice. Moral rigorism also persuaded Tertullian to join the Montanists and, finally, to found his own sect, the Tertullianists. But in spite of his leaving the Catholic church, his writings continued to be read, and they deeply influenced later Latin writers.

Cyprian: Africa and Rome

When the Decian persecution began (A.D. 250), the first edict was directed against the bishops. A few were executed (Fabian of Rome), some apostatized (Euctemon of Smyrna), and others fled. Among the latter was Bishop Cyprian of Carthage. He was a recent convert to Christianity, a member of the upper class who had become bishop only a few years after his conversion. During the persecution, when large numbers of Christians denied their faith, Cyprian tried to direct the affairs of his church through correspondence and messengers. After his return, he found that the confessors, that is, those who had confessed their faith and suffered imprisonment and torture, had claimed the right to remit apostasy and wanted to accept large numbers of lapsed Christians back into the church without further ado. They had even elected a rival bishop during Cyprian's absence. Supported by a synod of African bishops, Cyprian was able to prevail; only the legitimate bishop had the right of readmission, and each case should be decided individually, with specific periods of penance.

Meanwhile, the church in Rome had been split over the same question. Majority Bishop Cornelius advocated a lax policy in the readmission of lapsed Christians, while the rigorist minority, forming a separate group under Novatian, wanted to preserve the church as a community of pure saints (the Novatianists were also known as the "Pure";

Gk. *katharoi*). In spite of differences in this matter, Cyprian finally supported Cornelius. However, in A.D. 254, the next Roman bishop, Stephen, began to admit former Novatianists into the church, recognizing their baptism by Novatian as valid. His position was that the effectiveness of the sacrament depended upon Christ and not upon the purity of the minister, as long as it was formally correct. Cyprian insisted upon the more rigorous African position, demanding rebaptism in such cases—how could a heretic communicate the Holy Spirit to a baptized person?—and also questioned Rome's right of legislation in such matters without the consultation of a council of bishops. In the controversy that followed Stephen denounced Cyprian as Antichrist and also appealed to the passage in Matthew 16 about Peter's power of the keys—the first occasion for a Roman bishop to do that. But two African synods confirmed Cyprian's views, and many eastern bishops wrote in support of Cyprian. Stephen died before the conflict could be resolved (A.D. 256). The African view of the sacrament's dependence upon the purity of the minister emerged again in the Donatist controversy of the fourth century.

Cyprian's literary work is mostly related to his church-political activities; it consists of such writings as *On the Unity of the Church* and *On the Lapsed,* and of a large corpus of letters. His correspondence shows that he was a masterful politician who was able to direct church affairs with diplomatic skill and theological integrity. At the same time, he excelled as a teacher and pastoral counselor whose advice in theological, ethical, and disciplinary matters was sought by many other churches and bishops in East and West. When the persecution was renewed under Valerian in A.D. 258, Cyprian stood by his church and was executed by the sword. The report of his martyrdom was soon widely distributed together with his other writings, and it seems that his works enjoyed a greater popularity than those of any Christian writer before him.

CHRISTIANITY IN SYRIA, MESOPOTAMIA, AND PERSIA

Beginnings and the Apostle Thomas

Ancient traditions and legends about the beginnings of Christianity in eastern Syria, including a correspondence of Abgar V, ruler of Edessa and the Osrhoëne (the area between upper Euphrates and Tigris), with Jesus, have been interpreted as evidence for the establishment of a state church under Abgar IX *ca.* A.D. 200, and of the consecration of Palut by Bishop Serapion of Antioch as the first bishop of eastern Syria. More recent research has shown that the very first orthodox bishop of Edessa was Kune, shortly after A.D. 300, and that there is no evidence for the existence of orthodox churches in that area before the fourth century. However, Christian missionaries must have come to eastern Syria as early as the first century. Sayings of Jesus under the authority of Thomas were probably composed here into the *Gospel of Thomas.* It represents a Gnostic and ascetic Christianity advocating the ideals of poverty, virginity, and homelessness. That the authority of Thomas continued in this area is shown by the *Acts of Thomas,* written in the early third century—a book that shares the same religious ideals. By this time, Christian churches were established also in Persia and perhaps farther to the east (reflected in the reports in the *Acts of Thomas* about the apostle's travel to India). Other sects had also found their way to this area, probably the Marcionites and certainly the Jewish-Christian baptists called after their founder Elkasai, the Syrian prophet from the time of Trajan.

There is a striking predominance of ascetic ideals in Syrian Christianity. Syrian ascetics refused to be organized into corporate groups, and they did not admit married people to baptism. It is characteristic that even the fourth-century Persian bishop and sage Afraates did not allow marriage after baptism; married people were admitted only to associate membership of his church. This is probably a direct continuation of the Enkratite (abstaining) group founded by Justin Martyr's student Tatian after his return to his native Adiabene (east of the Tigris). The harmony of the four Gospels that Tatian composed (*Diatessaron*) became part of the Syrian canon of the New Testament and was still used by Ephrem (A.D. 306–377), the theologian of Syrian orthodoxy, for his commentary on the Gospel.

Bar-Deisan

The Christian philosopher Bar-Deisan (also known as Bardesanes), who lived in Edessa A.D. 154–222, does not seem to fit the general picture of Syrian asceticism. He was an Iranian nobleman who became the court theologian of Abgar VIII the Great, whom he converted to Christianity and whom he persuaded to issue legislation banning castration in honor of Atargatis, the Dea Syria. Bar-Deisan was a man open to the pleasures of the world and is said to have been a great archer. His writings demonstrate that he was a philosopher, apologist, and poet. His treatise against Marcion is lost, and so are the 150 hymns he composed. In an extant *Book of the Laws of the Countries,* which either he himself or one of his students wrote, the question of the freedom from fate as dictated by the stars is the central theme. Bar-Deisan tries to maintain the unity of creation and the freedom of the human will, refuting the thesis that people in the seven geographical areas of the world are subject to the seven planets and their laws. Rather, Christ's cross is the ordering principle which reestablishes the good creation that had been contaminated by the powers of darkness.

Mani and Manichaeism

Mani, the son of an Iranian nobleman, was born A.D. 216 in a district north of Babylon. With his parents he belonged to a sect of Christian baptists that has now been identified as the Elkasaite sect. He had received revelations from his heavenly "twin," and in A.D. 240, after Ardashir I, the first Sassanian Persian—after the overthrow of the Parthians—had been crowned in Ctesiphon (224/226), Mani received the heavenly command to proclaim his message. First he converted his parents, then he went to India (Pakistan), where he remained for one year. After his return, he was received by the Persian king Shapur I (A.D. 242–272). A vigorous expansion of the new religion of Manichaeism followed. But under Bahram I (A.D. 273–276) Zoroastrianism was established as Persia's state religion; Mani was arrested and died in prison (A.D. 277). Manichaeans were henceforth persecuted in Persia as heretics. The new religion, however, continued its expansion both east and west. Manichaean books, originally composed in Syriac by Mani and by his disciples, have been found in Turfan in central Asia as well as in Egypt. They are translated into Greek, Latin, Coptic, Persian, Arabic, Sogdian, Turkish, and Chinese. There are also numerous reports and polemics by Christian and Muslim authors.

Mani understood himself as the final divine messenger (after Noah, Abraham, Buddha, Zarathustra, Jesus, and Paul) and wanted to found a religion that incorporated the essence of Christianity, Buddhism, and Zoroastrianism. The basic structure of his religion, however, is Gnostic. In a complex mythical drama of the fight between light and darkness (elements of this myth are borrowed from Iranian and Gnostic religions), particles of light have been trapped by the powers of darkness. The powers are induced to pollute this light into the physical world, which has been set up as a gigantic cosmic machine in which a mechanical (for example, the revolution of the astral spheres) and biological process has the purpose of bringing the particles of light back to their origin. The community of the elect founded by Mani is at the core of this process. The elect must not hurt the light wherever it is encountered (in animals and plants). Its members, therefore, practice a radical asceticism. They are not permitted to have offspring and cannot even prepare their own food. A wider group of followers (the auditors) provides all services for the elect (the monks). The latter, known as lean, ascetic figures who even refuse bodily hygiene, are committed to frequent and extended periods of prayer, hymn singing, and literary activity (the Manichaeans have produced books of unusual beauty). In the West, Manichaean writings underwent Christianizing revisions. The Manichaeans even called themselves Christians. Manichaean churches were founded throughout the Mediterranean world as far as Spain; St. Augustine was a Manichaean hearer for ten years before his conversion to Christianity.

THE GREAT PERSECUTION

Prior Developments

The last four decades of the third century gave peace to Christianity and allowed an exponential growth in the church unprecedented in previous centuries. This was witnessed both in terms of growth in population—especially in the East—and, perhaps more important, in terms of securing an elaborate ecclesiastical infrastructure that provided a strong socioeconomic network within the Roman Empire itself. In the Decian-Valerianic persecution the damage done to the Christian churches had little effect upon the economy of the empire. But by the dawn of the fourth century the Christian church was interacting with so many levels of society that official persecution of the illicit cult would become an impediment to the stable flow of goods and services and affect the administration itself, the courts, and the army, thus crippling the entire empire.

In A.D. 261 Bishop Dionysius returned to Alexandria, having been exiled for four years. His major concerns were setting the date of Easter annually in his Festal letter and settling the disputes with Modalists in Libya. Here, Dionysius went so far as to deny that Father and Son were of one substance. Even Bishop Dionysius of Rome became involved in the controversy, and his letters show that the West had very little appreciation for Eastern theology that was dominated by Origen's influence.

The Origenists became aroused once more about the statements of Antiochian Bishop Paul of Samosata. Paul was of Syrian background, and his theology came to be recognized later as of the Antiochene school. According to Paul, Jesus was nothing more than an inspired human, not at all related to the divine Logos. Thus Paul was a radical Monarchian, professing a Trinity in name only. This scandalized the Alexandrian Origenists; after three Antiochian councils (A.D. 264, 265, and 268) Paul was formally deposed. The bishop, however, refused to leave the episcopal house. He was politically powerful, fulfilling important financial responsibilities at the court of Queen Zenobia of Palmyra, who then ruled her own empire in the eastern provinces. In A.D. 272 the emperor Aurelian decided that Zenobia's Palmyrene empire was too powerful to continue as a loyal buffer between Rome and Persia. Zenobia was defeated and Paul temporarily imprisoned. Three years later, however, he was once more residing in the episcopal house in Antioch. The Origenists appealed

to Aurelian to decide Paul's fate—the first time that Christians appealed to an emperor to decide an ecclesiastical controversy—and the diplomatic Aurelian decreed that the decision resided with the Roman and Italian bishops. Paul was ousted.

Other evidence from this period shows how permanently the church was becoming integrated into Roman society. Bishops like Paul were emerging as metropolitan leaders. It was through the strength of Alexandria's Bishop Dionysius that Egypt and Cyrenaica were united as a political entity. Christians were also prominent in all facets of imperial service, as the church historian Eusebius records (*Ecclesiastical History* 7.32.4; 8.11). In Rome parishes were organized within the city limits. The bishop financed these parishes and authorized the clergy to serve them. Growth in sheer numbers of Christians is most visible in the increase in Christian cemeteries in Rome.

With Diocletian's rise to power in A.D. 284, the church continued to flourish under his innovative administration. Diocletian combined his organizational skills and his tremendous energy in order to devise new patterns for the imperial administration; he restored public services and introduced a number of economic and military reforms. He seems to have had no qualms about the participation of Christians in all public services for the first twenty years of his reign. That Diocletian divided the empire through the creation of the tetrarchy—Galerius became his Caesar in the East, Maximian Augustus and Constantius I Chlorus Caesar in the West (A.D. 293)—had significant effects upon the course of the later persecution.

Immediate Causes

Historians can only speculate why Diocletian signed the first edict against the Christians in A.D. 303. Eusebius blames the Christians themselves for their laziness, petty quarrels, and mishandling of liberty, all of which brought on the wrath of God (*Ecclesiastical History* 8.1). The Christian Lactantius, who served as a teacher of Latin rhetoric at Diocletian's court in Nicomedia, wrote a bitter polemic against the diabolical ways of the tetrarchy and blamed its collective evil for the persecution (see his treatise *On the Death of the Persecutors*). The rulers had had considerable success in securing the borders of the empire. In A.D. 295 Constantius secured Gaul, Germany, and Britain. In 298 Diocletian suppressed an uprising in Egypt, and in the same year Galerius conquered Armenia and Media, reversing his earlier military humiliation by the Persian king Narseh. Diocletian was a very religious man and, as reported by Lactantius, did all he could to obtain the favors of the gods for the well-being of the state. When discussing the Christians at the court with his Caesar Galerius, the latter never hid his animosity toward the Christians; because they did not honor the gods, the empire was not secure. He repeatedly urged Diocletian to force all citizens to sacrifice. Diocletian was reluctant, realizing that unnecessary bloodshed would upset the peace of his realm. Unlike the Manicheans, some of whom he had executed, there were too many Christians. But two incidents seem to have convinced Diocletian that persecution was unavoidable.

In A.D. 302 at a public sacrifice, the diviner (*haruspex*) was unable to read the entrails, and Diocletian was told that the gods were impeded by the presence of "contrary influences," namely Christians. Diocletian was furious and ordered his entire court to sacrifice. But this incident sparked no official actions. Galerius, however, seems to have continued pressuring Diocletian to rid the empire of the Christians. Finally Diocletian consulted Didyma, the famous oracle of Apollo near Smyrna that—in concert with the Neoplatonists—had long since been in the service of anti-Christian propaganda.

Didyma answered that because of the Christians only lies issued from the tripod. This response seemed to have removed all doubts from Diocletian's mind.

The Persecution

On 23 February 303, imperial guards demolished the church in Nicomedia (İzmit). Thus began the Great Persecution. The first edict, issued on 24 February 303, called for the destruction of churches and the burning of the sacred books. Clergy who did not cooperate were imprisoned. All Christians were removed from public service and from the army. Sacrifice to the emperors was required from all free citizens involved in legal cases before a court of law (that is, Christians would lose their legal rights). A second edict followed in the summer of 303, calling for the arrest of all clergymen; as a result, prisons in some cities were overcrowded with bishops, deacons, and lectors. A third edict, of 20 November 303, was styled as an amnesty; it allowed the release of all clergy from prison once they had sacrificed—those who refused were to be tortured. In the West, only the first edict was enforced: some property was confiscated, both personal and ecclesiastical. In Constantius' provinces, some churches were destroyed, but executions were not permitted.

The second phase began when Diocletian became ill; he did not appear in public between 20 November 304 and 1 March 305. At some time during this period, a fourth edict was issued, apparently written by Galerius, ordering all Christians to sacrifice on pain of imprisonment, torture, and execution. This edict was enforced in all eastern provinces, but not in the West (with the exception of Africa). At this point Diocletian and his co-Augustus Maximian abdicated. Galerius and Constantius I became Augusti, but Maximian's son Maxentius and Constantius' son Constantine (later the Great) were passed over in the appointment of Caesars. Maximinus II Daia became Galerius' Caesar in the East. Both together continued the persecution with unrelenting zeal until A.D. 311 in the eastern provinces. In the West, however, the political developments that led to the ascendancy of Constantine virtually terminated the persecution in the western half of the empire with the retirement of Diocletian in A.D. 305.

In the third phase of the persecution (A.D. 305–311) economic and legal chaos spread through the entire East of the empire. In Egypt, where the governor Hierocles—a Neoplatonist—tried to enforce all edicts, the persecution led to open civil war in which even pagans supported the Christians against the government. In Asia Minor there was an instance in which the entire population of one town was executed. In Syria, according to the report of Eusebius of Caesarea Maritima, civil life broke down completely: Christian women were forced to serve in brothels, many men were sent to work in the mines. On the whole, there was never a systematic effort to punish all Christians. Rather, the persecution became a long chain of unpredictable attempts to enforce the edict, with many opportunities for cruelty and sadistic excess. Torture and execution were selective and served the display of hatred rather than the eradication of a wrong religious belief. At the end, the persecutors had become frustrated, and the Christians were far from being victorious. They had their martyrs, but also many much less distinguished survivors: bishops who had sacrificed or had willingly handed over the sacred scriptures (*traditores*), and many who simply escaped.

In A.D. 311, Galerius became very ill. On 30 April he issued an edict of toleration. It requested that the Christians pray for his health and urged that their intercessions be directed to the welfare of the empire. The edict foreshadowed the shift that was to come under Constantine: if the old gods could no longer function alone as protectors of the empire, the new God of the Christians might assume this role. Galerius died a few days later. However, his Caesar, Maximinus II Daia, renewed the persecution in the realm under his authority, especially in Syria and Egypt. Many who had so far escaped were now martyred. Maximinus also intensified his efforts to rebuild the pagan cults and supported anti-Christian propaganda—the pagan *Acts of Pilate* were composed at his instigation and had to be used as a schoolbook. Political events brought his efforts to an end: he fell in battle, fighting against Licinius, Constantine's ally.

CONSTANTINE I THE GREAT

In the meantime the young, ambitious, and politically astute Constantine, son of the deceased Constantius I Chlorus, declared himself Augustus in Eboracum (York) in Britannia (northern England). After years of political and military maneuvering, his only remaining enemy in the West was Maxentius, son of the former Augustus Maximian, ruling Rome and Italy. The confrontation was inevitable. In A.D. 312 Constantine defeated Maxentius at the Milvian Bridge leading into Rome. The senate confirmed his rank, and the new eastern Augustus, Licinius, joined forces with him. Constantine and Licinius met in Mediolanum (Milan) in A.D. 313 and jointly issued an edict of toleration for all religions, including Christianity. Church property was to be restored. Licinius remained co-Augustus until Constantine defeated him in A.D. 323.

The night before he went into battle against Maxentius, Constantine is reported to have seen a symbol in the sky with the words, "In this sign, conquer." Eusebius later interpreted this symbol to have been a "chi-rho" (the first letters of the word Christ). Constantine indeed adopted this symbol for his labarum (standard) and was victorious. What Constantine's religion really was at that time is unknown, although his mother Helena was a Christian and one of his sisters had a Christian name, Anastasia. It appears that the new emperor favored a combination of Sol Invictus and the Christian God. He respected both, honored Sol Invictus on his coinage, but was equally interested in church affairs and granted many privileges to the Christians. In fact, his respect for the church earned him the trust of the Donatists.

The Donatist Controversy

Because of the recent persecution, the church in North Africa was split. In A.D. 311 a certain Caecilius was consecrated bishop of Carthage by an assumed *traditor* bishop. The Donatists (later so called because of their bishop Donatus) refused to honor his clergy and sacrament. The violent controversy that ensued, however, involved more than formalities in the ordination of a bishop. North African Christianity, especially in Numidia, had become the heir of the ancient Punic worship of Baal-Hammon (Saturn in its romanized form) and Tanit (Celestis) and of its rigorous ritual that was connected with abstinence and fasting. As these beliefs had survived particularly in the lower classes, social forces combined with religious fervor as Africa became almost completely Christian between A.D. 240 and 270 (excavations have shown that votive offerings to Saturn cease completely during this period). The Donatists represented a socioreligious stratum of the society that now wanted to be recognized as the official church. Only the emperor could grant privileges; thus they appealed to him. In terms of church discipline, the Donatists continued the tradition of Cyprian (rebaptism of *lapsi* and reordination of clergy).

Bishop Miltiades of Rome investigated the dispute in A.D. 313 and decided in favor of the Catholics. Further appeals of the Donatists to Constantine and to a synod at Arelate (Arles) (A.D. 314) were rejected. Constantine tried to use force. In the end he gave up and granted toleration (A.D. 321) with an appeal to the churches not to anger the Lord with quibbling, but to pay him honor in unity of worship. Constantine took it as his divinely ordained duty to guard religious harmony. This self-imposed responsibility served only to frustrate him on more than one occasion.

A few years later Donatus, who was a great orator and charismatic leader, could claim that all Africa had been converted and that 300 bishops were following his command. But the social component of the movement led to further radicalization, which became its downfall. Donatist circumcellions (people who lived around shrines) became a menace to landowners and orthodox bishops alike. Donatus' appeal to the emperor Constans I in A.D. 346 resulted in his exile and in a new wave of persecutions of his movement, which soon collapsed in Carthage and the province of Africa, although the controversies continued; however, the Donatists remained firmly entrenched in Numidia.

Monasticism

Monasticism, another movement that had its roots in the religious and social developments of former centuries, emerged at this time. Christianity had not only changed outwardly in the time of expansion and persecution; it also changed inwardly. Origen, a century earlier, had set the example of the philosopher ascetic whose life is characterized by continence, frugality, apatheia, prayer, and divine contemplation. The expansion of Christianity in the third century had led to a relaxation of moral standards and a disappearance of the apocalyptic vision among the faithful. Syrian ascetics had been familiar figures for some time, and it was not rare in Egypt that people left their villages in order to escape from taxation and economic pressures (*anachoresis*). The protest against the laxity of the city and village churches became an additional motivation for flight into the desert.

The most famous of these anchorites, Antony, left Alexandria in A.D. 285 and stayed in the desert for twenty years. His example led to the formation of a new blend of asceticism and martyrdom, while the old combination of asceticism and education no longer served as an ideal. Antony had a thorough mistrust of Greek education, and his attitude quickly became the hallmark of Egyptian monasticism. Antony came out of the desert briefly in A.D. 305 and organized a group of hermits into a loose association, but soon retired again to the desert, where he remained until his death in A.D. 356. The Alexandrian bishop Athanasius wrote his *Life of St. Antony* four years after the death of his great friend. The monks of this time wanted to be martyrs and they took on all the imagery that had formerly been assigned to the martyrs: athletes, soldiers of Christ, demon slayers. With the end of the persecution the highest goal for a Christian became retirement to the desert in order to become a martyr of the spirit. The gifts of prophecy, assurance of salvation, foreknowledge of the hereafter, and contact with the spiritual world gave the monk authority above and beyond that of the ecclesiarchs. This created a permanent breach in the church and established a tension between the two poles of authority. The monastic establishment in Egypt defied the bishops as well as the tax collectors, and even the emperor himself. It would take the efforts of Basil of Caesarea (A.D. 330–379) to bridge the gap between this Egyptian monasticism and more practical, ecclesiastical monastic structures. But even with Basil's innovations, the tension between spiritual and ecclesiastical author-

ity would remain a permanent factor in the conflicts between the monks and the institutional church.

The Christian Emperor

When Constantine I granted the Christian clergy freedom from public service, he made them equals of the priests of the state cult: it was in the interest of the empire that Christian clergy should not be distracted from their service to God. Further privileges granted to the bishops—the right to act with legal power in cases of civil law (A.D. 318), the authority to certify the manumission of slaves (A.D. 321)—recognized that the churches had already built their own systems of social and legal services, sometimes under aristocratic leadership. In such cases, the bishop functioned as a patron. In the fourth and fifth centuries it became a rule that the bishops were taken from the class of the decurions. When Constantine strengthened the position of the bishops, he increased his own opportunities to influence the people; and when he made donations to the churches, he thereby supported the only functioning system of social services. The old aristocracy had failed, and Constantine knew it. Thus he relied more and more on the infrastructures provided by the churches. This earned him the resentment and hatred of the pagan representatives of the old aristocracy, but it did not yet make Constantine a Christian emperor.

Legislation that had a more obvious Christian motivation was rare before Constantine's victory over Licinius (A.D. 323). The observance of Sunday as a public holiday was introduced in A.D. 321, but it was still called Day of the Sun (it became the Lord's Day under Theodosius). Temples could still be dedicated to the emperor, but sacrifices and the dedication of new cult statues were no longer permitted. In A.D. 325 crucifixion was outlawed as a punishment, and gladiatorial games and fights of criminals with wild beasts were no longer allowed. The army became officially Christian; all soldiers had to recite a prayer "to the one God" every Sunday. The most visible symbol of the beginning of a new age that would become a Christian age was the building—at the small ancient seaport of Byzantium—of a new capital, one that would no longer be dominated by the monuments of pagan religion. Constantine's architectural masterpiece, the Second Rome (the term New Rome first appears under Theodosius), was dedicated as Constantinople in A.D. 330.

Constantine's personal life and actions are filled with ambiguity, and his motives are difficult to sort out. His life is characterized by jealousy and compromising actions. He felt justified in murdering his wife, Fausta, who allegedly was unfaithful. His son Crispus had protected her, so he suffered the same fate. Whether the emperor felt remorse for these actions cannot be ascertained. But such actions must not be used as the sole criteria for the assessment of the emperor's Christianity. He was a political person, and he clearly understood his political office as a God-ordained task. But he also accepted for himself the duties of an officer of the Christian church. His letters show that he gave advice to bishops and churches not simply for reasons of political expediency, but because he believed that such was his Christian calling. He also understood himself to be a Christian teacher and regularly preached from the Bible in services held at the imperial chapel. Constantine's baptism on his deathbed was a common practice in the fourth century and thus gives no clue to his private feelings.

Eusebius' *Life of Constantine* is a panegyric that describes the man to fit the author's political and theological idealization of the God-given emperor. Eusebius could not hide his genuine awe and appreciation of what he believed to be the fulfillment of God's plan that took place during his lifetime. He witnessed the unfolding of this plan from the victory at the Milvian Bridge to Constantinople's dedication, and his biographical work reflects this excitement. Eusebius eagerly bestows upon Constantine the role of universal bishop, since he bore the image of divine kingship. But he goes beyond the traditional panegyric in one way: he truly believed that the events of his day were proof that Constantine was divinely sent. Thus, his *Life* is a recording of the divine economy being realized in history.

THE TRINITARIAN CONTROVERSY

In his attempt to establish peace and unity in the African church, Constantine had been frustrated by a division that had its roots in the persecution. The Egyptian church, too, had not been able to emerge united from the trials of the persecution. Melitius, bishop of Lycopolis in Upper Egypt, had organized a network of a "church of the martyrs" with strict regulations for the readmission of those who had lapsed, thus defying the lax policies of the bishop of Alexandria. The Melitians controlled many bishoprics and an extensive network of monasteries. Although they did not trigger the Arian controversy, their repeated alliances with the Arians against the bishop of Alexandria—the leading defender of orthodoxy—aggravated the quarrel and prevented a political solution for many years.

In A.D. 318 Arius, a presbyter serving churches along the docks of Alexandria, was rallying his community to support his interpretation of the relationship between God the Father and Jesus Christ. The focal point of his thesis is summed up in the phrase, "there was a time when he [the Son] was not." He wrote catchy poems and hymns on this theme, and his theology caught on quickly in the community. Arius allowed the Son the title "God," but he qualified this by saying that his divinity must be understood in the moral sense only. The Son had a beginning. He was made out of nothing, not begotten but created, and mutable just like any other human being. Bishop Alexander, Arius' superior, condemned the teaching as heresy in A.D. 320.

But Arius was a student of the famous Antiochian theologian Lucian (martyred in A.D. 312), under whom many of the influential eastern bishops had also studied. Thus, he had many friends. When it became obvious that Arius' party was growing in numbers and conviction, Constantine called a council in Nicaea (İznik) in A.D. 325. Bishops from all over the Mediterranean met in this small town not far from the capital, Nicomedia. The council rejected Arianism as heresy, and the creed put forth was signed by all but a few radicals who were Arians. The procedures leading to the formulation of the creed are not quite clear, but it is evident that at some point the phrase "the Son is coessential [*homoousios;* also translated "of the same substance"] with the Father," was added, certainly with the emperor's approval. This term assured the Son's eternal generation and his coessential divinity with the Father. Arius and Bishop Eusebius of Nicomedia could not tolerate the nonbiblical term *homoousios;* they were banished. Constantine exhorted all present to subscribe to the creed and made the phrase *homoousios* the litmus test of orthodoxy.

The Victory of Arianism

Two years after the Nicene Council a reaction set in. Not coincidentally, Eusebius of Nicomedia was allowed to return to his see: his party's ability to win imperial patronage and to move court circles away from orthodoxy was remarkable. At the very same time, Athanasius—ardent advocate of the term *homoousios* at Nicaea, where he participated as presbyter—was elected bishop of Alexandria and was immediately opposed by the Melitians, who elected their own

bishop. But while Athanasius could strengthen his own position as popular spiritual leader, patron, and unofficial master of the largest city of the East, Melitians and Arians together made an alliance with the majority of the more moderate eastern bishops. Protracted and increasingly hostile maneuvers finally led to Athanasius' banishment to Treveri (Trier) (A.D. 335)—the first of five exiles. Arius would have been reinstated had he not died suddenly. Constantine himself had grown more and more impatient with the never-ending quarrels; he may also have come to believe that the orthodox position of the Nicene Creed was of little use for the establishment of the unity of the church. Indeed, in spite of his incessant efforts, the eastern church was now more seriously divided than in the years before the Council of Nicaea.

At Constantine's death in A.D. 337, Athanasius returned to his episcopal duties in Alexandria only to discover that Constantine's son, Constantine II, who had become the ruler of the East, was Arian and completely under the influence of Arius' friend Eusebius of Nicomedia, now bishop of Constantinople. Athanasius was exiled once again. At the Council of Antioch (A.D. 341) the Eusebians shifted their attack to the word *homoousios* itself. Subtlety and confusion reigned: *homoousios* was not actually condemned, since orthodox bishops were present, but mention of the word was so scrupulously avoided that the Nicene Creed was practically nullified. Two more councils, in Serdica and Philippopolis (A.D. 343), reissued this Antiochian Creed. However, Constantius now tried to achieve a reconciliation. Athanasius had received full support from the West when he was in exile in Rome and was recalled to his see in A.D. 346. A new turn came in A.D. 350 when Constans I, ruler of the West, was murdered. His Arian brother Constantius II was thus ruler of the whole empire. He moved his residence to Sirmium, where the Illyrians Ursacius and

1069

Valens, both students of Arius, became his court bishops. Many orthodox bishops were exiled; Athanasius fled into the desert. Others were willing to sign an anti-Nicene creed, which said that the Son was "not like" the father (*anhomoios*).

However, this radical Arianism offended even the more moderate Eusebians. Constantius desired to restore harmony within the Arian camp. The creed resulting from another series of councils, the Fourth Sirmium (A.D. 359), made no mention of "essence" (*ousia*) and maintained the clause "the Son is like [*homoios*] the Father in all respects." Jerome's famous statement refers to this period: "The whole world groaned in astonishment to find itself Arian."

Julian "the Apostate"

The victory of Arianism had been achieved solely through imperial support. When Constantius died two years after the Sirmium Creed, that support ended abruptly. His cousin Julian was the sole surviving member of Constantine's family. Once a student of philosophy at Athens, he had been appointed Caesar in Gaul in A.D. 355. In a conflict with Constantius about sending troops to the Persian war, Julian was proclaimed Augustus by the troops in Parisii (Paris). When he moved east to meet his cousin in battle, Constantius suddenly died. As soon as Julian's rule was confirmed in A.D. 361, he openly declared his paganism. No ecclesiastical party could expect imperial support. Athanasius returned to his see, but was exiled once more, this time by the pagan emperor as "an enemy of the gods."

Julian was probably a baptized Christian, but full of hatred for his imperial Christian relatives who had murdered his father and his brother. He had studied the Neoplatonists, was initiated into the mysteries of Eleusis and Mithras and was an admirer of the famous pagan orator Libanius of Antioch, as well as of Greek culture and its moral values. Immediately, he initiated sweeping reforms, in incredibly hectic activity. On the one hand, the Christians lost all of their privileges, were expelled from the Praetorian Guard, had to return all pagan property, and were excluded from teaching in public and rhetorical schools. On the other hand, pagan institutions were revived—there was even an attempt to rebuild the Jewish temple in Jerusalem, which had been destroyed in A.D. 70. Regular sacrifices were again encouraged, and pagan temples were requested to take over the social and religious functions hitherto controlled by the Christians. The emperor assumed the full duties of the *pontifex maximus* of the state. There was no open persecution of the church. Julian himself published tractates against the Christians and propagated a new pagan theology in his elaborate *Hymn to Helios.*

Why did Julian fail? This is one of the most debated questions. Half of the time of his short reign he spent in Antioch, preparing a campaign against the Persians and defending himself against those who ridiculed him because of his philosophical beard. His idealization of the pagan heritage of Rome led him into the pursuit of unrealistic goals. People were dependent upon the church's care for the poor, the widowed, and the orphaned. Since pagan priests did not know how to provide this care, there was a great deal of unrest. Julian wanted to bring back the ancient ideal of justice, but when an Arian bishop of Alexandria was slain by a mob, he refused to prosecute the guilty (even his friend Libanius disagreed). The pagan aristocracy was not able to rebuild the old system of patron and client in the cities—the backbone of the social stability of the empire. Bishops like Athanasius had taken over from their pagan predecessors. The most serious problem may have been Julian's war policy. It seems that the Persians tried to negotiate a peaceful settlement. But Julian wanted to enhance his image as the great conquerer of the eastern powers. Meanwhile, Germanic tribes invaded at the northern frontier. After less than two years as emperor, Julian died (A.D. 363) from a wound he had received in his unsuccessful Persian campaign. Athanasius visited the new emperor Jovian in Antioch and returned to his see.

The Council of Constantinople

The Trinitarian controversy was not really settled until A.D. 381, at the Council of Constantinople. It took the individual geniuses and the collective efforts of the Cappadocian Fathers to hammer out the consistent terminology that was to become the foundation of classical Trinitarian theology. Basil of Caesarea and Gregory of Nyssa were brothers in a large, wealthy Christian family in the province of Cappadocia. Gregory of Nazianzus grew up in a town in the same region, and became Basil's lifelong friend when they met at school in Athens. When Basil returned to Asia Minor, having traveled through Egypt and Syria, he and Gregory Nazianzus began a monastery in Neocaesarea (Niksar) in Pontus (northern Asia Minor). In A.D. 364 Basil was asked to become bishop of Caesarea, and he left his quiet monastic life for the arduous demands of church and politics.

The new Arian emperor Valens lost no time in trying to break the new orthodox stronghold in Cappadocia. When he endeavored to divide the diocese and to appoint new bishops so that the Arians would outnumber the orthodox bishops, Basil immediately consecrated his own bishops before Valens' hierarchs could arrive. Among these new bishops were his best friend, Gregory of Nazianzus, who became bishop of Sasima (later he was briefly bishop of Constantinople), and his younger brother, Gregory, who had to accept the bishopric at Nyssa. Basil died in A.D. 379, not witnessing the complete defeat of Arianism.

This defeat was secured, however, through Basil's theological contributions. In his tract *On the Holy Spirit* Basil states that God cannot be known in his essence (*ousia*) but only through the three individual existences (*hypostaseis*): Father, Son, and Spirit. All human beings can experience their energies and their operations. Each of the three individual existences shares the same essence with each of the other two, but has its own way of existence (*tropos hyparxeos*): the Father in the way of source and will; the Son in the way of generation, creation, and redemption; the Holy Spirit in the way of procession and sanctification. Basil also stresses that the three "coinhere" in each other. No *hypostasis* acts without the other two; they cannot be added together, since their essence is all the same.

In his *Five Theological Orations,* Gregory Nazianzus concentrated more on the unity than on the individuality of the three existences of the Trinity. He stressed the fact that if there was a time when the Son was not, then there was a time when the Father and the Spirit were not. His apophantic theological method became the model for all eastern Christian theology. Gregory of Nyssa dispelled the notion that God is a static entity. *Theos* was an action term, to be experienced by humankind. He is credited with the authorship of Basil's *Letter* 38, in which he likens the Trinity to a rainbow. There is one unity of the phenomenon of light and individual colors without distinguishable boundaries, yet they are thoroughly individual. For Gregory the three existences were three "hows," not three "whats." The formulations in the Constantinopolitan Creed reflect the theological thinking of all three Cappadocians.

The Council of Constantinople was convened by the emperor Theodosius I in May 381. It renewed the Nicene Creed, but differently worded; a brief section on the Holy Spirit was added. Among its canons was one that made the bishop of Constantinople, the New Rome, next in rank to the bishop of

Rome. Although this caused resentment in Rome—and in Alexandria—the creed itself quickly gained general recognition. Arianism had run its course. But meanwhile the Germanic tribes, ready to overrun the empire, were accepting the Christian faith in its Arian form. It took centuries in the West until Catholic Christianity could establish itself in central and western Europe under the leadership of Rome.

BIBLIOGRAPHY

CHRISTIAN BEGINNINGS AND THE EMERGENCE OF DIVERSITY

C. K. Barrett, ed., *The New Testament Background: Selected Documents* (1956); Walter Bauer, *Orthodoxy and Heresy in Earliest Christianity,* 2d ed. (1971); Gunther Bornkamm, *Paul,* D. M. G. Stalker, trans. (1971); Rudolf Bultmann, *Theology of the New Testament,* K. Grobel, trans. (1951); Ronald D. Cameron, ed., *The Other Gospels, Introductions and Translations* (1982); Werner Foerster, *Gnosis: A Selection of Gnostic Texts,* R. McL. Wilson, trans. (1972–1974); F. J. Foakes-Jackson and Kirsopp Lake, eds., *The Beginnings of Christianity* (1920–1933); Howard C. Kee, *The Origins of Christianity: Sources and Documents* (1973); Helmut Koester, *History and Literature of Early Christianity* (1982), and *History, Culture, and Religion of the Hellenistic Age* (1982); Werner Georg Kümmel, *Introduction to the New Testament,* Howard C. Kee, trans. (1975); James M. Robinson, ed., *The Nag Hammadi Library in English* (1977); Walter Schmithals, *Paul and the Gnostics* (1972).

THE DEVELOPMENT OF ECCLESIASTICAL ORGANIZATIONS AND NORMS

Charles Bigg, trans., *The Didache* (1922); Raymond E. Brown, S. S., *Antioch and Rome* (1983); Hans Von Campenhausen, *Ecclesiastical Authority and Spiritual Power,* J. A. Baker, trans. (1969); Henry Chadwick, *History and Thought of the Early Church* (1982); Virginia Corwin, *St. Ignatius and Christianity in Antioch* (1960); Robert M. Grant, *The Apostolic Fathers: A New Translation and Commentary* (1964–1968); J. B. Lightfoot, *Apostolic Fathers: A Revised Text with Introductions, Notes, Dissertations, and Translations* (1885–1890); Wayne Meeks and Robert Wilken, *Jews and Christians in Antioch* (1978); Morton Smith, *Clement of Alexandria and a Secret Gospel of Mark* (1973).

THE CHURCH AND THE WORLD AND WESTERN CHRISTIANITY

Leslie W. Barnard, *Justin Martyr: His Life and Thought* (1967); Timothy D. Barnes, *Tertullian: A Historical and Literary Study* (1971); Charles Bigg, *The Christian Platonists of Alexandria* (1886; repr. 1968); Peter Brown, *The World of Late Antiquity A.D. 150–750* (1971); Gerard E. Caspary, *Politics and Exegesis: Origen and the Two Swords* (1979); Henry Chadwick, *Early Christian Thought and the Classical Tradition* (1966); Jean Daniélou, *Origen,* Walter Mitchell, trans. (1955); Robert M. Grant, *Second Century Christianity* (1946), and trans., *Ad Autolycum by Theophilus of Antioch* (1970); Stanley L. Greenslade, ed., *Early Latin Theology: Selections from Tertullian, Cyprian, Ambrose, and Jerome* (1956); Henneke Gülzow, *Cyprian und Novatian: Der Briefwechsel zwischen den Gemeinden in Rom und Karthago zur Zeit der Verfolgung des Kaisers Decius* (1975); S. L. Guterman, *Religious Toleration and Persecution in Ancient Rome* (1951; rev. ed. 1971); John N. Kelly, *Early Christian Doctrines* (1958); Ramsey MacMullen, *Enemies of the Roman Order* (1966); Herbert Musurillo, *The Acts of the Christian Martyrs* (1972); Eric F. Osborn, *Justin Martyr* (1973); John Earnest Leonard Oulton, ed., *Alexandrian Christianity: Selected Translations of Clement and Origen* (1954); Jaroslav Pelikan, *The Emergence of the Catholic Tradition 100–600* (1971); Michael M. Sage, *Cyprian* (1973); Cyril C. Richardson, *Early Christian Fathers* (1953); Cullen I. K. Story, *The Nature of Truth in "The Gospel of Truth" and in the Writings of Justin Martyr* (1970).

CHRISTIANITY IN SYRIA, MESOPOTAMIA, AND PERSIA

Tjitze Baarda, *Early Transmission of Words of Jesus: Thomas, Tatian and the Text of the New Testament* (1983); Ronald D. Cameron and Arthur J.

Dewey, trans., *The Cologne Mani Codex* (1979); François Decret, *Mani et la tradition manichéenne* (1974); Gilles Quispel, *Tatian and the Gospel of Thomas* (1975); Kurt Rudolph, *Mandaeism* (1978); Geo Widengren, *Mani and Manichaeism*, Charles Kessler, trans. (1965).

THE GREAT PERSECUTION

Timothy D. Barnes, *The New Empire of Diocletian and Constantine* (1981); Pierre Bastien, *Le monnoyage de l'atelier de Lyon: de la réforme [monétaire] de Dioclétien à la fermeture temporaire de l'atelier en 316 (294–316)* (1980); Arne S. Christensen, *Lactantius, the Historian: An Analysis of the De Mortibus Persecutorum* (1980); William H. C. Frend, *Martyrdom and Persecution in the Early Church* (1965); Arthur J. Mason, *The Persecution of Diocletian* (1876); De Lacy Evans O'Leary, *Coptic Martyrs* (1937); Carol H. V. Sutherland, ed., *Roman Imperial Coinage 6: From Diocletian's Reform (A.D. 294) to the Death of Maximinus (A.D. 313)* (1967).

CONSTANTINE

Apostolos Athanassakis, *The Life of Pachomius* (1975); Timothy D. Barnes, *Constantine and Eusebius* (1981); Norman H. Baynes, *Constantine the Great and the Christian Church* (1931); Norman H. Baynes and Elizabeth Dawes, *Three Byzantine Saints* (1948); Peter Brown, *The Making of Late Antiquity* (1978), and *Society and the Holy in Late Antiquity* (1982); William H. C. Frend, *The Donatist Church* (1952); Robert M. Grant, *Eusebius as Church Historian* (1980); Robert C. Gregg, trans., *Life of St. Anthony and the Letter to Marcellinus by Athanasius* (1980); Arnold H. M. Jones, *Constantine and the Conversion of Europe* (1948; rev. ed. 1962); James Stevenson, ed., *A New Eusebius* (1960); Benedicta Ward, trans., *The Sayings of the Desert Fathers* (1975).

THE TRINITARIAN CONTROVERSY

Robert Browning, *The Emperor Julian* (1976); Robert C. Gregg, *Consolation Philosophy: Greek and Christian Paideia in Basil and the Two Gregories* (1975); Robert C. Gregg and Dennis E. Groh, *Early Arianism—A View of Salvation* (1981); Edward R. Hardy, *Christology of the Later Fathers* (1954); Bloomfield Jackson, *Saint Basil, De Spiritu Sancto*, in *A Select Library of Nicene and Post-Nicene Fathers of the Christian Church*, vol. 8 (1961); H. Lietzmann, *From Constantine to Julian, A History of the Early Church*, vol. 3, B. Woolf, trans. (1950); William G. Rusch, *The Trinitarian Controversy* (1980); James Stevenson, ed., *Creeds, Councils and Controversies* (1966); Monica W. Wagner, C.S.C., trans., *Saint Basil, Ascetical Works* (1950).

PRIVATE AND SOCIAL LIFE

Greek Education and Rhetoric

CAROLYN DEWALD

THE ART OF RHETORIC has two parts: the practice of formal oratory and the body of theory that purports to set out the rules for composing and delivering a successful speech. The practice of oratory was a fundamental part of ancient Greek culture for well over a thousand years, from Homer's day into the early medieval period. Even when the Greeks became a literate people, from the seventh or sixth century B.C. onward, their mode of intellectual exchange continued to be an oral one. The public and ceremonial life of the Greek community relied heavily on the exercise of traditional formal speech. The art, or *techne,* of speechmaking came much later, in the fifth century; but when it did, it rapidly evolved into a tightly organized body of material. This material in turn became the foundation for Western secondary education. This essay will sketch the history of the process: how oratory first became an art, with rules that could be taught, and then how this fact shaped the way that Greeks came to regard their cultural heritage and to transmit it to posterity.

Homer gives the first and most extensive picture of the role of formal, artistic speech in the Greek world of the eighth and seventh centuries B.C. In the Homeric poems, oratory is one of the two most important aspects of the aristocratic warrior code. A man had to learn to be both "a speaker of words and a doer of deeds" if he was to be accepted among the *aristoi,* the elite of his culture. Formal speech does not come adorned with an elaborate system of rules in Homer; several centuries later Plato made fun of contemporaries who insisted that Nestor and Odysseus were writing handbooks of rhetorical dos and don'ts under the walls of Troy. But the modern reader is at first startled by the number of contexts in Homer where we would expect informal conversation and instead find speeches: not just in embassies, group deliberations, and quasi-judicial hearings, but also when people meet on the battlefield or converse at home.

Homer distinguishes a variety of appropriate and inappropriate speaking behaviors. Nestor speaks with the honeyed smoothness and abundance appropriate to an elder statesman, Achilles with the passion of the aggrieved young warrior, Priam with the pathos of a soon-to-be-defeated king and grieving father, and Diomedes with the prudence of a man just coming into his own authority on the battlefield and in the council chamber. Inappropriate speaking styles also play an important part in the plots of the poems. The first two books of the *Iliad* display Agamemnon as a mediocre general and a mediocre speaker as well. He alienates his best warrior by intemperate and insulting speech in assembly; in Book Two, Odysseus must rescue the situation after Agamemnon's exhortation to the army has backfired and demoralized the troops. Sometimes the speaker's age prohibits him from speaking well. In Book Two of the *Odyssey* Telemachus calls an assembly. He begins eloquently enough but ends in a tantrum, throwing the speaker's staff to the floor. It is an effective ploy for stirring the pity of the audience; it is also however the act of a very young and frustrated man.

In the Homeric poems only the upperclass warrior has the right to use formal speech. Brutally evocative of this fact is the scene from Book Two of the *Iliad* where a commoner from the ranks, emboldened by conflict among the commanders, claims a freedom of speech to which he is not entitled. Thersites' arguments are on the whole quite pertinent, but his speech is disordered, and his peers laugh when Odysseus beats him about the head and shoulders and forces him to desist.

Like skill in battle, extraordinary skill in speechmaking is acknowledged as a gift of the gods. Athene gives it to Odysseus; Hesiod mentions that the Muses endow kings with persuasion (*peitho*) (*Theogony* 81). But some ability in the use of formal speech is necessary, precisely because it is the mark of one's membership in aristocratic culture. Those who have learned its implicit rules become part of the nexus of guest-friendships that link aristocrats from all corners of the Greek-speaking world. Odysseus is the clearest example of this. In Book Six of the *Odyssey* his speech to the princess Nausicaa at the beach convinces her that he is of her own world, even though he delivers it naked and matted from his struggles in the sea.

The Homeric poems suggest several patterns through which the archaic Greek youth learned to be a speaker of words and a doer of deeds. In some respects Phoenix, the tutor of Achilles, foreshadows the career of the tutor (*paidagogos*) and the teacher of letters (*grammatistes*) of the classical period. A man of good breeding encounters misfortune and must seek employment. He becomes a dependent in another noble household and because of his personal excellence becomes the young master's companion. The teacher of the young was never accorded high social status in Greek culture, because he was obliged to work for hire. From the beginning, however, he was expected to be a worthy model for his charge, and Achilles shows Phoenix the deference due to a beloved elder. The Homeric version is doubtless an idealized picture, but Sophocles' *Electra* in the classical period also testifies to the mutual affection that could bind a tutor and his youthful charge.

Other patterns of education are suggested in the Homeric poems. Another of Achilles' teachers was Cheiron the centaur. Cheiron suggests the seed from which the later model of the formal school would grow: a man outstandingly gifted in some important art to whom youthful princes would be sent by their fathers. There is in Homer still no suggestion of group instruction; the transmission of knowledge was an individual affair. Cheiron was himself a famous healer; the model of the youthful apprentice learning his skills from the master remained into Hellenistic times the customary way to teach complex skills, especially in such applied sciences as navigation, engineering, and medicine.

At least as important as these two models

(and probably more common in the actual world of archaic nobility) is the association of the young man with older peers. Athene herself accompanies Telemachus on his first visits as a guest-friend; from her assumed name, Mentor, comes one of our modern terms for guide and instructor. The part of the *Odyssey* labeled the Telemachia—the first four books—gives us some of the final stages in the education of the prince. Telemachus is exposed to a number of situations and is coached in how to handle himself in them. By the conclusion of the *Odyssey* he has learned to move in polite society and has become the representative of those rules in his own home. Natural ability and the chance to learn from imitation of worthy models were clearly the basis of all Homeric education; in the later classical period as well, even professional educators like Isocrates continued to consider aptitude and imitation far more important than formal instruction.

Before leaving Homer for later developments, two aspects of the general culture displayed in the Homeric poems are worth commenting on if we are to understand fully the future shape both of Greek education and of Greek rhetoric. First, there is from the beginning a close connection between fighting and formal speech. To be a good warrior implies that you can kill your opponent; to be a good speaker implies that your presentation of yourself in a formal setting will prevail. In argument, you will overcome your opponents; in epideictic settings, where oratorical skill is on display, you will impress your hearers and win them over, as Odysseus wins over the Phaeacians. Moreover, in an oral society strife is very much a potential part of group deliberations, where warriors decide on joint actions to undertake. Part of the need for a truly formal, courteous oratory came from the constant threat to group cohesiveness posed by the personal rivalries and bad feelings that

inevitably existed in such a competitive society. The first scene of the *Iliad* illustrates the potential danger; Achilles and Agamemnon quarreling in assembly almost destroy the Greek cause. Even the combined verbal skills of a Nestor and an Odysseus barely suffice to contain and to limit the damage. Later, as we see speech further formalized in the polis, the Greek city-state, it will never quite lose this aggressive, contest-oriented aspect of its origins. Its very formality is often what keeps public speech from breaking out into open strife; at the same time, the ability to handle the rules effectively becomes a part of the warrior's total aggressive capacity.

A second aspect of formal speech will assume more importance in the mid fifth century, but is present already in Homer: the connection between speech (*logos*) and deception. We feel vaguely uncomfortable at Odysseus' lying to his faithful retainer and winning a cloak from him before revealing his identity; like Telemachus we feel some discomfort and amazement at the delicate battle of wits between Odysseus and Penelope at their reconciliation. Even if formal speech is a device encouraging group solidarity, there is as well a deeper sense in which the manipulation of persuasive words to achieve one's ends leads to individual isolation and alienation. The individual hero stands alone and uses his wits against others, and he accepts a universe where others, whether men or gods, are likely to use their verbal skills to deceive him in turn.

This is true not only in Homer. In the anonymous *Hymn to Hermes* the infant god tells lies with all the panache and persuasiveness of an experienced criminal lawyer. In Hesiod's *Theogony*, Zeus uses *haimulioi logoi*, "wily words," to distract even Metis, the goddess of intelligence, so that he can swallow her whole. This awareness of, and pleasure in, the power of speech to beguile and deceive was later viewed by the Romans as one of the most characteristic and reprehensible of Greek traits.

Epic poetry played a significant part in determining the course of classical education and rhetoric. Homer himself became "the teacher"; throughout later Greek culture, Greek children would be given long passages from the *Iliad* and the *Odyssey* to memorize, and later Greeks claimed to find in Homer the whole of their society's value system. Homer had another, perhaps subtler, effect on the formal art of speaking. When rhetoric became a *techne,* in the fifth century, it showed from the beginning the influence of epic poetry. The high oratory of the fifth and fourth century, with its large and lofty vocabulary, extraordinary flexibility in word order, and almost poetic rhythms and turns of phrase, would not have been possible unless both speaker and audience had been raised on Homer.

Between the seventh and the fifth century the city-state replaced the home as the chief focus of political allegiance; religious cults and festivals were increasingly civic in orientation; the hoplite citizen army rendered the older mode of aristocratic single-handed combat obsolete. The increased importance of the citizen in the army, shoulder to shoulder with his peers, was gradually reflected in the increased importance of civic assemblies and in the necessity for powerful aristocrats to persuade as well as coerce, becoming in general more responsible to the needs of the common people. Both poetry and oratory played an important part in developing civic politics. Dionysius of Halicarnassus calls Alcaeus' poems (late seventh century B.C.) political rhetoric set to meter; Solon's poems from the same era are directed to both the external and internal political problems of Athens.

It was during the seventh and sixth centuries that formal education first appeared and that the citizen bodies of the larger Greek cities became literate. The two processes were not at first intimately connected. The traditional education of the Athenian child down to the later fifth century was not primarily an education in letters. Its purpose was rather to make available even to ordinary citizens the aristocratic pursuits in sports and music that had earlier been denied them. The Athenian child went at about age seven first to the gymnastic instructor, *paidotribes,* and then to the music instructor, or *kitharistes;* the teacher of letters, *grammatistes,* emerged only in the early classical period and initially was considered of lesser importance.

Nonetheless, if the orator Aeschines is right (*Against Timarchus* 7–9), Solon in the early sixth century required everyone by law to teach his sons letters; the development of ostracism by the end of the century suggests that some degree of literacy was by then taken for granted in Athens. Moreover, laws were written on stone in the central open space of the polis; the fact that a citizen could now read the laws of his city was instrumental in the development of a newly critical attitude toward tradition. Oral manipulation of law by interested parties (usually aristocrats) was no longer as easy as it had been in Hesiod's day; because the law was inscribed, it was no longer hallowed by tradition but had become a cultural artifact capable of being criticized and changed when it was no longer useful.

Writing also made possible self-conscious reflection of another sort. Philosophers, both in poetry and in the beginnings of artistic prose, began to reflect on the rules that order the natural and the human cosmos. Especially in the Greek-speaking cities of Asia Minor and southern Italy, Greeks began to describe foreign places and customs, perhaps to compile individual city traditions, and to record and systematize traditional myth. The changes in rhetoric that occurred in the fifth century should be viewed as one aspect of this larger social transformation—but an aspect that was itself to have revolutionary consequences. The change from *mythos* to *logos*—from a traditional society that transmitted its most important thought in terms of story and song to a society that argued, analyzed, and gave an account of itself in terms of science, philosophy, and history—had already begun by the time rhetoric became an art. It was largely in the terms invented by this new discipline, however, that the process was completed. For with the change to a self-conscious society that argued about and criticized the bases of its own knowledge about itself—what G. E. R. Lloyd calls second-level thinking—came the need for a self-conscious mechanism for transmitting that society's understanding of itself from generation to generation. The formal study of rhetoric and the development of the first formal literary education in the fifth century B.C. are intimately connected processes.

The Greeks themselves believed that the formal art of rhetoric began in Sicily, in the disturbances following the expulsion of the Syracusan tyrants in 467 B.C. Corax and Tisias are the names mentioned in the doxographic accounts as Syracusans who capitalized on the now urgent need for persuasive speech in the lawcourts and in the newly powerful democratic assembly by beginning to teach the art of speechmaking. We are not sure precisely what they did. Aristotle in the fourth century compiled a collection of earlier rhetorical theory that seems to have begun with Tisias. This became the standard collection of all early rhetorical theory, and later Roman and Greek writers seem to have read it. Since it was lost in late antiquity, we are dependent for our knowledge of the development of technical rhetoric on the comments made by authors like Cicero who had it available to them.

Generally attributed to Corax and Tisias is, first, the new idea of the art of speaking as a skill that can be reduced to rules and can

be taught. They may have acted as speechwriters for others or coached people in preparing speeches to be delivered in court and in the assembly. They wrote handbooks to be used in preparing speeches for courts of law and perhaps deliberative assemblies. Their most important theoretical advance was to make explicit something that good speechmakers had undoubtedly already intuitively discovered: a good speech is organized into several discrete parts, each with its own function. The four-part theory of judicial speech was quickly adopted as canonical and, with minor variations, lasted to the end of antiquity. A speech in a lawcourt was supposed to contain, first, an introduction that oriented the audience to the issues and made them well disposed to the speaker; then a narration that told the speaker's version of what had happened as clearly as possible; third, a section of argument, in which objections to the speaker's opponent were put forth and the stronger points in the speaker's own case developed; finally a conclusion, in which the speaker summarized the case. The theory as a whole was developed gradually; even later fifth-century Athenian speakers like Andocides did not fully exploit the use of narrative or conclusion. Other areas of importance to later rhetorical theory were also anticipated by the Syracusans. They paid some attention to style and discussed the use of arguments from probability—what was later to be called artistic proof. All of these observations, however, were apparently set out not in an orderly, analytical framework but as a series of prescriptions, each beginning, "You should . . ."

THE SOPHISTS AND THEIR CONTRIBUTION

The art of rhetoric invented by the Syracusans would have remained an obscure footnote in Greek intellectual history, however, had it not been joined to another, much larger social transformation that took place in Athens in the second half of the fifth century. The Sophists were intellectuals, chiefly from Ionia (Greek Asia Minor) and southern Italy, who congregated in Periclean Athens, drawn there by Pericles' own interest in their ideas and by the richness and power of Athens as leader of the Delian League. On the newly rich, powerful, and self-confident society of democratic Athens the Sophists had an astonishing impact. The boldness of their sociological and philosophical speculations makes them important for the intellectual history of their times; the rest of fifth- and fourth-century Greek philosophy cannot really be understood except in the context of the questions they raised.

At least as important as the intellectual content of their thought in making this movement revolutionary was their style—the way in which they chose to present themselves to Athenian society. They constituted themselves the first professional educators, teaching for pay a secondary and higher education to the Athenian young. One of the most controversial and politically important subjects they claimed to teach was the art of speaking in the courts and assemblies.

A general survey of the Sophists' contribution as intellectuals and teachers is in order before we turn to their direct contributions to rhetoric. G. B. Kerferd likens the Sophists to Thucydides' Sparta—if one looks at their remains, it is difficult to believe the impressiveness of their contribution. In part this is the result of the very revolution in thought that they engendered. As the precursors of the great age of the fourth-century schools, the Sophists did not yet have available to them structures for preserving and transmitting the bulk of their work in writing. It is not clear that they would have even understood the need to sum up their positions systematically in this way. Their approach toward each other was individualistic and competitive. Plato describes the personal rivalries pervading their discussions. Gorgias, in the dialogue named after him, is torn between his interest in Socrates' ideas and his practical sense that the onlookers (and potential paying customers) regard the conversation more as a wrestling match than as a joint disinterested search for truth. Later scholars felt the contributions of the Sophists had been superseded and that anything of value in them had been incorporated into the work of Plato and Aristotle. Most of our knowledge comes from late sources interested principally in other matters or from the Sophists' fourth-century successors, who were generally critical of Sophist accomplishments.

It was as a social and political phenomenon that the Sophists had their greatest impact, but it is important to stress the breadth of their interests in the other areas of early Greek speculative thought as well. Gorgias is depicted on Isocrates' tomb gazing at an astronomical sphere; he seems also to have been interested in problems of vision and to have held a theory of effluences similar to that of Empedocles (with whom, in one tradition, he is said to have studied). Hippias the polymath studied music, astronomy, and mathematics; in the *Protagoras* of Plato he holds forth on questions of natural science and astronomy. Prodicus seems to have been concerned with the nature of man; Antiphon considered cosmology and mathematics. As G. E. R. Lloyd points out, many of the early Hippocratic treaties on the body and medicine present themselves in the form of sophistic demonstration pieces (*epideixeis*); perhaps it is noteworthy that Gorgias' brother was a physician.

It was the Sophists' work in what we now call philosophy and the social sciences that stirred up the most controversy among their more conservative Athenian hosts. They seemed as a group all too willing to call into question established conventions of society, belief in the gods, and the rule of law. According to the composite picture presented by Plato and extant fragments of such great first-generation Sophists as Protagoras, Gorgias, and Antiphon, the Sophists distinguished what was natural, innate in human beings, from what was merely conventional. Justice, Protagoras claimed, was innate in all men—a tenet that certainly fitted the dominant ideology of Periclean democracy. Protagoras and Gorgias claimed also to be able to teach justice. The notion that becoming a good citizen was teachable was of course essential to the sophistic claim to teach the citizen young of Athens. The Sophists distinguished between what is naturally just and what is merely the result of local traditions; they gave display speeches celebrating the theme of Panhellenism. Many Athenians felt that in advancing such opinions and teaching them to the young, the Sophists were tampering with the foundations of a society for which they bore no personal responsibility and were leaving others to suffer the consequences. In the *Gorgias* and in the *Protagoras*, Plato draws a sharp contrast between Socrates, the Athenian stonemason concerned for the health of his city, and the Sophists, who are foreigners making money from their wits.

The content of their theories made the Sophists an easy target for prosecutions of impiety. More fundamental than their theories, however, were the changes that they were making in the very definition of how one went about thinking and arguing. As we have seen, the connection between speech, power, and deception was an old one in Greek poetry; some of the pre-Socratic thinkers had begun to argue in terms of ontology and epistemology. At least two of the outstanding Sophists among the first generation that came to Athens struggled seriously with issues of language, knowledge, and being that were raised but not sys-

tematically explored by earlier Ionian thinkers. Protagoras and Gorgias seem to have argued that language itself was a social artifact and that real knowledge was a hypothetical and perhaps unreachable state. In its place they postulated *doxa,* opinion, and the notion of the plausible or probable, *to eikos.*

What the Sophists represented as a social phenomenon was a crisis typical of the transition from a traditional to a literate culture. Traditional sources of knowledge—poetry, gnomic wisdom, legends, and semihistorical myths—no longer had the power to elicit unthinking belief. When the Sophists began to investigate the basis on which they were entitled to say that they knew something, they encountered the complexities of language and the problems of defining language, belief, and knowledge that continue to occupy philosophers today.

Their pessimism about the possibility of attaining real knowledge had implications for the way in which they conducted their discussions, both among themselves and with the Athenian citizens who became their patrons. The earlier model of speech as an *agon,* part of the warrior's competitive stance toward his peers, was developed by the Sophists into professional argumentation. Protagoras announced that there are two opposed arguments on any issue. Through a process of trial and error one tests successive positions, to see which is the more probable, that is, convincing. This process led to a much greater awareness, both in the Sophists themselves and in their audience, of argument as a skill with rules of its own. Better and worse arguments for any position could be found; the competing arguments, or *antilogikoi,* of the fifth century were produced to show how such arguments would enter in combat with one another. To some of their critics, the Sophists come to Athens and habituated the better born and more intellectual of the citizens to think that two positions can be taken on any issue; that what is required is not truth (since this is either relative to the speaker or entirely unattainable) but *doxa,* opinion; and that the weaker (worse) can be made the stronger (better) argument by the exercise of skills that they claimed to teach.

In the *Protagoras* and the *Gorgias,* Plato gives a vivid picture of the way the Sophists met Athenian citizens. They would come to the house of one of their rich and wellborn enthusiasts and hold forth, either in conversation or in a general lecture, to those who cared to come and meet them. This was bad enough. But the really serious issue at stake, in Plato's eyes, was their effect on the young. They claimed to be able to teach the young to be better citizens, both in private and as speakers in the Athenian assembly and law-courts. But in the eyes of Plato and other conservative Athenian critics, both the style and the content of the Sophists' teachings had an insidious effect. Under their tutelage young men at an impressionable age learned not to respect ancient Athenian tradition or their elders but to call all this mere convention; they also learned tools of argumentation that allowed them to overcome others in debate even if their cause would not in some way benefit the city. The same techniques that allowed them to shine in debate were used to revolutionize the traditional art of speechmaking. Eristic—disputational—skill and a self-conscious technique of manipulating words became increasingly necessary, if a speech was to carry conviction. The Sophists taught this skill to anyone who had the money to pay them. The popularity of the argumentative techniques that they developed generated its own innovative momentum. Once this new form of argumentation was accepted by the general population, those who refused to use it were increasingly at a disadvantage, both in their public role and in their private affairs as citizens.

The Sophists seem not to have concerned themselves with elementary education; this remained very much in the hands of the *paidotribes,* the *kitharistes,* and the *grammatistes.* But from the age of about thirteen to seventeen the wellborn Athenian youth increasingly went to a Sophist for his secondary education. We have some details of their procedure only for those outstanding figures who were taken seriously by Plato. Protagoras seems to have viewed his teaching principally as a matter of personal association, much as the earliest Greek educators had done. The young pupil attended the master and heard him deliver speeches in a formal expository style. Perhaps some of these speeches would be copied out and the youth set to memorize them; some have argued that Gorgias' *Encomium of Helen* and *Defense of Palamedes* are actually set pieces to be memorized, because they present in a highly artificial form arguments that the young pupil interested in learning to speak could commit to memory as a sort of paradigm, much as Phaedrus learns the speech of Lysias in the *Phaedrus* of Plato. The *Tetralogies* of Antiphon are perhaps another example of model speeches to be learned by students for their method of arguing probabilities. Some Sophists produced handbooks, though these apparently remained, like the earlier Syracusan contributions to technical rhetoric, a matter of almost random strings of observation and advice. Later educators made fun of their technique. Isocrates likens the Sophists' use of commonplaces to someone trying to teach the art of reading from the alphabet alone; Aristotle compares the practice of making the student memorize finished speeches to teaching the art of shoemaking by giving the apprentice shoemaker a pile of finished shoes.

G. A. Kennedy isolates four characteristics in the sophistic movement that formed the basis of their contribution to the developing art of rhetoric. First, there was the new rationalism of proof and argument. In the *Encomium of Helen,* for instance, Gorgias uses disjunctive or dilemma arguments, which offer an opponent alternatives but no chance of winning. Also used were *a fortiori* arguments and attacks on opponents for inconsistency and irrelevance. Intense interest was paid to *to eikos,* the probable; topics to be used in argument included expediency, justice, the possible, and the honorable. Second, the Sophists continued and elaborated upon the Syracusans' division of a speech into its component parts. Third, and very significant for the later history of Greek prose style, the Sophists experimented with various ways of making prose artistic. Gorgias in the *Encomium of Helen* celebrates speech as a magic that can enchant its hearers. Thrasymachus is said to have worked to specify the rhythms particularly appropriate in oratorical prose. Antiphon and a number of the other early Sophists relied heavily on antithesis to develop their arguments; Gorgias added kinds of clause parallelism and end rhyme like homoeoteleuton, isocolon, and parison. The prose of the Athenian historian Thucydides shows us that Gorgianic figures, as they were called, were very popular in the early years of the Peloponnesian War in Athens. We find them making their effect in drama as well.

The stylistic excesses of this first generation of experimenters quickly became outmoded; Gorgias himself was excluded from the later canon of classical models for good Greek prose. Nonetheless, these efforts, with their jingling end rhymes and the monotonous stiffness of their parallel clauses, were the direct precursors of the magnificent and supple oratorical periods of the great fourth-century speakers. Antithesis in particular—the most important of all the figures favored by the Sophists—was superbly designed for bringing out the muscularity of argumentative thought, as that generation defined it. Antithesis forced into the

structure of the very sentence the sense of contrast, of struggle and tension between competing ideas. The Sophists sought to rival the emotional power of verse but to do so through the ways of thought that prose favored and whose full expression only prose made possible.

Finally, the Sophists' attention to language also bore fruit in the new science of philology. Protagoras concerned himself with the division of four basic kinds of speech: request, question, answer, command; he also is said to have written on the correct use of words. This, as we see humorously displayed in the *Protagoras* of Plato, was also a concern of Prodicus, whose special focus was on synonyms and drawing fine distinctions between them. Again, we see in Thucydides the results of these stylistic adventures. He confidently exploits the astonishing capacity of the Greek language for abstract neologisms, coining new words to express the new discoveries of his generation about man as a social animal.

Much consideration has been given here to the Sophists because they were the thinkers who first defined themselves as intellectuals and made their living on the skills they claimed both to possess and to impart to others in a formal secondary education. G. B. Kerferd comments that their most marked single characteristic was a sustained attempt to apply reason to achieve an understanding of both rational and irrational processes. Their answers to various problems were no doubt naive or inadequate, but they certainly struggled with the complexity of the problems. As the group who popularized speechmaking as a systematic art in Athens, their revolutionary consequences were felt almost immediately. The Sophists forced into Athenian judicial and deliberative thought a new level of rigor, of argumentation, and of logical organization for a speech; they gave the increasingly discriminating audience of Athenian citizens a heightened appreciation both of argumentation and of style.

THE FOURTH CENTURY: PROFESSIONAL EDUCATION AND TECHNICAL RHETORIC

The great age of the Sophists ended with the Peloponnesian War (431–404 B.C.). During and after the war Athens lost the resources to support a large band of foreign intellectuals. Many Athenians blamed the course of the disastrous twenty-seven-year war on the teaching of the Sophists; Socrates was killed in 399 B.C. as a scapegoat for the whole movement. The legacy of the Sophists remained visible, however, in the distinctive developments of Athenian education and rhetoric.

In fourth-century Athens education became fully professionalized. Schools with professional teachers and curricula were founded, and from this point onward those schools became the principal way in which the young would learn what it meant to be Greek. Within them, training in the art of rhetoric became accepted as the apex of the male Greek youth's formal education. Our earliest extant handbooks of technical rhetoric date from this period; they represent a further stage in the transformation of rhetoric from a traditional art into what G. A. Kennedy calls a conceptual one. What had started in Syracuse as discrete observations about successful speechmaking was now evolving into a set of prescriptive requirements within an organized educational curriculum. These formed the standard of taste according to which the student learned to express his own thoughts and against which he learned to measure the oratorical and literary performance of others. Ultimately such prescriptions would severely diminish the spontaneity and vigor of Greek oratory and literary prose.

The effects of this process are not yet fully visible in the oratory and literary prose of the fourth century, however. The fourth century was also the great age of Athenian judicial and deliberative speechmaking. Orators began for the first time as a matter of course to edit and publish their most successful speeches. Moreover, the new stability of the professionally organized schools assured that these speeches would be studied and preserved. This concern with proper formal expression was part of a larger social movement created by the fact of widespread literacy and a secondary education that was literary in content. Educated fourth-century Greeks began to define their own cultural heritage as both a literary and a classical one; they increasingly saw themselves as the heirs of a great tradition that they had to preserve, cherish, and try to emulate.

These developments affect the nature of the material we encounter when we turn to the rhetoric and education of the fourth century. Our evidence is no longer scraps quoted by later authors, but a substantial extant corpus of prose writers setting out their own thoughts at length and in context. The focus here will be on only a handful of the most important educators and orators, in order to suggest the dominant lines of development that lead from the classical age to the Hellenistic world of the next three centuries. But the reader who wants to understand the complex tensions that define the fourth century as an age that looks both back and forward is strongly encouraged to turn to the texts themselves. We can still hear the voices of Isocrates, Plato, Aristotle, Lysias, and Demosthenes more or less as they intended; this fact more than any other suggests the extent of the cultural changes that had taken place.

Isocrates (436–338 B.C.) is the first of the great educators, the man who gave shape to fourth-century rhetorical education. He began his career as a professional speechwriter but, after studying with Gorgias in Thessaly, had opened a school in Athens by the late 390s. In many respects his school continued fifth-century sophistic practices. He taught principally by association, encouraging students to imitation. He seems to have been the only teacher, and the education he provided remained intensely individualistic. As in the case of the Sophists, at his death his school died with him.

Several aspects of his career, however, suggest the shape of future developments in Greek education. As an Athenian citizen Isocrates could possess property, and he ran his school in a private building near the Lyceum, a grove sacred to Apollo Lyceius and later used by Aristotle as the site of his research institute. Isocrates did not harangue his audiences in the gymnasia, the open areas in the city reserved for sports; by temperament he disliked the eristic and competitive model of the Sophists. He therefore fashioned a new and more dignified persona for himself as a gentleman who was also a professional educator and counselor of statesmen. His course was three or four years long, and he could charge 1,000 drachmas for it. Despite his complaints in the *Exchange of Property* (*Antidosis*), Isocrates became one of the wealthiest men in Athens through the success of his school, which he ran for fifty years.

Isocrates articulated the need for a formal secondary education, with a self-conscious theoretical underpinning and techniques of teaching more advanced than those used by the *grammatistes*. The contents of this education are described in passages scattered throughout his speeches; the speeches themselves were written in large part to advertise the virtues of the schooling he provided. To become the dominant educational theorist of his day, he was obliged to fight a battle on several fronts. He believed that he was fighting for the old, traditional culture of the polis against the modern technicians,

both among the Sophists and among the Socratic philosophers. He mocked both the excessive dependence on rules and handbooks of the Sophists, and the excessive claims of the philosophers—each one of whom, he pointed out, claimed to have discovered Truth but was unable to convince a single one of his fellow philosophers. He also disapproved of those, like Alcidamas, who claimed to teach and practice mere rhetorical improvisational ability. In this respect he believed himself to be an heir to Socrates, requiring rhetoric to be closely connected to the study and practice of civic virtue. Isocrates believed that exposure to the literature and history that embodied the great ideals of the past would inspire in the young would-be orator a desire to become a good and noble citizen. This is a far cry from the Platonic idea of the Good but represented the ordinary, intelligent fourth-century citizen's vision of achievable excellence. It bears comparison with the practical observations on training wives, children, dogs, and horses made by Isocrates' contemporary, the country gentleman Xenophon.

The training of Isocrates' school was a pragmatic one. He believed in a combination of talent, practice, and instruction—with instruction taking a distant third to the other two. In one respect, Isocrates' approach was Gorgianic. As the student progressively improved his abilities as an orator, he would also learn more about seizing the right moment (*ho kairos*) and advancing the right opinion (*doxa*) for the situation. Both touching and revealing is Isocrates' vanity about his pupils' importance as political figures in their states after leaving his school. He addressed three speeches to the royal house of Cyprus and the royal prince, Nicocles, who perhaps studied with him; the *Areopagiticus* and the *Exchange of Property* both deal at length with another pupil, Timotheus, the ill-fated architect of the Second Athenian League. The ancients took Isocrates' boasts on this score seriously, however; Cicero calls him the Trojan Horse out of whom came all the leaders of Greece.

Isocrates' reputation as a political and educational theorist would probably be higher if we did not have his twenty-one extant speeches. Isocrates wrote speeches that were really political pamphlets setting out his thoughts on the great issues of his day. He had neither the passionate logical clarity of a Plato, abandoning contemporary politics in his writings for the world of ideas, nor the passionate political goals of a Demosthenes. Instead, he seemed to treat each new event as it came as an opportunity to air his rather limited and conventional fund of wisdom. We see him moving from an appreciation of Athens as the rightful leader of Greece, to a request for the sharing of power between Athens and Sparta, to a reactionary desire for Athens to return power to the early fifth-century aristocratic council of nobles, to an enthusiasm for a number of fourth-century strongmen, culminating with Philip II of Macedon. If one tries to trace a political philosophy that would unite these disparate stances, it is hard not to feel with G. A. Kennedy that Isocrates already foreshadows in his writings the evils that rhetorical culture would bring to the Hellenistic world. Not only are his proposals inconsistent and often impractical; despite its purity of vocabulary and the amplitude of its periods, the style is diffuse and verbose. Dionysius of Halicarnassus later calls him the "slave of smoothness."

Neither as a political theorist nor as a moral philosopher was Isocrates one of the outstanding minds of his time. But he is a witness to the political crisis that beset the Greek polis of the mid fourth century. New solutions to old problems were obviously needed; Isocrates, at least, saw the urgency of the situation, and it is poignant that his work testifies so obviously to the poverty of the traditional political solutions available.

As an educator, however, he was to have an enormous impact on the shape that his culture took after him. He articulated the connection between personal and civic morality, the love of Greek literature, history, and culture, and the art of declamation that would remain the basis of Hellenistic and Greco-Roman secondary education. Dionysius of Halicarnassus generously sums up his contribution (*Isocrates* A): "Most significant of all are the themes upon which he chose to concentrate, and the nobility of the subjects which he spent his time in studying. The influence of these would make anyone who applied himself to his works not only good orators, but men of sterling character, of positive service to their families, to their state and to Greece at large. The best possible lessons in virtue are to be found in the discourses of Isocrates."

Plato's Academy was founded on the outskirts of Athens in about 387 B.C. He was not the only pupil of Socrates to found a school, but the form that his school took was unusual in that it was more than a group gathered around himself. The Academy, in fact, was organized into a community that became a school in the modern sense of the word and lasted after Plato's own death for several hundred years.

In three dialogues, the *Gorgias,* the *Protagoras,* and the *Phaedrus,* Plato criticized the fifth-century sophistic movement and the role of rhetoric within it. His critique of education, rhetorical and otherwise, was even more wide-ranging. It is important to distinguish Plato's opinions as an educational theorist from the actual practice of the Academy. Some of the distinguishing features of his educational theory, developed principally in the *Republic* and the *Laws,* never did find acceptance in a Greek context. His observations on the education of women, the existence of carefully supervised and gradated exercises from earliest childhood, and the moral obligation to banish epic and tragic poetry from the state have been of more interest to modern educational theorists than they were to his contemporaries or successors.

Some of Plato's opinions, however, did at least foreshadow significant trends in Greek education. Unlike Isocrates, Plato recognized the importance of intellectual aptitude, particularly aptitude in mathematics, as a basis for determining the student's fitness for higher studies. He also argued for serious mathematical and scientific courses within the secondary school curriculum. The state-supported educational and research institutions in the Hellenistic kingdoms and Roman world were first anticipated in Plato's writings, although it was Aristotle's school that provided the practical blueprint for them. Plato also argued for an integrated curriculum in secondary education, taught by permanent specialists. Plato's own model education split secondary schooling into three sections of three years each, with the focus principally on literature from ages ten to thirteen, music from thirteen to sixteen, and mathematics from sixteen until the commencement of compulsory military service, or the *ephebeia,* at about age eighteen. In theory, a Platonic education took a lifetime. One studied science from twenty to thirty and dialectic from thirty to thirty-five, and then spent fifteen years as an experienced administrator for the state. At age fifty, the Platonic student was theoretically ready for the vision of the Good.

These aspects of Platonic educational theory bore little resemblance to what went on in Plato's own school. The Academy was from the beginning a more elaborate institution than Isocrates' school. It consisted of courses offered in the public gymnasium dedicated to the hero Academus, and also on a small private estate that Plato owned nearby. Whether or not it was initially structured on the model of the religious community, *thiasos,* it became in practice a secular

intellectual community composed of both advanced and younger students. Plato himself was the scholarch, who set the problems and perhaps directed the discussions. Adherence to his own distinctive philosophy was not required; we know that Plato's successor as scholarch, Speusippus, did not believe in the theory of ideas. The teaching atmosphere was apparently quite open, quite different in this respect from older sectarian religious and philosophical institutions. Like their predecessors, the Sophists, members of the Academy often taught in public, in the state gymnasium of Academus from which the school took its name. Lectures were apparently regularly open to the public. Plato did not take fees from the members, although only those with independent means normally had the leisure to follow the full course of study offered.

The course in the Academy was not, like that of Isocrates, concentrated upon the art of the *logos.* Rhetoric was taught as a concession to its popularity, but it was not an essential subject of study. The focus of the education offered was upon knowledge for its own sake rather than success as a gentleman and citizen. Rigorous demonstration was required, and the structure was probably that of the small discussion group, with the advanced and more gifted students directing the discussion. There was no fixed age at which one entered or left the Academy; Aristotle began at seventeen and was a member to his thirty-seventh year. There was no fixed curriculum or degree to be achieved.

Plato held aloof from Athenian politics, not, like Isocrates, who had a speech defect, from an inability to speak, but rather, as he says in the *Seventh Letter,* from a deep pessimism about the possibility of good government, given contemporary Athenian conditions. The Academy was, however, not apolitical. The list of influential fourth-century statesmen produced was as impressive as that of Isocrates. By following Plato's and his pupils' involvement with the politics of Syracuse under Dionysius I and Dion, we can conclude with H. I. Marrou that the Academy became at times "a fraternity of political technicians who were able to take concerted action at any time." What Isocrates espoused by personal predilection was for Plato a carefully thought out program: training a cadre of experts who would guide the governments of their various states. This model was to become important in the world of the Macedonians and was followed particularly by the Stoics as consultants to the rulers of the Hellenistic East.

With Isocrates we have the invention of literary culture as the basis for a secondary humanistic education; with Plato we have the beginning of a genuine higher education, with its end the pursuit of knowledge.

The contribution of one other fourth-century theorist is fundamental if we are to understand the final shape taken by Hellenistic higher education and rhetoric. The Lyceum of Aristotle, although it did not have the long vitality of the three other Athenian Hellenistic schools, the Academy, Epicurus' Garden, and Zeno's Stoa, was the first genuine research institution, founded to gather, organize, and preserve human knowledge in all fields. Aristotle himself, as part of this larger effort, both gathered the remains of earlier technical studies of rhetoric and himself produced the most comprehensive survey of Greek rhetoric as an art.

Like the other schools, the Lyceum took its name from its site, in one of the three large public gymnasia in Athens. It was founded in 335, after Philip II's conquest of Greece at Chaeronea (338 B.C.) and Alexander's brutal destruction of Thebes. The scholars who gathered there under Aristotle's guidance were known as Peripatetics, probably after the *peripatos,* the shaded walk that was part of the gymnasium in the Ly-

ceum. Aristotle abandoned the use of dialectic and discussion as the way to knowledge. His theoretical model was more that of biology than mathematics, and he saw the need for empirical research. The Lyceum was founded to make possible the systematic collection of research material of all kinds. It required a cooperative rather than competitive spirit among its members in order to collect and classify information and publish the results in an organized form. Plato had called Aristotle "the reader," and Aristotle's school was apparently the first to recognize the value of organizing a library as part of a research institution's structure. J. P. Lynch points out that this is part of what made the Peripatetics so vulnerable to outside disruption in the third century; more than the other schools, they depended on unbroken continuity and security of physical setting, on the preservation of documents, specimens, and books. An achievement like that of the fourth-century Lyceum also counted on substantial subsidies on a scale not available to earlier educational institutions. Aristotle was himself wealthy; he was also supported by the resources and patronage of his former pupil, Alexander the Great.

The Lyceum was both more and less overtly political than either the school of Isocrates or Plato's Academy. On the one hand, the patronage of the Macedonians gave the Lyceum its start and helped to explain the later vicissitudes of its fortunes. But neither Aristotle nor most of his pupils were Athenian citizens, and the Lyceum produced no Athenian public figures or orators of note except for the late-fourth-century general and politician Demetrius of Phaleron. Demetrius, ruling Athens from 317 to 307, gave Aristotle's successor, Theophrastus, rights of property possession in Athens and thus assured the school's physical continuity. After Demetrius was exiled he went to Alexandria and there was probably instrumental in founding the city's famous Museum. It was at the Museum in the Hellenistic period that the crucial job of collecting, evaluating, and preserving the Hellenic past was accomplished.

Aristotle is said to have taught rhetoric while still at the Academy; neither the collection of rhetorical handbooks that he compiled, the *Synagoge technon,* nor the early dialogue that he composed on rhetoric, the *Gryllus,* has survived. We owe our knowledge of Aristotle's place in the history of rhetoric to his treatise, the *Rhetoric,* compiled from the lectures that he delivered in the Lyceum over a number of years. The *Rhetoric* is not directed to those who want to learn the art of speaking but is intended as a survey of the field as a whole. Written in three books, it is worth a brief summary here because the contents reveal what the technical study of rhetoric meant to the greatest classifier and organizer of fourth-century thought.

The first book defines rhetoric as a study of the available means of persuasion. These are three: the speaker persuades by displaying his own personal character (*ethos*), by stirring his audience's emotions (*pathos*), and by convincing his audience through persuasive argument. The two kinds of argument available to him are inductive, the use of the *paradeigma* or example, and deductive, the use of the rhetorical syllogism or *enthymeme.* Aristotle argues that rhetoric is in fact an aspect of dialectic, except that its premises (and therefore conclusions) are not universals but rather probabilities and signs. He then distinguishes the three kinds of rhetoric. Political or deliberative rhetoric concerns itself with exhortation and concerns the future; its arguments focus on expedience. Judicial or forensic rhetoric concerns itself with accusation and defense and concerns the past; its arguments focus on justice. Finally, epideictic, or ceremonial, or-

atory concerns praise and blame in the present; its arguments focus on honor and dishonor. Aristotle then sets out the subjects proper to each kind of rhetoric.

In the second book, Aristotle first discusses *ethos* and *pathos,* and defines the types of human character, the emotions, and the speaker's capacity to direct his speech appropriately. In this section particularly he is carrying out the program suggested by Plato in the *Phaedrus,* acknowledging that effective oratory requires a well-developed sense of psychology. Then he turns to forms of argument that he calls common to all oratory and again discusses the example, the *enthymeme,* and arguments of refutation.

The third book deals with style. It is the section of the *Rhetoric* that is both the most dependent on earlier rhetorical theory and the most influential in the later history of rhetoric. It fits in with a process already begun by Isocrates that Kennedy has remarked on: the tendency of the technical study of rhetoric to become more and more literary and less oratorical in its concerns. Aristotle stresses the stylistic virtue of clarity, although he also requires a speech to be appropriate to the emotion of the hearers, the character of the speaker, and the nature of the subject matter. He deals with impressiveness and correctness of language, with prose rhythm, and with the rhythmical verse unit called the period. He considers the elegance that antitheses, metaphors, riddles, puns, proverbs, and hyperboles bring to style. Only in chapter thirteen does he turn to the staple of earlier rhetorical theory, the parts of a speech. For Aristotle, the heart of a speech is statement and proof, although it also needs an introduction and an epilogue.

Friedrich Solmsen defines five areas in which Aristotle's *Rhetoric* is a significant achievement in the history of technical rhetoric. First, it represents a decisive break with the earlier sophistic and Isocratean organization of rhetoric around the parts of a speech. Aristotle focuses instead on its essential functions; a speech persuades by proving its points, stirring the emotions of its audience, and conveying a sense of the speaker's character. In discussing how to achieve these ends Aristotle looks first at the proofs themselves (that is, the material content of the speech), then at its style and its organization. Second, Aristotle makes rhetoric genuinely philosophical by concentrating in the first book on kinds of proof as the core of rhetoric. Before Aristotle, "commonplaces" had been ready-made arguments that a speaker could simply memorize and insert into his speech. Aristotle replaces these with abstract forms of argument capable of being adopted to any context. Third, in elevating *pathos* and *ethos* to the status of *pisteis,* kinds of proof on a par with argument, Aristotle points to the increasing sophistication of the psychological bases of effective oratory much practiced by fourth-century orators and revived by Cicero in Roman oratory. Fourth, Aristotle is apparently the first to define the three kinds of speech, each with its distinctive focus: deliberative, focusing on the good, judicial on the just, and epideictic on the beautiful. The Roman rhetorician and teacher Quintilian comments that it was due to Aristotle that this tripartite scheme became standard. Finally, Aristotle is the first to identify "virtues of style." Under his successor, Theophrastus, these developed into the canonical four virtues: correct language, clarity, appropriateness, and ornateness.

The *Rhetoric* of Aristotle seems not to have dominated Hellenistic rhetorical developments; later, through Cicero and Quintilian, some of its distinctive emphases reenter the mainstream of Greco-Roman rhetorical theory. If we compare Aristotle's *Rhetoric* to the other extant fourth-century treatise, the *Rhetoric to Alexander,* we see that Aristotle's work is not simply a compendium of contemporary fourth-century rhetorical theory but, rather, a consciously argued philosophical investigation of the nature of rhetoric: what kind of an art it is and how it functions.

In one respect, however, Aristotle's *Rhetoric* seems to have been a typical fourth-century product. Like the *Rhetoric to Alexander,* it is a dry, spare, technical handbook. It is difficult for the modern student not to be overwhelmed, even in the *Rhetoric,* by the impression of lists: the three kinds of oratory; the four parts of an oration; the three parts of rhetoric (which in the Hellenistic period would become five: invention, arrangement, style, gesture, and memory); the virtues of style (which would lead to the theory of three styles: grand, middle, and plain); and most of all, the apparently endless strings of itemized detail, arranged systematically under more general headings. In their emphasis on the right moment (*ho kairos,* the right moment, and *to prepon,* the fitting), Gorgias and Isocrates had at least recognized the element of creative spontaneity in great rhetorical prose. But as the study of rhetoric and its lists and rules became in the Hellenistic period the backbone of education, and as the opportunities for serious political and judicial argument diminished, technical rhetoric no longer simply instructed one in the art of delivering a convincing and stirring speech; as Kennedy comments, it showed instead "the beginning of the process of ossification which overtook all ancient creativity."

ORATORS AND ORATIONS

The fourth century is not just the age of the full development of technical rhetoric; it also produced great speeches. The oratory and the handbooks of the fourth century complement each other. No one ever learned to deliver a great speech from a handbook, but it is useful to be reminded of the precise and meticulous attention to detail that underlay the lively and self-confident artistry of fourth-century speechmaking. Ten orators became known sometime in the Hellenistic period as canonical; their works were preserved to serve as models for imitation for later would-be writers of good Attic prose. The list consisted of Antiphon, Andocides, Lysias, Isaeus, Isocrates, Demosthenes, Aeschines, Hyperides, Lycurgus, and Dinarchus. Of the ten, all but Antiphon spoke in the fourth century. The speeches of other orators were preserved only when their speeches were later attributed to one of the ten or through paraphrase or quotation in later savants like Dionysius of Halicarnassus, Philostratus, or Aulus Gellius. The extant corpus of fourth-century speeches is the heart of Greek rhetoric; what follows is a severely circumscribed version, arranged according to Aristotle's categories, of its highlights. The orators themselves and Kennedy's *Art of Persuasion in Greece* should be consulted by any student seriously interested in the genre. Its fascination is at once historical and literary: we hear a fourth-century voice trying to persuade, stir, and charm us as he recreates for us the argumentative context that preoccupies him. The best of these speeches—Lysias' courtroom speeches or Demosthenes' great political orations—strike us as both deeply familiar and at the same time deeply foreign to our modern mentality. Perhaps more than any other extant genre, they let us directly experience what it meant to be an educated fourth-century Athenian.

Judicial Speech

Werner Jaeger calls this branch of oratory "a native Attic vegetable." Great courtroom speeches come from the specifically Athenian convention that one had to speak on one's own behalf in the lawcourt. Hence arose the institution of the logographer or paid speechwriter. We do not know the specifics of his task, whether for instance he was expected to be an expert in the law or to specialize in certain kinds of cases. Judicial speeches written for others and published by Antiphon, Lysias, Isocrates, Demosthenes, Hyperides, and Dinarchus are extant.

In Antiphon's *Tetralogies* we go back before the extant handbooks to see three hypothetical murder cases sketched out, each stripped to its argumentative essentials. These show the fifth century's enthusiasm for argument from probabilities and the relative indifference to the ethical and emotional aspects of speechwriting. The *Tetralogies* lack a full narration, both because they are pattern pieces rather than actual cases and because most fifth-century oratory skimped this aspect of the speechmaker's art. In Antiphon's actual courtroom speeches we find the same tendencies, although they are offset by a vigor of expression and a freedom of arrangement in the parts of the speech that fourth-century orators often lack.

The speeches of Andocides (*ca.* 440–*ca.* 390 B.C.) are interesting because he was not a professional logographer but wrote and published several speeches defending his own behavior in the troubled years during and after the Peloponnesian War. Kennedy comments that his speeches show the difficulties that might beset an educated and noble, but not rhetorically sophisticated, late-fifth-century man in the courtroom. Andocides does not fully exploit the possibilities of using *ethos* and *pathos;* the tone at times is insolent, relying on the older style of displaying a "noble" character rather than the newer egalitarian and safely "democratic" one. He also fails to organize his speeches clearly and he uses old-fashioned proofs from direct evidence rather than the more sophisticated arguments from probability developed by contemporary teachers of rhetoric.

Lysias is the earliest and possibly the greatest of the fourth-century professional speechwriters. He was born in the 440s to a wealthy metic family that later suffered in the hardships of the Peloponnesian War. As a result he was forced to become a speechwriter to support himself. His Greek prose style became in the Greco-Roman world the very model of Attic purity. It is simple and relatively unornamented, although the rhythm and structure of his more complex sentences show a fourth-century suppleness. He is most innovative in his masterly exploitation of the character of the speaker as an important aspect of persuasion; in his speech *On the Cripple,* the language and the thought present the speaker not just as conventionally respectable and virtuous but as a full, definite, and idiosyncratic personality.

Epideictic Speech

Epideictic, or display, speech is the form of oratory closest in style and function to poetry; in late antiquity virtually all poetry came to be regarded as a subdivision of epideictic. It grew out of the archaic ceremonial poetry of praise and blame, and of the three ancient types of oratory it was always the least dependent on a democratic political context. Epideictic was from the beginning more literary than the other two kinds of oratory, judicial and deliberative; the orator's purpose was frequently to amaze his hearers by the eloquence of his style rather than to persuade them by argument. Epideictic speeches were already in the fifth century given at festivals and games and on various civic and private occasions. The fifth-century Sophists advertised their own skill at speechmaking by delivering display speeches in the gymnasia and agora of Athens and other large cities and to the assembled Greek world at the great games; they often extolled Panhellenism or delivered speeches in honor of mythological subjects. We still possess Gorgias' speeches in praise of Helen and Palamedes, and Antisthenes' on Ajax and Odysseus. Such speeches show us the mixture of serious argument, playfulness, and literary conceit that often characterized the genre—and which make it a taste acquired with difficulty by most modern students. The funeral oration is a subdivision of epideictic. We still possess in part or in whole funeral orations written by Pericles, Gorgias, Lysias, Demosthenes, Hyperides, and Plato in the *Menexenus.* Kennedy comments that we are moved especially by the funeral orations of Pericles and Hyperides because they are anchored in the real occasion, mourning the Athenian fallen, and least inclined to the elaboration of mythological commonplaces.

Later in its Hellenistic and Greco-Roman manifestations, epideictic would include speeches intended only as exhibitions of cleverness. But the greatest of all the epideictic speakers was Isocrates. His example should remind us that the line between epideictic and the other two genres of oratory is not always easy to draw, since judicial and deliberative speakers very often included long sections of praise and blame in their speeches, while many of Isocrates' speeches, like those of other epideictic speakers, were very often deliberative in intent.

Deliberative Speech

In the *Phaedrus,* Plato says that fifth-century politicians did not publish their speeches for fear of being considered Sophists. As Kennedy points out, the fifth century might well have produced even greater political oratory than the fourth century. We have in Thucydides ample evidence of the rigor and seriousness with which the Periclean democratic assembly disputed the issues confronting the city. The first extant deliberative speech that we know was actually delivered is that of Andocides, *On the Peace with Sparta,* arguing for his own return from exile. Like his earlier judicial speeches, this speech does not make use of either *ethos* or *pathos* as the fourth-century speakers were to exploit them.

With Demosthenes (384–322 B.C.) we come to the full artistry of deliberative prose. Demosthenes was apparently self-taught as an orator. His career, like that of Lysias and Isocrates, suggests how close the ties often were in the fourth century between early misfortune and the choice of a career as an intellectual. All three were young men of good family, forced by family misfortune to earn a living by their wits. Demosthenes began his career as a litigator, suing to recover the property that his dishonest guardian Aphobus had embezzled. Both his judicial and his deliberative speeches demonstrate Demosthenes' ability to use complex grammatical structures and prose rhythms to augment his arguments. His later deliberative speeches became in the Hellenistic and Greco-Roman periods the very model of the grand style. The language can become torrential, overwhelming the reader with all the power of the genre. Their impact is so great, however, because the power of the language is always harnessed to the political ends for which Demosthenes passionately argued. In his greatest speeches we follow the specifics of what Werner Jaeger calls "the death-struggle and transfiguration of the city-state"— the same fourth-century struggle to which Isocrates unsuccessfully tried to provide a theoretical and intellectual response.

Demosthenes' earlier speeches suggest that he was initially sympathetic to the conservative group around the fourth-century Athenian statesman Eubulus; like Isocrates he put emphasis on prudent fiscal policies and the protection of a healthy upper class as the only security for the Athenian state. From the beginning Demosthenes' speeches show an exceptional grasp of the complicated power relations that characterized mid-fourth-century Greek politics; Athens, Thebes, and Sparta had to preserve a balance of power in which no one state could dominate the others. Demosthenes' own politics, however, changed in the late 350s. The *Philippics* and *Olynthiacs* were delivered in order to rouse the Athenians from their torpor and indifference to the growing power of Philip II of Macedon and to avert the danger that Philip posed to the grain supply and Athenian territory in the northern regions of Greece. Demosthenes used deliberative rhetoric as a way to educate the Athenian people into understanding their own historical destiny and the obligations that their noble past had laid upon them. He discussed not just Philip's power but also the moral foundation from which all political power is earned and sustained. In his last and greatest speech, *On the Crown,* he assessed his life's work in the light of the defeat at Chaeronea and justified the moral necessity of his actions. Deeply influenced by the tragic vision of the fifth-century historian Thucydides, Demosthenes too argued for a vision of magnificent achievement even in defeat, to be handed to posterity. To Demosthenes, even though Philip had won it was important that at the last the ancient city-states had mustered the will to fight him. The Athenians who heard Demosthenes' defense agreed with him. His opponent, Aeschines, did not in this instance receive the requisite one-fifth of the votes and had to retire to Rhodes to avoid paying a substantial fine.

The career of Demosthenes shows the ambiguities that mark the whole of the fourth century as a transition point between the classical and Hellenistic cultures. Many scholars have argued that Demosthenes' campaign against Philip was from the beginning a quixotic one. In the changed conditions created by Philip's army, Demosthenes' vanity would not permit him to see that Athens was no longer the center of the world and that he himself was no longer essential to the well-being of Athens. To that extent he is a poignant figure, fruitlessly using the power of his oratory to celebrate a romantic and anachronistic set of political ideals. On the other hand, in political and personal failure Demosthenes himself became in many respects a model for the cultural world to come. His career exemplified the power that *tuche,* chance, would have in Hellenistic thought; for his cultural descendants he would embody the helplessness of the individual attempting to combat mighty and impersonal social forces—but also the integrity and the valor of the attempt to remain steadfast to one's heritage, even when it was not a sensible or easy thing to do.

Aeschines (*ca.* 390–*ca.* 320 B.C.) is worth brief consideration, too, for he provides a fuller view of the perils that beset fourth-century political speech. Where Demosthenes even in his enormous personal vanity was still a statesman, Kennedy comments that Aeschines exhibited "diversionary tactics, legalism, and a preference for vivid description over close logical argument." Like Isocrates, he foreshadows a Hellenistic tendency to find simple rhetorical solutions to complex political problems. It is possible that, as Demosthenes was later to argue, Aeschines' speech at Delphi in 339 B.C. had given Philip the opening he needed to bring his army into central Greece—and that Aeschines himself never did perceive the responsibility he bore for the consequences at Chaeronea the following year. But a more important point about deliberative oratory underlies the charges and countercharges of

this sort that Demosthenes, Aeschines, and other fourth-century orators hurled at one another. Ultimately Philip found the old Greek poleis so easy to conquer because they still clung, in their larger politics as in their speechmaking, to an intensely argumentative and individually competitive ideal. The citizen was expected to further the good of the polis—but his own worth was, just as Achilles' had been, dependent on his superiority in competition with his fellow citizens. The notion of public speech as part of the Greek male citizen's competitive arsenal did not disappear with the defeat of Athens by Philip in 338; but it had played a large part in the narrowly self-interested demagoguery that crippled fourth-century politics, and with the rise of the Macedonian kingdoms its more virulent forms gradually became anachronistic. Aeschines' attitude to political oratory, as opposed to politics, seems to have contained genuinely disinterested elements. Exiled in Rhodes, he gave as a display oration his earlier forensic speech *Against Ctesiphon,* to which Demosthenes' *On the Crown* had been the reply. When the Rhodians expressed astonishment that he did not win, Aeschines is said to have retorted, "You would not wonder if you had heard Demosthenes' reply."

A large part of the richness and fascination of extant fourth-century Athenian deliberative oratory comes from the fact that it gives us the drama of the end of the Greek city-state, enacted from the intensely engaged and self-interested vantage point of the orators themselves. After 338 B.C. Athenian democracy became obsolete as a political system. But as it was celebrated by the orator Demosthenes and by the educator Isocrates it became instead a state of mind—a cultural and humanistic ideal. Through the role it was to play in Hellenistic secondary education, this ideal would continue to nourish and shape the Greek and Roman worlds that followed.

The orations of the fourth century also provided a stylistic model for later Greek literary prose and gave the Hellenistic age significant aspects of its literary taste. They articulated an interest in personality and a private moral sensibility that would become quite important in the third century. Aristotle saw that *ethos* and *pathos* were essential to effective persuasion. Lysias, Isocrates, Demosthenes, and even lesser orators like Hyperides and Lycurgus present themselves and their clients as individual personalities with their idiosyncratic strengths and weaknesses in a way that reminds us of Theophrastus' *Characters* and Menander's domestic comedies.

Finally, the fourth-century Attic speakers gave to their successors a changed definition of what it meant to be Greek. They made the whole Greek cultural and political past, embodied in its literature and history, into something to which one could offer personal allegiance. Isocrates is often quoted for his dictum in the *Panegyricus* that "those are called Greeks who share our education and culture *(paideia)* rather than those who share a common race." The fourth-century orators began the practice that would last to the end of antiquity of looking to models from the historical past to find precedents for judgment and action in the present. Tradition was no longer a changing and living thing but, rather, was embodied in a clearly defined set of written documents from the past—documents that had to be studied before one could claim the right to participate in the tradition.

THE HELLENISTIC AND GRECO-ROMAN EDUCATIONAL SYSTEM

The conquest of Greece by Philip II and of the Persian Empire by his son Alexander meant both a decline of freedom and power within the old Greek cities and the opening of new horizons of wealth and opportunity in the newly Greek East. In Egypt and on the banks of the Tigris and Euphrates, Greek cities sprang up. In old Greece and in the new garrison towns, the local municipality continued to be the theater in which the individual citizen found meaning and importance in his life. But the trends we have seen in the fourth-century orators were accelerated; the culture was no longer experienced as something current, defined by one's family and polis. It increasingly became, as Isocrates and Demosthenes had defined it, a creation of the past, accessible to Greeks of the third century through books. This became even truer in the mid second century as the Greek kingdoms of the East became in turn subject to Roman hegemony and part of a larger Mediterranean empire. H. I. Marrou calls the Greeks in the Hellenistic and Greco-Roman period a "people of the book," "a scribal culture," and, most aptly, "a civilization of the *paideia.*" We will consider the implications of this process, starting with the details of the formal educational system, now firmly in place, and then turning to the technical rhetoric and the oratory that were in large part the results of this educational system.

We do not possess documents of Hellenistic educational theory, although it is significant that philosophers like Aristippus, Theophrastus, Cleanthes, and Zeno wrote treatises on *paideia.* The theory and practice of education was now a separate subject in itself and no longer, as it had been for Plato and Aristotle, one aspect of ethics and politics. The fairly consistent form of such scraps of Hellenistic school documents as we possess and the conservatism of the extant handbooks from the Greco-Roman period enable us to describe with some confidence the practical details of late Greek primary and secondary education.

Primary education occupied the years

from about seven to about fourteen. There seem to have been no formal grades as we know them; the freeborn Greek boy generally proceeded on to secondary education as soon as he had learned to read, write, and do simple arithmetic. Music and gymnastics continued to play a part in both primary and secondary education, but the most important component was now literary. The *grammatistes,* or primary school teacher, remained a private individual, paid by the parents of his pupils and generally considered of low social status. There were no regular intervals like our school week; municipal festivals and religious holidays punctuated the year in accordance with the monthly municipal calendar.

The apparatus of primary schooling was simple. The teacher's scroll contained all the graduated exercises, from the simplest to the most complex, and as the student advanced to each exercise he would copy it onto his own wax tablet. Reading and writing were the most important aspects of the elementary curriculum. The teacher would first teach the letters, then syllables, then monosyllabic and polysyllabic words, and finally short continuous passages. These were taught through a process of dictation, reading, and memorization; after the student had copied what the master directed he would try to reproduce it accurately. The third-century teacher had no more interest than his predecessors in child psychology or the reinforcement of learning through pleasure. The third mime of Herodas suggests the brutality of the process: the child simply endured until, by dint of repetition reinforced by the threat of punishment, he mastered one level and went on to the next.

Learning to read was more difficult for the Greek child than it is today. Punctuation was not used, and the letters of one word flowed continuously into those of the next, both in cursives and in capitals. Moreover, no grammar was taught (it seems not to have been

adopted as a school subject until the handbook of Dionysius Thrax came into use in the first century B.C.); for the third- or second-century schoolchild the words and passages of his textbook—often difficult or archaic to begin with—must have seemed nearly those of a foreign language. This was true even when his mother tongue was the most widely spoken Greek, *koine.* When, as in the newly Hellenized East, the child's mother did not speak Greek, the Greek learned at school was in fact a foreign tongue. The effects must have been similar to those created by the learned Latin of the Middle Ages and the Renaissance—good Greek became a language learned from male teachers, for the purpose of later public achievement. As such, it automatically distanced and perhaps even alienated the student from the states of mind and experiences expressed in his mother tongue. This estrangement contributed to the later tendencies toward formalism and classicism found both in Greek as a literary language and in the Greek education that trained the youth to use this language.

Secondary school lasted from about the fourteenth year until the *ephebeia,* discussed below. In secondary school the grammarian introduced the student to the classics of Greek literature. Alexandrian scholars and teachers of the Hellenistic period selected a canon of classical authors that became standard for the rest of antiquity. Homer and Euripides were the most important, but it also included Hesiod and Apollonius of Rhodes in epic; the lyric poets, including Callimachus; Aeschylus and Sophocles among tragedians; Menander and increasingly Aristophanes among comedians; and Herodotus, Xenophon, Hellanicus, and Thucydides in prose. The student generally met the fourth-century orators later, under the guidance of the rhetor, when he had himself begun the study of rhetoric in the *progymnasmata,* discussed below.

The procedure of learning to read the classics reinforced the experience of primary school in that the systematic and rather rigid curriculum gave little encouragement to individual taste, imagination, or enthusiasm. First, the content of the work to be studied was summarized; the student's text was then checked for correctness (essential in an era before the printed text); the text was read with attention to word division and, in poetry, scansion; and, finally, its literal and literary meaning were explained. In this last stage the grammarian would proceed much as in traditional translation courses today. Words and forms were studied and then names and places, with reference to relevant mythological and historical background. The literary criticism that finished the process was generally an investigation of the ethical lessons that the work possessed. This was of practical value, since it allowed the student to store the literary and historical examples upon which he would later draw when he advanced into making his own declamations under the supervision of the rhetor.

At the end of the grammarian's course the student was introduced to the first stages in the art of literary—that is, rhetorical—composition. The entire course was called the *progymnasmata*, and it continued under the tutelage of the rhetor to form the first part of higher education as well. We have the texts of *progymnasmata* from the first and second centuries A.D., written by Aelius Theon and Hermogenes of Tarsus, but the essentials were obviously in place much earlier. They continued, with minor modifications, to form the basis of Greek literary composition for the next thousand years.

In the *progymnasmata,* the student learned to reproduce good classical Greek and to handle the various aspects of rhetorical invention, arrangement, and style by proceeding through a series of exercises of gradually increasing difficulty. In the early stages, re-telling fables, telling fictitious stories or incidents from the past, and relating anecdotes about the doings and sayings of famous sages, he learned to handle narration: getting the details right, making it clear and interesting, pacing it so that the story was an intelligible whole with a point at the end. He also learned amplification, or where to expand, and he made sure that his language was free of barbarism and solecism. In the intermediate stages he learned to argue. He learned how to confirm or refute a variety of arguments, to handle the commonplace effectively, and to praise and blame famous literary and historical individuals from the Greek past. He was then taught to compare and contrast two or more individuals, and to deliver a convincing monologue by adopting a fictitious or historical persona. Like the commonplace, this would be useful in his later career as a speechmaker since it was an aspect of Aristotle's ethical proof, persuading the audience by constructing a likable and trustworthy persona for the speaker. The final stages of the course taught the student how to use all these skills in constructing his own speeches. He first learned to argue a thesis, or general moral point—whether, for instance, it was good to kill a tyrant, or to marry. Then he learned to argue the justice or injustice of some piece of legislation; this was often archaic or even imaginary, with bizarre provisions whose implications could be elaborated to tedious lengths. At the end he would be ready to write and deliver his own practice declamations.

If the student managed to stay the course, he also learned in the process of completing the *progymnasmata* to repress any tendencies he might have had to idiosyncratic expression or observation. What he learned—the sign, in his culture, of an educated man—was a formal and highly stylized means of self-expression and argumentation. What his peers would look for as the mark of his attainment was his ability to handle extremely traditional forms of speech and thought in a manner that formally adhered to the rules but, within these boundaries, found something interesting to say. These are indeed the traits of an "Alexandrian" art; our own age, in the grip of a very different set of artistic canons, finds them almost impossible to appreciate.

All of the seven liberal arts of Martianus Capella (fifth century A.D.) had been known and practiced in the Hellenistic world, but they did not form a systematic course of secondary and higher education until they were adopted in the medieval West. Of the trivium—grammar, rhetoric, and dialectic—the third was left to those who went on to study in the philosophical schools; for the quadrivium—geometry, arithmetic, astronomy, and music theory—we know of individual scholars who made substantial contributions, but there is little evidence that any of it was required for a normal Greek secondary or higher education. In mathematics, the student learned simple practical calculation and geometry. Indicative of the difficulty of teaching a genuine scientific education was the fate of astronomy. It was generally taught in the form given it by Aratus of Cilician Soli (third century A.D.), in a long and difficult poem focusing more on abstruse mythological conceits than on actual science. Those with a taste for real science learned it in apprenticeship to practicing scientists or in institutions of higher learning like the Academy in Athens or the Museum in Alexandria, where mathematicians and research scientists might work. The normal Greek secondary education remained predominantly literary and rhetorical—precisely because the art of rhetoric had been so well worked out that teaching it required almost no serious talent or sense of vocation on the part of the teacher. Inspired teachers of course existed, but it was the innate conservatism of the teaching profession that

kept the same system in place until virtually the end of antiquity.

The *ephebeia* deserves particular mention as the only official state-supported educational institution that existed throughout the Greek-speaking Hellenistic world. It began in Athens, probably in the fourth century, as a compulsory military service; but as this became irrelevant in the world of the Hellenistic monarchies, the *ephebeia* in Athens and elsewhere became a combination of literary, musical, and gymnastic courses offered to the city's aristocratic youth. Although in other cities the *ephebeia* often began at fourteen, in Athens it traditionally began at age eighteen. Often the facilities that supported the *ephebeia* were quite elaborate, with training grounds, lecture rooms, and even libraries attached.

A city official, the *gymnasiarches,* was appointed as overseer of the *ephebeia.* He was chosen from among the wealthiest and most important men of the city, and although he did not actually teach, he oversaw the courses, both athletic and literary, that the young men followed. He also supervised the appointment of teachers and the official competitions and city processions in which the youth of the city participated, and he was expected to contribute from his private resources for this purpose. This was a prominent example of *euergetism,* the system of private benefaction of public institutions that enabled Hellenistic and imperial cities to survive as cultural centers.

Of the content of higher education in the Hellenistic period we know relatively little, although here again we can once more extrapolate from the later period. The *meletai* or practice declamations that the student learned to deliver at the end of his school career did not only take place within the school; they also formed a prominent part of the public culture of the Greco-Roman world. Large cities had their own rhetors in residence, and we hear of competition between cities on this score, luring away one another's most famous teachers and speakers. Traveling orators also came through, giving short courses and public lectures. These were immensely popular, and in the second century A.D. they produced the cultural and political phenomenon known as the Second Sophistic, with star performers who attracted crowds in the thousands and represented their cities in diplomatic negotiations even with the emperor. Such men, like the earlier fifth-century Sophists, were often attended by groups of advanced pupils in training to be rhetors and Sophists themselves. Philostratus' *Lives of the Sophists* gives a vivid picture of the wealth, power, and prestige of the most eminent of these men.

Research institutions continued during this time to produce advances in knowledge, although the ancient world never fully developed either an understanding of scientific induction or a sense of the material benefits that greater technological understanding would bring. Many individual scientists practiced in their own fields, as engineers or doctors; some were employed by the Hellenistic monarchs as experts on warfare. As we have seen, it was a Peripatetic, Demetrius of Phaleron, who had counseled the Ptolemies in Alexandria on setting up the Museum in the late fourth century. This continued to be a state-supported center of research into the first century A.D.; the Library at Alexandria and libraries in other intellectual centers like Pergamum, Athens, Rhodes, Antioch, Berytus (modern Beirut), and Rome also attracted scholars to collect and edit texts and to publish the weight of their learning in commentaries.

Particularly in Athens, but also in some of the other great centers of learning, the philosophical schools continued to attract adult adherents. The fourth-century institutions of the Academy and the Lyceum were joined by the Garden of Epicurus, founded in 307/

306, and the Stoa, founded by Zeno about 300 B.C. These schools concerned themselves with ethical issues rather than with the kind of mathematical and scientific research that characterized the earlier Academy and Lyceum. Much of their energy seems to have been directed to controversy among themselves; this was perhaps an inevitable result of the personalism that, as Aristotle saw, was encouraged by the importance of individual association within the schools. Like the rhetors, some philosophers traveled from city to city; and like the rhetors they were generally attracted to the larger and wealthier urban centers, where they would hope to receive monarchical patronage or at least some support from the wealthiest of the local citizens.

HELLENISTIC AND GRECO-ROMAN RHETORIC

About the oratory and the technical rhetorical treatises produced in the Hellenistic period we have little information. One extant treatise in Greek, *Demetrius on Style,* was written sometime between the fourth century B.C. and the first century A.D.—we have so little of a context in which to set it that scholars still argue seriously for both extremes of dating. The fate of Hellenistic oratory was very similar. Philostratus, writing in the early third century A.D., gives almost no information about the centuries that fall between Aeschines in the fourth century B.C. and Nicetes of Smyrna in the first century A.D. From Cicero and other Latin authors we hear of a Hellenistic oratory called "Asianic"; the name most closely associated with it is that of Hegesias of Magnesia (modern Manisa, in western Asia Minor) of the mid third century B.C. This oratory seems to have flourished in the large cities of Asia Minor after the decline of oratory in Athens. There are no examples of it; we know of it because of a strong reaction against it in the first century B.C., when contemporaries of Cicero, labeling themselves Atticists, castigated Asianism for its unbridled and bombastic style.

During this time the trends in speechmaking noted at the end of the fourth century continued. With the loss of civic independence, there was no use for a powerful judicial or deliberative oratory in the Greek world. The speeches that continued to be given in courts and city council chambers were not intended to sway large numbers of citizens but to reach a single man or a small group of local notables; such speeches were not considered important enough to be published and preserved. The oratory that flourished was ceremonial; the audience's role was that of spectator rather than judge. Festival speeches, speeches at marriages, funeral orations, and the like continued to be given, as well as sophistic showpieces that were simply vehicles for displaying the speaker's cleverness as he orated on topics like baldness, a parrot, or malaria. Also increasingly popular were the *meletai* or practice declamations similar to those that a student learned to deliver at the end of his school career. These could be theses, arguing general propositions (Should one kill a tyrant?), or hypotheses, arguing the pros and cons of specific situations (Should Harmodius and Aristogeiton have killed Hipparchus?). The hypothesis in Greco-Roman times developed into the *suasoria,* or mock deliberative case, and *controversia,* or mock judicial case, the topics of which continued to be drawn from the famous moments of the classical Greek and also Roman past.

This tradition remained enormously popular to the end of the ancient world. It reveals the same mixture of artificiality, conventionality of form, and classicism of content that marks the system of education that produced it. Rhetors and their pupils argued supposed judicial speeches concerning lurid cases of abduction, rape, murder, and family betrayal; they delivered new versions of what Demosthenes said after hearing of the Greek defeat in the Lamian War, what the Spartans might have said to each other at Thermopylae, or what could have been said to Alexander as he was about to enter Babylon. As oratory became increasingly ceremonial and literary, divorced from present-day concerns and the contemporary language of the street, it lost its original functions as primary rhetoric. The content of the speech was no longer essential; even if a speech was actually delivered, it was now heard and admired for its style. Public oratory continued to serve serious political ends, but these were no longer closely associated with the speech's contents.

The technical developments in rhetoric that occurred in the Hellenistic period reinforced this trend. The general shape of the discipline had been fixed by the end of the fourth century; Hellenistic theorists filled in the gaps that Aristotle left, producing monographs on various individual topics. The details multiplied and the categories became more elaborate and rigid. Practicing rhetors generally continued to teach according to the old Isocratean method, requiring their students to imitate their example. Most of the treatises we know of were written in the philosophical schools.

The Peripatetics were the most interested in rhetoric. Theophrastus' treatise *On Style* was used by Cicero, and his theory of the four virtues of style—purity, clarity, propriety, and ornamentation—was influential in later Greco-Roman rhetoric. Theophrastus considered *schemata,* or figures, as important as diction. Although he listed only eight figures, it was the beginning of the long lists of figures of thought and speech that occupy much space in later handbooks. Theophrastus also wrote on delivery, following Plato's and Aristotle's recognition of the importance of psychology in persuasion; he analyzed the use of the voice and gesture to raise the emotions of the hearers and make them responsive to the speaker. Here too his work set the tone for the developments that were to follow: greater elaboration of detail within clear and teachable categories. Theophrastus' work is not extant. The one possibly Hellenistic treatise we do possess, also titled *On Style,* is ascribed to "Demetrius," but is almost certainly not written by Demetrius of Phaleron; it might be the work of a third-century Peripatetic. It illustrates several of the same trends: the growing importance of rhetoric as a literary rather than an oratorical discipline, and a tendency to lists of figures and precision of categories. Most of the treatise is structured around a discussion of four styles: the impressive, the elegant, the plain, and the forceful.

The Stoics also wrote rhetorical handbooks. Their chief interest lay in the technicalities of argument and in language theory. They studied grammar and diction and were particularly interested in word definition. They first distinguished the trope, or single word used in a novel way, from the figure, or group of words used for effect. Their larger influence on later Greco-Roman rhetorical theory was limited, according to Cicero, by their insistence on a straightforward and plain style of speech in which the facts of the case and the virtue of the speaker would argue for themselves. Their chief influence lay in the area of style; their studies contributed to the growing taste for purity and correctness that produced the Atticism of the first century B.C. The Epicureans and Academics were generally hostile to rhetorical studies, although a treatise on rhetoric by Philodemus, an Epicurean of the first century B.C., has been preserved in fragmentary condition among the papyri from Herculaneum. It is of interest as a non-Ciceronian source for the late Hellenistic philosophical objections to rhetoric. Like other Epicureans, Philodemus seems to have thought that no rhetoric except possibly epideictic could really lay claim to being a *techne:* both an art and a learned skill.

The Hellenistic handbook most important for later Greco-Roman theory seems to have been written outside the philosophical schools. Hermagoras of Temnos (*ca.* 150 B.C.) organized his discussion of rhetorical invention around *stasis* theory. He defined the *stasis,* or point at issue in a judicial case, as necessarily one of four kinds. One could argue the fact (he did not do it); one could admit the action but redefine it (it was not murder); one could argue that the act was morally justified even if technically a crime; or, finally, one could argue that the case was not being tried under the correct laws or in the correct court. A great deal of Hermagoras' theory can be reconstructed from the use made of it by Roman theorists, including the anonymous author of *Rhetoric to Herennius* (first century B.C.), Cicero, and Quintilian. Perhaps the Romans' initial enthusiasm for *stasis* theory came from its usefulness for actual judicial pleading. But *stasis* theory owed its enduring popularity to the fact that it helped the declaimer decide the specifics of what he wanted to argue in his imaginary productions.

In the early second century B.C. the Greeks came in increasingly intimate contact with the Roman Empire. As Horace put it, the Greeks took their captors captive; among educated Romans there was great enthusiasm for the Greek language and literature and for the rhetorical and literary education in which Greek culture had been preserved. In 155 B.C. the philosophical schools in Athens sent a delegation to Rome to protest the claims of rhetoric to provide higher education. The charge, formulated in terms reminiscent of Plato's *Gorgias,* was that rhetoric was not a *techne.* The philosophers protested first against the utility of handbooks, with their long lists of figures and increasingly detailed categories of analysis. They argued that good speeches had existed before such handbooks had been invented; one simply did not learn to speak well from them. They also protested the inclusion of theses, or general topics, among the practice declamations taught in rhetorical schools. Questions like whether it is wrong to kill a tyrant were, they claimed, actually philosophical issues that had been made by rhetoricians into empty vehicles for showing off one's style. The philosophers were not against all rhetoric; declamation had long been taught in both the Lyceum and the Academy, and the possibility of teaching epideictic oratory through lists and rules was generally conceded. But their concerns were real ones; and underlying the theoretical arguments, as in Plato's own day, was an economic and social issue: Who would provide the higher education for the newly hellenized and philo-Hellene Romans?

The quarrel between rhetoric and philosophy subsided; in the late republic and the early empire both were generously sponsored by the Romans. Vespasian in the first century A.D. set up state-supported chairs of both rhetoric and philosophy at Rome and Athens. Rhetoric continued to dominate secondary education; its lists and rules appealed to a Roman preference for the clear-cut, practical, and prescriptive. Moreover, since Greek was a foreign language learned at school, the questions of artificiality and loss of spontaneity mattered less than the fact that the new Greek education was clearly and systematically organized. The voices of some in the Greco-Roman period protested this state of things—for example, the shadowy Augustan teacher Theodorus of Gadara (Palestine), the philosopher Dio Chrysostom of Prusa (modern Bursa, Turkey), and the second-century satirist Lucian. But none of these critics really mounted a serious attack. Lucian's satire on rhetorical education does indeed mock the sterility

and vacuity of many aspects of the public oratory of the empire. What Lucian argues for, however, is not an abandonment of rhetorical education or oratory, but a return to the full, serious training of the good old days, when shallow flourishes and fifteen or twenty Attic words, a fancy cloak, and effeminate manners were not a substitute for real rhetorical skills.

Lack of space prevents us from discussing the technical treatises, rhetorical essays, and oratory produced in Latin by the generations spanned by the author of the *Rhetoric to Herennius,* Cicero, Quintilian, and Tacitus. As they themselves made clear, they wrote as students of an art that they had learned in Greek, in order to make it accessible to a wider Latin audience. Cicero and his successors struggled to shape the various strands of the Greek rhetorical tradition they had received into an intelligible whole. Cicero claimed that his own rhetoric was a blend of the Aristotelian and the Isocratean; both Cicero and Tacitus took trouble to explore at length the tension between the demands of substance and form in good oratory. In the West, it was through Latin transmission that Greek rhetoric came to influence the Middle Ages, although in the Renaissance the Greek authors again began to be read for themselves. In the Greek-speaking East, the tradition as we have sketched it remained the backbone of Byzantine schooling and literary life.

We have already noted the increasing concern of technical rhetoric with style. In the first century B.C. this concern, coupled with the classicism already inherent in Greek education, led to a movement called Atticism. It required a purification of the ornate literary language of the day and a return to the written Greek of the fifth and fourth centuries B.C. Many Romans and Greeks alike considered the ideal Greek style to be that of Lysias, clear, controlled, and simple, although Cicero protested that Demosthenes'

Greek was as Attic as that of Lysias. Atticism retained an enormous impact on the choice of vocabulary and sentence structure in spoken and written educated Greek through the second century A.D., and, in a modified form, it set the standards of taste for the Byzantine period as well.

Its most influential exponent was Dionysius of Halicarnassus, a Greek rhetor of the Augustan period who lived in Rome but wrote in Greek for educated Romans. A number of his treatises have been preserved, and they suggest the odd mixture of conventional rhetorical terminology and acute literary judgment that the study of rhetoric could create in the Greco-Roman period. As G. M. A. Grube comments, in Dionysius' hands the rhetorical study of style became a genuine literary criticism. Dionysius used his critical-rhetorical formulas to evaluate the style of an author rather than using authors only as examples of the formulas. He wrote short treatises on the style of Isaeus, Lysias, Isocrates, Demosthenes, Dinarchus, and Thucydides, and literary essays on composition and imitation. These latter works give the best clue to Dionysius' intentions. He undertook to analyze the prose style of some of the "best" authors so that would-be imitators would know what in their styles could be used and what should be discarded as idiosyncratic and not adequately classical. Imitation had meant the imitation of life for the age of Plato and Aristotle; to the atticizing Greeks of the Roman Empire it meant the self-conscious imitation of the vocabulary and sentence structure of a recognized canon of long-dead authors.

Longinus is an unknown author, probably of the first century A.D. Even more strongly than Dionysius, Longinus shows the creative use to which conventional rhetorical terminology could be put. In a relatively short treatise, *On the Sublime,* he made use of the same tradition as Dionysius to try to evaluate what kinds of qualities made up great-

ness of style. Although his work seems not to have created imitators in the ancient world, it was preserved and proved enormously influential in the seventeenth and eighteenth centuries for its recognition of some of the mysterious aspects of artistic genius. More representative of the tradition as a whole, and more important for the medieval future of Greek rhetoric, was the work of Hermogenes of Tarsus, perhaps to be identified with the second-century Sophist of that name described by Philostratus in *Lives of the Sophists.* Hermogenes wrote an influential revision of Hermagoras' *stasis* theory that continued to form the basis for discussions of invention in the Byzantine period; he also wrote a treatise on "ideas" or qualities of style, following in the path of Theophrastus and Dionysius. In Hermogenes we see sharply developed most of the trends that had begun in the Hellenistic period. His presentation is systematic, authoritative, prescriptive, and well illustrated by examples; his taste is classical, presenting Demosthenes as the model that combined all of the best qualities of style. Hermogenes was credited with a handbook of *progymnasmata,* and his works on style and *stasis* theory became the object of numerous Byzantine commentaries. It was through handbooks like his that the rhetorical culture we have described became the foundation for the preaching and teaching traditions of Greek and Latin medieval Christianity.

***

If one compares the rhetorical literature of the empire to that of the fifth and fourth centuries B.C., it is hard not to feel dismayed. In surveys of Greek literature, words such as "sterility" and "torpidity" occur with some frequency. At the beginning, the ability to speak well was part of the Greek citizen's competitive arsenal, a vital aspect of his role as a "speaker of words and doer of deeds." In the classical period, spontaneity and responsiveness were recognized aspects of the art of rhetoric. But in the late antique period rhetoric seems to have become instead a set of rigidly prescriptive rules by which one learned to speak and write in the idioms and with the assumptions of a vanished age. Rhetoric may seem at the last to have become a prison, forcing the style and substance of the past on a culture whose reality was now quite different. When we encounter a rare voice that seems to resist the well-worn commonplaces and obsessive stylistic concerns of Atticism—Longinus, perhaps, or Lucian—we feel that such voices should have been more influential among their contemporaries.

To understand the phenomenon, we must put aside our own tendencies to anachronism and look instead to the changed function of rhetoric within Greco-Roman culture in its own terms. As P. Bourdieu comments, "No one acquires a language without thereby acquiring a relation to language, . . . a certain manner of using the acquirement." The ceremonial rhetoric and the educational process that created and perpetuated the rhetorical style remained vigorous in the late antique period precisely because they formed such an essential part of its social structure. In the municipal oligarchies responsible for the continued economic and cultural vigor of the cities of the Greek-speaking East, the ability to declaim in a good Attic Greek and to write as though one were declaiming became a mark of class membership; for the gifted and ambitious seeking entry into the elite it was a mode of recruitment. For the larger urban society, rhetoric had important public and ceremonial functions. In a world where the individual citizen had less and less contact with the real centers of power, the rhetorical tradition remained a way to maintain a living connection with the classical past. The language and literature taught in the schools kept alive the values of the polis; a fierce conservatism of form and content were the cost of maintaining these values through long centuries in which they were not obviously necessary for political and economic survival. We owe to the generation of Demosthenes and Isocrates the invention of the concept of classical humanism; we owe to the rhetorical culture of the Hellenistic and Greco-Roman world the fact that it is still a living tradition.

BIBLIOGRAPHY

SOURCES

Dionysius of Halicarnassus, *Critical Essays*, S. Usher, trans., 2 vols (1974), "Isocrates" in vol. 1.

For convenient editions and translations of other ancient authors, see the bibliographies in D. L. Clark (1957), A. G. Beck (1964), S. F. Bonner (1977), and D. A. Russell (1981). Also helpful are H. L. Hudson-Williams (1968) and individual notes in G. A. Kennedy (1980).

STUDIES

G. A. Kennedy (1963 and 1980) and H. I. Marrou (1956) are the most basic and authoritative works on the topics covered in this article. Frederick A. G. Beck, *Greek Education 450–350 B.C.* (1964); Stanley F. Bonner, *Education in Ancient Rome* (1977); Glen Bowersock, *Greek Sophists in the Roman Empire* (1969); Pierre Bourdieu, "The Literate Tradition and Social Conservation," in Pierre Bourdieu and J.-C. Passeron, *Reproduction in Education, Society, and Culture*, R. Nice, trans. (1977); Donald L. Clark, *Rhetoric in Greco-Roman Education* (1957); Martin L. Clarke, *Higher Education in the Ancient World* (1971); Georges M. A. Grube, *The Greek and Roman Critics* (1965); H. L. Hudson-Williams, "Greek Orators and Rhetoric," in *Fifty Years (and Twelve) of Classical Scholarship*, 2d ed. (1968); Werner Jaeger, *Paideia: The Ideals of Greek Culture*, Gilbert Highet, trans., 3 vols. (1939–1944); George Alexander Kennedy, *The Art of Persuasion in Greece* (1963), *The Art of Rhetoric in the Roman World* (1972), *Classical Rhetoric and Its Christian and Secular Tradition from Ancient to Modern Times* (1980), and *Greek Rhetoric Under Christian Emperors* (1983).

George B. Kerferd, *The Sophistic Movement* (1981); Geoffrey E. R. Lloyd, *Magic, Reason and Experience* (1979); John P. Lynch, *Aristotle's School: A Study of a Greek Educational Institution* (1972); Henri-Irénée Marrou, *A History of Education in An-tiquity*, George Lamb, trans. (1956); Donald Andrew Russell, *Criticism in Antiquity* (1981), and *Greek Declamation* (1983); Robert Wayne Smith, *The Art of Rhetoric in Alexandria* (1974); Friedrich Solmsen, "The Aristotelian Tradition in Ancient Rhetoric," in *American Journal of Philology,* **62** (1941).

Roman Education and Rhetoric

CECIL W. WOOTEN

EDUCATION

Rome began its long history as a village of peasants on the banks of the Tiber, and the conservative outlook that one often associates with agrarian societies was to influence Romans for many generations to come. The virtues that were celebrated by the Romans were those of the peasant: fierce loyalty to the land, cooperation, simplicity, self-reliance and discipline, endurance of hard work and routine. Many Romans believed these values had been most responsible for Roman success, and it was only natural, therefore, that early Roman education should be directed primarily at preserving them.

In early Rome parents were their children's teachers, and the aim of early education was to initiate children into the Roman way of life, to pass on traditional customs and attitudes, to engender respect for these values, and to begin to make of children model Roman citizens. Early Roman education thus aimed at transmitting culture, not facts. Children were generally educated by their mothers until they were six or seven. In addition to trying to inculcate respect for traditional Roman attitudes, mainly through telling stories from Roman legend and history illustrating Roman virtues, mothers taught Latin and a certain amount of Greek.

At six or seven a boy's education passed into the care of his father, who became his tutor; and the basis of this next stage in his education was imitation. The child followed the father everywhere and was supposed to learn from his example. He assisted him on the land, since most early Romans were farmers, attended debates in the Forum or in the senate, and participated in religious ceremonies. In addition to instilling in the boy admiration for such typical Roman values as respect for authority and hierarchy, a sense of sacrifice and self-control, and a desire to serve the community in which he lived, the father also tried to inculcate respect for special family traditions. The Brutus family, for example, descendants of the Lucius Brutus who drove out the kings and set up the Roman Republic (*ca.* 510 B.C.), cherished traditions of tyrannicide that surely influenced Marcus Brutus when he became involved in the conspiracy to kill

Julius Caesar in 44 B.C. Portraits in stone of the family's ancestors, which were kept in the household, would have aided the father in this task; and Roman funerals, at which family members dressed as prominent ancestors, would surely have had a dramatic effect upon young boys. Polybius in his *Histories* (6.53–54) indicates their importance.

The primary goals of early Roman education were to provide children with a sense of tradition, to encourage them to think of themselves not as individuals but as continuators of the family and by extension the state, whose customs they must heed and ambitions they must promote. In essence, early Roman education encouraged the group ethic. In his biography "Cato the Elder" (*Parallel Lives,* 20.3–5, Bernadotte Perrin, trans. [1914–1926]), Plutarch describes very well the attitude of Cato, a traditionalist Roman of the second century B.C., toward the education of his son; and this attitude probably typifies that which had existed from early times:

> As soon as the boy showed signs of understanding, his father took him under his own charge and taught him to read, although he had an accomplished slave, Chilo by name, who . . . taught many boys. Still, Cato thought it not right . . . that he should be indebted to his slave for such a priceless thing as education. . . . He taught his son not merely to hurl the javelin and fight in armour and ride the horse, but also to box, to endure heat and cold, and to swim lustily through the eddies and billows of the Tiber. His history of Rome . . . he wrote out with his own hand and in large characters, that his son might have in his own home an aid to acquaintance with his country's ancient traditions.

Early Romans distrusted professional teachers. They felt that professionals would not be as concerned for the welfare of the child or for the very important business of training future Roman citizens, the inheri-

tors of the state, as their parents would be; and, consequently, professional teachers (usually non-Romans) were periodically expelled from the state by the censors on the grounds that they were a harmful influence on Roman society.

When boys passed into the care of their fathers, girls continued to be trained by their mothers in household tasks such as weaving and sewing. A Roman girl was usually married at age twelve or thirteen, at which time her education at home came to an end. A boy continued his education until the age of sixteen. Then, to mark the next stage of his education, there was a ceremony during which the boy discarded the toga bordered with purple, which children wore, and put on a pure white toga, which marked his new adult stage. The following year he was apprenticed to an older man, usually a friend of the family and prominent in the state, who prepared him for a career in public service, the preserve of the upper classes. This preparation was principally geared to training in public speaking, since many wellborn sons were destined for careers as courtroom advocates and politicians. Of this experience, Tacitus writes (*A Dialogue on Orators* 34, William Peterson, trans. [1914]):

> The youth had to get the habit of following his patron about, of escorting him in public, of supporting him at all his appearances as a speaker, whether in the law courts or on the platform, hearing also his word-combats at first-hand, standing by him in his duelings, and learning, as it were, to fight in the fighting-line. It was a method that secured at once for the young students a considerable amount of experience, great self-possession, and a goodly store of sound judgment: for they carried on their studies in the light of open day, and amid the shock of battle.

Political apprenticeship was generally followed by a year in the army training under an older man in preparation for the day when young men themselves might command troops.

In these last two stages of a boy's education, one sees again the importance of example in early Roman education and the almost constant emphasis in Roman thought on the value of old age and on the experience and wisdom that the young can learn from their elders. These comments apply, it must be noted, to the upper classes. Roman literature, the major source of information about Roman society, was produced by the upper classes and deals, for the most part, with their concerns. Very little is known about the much more numerous lower classes, and this is especially true for the early period of Roman history, when sources are generally sketchy. Upper classes tend to set trends that are followed by lower classes, and we can only assume that whatever education existed for the latter was modeled to a great extent on what was practiced among the upper classes.

By the middle of the second century B.C., the type of education based on the family and its traditions was no longer practicable. At the end of the First Punic War (241 B.C.), Rome acquired its first overseas province, the island of Sicily; by 146 B.C., the year in which Carthage in the West and Corinth in the East were both sacked by Roman armies, Rome had become the leading power in the Mediterranean. The circumstances of empire meant that fathers tended to be gone from home, employed in overseas armies or administration, and mothers became increasingly involved in political intrigue in the absence of their husbands, who until then had looked after family interests. In pursuing the pleasures of life that were made possible by the influx of wealth into Italy at this time, mothers were also less inclined to bother with their children's education.

Moreover, during the wars of expansion from 264 to 133 B.C. many slaves flowed into Italy as prisoners of war. Some, especially from the Greek-speaking East, were better educated and more cultured than their Roman masters. They assumed many of a Roman woman's duties, from the breast-feeding to early education of her child. Moreover, when Rome first began to have sustained contact with Greek culture, Romans began to be increasingly influenced by Greek ideas, including those relating to educational theory and practice. Romans may have sought to emulate Greek educational practice so that they as conquerors would not be less civilized and cultured than the conquered. Schools, with curricula based on Greek models, began to be organized, and young Romans, for the first time in Roman history, began to be educated by professional teachers, many of whom were Greek.

After the second century B.C., the following educational pattern emerged: a nurse, who was usually Greek, taught a child simple reading and acted as the child's tutor, guardian, and servant until he was sent to school. An unfortunate consequence of this procedure, in the eyes of many Romans, was that their children often assumed attitudes more typically Greek than Roman. Thus, Romans tended to become more individualistic and more skeptical of traditional values and attitudes than they had been before. The usual sense of moral rectitude and self-sacrifice began to be replaced by selfishness, exclusiveness, and egoism; and this change in Roman attitudes, some have argued, led eventually to civil wars and civil disturbances in the first century B.C. when Roman vied with Roman to advance private ambitions.

When a Roman child at the age of six or seven was sent to elementary school, he studied reading, writing, and arithmetic. School lasted for five or six years. Lessons generally started at dawn, were interrupted for lunch, and continued, at least during the winter months, in the afternoon. Students had every eighth day off, a short break in the winter and spring, and a long break in the summer, from the beginning of July until the middle of October.

Pupils sat on backless stools and supported writing materials with their knees. Writing consisted mostly of copying passages, often with the teacher guiding the child's hand so that he would form the characters correctly. In reading lessons the teacher taught the children to pronounce letters, then syllables, and then words. There was also much recitation. The child memorized the passages that he had been copying, which were often of moral value, and then recited them to the class. The teacher would then correct pronunciation and intonation. Arithmetic was usually basic, often consisting only of addition and subtraction.

The qualities most highly prized in a Roman classroom were powers of memory and imitation. There was some competition among pupils, but the primary incentive to excel came from the "stick and the carrot." Students who performed well were often given rewards, such as cookies or small cakes; and students who performed badly were usually beaten with a cane. Intellectual excitement and curiosity were little encouraged in a Roman classroom, which was typified by learning by rote and severe punishment for poor performance. Even after Greek influence had begun to affect the Roman character, this was the approved educational approach among conservative and authoritarian Romans.

Pupils from affluent families were often accompanied to school by a slave (*paedogogus*) who carried their books and helped with lessons; others were taught at home by slaves or private tutors. After the second century B.C., schools, which were generally private, became more common. They were usually set up by parents who pooled resources, but sometimes a wealthy benefactor would set up a school in his hometown for the education of local children. It was not until the time of Vespasian (second half of the first century A.D.) that the government began actively to support education, especially in the provinces, where schools were used as a means of spreading the Latin language and Roman culture. The emperors sometimes subsidized schools or established chairs and often supported education more indirectly by offering tax incentives to teachers who would settle in backward areas of the empire, especially in the western part. Many private citizens also followed the emperor's lead in supporting education.

In secondary school, the Greek-inspired curriculum emphasized literature. Since there was no Latin literature that could be considered "classical" (and therefore worth learning) until the middle of the first century B.C., Greek literature was chiefly studied. Consequently, until the time of Cicero most educated (upper-class) Romans were bilingual. After Cicero's time, enough good Latin literature had been produced that Latin authors, including Vergil, Horace, Livy, Sallust, and Terence, as well as Cicero, began to replace Greek authors in school curricula. Bilingualism declined as a result. The training in literature was not in fact what we would call "literary." Rather it aimed at teaching systematically the structure of language. To the practical-minded Roman the content of literature was considered secondary to the way in which ideas were expressed; and the real purpose of the study of literature was to teach students how to use language effectively, which, in the context of the Roman upper classes, meant politically, since the upper class's political activity was supposed to benefit the state.

Literary education was taught by reading aloud, reciting passages that had been memorized, and analyzing the grammar and syntax of particular passages. Teachers were so dependent on Greek grammatical theory that when discussing Latin texts they spoke about grammatical topics, such as the definite article, that did not even exist in Latin. In a typical class, the teacher read a passage out loud and then explained its general difficulties. Then a student read the passage, after which the teacher proceeded to analyze the text closely, line by line, stressing grammatical explanation, as today many classicists still do. Grammatical explanation was accompanied by allusions to mythology, history, geography, and science as they were reflected in the passage, mainly to relieve the tedium of continuous grammatical discussion; however, there was little or no attempt made to teach aesthetic or literary appreciation. What was valued in a teacher was his knowledge of the systematic structure of language and his control of the minutiae of a literary text. As Juvenal says (*Satires* 7.230–236, Peter Green, trans. [1967]), in discussing what is required of a teacher,

His grammar must be above cavil,
History, literature, he must have all the
  authorities
Pat at his fingertips. They'll [the parents]
  waylay him en route
For the public baths, and expect him to
  answer their questions
Straight off the cuff—who was Anchises' nurse,
  what
Was the name of Anchemolus' stepmother,
  and where
Did she come from? How old was Acestes
  when he died?
How many jars of Sicilian wine did the
  Trojans
Get from him as a present?

Such a close analysis of literary texts often degenerated into pedantry, but the Romans were fascinated by these scraps of useless knowledge and would probably have considered literary appreciation of the text even more useless, since they tended to think in concrete rather than abstract terms.

Some aspects of the secondary education curriculum borrowed from the Greeks, such as music, dancing, and athletics, were de-leted by the Romans. Music and dancing were deemed unmanly by most Romans, and they never really warmed to athletics as simply competition, as its main purpose was military. Rome's greatest accomplishment was to take the parts of Greek civilization that it assimilated, including its educational system, and establish it firmly throughout the empire, especially in the backward western provinces. By setting up schools throughout the empire, Rome completed the historic mission begun by Alexander the Great to spread Greek culture throughout the Mediterranean world. By giving the Western world peace and prosperity for more than 200 years, Rome created conditions in which Greco-Roman culture could take such firm root that it would become, with the Judeo-Christian tradition, one of the two major components of western European civilization. In all the provinces of the western empire, Romans, at first individually and then under the aegis of the state, set up schools where Latin and Greek were taught. The promotion of education by the Julio-Claudian, Flavian, and Antonine emperors continued a deliberate policy of romanization that was first actively pursued by Julius Caesar. In addition to setting up schools, the Romans also took as hostages the children of leading families in newly conquered territories and brought them up in Roman schools in Italy. This meant that when they returned home to assume leading positions in the community they were often more Roman than provincial and thus set the tone that others lower in the social scale could emulate.

RHETORIC

Roman higher education began at about age sixteen and was modeled, with certain exceptions, on Greek educational practice. The Greek system emphasized philosophy, history, and rhetoric. The Romans were suspicious of philosophy as being too intangible and too far removed from reality to have any practical social benefit, and as for history, they felt that young men growing up in a society as tradition-conscious as Rome would acquire a knowledge of Roman history without special training. Roman higher education, therefore, was restricted to the study of rhetoric, which greatly appealed to the Romans because of its practical benefits. It provided the individual with skills that were useful in a society where oral expression and the spoken word were the primary means of publicizing one's opinion and registering a social impact. (This was especially true for members of the upper classes, for all practical purposes the only Romans who reached this stage of education.) Moreover, since Roman society was firmly rooted in patron-client relationships, in which the patron was expected to defend his clients in court, it was important that members of families with a large clientele be well acquainted with rhetorical theory.

For many years Romans studied rhetoric in Greek. Although the first school of rhetoric conducted in Latin was set up by Lucius Plotius Gallus in 93 B.C., it was closed the following year, probably because the government was unwilling to make oratorical skill, a potentially powerful political instrument, too easily accessible to demagogues who might have threatened the prerogatives of the aristocracy. In the following decade, however, the *Rhetoric to Herennius* was written, perhaps by a certain Cornificius, and Cicero completed *On Invention.* These two handbooks made rhetorical theory available in Latin, and by the end of the century rhetorical education in Greek had been replaced to a great extent by instruction in Latin. This coincided with the development of Roman literature in Latin, and in 26 B.C. Quintus Caecilius Epirota became the first secondary teacher to lecture primarily on Roman authors.

Rhetorical theory, following the Greek postulators, was taught in order to refine the art of speaking. Teachers in the rhetorical schools broke the subject into a number of divisions. Invention dealt with the subject matter of speechmaking, with discovering what could be said and how arguments could be presented. Roman students learned the use of syllogism and induction and were taught how to appeal to an audience's reason (the logical proof), and to its passions (the pathetic proof), and how to inspire a favorable opinion (the ethical proof). The latter was especially attractive since Romans had so much respect for authority and hierarchy. A Roman orator would often attempt to convince his audience that his point of view should be accepted simply because of the trust that his own character inspired. This is why Cicero, for one, spends so much time in his speeches talking about himself.

Students also studied the essential arrangement of a model speech: the prooemium, which served to secure the interest or goodwill of an audience; the narrative, which set out the basic facts of the case; the confirmation, the purpose of which was to argue the speaker's own point of view; the refutation, which should refute the arguments of his opponent; and finally the epilogue, which was meant to summarize the case, inspire a favorable opinion, or, as often happened in Roman oratory, provoke an emotional reaction in the audience. Under the rubric of style students learned the virtues of style—correctness, clarity, propriety, and ornamentation—and were exposed to the concept of the three styles, the plain, the middle, and the grand. Finally, students of memory learned mnemonic devices to help them remember long speeches, and students of delivery were taught the techniques of delivering a speech.

Taking theories developed by the Greeks, the Romans contributed systemization and organization to the study of rhetoric and passed them on to western Europe in Latin. Quintilian's *Education of an Orator* (*Institutio Oratoria*) discusses the training of the orator from childhood to his higher education and is a detailed and clear compendium of most of the rhetorical theories that had been developed by the first century A.D. Cicero's *On Invention* dates from the preceding century.

One exception to the Romans' lack of original contribution may be noted. In the *Orator,* written in 46 B.C., Cicero identifies the three types of style, the plain, the middle, and the grand, with the three functions of the orator, to teach, to please, and to move, which he had discussed nine years earlier in his work *On the Orator*. The functions of the orator are analogous to Aristotle's proofs: logical (to teach), ethical (to please), and pathetic (to move). It was Cicero who first neatly argued that the plain style, which is conversational in tone, should be used to teach; the middle style, which depends on balance, parallelism, and figures of speech that are often associated with poetry, should be used to please; and the grand style, which uses figures of thought such as exclamations, anacoluthons (abrupt changes of grammatical construction), and rhetorical questions should be used to arouse the emotions. The most attractive aspect of this argument is that it defines the three styles, which are conceived of in different ways by different authors and are thus a source of some confusion, primarily in terms of function rather than in terms of form; and that is very helpful in trying to determine exactly what the three styles are.

The Roman system of rhetoric was designed to produce skilled orators. It was quite practical during the republic when there were democratic assemblies and free courts, where cases were tried before large juries that were susceptible to powers of persuasion. Under the principate, however, republican-style rhetoric and oratory became obsolete. The senate lost its real power, and it was reduced to rubber-stamping decisions made by the emperor. There was, consequently, no place for deliberative, or political, oratory, especially after Tiberius transferred elections of magistrates from the popular assembly to the senate, where the emperor's influence could be used to greater advantage. Moreover, many of the legal cases were now tried before the emperor himself, especially from Claudius' time onward, or before a single magistrate, an imperial prefect, where elaborate judicial oratory would be ineffective and inappropriate. Thus the imperial system took away much of the free life that had fostered republican, Ciceronian oratory. Romans, however, continued to study rhetoric in advanced schools, and despite the decline of its practical life, it flourished in a new, independent, self-centered activity.

Declamations had been used as rhetorical exercises to train students in lawcourt or political oratory and to keep already trained orators in practice. They were speeches on imaginary topics, often based on history or intricate legal points, and their appearance in Rome dates from the middle of the second century B.C. During the imperial period declamations became a form of popular entertainment, and in the hands of great declaimers, who were what we might call "concert orators," declamations became social occasions, sometimes attended even by the emperor. Schools of rhetoric often put on declamation recitals to display the abilities and talents of students and teachers. Since declamations no longer had any practical value, the themes became unreal, romantic, melodramatic, and farfetched.

There were two types of declamations. The *controversia* was a declamation in the form of a judicial speech, based on specific laws, often imaginary, and usually dealt with a complicated situation. Examples, taken from Clarke's *Rhetoric at Rome* (pp. 90–91), are translations of passages from Seneca the Elder's *Controversiae:*

> The law ordains that if a man catches an adulterer in the act and kills both parties he is free from blame. Another law permits a son to punish adultery on the part of his mother. A brave man lost his hands in battle; he caught his wife, who had borne him a son, in the act of adultery. He ordered the young man to kill them; he refused and the paramour escaped. The father disinherited the son.
>
> The law ordains that in the case of rape the woman may demand either the death of her seducer or marriage without dowry. A certain man raped two women in one night; one demanded his death, the other marriage.
>
> The law requires that a priestess must be chaste and undefiled, and born of chaste and undefiled parents. A certain virgin was captured by pirates and sold. Bought by a brothel-keeper, she was forced to prostitution. When men came to her she persuaded them to leave her untouched while giving the usual fee. A soldier came to her whom she was unable to persuade. He took her in his arms and tried to force her, and as he did so she killed him. She was accused and acquitted, then returned to her own, whereupon she tried to obtain a priesthood. Her claim was contested.
>
> A man was captured by pirates and wrote to his father asking to be ransomed. The father refused. The daughter of the pirate chief made the young man swear to marry her if he was set free. He did so. She left her father and followed the young man. He returned home and married her. An heiress appeared on the scene. The father ordered him to leave the pirate chief's daughter and marry the heiress. He refused, and was disinherited.

The examples show some favorite themes of these debates: rape, adultery, piracy, and loss of limb. Others were shipwreck, poisoning, and sexual abnormality. The makers of declamations excelled in the fantastic and melodramatic.

The *suasoria* was a type of declamation that dealt with a dilemma often confronting a historical or mythological character; it was basically deliberative oratory: Should Agamemnon slay Iphigenia to appease the winds? Should Caesar kill Pompey? Should Cicero burn his works to appease Antony? The speaker either addressed himself, pretending, for example, to be Agamemnon, Caesar, or Cicero, or took the role of an advisor to the character in question. An amusing example of a *suasoria* is found at the end of the *Satyricon* by Petronius Arbiter. In an attempt to drive off the legacy hunters who hope to inherit from him, Eumolpus, a disreputable old poet, stipulates that anyone who wants to inherit in accordance with the terms of his will must first eat a piece of his corpse. One of the legacy hunters addresses his colleagues in the *Satyricon* (141, William Arrowsmith, trans. [1959]):

> I am not in the least disturbed by any fear that your stomachs will turn. They will obey you quite without qualms so long as you promise them years of blessings in exchange for one brief hour of nausea. Just close your eyes and imagine that, instead of human flesh, you're munching a million [sesterces]. If that isn't enough, we'll concoct some gravy that will take the taste away. As you know, no meat is really very tasty anyway; it all has to be sauced and seasoned with great care before the reluctant stomach will keep it down. And if it's precedents you want, there are hundreds of them. The people of Saguntum [Sagunto], for instance, when Hannibal besieged them, took to eating human flesh, and did so, moreover, without the slightest hope of getting an inheritance out of it. And when a terrible famine struck Petelia [Strongoli], the people all became cannibals, and the only thing they gained from their diet was that they weren't hungry any more. And when Scipio captured Numantia, the Romans found a number of mothers cuddling the half-eaten bodies of their children in their laps.

This little speech illustrates the cleverness and ingenuity that are often found in rhetorical declamations.

Declamation was, above all, an exercise in

imagination. Its format was to propose a difficult case to the speaker and demand he make the most of it. Since the same topics were argued over and over, new possibilities of proof, exposition, presentation, and expression were constantly being demanded by an audience that had come to appreciate cleverness, subtlety, style, and artistic technique as virtues in themselves. The declaimer, who sought audience approval more than credibility, aimed to produce a speech that was more striking and ingenious than honest or believable. Declamations, therefore, were filled with "purple prose," picturesque descriptions of places and things, vivid portrayals of people in the grips of violent passions, and sparkling epigrams that stand out from the body of the speech as a whole. Augustus initiated a long period of peace and prosperity after almost a hundred years of civil turmoil. Nonetheless life became dull and humdrum. This is surely why the world of the declamation seemed so attractive. Interest in the farfetched, the melodramatic, and the unnatural must have been an attempt to escape from the boredom that many Romans must have felt during the Augustan Age.

Many criticisms could be leveled at declamations as they were practiced in the schools of rhetoric, and the Romans themselves were aware of them. A basic one was that declamatory exercises did not truly train students to become practicing orators. Encolpius, the rogue hero of the *Satyricon*, undercuts his own criticism by delivering what is in effect a declamation against declamations. He says at the beginning (1–2, Arrowsmith, trans.)

> No one would mind this claptrap if only it put our students on the road to real eloquence. But what with all these sham heroics and this stilted bombast you stuff their heads with, by the time students set foot in court, they talk as though they were living in another world. . . . We keep them utterly ignorant of real life.

All they know is pirates trooping up the beach in chains, tyrants scribbling edicts compelling sons to chop off their fathers' heads, or oracles condemning three virgins. . . . Action or language, it's all the same: great sticky honeyballs of phrases looking as though it had been plopped and rolled in poppyseed and sesame. . . . It was you rhetoricians who more than anyone else strangled true eloquence. By reducing everything to sound, you concocted this bloated puffpaste of pretty drivel whose only real purpose is the pleasure of punning and the thrill of ambiguity.

Seneca the Elder, in a somewhat more serious vein, reports the similar criticisms of Votienus Montanus, a famous orator in the Augustan Age, in the preface to Book Nine of the *Controversiae* (4–5, Michael Winterbottom, trans. [1974]):

> Students are so coddled and pampered in the exercises of the declamation school that they cannot tolerate noise, silence, laughter, even the open air. But no exercise is any use unless it very closely resembles the activity for which it is a preparation. . . . Men going out of a dark shady place are blinded by the dazzle of broad daylight; similarly as pupils pass from the schools to the forum, they are put off by the novelty and unfamiliarity of everything.

In spite of his criticism, Seneca nonetheless considered declamations important, for he collected many examples of them in his *Controversiae* and *Suasoriae* and thought that these would be useful in the education of his sons. Quintilian, on the other hand, argued that the study of speeches that had been actually delivered (especially from those trials where speeches delivered on both sides had been preserved), the writing of speeches concerning real court cases, and attendance at court would be better preparation than declamatory exercises (*Education of an Orator* 10.1.22–23).

Romans continued to practice declamations, evidently because they served a useful function. For, regardless of their fictitious themes and imaginary legal bases, declamations taught students how to analyze a situation in legal terms; and many of the cases are not as farfetched as critics claimed. As vehicles that encouraged students to think and express themselves clearly, they served a worthy educational purpose.

Declamations also exerted an important influence on Roman literature during the Silver Age (A.D. 14–138). Many of those traits that are most typical of Latin literature after Augustus, and which are now often labeled mannerist, can be traced back to the training that most Latin authors had received in declamations: the rhetorical cleverness, the striving for novelty and striking effect through exaggeration and an overabundance of detail, an obsession with style, elegance, wit, cleverness, and preciosity, often entailing a neglect of content, and a concentration on detail rather than the whole. Moreover, the interest in Silver Age Latin literature in the grotesque, the passionate, the distorted, and the violent is also reminiscent of what one finds in the declamations.

In fact, during the early empire the great declaimers were so famous and declamation so valued as a ticket to fame and success that basic principles of rhetoric began to be taught in the secondary school so that students could proceed directly to declamations when they entered the schools of rhetoric. Quintilian (*Education of an Orator* 2.1.3, H. E. Butler, trans. [1920–1922]) comments on this practice:

> Consequently subjects which once formed the first stages of rhetoric have come to form the final stages of a literary education, and boys who are ripe for more advanced study are kept back in the inferior school and practice rhetoric under the direction of teachers of literature. Thus we get the absurd result that a boy is not regarded as fit to go on to the schools of declamation till he knows how to declaim.

The rhetorical exercises that were taught by the secondary schoolteacher were primarily preliminary exercises known as *progymnasmata.* The most basic of these were the maxim, the fable, and the mythological narrative. Students were required to retell these in their own words and then to explain a story or proverb in a short essay. Then they would go on to write speeches in character, passages in which someone was praised or blamed, and short essays comparing two people or things. Later students were given topics to argue (such as whether one should marry or whether a wise man would enter politics). These were different from *suasoriae* in that they dealt with the question in general rather than as it related to a particular individual. Generally, in teaching these preliminary exercises the secondary schoolteacher would give the students a model, often written by himself, which the boys were supposed to memorize. Then they would try their own hand at a similar exercise.

Declamations are an obvious target of critical comment about Roman higher education; but the system in general is open to criticism, mainly because of the limited scope of the curriculum, which consisted only of rhetoric. Criticism of the whole system of higher education was voiced in antiquity, mainly by Cicero and his admirer Quintilian. Neither had much impact on the curriculum.

By the first century B.C. many treatises on rhetoric had been written dealing with all the various aspects of rhetorical theory, and rhetorical education tended to be restricted to a detailed study of the many technical aspects of rhetoric as they were expounded in these treatises. Cicero's *On Invention,* written when he was still a student and destined to become one of the major textbooks in the Roman schools of higher education, reflects very well the technical tradition that dominated Roman training in rhetoric. When he was older, Cicero realized that content was as important as form, that a truly great speaker must not only be educated in the technical aspects of the art of public speaking but also be generally well educated in the topics that he might be called upon to discuss. In *On the Orator,* written in 55 B.C., he tried to revive the Isocratean or Sophistic tradition of rhetorical education that was based on wide general learning in addition to the technical aspects of rhetorical theory. Cicero underlines the importance of general education, a major theme of the work, toward the beginning of this work (*On the Orator* 1.20, E. W. Sutton and H. Rackham, trans. [1942]):

> And indeed in my opinion, no man can be an orator complete in all points of merit, who has not attained a knowledge of all important subjects and arts. For it is from knowledge that oratory must derive its beauty and fullness, and unless there is such knowledge, well grasped and comprehended by the speaker, there must be something empty and almost childish in the utterance.

The topics that Cicero felt were most appropriate for the training of the orator were law, history, philosophy, and literature.

In *Brutus,* his history of Roman oratory and orators, written nine years after *On the Orator,* Cicero expounds (322, G. L. Hendrickson, trans. [1961]) upon the advantages to be derived from the sort of broad general education that he had advocated in the earlier work:

> I say nothing of myself; I shall speak rather of others. Of them there was not one who gave the impression of having read more deeply than the average man, and reading is the wellspring of perfect eloquence; no one whose studies had embraced philosophy, the mother of excellence in deeds and in words; no one who had mastered thoroughly the civil law, a subject absolutely essential to equip the orator

with the knowledge and practical judgement requisite for the conduct of private suits; no one who knew thoroughly Roman history, from which as occasion demanded he could summon as from the dead most unimpeachable witnesses; no one who with brief and pointed jest at his opponent's expense was able to relax the attention of the court and pass for a moment from the seriousness of the business in hand to provoke a smile or open laughter; no one who understood how to amplify his case, and from a question restricted to a particular person and time, transfer it to universals; no one who knew how to enliven it with brief digression; no one who could inspire in the judge a feeling of angry indignation, or move him to tears, or in short (and this is the one supreme characteristic of the orator) sway his feelings in whatever direction the situation demanded.

In spite of these eloquent appeals and the equally enthusiastic exhortations of Quintilian, Roman higher education in the next century continued to restrict itself almost exclusively to the study of the technical tradition in rhetoric. And those students, like Cicero himself, who wanted to complement their education were forced, after the completion of their higher education in Rome, to continue their studies in the east, usually in Athens or on Rhodes, where they could be exposed to the philosophical tradition that was so important a part of Greek education.

Individual weaknesses of higher education may be singled out for discussion, but in fact the whole educational system was vulnerable. An obvious fault was that the state never vigorously supported education and did not support it at all until relatively late. Education was never made compulsory. Moreover, the goal of the educational system remained limited, restricted almost exclusively to teaching literacy. Technology and the natural sciences were almost totally neglected, and little attempt was made to stimulate intellectual curiosity. This system remarkably suited the purposes of the Church Fathers—Christianity being the successor of Greco-Roman civilization—since a religion based on written revelation demands a certain level of literacy among its adherents. The church incorporated into its own educational practices much of the curriculum and many of the pedagogical techniques that had been practiced in Roman schools, thus completing, in the field of education, the romanization of western Europe.

BIBLIOGRAPHY

SOURCES

Cicero, *Brutus,* G. L. Hendrickson, trans., and *Orator,* Harry M. Hubbell, trans. (1939; rev. ed. 1961), *On Invention,* Harry M. Hubbell, trans. (1949), and *De Oratore (On the Orator),* E. W. Sutton and H. Rackham, trans., 2 vols. (1942); Juvenal, *The Sixteen Satires,* Peter Green, trans. (1967); Petronius Arbiter, *Satryicon,* William Arrowsmith, trans. (1959); Plutarch, *Parallel Lives,* Bernadotte Perrin, trans., 11 vols. (1914–1926); Quintilian, *The Education of an Orator (Institutio Oratoria),* H. E. Butler, trans., 4 vols. (1920–1922); Seneca the Elder, *Declamations* (includes *Controversiae* and *Suasoriae*), Michael Winterbottom, trans., 2 vols. (1974); Tacitus, *Dialogus (A Dialogue on Orators),* William Peterson, trans. (1914; rev. ed. by Michael Winterbottom, 1970).

STUDIES

Stanley Frederick Bonner, *Education in Ancient Rome* (1977); Martin Lowther Clarke, *Rhetoric at Rome* (1953; repr. 1966); Aubrey Gwynn, *Roman Education from Cicero to Quintilian* (1926; repr. 1964); George Kennedy, *The Art of Rhetoric in the Roman World, 300 B.C.–A.D. 300* (1972), and *Classical Rhetoric and Its Christian and Secular Tradition from Ancient to Modern Times* (1980); Anton Leeman, *Orationis Ratio* (1963); Henry Marrou, *A History of Education in Antiquity,* George Lamb, trans. (1956).

Folklore

WILLIAM F. HANSEN

THE IDEA OF FOLKLORE

Neither the Greeks nor the Romans had a concept or encompassing term for folklore as such, although they did recognize and have names for many of the traditional forms of expression that we now classify as genres of folklore. The term "folklore" only came into being in the mid nineteenth century. Its inventor, the Englishman William Thoms, intended it to replace "popular antiquities" and "popular literature," the phrases in use at the time.

In the years since Thoms wrote, it has been possible to distinguish several views as to what is, or should be, subsumed under the term "folklore." According to the narrow view, folklore is a synonym for oral literature, or as it is often called, verbal art, by which folklore scholars mean myths, legends, folktales, proverbs, riddles, and the like. In the middle view, folklore refers principally to verbal art and to folk beliefs. This is essentially the idea that Thoms advanced. In the broad view, folklore embraces, in addition to these forms, a number of other cultural phenomena, including traditional material culture. Limited space dictates that the present discussion confine itself to the narrower concept, that is, to traditional forms of Greek and Roman verbal art. Eight popular genres will be considered: fable, anecdote, joke, magic tale, novella, legend, proverb, and riddle.

Since we are not party to the live expression of folklore in Greco-Roman antiquity, we must reconstruct the experience from indirect sources of information. In many instances we possess ancient compilations of a particular genre of folklore, such as fables, from which it is possible to gain a good notion of the content and form of the genre. Compilations rarely prove helpful, however, in revealing much about what sort of person employed a particular form of folklore, under what conditions, and with whom. For contextual information we must draw upon other sources, the most important of which are the following: literary representations, as when Homer represents the bard Demodokos singing the risqué tale of the adultery of Ares and Aphrodite to an all-male audience, thereby lightening the mood of the guests following an angry exchange of words; literary uses, as when Cicero employs a particular proverb in a personal letter, much as (we may suppose) he might have employed it in a live conversation; written commentaries, as when Quintilian informs us that it is effective to use Aesopic fables in addressing country folk and uneducated persons, since they are especially receptive to this kind of story; and the fieldwork of modern folklorists, who are able to study live folklore in situ. With these aids, we can try to imagine contexts for texts that do not have them.

NARRATIVE FOLKLORE

Fable

After Odysseus returns from Troy to Ithaca, he comes disguised as an old beggar to the hut of the swineherd Eumaios, who takes him in and feeds him. In the evening the weather turns wet and windy, and Odysseus, hoping to induce his host to let him have the use of a cloak, announces that he is going to express a wish in the form of a story. He then tells how when he was a younger man at Troy he had participated in a surprise assault; the weather turned bitterly cold after the soldiers had encamped for the night, and he alone had neglected to bring a cloak with him. But he mentioned his plight to his commander, who cleverly devised a way for him to have the use of another man's cloak. Eumaios is delighted with the tale and provides his guest with warm clothing for the night (Homer, *Odyssey* 14.457–522).

This is a classic instance of what the Greeks called an *ainos,* or brief story that did not refer explicitly to the addressee but which the teller wished his hearer to interpret as though it did. The teller's principal intent was to convey a message indirectly,

not to recount a tale for its interest as a factual account of the past or for its own value as entertainment. The term *ainos* included the fable, for the fable was also a brief narrative of a past event, told to illustrate an idea that was meant to be understood metaphorically. That is, an *ainos* was not so much a story as a way to use a story. It was a traditional rhetorical device. The principal difference between the two kinds of *ainos* lay in their content. The man who employed the former kind of story had a traditional way of using nontraditional material; he invented a realistic tale of his own and reported it as something he had experienced, for which reason one could call it a "personal-experience fable." In contrast, the man who used the second, metaphorical, kind of story was usually employing traditional content in a traditional way, for he generally recounted a tale that was already part of his repertoire and frequently was familiar to his hearer as well. It was characteristic of these tales, as opposed to the personal-experience fables, that they were obviously fictitious: the actors were most often talking animals or plants. This kind of *ainos* the ancients associated with the name of Aesop.

Aesop was a historical person who lived in the early sixth century B.C. His fame lay in his skillful employment of fables in live contexts; he is not known to have written down any tales, nor is it likely that he did so. He did not invent the fable as a genre or even introduce it to the Greeks, for fables of the "Aesopic" kind were used by Greek poets before the time of Aesop. But eventually the Greeks, followed by the Romans, classified most fables of traditional or fantastic content as Aesopic; they often called them simply "Aesopic tales." Ancient Hebrew literature shows analogues to both the personal-experience fable (1 Kings 20:38–42) and to the Aesopic fable (Judges 9:7–

20), and fables of the Aesopic kind have been found in Mesopotamia on clay tablets dating to *ca.* 1800 B.C. A few of the Mesopotamian fables are identical to Aesopic tales in the Greco-Roman tradition. The Greeks seem to have adopted the idea of the fable from the East, and the Romans in turn got it from the Greeks.

The earliest example of a fable of the Aesopic kind in classical literature is told by the poet Hesiod in his *Works and Days* (202–212). While exploring the notions of justice and of insolence he recounts the *ainos* of the hawk who caught a nightingale. The victim cries piteously, but the hawk addresses her, explaining that it is of no use to scream, for he will do whatever he pleases with her; it is foolish for the weak to match strength with the strong. Hesiod then describes whom the tale applies to and how it applies, and continues his discussion of justice and insolence. His tale exemplifies the typical (but not invariable) form of the Aesopic fable. It consists of a single episode and focuses upon two actors, one of whom makes an epigrammatic statement in direct speech that concludes the tale and gives its point.

The literary use of the fable took a different turn in the late fourth century, when Demetrios of Phaleron made a written compilation of Aesopic fables. The work was meant as a source book for speakers and writers, the first such compilation, so far as we know, in the Greco-Roman world. The first writer to exploit the literary potential of a collection of fables was Phaedrus, who made a collection of Aesopic fables in Latin verse in the first century A.D. His reader was expected to read the versified tales consecutively and for their own interest, not to scan the collection merely to borrow a tale. The chain of literary fabulists thus begun continued through antiquity, into the Middle Ages and beyond, leading to many literary collections in verse and prose in a variety of languages, of which the best known in modern times is that of La Fontaine.

Anecdote

Although the oral anecdote no doubt flourished among the Greeks and Romans from time immemorial, like the fable it did not receive systematic attention from ancient writers before the fourth century B.C., when apothegms were mentioned by name for the first time and several compilations entitled *Khreia* (*Anecdotes*) were published. The earliest compilers were mostly philosophers, and the anecdotes concerned the doings and sayings of philosophers, whose teachings and personal character were thereby exemplified. Of course the living oral anecdote was not limited to philosophers, nor even to famous persons, and presently we hear of other compilations. Apothegms were also published as such. There are two extant collections attributed to Plutarch, *Apothegms of Kings and Commanders* and *Laconic Apothegms.* Published collections were drawn upon by writers of dialogues and of other literature that imitated live conversation, by biographers such as Diogenes Laertius and Plutarch, and by later collectors of anecdotes such as Aelian. The practice of publishing anecdotes continued among the early Christians, notably in the *Apothegms of the Fathers,* and was revived in the Renaissance.

An anecdote is a brief narrative in oral or literary tradition, or both, that tells of a memorable utterance, action, or experience of a named person on a particular occasion. Like the personal-experience fable, it is realistic and told as a true incident, although its verity is usually not insisted upon or debated. For example, Aristippos, "asked by Dionysios why philosophers come to the doors of the rich whereas the rich no longer come to the doors of philosophers, said,

'Because the former know what they need while the latter do not' " (Diogenes Laertius, *On the Lives of the Famous Philosophers* 2.69). Thus, like the Aesopic fable, the narrative usually provides the setting for a climactic remark or reply, except that in an anecdote the remark is usually clever or witty. When this is the case, we have the kind of *khreia* that was also an apothegm (Gk. *apophthegma*, Lat. *dictum*), or pointed utterance in a narrative setting. Most Greek and Roman anecdotes were of this sort.

Although a person might well recount one witty anecdote after another at a social gathering, as do the men in Macrobius (*Saturnalia* 2), one could also tell an anecdote to illustrate an idea or a person's character. Xenophon (*Hellenika* 2.3.56) tells how Theramenes, unjustly condemned to death, yelled out what was happening to him as he was being led away by his executioners. When one of the executioners told him that he would be sorry if he did not keep quiet, Theramenes asked, "And if I do keep quiet, then I won't be sorry?" Xenophon says he admires how Theramenes remained self-possessed and kept his sense of humor in the face of death.

Joke

Greek and Roman jokes were short, traditional comic tales, the principal object of which was to amuse. Thus: A fool's son was playing with a ball, which fell into a well. The boy looked into the well, saw his own reflection, and asked for the ball. When he complained to his father that he did not get his ball back, the father looked into the well, saw his own reflection, and said, "Sir, give the boy back his ball" (*Philogelos* [*Lover of Laughter*] 33). Another example: A Sicilian, whose friend was sadly telling him that his wife had hanged herself from a fig tree, said, "Let me have some cuttings from that tree

of yours to plant" (Cicero, *On Oratory* 2.69.278). The joke, like the anecdote, was a realistic tale, but its characters were generic types such as fools, seers, cowards, Sicilians, and the Abderites of Thrace, like the anonymous types of the Aesopic fable. That is, the joke was a realistic comic tale that made no pretense at all of being historically true. Ancient authors rarely recounted a tale that made no claim whatsoever to historicity for its own sake. That is why we have so many comic anecdotes but so few jokes. The difference between specimens of the two genres could lie merely in whether the incident was told about a historical person or not. Although both genres often took the form of a short narration capped by a memorable utterance, the anecdote more often culminated in a clever remark, whereas the punch line of a joke was more often offered by a fool. Neither the Greek terms (*geloion, asteion, khleue*) nor the many Latin terms (*ridiculum, iocus, dictum, facetia*) clearly distinguished the joke from related forms; these terms were used to refer to any funny tale or quip.

The joke, if not at home in most ancient literature, was welcome on social occasions that fostered an element of play, such as parties, where participants are often represented in literature as exchanging humorous stories. Xenophon in his *Symposium* describes a professional buffoon named Philip whose wit earned him a seat at a symposium, just as elsewhere parasites are represented as trading their wit or flattery for a meal. In the comedies of Plautus, parasites sometimes refer to books that they consult when they need good jokes. One such book has survived. It is the compilation of Greek jokes known as *Philogelos* (*Lover of Laughter*), a work of uncertain date (fourth century A.D.?) and authorship. Its jokes are grouped according to various principal characters (stupid men, misers, Abderites, and so forth) and are told with no elaboration;

the form is clearly that of a source book. Since the Plautine comedies were adaptations of plays of Greek New Comedy, which dates from the fourth century B.C., the original references to joke books were probably to Greek books that were in circulation at that time. From the Hellenistic period we also have fragments of a handbook of comic insults.

The genres of story that we have considered so far are all very short narrative forms that would seldom fill more than half a page in a modern book. They are usually mono-episodic tales with one or two important characters, one of whom usually concludes the tale by uttering a pointed statement that is summary (Aesopic fable) or clever (anecdote) or funny (joke). In contrast, the longer genres of oral narrative focused less on the climax of the tale than on the events themselves, which were developed for their own interest. These genres—magic tale, novella, legend—were commonly referred to simply by one or another general word for story or tale (Gk. *mythos, logos, historia;* Lat. *fabula, narratio, historia*). The longer the narrative genre, the vaguer the Greek and Roman vocabulary to distinguish or identify it.

Magic Tale

The magic tale, or fairy tale, is usually a long and complex story. In modern oral tradition, the magic tale consists of many episodes, the telling of which, depending upon the skill of the raconteur and the nature of the storytelling event, can actually last hours. The magic tale is therefore not a casual tale, like an anecdote, but is an elaborate narrative appropriate to an audience that is willing to sit back and attend to a long performance. Like the joke, it seeks to entertain and makes no claim to historicity. The characters are either unnamed or have conventional fairy-tale names like Jack or Hans; the locales are vague and unspecified; the world of the narrative contains unrealistic features such as magic objects, speaking animals, and supernatural spouses, helpers, adversaries, and tasks. The magic tale is the extended fiction, or romance, of oral story-telling.

Our best evidence for the magic tale in antiquity is found in Apuleius' *The Golden Ass* (*Metamorphoses*), where it is told that some robbers kidnapped a girl on her wedding day in order to exact a ransom from her wealthy parents. The men leave her in the care of an old woman, who, in her attempt to console and encourage the frightened girl, tells her the long and wondrous tale of Cupid and Psyche (4.28–6.24), a story of the difficult trials and eventual triumph of a beautiful princess. Although the tale has been modified in its adaptation to Apuleius' novel, familiar traits of the genre abide in the adaptation: the mostly anonymous cast of characters, the unnamed lands in which the action takes place, the elements of magic and wonder, the happy conclusion. This tale was fantasy to be enjoyed for its own sake. The narration is also long, requiring forty to fifty pages in a modern book. It is noteworthy that Apuleius represents both teller and hearer as being female, for this story, which in all its essentials is also known to modern oral tradition, is more often told by female raconteurs than by males; it is primarily a women's story.

As in the case of the joke, there is relatively little direct evidence for the magic tale in Greek and Roman literature, and probably for a similar reason; namely, that the magic tale did not purport to be more than an entertaining fiction, and so was regarded by most writers as a trite form of expression, not suitable to literature as they conceived of it. No collection of magic tales is known to have been made in antiquity, and perhaps none was made in Europe until the sixteenth century, when Straparola included some in *Pleasant Nights.*

Novella

A novella, or realistic folktale, was a traditional story that, unlike the magic tale, typically found its setting in the familiar world governed by the ordinary laws of reality. In his *Satyricon* (109–113), Petronius tells how persons aboard a ship fight, make peace, and celebrate their treaty with food and song. When after a while the party is becoming quiet, one of the men, Eumolpus, begins to comment upon the unfaithfulness of women, adding that he has in mind not the well-known women of the old tragedies and legends but something that has happened in their own time. All ears turn to him, and he tells of a woman of Ephesus who was famous for her fidelity to her husband, and when the man died she joined him in his tomb with the intention of following him in death. But she was seduced in the tomb by a soldier and even turned the body of her husband over to him in order to replace a missing corpse that the soldier was supposed to have been guarding. When Eumolpus finishes his story, the sailors laugh, one of the women blushes, and a man who evidently has once been cuckolded grumbles. If the tale of Cupid and Psyche was primarily a story for women, the tale of the widow of Ephesus was definitely a story for men.

Although a novella might circulate as the report of a true event, the relative importance of its possible historicity and of its intrinsic interest as a romantic or comic or tragic story varied. In the present instance, Eumolpus announces that the events took place in the recent past in Ephesus, but he makes little effort to convince the others that the events have really occurred. He does not name names or explain how he himself came to know of the events. His purpose is not to put forth a serious argument about the character of women founded upon historical fact, but to tell a realistic story that amuses the men and teases the women, and that gains piquancy from its being touted as a true account. The credence given to different novellas was probably comparable to that given to different anecdotes, and, indeed, the ancient novella might be described as an extended anecdote. In structural complexity, the story of the widow of Ephesus was about midway between an anecdote and a magic tale; in Petronius' narration, it requires about three pages of text.

Collections of novellas, sometimes combined with other genres, were made in antiquity and in the Middle Ages, and as a literary form the novella blossomed again in the early Italian Renaissance. An influential collection of ribald novellas in antiquity was the *Milesian Tales* of Aristeides of Miletos (*ca.* second century B.C.); it was translated into Latin, but neither the original nor the translation has survived.

Legend

The legend is a traditional story, told as a report of actual events, in which the principal characters are human beings. It is a somewhat cumbersome scholarly category since it includes many kinds of story found throughout ancient literature; both the anecdote and the novella, when historicity was emphasized, might be considered varieties of the legend. Many legends were simply narratives of a remarkable but more or less realistic incident. Thus, an etiological legend attached to the Greek town with the curious name of Ophiteia (Snaketown) tells how a man once killed a snake that seemed about to attack his son but, as it turned out, had been guarding him from a wolf; the grateful man gave the snake funeral rites (Pausanias, 10.33.9–10). Probably this story was only told when someone, such as the traveler Pausanias, asked how the town came to have so strange a name. A remote element of the supernatural was present in the many legends in which cleverly ambiguous or unclear oracular responses were given to inquirers, especially at the oracle of Apollo at Delphi. The supernatural element, such as it was, belonged to a familiar institution: people did obtain oracular responses in real life, although the actual responses were not riddling or deceptive.

Legends of direct encounters with the supernatural stand apart from these stories as being more wondrous and therefore more controversial. No one discussed the supernatural elements of a magic tale for their possible verity because it was clearly understood that the tale was intended as pure fiction; but it was equally clear that the legend of supernatural encounter was not so intended. In such legends, the supernatural was taken seriously. Anticipating skepticism from his hearers, a teller usually took pains to give his narrative credibility. Thus, in Phlegon's report (*Marvels* 1) of the return to life and second death of a deceased girl, the teller provides details of names and places and claims that he himself, as a local official, had been present soon after the event and participated in the investigation. Here the narrative is told in the first person, as also happens in a legend-telling session in Petronius (*Satyricon* 61–64), in which two uneducated freedmen narrate accounts of a terrifying supernatural encounter each has had, Niceros with a werewolf, Trimalchio with witches. Niceros, expecting his more educated listeners to scoff at him, repeatedly asserts the truth of his report, and Trimalchio also feels impelled to add that Niceros is an absolutely reliable man. This kind of legend was a vehicle for the expression and transmission of folk beliefs in supernatural phenomena.

Legends of the deeds of prominent families in early Greece and Italy are usually classified, together with myths, as mythology, so I pass them over here.

Proverb and Riddle

The kinds of proverb and riddle circulating in antiquity are too many to enumerate here; some representative examples must suffice. The proverb (Gk. *paroimia;* Lat. *proverbium, adagium*): "One hand washes the other" (Petronius, *Satyricon* 45.13); the proverbial phrase: "You're teaching a dolphin to swim" (Zenobios, 3.30), used about someone teaching another person something he already knows; the proverbial comparison: "whiter than snow" (Homer, *Iliad* 10.437); the Wellerism: " 'Not so bad after all,' said the man who threw a stone at his dog but hit his stepmother" (Plutarch, *Moralia* 6.467c); and the fable-proverb or short fable: "A mountain was in labor, then gave birth to a mouse" (Diogeneianos, 8.75), a form intermediate between the proverb and the fable that the Greeks probably borrowed from the Near East.

An example of a frequently cited riddle (Gk. *ainigma, griphos;* the Romans used the Greek terms) is: "A man and not a man killed a bird and not a bird, sitting on wood and not on wood, with a stone and not a stone" (Athenaios [Athenaeus], *The Learned Banquet* 10.452c), for which the solution is eunuch, bat, fennel, pumice. The Greeks also devised mythological riddles (like the biblical riddles of later tradition), rebuses (visual conundrums), and mathematical and verbal puzzles. Riddles played an unusually important role in traditional story, from the riddle of the Sphinx in the Oedipus legend to the many oracle legends in which the oracular message was really a riddle that the inquirer had to solve.

Although proverbs and riddles had a number of poetic features in common, such as a frequent use of metaphor, their functions were virtually opposite, for the application of a proverb had to be clear to the hearer if it was to be effective, whereas a successful riddle was one in which the hearer could not perceive the referent. Riddling was a common game at Greek symposia. One person posed a riddle, and the others offered their solutions one at a time; there were traditional rewards and punishments for winners and losers. In contrast, the proverb was a conversational genre, likely to appear in informal discourse, especially in the speech of the less educated. Thus, in the *Satyricon* (62.12), the freedman Niceros uses a proverbial comparison in the course of relating the frightening experience he has had: "As soon as it was light outside I ran from the house *tamquam copo compilatus*" (like a swindled innkeeper, that is, as fast as an innkeeper chasing a nonpaying customer). Niceros' comparison gains poetic effect from its concision and alliteration, while its imagery reflects his humble background.

The Greeks characteristically showed more interest than the Romans in proverbs and riddles. Aristotle—who can be called the father of folklore studies—devoted some time to the riddle, and his student Klearchos wrote a book *On Riddles,* of which fragments survive. Aristotle's own *Proverbs* (*Paroimiai*) has not come down to us, but other scholars presently made compilations of and commentaries on Greek proverbs and proverbial expressions (the two were usually not distinguished in antiquity), and Byzantine scholars continued the tradition. Few collections of Roman proverbs were made, and none has survived, a lack that in the sixteenth century Erasmus of Rotterdam tried to make up for in his *Thousands of Proverbs* (*Adagiorum Chiliades*). We do, however, possess a collection of Latin riddles, made by Symphosius (late fifth century A.D.?). It was highly esteemed in Europe throughout the Middle Ages and influenced medieval riddle collections.

FINAL OBSERVATIONS

The eight genres of folklore surveyed here illustrate traditional verbal resources that were available to bearers of Greek and Roman culture, although not to all of them, for some items circulated mostly through male conduits, others through female conduits, and still others through conduits characterized by education or age or personality or geography. In short, Greek and Roman folklore was not something every Greek and Roman inherited automatically or shared equally. Nor did different forms of folkloric expression perform one and the same function. Joking and riddling belonged to symposia and other playful gatherings, whereas genres such as the anecdote, the fable, and the proverb normally colored informal conversation, and the longer narrative forms such as the novella and the magic tale tended to be performance pieces.

The most noticeable influence of ancient folklore has not been upon folklore itself but upon literature and scholarship. Numerous Greek and Roman tales are still familiar to readers today from ancient or modern literary treatments, and the collecting and theorizing that flourished in Greece in the fourth century B.C. stimulated the collectors and thinkers who followed. Finally, we remain participants in ancient folklore to the extent that we continue to regard many ancient folkloric narratives as true or quasi-true accounts, just as many ancients did before us, and perhaps for similar reasons. We want the Pythia to have uttered obscure oracles in a state of divine frenzy; we want famous persons to have been so anecdotally clever; and we want the old legends to have been history.

BIBLIOGRAPHY

SOURCES

Claudius Aelianus, *Varia Historia,* Mervin R. Dilts, ed. (1974), a collection of Greek anecdotes; Aesopus, *Aesopica: A Series of Texts Relating to Aesop or Ascribed to Him or Closely Connected with the Literary Tradition that Bears His Name,* Ben E. Perry, ed. (1952); Apuleius, *Metamorphoses* (*The Golden Ass*), Pierre Grimal, ed. and comm.

(1963), Latin text of the tale of Cupid and Psyche, with French commentary; Athenaeus, *The Deipnosophists* (*The Learned Banquet*), Charles Burton Gulick, ed. and trans., IV (1930); *Babrius and Phaedrus*, Ben E. Perry, ed. and trans. (1965), texts of the two fabulists together with English summaries of the fables in Perry's *Aesopica;* Marcus Tullius Cicero, *Rhetorica*, A. S. Wilkins, ed., I (1902); Diogenes Laertius, *Vitae Philosophorum* (*Lives of the Philosophers*), Herbert S. Long, ed., 2 vols. (1964), anecdotal biographies; Alexander Giannini, ed. and trans., *Paradoxographorum Graecorum Reliquiae* (1966), Greek texts with Latin translation of Phlegon and the other Greek paradoxographers.

Herodotus, *Historiae*, Karl Hude, ed., 2 vols. (1908, 3d ed. 1940), many novellas and legends; Léopold Hervieux, ed., *Les fabulistes latins depuis le siècle d'Auguste jusqu'à la fin du moyen âge*, 5 vols. (1893–1899), the Latin texts; Hesiod, *Works and Days*, Martin L. West, ed. and comm. (1978); Homer, *Opera*, Thomas W. Allen, ed. (1908; 2d ed. 1917, 1919), vols. 3 and 4 are the Greek text of the *Odyssey;* Ernst L. von Leutsch and Friedrich W. Schneidewin, eds., *Corpus Paroemiographorum Graecorum*, 2 vols. (1839–1851); *Supplementum* (1961), texts of the ancient and Byzantine Greek writers of proverbs; Machon, *The Fragments*, Andrew S. F. Gow, ed. and comm. (1965), a collection of versified Greek anecdotes; Ambrosius Macrobius, *Saturnalia*, James A. Willis, ed., vol. 1 (1963), book 2 contains witty anecdotes.

Raymond T. Ohl, ed., trans., and comm., *The Enigmas of Symphosius* (1928), a collection of Latin riddles in verse; August Otto, ed. and comm., *Die Sprichwörter und sprichwörtlichen Redensarten der Römer* (1890), a compilation of Latin proverbs with commentary; William R. Paton, ed. and trans., *The Greek Anthology*, V (1918), book 14 contains a collection of Greek riddles and puzzles; Herbert W. Parke and Donald E. W. Wormell, eds., *The Delphic Oracle*, II (1956). Greek and Latin texts of the oracular responses; Petronius Arbiter, *Satyricon*, Konrad Müller, ed. (1961); Pliny, *Natural History*, Harris Rackham, William H. S. Jones, D. E. Eichholz, eds. and trans., 10 vols. (1938–1963), a compendium of ancient folklore of all kinds.

Plutarch, *Moralia*, W. Nachstädt, W. Sieveking, J. Titchener, eds., II (1935), texts of Plutarch's apothegms, with references to parallels; Reinhold Strömberg, ed. and comm., *Greek Proverbs: A Collection of Proverbs and Proverbial Phrases which are not Listed by the Ancient and Byzantine Paroemiographers* (1954), complements Leutsch and Schneidewin, above; Andreas Thierfelder, ed., trans., and comm., *Philogelos: Der Lachfreund von Hierokles und Philagrios* (1968), text of the Greek joke book with German translation and commentary; Xenophon, *Opera*, E. C. Marchant, ed., 5 vols. (1900–1920).

STUDIES

Roger Abrahams, "The Complex Relations of Simple Forms," in *Genre*, 2 (1969); Dan Ben-Amos, "Toward a Definition of Folklore in Context," in *Journal of American Folklore*, 84 (1971); Richard H. Crum, "Additions to the Bibliography of Greek and Roman Folklore," in *Classical Weekly*, 42 (1948–1949), complements McCartney, below; Linda Dégh and Andrew Vázsonyi, "Legend and Belief," in *Genre* 4 (1971), and "The Hypothesis of Multi-Conduit Transmission in Folklore," in *Folklore: Performance and Communication*, Dan Ben-Amos and Kenneth S. Goldstein, eds. (1975); Richard M. Dorson, ed., *Folklore and Folklife: An Introduction* (1972).

Joseph Fontenrose, *The Delphic Oracle: Its Responses and Operations, with a Catalogue of Responses* (1978); Edward S. Forster, "Riddles and Problems from the Greek Anthology," in *Greece and Rome*, 14 (1945); Reinhard Häussler, ed., *Nachträge zu A. Otto, Sprichwörter und sprichwörtliche Redensarten der Römer* (1968), complements Otto, above; Elizabeth Haight, *The Roman Use of Anecdotes in Cicero, Livy, and the Satirists* (1940); William R. Halliday, *Greek and Roman Folklore* (1927), represents the middle view of folklore; William F. Hansen, "An Ancient Greek Ghost Story," in *Folklore on Two Continents: Essays in Honor of Linda Dégh*, Nikolai Burlakoff and Carl Lindahl, eds. (1980), and "The Applied Message in Storytelling," in *Folklorica: A Festschrift for Felix J. Oinas*, Egle V. Žygas and Peter Voorheis, eds., *Indiana University Uralic and Altaic Series*, 141 (1982); *Journal of Folklore Research*, 20 (1983), contains several studies on ancient Greek folklore.

Rudolf Kassel, "Reste eines hellenistischen Spassmacherbuches auf einem Heidelberger Papyrus?" in *Rheinisches Museum für Philologie,* **99** (1956); Jan Kindstrand, "The Greek Concept of Proverbs," in *Eranos,* **76** (1978); Eugene S. McCartney, "A Bibliography of Collections of Greek and Roman Folklore," in *Classical Weekly,* **40** (1947); Konrad Ohlert, *Rätsel und Rätselspiele der alten Griechen* (1886; 2d ed. 1912); Alice S. Riginos, *Platonica: The Anecdotes Concerning the Life and Writings of Plato* (1976); Alex Scobie, "Story-tellers, Storytelling, and the Novel in Graeco-Roman Antiquity," in *Rheinisches Museum für Philologie,* **122** (1979); Sandra K. D. Stahl, "The Oral Personal Narrative in its Generic Context," in *Fabula,* **18** (1977); Sophie Trenkner, *The Greek Novella in the Classical Period* (1958); Otto Waser, "Volkskunde und griechisch-römisches Altertum," in *Schweizerisches Archiv für Volkskunde,* **20** (1916), represents the broader view of folklore.

Athletics

DAVID C. YOUNG

INTRODUCTION

When his best friend Patroklos lies dead and unburied, Achilles acts as Homer thought appropriate. He calls the Greeks together for athletic contests. The heroes of the Trojan War put down their swords and contend for prizes in events such as footracing and wrestling. These are the funeral games of Patroklos (*Iliad* 23). The chariot race is an exciting affair as rival chariots jostle one another, drivers cry "foul," and one spectator offers to bet on the outcome. In the footrace Odysseus wins when Oilean Ajax trips into a manure pile. Ajax can blame his bad luck on Athena, an expedient not possible for modern runners. We may think a funeral a strange occasion for athletics, but will be more surprised by the value of the prizes, especially if we still believe ancient athletes were amateurs who refused all material gain.

The richest prizes go to the charioteers. The winner receives a slave woman and a large caldron of costly metal. A caldron "valued at twelve oxen" goes to the winner in wrestling. In the footrace first place wins a chased silver bowl, "the finest on earth"; second wins an ox, and third a half-talent of gold. These are fictitious games of mythical heroes, but they reveal the basis of historical Greek athletics.

Perhaps nothing else is more distinctive of ancient Greece than athletics. Barbarians did not have them. Other things we associate with Greece—democracy, tragedy, black-figure painting—were localized matters and did not last long. But athletics thrived throughout the Greek world from the dawn of recorded history to the end of antiquity. They lasted until barbarians overran Greece and Christianity, hostile to athletics anyway, replaced pagan institutions. The last Olympics took place in St. Augustine's time; they were banned by Emperor Theodosius I in A.D. 394.

The first Olympics antedated Homer, and the origins of Greek athletics are lost in prehistory. Some scholars think that Mycenaean Greeks practiced athletic events. Boxing certainly goes back to the Bronze Age. A fresco from Thera depicts boxing as early as 1600 B.C. There was boxing in Minoan Crete and in the Greek Dark Age, but we know little more. Wrestling, footracing, archery and spear throwing might have existed in the Bronze Age. But no discuses or jumping weights have turned up at Mycenae or Tiryns, nor is it likely that they will. When his heroes hold games, Homer probably gives us a picture of athletics in his own day, five centuries after any Trojan War.

It is tempting to see the very origin of Greek athletics in funeral games like those of *Iliad* 23. Ancient sources attribute more than thirty funeral contests to the prehistorical period. Homer mentions several others. At Olympia, Pausanias saw an ancient chest that depicted athletic games held upon the death of Pelias, Jason's nemesis who had forced his quest of the Golden Fleece. Poetry and music could join athletics on the program. Hesiod proudly claims he himself won the poetry prize at Amphidamas' funeral games. The tradition of funeral games continued into classical times.

Yet not all early athletics were connected with funerals. In *Iliad* 22 the poet contrasts large prizes for charioteers at a contest "when a man has died" with a smaller prize given at some footrace—an oxhide or a sacrificial animal. He clearly knew athletics apart from funerals. And in *Odyssey* 8, Homer presents athletic contests that are neither funereal nor religious. When the Phaeacians welcome Odysseus to their utopian island, they hold athletic games in his honor. At first Odysseus declines to take part, but when taunted with a charge that he may not be an athlete, he lets fly a discus throw that sets a new Phaeacian record. The Phaeacian games are unusual because they offer no material prizes and no chariot race; otherwise they seem much like those in *Iliad* 23, and much like what athletics must have been in Homer's time. The Phaeacians even include a long jump, absent in the *Iliad.*

In historical times Xenophon's band of Greek mercenaries, like the Phaeacians, need no funeral or religious occasion for games. For the sake of nothing but the contests themselves they—like their ancestors of *Iliad* 23—take time out from a rugged military campaign in Asia to hold an athletic meet.

Even if the origins of Greek athletics were secular, the great athletic contests of Greek history were attached to religious festivals. The oldest and most prestigious were the games held at Olympia in the northwest Peloponnese. Most Greek historians dated the Olympics from the year we call 776 B.C. A few authors, ancient and modern, wish to place their beginnings centuries earlier, in the Mycenaean age, but archaeology supports no date earlier than 776. We may then reckon that the second Olympiad took place in 772, the third Olympiad in 768, and so on.

Ancient accounts of the Olympics' genesis are so long after the event and so colored by local politics that we cannot trust them. Similarly, Pausanias offers a timetable listing the year in which each event was held for the first time. But this list is doubtful on several accounts. For one thing, it is hard to believe, in light of the early evidence, that there were no boxing or chariot contests at Olympia until the 680s, when Pausanias dates their inception. We shall never know exactly which events the first Olympics contained. But we do know the full program a century after that, and that program remained the same, with only minor changes, from the mid sixth century on.

The track events were just three: short, middle, and long distance races. There was an all-around contest, the pentathlon, or "five-event" match. It included the three field events, long jump, javelin, and discus, a short footrace, and wrestling. Like the short footrace, wrestling was also held as a separate competition for specialists, apart from the pentathlon.

Two other combative events pitted one contestant against another. These were boxing and another, even more dangerous event called the *pancration,* a no-holds-barred "anything goes" fight. There were equestrian events, as well. The regular mounted horse race was called the *keles;* the *harma,* the most spectacular event in antiquity, was a race for chariots drawn by teams of four.

A few events were added over the centuries. About 520 B.C. the officials instituted a middle distance race in which the runners competed in armor. Contests for announcers and trumpeters began in the 390s. Several new equestrian contests were added, some of which were later dropped. Yet the small group of events noted above practically comprises the whole Olympic program.

There were no ball games, no team games. In fact there were no "games" at all, nothing that the Greeks would call "games" or "sports." The term "Olympic Games" is our own invention. The Greeks used only the words *agones* and *athla,* "contests." They indeed had team games and ball games, but they never thought to include them in their major athletic festivals. For ball games were "play" to the Greeks, what we originally meant by "sport"—diversion and recreation. Greek athletics were never conceived that way. The word they used for athletic festivals, *athla,* connoted besides prizes and contests only struggle and toil, suffering or even pain. And Greeks tended to view that struggle as an individual one, not a team effort.

In the first century of the Olympics they were not truly Panhellenic. Almost all the victors came from the Peloponnese; at first, even from its western region. But by their centennial, the Olympics had seen victors coming from Athens, and athletes had come from as far away as Ephesus in Ionia, on the coast of modern Turkey. By 600 B.C., although most victors still hailed from Sparta and other Peloponnesian cities, Athens was well represented. Contestants had begun to arrive too from Magna Graecia in the west,

Greek Italy and Sicily. And more came from the east. Thereafter the Olympics were truly Panhellenic, even if athletes from Magna Graecia dominated in the next two centuries, and those from Egypt and Asia Minor were to prevail over the last centuries of the Games.

Shortly after 600 Greece suddenly became a nation of athletes. Other major athletic festivals sprang up as if sown by a single wind. In 582 the Pythian Games were instituted at Delphi in a festival honoring the god Apollo. Two years later another Panhellenic meeting was born at Isthmia, near the crossroads between Attica and the Peloponnese. The Isthmian Games honored Poseidon. In 573, less than another decade, the last of the Big Four contests, which the Greeks called "Crown Games," began at Nemea, another northern Peloponnesian site. Like that at Olympia, the Nemean festival was held in honor of Zeus.

A few years later, in 566, Athens followed with its own contests, the Panathenaic Games in honor of Athena. A score of less prominent festivals could date from this period or the next few decades. Perhaps a modern analogy helps to explain how such athletic fever could spread. There were neither formal baseball rules nor organized adult baseball clubs in the United States until 1845. But by 1857 there were more than twenty organized teams. By 1864 some players were paid. And in 1869 the first wholly professional team toured from coast to coast, playing about sixty games before 200,000 paying spectators. Baseball soon became the national game.

From the early sixth century B.C., then, athletic games were widespread and integral to Greek culture. They find frequent mention in sixth-century literature, and figure prominently in art. Much of our information about athletic technique comes from scenes on early vases. They show boxers' hand coverings, and how wrestlers countered their opponents' holds. Art also proves that athletics were major spectator events in the early sixth century. Pausanias describes the spectators on that early chest he saw at Olympia which showed the funeral games for Pelias. And a noted fragment of a vase painted by Sophilos represents the heroes at Troy sitting calmly—on neatly made ascending rows of seats—as they watch the funeral games of Patroklos. This painting, experts say, dates from about 580 B.C., but it looks much like any crowd scene in a stadium today.

Where did Sophilos learn of spectators seated neatly at athletic games? Not from Homer's account of Patroklos' games, for he says nothing of seating. Olympia might have suggested the scene we find. There, as on the vase, a raised embankment for seating separated the equestrian events in the hippodrome from the athletic stadium proper. Perhaps Sophilos places Patroklos' games in something like the early panathenaic stadium, for Athens' great festival began during Sophilos' career. But whether Athens, Olympia, or another site was in the artist's mind, the painting makes the answer to one question quite clear: athletics were in the early sixth century a serious, organized adult activity that drew numbers of spectators. Those who object, as did Tertullian and the classical scholar E. N. Gardiner, to spectator interest in athletics will find no refuge in archaic Greece. And no matter what Gardiner might say or wish, Sophilos represents something more than a few nobles at play.

The major festivals were joined by many lesser games that met annually or biennially at Thebes, Rhodes, Sicyon, Pellene, and other places. Athletes could compete almost continually from spring through fall. And a staggered sequence of the Big Four afforded them at least one of these great games annually. If we start with any Olympic year, such as 476, the sequence worked as follows:

476 Isthmian Games, Olympic Games
475 Nemean Games
474 Isthmian Games, Pythian Games
473 Nemean Games

In 472 the cycle would begin again, with Isthmians and Olympics once more. The cycle of four was called a *periodos* (circuit). An athlete who won in each of its four games earned the coveted title *periodonikes* (victor of the circuit). There follows here an analysis of the common events of the circuit, and a look at some prominent athletes who competed in them.

RUNNING EVENTS

The shortest race was the *stade*, a sprint one length of the stadium track, 600 Greek feet. That distance varied slightly from place to place, for the Greeks did not have standardized measurements. At Olympia the stade was 192 meters long, corresponding to our 200-meter or 220-yard dash. The *stade* was the most prestigious athletic event, and for it alone we possess a list of victors that is nearly complete, from 776 B.C. to A.D. 217. But the winning runner did not have the year named after him, as some say. Rather, the *stade* victor's name was the first listed in the Olympic summaries. Since the Olympic Games were an ancient Panhellenic institution with continuous records, later Greek historians found it useful to correlate sundry events with "the year so-and-so won the *stade*."

Many *stade* runners also competed in the *diaulos* event, a race two lengths of the stadium, about 440 yards (400 m). Since the Greek stadium was longer than ours but far narrower, it had no gentle turns. Each *diaulos* runner must have turned sharply at the far end, to return in the same or an adjacent lane. The *hoplites* or "race in armor" was the same length. The exact distance of the "long race," the *dolichos,* is unknown, but it was probably nearer to our 5,000-meter than our 1,500-meter or mile run.

Techniques of running obviously remain the same. Sprinters and distance runners in Greek art look just like their respective modern counterparts. Distance runners have the same relaxed arm carriage, sprinters lean with raised arms at the finish. But all runners, even sprinters, used a standing start. The crouched start of modern sprinters is less than a century old. The remains of starting lines at the Greek sites are Hellenistic or later. They consist of long, low stone sills with horizontal grooves, and holes for vertical posts. Most probably held a system of individual starting gates, but their operation is not clear.

Greeks had no stopwatches and preserved no marks of time or distance. To beat his competitors was an athlete's goal. But records were carefully kept and coveted, all set on the basis of a unique combination of victories. "First" or "only man on earth" is the language of these records, which begin in the sixth century. The best record for total Olympic running victories was set by Leonidas of Rhodes in 152 B.C. He won his fourth Olympic 200-meter crown in a row—and he won the 400 and the race in armor at each of those Olympiads as well. Perhaps the most impressive running record was set by Polites of Caria in A.D. 69 when he won the 200, the 400, and the *dolichos,* all in a single Olympiad. Our own Olympics have not seen so versatile an athlete, able to be both the best sprinter and the best distance runner. But few new combination records remained to be set by A.D. 69. And perhaps within 800 more years we too shall see the likes of Polites.

In modern times New Zealand, Finland, and Kenya have produced more than a proportionate share of distance runners. In an-

tiquity the mother of distance runners was mountainous Crete. A hint comes as early as *Odyssey* 13, which refers to footraces on the island. In 472 a Cretan named Ergoteles won the Olympic *dolichos.* But he did not compete for his native land. He ran for a Sicilian city, Himera. Political discord had driven him from Crete. Himera offered him citizenship and land. The transplanted Cretan did not win in the Olympic Games of 468, but he retook the Olympic crown in 464. His adult Pythian victories began in 478, so he was in his middle thirties when he won his second Olympic title.

We lack good records of the *dolichos* from 468 to 452. But in 448 another Cretan, Aegidas, won the race. We do not know who won it from 444 to 400, but in 396 the *dolichos* winner again comes from Crete, and the next known winner is the Cretan Sotades, in 384. Sotades won again in 380, but not running for Crete; like Ergoteles he switched national allegiances. He competed for Ephesus in Asia Minor—which city, we are told, offered the Cretan champion a lot of money. And when Xenophon's mercenaries stop to hold those games in Asia, typically "more than sixty Cretans competed in the *dolichos*" (Xenophon, *The March Up Country* [*Anabasis* 4.8.27]).

WRESTLING

No ancient event drew so many casual participants as wrestling (*pale*). Men who never competed in a festival met their friends for a bout at the local *palaestra.* Even Socrates wrestled until well along in years. But as the normal weekend tennis player today could not win a point against a Wimbledon champion, so the casual wrestler would have won no falls against the seasoned professional wrestler of the Greek circuit.

Ancient wrestling was a highly technical

contest of sophisticated holds, counter-holds, and throws. The bout turned on technique, balance, and strength. The object was to throw one's opponent three times onto the soft sand wrestling surface. A "throw" was called when a contestant's back, thigh, or shoulder touched the sand. Wrestlers prided themselves on winning "without a fall" being scored against them.

No ancient athlete impressed the Greek public and later Greek memory more than Milo of Croton (Crotone) in south Italy, a wrestler. Centuries after his death he was the object of fable and fantasy, and Greeks never tired of Milo tales: he would stand on a greased discus, and no man could push him off; he snapped headbands with the muscles of his temples; he ate a whole bull at one sitting and drank gallons of wine every day. In Croton's great battle against Sybaris (the story goes) he led the rout of the enemy—armed with a club and clad in a lion skin, like Herakles—wearing all his Olympic crowns. He was a devotee of Pythagoras, and that famous mathematician-philosopher died in an accidental fire at Milo's house.

None of these stories is likely true, but Milo's authentic exploits are even more impressive. He won at least six Olympic crowns in his event, five in the men's category. He reigned as Olympic wrestling champion for two decades, 532–512, a record never broken. He had seven Pythian crowns, and was the men's Pythian champion for twenty-four years. His Isthmian victories were ten, the Nemeans nine. He was over forty when finally forced into Olympic retirement, beaten in 512 by a fellow Crotonian. But he retired *periodonikes* five or six times over. What a wrestler he must have been!

Pentathlon and Field Events

Homer gives the javelin, discus, and long jump each as an independent competition,

and Greek literary tradition states that they were once held separate from one another. Yet throughout the historical period these field events existed only within the pentathlon, joining special pentathlon *stade* and wrestling contests to make up the five events. As in our decathlon, each pentathlon entrant competed in each event of the program. The exact order of the five events is unknown, except that wrestling was certainly last.

The long jump presents special problems. Two texts from late antiquity report jumps that exceed fifty feet. The modern world and Olympic record, set by Bob Beamon in 1968 (and which many think the best athletic feat of our time), is 8.9 meters (about 29 ft.). How could the Greeks jump so much farther? That question has given rise to many theories about the ancient jump. Most modern scholars conclude that it was not a single leap, but a series of jumps. The notion that the Greek event was a triple-jump long held sway. But many recent writers accept Joachim Ebert's puzzling theory that the ancient event consisted of a series of five standing jumps. We do not need such expedients, or further speculation. Reports of ancient jumps beyond fifty feet are almost certainly errors or exaggerated fancy. They come from no authors or records contemporary with the supposed prodigious leapers, Chionis in the sixth century, and Phayllos in the fifth. They come from untrustworthy sources many centuries later. We do not believe that Milo actually ate a whole bull for one dinner, or that Babe Ruth hit a baseball a literal mile. We do best to discount the reports of jumps of fifty-plus feet, and to believe in a single running jump much like ours. Vase paintings, in fact, make a running jump certain. Once airborne, Greek long jumpers look just like ours, with an important exception: they carry jumping weights that the Greeks called *halteres.*

The *halteres,* prominent in art and excavated at the sites, came in pairs, one for each hand. Made of stone or lead, these objects vary in weight but most are about five pounds. Aristotle says they increased the jumper's distance. In modern experiments, athletes find the *halteres* a hindrance. But ancient athletes developed their jumping technique over centuries; perhaps we should not expect to replicate it in a few hours. The vase paintings suggest part of a solution: flute players normally accompany the jumpers, no doubt setting a rhythm to which the athlete swung the weights and marked his stride. We have a report that in 1854 an English jumper who had mastered the use of the weights leaped 29 feet, 7 inches, just over Beamon's astounding modern mark. We may tentatively conclude that ancient athletes could jump beyond thirty feet, but not beyond fifty.

Greek javelin throwers, too, used a style just like ours, with one notable exception. Again they used mechanical aid. They wrapped a leather cord (*ankyle*) several turns around the javelin (*akon*), and put two fingers through a loop at the other end. As the shaft left the athlete's hand, the thong lengthened the arc made by his arm, giving more thrust to the throw and thus increased distance. Further, as the cord unwound, it spun the javelin, and the rifling effect made it fly truer. Here modern experiments succeed. The *ankyle* increases distance, and the javelin lands on point more often. Our javelin records are now well over 300 feet (91 m); ancient Greeks probably threw farther. With a stadium twice as long but half as wide as ours there would be no danger to the crowd—if the throws were straight.

Other societies have had running, wrestling, and spear-throwing contests of some kind. But the discus was exclusively a Greek event until A.D. 1896. The modern Greeks revived the discus throw for the first modern Olympics at Athens in 1859, and included it in their excellent national Olympic Games

of 1870. It became a standard event in modern Greek athletics. The rest of the world adopted the discus throw after the first modern International Olympic Games held in Athens in 1896.

Archaeology has given our museums some ancient discuses. They are made of stone or bronze, and vary greatly in size and weight. But the size most commonly found at Olympia is about the same as our own. Indeed the modern discus was patterned after an ancient discus found at Olympia. Because modern Greek officials misunderstood the stance of Myron's famous statue of a discus thrower, and because the event was foreign to most athletes, effective technique was slow to develop in modern times. At first athletes did not spin with the throw, to make use of centrifugal force. Distances in 1900 were about half as far as now. Classical scholars of that period assumed that ancient athletes knew no better, and write as if they too threw with feet planted. But the evidence suggests that the ancient Greeks did spin fully as they threw and probably used a technique much like that used today.

The Greeks have left no explanation how they determined the pentathlon victor. There is no evidence for point values assigned to each athlete in each event, as in our decathlon; nor for points assigned the athletes' relative rank in each event. There are only a few hints at a solution. Any athlete who won three events was declared winner, even if the fourth and fifth events had not yet been held. An athlete could finish second in the first four events, yet still reach the wrestling finals, which determined the all-around victor. Of many theories so far proposed only one does not clash badly with this evidence or common sense: each athlete was in an individual best-of-five contest with each of the other contestants. When any athlete bettered another in three events, the latter retired defeated. Many difficulties remain even with this theory, which is no more than an expedient proposal.

Several recent writers argue that antiquity esteemed its pentathletes less than athletes who specialized in the other events. But they rely on nothing but the relative value of cash prizes awarded at some local games in Asia Minor during the Roman Empire. In classical Athens the pentathlon prize is as large as the prize for wrestling or boxing. Aristotle speaks of pentathletes in glowing terms. An early artist represents the pentathlete Phayllos on a vase, and the Athenian comic dramatist Aristophanes viewed him as proverbial for his speed. After retiring from competition Phayllos provided and commanded the only western Greek warship to fight at the battle of Salamis.

Another pentathlete, Ikkos of Tarentum, (Taras, Taranto) in south Italy, made another kind of name for himself. An Olympic champion early in the fifth century, he later became a successful coach—"the best of his time," Pausanias says. The Olympic pentathlon victors of 476 and 472 were from Tarentum, no doubt his pupils. Plato implies that Ikkos wrote a book about athletics, and ranks him in athletic training where he ranks Homer and Hesiod in poetry. Sadly, we have not a word of Ikkos' book. But ancient coaches, we know, cared as much about diet and exercise as technique, and there was a close connection between medicine and coaching. The noted trainer Herodicus is credited with first teaching Hippocrates medicine. Others such as Melesias, a wrestling coach, were known mostly for success. Students of Melesias won at least thirty victories in the Big Four.

BOXING

There were no weight divisions in Greek boxing. Only large, strong men could win at the higher levels of competition. There were no rounds, no winning by decision. A match ended only when one fighter knocked the other out, or one man signaled his own defeat by raising his index finger. Vase paintings show all blows being thrown at the head. We see no evidence of body punching or infighting in a normal bout. In the early centuries boxers wrapped soft leather strips around their knuckles to protect their hands, not to soften the blows. Their fingers were left free, perhaps to fend off blows more easily.

The "soft thongs" later developed into a more brutal device, the "sharp thongs." These were gloves pulled over the wrist, knuckles, and forearms. The fingers were still uncovered, but over the knuckles, the hitting surface, lay strips of hard leather. They could do ready damage to a boxer's face, and antiquity had its cauliflower ears and punch-drunk fighters. One jokester notes that, although Odysseus' dog recognized its master after an absence of twenty years, the boxer Stratonikos could not recognize himself in a mirror after just one bout.

For all its brutality boxing could occupy a respected family man. Diagoras was, Pindar says, "gigantic." A native of Rhodes, far from mainland Greece, he spent much of his time away from his family competing at Thebes, Aegina, Argos, Athens, Isthmia, Nemea, Delphi, and the rest. He capped his distinguished career by winning the Olympic boxing title in 464. Pindar celebrated the occasion in song. But Diagoras was no youngster by then. He was the father of two or three children. Within sixteen years two of his sons were crowned Olympic champions in their own right. His daughter bore two more Olympic victors to the family. Diagoras became proverbial as a man with a happy life. He exemplified a view of blessedness founded upon success in athletics and children, an ideal Pindar (*Pythian* 10) expressed almost thirty years before Diagoras' Olympic victory:

Blessed and celebrated in song is the man, who, prevailing by excellence of hands or feet, wins the greatest of prizes with courage and strength, and lives to see his young son duly crowned victor at the Pythian Games.

Even better, Diagoras' family was fully Olympic.

Pancration

Pancration means "any form of power." It was an event even more dangerous than boxing, for it combined boxing with wrestling and added a strong element of street fighting. No blows or holds were barred except biting and eye-gouging. Again there were no weight divisions, but tough, gritty men sometimes won against far bigger opponents. Again there were no rounds, but such unrestrained fighting no doubt ended in rather short bouts. There are only a few reports of fatalities, as in boxing—not so many as one expects from such an event. Good athletes obviously signaled defeat before they were seriously injured. Yet later Greeks cherished the tale of Arrhichion. In 564, the story goes, Arrhichion succumbed to a fatal chokehold just as his opponent gave up, writhing in pain from the toehold that Arrhichion applied with his dying gasp. The officials gave Arrhichion a posthumous victory. It was his third Olympic victory and last match.

Arrhichion's story seems rather embroidered. History tends to outstrip legend. Theogenes of Thasos was both pancratiast and boxer, never beaten in the latter event. His twenty-two-year career brought him more than 1,300 victories as he toured the circuit, master of two tough events. Among his records: first to win both boxing and *pancration* at the Olympics; first to win both boxing and *pancration* at the Isthmian Games (he did it twice). That Isthmian record lasted for two and a half centuries until Kleitomachos

of Thebes set a new one: victor in boxing and *pancration*—and also wrestling—all in one day. Like several other early athletes Theogenes received cult worship in his hometown several centuries after his death.

EQUESTRIAN EVENTS

The owners of the stable, not the jockeys or charioteers, were the victors of record in equestrian events. Racing stables were very expensive in antiquity, and horse and chariot racing were in the hands of the rich. A champion racehorse was as costly then as it is now, and the expense of upkeep was greater. The most successful ancient stable belonged to Hieron I, monarch of Syracuse, Sicily, one of antiquity's most populous and powerful cities. He owned the renowned racehorse Pherenikos, "Bring-victory." Hieron won the Pythian horse race in 478 and 474, the Olympic horse race in 476 and 472, the Pythian chariot in 470, and the most prestigious event of all—outranking the *stade*—the Olympic chariot in 468. Pindar wrote four poems to celebrate these victories; Bacchylides wrote three more. Other chariot victors at the Olympics tend to be monarchs or wealthy politicians, such as Alcibiades. Yet the people of Argos found a way to break this monopoly of the rich in 480 and 472, when they somehow pooled their resources and won with an "Argive people's entry."

OTHER EVENTS AND PRIZES

If we hesitate to call horse races "athletics," music, to us, is wholly another matter. Yet several ancient meets featured musical events, that is, contests in flute playing and kithara singing. The kithara was a stringed instrument that the musician played to accompany his singing. Plato even calls the musicians "athletes," which meant "contestants for a prize," whether musical or physical. One Pindaric ode honors a victorious flautist. Musical contests were integral to the Pythian and panathenaic games, but none took place at Olympia, Isthmia, or Nemea.

The Olympics had only two age divisions, boys (under twenty?) and men. Elsewhere, as at Nemea and Athens, there were three: boys under eighteen, youths eighteen to twenty, and men. There is no good evidence that women or girls competed as athletes at the international festivals in archaic, classical, or Hellenistic times. Early Sparta and perhaps other cities held something like intramural races for girls. And women victors in chariot races are known at Olympia and Athens starting in the fourth century. The first was Kyniska of Sparta, Olympic chariot victor about 396. But these women merely owned the winning stable. They did not drive or compete themselves.

The first cogent evidence for women's physical athletics comes from Delphi in the mid first century of our era, when a proud father catalogs his daughters' success. Their victories include the *stade* race in the Pythian, Nemean, and Isthmian Games. One daughter's record—"first young woman ever to win the *stade* at both Pythian and Isthmian Games"—interests us on two accounts. First it proves that females did compete and win at these major games; second that women's competitions there had not occurred for long. Otherwise so simple a record as back-to-back Pythian and Isthmian victories would have been set long before. Pausanias in the next century tells of competitions for maidens at the Heraia festival at Olympia. It seems that girls' or women's competition did not exist on an international scale until after the birth of Christ, but spread in the early Roman Empire.

Some cities cultivated athletics more than others. For about a century Croton, a Greek colony in Italy, won far more Olympic victories than any other city. But its athletic domination suddenly ended in 480. We know not why. Perhaps state funding disappeared, and it could no longer recruit. Croton's defending Olympic 200- and 400-meter champion Astylos moved to Syracuse. Croton never won another major victory.

We know almost nothing about how officials chose contestants, and little about how they organized the meets. At Athens a board of ten arranged for the various events and distribution of the prizes. It required a large budget, which was provided by a direct tax on wealthy citizens. The organizers of the Big Four gave no prizes of value, only a symbolic crown. But we must not misconstrue these symbolic prizes as indicators of amateurism. No amateur ever competed at Olympia or Delphi. Despite much modern nonsense about ancient "amateurism," the Greeks had no word for it. In both origin and practice Greek athletics had prizes at their heart.

No rule prevented an Olympic victor from taking cash rewards elsewhere, then competing at Olympia again. In the early sixth century Athens paid a cash prize of 500 drachmas to any Athenian citizen who won at Olympia. An annual crop worth that much placed a landowner in the wealthiest census class. In buying power the money equaled about fourteen years' wages for a workingman. Some other cities seemed to follow the same policy. In fifth-century Athens victors at any of the Big Four games received, among other things, free meals at public expense for life.

Yet athletes did not rely on the Big Four. The other festivals paid directly, sometimes in cash but more often bowls of precious metal or large caldrons as in the *Iliad.* At Athens victors in each event won large amounts of olive oil, which they could sell on the export market. The winner of the *stade* received 100 amphorae of oil worth at least 1,200 drachmas in the classical period. So much money could buy several houses or half a dozen slaves. A carpenter or mason worked almost three years (847 days) to earn as much. Second in the *stade* was paid oil worth half a year's wages. The youths' and boys' categories paid lesser but substantial amounts. We wince when our superstars of the track earn five or six thousand dollars for one appearance, but a seventeen-year-old boy in Plato's Athens could win a prize worth more. Musicians' prizes were even greater, cash and silver outright. They had no need to sell oil. First place for singing musicians won more money than a carpenter earned in three and a half years. Even fourth place won a cash prize worth about a year's wage.

Money obviously was not everything. Athletes enjoyed many nonmaterial rewards. The public adulated its superstars then as now, but the limelight lasted longer. Statues of great athletes lined the sites at Olympia and Delphi in a kind of hall of fame. Pausanias saw statues 700 years old. Many athletes found a leading poet, such as Pindar, to celebrate their victories in a choral song. These commemorative poems entered the world's great literature, preserving some athletes' feats and moments of glory to this day.

A few ancient philosophers such as Xenophanes and Socrates complained about the attention and wealth that the athletes received. But they never questioned the athletes' integrity or right to profit from their skill. Our aversion toward athletic money is the irrational legacy of the modern movement called "amateurism." Originating in Victorian England, its aim was to restrict competition to the upper class.

If we set aside any prejudice, money has little to do with the question of excellence. No one claims the music of Mozart or by a concert artist such as Isaac Stern is tainted because they accepted money for it. When a reporter asked Willy Stargell how much money he made in baseball's 1979 World Series, he replied, "I don't know. I just wanted a chance to play my best against the best. This is the World Series. I would have played for free." Ancient Olympic athletes, no matter how well paid, would surely have answered much the same way.

BIBLIOGRAPHY

SOURCES

Sextus Julius Africanus, *Olympionicarum Fasti,* I. Rutgers, ed. (1862; repr. 1980); Pausanias, *Guide to Greece,* Peter Levi, trans., vol. 2 (1971); Pindar, *Victory Songs,* Frank J. Nisetich, trans. (1980).

STUDIES

Ludwig Drees, *Olympia: Gods, Artists, and Athletes* (1968); Joachim Ebert, *Griechische Epigramme auf Sieger* (1972); Moses I. Finley and H. W. Pleket, *The Olympic Games: The First Thousand Years* (1976), the best introduction to the subject; E. Norman Gardiner, *Greek Athletic Sports and Festivals* (1910), an earlier, more detailed version of the previous entry, and *Athletics of the Ancient World* (1930; repr. 1978); Harold A. Harris, *Greek Athletes and Athletics* (1964), and *Sport in Greece and Rome* (1972); Theophil Klee, *Zur Geschichte der gymnischen Agone an griechischen Festen* (1918; repr. 1980); Rudolf Knab, *Die Periodoniken* (1934; repr. 1980); Johann H. Krause, *Olympia* (1838; repr. 1972).

Stephen Miller, *Arete: Ancient Writers, Papyri, and Inscriptions on the History and Ideals of Greek Athletics and Games* (1979); Luigi Moretti, *Olympionikai* (1957), an indispensable list of all known ancient Olympic victors, their dates, and a summary of the evidence for each victory; Roberto Patrucco, *Lo sport nella Grecia antica* (1972); H. W. Pleket, "Games, Prizes, Athletes, and Ideology," in *Stadion,* 1 (1975); Michael Poliakoff, *Studies in the Terminology of Greek Combat Sports* (1982); Rachel Robinson, *Sources for the History of Greek Athletics* (1936; repr. 1979); Lynn E. Roller, "Funeral Games for Historical Persons," in *Stadion,* 7 (1981); Thomas F. Scanlon, *Greek and Roman Athletics, A Bibliography* (1984); Constantinos Yalouris, ed., *The Olympic Games throughout the Ages* (1976); David C. Young, "Pindar," in T. J. Luce, ed., *Ancient Writers: Greece and Rome* (1982), and *The Olympic Myth of Greek Amateur Athletics* (1984).

Greek Spectacles and Festivals

ROBERT GARLAND

ORIGINS

Greek festivals varied enormously in size, importance, and popularity. At the top end of the scale there were the great interstate festivals, such as those celebrated at Delphi, Isthmia, Nemea, and Olympia, which attracted Greeks from all over the Greek world, while at the lower end there were the village or deme festivals, which had only a local significance. Judged overall, festivals constituted an essential ingredient of the Greek way of life, being occasions when large numbers of people would assemble to express and reinforce their corporate identity by recognizing ties of common worship. Many of the most important festivals, such as the Eleusinian Mysteries, were celebrated at only one center. A few were dispersed throughout the Greek world, such as the Thesmophoria, whose celebration is attested in at least thirty cities in mainland Greece, Asia Minor, and Sicily. Others had a tribal following, such as the Karneia, whose popularity among Dorians is demonstrated by the existence of the month Karneios in most Doric calendars.

It has to be admitted from the start that we are very imperfectly informed about the precise nature and significance of even major Greek festivals. Much of the evidence concerning the details of ritual procedure postdates their demise, and even where a rare contemporary account throws some incidental light on the subject, it is never adequate to the task of explaining what a festival really signified to the participants or the quality of the experience that they obtained from it. Characteristic but by no means constant features include: the formal procession to the deity's shrine with ritual stops along the way; the singing of hymns by organized choirs; the decorating of a wooden object that in some sense symbolized or contained divinity; competitive athletic, musical, and dramatic events; and finally, most essential of all, the blood sacrifice of an animal upon an altar in front of the deity's shrine and the subsequent distribution of meat among the officiating priests and worshipers.

Respect for the festivals of other communities was a principle of Greek international law, although not invariably upheld. Xenophon (*A History of Greece* [*Hellenika*]

4.4.2) records an instance when *ca.* 393 B.C. a massacre was carried out in Corinth on the last day of the Festival of Artemis Eukleia because the perpetrators of the deed "thought that on that day they would apprehend and slaughter the greatest number of people in the marketplace," an action condemned by Xenophon as displaying "a contempt for religion and a total disregard for all the conventions of civilized life." A festival once begun was rarely interrupted, even when disaster struck. Xenophon (*A History of Greece* 4.4.16) reports that when the news of Sparta's defeat at Leuctra arrived during the celebration of the Gymnopaedia in 371 B.C., the ephors did not interrupt the performance that was taking place, but simply announced the names of the dead and ordered that there should be no lamentation. A rare exception to this rule occurred in 335 B.C. when the Greater Mysteries were cut short at Eleusis following the announcement of the destruction of Thebes by Alexander, in order to enable the Athenians to prepare for an expected siege.

PANHELLENIC FESTIVALS

The most popular and most prestigious Greek festivals were the great interstate or Panhellenic games, each associated with a shrine of national importance. The first to be founded were the Olympic Games in 776 B.C. This was originally a local event which subsequently became "panpeloponnesian," and ultimately a focus of athletic activity throughout the Greek world every four years. Each Olympiad was announced by officials known as *spondephoroi*, who declared Olympia sacrosanct, forbade the entry of any army into its territory, and called for a sacred truce everywhere for one month. In due course there arrived delegations of sacred envoys called *theoroi*, who at the festival offered sacrifice in the names of their cities.

The next interstate festival to be founded was the Pythian Games at Delphi in 582 B.C., also quadrennial. This was followed a year later by the biennial Isthmian Games at the Isthmus of Corinth in honor of Poseidon and, from 573 B.C., by the Nemean Games at neighboring Nemea in honor of Zeus, also biennial. Thus by the middle of the sixth century B.C. there came to be established the so-called *periodos,* or cycle of games, at least one of which was held every year. All four offered only a wreath as a prize, the Olympic wreath being made up of branches from the sacred olive tree growing in the sanctuary precinct. All were managed locally by the neighboring community and partly owed their importance to their distance from powerful political centers. The Olympic Games, for instance, were administered by the Olympic Council, which was composed exclusively of the Eleans, in whose territory Olympia was situated. Eleans also made up the board of judges, or *hellanodikai,* who enforced penalties on those who violated regulations. Only the Pythian Games, being subject to the deliberations of a contentious league of states known as the Delphic Amphictyony, fell in 347/346 B.C. into the hands of Philip II of Macedon, who now celebrated them in his own name in order to legitimize his military presence in central Greece.

Equally Panhellenic in character, but without accompanying games, were the Eleusinian Mysteries, originally independent but from the sixth century B.C. onward centrally administered by the Athenian state. Their public aspect can be reconstructed with some certainty, its central features including the transport of sacred objects in a large procession from Athens to Eleusis and a ritual bath in seawater at Phaleron on the Attic coast. The precise nature of the Mysteries themselves, however, eludes us, since the divulgence of their secrets was deemed a capital offense by the state. In the words of the Homeric *Hymn to Demeter* (473 ff.), "To the kings . . . Demeter showed the conduct of her rites and taught her rituals, . . . terrible mysteries (*orgia*) which no one can violate or pry into or utter." The climax of the festival seems to have been a solemn rite performed inside a building known as the Telesterion, or hall of initiation. Initiation was in at least two stages, *myesis* and *epopteia,* and included the revealing of sacred objects by the high priest, or *hierophant,* an experience judged to be so intense that it guaranteed those privileged to witness it a blessed life in the hereafter.

ATHENIAN FESTIVALS

The only Greek state whose festival calendar can be reconstructed in any detail is that of Athens. The religious year began around the time of the summer solstice in late June and consisted of twelve lunar months, each twenty-nine or thirty days in length. It was quite separate from the civic year, which was based on a division of the calendar into ten *prytanies,* according to the length of time the councillors of each of the ten tribes presided over the council. Probably some set of regulations setting out the city's religious obligations was included in the law code introduced by Solon, but our knowledge of it is slight. At the end of the fifth century B.C. a lengthy revision of the festival calendar took place under the supervision of an official transcriber called Nikomachos. That such an undertaking was judged necessary reflects the complexity of Athenian religious practices at this date, which had been growing steadily as new cults from abroad gained official acceptance from the state.

The first eight days of the month were taken up with monthly festivals, mostly devoted to the celebration of divine birthdays. Athena's birthday was honored on the third, Artemis' on the sixth, and Apollo's on the seventh. The first day of the month was called Noumenia, new-moon day, judged to be "the holiest of all days" (Plutarch, *Moralia* 828a). It was an occasion when a large market was held in Athens and when a honey cake was put out for the sacred snake that was believed to guard the Acropolis.

In addition to the monthly festivals, there were the annual festivals. These accounted for some ninety days of the calendar in all. As a group, the most prominent and numerous were the agricultural festivals held mainly in honor of Demeter and Dionysos, which highlighted the critical moments in the farmer's year. Interestingly, most emphasis was placed not on the harvest but on the sowing time, which may either indicate that crop gathering is not a period of special anxiety requiring the propitiation of the gods, or else, as Aristotle (*Nikomachean Ethics* 1160a) pragmatically suggested, that an agricultural community is simply not at leisure to engage in festival activity at the time of harvesting.

Festivals with a strong agricultural element include the Thesmophoria, a women's festival in honor of Demeter celebrated in the fall when the putrefied remains of pigs that had been thrown into subterranean caves were brought up, placed on an altar, and mixed with seed grain, a ceremony evidently intended to assist the germination of the grain; the Oschophoria, a vintage festival so named from the fact that two youths of noble families carried vine branches known as *oschoi* laden with grapes; the Haloa, a women's festival of Demeter celebrated in Eleusis in midwinter at which pastry objects in the form of phalluses were eaten; the Rural Dionysia, held in a number of Attic demes around the time of the Haloa, when a giant phallus was borne aloft in procession; the Anthesteria or Flower Festival, celebrated in early spring, when wine jars containing newly fermented wine were opened and ceremoniously blessed by Dionysos, god of wine; the Thargelia, in honor of Apollo, which took its name from the fact that first fruits (*thargela*) in the form of a pot of boiled vegetables were offered to the god on this day, while a human scapegoat was ritually beaten and driven out of the city; and finally the Pyanopsia, named after *pyanos,* a boiled bean, when olive branches called *eiresionai* laden with wool, fruits of various kinds, cakes, wine, and oil flasks, were borne by children in procession and hung up on the front door of every Athenian home.

Although the promotion of fertility, both human and vegetative, may have been the chief purpose behind the majority of ritual activity carried out in connection with these festivals, closer inspection reveals in many cases puzzling complications. The Anthesteria, for instance, which lasted three days and was in essence a cheerful feast of Dionysos, ended somberly with a day of evil omen devoted to the cult of the dead, especially to those who had perished in Deukalion's flood. On this day, known as Chytroi from the fact that pots (*chytroi*) of porridge were offered to the dead, ghosts were believed to leave their graves and wander abroad. Precautions against their noxious presence included chewing buckthorn and smearing the doors of one's house with pitch. What seems to have happened is that two quite separate festivals merged, perhaps for no better reason than that they occurred at about the same time in the year.

It is noteworthy that many of the festivals devoted to Demeter were celebrated in secret by women. The traditionally close association between women and fertility may partly account for this phenomenon, but it should be borne in mind that festivals of this kind served as the only regular occasions when Athenian women could freely consort together outside the home. Quite likely, too,

the coarse jesting among women known as *aischrologia,* which formed an element in certain Demeter festivals, was allegedly done in remembrance of the time when the goddess was made to laugh while grieving for the loss of her daughter Persephone, and was intended—or at least served—to facilitate psychological release from the repressiveness of normal domestic life.

A second category that serves to link together aspects of a number of Athenian festivals has to do with the recognition of age distinctions or rites of passage. The Apatouria was a festival celebrated by hereditary associations called phratries, or brotherhoods. Its third and final day was the occasion when male children soon after birth, young male adults, and newly married wives were officially registered in phratries. It was called Koureotis, or the Day of Hair-Shearing, after the ceremony that symbolized the transition to new status. Formal admission into the religious community took place on the second day of the Anthesteria, known as Choes (Cups), when Athenian infants in their third or fourth year would be presented with an individual *chous* (jug) and experience their first taste of Dionysos' gift. Finally, for young girls there was a festival called the Brauronia, or festival in honor of the Artemis of Brauron in Attica. It included a ritual dance or pantomime, when girls aged between seven and eleven dressed up in saffron robes and "acted the she-bear," believed in some way to have symbolized the transition from childhood to puberty.

A third category of festivals included those that had to do with the dead. In addition to the last day of the Anthesteria, already noted, there was also the Genesia, said by Herodotus (*Histories* 4.26) to be "known to all the Greeks." This was originally a private festival celebrated on the deceased's day of death, which later, following Solon's reform of the religious calendar, became a national day of remembrance for all the dead. Another such festival was the Nemeseia, held at night, which as its name (from *nemesis,* vengeance) suggests, was probably intended to placate the angry dead.

One of the most solemn and at the same time most spectacular events in the Athenian calendar was the annual ceremony for the war dead, the *taphai,* which took place at the end of the campaigning season (that is, early winter). As is made clear from Thucydides' famous description (*History of the Peloponnesian War* 2.34), this event was remarkable in achieving a harmonious balance between the claims of the family and those of the state, to each of which it gave an equally leading role:

> Three days before the ceremony the bones of the fallen are brought and put in a tent which has been erected, and people make whatever offerings they wish to their own dead. Then there is a funeral procession in which coffins of cypress wood are carried on wagons. There is one coffin for each tribe, which contains the bones of members of that tribe. One empty bier is decorated and carried in the procession: this is for the missing, whose bodies could not be recovered. Everyone who wishes to, both citizens and foreigners, can join in the procession, and the women who are related to the dead are there to make their laments at the tomb. . . . When the bones have been laid in the earth a man chosen by the city for his intellectual gifts and for his general reputation makes an appropriate speech in praise of the dead and after the speech all depart.

Panathenaia and City Dionysia

Undoubtedly the grandest and most lavish Athenian festivals were those based in the city, principal of which were the Panathenaia and the City Dionysia. The Panathenaia, or All-Athenian Festival, was held annually on the official birthday of the city's patron goddess, Athena. Once every four years it was celebrated with special

pomp and circumstance, and it is this occasion that forms the subject of the Parthenon frieze now in the British Museum. The Great Panathenaia began with a procession that started outside the city at the Dipylon Gate and proceeded through the Agora along the Panathenaic Way in the direction of the Acropolis, its final destination. Many different groups of the citizen body participated, including a large military contingent. The formal nature of the procession is indicated by the fact that various age groups were assigned specific roles. Thus young girls carried on their heads either baskets containing barley meal for sprinkling on the sacrificial victims, or cushioned chairs for gods to sit upon; young men carried water pitchers; and old men held olive branches sacred to Athena. Resident non-Athenians, metics, were also allocated a role as bearers of offering trays. The rear was probably brought up by freed slaves and non-Greeks who carried branches of oak trees. Possibly at the head was a ship mounted on wheels, which, in place of a sail, had a woolen robe known as a peplos rigged to its mast. The ceremonial peplos was especially woven every four years to clothe a venerable image of the goddess Athena that was housed on the Acropolis and was believed to have dropped from heaven. Strange as it seems, the removal of the goddess' old peplos combined with the presentation to her of the new one constituted the most sacred and solemn moment in the whole proceedings. The procession also included a herd of cows that were sacrificed on Athena's altar. The meat was then burnt, and after the goddess had received her portion the rest was distributed among the whole population down at the Dipylon Gate where the procession had begun. Individual and team events modeled on the Olympic Games also formed a major part of the Panathenaia. They included a recitation of the works of Homer, flute and harp contests, a variety of athletic and equestrian events, a dance event, and a naval competition among the ten tribes. Many of the events were open to foreigners as well as Athenians. Athletes were awarded panathenaic amphoras containing olive oil, bearing the inscription "One of the prizes from Athens."

The origins of the panathenaic festival are not known, but its promotion to the rank of Athens' premier festival was undoubtedly due to Peisistratos (Pisistratus), tyrant of Athens around the middle of the sixth century B.C., whose policy was to foster a spirit of unity among the population at a time when faction was rife among aristocratic kin groups, or *gene*. Clearly as well it was his intention to make it a rival to the Panhellenic festivals, though this it did not become. In the following century the Great Panathenaia was used as an instrument of imperialist propaganda when in 425/424 B.C. the city passed a law requiring that each of her allies should contribute a cow and a suit of armor as an offering, which was imposed with the same threat of penalty as failure to pay the tribute money.

Peisistratos' further aim of reconciling the urban and rural population of Attica is revealed by his interest in Dionysos, in whose honor the Great or City Dionysia was established. This was an occasion when competitions of dramatic and lyric poetry were performed in the theater of Dionysos on the south slope of the Acropolis. Here were staged works that rank among the greatest achievements of Athenian culture, namely the tragedies of Aeschylus, Sophocles, and Euripides, and the comedies of Aristophanes. Admission to the theater was probably by ticket: small discs of lead have been discovered that may have been seat tokens. The price of admission was originally two obols a day, but from the fourth century B.C. and possibly earlier the state treasury paid

for the seats of citizens out of a special festival fund called the *theorikon*. It has been estimated that some 1,500 persons were needed to stage the City Dionysia with its numerous choruses (nine for tragedy alone). From the financial outlay needed to put on such a program, it is abundantly clear that drama occupied a central position in Athenian culture.

The opportunities that such an occasion afforded for advertising Athens' artistic leadership, no less than her political supremacy, were certainly not overlooked. It was to the City Dionysia, which coincided with the beginning of the sailing season in Greece, that Athens' allies brought their tribute money, which was proudly displayed in the theater (Isocrates, *On the Peace* [*De Pace*] 82). At the same time, orphans of those who had died fighting for their country paraded in battle gear and received the blessing of the people. In view of the fact that the City Dionysia was open to all, there could hardly be a more politically charged demonstration of Athenian cultural prestige, military might, and public spirit, all clearly intended for consumption both at home and abroad. This festival may be interestingly contrasted with the exclusively Athenian Lenaia, which also included dramatic contests but which was celebrated in midwinter with only citizens in attendance.

The responsibility for the organization of all these festivals was divided among a large number of magistrates, all of whom, by the fifth century B.C., were annually elected. The chief of these was the king archon (*basileus*) who, in the words of the Aristotelian *Constitution of Athens* (57.1), "administered all the traditional sacrifices." The Great Panathenaia was so complex in its arrangements that it was organized by ten *athlothetai*, or superintendants of the boards. Another decemviral board, the *hieropoioi*, or overseers of sacred rites, was put in charge of the other quadrennial festivals. Final control, however, remained with the demos, or people, who met in assembly to scrutinize the conduct of the officials responsible and at the same time to hear complaints against individuals for misconduct during a festival.

FESTIVALS OUTSIDE ATHENS

As well as festivals that came under the purview of the Athenian state, countless others were celebrated in the 140-odd demes spread throughout Attica. Of these the most popular was the Rural Dionysia, whose importance for Athens' country population is well demonstrated in Aristophanes' comedy *The Acharnians.* Though our present knowledge of deme festivals is slight, religious calendars have been found from which a picture is beginning to emerge of the extent of festival activity at local level: the deme of Thorikos, for instance, lists forty-two gods or heroes in its calendar, each of whom was annually in receipt of cult activity.

Athens' large number of festivals prompted one ancient writer to inquire how it was possible to conduct public business in the city with so many interruptions (pseudo-Xenophon, *Constitution of Athens* 3.2). In fact the "days of release" (*aphesimoi hemerai*) accounted for some sixty days annually, when most, if not all, legal and political business was suspended. On the other hand, if any crisis arose requiring urgent attention, the archon had the right to intercalate one or more days into the year, a device that happily prevented any conflict arising between the religious and secular concerns of the state. Not all Greek states were equally pragmatic, however. The people of Amyklai near Sparta are reported as regularly returning home when campaigning abroad "to celebrate the Hyacinthia and sing a hymn to Apollo" (Xenophon, *A History of Greece* 4.5.11), and it was religious scruples, too, that prevented the Spartans from assisting

the Athenians at the battle of Marathon, which coincided with the Karneia festival, for they could not march until the full moon (Herodotus, *Histories* 6.106; 7.206). Probably no other Greek state had such a full and varied festival program as that of Athens. Certainly Pericles regarded it as a mark of his city's uniqueness that there were "such a vast number of outlets for relaxation through annual games and sacrifices" (Thucydides, *History of the Peloponnesian War* 2.38.1).

Among the festivals of Sparta, with whom, incidentally, Pericles is contrasting Athens in the passage, the Hyacinthia was of particular interest in that its first half was an inversion of the usual practices at Greek festivals, since no garlands were worn, no hymn was sung, and the food was extremely plain. Halfway through, however, the atmosphere suddenly changed: a hymn was sung, a large procession took place, "and the whole city was given over to the bustle and gaiety of a festival" (Athenaeus, *The Learned Banquet* [*Deipnosophistai*] 139d). Other important Spartan festivals were the Gymnopaedia, or Festival of Naked Youths, held in high summer, which tested the physical endurance of boys to the limit; and the Karneia (Carnea), a vintage festival at which youths called *staphylodromoi,* or "grape-cluster-runners," pursued a garlanded man who somehow acted as a scapegoat, while at the same time model rafts were borne in procession, perhaps commemorating the legendary crossing of Dorians into the Peloponnese.

FESTIVALS OF THE HELLENISTIC AGE

The Hellenistic world, inaugurated by the conquests of Alexander, saw an influx of new religions into a much enlarged Greek world. In the third century B.C. Alexander's empire fragmented into three great territorial states, each ruled by a monarchy: the Antigonids in Macedon, the Ptolemies in Egypt, and the Seleucids in Syria, Mesopotamia, and Iran. These states, being accidental rather than natural formations, were inherently unstable, consisting as they did of a heterogeneous mixture of Greeks and Macedonians alongside the indigenous populations. One of the methods by which the successors of Alexander sought to unify their kingdoms was the introduction at their royal capitals of grandiose ceremonials. Perhaps the most magnificent of these was the Great Procession held by Ptolemy II Philadelphus in Alexandria in 271/270 B.C. No fewer than 57,600 infantry and 23,200 cavalry are said to have participated in the procession, which also included "a golden phallus, 120 cubits long and 6 cubits in circumference, painted and bound with golden fillets and provided with a gold star at its extremity" (Athenaeus, *The Learned Banquet* 201b–f). Permanent festivals, both biennial and quadrennial, were also established at this time under royal patronage and for royal propaganda. The most ambitious was the Ptolemaia, inaugurated by Ptolemy II in 279/278 B.C. in honor of his deified father. A decree passed by the Island League, comprising many of the smaller islands of the Aegean, records the League's recognition of the festival as equal in status to the Olympic Games (*isolympia*).

It was not only the Hellenistic kings who recognized the propagandist value attaching to festivals. The Greek states were quick to appreciate the political advantage to be derived from spontaneously voting sycophantic honors to a living ruler. The first Hellenistic king to be so honored was Antigonus I, for whom an annual sacrifice, competition, and wreath-wearing ceremony was instituted by the city of Scepsis in 311 B.C. Moreover, now that the Macedonian conquest had deprived the Greeks of the traditional outlet for the competitive spirit through perpetual warfare, they vied with each other instead in sponsoring spectacular new games which they sought to elevate to the dignity of international festivals. The number of such festivals now increased considerably, as did the length of their programs, which came to include, in addition to traditional dramatic and sporting events, epic verse composition and declamation, and panegyrics in both verse and prose. The latter, being composed for the god in whose honor the games were held, were frequently addressed to the king, and later, when Greece was absorbed into the Roman Empire, to the emperor, as a way of currying favor with the authorities.

A new feature of the Hellenistic world was the emergence of a class of professional entertainers who provided the specialist functions that the increasingly elaborate and sophisticated ceremonials now demanded. Particularly notorious were the guilds of professional actors known as the artists (*technitai*) of Dionysos, the ancient forerunners of the medieval troubadours, who moved around the festival circuit and whose reputation for immorality was so widespread that it became the subject of a well-known rhetorical exercise for school children: "Why are the artists of Dionysos mostly scoundrels?" (Aristotle, *Problems* 956b11). The same period saw the increasing professionalization of sport. A later second-century B.C. inscription set up by the Guild of the peoples of the Chersonese (Gallipoli peninsula) provides some insight into the number of international festivals at which athletes could compete in this era. It celebrates a certain Onasiteles who was victor at the Isthmia, the Nemea, the Asklepieia in Kos, the Dorieia at Knidos, the Dioskoureia, the Herakleia, the Tlapolemaia, the Poseidania, and the Halieia.

POSTHELLENIC CELEBRATIONS

Greek festivals and spectacles continued to be celebrated in the Roman era, although they increasingly came to reflect the preoccupations and interests of the occupying power. Thus, for instance, Romaia, or festivals in honor of Rome, were established throughout the Greek world from 189 B.C. onward, while festivals such as those in honor of Artemis Orthia at Sparta, the Eleusinian Mysteries, and the Olympic Games remained popular and enjoyed imperial patronage until the end of the second century A.D. In A.D. 391 the edict of Theodosius I the Great prohibited all pagan festivals throughout the empire, although it is possible that the Olympic Games had come to an end more than a century before.

CULTURAL FUNCTIONS OF GREEK FESTIVALS

No description of ancient festivals is complete without an attempt to understand the value and meaning for the participants of the repetitive rituals that occupied so large a part of their yearly routine, and that, in purely economic terms, constituted the highest recurrent item of state expenditure after war. At the same time the effort to provide a coherent explanation out of the mass of conflicting, partial, and highly incomplete data that survives from the Greek world on the subject is to enter one of the most contentious areas of current scholarship.

The Greeks were proponents of the myth and ritual theory. That is to say they explained the origins of obscure ritual practices by means of an etiological myth. The custom of throwing piglets into subterranean caves sacred to Demeter probably at the Skirophoria was, for instance, rationalistically explained as a way of honoring the swineherd Eubouleus who, along with his herd of pigs, was swallowed up in the same chasm as Persephone when she was abducted to Hades by Pluto (scholiast on Lucian, *Prostitutes' Dialogue* 2.1).

Influential in recent times has been the structuralist school associated with the name of Claude Lévi-Strauss, according to which religious activity is seen as a way of reinforcing the unity and structure of the social machine. Structural anthropologists lay great emphasis on the presence of elements such as role reversal, opposition, and inversion, which constitute a marked feature of a number of Greek festivals. At the Athenian Oschophoria, for instance, two young men dressed up as women, the herald did not himself wear a garland but placed it on his staff, and a ritual shout was uttered that expressed a mixture of hilarity and pain. Such inversion of natural behavior, it is argued, performed the socially useful function of resolving or at least palliating the contradictions inherent in human experience, by setting up a dramatized model through which these contradictions could be acted out.

Another explanation is that many festivals came into being as the result of some catastrophic event that left a permanent scar on the cultural consciousness. An example is the Gymnopaedia, possibly instituted under the impact of the Spartan defeat at the battle of Hysiai, in 669 B.C. The ritualized activity, which in certain stereotypical sequences (the Hyacinthia or the Christian Easter), passes from hopelessness to rejoicing, may then be said to create "a concentration and shift of anxiety from reality to a symbolic sphere which makes it possible to handle anxiety to some extent . . . and which thus presents a model of how to overcome" (Burkert, 1979, p. 50).

Conversely, other festivals, particularly those established in historical times, celebrated national success, such as the Eleutheria, or Festival of Liberty, founded in 335 B.C., commemorating the victory over the Persians at Plataia more than one-and-a-half centuries earlier, or the Soteiria or Festival of Deliverance, established by the Aetolians in commemoration of their defeat of the Gauls who attacked Delphi in 276 B.C.

Hypotheses may also be sought for the generic features of Greek festivals. An evolutionist explanation of the competitions that formed so large a part of festival activity is that they developed out of the communal ecstatic dance. Ritual dances themselves, which continued to be performed in many festivals, may have acted as a form of social control, being a way of redirecting destructive urges. The fact that Greek athletes performed naked may be interpreted as a way of proclaiming "Greekness," and hence of reinforcing group identity and racial exclusiveness, since barbarians regarded nakedness as something shameful (Herodotus, *Histories* 1.10.3). Another feature, the procession, was clearly intended, on one level, to be a reenactment of the deity's first arrival in the community, often achieved, it is suspected, in the face of conservative opposition (see Euripides' *The Bacchants* [*Bacchai*], *passim*). On another level, however, processions had political value, being symbolic of the ascendancy of the state over its outlying sanctuaries, as for instance in the case of Athens, whose control over the sanctuary of Eleusis was possibly formative in the foundation of a centralized Athenian state.

In conclusion, no single unifying explanation can account for the diversity of social behavior that Greek festivals generated. Rather, each festival should be regarded as containing within itself a plurality of competing but partly allied codes or messages out of which the individual participant selected whatever for him had most meaning.

BIBLIOGRAPHY

SOURCES

Aristotle, *The Athenian Constitution*, P. J. Rhodes, trans. (1984); Athenaeus, *The Learned Banquet* (*Deipnosophistae*), C. B. Gulick, trans., 7 vols. (1927–1941); Michel M. Austin, *The Hellenistic World from Alexander to the Roman Conquest: A Selection of Ancient Sources in Translation* (1981); Herodotus, *The Histories*, Aubrey De Selincourt, trans. (1954); *The Homeric Hymns*, Apostolos N. Athanassakis, trans. (1976); Pausanias, *Guide to Greece*, vol. 1 (Central Greece), Peter Levi, trans. (1971); Plutarch, *Moralia*, Frank C. Babbit, trans., 15 vols. (1927–1976); Thucydides, *A History of the Peloponnesian War*, Rex Warner, trans. (1954); Xenophon, *A History of Greece* (*Hellenica*), Rex Warner, trans., intro. and notes by George Cawkwell (1979).

STUDIES

Walter Burkert, *Structure and History in Greek Mythology and Ritual* (1979), and *Greek Religion Archaic and Classical* (Eng. trans. 1985); Ludwig Deubner, *Attische Feste* (1932; repr. 1966); R. Gordon, ed., *Myth, Religion and Society* (1981); Geoffrey Stephen Kirk, *The Nature of Greek Myths* (1974); Claude Lévi-Strauss, *Structural Anthropology* (1963), and *Mythologiques*, 4 vols. (1964–1972), the first two volumes are available in English as *The Raw and the Cooked* and *From Honey to Ashes*, John and Doreen Weightman, trans. (1969, 1973); Jon D. Mikalson, *The Sacred and Civil Calendar of the Athenian Year* (1975), and "Religion in the Attic Demes," in *American Journal of Philology*, **98** (1977); August Mommsen, *Feste der Stadt Athen im Altertum* (1898); George E. Mylonas, *Eleusis and the Eleusinian Mysteries* (1961); Herbert W. Parke, *Festivals of the Athenians* (1977); Arthur W. Pickard-Cambridge, *The Dramatic Festivals of Athens* (1953; 2d ed. rev. by John Gould and D. M. Lewis, 1968); A. Schacter, "Cults of Boeotia," in *Bulletin of the Institute of Classical Studies*, **38**, 1 (1981); Frank W. Walbank, *The Hellenistic World* (1981).

Roman Games

JOHN H. HUMPHREY

ANY SURVEY OF ROMAN SPECTACLES and festivals must focus above all on the games, the *ludi* and the *munera,* which were such a preoccupation for the inhabitants of Roman towns from one end of the empire to the other. The contrast between Greek and Roman games could hardly be more striking. In Greece the games were essentially athletic competitions in which freeborn male citizens of individual Greek city-states (poleis) competed with one another for symbolic and (in most cases) monetary prizes. To compete at Olympia one had to be Greek-speaking and born of legitimate Greek parents (judges checked the credentials of entrants). Greek society placed high store upon individual athletic excellence (*arete*), and although winning was not the sole end of competing, it was by far the most important. The typical events of the four Crown games (Olympia, Delphi, Isthmia, and Nemea) included short- (*ca.* 190 m), middle- (*ca.* 380 m), and long-distance running events, the pentathlon (which consisted of sprint, javelin, wrestling, long jump, and discus), the three heavy events of boxing, wrestling, and *pankration* (a combi-

nation of both, plus kicking), and equestrian events such as two- and four-horse chariots and ridden horse racing. Games were held at sanctuaries, either annually or every four years, and remained essentially religious celebrations. Greater attention was paid to the needs of the athletes and competitors than to those of the spectators: thus, stadia or hippodromes with permanent seating were rarely provided, the spectators having to sit on the banks, and sanitation was nonexistent, as were accommodations for any but the most distinguished visitors.

At Rome, on the other hand, athletic games in the Greek style were slow to arrive, and when they did, they never matched other events, such as chariot races, theatrical performances, gladiatorial contests, and hunts, in popularity. Competitors were almost always slaves or criminals, not freeborn Roman citizens (who were stigmatized if they appeared in the arena). Many competed of necessity, not by choice. Similarly, the participants primarily performed not for themselves but for the organizations to which they belonged (as property, not members)—whether circus faction, gladiatorial school, or troupe of hunters. At Rome, prizes were not merely symbolic, as they were in the Olympic Games: competitors performed for financial gain, often considerable sums. Roman sports were also much more dangerous than Greek games, where deaths rarely occurred, and then only in the heavy events (chiefly boxing). Much of the appeal of the Roman games was that the crowd went expecting to see the bloodshed, if not the death, of animals and humans, but this was not the motivation for attending Greek games. A second great attraction of the Roman games was the betting. Only one event—chariot racing—was almost equally popular in both Greek and Roman games, but even here the differences outweighed the similarities. At Rome, games were held not only on the anniversaries of temples and cults but also on many other occasions, justified by pretexts that might have little to do with religion proper. The sheer number of days devoted to one type of game or another, not only at Rome but also in smaller towns around the empire, far exceeded anything known in the Greek world. Although religious in origin, the Roman games quickly became more of a secular and political phenomenon. Emperors and magistrates or wealthy benefactors went to considerable pains to provide lavish accommodation for the spectators, ensuring that they had the best view amidst considerable comforts and amenities while watching events that unfolded in an architectural context no less carefully devised to enhance and facilitate the events to the maximum degree possible. The Roman games were above all spectator sports designed for the entertainment of the masses. Unlike modern American spectator sports, they centered on the efforts of individual competitors; they were not team sports.

At first special votive games were held in connection with triumphs, but from 366 B.C. they seem to have been increasingly linked with particular Roman festivals. First came the annual Ludi Romani, part of the festival of Jupiter, Juno, and Minerva, centering on the thirteenth of September, the day of the dedication of the Capitoline temple, when there was a feast of Jupiter there for senators. During the late third and early second centuries B.C. several other festivals with games were introduced, or games were added to existing festivals in honor of Apollo, Cybele, Ceres, Flora, and Jupiter again in the case of the Plebeian games. Later games were often added by emperors to commemorate victories, anniversaries, births, accessions, and deifications. Some of the games established during the republican period were introduced to avert a crisis to the state or to secure the blessing of the gods. The religious connection was further emphasized by the processions that went to the theater or circus carrying images of the gods raised aloft. At these festivals games in the theater (*ludi scaenici*) typically occupied several days, the final day or days being reserved for performances at the circus (*ludi circenses*). The other types of games (*munera*) had a different origin.

The Roman games may best be examined by considering in turn each of the major building types and the sports for which they were specifically designed. Circuses were primarily intended for chariot racing, although battles, tournaments, athletics, and hunts were also held there (particularly in the late republic and early empire). Amphitheaters chiefly exhibited gladiatorial combats (gladiators normally fought in pairs) and wild beast hunts. Theaters were used at first for serious drama and Atellan farces but soon came to exhibit chiefly mime and pantomime. Stadia exhibited athletics, and naumachiae were built for mock naval battles and displays.

CIRCUSES AND CHARIOT RACING

The most popular sport was certainly chariot racing, held as early as the Etruscan period in the area of what became the Circus Maximus in the valley between the Palatine and Aventine hills. That circus evolved over many centuries from something that must have closely resembled a Greek hippodrome (having a flat grassy arena and adjacent slopes on which spectators sat) until its form was crystallized by two major reconstructions, the first by Julius Caesar and/or Augustus, and the second by Trajan in the early second century A.D. In its final form, its arena took the form of an elongated oval 612 yards (560 m) long and 93 yards (85 m) wide, with one end open and flattened: here were located the starting gates (*carceres*). The enormous length of the arena was divided down the middle by a barrier (*euripus*), which had turning posts (*metae*) at either end, around which the chariot teams raced. At the opposite end from the starting gates, in the middle of the semicircular end of the building, stood the monumental Arch of Titus (constructed A.D. 80–81). The entire circus, save for the open end at the gates, was ringed with stands; after Trajan's additions, the seating capacity was perhaps close to 170,000.

Although few parts of the Circus Maximus are visible today, earlier excavations, the evidence of the *Forma Urbis Romae* (the marble "map" of Rome dated to the early third century A.D.), and more fully excavated circuses in the provinces show that this and other monumental circuses were carefully designed for the particular sport of chariot racing. Efforts were made to ensure that the teams all traveled the same distance by arranging the twelve starting gates along a shallow arc that pointed toward the track on the right of the arena. The line of the barrier was angled so that the end lying nearest to the starting gates was positioned to the left of the arena's axis: this refinement equalized the opportunity for those teams that had drawn outside positions at the start by reducing the angle at which they had to turn when they reached the turning post.

When the race was begun, the gates were opened mechanically by an attendant who, from a perch on the upper story, pulled a lever that operated a catapult system. The catapult jerked out the latches that held shut the pair of wooden gates in front of each stall. The removal of the latches permitted the gates to fly open, since the gates themselves were held in a state of tension by twisted sinews attached to the piers behind. (The functioning of this catapult mechanism has been reconstructed on the basis of gates that have survived from the circus at Lepcis [Leptis] Magna in Tripolitana, Libya.) This mechanical system eliminated the possibility of bribery of attendants who might otherwise have been employed to open the gates.

Once in the gates—positions were drawn by lot from a lot machine—the chariot teams waited for the signal of the start, the dropping of a white handkerchief (*mappa*) by the presiding magistrate who sat in the box or tribunal built over the gates. At this signal the gates were flung open and the teams, which raced counterclockwise, charged toward the right side of the arena, following lanes marked with chalk for about 186 yards (170 m), until they reached the beginning of the barrier. A white line drawn across the track at this point signaled the charioteers that they could leave their appointed lanes and move into any lane they wished, presumably the inside of the track, the favored position because it offered the shortest lap distance. The race continued for seven complete revolutions. At the completion of the last lap, instead of returning down the track to the starting gates, the teams would round the turning post and head back up the track on the right side of the arena toward the finish line, roughly two-thirds of the way up this side. Here was located the box of the umpires who officially judged the winner. Behind them rose the temple of the Sun and Moon, the Sun being the god to whom the circus as a whole was consecrated. On the opposite side was the emperor's box (*pulvinar*), which also held the images of the gods that had been paraded around the arena before the race began. Augustus was responsible for building the *pulvinar*. Thus here, at the finish, the emperor, his family, and the images of the gods were placed in alignment with the temple of the Sun and Moon.

The Circus Maximus, like other monumental circuses, was elaborately decorated, particularly the gates and the *euripus*. The latter, whose design seems to have been perfected only during the first century A.D., consisted of a series of water basins out of which rose a variety of monuments and fountains. At the midpoint was an obelisk Augustus had brought from Egypt in 10 B.C. and had dedicated to the Sun. (A second obelisk was added in A.D. 357.) Laps completed by competing teams were counted by ornamental eggs (sacred to the Dioscuri) and dolphins (sacred to Neptune), which were lowered in the case of eggs or turned in the case of dolphins. Later the dolphins became a fountain, spouting water into the basin below. The *euripus* also contained a colossal statue of Cybele riding on a lion, altars, statues on columns (including several of Victory), and small shrines and pavilions. The turning posts, situated at each end of the *euripus,* consisted of three tall cones on a semicircular plinth; below the plinth at one end was the ancient shrine of Consus, an agricultural deity. Standing within the arena at the semicircular end of the circus was the temple of Murcia (Venus) within an enclosure, while a second set of eggs and another small pavilion stood at the other end near the starting gates.

The Circus Maximus was the only important circus in Rome. The Circus Flaminius, located in the southern part of the Campus Martius, was never built up as a monumental circus and was rapidly encroached upon by other buildings, leaving only a small piazza where obscure horse races (*ludi taurii,* in honor of the gods of the underworld) were held from time to time. Gaius (Caligula) and Nero, both fanatics of the circus, developed a circus in the imperial gardens on the Vatican Hill, chiefly so that they could themselves practice driving chariots, but it was probably not used for spectacles after Nero's death. The circus near the Sessorian palace on the southeast edge of the city was probably built by Caracalla and Elagabalus, two other emperors with a passion for chariot driving, but it too probably soon passed out of use and was then cut by the city wall.

Unlike the Greek games, where private individuals entered chariot teams in their own names (although often leaving the driving to one of their slaves), at Rome—from at least the first century B.C.—it appears that the races were in the hands of professional organizations, the circus factions (earlier we may assume that races were held after the Greek model). The factions were run as business ventures by private individuals (*domini factionum*) who hired out horses, charioteers, and all the necessary equipment to the sponsors of the games (*editores*). Each of the four factions (red, white, blue, and green) had its own stables and headquarters located in the southern part of the Campus Martius. Each faction employed, in addition to charioteers, a large number of specialized personnel concerned with the recruitment and training of drivers and horses and the maintenance of stables and horses, as well as numerous arena hands. There were *sparsores,* for instance, whose duty was to throw water on the heads of the horses to keep the dust out of their eyes and refresh them, and *hortatores,* who acted as cheerleaders or pacemakers, and who worked on foot or on horseback.

Factions actively competed with each other for the best charioteers, some of whom might race for three or four different factions during their careers. Presumably the contracts gave the charioteer a certain percentage of the winnings, and some became enormously wealthy, as the inscriptions on their tomb monuments make clear. One of the best known is Gaius Apuleius Diocles, a Spaniard by birth, whose racing career lasted for about twenty-four years, mostly during the reign of Hadrian; he entered a total of 4,257 races and won 1,462. The factions, which were present in the major cities of the empire, apparently obtained their racehorses mostly from private stud farms, of which several are attested in North Africa and in Spain. Other well-known breeding areas included Sicily, southern Italy, and Cappadocia (eastern Asia Minor).

In smaller towns, where the factions were not established, it was probably the *editor* or benefactor who recruited the teams from local stud farms, or races might have been provided by the horse breeders themselves who desired to train their animals. Many smaller towns could not afford monumental circuses but made do with level fields (which might revert to pasture or agriculture at other times of the year). A monumental circus was probably the single most expensive public building in Roman times and thus tended to be the last to be added to a city's amenities. By the fourth century A.D. the factions' monopoly of the provision of teams in the major cities had passed to the emperors, who wished to control the political benefits that providing the races carried. Thus, direct management of the factions was removed from the hands of businessmen and given to what Alan Cameron (1976) calls player managers (*factionarii*), normally the senior charioteers in each faction. Horses were largely provided from the imperial stables.

Almost everyone who attended the races supported a particular color, emperors included. They also followed the careers of various charioteers and horses (whose names were well known) in enormous detail. Passions ran high; curse tablets were frequently inscribed and buried in order to bring about the downfall of a rival. By the mid fourth century circus races at Rome were held during sixty-six days of the year, and there were normally at least twenty-four races each day. Only at circuses could women sit next to men, and no sector of the population was excluded. Senators and knights (*equites*) were given their own seats at least by the time of the early empire. Under the stands could be found shops of many kinds and public latrines. Because these were great public events, political demonstrations often erupted.

THEATERS AND THEATRICAL PERFORMANCES

By far the largest number of *ludi* took place in the theaters (101 days by the mid fourth century A.D.), doubtless because they were cheaper to stage than chariot races, fights, or hunts. Although the *ludi scaenici* are attested as early as 364 B.C., Rome received its first permanent theater relatively late due to the reluctance of the senate to permit the people to be seated at public gatherings, on the pretext that it would be injurious to the public character. Before that time dramatic performances were given in temporary theaters or on temple steps.

Rome eventually possessed three permanent stone theaters, all in the southern part of the Campus Martius. The first, that of Pompey, dedicated in 55 B.C. with elaborate games, was justified as "a temple of Venus under which we have set stone seats." In fact, the theater was more important architecturally than its temple. It was part of a large dynastic complex of buildings intended by Pompey to restore his political fortunes; it included a large portico with a garden (the first public park in Rome), located behind the stage and adorned by statues representing the nations he had conquered or depicting subjects linked with the world of the theater. (Vitruvius, in his ten books *On Architecture,* had prescribed a portico to protect spectators in the event of rain.) More extensive ruins have survived of the Theater of Marcellus next to the temple of Apollo. It was built by Augustus, who dedicated the theater in 13/11 B.C. to Marcellus, his nephew and son-in-law who had died in 23. The semicircular cut-stone facade, which buttressed the seating tiers, is well preserved to the top of the second story, preserving two arcades, the lower decorated with Doric and the upper with Ionic half-columns. This design was influenced by the late republican sanctuaries in Italy and would in turn influence other entertainment buildings, including the Colosseum. A third example, the Theater of Balbus, is also Augustan (13 B.C.), having been built from African booty acquired by Lucius Cornelius Balbus, a Spaniard. The seating capacities of these three theaters ranged from about 7,000 to 17,000.

However, a clearer impression of Roman theaters may be obtained by studying the provincial theaters at Lepcis Magna and Sabratha in Tripolitania, Arausio (Orange) in Gallia Narbonensis (Provence), and Aspendos in Pamphylia (southern Turkey). They show that Roman theaters differed considerably from Greek: a low and deep stage was dominated by the *scaenae frons,* a massive backdrop comprising a stone wall that protruded and retreated in many rectangular and curvilinear shapes, the whole clothed with a three-story columnar screen. Statues were placed between the columns, while the front of the low stage was often decorated with reliefs. Statuary, altars, and inscriptions were placed at many other points. The semicircular seating area (*cavea*) was joined to the stage building to create a fully enclosed and unified building, over which there was a wooden roof and an awning. The Roman orchestra was a semicircle, not a full circle as in the Greek theaters, and was used for the seats of dignitaries, which were carried in; the action was restricted to the stage alone. Roman theaters made use of a natural hill slope for the seating if one existed (as in Arausio), but more frequently were built on vaulted substructures. An interesting detail is the use of bronze vessels (recommended by Vitruvius) among the seats to improve the acoustics.

Performances in theaters came to cater more and more to the public taste—and to the lowest common denominator at that—in order to ensure a good-sized audience. Although high-quality plays by such writers as Plautus and Terence, often based on Greek models, were produced, particularly during the second century B.C., the audience was usually impatient and easily bored, and consequently mime and pantomime soon took over as the most popular forms of theatrical entertainment. Mime plays could be blasphemous, immoral, and obscene, and only here (and, rarely, in pantomimes) could female parts be played by females. They were much attacked for their obscenity and blasphemy by Christians (starting with Tertullian). The subject of the mimes was the everyday life of the common man, particularly sudden changes in material fortune and what might be called bedroom farce. They were accompanied by music and songs. Mimes, like the Atellan farces (named after the village of Atella, north of Neapolis [Naples]), often included allusions to current events and imperial goings-on. Actors did not wear masks but made heavy use of facial expressions.

Pantomime was more sophisticated, and actors were generally called upon to change masks for each of the multiple characters they portrayed. These performances resembled ballet dances in which performers combined dancing and acting skills with expressive movements of their hands and heads, all accompanied by music and singing by others. They usually acted out Greek myths. Pantomime achieved great popularity under Augustus and continued to be important in the late empire, particularly in the East. Lucian commented favorably on pantomime in *On Dancing* (*Peri Orcheseos*) (see Kokolakis, 1959), although others were more critical. Training schools are known to have existed.

In general, actors, like charioteers, were not considered respectable, most being slaves or freedmen; however, there were important exceptions, such as Quintus Roscius Gallus, a friend of Cicero. Any Roman citizen who appeared on the stage was stigmatized, and actors were banished at various periods. Successful actors could become very wealthy and some developed close links with emperors and their families (Mnester with Gaius and Messalina), although these friendships could not protect them from harm if they caused displeasure, particularly if they satirized emperors. A few emperors, of whom Gaius and Nero are the most famous, appeared on the stage as actors and singers, and Nero used professional claqueurs from Alexandria. Political disturbances, due particularly to the theater factions that supported rival actors, were much more common in the theater than in other entertainments.

AMPHITHEATERS AND GLADIATORIAL GAMES

Gladiatorial games (*munera*) had a completely different origin from the *ludi*. At first, beginning in 264 B.C., they were held in connection with aristocratic funerals. Only later were they held without a funerary pretext, but they were almost never incorporated into the *ludi* in honor of various gods; consequently, they occurred less frequently than theater and circus performances. The amphitheater was the building form specifically developed to house gladiatorial fights, but, like the theater, the amphitheater arrived late in the city of Rome. Since the Greeks developed no sport resembling gladiatorial games, they naturally had not devised a building type for the Romans to copy. It was evidently in Campania, where some famous gladiatorial schools were located, that this particular building type was developed. Oval in shape, with seats around the full circumference, it was banked steeply so that even spectators in the topmost tiers would have a good chance of seeing the details of the fighting. Early amphitheaters, such as the well-preserved example at Pompeii (*ca.* 80 B.C.), made extensive use of earth banks for the seating, and this design was followed by later provincial amphitheaters when possible. The Pompeii amphitheater is important because it shows how the early amphitheaters lacked substructures below the arena, and contained only a few passages below the seating; access to the upper seats was by way of staircases attached to the outside facade. There is ample evidence that there was an awning over the seating (which can also be seen in a well-known wall painting, illustrated in Rainer Graefe's *Vela erunt* [1979]).

In Rome the first permanent amphitheater dates to the reign of Octavian just before he took the title Augustus (29 B.C.); it lay in the southern part of the Campus Martius, not far from the three theaters and close to the Tiber. Previously, gladiatorial fights had been staged in the Forum Romanum, the Circus Maximus, the Forum Boarium, or the Saepta Julia (located in the Campus Martius). Nero then built (A.D. 57) a wooden amphitheater, which in turn was superseded by the massive Flavian Amphitheater, better known today as the Colosseum. This was begun by Vespasian on the site of the artificial lake of Nero's palace, the land of which Vespasian and subsequent emperors returned to the people. This four-story structure was dedicated with elaborate ceremonies in 80 by Titus, although it was only completed under Domitian when subterranean galleries were built below the arena. The arena was 94 yards (86 m) long and 59 yards (54 m) wide; the overall dimensions of the Colosseum were 206 yards (188 m) by 171 yards (156 m).

The Colosseum is a most sophisticated structure. The stages of its construction were arranged so that several different parts could be worked on simultaneously, and the materials used at the various levels were carefully graded. It was designed specifically to allow spectators (capacity was about 50,000) to reach their seats and to exit as efficiently as possible and to permit gladiators and animals to enter into the arena as expeditiously and safely as possible at just the right moment. Thus below the wooden arena floor was built a two-story substructure that contained ramps, cages, and pulley-drawn elevators from which animals could emerge through trapdoors into the arena. The massive arcaded facade, which stood about 164 feet (50 m) in height and which was decorated in the traditional classical orders, consisted of a double ring that buttressed the steeply rising tiers inside. Seven-

ty-six numbered entrances led spectators via a series of tunnels, ramps, and stairs to their assigned sections. Access to the various sections was carefully planned so that the social classes remained segregated even while entering. The seating tiers themselves were organized hierarchically with senators followed by knights at the front, other groups in the middle tiers, and women in the wooden section at the top. Others stood on the roof. The emperor or the games-giver (the *editor* or *munerarius*) had his own box; it faced the box of the city prefect. Elaborate stage settings, with trees, rocks, life-size models of ships and natural features, and scaffolds were sometimes brought in to heighten a spectacle's realism. The Colosseum exerted a strong influence on the building of monumental amphitheaters throughout the empire, as did the Circus Maximus on other circuses.

Our knowledge of the organization of the gladiatorial games has been greatly enhanced by a recent study by Patrizia Sabbatini Tumolesi (1981) of advertisements (*edicta*) painted on the walls of buildings at Pompeii. Gladiatorial and other games were often required as part of a magistrate's responsibility, although they might also be given by nonmagistrates in hopes of furthering their political ambitions. The games-giver was often personally involved with the preparations, making use of trainers (*lanistae*) as intermediaries, and being responsible for pairing each set of gladiators. In this latter he would try to match the combatants as evenly as possible. Announcements of upcoming games, which usually acclaimed the games-giver, gave the reason for holding a game, the name of the games-giver, the number of gladiatorial pairs to fight, the location, date, and number of days devoted to the show, and special features such as awnings or the distribution of tokens redeemable for gifts or prizes. The program itself might also be posted, as occurred at Pompeii, and it is likely that programs, made of papyrus, were sold to the public during the games.

The fight was preceded by a parade of gladiators and by a banquet for the fighters and the condemned men who had been sentenced to die in the arena. The banquet was held on the evening before the games, and the public could attend. A portrayal of such a banquet is found on a famous mosaic from Thysdrus (El Djem, in Tunisia).

The shows, normally held in the spring or early summer, were composed of several different elements. In Rome gladiatorial fights might be spread over several days, followed by a day of animal hunts and combats (*venationes*); or the hunts might occupy the mornings, followed by a midday pause or special midday show, and then gladiatorial pairs in the afternoons. By the end of the first century A.D. animal hunts were regularly joined with gladiatorial fights in the same show. The midday show might feature clowns or other comic turns, the distribution of presents, or public executions of condemned men. The pre-show feature was a procession (modeled on the circus procession) of the participants—including the condemned men in vehicles—who followed the parading of the images of gods.

Gladiatorial contests consisted of hand-to-hand combats. In Rome there were normally no more than 120 such pairs fighting in any one *munus*. Outside Rome from twenty to fifty such pairs might fight in one set of games and five to ten pairs on any one day. There were several different types of gladiators, distinguished by their costumes and weapons, and gladiators with complementary techniques and weapons would usually be paired. During arena combats two judges (*summa rudis* and *secunda rudis*) wielded long sticks to separate the fighters if need be, and an orchestra of musicians played trumpets, horns, and a water organ to dramatize the spectacle. A herald and bearers of placards communicated messages from the games-giver to the spectators, while attendants raked the bloodied sand and carried away the dead or wounded in barrows or on stretchers. One of these wore the mask of Charon; others wore masks of Mercury and held red-hot metal staffs (*caducei*) to ascertain whether those condemned to die were in fact dead. Other employees were responsible for preparing the machinery and props used as scenery and equipment.

Before the fight started, the games-giver would inspect the weapons; rods, whips, and red-hot plates were prepared to be used on gladiators who did not fight wholeheartedly. After a warming-up period, he would then give the signal for the fight to begin. (There is no evidence, incidentally, that the combatants normally saluted the president with "Hail, Caesar, those about to die salute you.") There were breaks in the course of the fight during which the fighters might be treated by their attendants. Gladiators fought until one of them raised a finger (*ad digitum*) as an admission of defeat and request for *missio,* permission to depart alive— or until one or both fell dead. (Occasionally fights were staged that did not allow the opponents to surrender.) When a gladiator surrendered, he threw his weapon to the ground or adopted a pose of submission, and the judge then had to ensure that the opponent did not strike. The decision of life or death was taken by the games-giver, but in this matter he normally followed the wishes of the crowd; thumbs down (*pollice verso*) meant they were against *missio*. The decision could also be left to the victorious gladiator.

It would appear that the duel itself—the skill that individual fighters displayed as swordsmen or fencers—was not what entertained the public. Rather, the spectators appeared more interested in the outcome, specifically the fate of the loser and how he would accept the death sentence. Representations of this scene show him acquiescing passively in his fate. The victor then received his palm and crown and prize money, and circled the arena to receive the ovation of the crowd.

Gladiators were normally slaves, but the arena also provided a means for getting rid of unwanted social elements. Prisons for long-term detention of criminals did not exist in the Roman world, and those guilty of capital crimes were often sentenced to be sold to a gladiatorial school or to die in the arena within a specified period of time. Thus criminals, informers, and prisoners of war provided a steady source of manpower for the games. But they should not be confused with the group of skilled gladiators who fought with weapons, who earned considerable fortunes, and who were under no life sentence. Indeed, most gladiatorial contests did not end in the death of one or the other, and gladiators who were popular or who had put up a good fight were frequently spared. Trained gladiators did not normally fight more than about twice a year, and it was a very successful gladiator who completed a career of fifty fights before he retired.

Gladiators lived in barracks in small cells; their living conditions were poor. Rome possessed four gladiatorial schools, of which the Ludus Magnus, next to the Colosseum, has been largely excavated. The excavations show that the cells opened off a rectangular portico; a small training arena within the portico was designed like a miniature amphitheater, with seating around. Each gladiatorial school specialized in different methods of combat. No privately owned schools were permitted in Rome after the Julio-Claudian period (ca. A.D. 68), the emperor retaining a monopoly. The gladiatorial support organization in Rome included a hospital, an armory, a building for stripping the weapons off dead gladiators, another for sharpening weapons, and another for housing stage machinery, as well as a camp for the

sailors who operated the awnings that could be drawn over the Colosseum.

ANIMAL HUNTS

An even more extensive support organization was required for the animal hunts (*venationes*). During the period of the republic, rare animals were usually brought to Rome purely for display, but beginning with the massive shows staged by Pompey and Caesar in the middle of the first century B.C., animals were made to fight each other or humans for the enjoyment of the crowd. To cater to this taste there developed in provincial areas, where animals lived in the wild, a sophisticated network of agents, trained hunters, land transporters, and shippers. Others were responsible for the welfare of the animals while in transit or in holding camps prior to the day of their exhibition. The practical difficulties involved in bringing these beasts to Rome (the shipments included both aggressive animals such as lions, tigers, leopards, panthers, bulls, bears, elephants, and hunting dogs, and animals used as prey, such as gazelles, deer, ostriches, and goats) are well illustrated in the letters of Quintus Aurelius Symmachus, a statesman of the late fourth century A.D.; some animals died en route or were so weak that when they finally arrived in the arena they could not fight. (Starvation to make the animals more aggressive was not unknown.) The best visual documentation of the support organization, capture, and transport of animals to Rome is found on the Great Hunt mosaic from the villa at Piazza Armerina, in Sicily, which depicts vivid scenes of the capture and transport of animals. From this and other hunt mosaics it can be seen that hunters, setting up nets in advance, would sweep across the countryside on horse or on foot, driving scores of animals before them, and luring them into cages that were ready to transport them live to wherever they were needed.

Once in the arenas, animals were pitted against troupes of trained hunters, several of which are known from North African mosaics, or against each other (a frequent pairing was a bull and a bear); alternatively, animals were set loose on exposed and un-armed criminals who were tied to a stake and then wheeled out for mauling. More rarely, animals were used to perform circus tricks (a troupe of bears is known to have performed at Carthage). The different types of perfor-mances with animals are well illustrated on a mosaic from the villa at Zliten (near Lepcis Magna). A mosaic from Sicca Veneria (El Kef) in Tunisia shows hunters leading hounds into an arena to attack scores of os-triches and gazelles, none of them able to fight back. Another from Smirat, Tunisia (located between El Djem and Sousse), shows a troupe of hunters, each one fighting a leopard; a long inscription in the center records the generosity of one Magerius, who was pressured by the crowd to pick up the cost of the games.

CONCLUSION

Of the major types of entertainment in Rome, it is easiest to understand the attrac-tions for Romans of chariot racing, a sport that is intrinsically suspenseful and exciting, made more so by the partisanship of support-ers of different factions and by the oppor-tunities for betting. That was the sport, too, against which Christian writers had the least vehement objection. Christian condemna-tion of the theater, with its performances featuring moral turpitude and depravity, not to mention nudity and sexual license, was stronger. From today's vantage point, it is the cruelty and undisguised killings in the arenas of both humans and animals that are most difficult to comprehend. They cannot simply be regarded as the result of escapism, satisfying the need to take one's mind off the misery and squalor of daily life. Keith Hop-kins (1983) and Georges Ville (1981) have recently tried to understand this phenome-non. With regard to the great pleasure the Romans took in watching the slaughter of men and animals, Hopkins draws attention to the fact that Rome was a warrior state, where decimation of an army unit—the planned one-in-ten thinning of ranks—was an accepted practice, and sees the arenas as "artificial battlefields set up in their towns in memory of their warrior traditions." Brutal-ity was built into Roman culture, and the popularity of these shows was a "by-product of war, discipline, and death." Furthermore, spectacular punishments in the arena not only were a way of dealing with criminals but also helped reinforce law and order. Hop-kins also suggests that the social psychology of the crowd "helped relieve the individual of responsibility," and that, psychologically, some spectators could identify "more read-ily with the victory of the aggressor than with the sufferings of the vanquished." The games provided a psychic and political safety valve for the population, for "what-ever happened in the arena the spectators were always on the winning side."

Contemporary objections to the games were infrequent, and those that were raised seem to miss the main point. Less substan-tial objections, made by members of the upper classes, focused on the pointlessness or excessive cost of such shows; or they con-sidered the games to be boring and monoto-nous (but not enough to stop them from attending). However, the upper classes also argued that these shows were good for the masses. Occasionally we do find written ob-jections to the inhumanity of the *munus*. Cicero (*Tusculan Disputations* 2.17.41) dis-played some pity for the gladiator if he was innocent, but generally he regarded the arena as good discipline. Seneca the Younger (*Letters* 1.7.3–5; 18.103.2; 15.95. 33) was more concerned about the spectator who might be corrupted by watching. No one questioned the morality of the games. On the contrary, there are many indications of acceptance of and even enthusiasm for the institution by the upper classes. As Ville (1981) points out, it was "the aristocracy which organized and financed these *munera,* who presided and who exercised the right of life and death, who had control of the best seats and who made of the amphitheater a microcosm of the Roman city in its hierarchical arrangements" (p. 456). The state and the emperor sanctioned the games.

There must nevertheless have been some ambivalent feelings felt by the people. They cannot have been unmoved as they watched fellow citizens being killed before their eyes, and at least one instance of a general revulsion is recorded. During the elaborate games staged by Pompey, the elephants, which were being mercilessly hunted down and slaughtered, cried out in pain, at which point the crowd, bursting into tears, rose in a body and invoked curses on the head of Pompey. Yet elephants were perhaps a special case, engendering more sympathy than most animals or even than most humans. The enormous numbers of animals slaughtered at the dedication of the Colosseum (5,000 in 100 days) or at Trajan's games (10,000, as well as 10,000 gladiators) have not registered a single negative comment in our sources. There were objections made to the training of lions to eat humans. (It was apparently all right for animals to kill defenseless humans, but to eat human flesh transgressed the bounds of decency.)

In general, the ambivalence that some of these sights probably prompted was satisfied by a public attitude that viewed the performers—the fighters—as impure, rather than the institution itself. Feelings of commiseration for the cruel lot of the gladiators

intervened only at a later date, after the official establishment of Christianity. But Christianity too was more concerned with the effect of watching such spectacles upon the soul of the spectator, although it also made it unthinkable to take pleasure in watching the suffering of another human being, and this ultimately brought about the termination of the games. Looked at as a whole, the Roman games are a microcosm of Roman society. They were used as a political forum, in the absence of any more democratic institutions, where the people could make their views known on a wide variety of topics, and they were used by the emperor and the upper classes as an instrument of control. They reflect the strongly hierarchical nature of that society, and the study of them forms an indispensable part of our effort to understand that society.

BIBLIOGRAPHY

GENERAL

John P. V. D. Balsdon, *Life and Leisure in Ancient Rome,* 2d ed. (1974); Monique Clavel-Lévêque, *L'Empire en jeux: Espace symbolique et pratique sociale dans le monde romain* (1984); Ludwig Friedländer, *Darstellung aus der Sittengeschichte Roms,* 7th ed., L. A. Magnus *et al.,* trans., as *Roman Life and Manners Under the Early Empire,* vol. 2, 4 (1908–1913); Howard H. Scullard, *Festivals and Ceremonies of the Roman Republic* (1981); Paul Veyne, *Le pain et le cirque* (1976).

CIRCUSES AND CHARIOT RACING

Alan Cameron, *Porphyrius—The Charioteer* (1973), and *Circus Factions: Blues and Greens at Rome and Byzantium* (1976); John H. Humphrey, *Roman Circuses: Arenas for Chariot Racing* (1986); Elizabeth Rawson, "Chariot-Racing in the Roman Republic," in *Papers of the British School at Rome,* **49** (1981).

THEATERS AND THEATRICAL PERFORMANCES

Margarete Bieber, *The History of the Greek and Roman Theatre,* 2d rev. ed. (1961); John A. Hanson, *Roman Theater-Temples* (1959); Minos Kokolakis, *Pantomimus and the Treatise Peri Orcheseos (De saltatione)* (1959).

AMPHITHEATERS, GLADIATORIAL
GAMES, AND ANIMAL HUNTS

J. K. Anderson, *Hunting in the Ancient World* (1985); Andrea Carandini, Andreina Ricci, and Mariette de Vos, *Filosofiana, The Villa of Piazza Armerina: The Image of a Roman Aristocrat at the Time of Constantine* (1982); Katherine M. D. Dunbabin, *The Mosaics of Roman North Africa: Studies in Iconography and Patronage* (1978); Rainer Graefe, *Vela erunt: Die Zeltdächer der römischen Theater and ähnlicher Anlagen* (1979); Keith Hopkins, "Murderous Games," in *Death and Renewal* (1983); George Jennison, *Animals for Show and Pleasure in Ancient Rome* (1937); Louis Robert, *Les gladiateurs dans l'Orient grec* (1940); Patrizia Sabbatini Tumolesi, *Gladiatorum paria* (1981); Jocelyn M. C. Toynbee, *Animals in Roman Life and Art* (1973); Georges Ville, "Les jeux de gladiateurs dans l'empire chrétien," in *Mélanges de l'École française de Rome* **72** (1960), and *La gladiature en Occident, des origines à la mort de Domitien* (1981).

Greek Associations, Symposia, and Clubs

NICHOLAS R. E. FISHER

INTRODUCTION

This essay on Greek society and the companion essay ROMAN ASSOCIATIONS, DINNER PARTIES, AND CLUBS seek to illustrate and illuminate important aspects of the prevailing patterns of social life in ancient times, by concentrating on two related institutions: the symposium, or drinking/dinner party, and the voluntary association or club. Both were central to life in the Greek city-states and the Greek cities of the Hellenistic world, and reveal much of what was most distinctive about ancient Greek social forms and relations.

In most, if not all, societies, social relationships of all sorts tend to be sanctified and solidified by a shared taking of food and drink; but in few societies have celebrations of shared eating and drinking been so highly valued, so idealized and stylized, so widely practiced at many levels, and so significantly used as occasions for philosophical, political, and moral discussions and their reflections in poetic and prose literature. The list of major Greek authors who wrote for or about symposia is long and impressive, and

includes almost all the lyric and elegiac poets and the epigrammatists, philosophers like Plato, Xenophon, and Aristotle, satirists like Lucian, and, at greatest length, scholarly belletrists like Plutarch and Athenaeus. Athenaeus, a Greek Sophist from Naucratis in Egypt, wrote in the early third century A.D. *The Learned Banquet* (*Deipnosophistai*), an account (of which we have a partially abbreviated version, in fifteen books) of an alleged learned symposium of Greek and Roman scholars. This work discusses all aspects of the Greek symposium as a central feature of cultivated life, following, in the sequence of topics discussed, the usual order of a real symposium, and it includes a vast array of lengthy quotations from earlier poets, historians, philosophers, and other writers on a wide range of sympotic customs and developments. Athenaeus will be cited more than any other author in what follows, but recognition of the symposium's importance in Greek life and evidence for its development are to be found throughout our evidence for Greek society.

The part played in Greek cities by a wide variety of voluntary associations, based on ties of shared cult, political interests, occupation, neighborhood, and social needs and pleasures (usually a combination of more than one of these) was very great and increased steadily; it is illuminated in part by literary evidence, but much more by the innumerable meticulous records of these associations inscribed on stone. Different types of associations found members among different levels of ancient societies and could at different times raise varied political problems. As the cities of archaic and classical Greece oscillated between forms of oligarchy, tyranny, and democracy, political dangers could be perceived to come from the *hetaireiai,* essentially small groups of activists seeking to win advantages or power for themselves, and adopting oligarchic more often than democratic stances.

In this account greatest attention has to be paid to the institutions and behavior of the leisured classes at all times: the people of wealth and power, the setters of cultural and literary fashions and styles, and those with whom our sources are most concerned; but the involvement of more ordinary people in cult groups and clubs, and in dinner parties, is not ignored. These institutions are, like ancient societies in general, very heavily male-dominated, but the types and degrees of participation in them by women are also considered. In this respect a significant difference can be found between the cultivated societies of Greece and of Rome.

ARCHAIC GREECE

The Dark Age and Homer: Social Groups and Feasts

The nature of social organizations and gatherings in the Greek Dark Age (1100–800 B.C.) during the period of the rise of the Greek city-states (poleis) is extremely obscure and controversial; however, three

points of importance to this study can be firmly made. First, social organization was usually complex, as groups of different types flourished inside these growing communities; second, most, if not all, of these groups defined themselves, at least in part, in cult terms, reinforcing their identities through shared sacrifices to particular deities; and third, such gatherings regularly involved shared feasting on the sacrificed meats and shared drinking of wine.

As the poleis developed, membership in these communities was most commonly organized on the basis of "tribes" (*phylai*), groups that claimed to be descent groups; often there is also evidence for subdivisions of the tribes called phratries (*phratrai* or *phratriai,* literally "brotherhoods," from the basic Indo-European term [*phrater*] for brother). The idea of such divisions of a community is certainly ancient; the standard term for a natural brother in Greek has become *adelphos,* not *phrater,* and among the various, scattered Dorian poleis the same three tribal names recur with regularity, whereas the Ionian cities usually had four tribes, and the same names are used, although with less regularity. But the composition of such bodies is most unlikely to have remained undisturbed through the confused periods of migrations and resettlements of the Geometric period, and it is noticeable how small a part is played by tribes and phratries in the Homeric poems, and how absent they are from those parts of Greece that remained loosely organized as "tribal states" (*ethne*) and did not develop as poleis. As each polis developed, pseudokinship groupings re-formed, with their cults, festivals, and initiation rituals, probably as part of a process whereby landowning aristocrats attempted to organize their followers and arouse loyalty among them, and the peasants sought protection and some sense of reciprocal community feelings. These groups were accepted as the constituent units of the polis community as a whole, regulating polis membership through their incorporation procedures.

These were far from the only active social groups, however, since scattered later sources preserve the memory of a great many other types of associations, based on localities, cults, supposed kinship bonds, or shared occupations or activities; in particular the younger aristocrats seem to have formed bands for the purposes of hunting, fighting, or piracy. Whether such bands had a connection with the development of phratries and further subdivisions of phratries remains at present an open question.

The festival and the feast were the common activities central to all these groups, and featured communal eating and wine drinking. Some feastings also appear to have involved the whole community, often on an egalitarian basis, and in connection with the celebration or encouragement of crop production. But most groups were variously exclusive, with a defined membership; they were normally also exclusively masculine or feminine, the majority no doubt restricted to males. Many of these seem to have involved complex rituals of initiation of boys and, to a lesser extent, of girls into adulthood and their respective roles in society; these rituals, with characteristic three-stage patterns of separation, marginality, and incorporation, seem likely to have been the primary setting for the socially approved forms of homosexual relationships between boys (those passing through the initiatory process), and young men (those who have recently passed out of it).

The Homeric poems form the most substantial body of evidence for the social organizations and social values of the Dark Age, although it is highly disputable whether they represent the conditions exclusively of any single period. For our purposes, however, they do well illustrate a number of features of early archaic social life, and in particular the central role of feasting. Many different types of feast are recognized in the epics; when the disguised Athena comments in the *Odyssey* (1.225–226) on the grossly insulting manner in which the suitors are feasting, ignoring their supposed host Telemachos and his new guest, she asks him, "What feast, what gathering is this? What is your concern with it?/A banquet, or a wedding? It is certainly no communal meal [*eranos*]." The point here is that Athena, even in her pretended ignorance of the situation, can see that something abnormal is going on. There are many types of social occasions that demand a formal shared meal, both those given by a single host and the *eranos,* a meal to which all contributors bring equal contributions; but this disorderly group neither allows the expected host, Telemachos, to command authority nor observes the appropriate behavior when a strange guest arrives.

Naturally, the sort of feasts most often portrayed in the *Iliad* and the *Odyssey* are those of the king for his companions and guests in the royal halls (or in the great tents, when on campaign at Troy). Their essence, and their social value, are well illustrated by the appropriate words of Odysseus to his model host, King Alkinoös of the Phaeacians (*Odyssey* 9.5–10):

> No social event, I do think, has more
>   shared pleasure [*charis*]
> than when good cheer [*euphrosyne*] has a
>   hold on all the people,
> and the banqueters in the halls are
>   listening to the bard,
> sitting all in order, and at their sides the
>   tables are full
> of bread and meats, and drawing the
>   strong wine from the mixing bowl
> the wine-pourer carries it around and
>   pours it in the cups.

The feasters sit on chairs or benches and eat quantities of meats, cooked on spits, and bread; wine is served with the food, but wine drinking may continue afterward, as may the musical entertainments, dancers, acrobats, choral singers, or the recitations of a bard. These are essentially all-male occasions, although not as exclusively as the later Greek symposia. Queens like Arete among the Phaeacians and Helen at Sparta may be somewhere on the scene, or assist in the pouring of libations and the preparation of the wine; Penelope may make dramatic entrances at Ithacan feasts; but they do not seem to participate fully in the eating and drinking.

Banquets may be given by kings and their accompanying nobles (*aristoi*) and companions (*hetairoi*) to each other in turn, as among the Phaeacians (*Odyssey* 8.37 ff.), or as Telemachos is imagined as doing by his dead grandmother (11.185–187), or as Telemachos himself suggests the suitors do instead of infesting his house (2.139–140). Feasts may also be offered, and in some sense funded, by the community as a whole for the honor of the kings and nobles, the best fighters and bulwark of the community (*Iliad* 4.257 ff.; 4.343 ff.; 17.248 ff.; and the most famous case, of the special feasting privileges given to Sarpedon and Glaukos in Lykia, 12.310 ff.). But the chief king of the community must, of course, himself show exceptional generosity in giving feasts and gifts to his local aristocrats, to his personal band of fighting *hetairoi,* to guests, and at times to the people as a whole (*Iliad* 9.68 ff.; *Odyssey* 4.5 ff.). Reciprocal feastings of these various types form an essential part of the economic and social relations between kings, nobles, and people that are presupposed in the poems.

The essential values of the shared feast are the containment of undue competition or violence and the sharing of pleasures; the two Greek terms *charis* and *euphrosyne,* found together repeatedly in praises of the symposium for centuries to come, convey both the sense of reciprocal good will, fun, and equality of the single feast of the moment and also the idea of a more permanent reciprocity, the promise of future feasts where guests will become hosts, and of the uniting bonds of friendship and loyalty, regularly renewed. The proper giving of hospitality is in fact the central moral theme of the *Odyssey;* it connects on the one hand the incessantly unreciprocal and humiliating feasting of the suitors at the expense of the house of Odysseus with the grossly unhospitable behavior of the Cyclops, and on the other hand the examples of proper feasting in Pylos, Sparta, and the land of the Phaeacians with the restoration of order and harmony in Ithaca. In the *Iliad,* too, issues of the sharing of meals, of when and with whom to eat, can be moments of the greatest moral significance and emotional tension, the epitome being the final shared meal of Achilles and Priam in Achilles' tent (*Iliad* 24).

Archaic Aristocracies: The Symposium

The full forms and rituals of the classic Greek symposium developed, it seems, among groups of aristocratic *hetairoi* (perhaps to be seen as the descendants of the Homeric and earlier warrior bands) toward the end of the seventh century B.C. or earlier. The symposium quickly established itself as one of the major defining elements in Greek social life (as did the practice of naked exercising and athletics in the gymnasium), and it will now be briefly described.

One central feature, like many innovations in Greek culture at this period (*ca.* 750 B.C.), came from the Near East: the practice of reclining on couches. (The prophet Amos, in the Old Testament, Amos 6:4, warns against those who recline at banquets among the decadent Samarians in Palestine, and Athenaeus, 428b and 459–460, shows consciousness of the change in Greek life.)

In due course it became a sign of a conservative backwater (as noted in Athenaeus, 143e) if men still sat at formal dinner or drinking parties, private or public, as they apparently did in Crete. Reclining figures at banquets appear first on Corinthian vases about 600 B.C., then regularly on Attic vases, paintings, and reliefs, and at around the same time in the work of the lyric poets, first perhaps in the lines of the Spartan poet Alcman ("Seven couches and as many tables laden with poppy-seed rolls, and linseed and sesame, and honey-cakes among the cups"; Page, *Poetae Melici Graeci* frag. 19). The main features of the symposium are clearly found in the fragmentary remains of Alcaeus' poems (Lobel and Page, *Poetarum Lesbiorum Fragmenta*) on conviviality and love: the word *symposium* for drinking together (frag. 368); reclining, with cushions around the head, by the fire with the rain outside (frag. 338); the mixing of the wine (frag. 346); the drinking to excess, and to command (frag. 332); the moralizing belief that wine shows the nature of a man (frag. 333); and so on.

But the single text from the archaic period (*ca.* 750–*ca.* 480) that best shows the main features of the aristocratic symposium and the moral seriousness and its social importance is the elegiac poem on the subject of the "good symposium" by Xenophanes of Colophon in Asia Minor (*ca.* 570–478), the traveling philosopher and moralist. It will serve well as the starting point for the description (from Athenaeus, 462c):

Now the floor is made clean, so are the
    hands of all and the cups; a slave
    sets round the woven garlands,
another hands around sweet-smelling
    myrrh in a saucer; a mixing bowl
    [*krater*] stands full of good cheer
    [*euphrosyne*].
Another wine is prepared, which claims it
    will never let us down, soft-tasting in
    the jars, with a bouquet of flowers.

In the middle of the room frankincense
    sends out holy scent, and there is
    cold water, sweet and pure.
The brown loaves lie ready, and the
    honorable table heavy laden with
    cheese and thick honey.
The altar in the center is covered all
    around with flowers, song and
    festivity [*thalie*] fill all the hall.
First it is right that the men of good
    cheer sing a hymn to the god with
    respectful tales and pure speech,
pouring libations and making prayers to
    have the power to do what is right
    (for that is what it is preferable to
    pray for,
not acts of insolence [*hybris*]); one should
    drink as much as one can hold and
    reach home without an attendant,
    unless very old.
One should praise that man who, while
    drinking, expounds brave deeds, so
    that men's memories and energies
    shall be for excellence,
not retailing the battles of the Titans or
    the Giants, nor of the Centaurs,
    inventions of our predecessors,
nor the violent civil wars [*stasis*], in which
    there is nothing good; men must
    always keep a good concern for the
    gods.

First, as an abundance of literary texts and visual evidence makes plain, the symposium is a characteristic activity of free adult males and, above all, of the wealthier or more aristocratic classes. To be permitted to join, as a reclining member, is indeed one of the signs of manhood, regulated in different ways in different states. This is clearly assumed by Aristotle, who urged in his *Politics* (1336b20–24) that young men should not watch performances of comedy or iambic verses (which might be obscene or scurrilous) until "they reach the age at which they are permitted to participate in the reclining [at symposia] and getting drunk, by which time their education will have made them completely immune to the harm of such things." Among the Macedonians no one could recline at a banquet until he had speared a boar without the use of a hunting net, meaning he had killed in a hunt in the approved adult, nonadolescent manner; the custom emphasizes the connections between manhood, hunting, and communal banqueting. Freeborn boys might nonetheless be present at at least part of a symposium, as a major part of the educative and socializing process. In archaic societies, as in Lesbos, aristocratic young men served as wine pourers, as Sappho's brother did in the town hall at Mytilene; or they might sit decorously by their elders, as Autolykos the beautiful boy sat by his father, while the others reclined, at the symposium given by Autolykos' lover Kallias. (He also leaves just before the sex cabaret at the end, Xenophon tells us in *Symposium* 1.8 and 9.1.) Hence the elegiac "advice" poetry characteristic of the archaic age, much of it associated with the name of Theognis of Megara and itself designed to be recited at symposia, can often be directed to a young man imagined as sitting among the "good men" and learning proper behavior from them.

Respectable women did not attend the male symposium at all; the women present were those serving the enjoyment of the men in various ways. Hence, in classical Athens, Isaeus (*On the Estate of Pyrrhus* 3.14) can remind a jury that "married women do not go with their husbands to dinners, nor think it right to join in dinners with strangers present, especially chance guests"; for him, as for Apollodoros in his speech against Neaira (pseudo-Demosthenes, 59.33–34, 48), evidence that a woman participated in symposia, let alone the subsequent revels in the streets or promiscuous sex, suffices to prove her a courtesan (*hetaira*), not a wife. As a result of these rules, one often cannot be sure of the social status of many of the young men or boys seen on black- or red-

figure vases in sympotic scenes, whether innocently serving or being courted or groped; but the women in similar scenes, clothed or not, handling flutes or being manhandled, fall necessarily into the various categories of the disreputable.

This exclusion of respectable women from symposia had significant consequences for the design of Greek houses and the articulation of the distinctions between public and private, and male and female space. Alcaeus portrays a symposium in a Homeric-style great hall, surrounded by weapons on the wall, which he and his companions envisage using very soon (Lobel and Page, frag. 357; Campbell, frag. 140); thereafter (as the military role of the aristocrats had ceased to be paramount, and armor disappeared from urban life) many ordinary houses develop a standard pattern, with a rectangular room, usually near the front door, designated as the "men's room" (*andron*), while other more remote areas would be distinguished as the "women's area" (*gynaikonitis*). The *andron* would be the most highly decorated room, often with a stone or mosaic floor (to facilitate the clearing up of sympotic messes); it was often designed for a system of couches arranged around the walls, with the door off center; the place of honor was at the right of the door, and the last place, the host's, at the left. Couches would normally accommodate two (and a gate-crasher on occasion; Plato, *Symposium* 213c), and cushions made reclining (on the left elbow) more comfortable; individual tables held dishes of food, perfumes, and flowers. In smaller houses an *andron* might only have three couches, whence the term *triklinon* (and subsequently *triclinium* in Latin) for a dining room; larger rooms are widely attested, and the public dining rooms in town halls and sanctuaries, imitating this pattern, often had an eleven-couch arrangement. Thus the main dining room of the standard Greek house in the classical period was an off-limits area for the respectable women of the house when in use, and can be seen as separate both from the private world of the household and the fully public world outside.

Symposium means "drinking together"; the main eating (in contrast to the Homeric pattern) is disposed of quickly, then tables are cleared, floor, cups, and guests are washed, and the all-important mixing of the wine in the krater takes place. The Greeks preferred to drink their wine heavily diluted; it is uncertain whether this is because the combination of climate, soils, and techniques tended to produce heavy, sweet wines of variable quality that were thought to be improved by dilution, as also with various additives like resin, gypsum, or brine, or because they liked to drink so much at their parties, which were often held in hot weather. Typically, however, they made a moral issue of their practice, regarding abstinence as bizarre, and drinking unmixed wine as abnormal and characteristic of "barbarians" or of mythical creatures like the Centaurs; drinking too much unmixed wine, they seem to have believed, was likely to make one mad. At all events, the start of the symposium, Athenaeus reports (430–431), involved a decision on the measures to be mixed, normally a collective decision, binding on all the company: a mixture that, with compulsory toasts, was sure to lead to drunkenness, or measures for more moderate drinking. Symposia often elected a leader, not necessarily the host, who might be called "king" (*basileus*) or *symposiarchos,* and who might pass "laws" for the company (a discussion entitled *What Sort of Man the Symposiarch Must Be* is found in Plutarch, *Moralia* 620–622b); the parody of the language and the procedures of more serious political life is characteristic.

Wine drinking was considered an essential part of civilized Greek life, and played a compulsory role in most festivals and sacrifices. Greeks tended to define the hallmarks of ideal, civilized male behavior in contrast with opposing behavior of barbarians, animals, or, to a lesser extent, women; it is not surprising that in addition to excluding respectable women from symposia Greek men made some attempts to restrict or control female drinking in general. A very few Greek cities (Miletus, Marseilles, and South Italian cities) are said to have forbidden wine drinking to women altogether (Athenaeus, 429; 440–441), although one may doubt if the laws were very stringently enforced. But most states permitted it or even encouraged it at certain festivals; nonetheless a familiar double standard operated, as women were supposed to be more susceptible to drink-loving and drunkenness, and husbands were expected to keep a stern eye on their wives' habits, and the keys of the wine cupboards.

Returning to the symposium and Xenophanes' poem: the atmosphere at the start of the drinking proper seems to be a mixture of religious solemnity and anticipatory festivity; usually a libation of pure wine is poured to the Agathos Daimon (Good Spirit) at the end of the eating, then follows a triple libation to Zeus Olympios, the Heroes, and Zeus Soter (Savior), a personal prayer, and a paean sung to Apollo. Clearly, at least at the start, the communal drinking continues to be felt as a sacred act of communion. Yet another set of deities or moral concepts presides, in theory at least, over the subsequent hours of enjoyment: the Charites (Graces). *Charis* is a concept that combines the idea of reciprocal good or generous behavior (gifts, thanks, countergifts, services) with the sense of goodwill and the aura of charm or beauty that should accompany such acts of harmony and fellow feeling as shared feasting, dancing, or lovemaking. There were three personified Charites, Euphrosyne ("Good Cheer" or "Goodwill"), Thalia ("Abundance," "Feasting"), and Aglaia ("Adornment"); they (especially *euphrosyne*) and *cha-*

ris itself appear repeatedly in the many descriptions of the ideal symposium.

Good advice is often not taken; the Xenophanes poem shows the moral ambivalence of the symposium, poised between the opposed ideas of harmonious *charis,* and quarrels and hybris (insolence). The poet calls for moderate drinking, for entertainment that emphasizes through songs and poetry the good deeds of men, not, either in mythological or contemporary vein, battles, drunken conflicts (the Centaurs), opposition to the Olympian gods, or violent civil conflicts (*stasis*); and he calls for prayers for justice, not for hubris. Hubris is behavior designed seriously to insult or dishonor others, often expressed in violence, and often, naturally, aggravated by drink. Two other verse passages, quoted by Athenaeus (36b–d), schematically portray the stages of the normal symposium in ways that further bring out these contrasts. A fragment from an epic poem by Herodotus' uncle Panyasis assigns the first two (harmonious) drinking rounds of the symposium to the Graces, the Hours, Dionysos, and Aphrodite; thereafter if one stays and drinks on, there comes hubris and ruin (*ate*); Dionysos himself speaks, in a fragment of a fourth-century Attic comedy, of a series of mixing bowls: three good ones ("for *euphrones* men"), health, love and pleasure, and sleep; then, for those not sensible enough to go home, comes hubris, a shouting *komos* (drunken procession to a new party, or to serenade a beloved), black eyes, a legal summons, biliousness, madness, and the throwing of furniture.

Hubris and its attendant disasters may affect a symposium in two ways. The first arises naturally from the forms of enjoyment commonly favored by those whose desire for fun was scarcely satisfied by decorous recitations of moral poems and praises of good deeds. As suits such a competitive society, a variety of sympotic contests is attested in the archaic and later ages. Many still involve music, singing, and poetry, competitive improvisations of songs or verses on set themes, or quotations of existing poems or songs, such as those of Alcaeus, Theognis, Solon, or Anacreon, or the shorter anonymous roundels often called scolia (Athenaeus 694c ff.). Themes may be political, religious, moral, abusive, or erotic. Physical contests were perhaps even more popular, and they too tended to involve parodic, playful imitations of more serious feats performed in theaters, stadia, or gymnasiums: many forms of dancing (often doubtless buffoonish and/or erotic), balancing exploits, and, most famous, the game called cottabus (*kottabos*), said to have been invented in Sicily, as were many gastronomic and sympotic refinements, which involved flicking, with an elegant action, the dregs of wine from one's cup at a target (Athenaeus, 427d; 666d–668e). Such games could be played for a variety of appropriate prizes, such as delicacies, clothes, or the favors of attendant girls or boys. One might also call out as one threw the name of one's boy- or girlfriend: hence the dramatic twist when in 404 Theramenes flicked the dregs of his hemlock in bitter "love" for Critias, his former colleague among the Thirty Tyrants in Athens who had ordered his execution. This was the same Critias who seems to have written much about sympotic customs in his political works and his work on inventions, in which he ascribed cottabus to the Sicilians (Xenophon, *History of Greece* [*Hellenica*] 2.3.56). All such competitive games must on many occasions have led to insults and fights, going beyond the tolerable limits of *euphrosyne*—much as those limits will have varied among different groups.

So, even more frequently, must sexual rivalries at symposia have led to trouble. Dionysos and love combined easily, and both the archaic and classical sympotic texts and the innumerable illustrations on vases teem with heterosexual and homosexual desires and activities, even if it is often hard to decide which of the varied portrayals of positions and numbers of participants represented common realities and which artists' or patrons' fantasies. But a distinction must be insisted on. A *hetaira* (courtesan), the most independent of the various categories of disreputable women present at symposia, may indicate even by her name (the feminine of *hetairos*) some claim to be taken as a genuine "companion," able to give and receive some affection or love, and in some cases exercise some choice in whom she sleeps with. But male relationships between a "lover" in his twenties and a "beloved" in his teens, of the same status and class, clearly surpass those with *hetairai* in romanticism, intensity, and political and social significance. From at least the sixth century in Athens and elsewhere, the strict connections of such relationships with initiatory rituals into groups like the phratries slacken, and the contexts of the pursuit, gifts, advice, and consummation become above all the gymnasium by day and the symposium in the evening. With this shift the complex double standards of the optional relationship develop, whereby pursuit and romantic expressions by the lover are approved, but the beloved should not seem overly keen and should certainly avoid any "feminine" submissiveness. Both modes, however, would be likely enough to produce quarrels and violence at a symposium, and many references in the literature—especially lawcourt speeches—treat fighting by drunk young men over either *hetairai* or boys as normal and frequent, although the quarrels often ended up in court.

The symposium may develop, second, into a drunken procession through the streets, a *komos*, in search of new girls or boys, a fresh party, or just rowdy "fun"; the *komos* members would often take their mixing bowls, torches, garlands, and musical accompaniments along with them. This stage is perhaps even more likely to provoke fights and hubris, not only among revelers or rival *komos* bands but in the form of assaults on innocent passersby.

It would be difficult to overstate the importance of the symposium as a social form as it developed in the archaic age in Greek cities and continued for many centuries. In Greek art, nearly all the shapes of painted pottery were designed for the drinking party: mixing bowls, cups, wine amphorae, jugs, wine or water coolers, perfume holders. The pictures on the vases regularly show sympotic and *komos* scenes, or reflect the same themes of education, drinking, and the tension between *charis* and hubris that pervades archaic poetry. Funerary art, too, reflects this predominance: Greek aristocrats in the archaic period liked to be represented in death enjoying the pleasures of the symposium, accompanied by their male companions, or by their seated wives and children, and the custom spread to southern Italy and Etruria, as did so much of the pottery.

Clubs, "Hetaireiai," and Politics in Archaic Greece

A law of Solon's concerning Athens in the early sixth century lists a number of social groups and organizations, quoted by Gaius (47.22.4), and rules that their own internal regulations are to be considered binding unless they contradict the city's written laws. The groups listed are the *demos* (people, here probably meaning members of the village community), phratry members, hero-cult associates (*orgeones*), members of cult associations with a kinship basis (*genos*), members of a dining club (*syssitoi*), members of a burial association, members of a cult association (*thiasos*), and those who have joined together for the purpose of piracy or trade. More will be said about some of these associations later, but it is certainly noteworthy that all these different types are recognized by the law at this date, and that criteria for the formation of groups include kinship or pseudokinship (*genos,* probably phratry; and some *orgeones* groups and *thiasoi* were later, at least, constituent parts of the phratries), shared cult activities (all *orgeones* groups and all *thiasoi* whether kin or voluntary associations), shared social activities, and occupational cooperation.

While some of these groups must have involved many of the poorer members of the communities, and no doubt all of them solidified their bonds by cult sacrifices and shared meals (all perhaps beginning to imitate as best they could the sympotic styles of the aristocracy), it remains the upper classes, organized above all for social and political purposes in bands often called *hetaireiai,* whose activities can be glimpsed in our sources. Two examples, from Lesbos and Athens, will demonstrate the social tensions and political changes with which they were involved.

The combination of the fragments of Alcaeus' poetry and a few comments by later authors show that Mytilene, chief city of Lesbos, suffered considerable turmoil in the late seventh century; a detailed picture is irrecoverable, but some features of the struggles are revealing. We hear of a noble group claiming common ancestry (the Penthelidai), whose favorite method of demonstrating their power is said to have been "going around and beating people with clubs," presumably after a good symposium (Aristotle, *Politics* 1311b.23 ff.). Decades of civil disturbance followed, with alternating periods of oligarchic rule and unsuccessful tyrants, in all of which Alcaeus and his *hetairoi* participated with vigor and venom before one of his former colleagues, Pittakos, won the support of the people as a whole and became *aisymnetes* (elected ruler), with powers to pass laws and to rule. The laws we hear of show him attacking the distinctive showiness and pleasures of his fellow nobles; sumptuary laws imposing double penalties for offenses such as assault committed when drunk hit hard at the antisocial sympotic hubris still characteristic of the likes of Alcaeus and his companions (Aristotle, *Politics* 1274b17 ff.).

Mytilene around the end of the seventh century provides also the best evidence for archaic female organizations, in large part modeled on the male. It is a controversial matter, but it does seem probable that Sappho's powerful and tender poems of her love for a succession of younger girls were written about, and perhaps for, some form of approved cult association (*thiasos*), probably with an initiatory background and a perceived socializing function for the girls; there is also some evidence (presented by Dover, 1978) for girls' "beauty contests," probably for selection for ritual processions and chorus. The descriptions in her poems of shared feasts and drinking, of luxurious lying on cushioned couches, with dances, garlands, and perfumes, of sexual rivalries and emotions, are in many ways close to the homosexual male symposium, but on analysis they display strikingly different conceptions of love and sensuality.

It is in Athens between the late seventh and the fifth centuries that the interrelationship of *hetaireiai* and political change can best be seen. The first attempt at a tyranny in Athens was mounted about 630 by one Kylon who, in Herodotus' words (*Histories* 5.71), "grew his hair long with a view to a tyranny, and gathering a *hetaireia* of his agemates, tried to seize the Acropolis," but foundered through lack of popular support. The crisis that brought Solon into office as lawgiver and mediator some forty or fifty years later had many facets, not least of which were forms of economic exploitation of the poor by the rich. But in the poems in which, as Aristotle says, Solon blamed the rich for all the troubles, he not only attacks their insane desire for wealth at all costs, but also claims that they will suffer grief "because of their great hubris; for they do not know how to control their excess, nor to conduct properly their existing good cheer [*euphrosyne*] in the calm of the feast" (West, frag. 4.8–10). His subsequent legislation, like that of Pittakos, seems to have contained attempts to curb such tendencies to arrogance and violence, as well as to cure the economic discontents and increase political participation. He too imposed restrictions on expenditure at funerals and on female displays of luxury (Plutarch, *Parallel Lives,* "Solon" 21), and very probably created the law making an act of hubris against a person of whatever sex or status a serious public offense, with the penalty due to the state and prosecution open to any citizen. Solon and the law recognized that acts of hubris might be committed by members of a demos against the nobles, but from Homer until centuries later, the characteristic forms of hubris are the acts of insolence and contempt for one's inferiors indulged in by the leisured classes. It is one of the signs of the strong community spirit and propensity toward citizen democracy that Athens felt and accepted the need to legislate against it.

Under the period of the tyranny of Peisistratos and his sons, active political involvement (let alone military deeds) were necessarily diminished, and the aristocratic *hetairoi* seem to have devoted themselves more insistently to sport, poetry, and pederasty at the tyrant's court, in their own houses, in the international arenas of the Panhellenic games, or among their foreign friends. The failure of the tyrant's sons to avoid hubris against young aristocrats produced the failed, romantic plot of Harmodios and Aristogeiton, the pair of wronged lovers, to end the tyranny, and, less directly, the more successful attempt put together by other Athenian houses, notably the Alcmaeonidai, and foreign allies from Sparta. But renewed factional competition between aristocrats and their bands of *hetairoi* induced one Alcmaeonid, Cleisthenes, as Herodotus put it, to "take the demos into his *hetaireia*" (*Histories* 5.66), and by his complex and farsighted reforms to bring Athens vastly nearer to being a democratic and more open society.

Archaic and Pseudoarchaic Societies: Crete and Sparta

Well into the classical period, the various city-states of Crete and the powerful state of Sparta seemed to display a set of stable social institutions that were designed to create an unusual degree of cohesion and discipline. This was done by means of a diminution of family life and discouragement of other voluntary associations, and a concentration on tightly structured, single-sex, age-differentiated groups that trained, competed, and ate together. Contemporary Greeks assumed these similarities arose from common (Dorian) origins, although they differed on who most influenced whom, and both social systems fascinated those living in more open societies, most evidently upper-class Athenians in the late fifth century, such as Critias. It is also striking how much serious critical analysis is devoted to Spartan and Cretan customs in the political theory of Plato and Aristotle (especially Plato's *Laws* and Aristotle's *Politics,* Book Two), and, in particular, the prominence (in the first books of *Laws*) given to the issues of common meals (*syssitia*) for the citizens, the educational value of communal drinking, controlled drunkenness, and homosexuality. They form the foundation for the ensuing general discussions of law and morality.

Our information on the Cretan institutions derives above all from a lengthy account by the fourth-century B.C. historian Ephoros (as summarized by Strabo in Book

Ten of his *Geography*), supplemented by the surviving law codes of various cities, especially Gortyn. Ephoros' account, already itself influenced no doubt by political theory in Platonic and other circles, is anything but a complete account of social life in the different Cretan cities, but the details do inspire confidence that genuine archaic rituals and customs are being reported, and that they were of greater significance in classical Crete than comparable rites elsewhere. All males had to spend much of their lives in collective military training and hunting, and take meals together in the messes, called in Crete (as in early times in Sparta) *andreia* (men's houses—contrast the private *andron* in other states). Age distinctions were very clearly marked. Boys, grouped, as in Sparta, in *agelai* ("herds"), had to eat in the messes seated on the ground, where the men sat on benches; the boys were toughened by having the same shabby clothes winter and summer, and waited on the men. They then embarked on a complex sequence of "rites of passage," culminating in a ritualized, semipublic homosexual "rape" and initiation, in which it was a matter of considerable shame for a boy of good birth and tolerable appearance to fail to find an "abductor." The couple spent some time together hunting, exchanging presents, and lovemaking, after which the lover (called the *philetor*) incorporated the beloved (called *parastatheis*, "stander-by," and then *kleinos*, "well-known") into his *andreion*, and gave him three significant presents symbolizing his new status: a suit of armor, an ox to sacrifice, and a drinking cup. When young men passed out of their "herds" each group in turn had to contract marriages simultaneously, although they did not necessarily set up homes at once.

In the case of Sparta we can see much more clearly how similar rituals and regulations—in origins no doubt not unlike those in a great many other poleis—were not merely continued when they declined in importance elsewhere, but were rigorously strengthened and reorganized to defend the peculiar economic and political system that Sparta developed from the seventh century onward. So the social system of late archaic and classical Sparta put its sons through a brutalizing, regimented system designed to equip them to uphold Sparta's military preeminence and her control over the Helots; to those ends it adapted carefully the messes, age-class training, rites of passage, and much else. Thus from ages seven to eighteen Spartiate boys, almost entirely separated from their parents, learned their military and athletic skills and a narrow, conformist ideology in their succession of age classes, and the closest individual relationship for most of that time will have been an "educative" homosexual bond with a lover, functioning as a surrogate father and probably neglecting his own young wife (Plutarch, *Parallel Lives*, "Lycurgus" 17–18).

In an atmosphere of intense competition to excel in these limited and compulsory activities—reinforced by much corporal punishment—the boys attended one of the formal messes (called in the classical period *syssitia* or *phitidia*), sitting, rather than reclining, or serving the wine, and hoping no doubt to be admitted as full members (but the blackball system of voting could exclude inadequate performers or nonconformists, at least from the more exclusive *syssitia*). In the most bizarre twist of older ritual (again reported by Plutarch in "Lycurgus" 28) the top 300 of those in their twenties formed an elite corps, the knights (*hippeis*), who spent part of their time living rough and hunting by night in the wild countryside, as if in a traditional rite of passage of youths on the margins, in isolation from the community; but they appear to have been engaged in spying on, hunting, and killing any Helots they caught, and by day also disposing of any Helots in the fields likely to cause trouble. In the *syssitia,* by tradition, food was not elaborate ("black broth") and drunkenness and hubris strongly discouraged; but we hear also that the prestige of individual members could be enhanced if they contributed extra produce from their fields, or from the chase, and one is tempted to wonder if the standard topics of conversation ("recounting citizens' honorable deeds") always managed to avoid political or personal conflicts. Other entertainments, again according to the versions in our sources, featured warlike dances and constant recitation of the songs of the inspiring Spartan poet Tyrtaeus, both at home and on campaigns.

As far as one can tell, Spartan society achieved greater success in discouraging the potentially disruptive (or invigorating) activities or loyalties of family life and of voluntary *hetaireiai* or other associations than it did in creating a wholly harmonious community, even among the Spartiates; economic and social tensions and conflicts and contradictions in the system were serious and endemic, and contributed to the disastrous loss of both manpower and power in the fourth century. The fact that for Spartiates there was only one set of institutions that could grant social identity, respect, or enjoyment meant that those who failed, for economic reasons or through cowardice, bad luck, or failure to conform—those who were thus forced to join the varied ranks of the "dishonored"—are likely to have experienced extreme bitterness or despair. In Xenophon's account in *Hellenica* (3.3.5–7) of the abortive rebellion of Kinadon, it is the disgraced categories of the "inferiors" as well as the Helots, freed Helots, and *perioikoi* (the subject people of Laconia) who would allegedly all "be glad to eat the Spartiates raw."

CLASSICAL GREECE: ATHENS

The nature of our evidence compels us to concentrate on Athens if we are to attempt some understanding of the complexities of social life in the more advanced Greek poleis; yet Athens, although innovative and influential, was scarcely typical. In contrast to Sparta, Athens was a relatively open society; in contrast to many others, a fairly stable community under its democracy, though not without its own tensions and contradictions. From the time of Solon the city recognized the existence of a great variety of associations and clubs. Aristotle, who criticized the Spartan system for its monolithic concentration on military values (*Politics* 2.9), realized that in a city like Athens a number of different types of groupings were all essential parts of the community, existed for different purposes, and produced different types of relationship, different degrees of affection or friendship, and different claims, duties, and loyalties (which he spelled out in *Nicomachean Ethics* 8.9). Athens, for all its faults, maintained a fair balance of freedom of thought and association for its male citizens, with compulsory membership in a number of bodies (among them phratries, demes, and tribes) that on the whole reinforced the cohesive "democratic" ideology of the society. This combination of freedom to spend one's leisure as one chose and to choose one's associates and one's loyalties with only the imposition of some community duties and festivities has no small part to play in the explanation of Athens' remarkable political and creative achievements.

Public Banquets and Feasts

Unlike Sparta, Athens did not compel its citizens to dine regularly in common messes, but virtually all the social units, public and private, offered feasts and drinking sessions to their members intermittently, and the types of public meals and public nourishment offered by the polis to all citizens and to particular individuals reveal something of the democratic ideology. Near the start of Book Five of *The Learned Banquet* (185c–186b), Athenaeus adduces various examples of the social value of symposia and dinners (*deipna*), and compliments the "old lawgivers who made provision for the dinners that exist now [in Athens], and established the dinners of the tribes [*phylai*], the demes, the cult associations, the phratries, and the *orgeones*"; he then mentions decent and ideal symposia conducted by the philosophical associations established on the original model of Plato's Academy and ends by referring to the joint meals taken by the standing members (*prytaneis*) of the council. At many publicly organized religious festivals feasting for all participants on the sacrificed meats was a popular feature. So the "tribes" dinners in this passage must refer to the great public feasts (*hestiaseis*) at the City Dionysia and the Panathenaea, organized on a tribal basis and financed as a liturgy by a wealthy member of the tribe; the local demes maintained a great many smaller sacrifices and festivals and produced meals for demesmen at many of these. These units were the "new" tribes and demes of Cleisthenes' reforms of 508; the older phratry organization maintained considerable vitality as a focus of all Athenians' social identity, and even if no longer required by strict law, membership in the phratry was a valuable indication of legitimacy and must have been virtually universal for male citizens. Boys would be brought to the attention of the phratry when two years old and formally admitted at around sixteen, in both cases normally at the chief phratry festival of the Apaturia (itself a lively affair, with the boys showing their paces with recitations of poetry and much eating of sausages); a girl, if not a formal member, would be "acknowledged" by her husband's phratry, when he gave her a feast to indicate the marriage. The *thiasoi* and *orgeones* groups mentioned in the Athenaeus passage are probably also related to the phratries, since

many smaller subgroups of phratries existed under such titles, sacrificing to particular cults and reinforcing their sense of citizen identity; they too held regular dinners and maintained their membership lists.

The Athenian equivalent of the adolescent rites of passage seems to have been focused on the phratry organizations before 508 and closely linked to certain myths of the Apaturia. After Cleisthenes, the *ephebeia*, while retaining some ritual elements, became a two-year period of patrolling frontiers and learning aspects of civic life either for all citizens, or perhaps just for those likely to be eligible for service as hoplites in the army (this is disputed), which started just as one was admitted at eighteen to membership in the deme. It was then given a tighter, more rigorously military organization under the orator Lycurgus' influence in the 330s (before being changed again in the Hellenistic period). Ephebes, boys aged eighteen or nineteen, lived a somewhat regimented life, messing and training together for part at least of the two years, but the training and the discipline were not at all as severe as in Sparta.

Regular meals at the state's expense were, broadly, of two types. The fifty members of the standing committee of the council (*prytaneis*), who had to be present at all times at the heart of the city, ate in the tholos in the agora. The *prytaneion* (city hall), however, to the northeast of the Acropolis, offered meals to various honorands. Distinguished visiting foreigners, such as ambassadors, were offered *xenia* (hospitality), the city's ambassadors were welcomed home with "dinner," as new citizens were welcomed to city membership also with "dinner"; all were probably given the same meal. But permanent rights to free meals at the polis' expense in the prytaneion were granted only to a very restricted number of the polis' benefactors, according to somewhat aristocratic criteria, at least until the period of the Peloponnesian War: victors at the Olympic Games, certain religious officials, or direct descendants of Harmodios and Aristogeiton, the tyrant-slayers. In the 420s it became the practice to extend the honor to generals who had achieved notable victories, although the granting of the honor in particular to Cleon caused offense. Socrates' proposal at the end of his trial that he be granted this privilege should be seen as bizarre and quite out of the question. The "democratic" mode of state sustenance was not in the form of shared meals, but rather grants of money, either pay for those who served on the council or the juries or held other offices, or the general distribution of relatively small amounts of money to all citizens (the *theorikon*), made at the time of the festival of the City Dionysia so they could be used, if desired, to buy tickets for the theatrical contests.

Private Symposia

The favorite mode of evening entertainment among groups of friends, at least in the more wealthy circles, continued to be the symposium, ending usually in a *komos;* and it continued to produce serious political and legal effects. The question of the diffusion of the habit of sympotic behavior down the social scale is difficult to answer. When Socrates and his interlocutors consider in Plato's *Republic* (372d–e1) whether their imaginary city should be given what Glaukon, for one, regards as merely reasonable elements of comfort and pleasure, it is the essential features of the symposium —reclining on couches, tables for the food, tasty foods, perfumes, *hetairai*, confectionary—that are mentioned first. Are these the tastes merely of the Platonic circle—the upper classes—or do such priorities spread more widely, even if fulfilled less frequently? Many jokes and scenes in Aristophanes and the fragments of Old and Middle

Comedy seem to assume a general awareness of sympotic customs and songs (for example, *Acharnians* 971ff.; *Knights* 529 f.; *The Peace* 341–345). But the single scene in Aristophanes' *Wasps* (1122 ff.) that is built on the idea of the institution extracts extensive humor from the supposition that the old, jury-loving Philocleon, whose son Bdelycleon wishes to equip him for high society, knows absolutely nothing about it: Philocleon has to be taught how to recline, how to wear smart clothes and shoes, and how to admire the bronze ornaments, painted ceilings, and tapestries in the hall and the *andron*. When he gets to a symposium attended by many upper-crust Athenians, he does indeed get unpleasantly drunk and shows great hubris, but his hubris is of a much coarser and cruder variety, like that of a nouveau riche, an overfed donkey, or a rustic; nor has he learned the aristocratic, insouciant charm to deal with the bystanders he has outraged on his progress home in a *komos*. These scenes suggest that full-scale sympotic behavior was felt to be characteristic of the upper class and the political "establishment" of top people (Cleon, Philocleon's hero and the leading "demagogue," is envisaged as present at one in *Wasps* 1220), and that some of the poorer citizens, even if they lived near the city, were totally ignorant of the procedures involved. But such ignorance was perhaps unusual, and many of the hoplite class, at least, may well have conducted reclining drinking parties with their friends in imitation of the rich, when they could afford it. Wine and most types of pottery were not expensive; the very rich preferred to use the more highly valued gold and silver drinking ware (Plutarch, *Parallel Lives,* "Alcibiades" 4). It is notable that in the fourth century B.C. the price of an evening's hire of flute, harp, and lyre girls was regulated (two drachmas maximum), and competition for a particular artiste had to be settled by lot. (Plato in *Protagoras* 347c–e talks of "symposia of cheap and ordinary people" who spend money on flute and dancing girls because they lack the sophistication and education to make their own entertainment.) It looks as if the law was concerned to keep the price of a reasonable symposium within the reach of many, even the majority of citizens (or their groups and clubs); these provisions do not resemble sumptuary legislation, which restricted the gross expenditure of the very rich.

No writer probably illuminated the sympotic activities of the Athenian upper classes in the mid fifth century more than Ion of Chios. The elegiac fragments (found in Athenaeus 447f., 463b) of this versatile aristocrat and author contain praises to "King Wine" and Dionysos, "lord of good-hearted symposia, . . . presiding over noble deeds, to drink, to play, to have just thoughts." In the manner of the Xenophanes poem, Ion in another poem sets up a symposium, apparently in the presence of the Spartan kings, and, using gold and silver vessels, he organizes the mixing of the wine, the singing, dancing, games, and jokes that those who have wives waiting for them at home should drink more nobly than the others. This combination of self-satisfied drinking and playfulness is found in the extracts that we have from Ion's innovative prose work *Visits* (*Epidemiai*), reminiscences of his social meetings with famous figures of the Greek world, which must have revealed the evening activities and values of the "international aristocracy" as the poems of Pindar do the favorite daytime contests of the gymnastic and athletic games. One passage reported by Plutarch (*Parallel Lives,* "Cimon" 9) shows Cimon, Ion's friend and hero, excelling at a party in Athens both at singing and at storytelling, recounting a famous stratagem of his of booty division at Byzantium. Another text recorded by Athenaeus (603e–604d) shows Sophocles at a party in Chios, there as one

of the Athenian generals against Samos in 440, displaying his "strategy" by scheming to chat up and steal a kiss from a beautiful, shy boy wine pourer, while scoring with witty quotations off the man sharing his couch, a schoolmaster from Eretria. No text better reveals the playfully competitive and cultivated conversation, the adaptation of serious issues and ideas to frivolous pursuits, and the romantically homosexual atmosphere of the classical symposium.

But the fullest portraits of upper-class Athenian symposia are the two Socratic works that properly established the banquet as a prose literary form, allowing the opportunity for philosophical explorations. Plato's *Symposium* is the most brilliant picture of Athenian high society, and Xenophon's *Symposium* is perhaps the most revealing; both were written in the first half of the fourth century, but are set in the tense years of the Peloponnesian War. Plato's symposium starts relatively sober, and the flute girl is dismissed to "play to herself if she wishes, or to women within." The subject of the successive, mildly competitive set speeches, suitably enough, is Love (Eros), and as in many of the early Platonic dialogues set in the gymnasium, all the participants (except Aristophanes) assume that it is homosexual love that is worthy of praise and philosophical discussion. This and much other evidence demonstrates that the development of literary and rhetorical techniques for the exploration of serious issues in prose, characteristic of the Sophist movement, had produced additional modes of intellectual games at the party. Despite the guests' resolutions, the sudden entry of Alcibiades playing the role of the uninvited guest, on a *komos* from another party, prompts the beginning of deeper drinking, and the drunk Alcibiades forces the tone of the conversation to more personal, more suggestive paths; yet his humorous exploration of Socrates as a "lover" reinforces the serious message of the philosopher's commitment to self-control and education.

Xenophon's *Symposium*, intellectually on a much lower level, still features competitive, sophistic, and playful discussions, on themes such as "what each guest most values." Less high-mindedly, they drink heavily from the start (2.27), and their host Kallias, one of the richest Athenians of his day, much known for his extravagance and hospitality to visiting Sophists, provides regular appearances by the cabaret of a Syracusan manager, a flute girl, and a couple of acrobats/dancers/sex-show artistes, whose final erotic performance allegedly produces the result that the married men hurry home to their wives and the bachelors resolve to get married.

The uninvited guest in Xenophon's banquet is a self-styled comic who makes a habit of turning up early at parties and gets admitted for the sake of his jokes and buffoonish dancing. The figure of the "parasite" (the term became standard in the fourth century, derived from a title of certain official participants at sacrifices or banquets with gods), the man who managed to attend many dinner parties without either paying his contributions to joint dinners or giving reciprocal parties of his own, became a stock figure in Greek (and Roman) comedy. (For an extended discussion with innumerable quotations, see Athenaeus, 234c–262a.) He seems to have had some basis in Athenian social life, and may possibly have had an origin in a more pervasive clientlike set of relationships in earlier times. The parasite in comedy tends brazenly to justify what is normally perceived as a shameful and servile way of life, and in fact and in comedy may belong to one of two broad types. The "jester" aimed to wangle invitations to any party by offering jokes or other services; the "flatterer" attached himself to one rich or influential man, praising him and running errands for his dinners. Junior politicians, making speeches or drafting motions in support of more established men, found themselves labeled flatterers or parasites.

Greek parties still maintained the strict distinction between the eating and the longer or more important drinking stages, but the dishes at the one, and the snacks, fruit, cheeses, and cakes at the second grew steadily more elaborate and expensive throughout the classical period. The Boeotians, the Thessalians, and above all the Sicilians were famous for their luxury and rich foods. So Plato's examples of luxuries in the *Republic* (404d) refer to Syracusan tables, Sicilian varieties of dishes, Corinthian girls, and Athenian cakes; he (or one of his supporters) complains in his *Letters* (7.326b) of the so-called "blissful life" in the Syracuse of Dionysios I (r. 406–367), consisting of two huge meals a day and loads of sex all night. In this regard, among many gastronomic books written in the fourth century the most famous seems to have been one written in mock epic verse by Archestratos of Gela, in Sicily; Athenaeus preserves about fifty extracts, from which it emerges that although there was particularly elaborate treatment of fish dishes (which played a major part in Greek cuisine), meats, desserts, garlands, perfumes, wines, and sympotic etiquette were scarcely neglected.

Unrestrained devotion to the life of luxury among kings or aristocrats who could afford it did not lack serious political consequences in this period, as earlier. In general, political philosophers such as Plato, Isocrates, or Aristotle and still more moralizing historians like Theopompos and Ephoros delight in showing, how excessive *tryphe* (luxury) can in itself produce envy and discontent if extremes of wealth are too great and palliative measures are not taken, and even more how if *tryphe* were to lead rulers or ruling classes to acts of outrage (*hybris*), this would be likely to inspire successful coups or even divine retribution (for instance, Aristotle, *Poli-*

tics Book Five, and the many examples in Athenaeus, Book Twelve). As far as Athens is concerned, we can see how such dangers were faced, with at least partial success.

In the first place, rich men who spent very large sums on private luxuries, such as symposia, *hetairai*, or boys, or on their houses, paintings, carriages, or clothes for their wives, could incur considerable social disapproval, which could count against them in the courts if it was suggested that they were seriously dissipating their basic wealth, to the detriment of their heirs; or if it was shown that they were also grossly underspending on what was due to the city in property taxes or in liturgies, that characteristic Athenian institution that introduced some degree of democratic control into the hitherto aristocratic practices of voluntary spending on the community's defense and festivals without removing the voluntary and honorific elements.

Second, the danger of hubris arising from the drunken excesses of symposia or from other expressions of contempt of the rich for the poor was supposedly met by the law against hubris, backed up by other laws against assault and criminal damage. The final scenes in Aristophanes' *Wasps,* where Philocleon, drunk, incurs rows and threats to bring prosecutions for hubris and fails to disarm his victims through his lack of charm, suggest that many aristocratic young vandals did often calm innocent sufferers—who may also have wished to avoid the troubles of a lawsuit and realized the difficulties in gaining a conviction in a most serious charge over aristocrats who would deny damage, laugh the whole thing off, and plead their and their ancestors' previous records of military service and liturgies. In fact, cases of hubris—a very serious charge—seem to have been rare in the courts; more common were charges of assault, where one could employ all the language of hubris to attack one's rich assailant and hope to win

financial recompense as well as satisfaction. These laws as a whole offered some protection and probably had some deterrent value, although in general the ambivalence of the attitudes of the poor toward the goings-on of the rich, and the natural advantages the rich enjoyed in the courts, may indicate that in practice, even in democratic Athens, rich drinkers were able to get away with a good deal of violence and mayhem.

"Hetaireiai" and Politics

So far we have considered casual symposia of friends, often arranged on the day, hosted by one man, or financed by equal contributions from all (the *eranos*); such gatherings may play with serious themes, but they are essentially occasions of fun and relaxation from work or politics. But groups of political activists continued to form *hetaireiai* composed of men, usually about the same age, who spent much of their lives together in the gymnasium and at symposia and from time to time engaged in mutually advantageous political or legal planning and activities. Adapting themselves to the procedures of the democracy and the need for open rhetoric, such groups operated within the political system and more or less within the law to aid each other's careers for most of the period of the democracy. The connection between political groups and the aristocratic leisure style of symposia is clear in a sentence of Plato's, written in the early 360s: "True philosophers know nothing of the agora, the lawcourt, the council chamber or any other public building, or laws; the enthusiasms of *hetaireiai* for offices, their meetings, dinner parties, and their *komoi* with flute girls, do not occur to them even in dreams" (*Theatetus* 173d).

Their activities much of the time may have been relatively harmless. But the Athenian demos could be suspicious of the plots and the values of such *hetaireiai*; at times absurdly, it seemed to Aristophanes in the 420s as he mocked tendencies to suspect tyrannical ambitions if a man bought expensive fish in the market (*Wasps* 488 ff.). But in a sense the demos was proved right in the next decade. Alcibiades was the most extreme case of someone who tried to combine playing the democratic political game with panache, energy, and great expenditure of wealth, and pursuing a fundamentally undemocratic and hubristic life-style. This came to a head in the year of the Sicilian expedition (415 B.C.), as the fashionable activity at many symposia of Alcibiades' and other sets became the parodic performance of the secret Eleusinian Mysteries, acts that betrayed both an aggressive, but perhaps not wholly assured, atheism, and an urge to mock and to risk offending the deepest religious and communal feelings of ordinary citizens. (The acts were done "in hubris," as Thucydides said in *History of the Peloponnesian War* 6.28.) There was also the contemporary formation of a drinking club provocatively called the *Kakodaimonistai* that honored an invented Evil *Daimon,* in place of the Good (*Agathos*) *Daimon* to whom all orthodox symposia offered a libation, and ostentatiously paraded its atheism (Athenaeus, 551e). But it was the political vandalism of another *hetaireia* in 415 that brought disaster on Alcibiades' balancing act and on the Athenians. The club to which Euphiletos and the orator Andocides belonged decided at one evening's drinking session to disrupt the forthcoming expedition to Sicily by mutilating all the little statues of Hermes outside peoples' houses throughout the city, as a pledge of their members' loyalty and commitment to antidemocratic action (assuming a fair amount of truth in Andocides' later account, in *On the Mysteries*). In the resulting outcry, allegations about the mystery parodies were made that, thanks to his opponents, led to Alcibiades' removal from command and contributed not a little to the failure of the expedition. A few years later the existing oligarchically minded *hetaireiai* were effectively organized into a conspiracy that created, through intimidation, terror, and murder, the atmosphere to force the Athenian Assembly to vote at Colonos for a less democratic system. The clubs were the victims of something of a democratic backlash in the years 410–405 when, probably, a consolidated law of impeachment was passed, including the clause "if anyone joins anywhere with others for the purpose of the dissolution of the democracy or forms a political society [*hetairikon*]" (Hyperides, *For Euxenippos* 7–8). The clubs then used the same techniques to assist in the establishment of the narrow oligarchy of the Thirty Tyrants in 404.

But the behavior of the 404/403 oligarchy so discredited oligarchy, and the restored, more forgiving and moderate democracy established itself so effectively, that the political clubs were allowed to operate, indulging in various "dirty tricks" from time to time and displaying a somewhat antisocial ethos without being regarded as a major threat. Elsewhere in Greece, where political discord and civil war were more regular occurrences, the formation of *hetaireiai* could be regarded as more dangerous by whatever form of government was in power.

Cult and Social Associations

Evidence suggests that an increasing number of social and religious clubs claimed membership from citizens and noncitizens throughout the classical period, followed by a huge explosion of such groups in the Hellenistic period throughout the Greek-speaking world. The evidence, however, is almost entirely epigraphic, and hence derives from the habit of the clubs themselves, following the practice of the Athenian democracy, of recording their decisions, regulations, and honorary decrees on stone. This habit grew through the fourth century, spreading from Athens; only a small fraction of the vast numbers of such records actually inscribed still exists. Nonetheless the impression of an increasing complexity of associations is justified.

Some associates, called either *orgeones* or members of a *thiasos,* were held to be part of a phratry, and hence descent groups, exclusively male citizens; others, *orgeones* or members of a *thiasos* or *eranos,* might be exclusively citizens, exclusively metics (immigrants), or of mixed membership. What all such groups tend to have in common is a cult basis, a shared meal (at least annually, often more frequent), an elected organizing official or two, a shrine or cult premises, often with dining room and sometimes with a plot of land that could be leased out to provide income, and some limited concern for the well-being of members.

An interesting example of a group of *orgeones,* probably part of a phratry, is illuminated by a series of inscriptions and some additional literary evidence concerning Sophocles, who was a prominent member. Originally they honored an obscure healing hero called Amunos; in 420, after a visitation of plague, moves were made to introduce into Athens a cult of the more famous healing deity Asklepios (Asclepius) from his center at Epidauros. After lodging for a time in the shrine of the Eleusinion on the Acropolis, the god, with his sacred snake and accoutrements, was given a permanent home with Amunos in his shrine near the theater of Dionysos. (In these matters Sophocles had lent a helping hand.) The *orgeones* offered cult to Amunos and Asklepios together in their enlarged shrine, and after Sophocles' death they created a new hero, Dexion (the Welcomer), to represent Sophocles in his capacity as host of the god; Dexion's shrine abutted the main one. Although the state took over aspects of the Asklepios cult at some point in the fourth century, the *orgeones* were still found maintaining their shrines to the three deities and organizing their annual reunion meals later on in the century. Of a group of *orgeones* devoted to a very obscure hero called Egretes, we learn from a lease inscription dated about 306/305 B.C. that the organization possessed some buildings and a shrine, and these had to be opened up and provision made for the annual banquet in the autumn with two sets of three couches each (indicating a minimum membership of twelve).

The introduction of new cults into Athens from elsewhere in the Greek world or beyond was a continuous process, and it often involved the creation or acceptance of new organizations and the granting of a shrine. In a major exceptional case, the rites of the Thracian goddess Bendis, two separate groups of *orgeones* were approved by the state, perhaps in 413/412 when Athens was considering using Thracian mercenaries, and were given the task of organizing two lavish processions annually from the city to Piraeus (which, being a port, was often the main center for foreigners and their cults), a torchlit horse race and a feast for all. One group was solely Thracian in composition, and formed presumably the main focus of Thracian identities in Athens; the other group was Athenian. Other foreign groups might simply be granted the right to own land for the foundation of a shrine to their chosen deity; so an inscription of 333 B.C. records an Athenian decision to grant permission to men from Citium (Kition) in Cyprus to buy a plot for a shrine to "their" Aphrodite, citing the precedent of Egyptians who had already founded their sanctuary to Isis. No doubt such organizations of particular groups of foreign merchants and visitors provided opportunities for nostalgic, identity-reinforcing reunions, aid for members in legal or other difficulties, and sources of useful information for Athenians privately or publicly about members of particular ethnic groups.

Other cults, many with foreign origins, led to the formation of groups with less official backing, and occasionally they incurred some disapproval and even legal opposition; not coincidentally, perhaps, membership in such cults often breached barriers between citizens and foreigners and broke down rigid role distinctions between men and women. A passage of Aristophanes' *Lysistrata* (387–389) is revealing, wherein an elderly, respectable official of the polis reacts to the pacifist rebellion of Lysistrata and her women associates by assuming it is another case of a disorderly and emotional cult indulged in by women: "Has the luxury (*tryphe*) of the women flared up again then, the tambourine-beatings, and their constant Sabazios rites, and the Adonis ritual, the one up on the roofs?" It is well known that women played a very substantial part as priestesses and participants in many of the state-approved festivals, and some festivals were restricted to them; but it may in general be said that they were given ritual functions that in the end reinforced their supposed natures and their social roles as wives and mothers, even if at times this was achieved by means of temporary reversals of norms or by ritual obscenity. For example, in the major Demeter festival of the Thesmophoria, married women of citizen families spent a few days encamped together, ritually separated from their homes and from sex, organized in official deme contingents and engaged in a grisly rite with decayed pigs, snakes, and phallic cakes in pits; afterward they returned home, equipped to improve the fertility of the seed for the autumn sowing and their own chances of procreation of legitimate children. But the female-dominated groups celebrating the eastern Adonis rites formed a marked, even systematic contrast. Private, informal groups of women, both of citizen

families and *hetairai*, lamented the early death of the passionate lover Adonis and imitated it by growing Adonis gardens, potted plants, and vegetables that were forced to flower and wither in the midsummer heat in a few days as symbols of passion and sterility; they also held mixed parties. The whole ritual joined the different, rigidly separated categories of women together in a bittersweet fantasy celebration of the independent, sexually free life they were not permitted to have. Respectable men tolerated this brief outlet without, it seems, fully approving of it.

In a somewhat similar fashion one may contrast different types of Dionysiac rites. The state-regulated festivals of Dionysos in Athens seem to lack the ecstasy and excitement supposedly characteristic of that god's cult, whether or not women were permitted to share in the drinking contests of the new wine festival of the Anthesteria (the point is disputed). Some Athenian women may have joined, every two years, in the Delphic maenadic excursions to the mountains where again the extent of genuine ecstatic wildness or of drinking is somewhat unclear. But many private Dionysiac *thiasoi* were clearly active, often practicing "mysteries" and initiation ceremonies, and involving men and women together (Aristophanes, *Lysistrata* 1 ff.; *Frogs* 357; Plato, *Phaedo* 69c). The similar rituals of the Phrygian god Sabazios are attested in Athens not only in Aristophanes, but also in the attacks on the disreputable activities of Aeschines and his mother, which presumably took place in the 380s, although uttered by Demosthenes in 343 (19.199, 281) and in 330 (18.259 f.). These Sabazios mysteries involved the handling of sacred (if tame) snakes, the purifying and initiating of candidates with mud and bran, readings from sacred (Orphic?) books and promises of a better life, and wild ecstatic cries.

Once more, attitudes were clearly ambivalent toward the introduction of foreign cults and associations. On the one hand the openness of the polytheistic system and of much of Athenian society encouraged acceptance, and some of the cults filled convenient religious or emotional gaps and were widely popular. But disapproval of their disruptiveness could easily be aroused among an audience at the comedies and among juries, and the "introduction of new deities" could form part of a serious prosecution in the courts. Socrates, whose talk of his private voice, his *daimonion,* led to this being added to the charges of corrupting the young, refused to plead for mercy with any of the usual rhetorical techniques; but when one of the most famous *hetairai* of her generation, Phryne, was accused of impiety by one Euthias, perhaps in the 340s, it was a different story. The indictment was that she had indulged shamelessly in *komoi,* had introduced a new god called Isodaites—apparently another god whose cult involved mysteries, popular with "common women and those of low character"—and organized illegal *thiasoi* of men and women together; but her acquittal was assured when the orator Hyperides, speaking on her behalf, caused her suddenly to reveal her breasts in court (Athenaeus, 591e).

Many associations, however, served essentially social purposes, even if they had a cult basis. It is noticeable, however, that economic or benevolent assistance seems on present evidence a fairly negligible feature in classical Athens, and likely to be found, if at all, more in the metics' associations than those of citizens. The term *eranos,* used in reference to benevolent associations, is revealing. It is still used, as in Homer, to indicate the sort of dinner or symposium to which each member brings his own contribution. It also refers frequently to a form of financial assistance that may be appealed to by people in difficulties, an interest-free loan collected on one's behalf by a circle of friends. (In a further development it became a sum of money collected by the acquaintances of a slave and used to buy his or her freedom, also to be paid back over a period of years.) But these are ad hoc friendly arrangements; and although the use of the term *eranos* for a club or association came into fashion toward the end of the classical period, it is not necessarily the case that mutual financial assistance was more prominent in them than in other types of associations. Concern for the proper burial of *thiasos* members is attested in some documents dated to the early third century B.C., and it may have been both a more general and an earlier phenomenon; but citizens at least would look first to their relations, phratry members, and their deme to ensure a decent funeral.

The last type of association that deserves mention is also included in Athenaeus' list cited at the beginning of this section. The philosophical schools founded as a direct continuation of Socrates' informal teachings at gymnasiums and symposia institutionalize elements of both settings. Both Plato and Aristotle based themselves at pleasant suburban public gymnasiums (the Academy and the Lyceum), and buying (Plato) or leasing (Aristotle, who was a metic) some adjoining land and buildings, created all-around educational establishments open to serious students; the tendency to classify them legally as cult *thiasoi* is perhaps a modern exaggeration, but they did both contain a shrine to the Muses and an altar, and both provided regular, usually serious and sober symposia. Their relations with the government of the polis fluctuated. Plato and his Academy, which sent out many to engage in politics, were tolerated despite their criticisms of democracy; Aristotle's and his successors' closeness to Alexander and other Macedonian rulers gave the Lyceum a more stormy passage. Aristotle thought it best to leave Athens on Alexander's death; Theophrastos, his successor, held influence under the regime of his former pupil Demetrios of Phalerum (and was permitted to buy the land and buildings of the school), and survived a legal threat when democracy was restored in 307. The defeat of the law requiring that philosophical schools be expressly approved by the polis in effect maintained the rights of freedom of association established by Solon.

THE HELLENISTIC WORLD

In dealing with the immensely complex and pluralist societies of the many Hellenistic kingdoms, this survey must restrict itself to consideration of the dominant political and cultural groups, the courts of the kings themselves, and the elites of the Greek and hellenized cities, where continuities with the world of classical Greece and anticipations of that of Rome can best be observed. The main concern will be to suggest the major roles played in urban social life by private symposia, dinners, and public banquets, and the growing importance of a great variety of voluntary clubs and associations.

Courts, Symposia, and Luxury

The Macedonian kings always claimed to be Greek, and from at least the fifth century onward their pursuit of the traditional activities of warfare, hunting, and feasting were open to influences from the Greek cities. So they adopted the practice of reclining at parties, and filled their halls with Greek actors, *hetairai*, comedians, dancers, and top cultural figures; so, for example, Archelaos at the end of the fifth century persuaded Euripides and his fellow poet Agathon (the host in Plato's *Symposium*) to stay at his court (though he failed with Socrates); Aristotle spent many years as the tutor of the young Alexander, and his nephew Callisthenes ac-

companied Alexander on his expedition as court historian. But the atmosphere at the Macedonian court could alarm Greeks, for various reasons.

Some objected to a high degree of luxury and self-indulgence; the historian Theopompos characteristically made Philip II the major figure of the *Philippica,* the continuation of his Greek history after about 360, but he engaged in lurid abuse of Philip's womanizing and drunken depravity, for which he was severely taken to task by the later historian Polybius. In particular, the Macedonians seemed to the Greeks to go in for especially heavy drinking, often of unmixed wine. The reason for this may have been that their soil produced better-quality wines even then, and they saw less need to make a great fuss about diluting it. More seriously, Macedonian banquets were also frequently the scenes of violent quarrels and insults, which were followed by deep resentments and even murders, or attempted murders. So Euripides was granted the opportunity to flog one of the royal pages, when accused by him of bad breath at a symposium; the pages, upset by Archelaos' insulting treatment of them, attempted an unsuccessful plot against him, although he was their lover; and Philip II, after several spectacular drunken rows at state banquets, was killed in 336 B.C. by one Pausanias, who had been subjected to a drunken mass rape by Attalos and his men, which had gone unpunished.

These traditions were fully carried on by Alexander, both on campaign and in the palaces of Pella, Babylon, and Susa. He conducted regular, lavish sympotic entertainments, often lasting all night and featuring varied entertainments, including jugglers, actors, competitive quotations from Homer, set debates, and, of course, excessive drinking. The standard participants would be the central group of his sixty or seventy followers, the companions or *hetairoi,* mostly Macedonian nobles and friends from whom he selected his most reliable generals and administrators; many more were present on the bigger occasions. Alexander's banquets and drinking parties were important events for relaxation and renewal of the ties of friendship and privilege between king and companions, for jockeying for precedence and favor, for exploration of strategies and policies; but they frequently erupted in conflict or violence due to personality clashes, policy disagreements, drink, and jealousies. Thus it was at symposia that the decision was taken to burn Persepolis (according to one source), that Kleitos (Clitus) was killed by Alexander, and that the issue of *proskynesis* (obeisance) provoked Callisthenes' opposition and led to his death.

As they tried to stabilize their spear-won kingdoms, Alexander's successors developed increasingly elaborate courts at which the central supporting roles were played by the "friends" (*philoi*), almost exclusively Macedonians or Greeks, since the successors showed no desire to follow Alexander's policy of involving Persians at the top levels. These "friends" (or sometimes "relatives," or "first and honored friends," as hierarchical protocol advanced), appointed personally by the king, were trusted advisers and administrators, and naturally were regular guests at royal banquets. Hellenistic historians and gossip writers delighted in stories of the pomp, luxury, or debaucheries of the kings; the themes of luxury and its dangers gained in popularity. Some kings earned reputations as persistent voluptuaries. Demetrios I Poliorketes, the king of Macedonia, for example, held symposia at which the famous Athenian *hetaira* Lamia entertained and was entertained, and which were allegedly the scenes of notable dishes, drinking, and dirty jokes; according to Athenaeus (614e–615a), Demetrios and Lysimachos, king of Thrace, exchanged insults on the relative excesses at each other's courts. Ptolemy II Philadelphos had so many

mistresses that they could be listed in the memoirs of Ptolemy VIII Euergetes, whose own gluttonies earned him the nickname "Potbelly" (Physkon). Other monarchs, not generally renowned for luxury, gave notable symposia on occasions: for example, Ptolemy I Soter (Egypt) and Antigonos II Gonatas (Macedonia), who at times induced his Stoic friends Zeno and Persaios to join in less intellectual pastimes, and, according to Athenaeus (603e), took Zeno on a *komos* in pursuit of a pretty boy musician. In entertaining Persaios and some visiting Arcadian ambassadors at a daytime banquet, Antigonos brought in topless Thessalian dancing girls and a flute girl at whose "auction" the philosopher himself, it seems, became involved in a violent episode. Persaios later apparently told the story himself, justifying sympotic excesses on the right occasions, in his "sympotic memoirs" (Athenaeus, 607a–e). A more bizarre style of entertainment was favored by Antiochos Epiphanes IV of Macedonia, who, like Nero, liked to go slumming, chatting with the goldsmiths, drinking in bars with casual visitors, and going on *komoi* with wild young men.

The tradition of literary and philosophical discussions at symposia was kept equally flourishing by many of these monarchs, especially those like the first two Ptolemies and Antigonos Gonatas, who were major patrons of the arts and sciences. A particularly revealing text here is the "letter of Aristeas to Philocrates," a work written by an Alexandrian Jew, perhaps in the middle of the second century B.C., and quoted by Athenaeus, which purports to be an account of the authorization of the Greek translation of the Old Testament (the Septuagint), following a seven-day intellectual symposium at which Ptolemy II Philadelphos put seventy-two Jewish sages through their paces; each "guest" responded to a moral, philosophical, or political question with an appropriate mixture of Hellenistic and Judaic sententiousness. Not only is the symposium felt to be the proper setting for this sort of imaginary royal reception and decision; many of the questions explicitly concern the value and the conduct of courtly symposia.

But the fullest surviving description of a luxurious banquet concerns one hosted not by a king but by a Macedonian noble, eager like many to display conspicuously the vast wealth accrued from the conquests in the East. The story was told in a variation of the literary form of the symposium, the "Sympotic Letters," in which a Macedonian, Hippolochos, and a Samian, Lynkeus (the brother of the sensationalist historian Duris and a pupil of Theophrastus), published exchanges of letters in which each described the lavish dinner parties they claimed to have attended. Hippolochos went to town on the wedding feast of one Karanos, of which Athenaeus gives an extended résumé (128–130d). In elaboration, playful theatricality, and profusion of wealth it goes beyond what was conceivable in classical Greece, and fully anticipates later Roman parties. The guests, all male, were deluged throughout with offers to accept and take away cups, tiaras, and the like of great value. Huge platters of rich, elegantly cooked dishes of fowl, fish, and meat followed in quick succession; the showpiece was a large roast pig whose belly was filled with thrushes, ducks, warblers, eggs, oysters, and scallops. Serious drinking accompanied the eating; the varieties of wine, some warmed, were mostly drunk with little or no water added. Troupes of entertainers came on at regular intervals—musicians, obscene male dancers, naked female jugglers, sword dancers, fire-eaters, and tableaux featuring choral singers. The end of the serious eating and the start of the symposium proper was marked, in Macedonian style (used also by Alexander), with the sound of a trumpet; and drinking of mixed wine and eating desserts was accompanied by the jokes and dancing of an elderly Athenian comedian and his wife.

Benefactions, Social Life, and Associations

The description of Karanos' feast, exceptional and highly exaggerated as it is (and hence no sort of basis for describing "normal life," even of the nobility) contains in the display of gross self-indulgence an element of avoidance of envy by wealth redistribution. The payoff of the story is that as they left the guests were sobered by the realization that what they were carrying away with them was the basis, if (or when) invested in land, slaves, or houses, of luxury for themselves. The supposed solidarity of the shared meal combined with more permanent benefactions became a major expectation by at least the Greek communities in the cities of their kings and upper classes. While "democracy" became the favorite title of orderly, limited self-government of the cities, and whatever the vitality of the popular assemblies and lawcourts, where they functioned, it is nonetheless true that ordinary citizens were heavily dependent on the largesse both of the ruler (monarch or protector) and of the wealthiest citizens. The holding of the main offices, of priesthoods, and the performance of liturgies, functions that were clearly separated in the classical Athenian democracy, tended to converge. Unable to compel the rich to perform liturgies, less able to serve as officials themselves, the poorer citizens assigned considerably more power and gave lavish public honors to their internal and external benefactors and "saviors"; they looked in return for generous "gifts" to enable them to exist, to carry on their characteristically Greek way of life, and to enjoy, at times of festivals, some form of genuine community spirit.

Thus the greatest benefactors, the kings, offered from time to time gifts of grain, assistance with the grain supply, or famine relief; they founded schools, stoas, gymnasiums, or theaters; they also subsidized the celebration of existing festivals, and added to the complexity of religious and social life with the "encouragement" of many new games and festivals in honor of their own dynasties. The most spectacular royal festival was unquestionably the Ptolemaia, instituted in 279/278 B.C. by Ptolemy II Philadelphos in honor of his father, Ptolemy I Soter, as a quadrennial festival explicitly intended to match the old Olympic Games, which sacred representatives from all over the Greek world were invited to attend. In addition to the days of athletic, musical, and dramatic contests, the Ptolemaia provided a colossal general feast for all the inhabitants of Alexandria, visitors, and soldiers, with especially luxurious provision for selected guests who were assigned the hundred gold couches in the palacelike marquees ornamented with columns, canopies, and statues and filled with flowers. Even more impressive was the great procession, consisting of a formidable military parade, complete with exotic animals from Ptolemy's zoo and a joyous succession of floats with revellers and choruses, of which the central theme was the celebration of Dionysos as patron of drama, forerunner of Alexander and Ptolemy I, conqueror of the East, tamer of animals, and above all creator of wine. Suitably lavish distributions of this product (Egyptian wine production was greatly encouraged by the Ptolemies) were no doubt essential to the enjoyment of the whole show. From the description in Athenaeus (196a–203d) and even more from the more famous literary description of the attendance of two Syracusan married women living in Alexandria at the music and tableaux of a festival of Aphrodite and Adonis put on in the palace by Queen Arsinoë II (Theocritus, "The Women at the Adonis Festival"), some feeling can be had for the functions of such roy-

ally sponsored holidays and ceremonies in the lives of at least the Greek middle classes in these cosmopolitan cities. With their military might and vast wealth, such festivals impressed and evoked awe, creating a brief sense of sharing and familiarity along with the realization of the gulf between rulers and the ruled: "Everything's grand in grand houses," is a comment (24) in "The Women at the Adonis Festival." They reminded the Greek elite class that it shared a common culture with the rulers, separate from the "natives" (even if Theocritus pokes some elitist fun at the vulgarity and clichés of the show and the women's remarks); the festivals enriched people's humdrum lives with color, vicarious luxury, and escapist fantasy, for which the Adonis cult was especially suited.

Other dynasties displayed the same lavish concern for games, festivals, and public feasting, if rarely quite on the same scale. It may be noted, however, that even in the period of relative decline the Seleucid kings came close to Ptolemaic grandeur. There was the grand procession of Antiochos IV (175–164 B.C.) at Daphne (a garden suburb of Antioch in Syria), followed by thirty days of games, and banquets with one day a thousand and another day fifteen hundred *triclinia*, where fountains flowed with wine (Athenaeus, 194c–195f). Already by this date (166 B.C.) mutual imitation between Hellenistic kings and Roman generals is in evidence. Antiochos was concerned to rival the triumphal games held by Aemilius Paullus at Amphipolis (in Macedonia) in 167, and the military emphasis in the procession at Daphne was probably due to the Roman triumph; the presentation of gladiatorial combats by Antiochos anticipated the general introduction of this characteristic feature of Roman life into the Greek-speaking world by a century or more. Regular royal feasts for the inhabitants at least of the Syrian cities later in the second century are also attested in a number of fragments (Athenaeus, 210c–e) of the great historian Poseidonios, who grew up himself not far away.

The cities depended even more on the regular financial services of their own citizens, the liturgy performers, and holders of priesthoods and offices. The lengthy, often verbose and florid inscriptions in which the communities record their gratitude and hope to encourage others to display the same honor-seeking munificence (*philotimia*) show the same types of benefactions and the same priorities as do the royal gifts. Gifts or loans of cash and assistance with grain supplies recur; very frequent too is the provision of public sacrifices and banquets, which may be of less lasting economic or educational value than other benefactions, but their value in maintaining the community's religious and social solidarity—and some political cohesion—should not be underestimated. Benefactors might enable traditional sacrifices and festivals to be restored and be celebrated particularly well by adding extra banquets for the citizens; they might also add to the number of existing festivals, through, for example, the posthumous creation of a hero cult for a member of the benefactor's family, marked by an annual contest and banquet, an occurrence attested for a city on the small island of Amorgos in the second century B.C. General rules affecting admission to such banquets in the Hellenistic period seem to preserve the idea of the city as the equal club of male citizens; although visitors as well as resident foreigners were admitted to banquets fairly readily, women and slaves could attend only very exceptionally. (In the Amorgos text, places were assigned for citizens, resident and visiting foreigners, and for Romans and their wives.)

Hellenistic cities took great care for the provision of educational and physical services for their younger citizens (or at least the better-off among them), so that the twin institutions of the gymnasium and the *ephebeia* became the hallmarks of hellenization and were especially popular focuses of benefactions. It was apparently the introduction in Jerusalem under Antiochos IV of a gymnasium, with its band of *ephebi* wearing broad sun-hats, that was a major irritant in the nationalist unrest that led to the Maccabean revolt (1 Maccabees 1:10 ff.; 2 Maccabees 4:2). Gymnasiums, which were in effect leisure centers, with stadia, training grounds, wrestling grounds, baths, and lecture rooms, were not only available to all, but also constituted one of the prime centers of the daytime social life of young men; moreover, they developed as places of secondary or tertiary education. At Athens, for example, the two-year *ephebeia* became, first, in the 330s, a more systematic and intensive program of military training and athletics, with some attention to civic patriotism; and second, as citizen militia became obsolete, changed again into a voluntary educational "school" for wealthier boys, with much greater emphasis on athletics and sports, and some—at times perhaps lukewarm—attention to philosophy. (One of the many inscriptions praising the conduct of the ephebes and their officials records that they "stuck it out attending the classes of Zenodotos . . . and all the other philosophers in the Lyceum and the Academy throughout the whole year"; cited in Wycherley, 1978.) This pattern became normal throughout the Hellenistic world and extended even as far as Aï Khanum in northern Afghanistan, where a gymnasium has been excavated; in it an inscription records that Clearchus, probably the Aristotelian philosopher, caused the inscribing of about 140 maxims of Delphic wisdom. Associations of young men (*neoi*) mushroomed, to provide clubs for the gymnastic and social activities of those in their twenties; younger boys too might receive some of their education in these institutions, and some of these "schools" offered some education to girls as well. Gymnasiums of these complex types needed careful regulation; a particularly elaborate city law concerning the management of a gymnasium in Beroea (Verria) in Macedonia was recently published by M. M. Austin (1981).

Historical sources also confirm the centrality of symposia and gymnasia in urban life. Another fragment of Poseidonios (Athenaeus, 210e–f) disapprovingly records the decadence of Syrians for "using the gymnasiums as if they were merely baths" and devoting themselves entirely to their eating and drinking associations; rather later, the Jewish philosopher Philo, praising the sobriety and spirituality of a Jewish ascetic community in *On the Contemplative Life* (40–56), contrasts it extensively with the sympotic excesses of ordinary inhabitants of Alexandria; in particular, he describes the drunken, violent, ignorant hubris of the nocturnal revelers as a horrible parody and perversion of the legitimate, sober, and manly activities in the daytime gymnasium. The Alexandrian scholar-poets provide more individual (and psychologically intriguing) pictures, although problems of literary convention complicate interpretation. It is worth noting that the third-century B.C. critic and poet Callimachus used the symposium at least twice in his *Aetia* as a transitional device, describing how a chance meeting and serious questioning (instead of heavy drinking) led to interesting accounts of the origins of local cults. We can see how the major development of the epigram, especially the erotic epigram, in the hands of poets like Asclepiades (*ca.* 290 B.C.) portrays a cosmopolitan world full of symposia, *komoi,* and varied heterosexual and homosexual activities and emotions. In this world, unlike that of classical Athens, there is no longer the strict distinction at symposia between respectable women and *hetairai* and

others; it is a much more complex and "modern" world where girls as well as boys may choose to flirt, to fall in love, or sleep around without necessarily being treated as prostitutes. Above all we can see in the poems of Theocritus (*ca.* 270 B.C.) not only such a (comparatively) liberated girl causing a disturbance at a rustic symposium through her shifting affections ("The Love of Cynisca"), but also a sensitive exploration in "The Spell" of the tragic emotions of the girl Simaitha, a respectable virgin living (very oddly and probably unrealistically) almost on her own with no means of support, who falls in love with the athletic star from the gymnasium and is of course betrayed by him.

The theater too was an essential leisure institution in all the cities, providing dramatic entertainment (especially the classic Athenian repertoire), musical dancing, and choral shows as part of many festivals. The steady growth of professional, often "international" associations, still with a cultic foundation, is remarkably strong in this area, as the associations of the "Artists [*technitai*] of Dionysos" developed in the third century B.C. into four large well-organized bodies, serving the festival needs of wide areas (Athens, Egypt, Isthmos/Nemea, and Ionia and the Hellespont are the titles of the troupes). The many records of their events and of the negotiations—not always amicable—with cities and kings show their importance in Hellenistic cultural life, even if they enjoyed a somewhat raffish reputation.

A vast proliferation of types of "private" associations is one of the main features of Hellenistic social life. In the sphere of high culture, besides the Artists of Dionysos and professional poets' clubs, the flourishing philosophical schools and cult associations in Athens served as a model for the institutional organization, often under royal patronage, of poets, philosophers, or other intellectuals. Most famously this resulted in the creation of the Mouseion (Museum) of Alexandria. Other urban occupations are by this time well represented. Mobile groups like traders and shipowners developed particularly impressive and long-standing associations, uniting, for example, traders from one area who regularly did business elsewhere. Delos provides both inscriptional and archaeological evidence for well-funded associations of merchants from Tyre, who met to honor "Herakles" (that is, the Semitic god Melkarth), and for the Poseidoniastai of Berytus (Beirut), who were permitted after a time to erect a sumptuous club building. In the cities there are attested innumerable clubs of fairly specialized workers in clothes manufacture, metalworking, and food supply, of food retailers, barbers, carters, and many others; no doubt in many cities these would largely operate as neighborhood groups as well. In addition, the old associations in the Greek cities did not lose their vitality, nor in many cases their exclusiveness; *thiasoi* dedicated to particular cults and groups of adolescents and young men cropped up everywhere. These associations had in common a central and supportive religious element that, as expressed through sacrifices, banquets, and drinking parties, many then and now would see as their primary function. The regulations of such clubs pay great attention to the need for members to keep to orderly and civilized behavior at their meetings, and avoid insults and hubris. Many clubs showed a wider concern for the well-being of members, and often for their funerals, but there is no good evidence for even the associations of traders or manufacturers acting collectively in pursuit of their joint economic interests. What they did go some way toward achieving was some sociable mixing of citizens and foreigners, and even of freemen, freedmen, and slaves, through common membership in the same clubs (especially cult associations),

particularly in the great ports and cosmopolitan cities. It seems not so much that the cults, loyalties, and associations of the old polis disappeared, to be completely replaced by new gods and associations—indications of rootless alienation—but rather that the new associations resulted from a lessened political power and partial or complete dependence on rulers. The opportunities of elite formation and wealth through hellenization produced both a greater stress on certain partially redefined polis institutions and values and the development and acceptance of a number of new ideas, institutions, and clubs that went beyond the bounds of the polis.

The position of women in these changes remains obscure. Although respectable wives seem in many places not to have attended dinner parties (Cicero, *Verrine Orations* 2.1.66 ff., had need to explain this peculiarity to Roman jurors), there is evidence that not all women at parties in Alexandria and other cities were *hetairai* or prostitutes, and the powerful queens were not so self-effacing. Under the Roman Empire, although women might regularly only appear in public veiled, their prominent roles in cult and festivals increased. Women clearly have greater rights of property ownership than they had in classical Athens, and the wealthiest of them seek to acquire honor by acting as benefactresses, liturgists, priestesses, founders of memorial associations, and even magistrates; but their rights are anything but absolute, and the praise for their generosity often stresses their female qualities as well as their *philotimia*. Curiously, while in general Athens seems still to be more restricted in the opportunities and expectations given to women than other cities, Athenian women are more widely attested as members, along with men, of various types of associations. Here too the overall picture is one of complexity, and no little contradiction.

BIBLIOGRAPHY

SOURCES

Andocides, *On the Mysteries,* in *Minor Attic Orators* I, K. J. Maidment, trans. (1941); *The Letter of Aristeas,* Henry G. Meecham, trans. (1935); *Lettre d'Aristée à Philocrate,* Andrè Pelletier, ed. (1962); Aristophanes, *Comedies,* David Barrett, Alan H. Sommerstein, trans. (1964–1978); Aristotle, *Nicomachean Ethics,* Harris Rackham, trans. (1926), and *Politics,* Harris Rackham, trans. (1932); Athenaeus, *Deipnosophists* (*The Learned Banquet*), Charles B. Gulick, trans., 7 vols. (1927–1941); Aulus Gellius, *The Attic Nights,* John C. Rolfe, trans., 3 vols. (1927–1941); Callimachus, *Aetia,* Constantine A. Trypanis, trans. (1958); D. A. Campbell, trans. and ed., *Greek Lyric I: Sappho, Alcaeus* (1982); Herodotus, *Histories,* C. Hude, trans. (1908), Aubrey De Selincourt, trans., 2d ed. (1972); Homer, *Iliad* and *Odyssey,* T. W. Allen, ed. (1902–1908), Richmond Lattimore, trans. (1951, 1967); Hyperides, *For Euxenippos,* in *Minor Attic Orators* II, J. O. Burtt, trans. (1954); *Inscriptiones Graecae,* 14 vols. (1873–); Isaeus, Edward S. Forster, trans. (1927); Josephus, *Jewish Antiquities,* H. St. J. Thackeray *et al.,* trans. (1930–1965); Richmond Lattimore, *Greek Lyrics* (1955); Edgar Lobel and Denys L. Page, eds., *Poetarum Lesbiorum Fragmenta,* (1955).

Lucian, *Carousal, or the Lapiths* (*Symposium*), in Lucian, A. M. Harmon, *et al.,* trans., 3 vols. (1913–1967); Philo, *Flaccus* and *On the Contemplative Life,* in Philo, F. H. Colson, G. H. Whittaker, trans., vol. 9 (1941); Plato, *Laws,* John Burnet, ed. and T. J. Saunders, trans. (1907), *Protagoras,* John Burnet, ed. (1903), *Republic,* John Burnet, ed. (1903), H. D. P. Lee, trans. (1955), *Symposium,* K. J. Dover, ed. (1980), and *Theaetetus,* John Burnet, ed. (1900); Plutarch, *Parallel Lives,* Bernadotte Perrin, trans., 11 vols. (1914–1926), *Symposium of the Seven Wise Men,* in *Moralia* vol. 1, Frank C. Babbitt, trans. (1928), and *Sympotic Questions* (*Table-Talk*), in *Moralia* vols. 8–9, Paul C. Clement, *et al.,* trans. (1961–1969); Strabo, *Geography,* Horace L. Jones, trans., 8 vols. (1917–1932); Theocritus, *Theocritus,* A. S. F. Gow, ed. (1950); M. L. West, ed., *Iambi et Elegi Graeci,* 2 vols. (1971–1972); Xenophon, *Hellenica* (*History of Greece*), E. C. Marchant, ed. (1900), Rex Warner, trans. (rev. ed. 1978), and *Symposium,* O. J. Todd, trans., (1922).

SOURCE BOOKS

M. M. Austin, *The Hellenistic World from Alexander to the Roman Conquest* (1981); M. M. Austin and P. Vidal-Naquet, *Economic and Social History of Ancient Greece* (1977); Mary Lefkowitz and Maureen B. Fant, *Women's Life in Greece and Rome* (1982).

STUDIES

Archaic and Classical Greece

John Boardman, *Athenian Black Figure Vases* (1974), and *Athenian Red Figure Vases: The Archaic Period* (1975); George M. Calhoun, *Athenian Clubs in Politics and Litigation* (1913); W. Robert Connor, *The New Politicians of Fifth Century Athens* (1971); J.-M. Dentzer, "Aux origines de l'iconographie du banquet couché", in *Revue archéologique,* 2 (1971), and *Le motif du banquet couché dans le Proche-Orient et le monde grec du VIIe au IVe siècle avant J.-C.* (1982); Marcel Detienne, *The Gardens of Adonis,* Janet Lloyd, trans. (1977); K. J. Dover, *Greek Homosexuality* (1978); Moses I. Finley, *The World of Odysseus* (1956; 4th ed. 1977); N. R. E. Fisher, "Hybris and Dishonour I," in *Greece and Rome,* 23 (1976); Louis Gernet, *The Anthropology of Ancient Greece* (1981); Giuseppe Giangrande, "Sympotic Literature and Epigram," in *L'Épigramme grecque,* Entretiens sur l'antiquité classique, 16 (1968); Sally C. Humphreys, *Anthropology and the Greeks* (1978), and *The Family, Women and Death* (1983); Catherine Johns, *Sex or Symbol: Erotic Images of Greece and Rome* (1982).

J. Martin, *Symposion, Die Geschichte einer literarischen Form* (1931); Peter von der Mühll, "Das griechische Symposion," in *Ausgewählte kleine Schriften* (1975); Oswyn Murray, *Early Greece* (1980), and "The Greek Symposion in History," in *Tria Corda: Scritti in onore di Arnaldo Momigliano* (1983); W. J. Slater, "Peace, the Symposium and the Poet," in *Illinois Classical Studies* (1981); R. A.

Tomlinson, *Greek Sanctuaries* (1976); Pierre Vidal-Naquet, *The Black Hunter* (1981, Eng. trans. 1986); Michael Vickers, *Greek Symposia* (1978); Susan Walker, "Women and Housing in Classical Greece," in *Images of Women in Antiquity* (1983); Jack Winkler, "Garden of Nymphs: Public and Private in Sappho's Lyrics," in Helene Foley, ed., *Reflections of Women in Antiquity* (1981).

The Hellenistic World

Eugene N. Borza, "The Symposion at Alexander's Court," in *Ancient Macedonia,* **3** (1983); Alan Cameron, "Asclepiades' Girl Friends," in Helene Foley, ed., *Reflections of Women in Antiquity* (1981); John K. Davies, "Cultural, Social and Economic Features of the Hellenistic World," in *Cambridge Ancient History* **7**, pt. 1, 2d ed. (1984); C. A. Forbes, *Neoi: A Contribution to the Study of Greek Associations* (1933); Frederick T. Griffiths, "Home before Lunch: the Emancipated Woman in Theocritus," in Helene Foley, ed., *Reflections of Women in Antiquity* (1981); Arthur E. Hands, *Charities and Social Aids in Greece and Rome* (1968); Alex Hardie, *Statius and the Silvae: Poets, Patrons and Epideixis in the Greco-Roman World* (1983); A. H. M. Jones, *The Greek City* (1940); Arthur D. Nock, *Essays on Religion and the Ancient World,* 2 vols. (1972).

Franz Poland, *Geschichte des griechischen Vereinswesen* (1909); Claire Préaux, *Le monde hellénistique,* 2 vols. (1978); E. E. Rice, *The Grand Procession of Ptolemy Philadelphus* (1983); Mikhail Rostovtzeff, *The Social and Economic History of the Hellenistic World,* 3 vols. (1941; 2d ed. 1953); W. W. Tarn, *Antigonus Gonatas* (1913); M. N. Tod, *Sidelights in Greek History* (1932); Riet Van Bremen, "Women and Wealth," in *Images of Women in Antiquity*, Cameron and Kuhrt, eds. (1983); F. W. Walbank, *The Hellenistic World* (1981); Richard E. Wycherley, *The Stones of Athens* (1978); E. Ziebarth, *Das griechische Vereinswesen* (1896).

Roman Associations, Dinner Parties, and Clubs

NICHOLAS R. E. FISHER

INTRODUCTION

This essay has been written in close connection with the essay GREEK ASSOCIATIONS, SYMPOSIA, AND CLUBS, and is in turn intended to demonstrate and illustrate the fundamental importance of these types of social institutions in urban life at different periods in Rome and the Roman Empire. Given the complexities of social life in all the very different areas that the Romans came to govern, the account cannot be comprehensive; it offers instead glimpses of certain selected periods (early times, the second century B.C., the late republic, and the early empire), and concentrates on two major themes: the steady hellenization of many aspects of Roman social life, in particular the life-styles of the very rich and their dinner parties; and the steady growth of voluntary clubs and associations, and their intermittent political significance.

Some points of comparison and contrast with the depiction of Greek social forms offered in the companion essay should be made at the outset. The social importance of the shared taking of food and drink is no less

great in Roman than in Greek life; and here too one major indication of this importance is provided by the constant use in Roman literature of the dinner party or the Greek-style symposium as the focus of moral discussions, pursuits of love and sex, revelation of social distinctions and individual characters, and academic disputations. Works that contain significant discussions or portraits of dinner or drinking parties include poems by Catullus, Horace and the elegists, the letters of Cicero and the younger Pliny, the novel of Petronius, and the scholarly writings of Aulus Gellius and Macrobius; they will be much cited and used in what follows.

While the Romans were from earliest times conscious of the debt owed by their increasingly sophisticated social life to Greek models, their standard dinner parties (*convivia*) differed in some important respects, especially the much greater emphasis on food (anticipated here by the kings and aristocracies of the Hellenistic world), and the more extensive participation of respectable women; the contrast between Greek and Roman practice in this respect is effectively made by Nepos, in the preface to his biographies of Greeks and Romans.

As in Greek and Hellenistic cities, membership in one or more of the many different types of clubs and associations was evidently of the very greatest importance for city dwellers of most levels of society in Italy and the Roman Empire; evidence from both literary sources and innumerable inscriptions suggests how much such clubs contributed to the sense of identity, leisure activities, and security of individuals in an uncertain and often hostile world. In the securely oligarchic world of the Romans, the political dangers of associations were not perceived, as in archaic and classical Greece, as the power drives of the aristocratic *hetaireiai* (small activist groups seeking advantages for themselves), but as the threat of unrest, dissent, and disorder among the lower orders of society, arising spontaneously or fomented by seditious leaders.

EARLY ROME AND THE ETRUSCANS

The complexity and variety of the forms of social organizations in Rome during the period of the kings and the young republic should not be underestimated. Family ties were strong, and the pseudokinship groupings, the gentes, appear to have involved all citizens (the laws of the Twelve Tables of 451–450 B.C. assume that all are members of a gens, a clan) and political and military cooperation between all members of a gens is attested. Reciprocal relationships between patrons and clients of various types seem to have been of great significance (as they probably were in the Etruscan cities) in the normal preservation of aristocratic control. A regular feature of the first sixty years of the republic (*ca.* 510–450 B.C.) seems to have been wars or raids conducted by semiprivate groups of gentes with their clients; in

about 479 the Fabii allegedly undertook a war with the city of Veii (Livy, 2. 48 ff.), and a recently discovered dedication to Mars, found in the city of Satricum (Conca) in southern Latium, set up by the "Companions [*sodales*] of Poplios Valesios" about 500, may represent raiding activities of such a gens group (the leader may well be the famous Publius Valerius Poplicola, consul four times in the first years of the republic, or one of his relatives), or it may represent the activities of a group of young men who were engaged in "rite of passage" raiding, a suggestion put forward by H. S. Versnel (1980). Many other overlapping distinctions between bewilderingly diverse categories of citizens complicated political life, especially in the period of the "Struggle of the Orders" of the fifth century. There were also a number of ancient priestly colleges of *sodales,* among them the Arval Brethren, the Luperci, and the Salii, which performed ancestral rituals and shared their common banquets; and the introduction of new cults and the dedication of new temples may also have produced new collegia or sodalities (*sodalitates*) responsible for the rites, such as the collegium of Mercuriales associated with the temple of Mercury, established in the 490s. Whether these had any connection with an association of merchants (*mercatores*), as Livy (2.27) implies, is doubtful, but associations of men based on shared occupations, common cults, and/or shared localities were probably well established by the middle of the fifth century in Rome. (The traditional attribution of their introduction to the legendary second king of Rome, Numa Pompilius, probably has little genuine tradition underlying it.) The Twelve Tables contained a law of essentially the same form as Solon's: it granted legal validity to regulations passed by *sodales* or members of a collegium, provided they did not conflict with public law.

From the earliest regal period the social

life of the Romans, especially that of the upper classes, must be seen in terms of their responses to outside influences, above all to the Etruscans (themselves very greatly influenced by the Greeks) and to the Greeks in southern Italy. The material remains of the Etruscan cities from the seventh to the fourth centuries B.C., in particular the grave reliefs and wall paintings, give a strong impression of a leisured aristocracy who preferred to be remembered enjoying themselves at a banquet, reclining in Greek fashion amid luxury. But in contrast to Greek custom, men and women—clearly on many occasions husbands and wives—recline equally together, and the emphasis is patently on the shared intimacy of the couple. Greek writers of the fourth and later centuries appear to confirm this Etruscan "peculiarity" in their condemnation of Etruscan luxury and debaucheries (with lurid descriptions of naked serving girls and wife-swapping orgies), which is likely to be typically Greek misunderstanding and denigration of their neighbors (and of which Theopompos, Timaios [Timaeus], and Poseidonios were guilty, as passed on by Athenaeus in *The Learned Banquet* 153d–154a; 517d–518a).

The early Romans adopted and adapted many major features of Etruscan culture, especially no doubt in the period of her Etruscan kings (the alphabet, many gods, their statues and temples, town-planning, the entrail-reading *haruspices,* the triumph, public games), but Rome remained a Latin, not a fully etruscanized or grecized city, and after the expulsion of her kings Romans remembered their Etruscan luxury, arrogance, and licentious women. The legend of Lucretia and Sextus Tarquinius, for example, first shows the young royal princes drinking in great luxury and discussing their wives' virtues; second, it contrasts the wives of the Etruscan princes, who frolic at a luxurious dinner party (*convivium*), with the noble Lu-

cretia, who works hard at spinning; and third, it focuses on Lucretia's honorable decision to commit suicide rather than live with the shame of having been raped by Tarquinius (Livy, 1.57 ff.).

Romans shared the Etruscan practice of permitting wives to attend dinner parties. At first, they later asserted, men and women both sat on chairs in the main room (atrium) of the house; later, but certainly by the second century B.C. if not earlier, men took to reclining, and the increasingly elaborate (and Hellenistic) town and country houses contained one or more specialized dining rooms (*triclinia*). For a period women still allegedly had to sit while men reclined, but by the late republic, at least, they too were able to lie down in equality, as Cicero tells us in *Letters to Friends* (9.26). Traditional practice, moreover, gave boys a separate, inferior role at dinners, sitting on the arms or at the feet of chairs or couches, or acting as wine pourers on private and public occasions (*cf.* Suetonius, *Lives of the Twelve Caesars,* "Augustus" 64; "Claudius" 32, where both emperors maintained the old-fashioned customs; Athenaeus, 425a). The few traditions that survive of early Roman *convivia* preserve above all the memory that, as in various archaic Greek states, patriotic songs were sung in praise of famous ancestors, either by young men or by adult males. Some archaic banquets in Rome may thus have performed an explicit "educational" role for young men, although the intensely homosexual atmosphere of Greece is not securely attested.

Finally, reconstruction of attitudes toward wine drinking in archaic Rome is problematic. Athenaeus in *The Learned Banquet* seems to offer diverse accounts; first he asserts that in Rome (as in a few Greek cities) women were totally forbidden wine, as were men under thirty (429b), but a little later he quotes Polybius to the effect that women were forbidden wine (a wife was not allowed access to the household wine stores, and had to kiss her husband and his relatives at least once a day for them to check her breath), but could drink *passum,* a sort of sweet raisin wine. Aulus Gellius (in *Attic Nights* 10.23) more precisely reports traditions that women were forbidden pure wine (*temetum*) (he also mentions the breath test), but could drink raisin wine and a sort of marc (*lora*), or else a wine spiced with myrrh. Archaeological evidence of the seventh century in Rome suggests that from the time that wine and viticulture were imported into Latium (traditionally associated with Numa Pompilius, 714 B.C.) aristocratic women could be buried with wine amphorae and cups. Perhaps, then, pure wine was not at first given to women because it was used especially for sacrifices and women had little sacrificial role. (As the exception that "proves the rule," in the married women's festival of the Bona Dea women could use wine in the sacrifices, but had to call it milk: Plutarch, *Moralia* 268e.) However, mixed wine of various types was allowed. Later, for example at the time of the Elder Cato (second century B.C.), in response to criticisms by Greeks of Roman women's sympotic drinking and to the growing tensions among the aristocracy, Roman men seem to have attempted to restrict their women's drinking, in part by "reinterpreting" their ancestral traditions; in the long run, this had little effect.

THE MIDDLE REPUBLIC: HELLENIZATION AND TRADITION IN THE AGE OF CATO

By the first half of the second century B.C. the progress of hellenization of all aspects of life in the increasingly powerful and wealthy city of Rome was far advanced, and it produced confused reactions. Looking back later, after the "decline" of the republic, many Romans seeking easy, moralizing causes for its failure liked to pick on specific moments when luxury and avarice took hold of the Roman character. Livy, for example, picked the year 187 B.C., when the army of Manlius Vulso returned from Asia with the habits and equipment of eastern luxuries. Livy's list is made up of the accoutrements of the Hellenistic symposium: couches, coverings, side tables, sideboards, lute and harp girls, and other convivial fun and games. The greater elaboration of banquets led to an increased prestige and value for cooks. Polybius, a second-century eyewitness, claims that many of the young men of his friend Scipio Aemilianus' generation had learned from the wars in Macedonia to waste their energies on boyfriends, *hetaerae* (as the Romans spelled it), musical entertainments, and drinking parties, that this Greek luxury was spreading wildly, and that Cato had declared in a public speech that the republic was in decline when a pretty slave boy cost more than a plot of land and jars of salted Black Sea fish more than plowmen. Other indications of these hellenizing tastes include the fact that the epic poet Ennius (239–169 B.C.), heavily influenced by the great Alexandrian writers, also produced a translation of the cookery poem of Archestratos of Gela sometime after 189 B.C., and the presentation in Plautus' adaptations of Middle and New Comedies of young men's debaucheries, parties, *hetaerae,* and parasites in an indissoluble mixture of Greek and Roman elements. This was a world in which the very word *pergraecari* (to behave in a very Greek way) meant in effect the enjoyment of dinners, drinking parties, and women (for example, in *The Haunted House* [*Mostellaria*] 22 ff.); the amounts of meat and fish regularly consumed reflected what was available in Rome rather than in classical or Hellenistic Athens. One should also mention the increasing lavishness of town houses, and the beginnings of the great mushrooming of luxurious villas for the Roman elite, above all along the Campanian coast, itself full of cities that appeared even more Hellenistic than Rome in their institutions and available amusements.

But opposition to these developments was widespread and could result in political acts and legislation. In Cato's notable censorship (184 B.C.), he expelled seven senators from the senate, among them a distinguished ex-consul, Lucius Quinctius Flamininus. Cato alleged that while on campaign in northern Italy, Flamininus had executed at a dinner party a Celtic chieftain to gratify the casual wish of his Carthaginian boyfriend, who reproached Flamininus for having caused him to miss out on the gladiatorial shows in Rome (Livy, 39.42 f.; Cicero, *On Old Age* 42 has a slightly different version). Flamininus' display was not an isolated act of sympotic brutality (although it was felt as a shocking abuse of power); later historians assert that beginning in Campania (where gladiatorial games first began) and spreading to Rome, it became a habit to hire a few gladiators to enliven after-dinner entertainments at private functions with blood and death.

More generally, Cato the Elder said in Plutarch's *Parallel Lives* ("Cato the Elder" 16) that when he became censor he intended to apply "surgery and cautery to the hydra-like *tryphe* [luxury] and softness" and to match his hostility to many forms of luxury and extravagance among the ruling class, which led to political corruption and the dissipation of estates, with a general and often inconsistent hostility to many forms of Greek culture (such as philosophy and medicine) that were also gaining support in Rome. He was not alone; the century would see a succession of sumptuary laws attempting to regulate expenditure on extravagance (in 182, 161, 143, 131, and 115 B.C.), which, although they all proved impossible to implement, must have been popular among both the senators who proposed and supported them and the people who voted for them. A variety of motives may be suggested. There was some moral opposition to luxurious extravagance in itself; there was a desire to reduce electoral "corruption" by restricting the number one could entertain at feasts and dinners (for example, the lavish feasts the rich gave for their weddings, funerals, and coming-of-age ceremonies, or to celebrate entering public office); and there may have been a feeling that it was desirable to reduce the burden for the oligarchy as a whole of having to keep up with the bigger spenders. Many of the poorer citizens, as Cicero makes clear in *For Murena*, preferred to see the surpluses of the rich spent on public buildings and shows than on these forms of private luxury and patronage.

The festivals and shows, celebrated with increasing lavishness, formed an essential element in the aristocrats' competitive drive for office and honors. There were many regular festivals, processions, and games in the Roman calendar, involving on occasions Greek-style athletics and chariot racing, and nearly all culminated in public banquets. The increased need for these to be organized led in 196 B.C. to the creation of a new "collegium" of priests (*epulones*) specifically for this task; many of the regular shows and games were in the charge of the magistrates called aediles, who had to decide by how much to supplement the state funds for the purpose out of their own pockets in the interests of furthering their popularity and careers. In addition, military success produced the grandest and most extensive of all displays in the form of the triumph, accompanied often by theatrical shows and votive games. A continuing hostility to the extent of the expansion in these areas too is shown by the fact that proposals to build a permanent theater for the many different types of drama and mime now popular were blocked in 154 B.C. In fact it was not until Pompey's great theater complex, dedicated in 55 B.C., that Rome had more than the increasingly elaborate temporary structures for drama.

It must be stressed, however, that at the theater, the games, and the public banquets, status distinctions were in Rome rigidly insisted on, if perhaps less so in the Campanian cities. (Suetonius, in *Lives of the Twelve Caesars,* "Augustus" 44, says that Augustus was shocked that senators could not find a seat at the theater in Puteoli.) In Rome, and everywhere, after Augustus had a senatorial decree passed, front seats were reserved for senators; after 67 B.C. the knights (*equites*) had fourteen rows of seats reserved for them. And some "public banquets" were in fact restricted to senators, while at others senators dined at their own separate tables, no doubt on superior fare. More than was the case in most Hellenistic cities, public feasting in Rome tended to emphasize the importance of the preservation of status distinctions, and the special honor of the individual responsible for the provision of the meal, as well as the creation of the sense of a harmonious community.

The steady proliferation of voluntary associations (collegia) can be confidently assumed during the long development of the republic, although it cannot be fully attested; presumably, too, such clubs often served a variety of purposes—occupational associations, cult groups, social and drinking clubs, and burial clubs. The major scandal involving the Bacchanalia groups in 186 B.C. indicates the spread of a particular type of Hellenistic cult throughout Italy, and of the Roman government's response to what it felt to be a serious threat to social order. Allegedly, the secret Bacchic mystery cults, spreading from the most hellenized cities of the south, involved initiation rituals, especially of children, and the usual mixture of drunken sexual orgies and human sacrifice. What seems new about these cults is that the

"cells" of Bacchic *thiasoi* (cult associations) demanded a considerably greater commitment to a "new" life, through oaths, initiations, and separation from family and local community, than did other locality- or trade-based collegia, or most optional cults. Moreover, they involved completely mixed groups, male and female, slave and free, with two sets of officials (modeled here on the collegia organizations), the "priests" and "masters" (*magistri*) who could be either male or female. (In the many Dionysiac cults in the Hellenistic cities *thiasoi* were usually either solely male or solely female.) Deciding that the cults constituted a major threat to community life and values, and probably to the usual political control of public meetings as well, the government suppressed the current groups brutally and swiftly, no doubt with the support of the oligarchic leadership in Rome and its allied cities and of sufficient numbers of volunteer citizen and allied militia. Also passed were measures designed to ensure that such "dangerous" mixed groups could not form again; limited groups were permitted, on application for a license from a praetor, but they could not have oaths, male priests, "masters," or common funds. Whether or not we should suppose these stringent regulations to have been totally enforced, the Romans seem satisfied that the dangerous aspects of the cults were removed.

THE LATE REPUBLIC

Daily Life, "Convivia," and Luxury

By the time of the political struggles of the last generation of the republic, a mass of evidence, provided above all by the works of Cicero, makes clear that an extremely luxurious living was readily available to the rich and leisured classes, in their town houses or country villas. Most of the ingredients of such living were perceived as being Greek or Hellenistic, and many of them were provided by those of Greek or eastern origin, at least by name or pretension. The Roman day was dependent on the hours of daylight, since the available oil lamps and candles gave a poor and smoky light (and eye diseases were common). Hence, rising at or even before dawn was standard, and the long hours of the morning, for men of leisure and wealth in Rome and other cities would, after a light breakfast, normally be taken up with financial, political, or legal activities, and with attending to calls from friends, clients, and petitioners. After lunch (*prandium*), not usually a matter of entertaining or many courses, and perhaps a siesta in hot weather, the rest of the day might normally (except for those devoted to work like Pliny the Elder) be given up to leisure and more or less civilized enjoyment by means of Roman equivalents of the Greek gymnasium and symposium. The Romans appear to have regarded the Greek emphasis on athletics, wrestling, and gymnastics as soft and insufficiently military as physical exercise. They tended to exercise and train in open-air parks like the Campus Martius, and their "leisure centers" tended to be called "baths" (*balneae, thermae*), which, while they might also provide art galleries, bars, snack bars, and general areas for ball games, conversations, and exercise, concentrated on the due process through warm bath, hot bath or sweat room, cold bath or swim, to toweling down, oiling, and being scraped with a strigil. Baths, whether small, functional, and privately owned, or large-scale centers given to a city by noble or imperial benefactors, were an essential feature of urban life throughout the empire; and the better-appointed country villas too had their own bathing facilities.

After the baths, those with leisure might devote the rest of the day to dinner (*cena, convivium*), and subsequent drinking sessions (sometimes called *comissationes*, the equivalent of the Greek *komoi*). The dinner itself was eaten by guests reclining, usually three to a couch, with three couches arranged around the low tables on which the dishes were placed. A broad division of courses into three stages was also standard: *gustus* (hors d'oeuvres), tasty snacks of olives, shellfish, or vegetables; the *cena* proper, a variety of substantial meat and fish dishes, served together or in sequence; and the *secunda mensa*, the dessert, usually fruits and nuts. The dinner party as a whole played as central a part in Roman leisured life and culture as did its equivalents in Greek, and dinner parties varied greatly in tone and atmosphere.

At the more respectable level, Cicero's letters, especially those to his good friend Papirius Paetus, who lived in Naples, are most informative. In the last such letter to survive, written in January 43 B.C., Cicero tries to rekindle Paetus' enthusiasm for the humane pleasures of dinner parties, and points out that the Latin term *convivium* means literally "co-living," in contrast to the Greek terms *symposion*, "co-drinking," and *syndeipnon*, "co-dining," and that this reflects a proper understanding that what matters most is the social harmony, expressed in the relaxed and friendly conversation (*Letters to Friends* 9.24). The social and political functions of these convivialities and exchanges of hospitality were very great. They developed and cemented reciprocal and equal friendships among the top elite in Rome and in other oligarchies; they also helped greatly to smoothe contacts and relationships between the Roman nobility and lesser notables or the municipal nobility. Thus a private dinner party at Rome might easily combine "harmony" with an insistence on clear status distinctions. Cicero, indeed, could display a most distasteful disdain on being asked to dinner by a municipal gentleman of whom he has never heard

(*Letters to Friends* 7.9; 7.16); and parties would have many clearly indicated as "lesser" guests—often known as "shadows" (*umbrae*)—"hangers-on" of important guests, or those used as reserves if the more distinguished guests failed to turn up.

Even in Cicero's circle some attention to gastronomic refinements was usually de rigueur, regardless of all the talk of the importance of conviviality. Excesses in this area might be widely condemned, most famously those of Lucullus, at whose gourmandizing, luxury villas built into the sea, and fish ponds for breeding special fish Cicero and others might sneer. Plutarch, in *Parallel Lives,* "Lucullus" 39–41, has some revolting anecdotes of Lucullus' elaborate habits even when dining alone or just with Pompey and Cicero. But Cicero, when attacking Lucius Calpurnius Piso in the courts in 55 B.C., takes an illuminating line. Piso maintained, as was well known, a close friendship with a Greek Epicurean poet and philosopher, Philodemos of Gadara, whose elegant poems include an invitation to Piso to a simple dinner, and also several descriptions of erotic symposia and activities (his theoretical writings include discussions of the correct behavior at symposia). Cicero exploited this relationship grossly by asserting that Philodemos corrupted his art by describing the details of Piso's "lusts, sexual excesses, varieties of dinners (*cenae*) and parties (*convivia*), all his adulteries" (*Against Piso* 70); but he also attacked the poverty of Piso's dinners, alleging that they failed to reach an acceptable standard of elegance, consisting of platefuls of rancid meat with no fish, shellfish, or home-baked bread, and where cheap wine was served by elderly, dirty slaves to guests crowded five to a couch. The tone of the invective suggests that Cicero may have expected his upper-class audience and readership to be more outraged by Piso's penny-pinching sordidness at the table than by his sexual excesses.

So Cicero himself, though certainly no voluptuary, showed when entertaining Caesar and his dictator's entourage in 45 B.C. that he "knew how to live" (*Letters to Atticus* 13.52); his villa at Cumae (in Campania), not one of the most luxurious, was able to accommodate Caesar and his entourage in four separate dining rooms, arranged according to strict hierarchy, with varying meals to match, so that the lesser freedmen and slaves "lacked for nothing," and the smarter people were given an "elegant" meal and the top triclinium a thoroughly sumptuous and well-prepared banquet. Cicero's letters to Paetus of about the same time indicate he could throw himself with above-average enthusiasm into the tasting of new gourmand dishes at various parties; in many of these letters there are amused references to the recent sumptuary laws of Caesar restricting the amounts that could be spent at individual dinner parties, perhaps as part of the attempt to reduce the danger of the upper class burdening themselves with debts and so favoring subversive action. As Caesar is said to have realized, these were hard to enforce, and no more successful than any others (Cicero, *Letters to Friends* 7.26; *Letters to Atticus* 13.7). One letter tells of an official dinner of the augurs at which the experimental dishes with fungi and special sauces may have kept within the new law, but gave Cicero a nasty attack of diarrhea; a report of the official meal of the pontifices in the late 60s B.C., preserved in the writings of the late sympotic author Macrobius (*Saturnalia* 13.3.12), gives a good idea of the range of dishes, the varieties of shellfish, fish, fowl, and meats, earlier served at major dinners.

At private dinner parties guests might not always know in advance who the other guests might be, or even what type of party it would turn out to be; hence many poems that use the "invitation to a party" motif often show an apparently scrupulous concern to specify in advance the scale of the occasion, the types of women likely to be present, the degree of luxury or simplicity of food, wine, or perfumes, and the degree of seriousness or frivolity to be expected. Cicero writes to Paetus of his surprise at one party to find the woman Cytheris reclining by the side of his host, Volumnius Eutrapelus; she was one of the most notorious and entertaining women of the sophisticated demimonde of the time, a mime actress, freedwoman, and mistress of Mark Antony and the elegiac poet Cornelius Gallus (his "Lycoris"). Cicero seems only moderately shocked and really quite amused at being asked to join such company; he tells Paetus (writing the letter during the long party itself) that he's really not very interested in that sort of thing, and most enjoys making his famous jokes at parties (*Letters to Friends* 9.26).

Respectable dinner parties at Rome give less of an impression than do those at classical Athens of a relentless substitution of parodic, humorous competitions in place of the serious, public discussions of issues; theoretical discussions of the ethics of dinner party behavior in the late republic emphasize humane, cheerful, and amicable conversation. Accordingly, Cicero's general rules for conversation advise agreeable discussions of domestic matters, politics, the arts, and learning, avoiding backbiting and boasting (*On Duty* 1.134–135). And Aulus Gellius in *Attic Nights* (13.11) summarizes the rules of etiquette contained in a section of Varro's *Menippean Satires* called "You Don't Know What the Late Evening Will Bring": These include the recommendation that the number of guests should not be fewer than the number of Graces (that is, three) and not more than the number of Muses (nine), obviously deities chosen as much for their appropriate associations as for their numbers; that the group, time, place, and preparations should all be carefully planned, and the conversation kept

cheerful and free from tension, combining the pleasant and the useful; similarly, readings from books should present material both edifying and enjoyable. The habit of discussion of all matters, including politics, at dinner parties was felt to be an essential element of "liberty," the sense of the right to rule, and live as they determined, enjoyed by the Roman republican upper class. Thus Cicero in 59 B.C., when the measures of the First Triumvirate were beginning to destroy this political liberty, could report that "under this oppression, at least in social gatherings and at dinner parties [*in circulis et conviviis*, a frequently recurring phrase, found also in Tacitus, *Annals* 3.54] conversation is freer than it was before" (*Letters to Atticus* 2.18); but when he entertained Caesar, then dictator, at Cumae, he told Atticus that the conversation avoided any serious matter, and the guest was one to whom one did not say "come again." The threat to uninhibited leisured conversation was a not inconsiderable part of the deprivation experienced by Cicero and his friends under the dictatorship, driving him to incessant work on his theoretical writings and to an unusual interest in gastronomy.

As in Greece, however, most parties were probably a good deal more riotous and dissolute than those that Cicero and Varro usually attended. One may have to discount some exaggerations in the abusive pictures created by the attacks of Cicero on Catiline's, Clodius', or Antony's debaucheries (*e.g.*, *Against Catiline* 2.22 ff.; *Letters to Atticus* 1.16; *Philippics* 2) or the obscene exchanges between Antony and Octavian in the 30s (recorded by Suetonius in *Lives of the Twelve Caesars*, "Augustus" 69); one also has to be aware of some stylization in the many sympotic poems of Catullus, Horace, and other poets. But a consistent and coherent picture does emerge of the upper-class life of luxury and enjoyment, indulged in above all by many of the young; primary elements of this life can be found mentioned in Cicero's speech *For Caelius* (35), which has necessarily to combine an attack on the allegedly gross and shameful promiscuity and incest of Clodia with an indulgent defense of the moderate sowing of wild oats by his client and friend Caelius Rufus: Caelius has to face charges of a life devoted to "lusts, love affairs, adulteries, [spells at] Baiae, beach parties, dinner parties, revels [*comissationes*], singing parties, musical parties, parties on boats." The major elements of this life of fun and luxury can be shown to be felt as Greek, or Hellenistic, and it is a mistake to attempt to draw clear distinctions between Roman "life" and Greek "literature" when discussing the use of these elements in Roman poetry. Elegant party-goers of both sexes paid great attention to hairstyles and clothes—for men, good quality togas or, in the heavily Greek atmosphere of the Campanian resorts, heavy, lightweight, or Greek-style cloaks; for women, brightly colored (perhaps in Tyrian purple) or see-through dresses, often called Coan "silks." Jewelry, pearls, gold, and silver might all be prominently worn, displayed, eaten off, or drunk from; perfumes and hair oils were also essential.

Architectural developments in luxury houses and villas reveal the importance of dining in the lives of their owners, and the developing elaboration and theatricality of the settings. The grander the house, the more *triclinia* it would have, suitable for different seasons; these might be in the garden, shaded by pavilions or pagodas, placed with open, shaded access to the outdoors, or in the house, but exposed to the winter sun. As we see from the large houses and villas discovered in places such as Pompeii, Herculaneum (Ercolano), Stabiae (Castellammare di Stabia), Oplontis (Torre Annunziata), and Rome, rustic views and the garden atmosphere were strongly cultivated, not only through access to the sights and smells of the flowers and to country or sea vistas, but also through elaborate wall paintings of idyllic landscapes. Alternatively, wall decorations, especially in the so-called second Pompeian style, featured elaborate architectural stage settings admirably suited to creating the impression for the guests of being part of a grand show, as the host might provide his choice from a wide variety of available entertainments.

Such entertainments included dicing and other forms of gambling indulged in not only by the notoriously dissolute like Catiline and Antony but by many others, including the emperors Augustus and Claudius, despite the existence of laws forbidding it. Prominent also were musical turns and dancing, performed either by guests or by hired professionals; there might be jokes and gossip from "wits" (*scurrae*), the equivalents of Greek parasites; poetry or prose readings, possibly from the host's works or those of his friends or clients; or performances by actors, mimes, acrobats, jugglers, strippers, clowns, or jesters. Many of these professionals would also be available for sexual services, and might be loosely described as *scorta*, "tarts," a term often used by Catullus and Horace. The sexually charged atmosphere of many a *convivium* was doubtless enhanced by visual stimuli, in the form of erotic or pornographic wall paintings, wine bowls, cups, and other ornamental or useful objects. Hence many a party must have ended with lovemaking, among the guests or between guests and "professionals," or else with bands of drunken males sallying forth to seek admission to their mistresses' houses, to find other parties, or to cause trouble. For Romans as for Greeks the drunken procession to a new party or to serenade a beloved was a feature of urban life, and the stylized basis of many Latin poems on the theme of the "excluded lover" lamenting outside the beloved's door.

Such sexual and romantic activity was

predominantly heterosexual in Roman society; the religious and educational traditions appear not to have provided a solid base for the legitimation of intense homosexual relationships, and orthodox opinion tended to disapprove of such emotions as typically Greek and decadent. In fact, however, even if the usual belief that homosexual acts between free males were prohibited under a *Lex Scantinia* is correct, which is far from certain, the law was certainly hardly, if ever, used; by the late republic, sexual exploitation of pretty boy slaves by young masters was extremely common, and affairs between free males, disapproved of by many, were fashionable and popular, especially among those most given to the life of Hellenistic culture, luxury, and poetry writing. But in Rome, unlike classical Greece, it was affairs with various types of sophisticated and cultured women that best offered opportunities for shared depth of passion and suffering by rejection, and provided the material for most of the poetry of Catullus and the elegists. Relationships with boys and with professional women of lower status were common enough in life and poetry, but generally they were regarded as involving fewer emotional demands (for example, Horace, *Satires* 1.2).

The one essential for parties of all types was wine. Originally Greek wines commanded the highest prestige and price, and the elder Cato in his work *On Agriculture* gave advice on how to produce passable imitation Coan wine on Italian soils. Good quality Italian wines, created perhaps by the application of Greek techniques, began to rival the Greek wines. Toward the end of the second century B.C. vintages began to be marked on the jars, and wine snobbery began in earnest; more intensive production of Italian vin ordinaire was subsequently developed to serve the growing demand in the army and the cities. Like the Macedonians, the Romans in general seem more flexible on the questions of pure or mixed drinking. In Greek-style sym-

potic poems and probably at Greek-style symposia the games played were of group decision, under the guidance of a symposiarch, but at many parties the choice as to how heavily to drink was left to each guest. Romans seem to have become increasingly fond of varying forms of mixed wine, warming themselves in cold or chilly weather with mulled wine, a wine mixed with honey, hot water, and spices; like the Greeks, they liked to cool themselves in summer with wine mixed with cold water from streams or wells, or, more expensively, with ice or snow brought down from the mountains packed in straw or cloth.

Collegia and Politics

The majority of evidence for the organization and activities of the many different types of associations and clubs throughout the Roman Empire comes from the imperial period and will be considered later. Here it is enough to indicate the role played by these essential features of urban social life in the complex political life in Rome of the last generation of the republic, and the resulting attempts to control them. The main bases of Roman clubs were, once more, local, religious, and occupational; since many occupational groups—shopkeepers, craftsmen, and many more—tended to congregate together, and a cultic function was ubiquitous in such organizations, no hard-and-fast distinctions between these types can be drawn.

In Rome and in other cities such organized groups and their leaders naturally could form the basis of political appeals and activities. The electioneering pamphlet attributed, probably correctly, to Cicero's brother Quintus advises Cicero as a candidate for the consulship "to take account of the whole city, of all the collegia, the *pagi* [the ancient districts just outside the old city], and the *vici* [the wards of the city itself], and if you win their leaders to your friendship, you will easily gain the rest of the crowd through them" (*On Canvassing for the Consulship* 30, Lewis and Reinhold, 1951) Candidates sought election through personal appeals for "friendship" from a great many groups and individuals, using all the available mechanisms in a society largely built on varieties of patron-client relationships. Among these, the clubs and neighborhood groups were clearly not to be neglected (even in the imperial period, the prominent graffiti in Pompeii showed that occupational collegia supported particular candidates in local elections). In Rome, the organizations of the *vici,* who were responsible for celebrating the Compitalia, festivals of local "blocks" held on street corners at the beginning of January, were held to have been the focus also of political riots and unrest in the years 67–64 B.C., and a strong senatorial reaction was produced in 64 suppressing all collegia not held to be in the public interest; many occupational groups must also have been affected. The attempts by Lucius Sergius Catilina (Catiline) between 66 and 63 to arouse the support of the urban poor were relatively unsuccessful, but Clodius in 58 started by reactivating many collegia-type organizations informally and illegally and had a law passed restoring the rights of free association. He then attempted to build a political career in part on the base of systematic support among the various collegia, given a stiffening of military-style organization and an infusion of money. Clodius' overtly political use of the collegia as sources for his vocal and violent support, and the recruitment in retaliation of gangs of gladiators and rural clients by Milo, Sestius, and others, created the climate of urban violence and disruption of elections characteristic of the 50s B.C., culminating in Clodius' murder and the following riotous burning of the senate building in 52. Clodius' gangs may have included shady politicians, ex-centurions, and gladiators, but the core of his support seems most likely

to have been the associations of local residents, craftsmen, and shopkeepers, and many (perhaps most) freedmen, who were persuaded that Clodius' populist policies had more to offer them than the orthodox senate-dominated policies had ever done.

The senate attempted once more to restrict the operations of these clubs in 56 B.C., and in 55 Crassus as consul passed a law specifically aimed, it seems, at *sodalitates* or any association active in attempting to influence elections by bribery or other means. It must be doubted whether these measures had any effect in the growing anarchy of these years. After the civil war of 49–45, Julius Caesar's aims were to restore order in the capital and to focus the loyalties and claims of the urban poor directly on himself, and hence the habit of free association could not be permitted to continue: Caesar forbade "all clubs except those of ancient constitution" (Suetonius, *Lives of the Twelve Caesars,* "Julius Caesar" 42). How precisely that was interpreted, and if it was seriously implemented, is unclear, though Josephus attests in *Jewish Antiquities* (14.10.8) that Jewish associations were specifically permitted to continue. As we shall see, the political implications of collegia continued to create alarm among the subsequent emperors.

THE EARLY EMPIRE

Augustus' Reforms, and Luxury and "Convivia" in Augustan Life and Literature

Augustus' personal seal was in the form of a sphinx, and his policies, personal life-style, and the responses they produced among the leisured classes are all appropriately complex and ambiguous. Augustus liked to create an impression of public grandeur, but lived with personal frugality and old-fashioned Italian morality. He boasted that he "had found Rome a city of brick and left it a city of marble" (Suetonius, *Lives of the Twelve Caesars*, "Augustus" 28). He himself lived in a single house on the Palatine, formerly the possession of the orator Hortensius Hortalus, with extremely simple furniture, according to Suetonius ("Augustus" 72–73), and had some relatively small-scale villas to retreat to in the towns near Rome or on the Campanian coast. Most of the great building schemes undertaken by him, by Agrippa, and by others of his family—the temples, piazzas, porticoes, baths, and parks—were made available for the use of the citizens at large. Augustus also notoriously attempted to restrict luxurious expenditure on such things as dinner parties and wedding feasts with a new set of sumptuary laws, and made a succession of assaults on upper-class "immorality" and childlessness with complex legislation penalizing adultery and encouraging marriage, the production of children, and the stable transmission of property and status through both inducements and penalties.

A concrete example illustrates the interconnections of these themes. One of Augustus' oldest friends and supporters, the very rich parvenu knight Vedius Pollio, suffered a severe reprimand at Augustus' hand when at a dinner party at his luxurious villa "Care's Ease" (Pausilypon) Pollio tried to throw a slave to man-eating lampreys in his fish ponds for having broken a crystal goblet. Augustus insisted that the slave be pardoned, the rest of the crystal service smashed, and the ponds filled in. In spite of this rebuke, when Pollio died in 15 B.C. he left his estates to his friend. Augustus accepted the villa, which remained an imperial estate for more than a century, but the huge and lavish town house was pointedly razed to the ground, and in its place was erected a public colonnade, with gardens planted with trellised vines and a picture gallery, and at the center was a shrine dedicated to the goddess Concordia. It was called Livia's

Portico, and the shrine to Concordia was instituted on 11 June 7 B.C., the date of the festival of Mater Matuta, celebrating marital unity and the proper production of children. Thus, as Ovid's comments in *The Roman Calendar* (*Fasti*), bring out (6.637 ff.), in place of one of the greatest monuments to private extravagance and excess was erected a complex of buildings for public use and delight, which also, through the shrine to Concordia and the name of the patron Livia, reinforced the ideals of Augustan policies for religious revival, marriage, and the family; for Livia, though in fact she had two husbands, and failed to bear Augustus a child, was publicly proclaimed as the ideal standard-bearer for these policies, the productive wife of a sole husband.

But such policies could not be presented without ambiguities, and may have had little practical effect. Even closer to Augustus than Vedius Pollio was Gaius Maecenas (d. 8 B.C.), the "knight descended from Etruscan kings," whose effeminate and luxurious life-style and literary tastes were well known. Farther up the Esquiline from Pollio's house, Maecenas improved the city by building over the public burial ground, which was a gruesome place with mass paupers' graves and witches (graphically depicted in Horace's *Satires* 1.8). Maecenas created his famous gardens there, which in part at least were open to the public. But there too were his very grand and tall mansion, his pool (the first heated swimming pool in Rome), and a sumptuous "dining hall" in the gardens, with elaborate trompe-l'oeil garden painting on the walls and a graffito on an outside wall, in the form of a *komos* epigram by Callimachus, asking forgiveness for the excesses brought on by the twin powers of Love and Wine: an ideal setting for elegant, Greek-style symposia. The mansion and the private gardens became the emperor's property on Maecenas' death. More important, many of Augustus' buildings would have been understood as a proc-lamation of an "imperial" personality cult as much as a restoration of "republican" ideals and religion, particularly the highly complex and elaborate development in the Campus Martius, formed by the interrelationships of the Ara Pacis, the huge obelisk/sundial, and Augustus' own mausoleum. (So, too, the Palatine complex, which united imperial residences, the temple of Apollo, libraries, and other buildings.) While many of the rooms and buildings would offer public access, the whole portrayed a genuinely "pala-tial" image, and went some way toward as-sociating the princeps and his family with the gods.

These ambiguities could be seized upon or alluded to by the Augustan poets, espe-cially those working in genres that had natu-ral affinities with sophistication, Greek tastes, and sexual permissiveness. For exam-ple, Propertius, in the persona of a passion-ate romantic but poor lover-poet, complains in one poem that his mistress has departed with a richer, coarser lover and blames the excessive taste for eastern jewelry among women (*Elegies* 2.16.19–22):

I wish that no one at Rome was rich, and
    that the leader [*dux*] himself was able
    to live in the thatched cottage.
Nowhere then would there be girlfriends
    greedy for presents, and a girl would
    grow gray staying in the same house.

The irony is complex and pointed; if the *dux* (certainly not Augustus' favorite title) really lived in Romulus' carefully preserved thatched cottage on the Palatine, if he were really to set an example of simplicity and frugality (instead of merely pretending to), then others might follow his example, and poor lovers could enjoy their life of "illicit" love more securely. Ovid went further in the *Art of Love* and paid for it eventually, at least in part, at the hands of a tired and embit-

tered Augustus. The poet praises explicitly the delights of luxury and all the cultivated arts of adornment and pleasure, and exults that he did not live in a less cultured age (3.101–128); most of Book One, for exam-ple, is devoted to instructing men where and how to pick up girls from a huge and varied selection of desirable and available beauties. Here it is noticeable how, among the most suitable places, Ovid seems to delight in mentioning Augustan buildings and areas that have associations that ought to be con-trary to his purposes: for example, Octavia's portico, dedicated to her son Marcellus, in whom Augustus had placed such hopes be-fore his early death in 23 B.C.; Livia's por-tico; and the temple of Apollo and the librar-ies on the Palatine. Subsequently, Ovid, like Propertius, recommends picking up girls at the emperor's own shows and his grandiose triumphs; although Ovid attempts to con-fuse the message by including formal pas-sages of Augustan encomia and by asserting that his material is based on affairs with un-married, not respectable women, one can well understand how the work disappointed the emperor and rankled him, as well as real-ize that he would have been reluctant to act against the poet on its offensiveness alone.

Convivia remained a central part of lei-sured life for those who accepted the official Augustan values as much as for those who tried to evade them. Emperors naturally liked to set patterns by their examples as well as by their precepts, and to some extent clearly did so; hence, rightly, the imperial biographer Suetonius regularly included discussion of his subjects' behavior on the dining couch as much as in bed or at the shows. He records in *Lives of the Twelve Caesars* ("Augustus" 73–82) that Augustus gave formal dinner parties frequently, pay-ing due attention to rank and rarely if ever admitting freedmen; courses were three or, on special occasions, six. Augustus excelled at drawing silent or whispering guests into the general conversation, introduced musical or circus entertainers, delighted in gambling, and played elaborate games of auctioning unseen articles of unequal value. In sum, the picture thus given is that Augustus displayed elegance without excessive extravagance, was sparing personally in what he ate and drank, and above all displayed the appropriate virtue of "civility" (*comitas*). The problem at these formal banquets was to reconcile the need to display graduated patronage to large groups of people by the distribution of food, drink, and "friendship" with the need to impress guests with genuine conviviality and equality appropriate to the symposium or the *convivium* proper. One may legitimately wonder if Augustus in fact achieved the ideal balance as often as Suetonius suggests, and also whether he did not also on occasion—and perhaps especially when away from the residence on the Palatine—dine more informally with guests he chose for himself.

A fairly frequent guest of Augustus' was Horace (65–8 B.C.), the official poet for the Secular Games of 17 B.C. The importance of symposia and *convivia* in all the varieties of Horace's poetry can hardly be exaggerated. Many of his poems are stylized invitations to Augustan top men, especially his friend, patron, and mediator with the princeps, Maecenas; many promise that the poet will celebrate a public or private occasion with a suitable party, and many more offer ironic or perceptive descriptions of sympotic conversations and behavior. On the whole, in the more conversational genres of the *Satires* and the *Epistles* the settings are decidedly down-to-earth and Roman, with greater emphasis on the quality of the food, the social relationships of the participants, the theatrical entertainments and jests, and the moral value of the symposium. In the *Odes* the settings are more systematically those of Greek-style symposia, with scarcely a mention of dinner, although the types of wine to

be drunk are dwelled upon at length. While displaying awareness that his richer friends such as Maecenas regularly drink the best wines and vintages, he too shows connoisseurship in the choice of fine jars for special occasions as well as an awareness of the right perfumes, unguents, flowers, locales, and modes of drinking. Women at Horace's dinner parties in the *Odes*, with the puzzling exception of Licymnia in *Odes* 2.12, are Greek in name and a regular part of the pleasures of the occasion. But the poet avoids passionate intensity or lasting commitment, instead choosing friendly relations with semiprofessionals, or else comments with detached, experienced irony on the absurdity or fickleness of love's passions as experienced by him or witnessed in others. But the setting of the idealized symposium also enabled Horace to explore the themes of the renewal or reinforcement of friendships, the dangers of excessive luxury and building of villas, the desirability of surrender to moderate drinking and pleasures in general or in the deserved intervals of political life, and the acceptance of the vicissitudes of fortune. In fact, as his claim to be the "Roman Alcaeus" suggests, Horace uses the world of the Greek symposium as it has been transferred to Rome. For him this was the preferred location from which he, the son of a freedman but a poet of the highest ambition, can speak of his relations of near equality with the famous and powerful and address the Roman public with some authority on social or moral matters. The setting also helps to legitimate his personal life-style, permitted by Augustus and Maecenas, of comfortable, unmarried, and moderately pleasurable leisure.

Not everyone followed Augustus' and Horace's examples and precepts; wilder parties and life-styles remained popular from the senatorial class down, and are well reflected in the love poets. The fact that not even the imperial family was exempt from such activities, in the sophisticated forms adopted by the elder and younger Julias, brought the various tensions of the reign into the open in the scandals of 2 B.C. and A.D. 8. If there is any truth in the anecdotes and allegations of the elder Julia's jokes and japes (recorded by Macrobius, 2.5), she associated with the fashionable young aristocrats in conspicuous *convivia* and luxury, in blatant contrast to her father's wishes. The official version had it that when she took to conducting *convivia* and *comissationes* with her lovers on the Rostra in and around the Forum Romanum, Augustus could hide the truth from himself no longer and banished her to a small island.

The love poetry that was doubtless most popular with these circles regularly asserts the close connections between Love and Bacchus for the enjoyment of the life of pleasure or of the intensity of passion, in sharp contrast to the less desirable or admirable life of military and political service. The elegiac poets profess to be relatively poor, and therefore forbear to describe choice vintages or elaborate food at their parties; but the settings of their poems are often enough drinking parties and drunken *comissationes* in the streets, or to their mistresses' doors, intimate parties with the beloved or with her rivals, country picnics, or revels in resorts like Baiae. Ovid's poems provide the most realistic details. One of his *Amores* (1.4) anticipates that the poet will attend the same *convivium* as his mistress and her husband, and runs through the probable actions and emotions. The picture is of a sizable gathering, of much drink, and a very loose atmosphere; both sexual fondling between lover and mistress as guests leave and more serious contact between those sharing the same couch seem eminently conceivable. In Book One of the *Art of Love,* Ovid naturally suggests that one may also meet suitable girls at *convivia,* when drink aids passion and seduction (although it may im-

pair judgment), and later in the same book he gives more detailed advice for appropriate behavior: signaling to the mistress, making friends with the husband, avoiding the violence that mars many a party (and the example, familiar in Greek sympotic poetry, of the Centaurs is used), and singing, dancing, and seductive talk are all recommended.

Public and Private "Convivia" in the Early Empire

Naturally enough, all emperors continued to set fashions (or shock opinion) by their dinner party habits, but practice varied on the matter of giving large-scale formal dinners (*cenae rectae*), at which guests had simultaneously to receive entertainments and gifts appropriate to their status and yet share in a supposed general sense of equal and harmonious feasting. Emperors down to Nero all gave formal dinners —for example, Tiberius would cut costs by serving leftovers, and Gaius (Caligula) aroused scandal by displaying prominently below him his sisters, with whom he was supposed to have incestuous relations. Nero, however, chose to emphasize the redistributive aspect by substituting *sportula,* a handout of food or money, for the formal dinners (Suetonius, *Lives of the Twelve Caesars,* "Nero" 16); but Domitian reversed this policy (Suetonius, "Domitian" 7), and the huge public banquets of his reign on the occasions of festivals and games received elaborate, flattering descriptions from contemporary poets. These descriptions emphasize the creation of social harmony and shared hospitality, yet it remains equally clear that those of higher status were granted better seats and larger baskets of food. The scale and settings of the feasts (such as Domitian's huge hall in the newly enlarged and rebuilt "palace," or the Colosseum) ensured that while all might see the emperor on his raised dais, only a few select guests would have a chance of engaging him in conversation (as, for instance, Statius mentions in *Silvae* 1.6; 4.2; and Martial in *Epigrams* 8.50). Further, if the upper classes turned up in force to see and be seen, then there can in fact only have been places for a very small proportion of the free poor, however large the gathering for a common meal. The whole effect must have been a reinforcement of the social hierarchies and of the ideological dominance of the emperor, while also offering some slight redistribution of wealth and a not totally false impression of civility and temporary conviviality.

The upper classes in Rome and other cities of the empire used similar techniques and were similarly affected by imperial switches of policy. Clients of rich men might in different periods be offered regular handouts (*sportula*), during morning calls or while attending a great man at the baths, or might hope for regular invitations to dinner parties, and then grumble if offered inferior wine, food, or seating; Juvenal's *Satire* 5 and Pliny the Younger's *Letters* (2.6) contain protests at the habit of differentiated menus and wines. In Rome the large-scale offerings of public largesse and shows were virtually monopolized by the greatest benefactor, the emperor himself. However, throughout the cities of the western provinces, as earlier, and continuing throughout the East, there was plenty of scope for the public-spirited and honor-seeking landowners and local elites to found temples, schools, libraries, and other public works, and also to distribute wealth in the form of public dinners or *sportulae* on the occasions of festivals, dedications of buildings, birthdays, coming-of-age ceremonies, marriages, or posthumous celebrations of a benefactor's birthday. Here again, on the basis of massive inscriptional evidence, it seems that in the western provinces the Roman habits of fairly strict observation of social hierarchies in the distribution of food or money are preserved;

members of the local councils receive the most, priests of the cult of Augustus (*augustales*) somewhat less, and ordinary citizens considerably less again. Women belonging to the relevant categories are sometimes omitted altogether, or if included they are usually wives of councillors and receive smaller gifts than their husbands.

The informal dinner parties of the emperors also set the fashion, and were given to gain favor among the various classes and to project a general and desired imperial image. One theme in the histories of "bad" emperors (as related by Suetonius and by Cassius Dio in his *Roman History*) is the terrifying combination of conviviality and the arbitrary exercise of power; so Gaius (Caligula) explained his burst of laughter to the consuls reclining next to him by revealing the sudden thought that he could have their throats cut on the spot; and thus Domitian made prominent senators and knights endure a night-long funeral banquet in a pitch-black room, with black couches, food, dishes, and individualized gravestones for company, before releasing them and sending presents after them. A second major theme is the extent of extravagance, luxury, and hellenization indulged in or sedulously avoided by various emperors; often a progression could be traced from initial good intentions and sumptuary legislation to gross self-indulgence, open or disguised. Tiberius began with an ostentatious display of parsimony and some interest in restricting extravagant purchases, although according to Tacitus (*Annals* 3.54) he expressed well-founded doubts on whether sumptuary legislation was desirable or could be effective (even those, he held, who "in social gatherings and at dinner parties" clamored for restrictive action would complain more loudly if laws were passed). But rumors of drunkenness and of *convivia* indulgences became increasingly insistent and convincing the more Tiberius shut himself away in

Campanian villas and finally on Capri. Whatever the truth of the wilder allegations made by Suetonius, persistent and increasing tastes for gourmet food and Hellenistic poets, scholarship, and games, for Greek astrologers and companions, and probably for Greek or grecizing boys as well, seem well enough attested. Gaius, according to Suetonius, was a "monster," who displayed the grossest and most public forms of extravagance, sexuality, and cruelty "even when he was relaxing and devoting himself to fun and feast." Claudius was held to be excessively fond of eating, drinking, and dicing, the most famous feasts of his reign being the extraordinary wedding revels and bacchanalia indulged in by his wife Messalina and her last lover Silius, which hastened their discovery and deaths. Nero's principate showed him gradually unfold into the apogee of extravagant and showy hellenization, scandalizing respectable Roman society above all by his obsession for entering public competitions as a musician, actor, and chariot racer, first in Naples, then Rome, and finally on a visit to Greece itself. His banquets were equally lavish, imaginatively elegant, and depraved (for a time under the expertise of Petronius), and open to public gaze, while, like Antiochos IV, he also had a taste for disguise and for roaming the bars and streets of the city looking for excitement and violence.

After Nero's death and the end of the Julio-Claudian era, a marked change of tone toward the more luxurious of Hellenistic practices was established with some success at the top of Roman society. From Vespasian to Trajan, that is, in the period A.D. 69–117, emperors made considerable efforts (and only Domitian totally failed) to establish a contempt for luxury and respect for the regular maintenance of harmonious, tension-free, cultivated dinner party relations, above all with the respectable upper classes. Such an achievement is proclaimed loudly in Pliny the Younger's *Panegyric* (47–49), and reinforced in a letter he wrote of a few days spent hearing legal cases in Trajan's coastal villa at Centum Cellae (Civitavecchia) near Ostia, where he purports to be delighted with the simplicity and charm of the evening dinners, with recitations or agreeable conversation, nothing excessive in the food and drink for a princeps, and gifts for all on leaving (*Letters* 6.31). Tacitus explains the change in tone in terms of the final demise of the old noble families of the "republic," in whom the luxurious Hellenistic habits and a willful contempt for traditional values were most deeply embedded, and the rise to the top of a new municipal and provincial class, under the powerful influence of Vespasian (and, one can add, in reaction against the final excesses of Nero).

Architectural developments in the design of *triclinia* in the early empire can also be identified, once again under the guiding influence of imperial innovation. Increasingly, it appears, the impression sought in the grander dining rooms was that of a great natural display or a theatrical tableau, and the placement of couches might well ensure that the most privileged guests had the finest views. Pliny the Younger makes a point of mentioning in his *Letters* (2.17) the splendid, contrasting views to be obtained from the different dining rooms of his coastal villa, also near Ostia. But two imperial settings may also be mentioned. Tiberius was fond of dining in a highly baroque and elaborate grotto setting at Spelunca (Sperlonga) on the Tyrrhenian coast (he nearly died during one dinner when part of the rock collapsed). Recent archaeological work there has revealed a *triclinium* built out on an artificial island, facing a huge cave inland decorated with carefully placed Rhodian baroque sculptures (from the same artists as the *Laocoön*) portraying four horrific scenes in the life of Odysseus that emphasize that hero's many-sidedness, his cunning, treachery, courage, and loyalty. It seems the perfect dining environment for the secretive, scholarly, and devious emperor. Second, Nero's Golden House, with its lakes, park, and wildlife—a remarkable and obnoxious attempt to bring the country into the heart of Rome—contained no doubt a great many *triclinia,* according to Suetonius, with ivory ceilings from which roses and perfumes fell onto the guests; the octagonal and domed central dining room possessed a revolving ceiling that reflected the movements of day and night and the seasons. Guests in such a room became, perhaps, the spectacle themselves, the center of the world.

In the extant literature from the first and second centuries A.D., the significance and the tensions of the dinner party in social life in the Greek and Latin parts of the empire are reflected even more substantially than before. Only a few examples can be given here. The letters of Pliny the Younger carefully and elegantly reveal, among other chosen aspects of his political and social life, the appropriate attitudes toward the functions and styles of convivial dining. One such letter (9.36) describes the daily routine followed on one of his country estates: exercise and a bath would be followed by a "simple" dinner with the wife or a few friends, accompanied by entertainments such as readings of books, performances of comic plays, or musical turns. In another letter (1.15) he presses a reluctant friend to accept such an invitation, jocularly contrasting his offerings of hors d'oeuvres, snails, eggs, lettuce, wheat cakes, chilled wine with honey, a comic play, book reading, or music with the more lavish attractions of oysters, sows' innards, sea urchins, and Spanish dancing girls that the friend might find elsewhere, and seriously pleads the greater claims of the easygoing fun and simplicity of his dinners. On other occasions Pliny deprecates elaborate circus acts at dinners, let alone the practice of maintaining one's own troupe of pantomimists that distinguishes the formidable elderly lady Ummidia Quadratilla's determination to uphold the decadent standards of Neronian society in a more sober age; or he praises the surprisingly deep literary scholarship and command of Greek as well as of Latin displayed by a retired and reclusive equestrian military officer when entertaining Pliny on his farm in central Italy. He records a dolphin story heard at one dinner, and reports his pleasure at being recognized at a dinner as a famous orator by a man visiting Rome from an Italian town. Finally, in the most explicitly persuasive letter on these themes, he attacks the so-called "elegant economy" practiced at dinner parties whereby two categories of "friends" are distinguished and freedmen are relegated to a third, each category being given different amounts and quality of fare; it is better, Pliny urges his "promising young friend," Junius Avitus, to serve the same relatively cheaper fare to all so that the ideal of convivial equality is preserved (*Letters* 2.6).

Although the humiliating aspects of many Roman dinner parties and the nasty games at the expense of clients, freedmen, and inferior guests provided the material for much satirical exploitation in the poems of Martial and Juvenal, many of the occasional poems of Martial and Statius were composed at and/or about the *convivia* of their patrons. The phenomenon is also explored from a different angle in an entertaining piece by Lucian (d. A.D. 180) called *Salaried Posts in Great Houses.* Whereas Martial and Juvenal often appear to sneer at the various types of Greeks and orientals seeking to climb in Roman society, Lucian's piece describes the indignities suffered by Greek philosophers and rhetoricians who accept posts in great Roman households as tutors and intellectual experts. The main humiliations are inflicted at the large *convivia;* the intellectual may be welcomed on first arrival with the place of honor, and suffer jealous grumbles from other clients, but he quickly sinks to a lowly spot among the clients, freedmen, tame wits, and parasites (*scurrae*), receiving little decent refreshment and a mass of gleeful, philistine sneers from his patron and other guests. But Lucian's satire, like that of Martial and Juvenal, can be impartial; another highly amusing work, *The Symposium, or the Lapiths,* offers a philosopher's symposium in the Platonic tradition, but this party of famous representatives of the major philosophical schools and other scholars gathered for a wedding banquet swiftly degenerates into a parade of greed, drunkenness, lust, and professional jealousies, and the traditional dangers, symbolized as ever by the wedding fight between Lapiths and Centaurs, are not avoided, as the various squabbles over food end in multiple clashes.

But many other Greek writers, with their high-level contacts in the Roman world, added more positively to the literary and philosophical sympotic genre. We may mention two lengthy works that proclaim the central functions of the symposium for the Greek upper class to be the strengthening of their political and social relations with eminent Romans, displaying the fruits of their literary and philosophical studies, and retaining their sense of a link with the classical past. The nine books of Plutarch's *Symposiac Questions,* dedicated to a close friend and eminent man, Sosius Senecio, twice consul under Trajan and a philhellene perhaps of eastern origin, purport to record interesting conversations held at a large number of banquets and symposia in Rome and in various cultural centers in Greece on the occasions of private celebrations, public festivals, and games. Of the ninety-five sections of the work (several of which form part of a chain of discussions on a single occasion), well over half concern topics directly to do with the symposium, such as the role of the sym-

posiarch, the preparation of food and drink, the use of garlands, the ethics of the selection of guests, the acceptability of serious political discussion, the appropriate types of conversation and jokes and the avoidance of offence and hubris, the physiological effects of food and drink, and the apt use of literary quotations. Many other topics arise from the settings of the party (such as athletic festivals, the ephebes' display in Athens, wedding parties, and so on). The scenes regularly show Greeks and Romans conversing together, and not infrequently Greek and Roman customs and linguistic terms are compared and contrasted, although overall it is Greek culture and literature that plays the dominant role. While the general effect (and obvious purpose) is the appearance of a shared world of polite letters and sympotic conversations and friendships, the underlying tensions in the power relationships can occasionally be glimpsed. For example, while the habit of guests bringing their own hangers-on along to a symposium is on the whole deprecated as against the spirit of free and easy equality, it is recognized that foreign dignitaries (that is, Romans) must be permitted to bring whom they choose. As a work providing a mass of detailed evidence for proper sympotic behavior and as a storehouse of literary quotations, the book is surpassed only by Athenaeus' *The Learned Banquet,* which, for all its colossal learning and usefulness in preserving fragments of lost authors and discussions of sympotic practice and theory, is a vast monument to the scholarly pedantry of its age.

By far the most vivid, subtle, and enjoyable depiction of a fictional banquet during the period of the Roman Empire is the "Dinner with Trimalchio," the most substantial surviving episode of Petronius' great novel, the *Satyricon.* The scene is the hugely lavish and vulgar hospitality of the freedman Trimalchio, at the baths and then at length in his mansion in a Campanian

"Greek city," almost certainly Puteoli. The house, Trimalchio boasts, was substantially rebuilt by him and is now equipped with four dining rooms, twenty bedrooms, two marble colonnades, and so on. Most of the other guests are also self-made, self-important freedmen; Trimalchio's wife, Fortunata, and several other wives are present. The contrasting characters of the narrator Encolpius, his two companions Agamemnon and Ascyltos, and his boyfriend Giton (better educated, possessing a veneer of snobbish sophistication, but shallow and cynical) provide many of the tensions of the dinner. Much of the satire is directed at the gross extravagance, theatrical display, and grotesque cultural pretentiousness of the dinner and accompanying entertainments. Dishes repeatedly belie their first appearances and disgorge unsuspected riches (as when a pig appears not to have been gutted and the cook is about to be whipped, the pig is slit open to reveal cooked sausages and blood puddings).

The episode also illustrates that "entertainment" is likely to take the form of staged trials of slaves or phony quarrels in order to display Trimalchio's sense of fun and humane fellow-feeling or that accounts might be presented so that the vast extent of Trimalchio's estate can be revealed. In the constant mythological, musical, and literary performances and by jokes and allusions to the host's artistes, Trimalchio and his guests are alike ridiculed for their unnecessary elaboration and their gross ignorance or incompetence. Nonetheless, in their set speeches and general conversation the freedmen reveal not only a fair amount of crudity, vulgarity, pretentiousness, devotion to money-making, and obsession with food, witchcraft, and death, but also a hard, earthy, touching honesty and vitality that contrasts favorably with the flashy and cheap amoralism and superficiality of the narrator and his supposed pals.

The "Dinner with Trimalchio" is a major, ironic, "realist" contribution to the sympotic genre, going well beyond Horace's treatment of the meal of the nouveau riche Nasidienus (*Satires* 2.8), and echoing at times the philosophical strands of the tradition; the long set-piece speeches of the various freedmen and the entry of the drunken central character Habinnas from another party seem equally to recall the techniques of the Platonic *symposion*. Like the work as a whole, as far as we can judge it, the "Dinner" episode displays in literary form of extreme skill and sophistication the same taste for experiencing the varieties of high and low life in Rome and the Campanian cities prevalent in Nero's circle; for us it represents the fullest and most subtly differentiated depiction of many aspects of social and economic life in Nero's Italy, and it is fitting, if somewhat fortuitous, that the central portion of what happens to have survived from a mammoth work is a set-piece portrayal of an elaborate dinner party.

Collegia and Associations in the Early Empire

Associations of many types, in Rome and throughout the empire, flourished even more vigorously than before, although many types continued to attract suspicion and suppression from the authorities; they form one of the most visible and significant features of social life in the cities of the empire for many different classes of people. At the higher levels, the ancient priestly collegia in many cases retained important functions and activities, even after they were usefully reorganized by Augustus as part of his major religious and social reforms; so the Arval Brethren, a "club" of moderately distinguished upper-class Romans, although reconstituted radically, continued for centuries to perform their rituals, eat their dinners, and record their acts. Poets, apparently sometimes associated with scribes and other minor officials who performed services for the magistrates, met in a collegium or a succession of collegia from the time of the middle republic (late third century B.C.) to the early empire. The officials who worked for magistrates as lictors, scribes, or messengers (collectively known as *apparitores*, having attained their largely sinecure posts through patronage), formed a significant class of upwardly mobile, relatively cultivated, and ambitious individuals, and no doubt the meetings of their various collegia, as well as their private *convivia,* reinforced their sense of position and their social contacts. Augustus seems to have tightened up the hierarchies of such bodies, and sought to reorganize the hitherto subversive local associations in Rome so that they conducted orderly and proper festivals, games, and banquets. Thus the cults of the Compitalia became official state cults, and were linked to the cult of the Lares (household gods) and the Genius (guiding spirit) of Augustus himself.

Outside Rome, in the cities of Italy and the western provinces, the organizations of the *augustales* developed rapidly from the time of Augustus onward, presumably with full encouragement from the emperor, although the degree of local variations in their structures suggests that it was not necessary to direct their formation from the center. These were groups of wealthy individuals, predominantly freedmen, who were selected (sometimes by the local town councils), often in annual boards of six, to form a collegium and to perform ceremonies connected with the imperial cult. They will have demonstrated their suitability for selection by public benefactions and been expected to continue to display their public spirit in the forms of games, public feasts, dedication of statues, temples, and so on; the reward will have been a recognized place in society, especially desirable for rich freedmen who were debarred from holding office as magistrates or on the official town councils. The institution of the *augustales* seems to have flourished first and with special vigor in the cities around the Bay of Naples (the setting of the *Satyricon,* in which the status of Trimalchio and two freedmen as *augustales* is notably mentioned), an area known for its economic prosperity, numbers of slaves and freedmen, openness to Greek and oriental influences, leisured life-style, and importance for the emperors' economic concerns. It is likely to have been a major force in providing successful freedmen and some freeborn men as well with a focus for their ambition for status; it would have helped the emperor to consolidate his position as the chief source of loyalty, devotion, and patronage; and it no doubt operated as a force for political and social stability in an often turbulent area.

Organizations of young men were also not neglected by Augustus. Associations of young men existed in varying degrees in Italian cities during the republic in not dissimilar forms from the *epheboi* and *neoi* groups in the Hellenistic world, and they may indeed have been subjected to Greek and Etruscan influences from early times. In Italy, though, such groups seem to have shown a greater interest in hunting, horseback riding, and military training than in athletics and the gymnasium. Augustus developed, standardized, and extended these traditions, typically using apparently conservative means to preserve his new order. In the capital, the young knights (*equites,* that is, sons both of senators and the class of knights) led the way, encouraged to exercise regularly on horseback in the Campus Martius, to parade in cavalry squadrons, and to present equestrian skills in the allegedly ancient horseback show called the Lusus Troiae, the Game of Troy, for elder and younger boys, including young "princes." *Collegia iuvenum,* colleges of young men, now become widely attested throughout the cities of the romanized western provinces, and they provided opportunities for the sons of the local nobilities and prosperous classes to train and play together, to participate in many civic cults, and to be seen to be ready to start their military and/or political careers. These bodies of young men were equally encouraged to provide public displays of their skills, often, it seems, giving competitive shows of hunting and gladiatorial fighting between contingents of different towns, in theaters and amphitheaters. These shows seem to have been encouraged even when emperors from Augustus on were trying to ban senators and knights from voluntary participation in stage shows and gladiatorial contests. But the bans, like sumptuary laws, seem to have been ineffective, and the apogee of such appearances was of course reached with the theatrical, circus, and gladiatorial activities of Nero.

Toward the other, less officially guided associations Augustus and subsequent emperors maintained the suspicious and cautious approach of the republican senate. Augustus seems to have repeated Julius Caesar's law, "abolishing all collegia except those which were ancient and legal" (Suetonius, *Lives of the Twelve Caesars,* "Augustus" 32). Subsequent policy, as finally formulated in the *Digest* (the compendium of classical jurisprudence), amounted to a permanent imperial injunction against all electoral clubs (*collegia sodalicia*) and associations formed by soldiers inside their camps, and requiring provincial governors to keep an eye on all associations "of the lesser orders" (the *collegia tenuiorum*). In general, to exist all associations had to seek approval from the senate or the emperor. Clubs that existed for essentially religious, social, or funerary purposes (often all three combined) were normally approved as a matter of routine, and doubtless many more operated without seeking formal permission, especially in the

provinces. Of the innumerable inscriptions recording the activities of these associations the most informative is the long document (Dessau, *Inscriptiones Latinae Selectae* 7212) of the "benevolent" collegium of Diana and Antinous (the dead, deified favorite of Hadrian), formed in the city of Lanuvium (Lanuvio, in ancient Latium) in A.D. 133. It quotes the senatorial permission authorizing the club to ensure the proper burial of its members, provided that members pay their dues no more than once a month for performing their rites and meet no more often than once a month to pay the dues.

Problems nonetheless arose fairly often with such clubs. Tiberius worried about some foreign cults, and particularly the rites and organizations of the Jews; Gaius agreed to the Alexandrians' persecution of the Jews, but permitted some clubs to be formed, which Claudius then suppressed while undoing Gaius' hostile acts against the Jews. In A.D. 59 there were serious riots at Pompeii during some gladiatorial contests, in which passionate rivalries between Pompeians and the visiting crowd from Nuceria Alfaterna (Nocera Inferiore) were aroused, and many were killed. The senate responded fiercely, banning any such shows in Pompeii for ten years and disbanding the collegia that had formed against the laws; which these were is not clear, but they may have been unofficial "fan clubs" supporting bands of gladiators (or *iuvenes*). The ban had little effect, and collegia of various cultic and occupational types continued actively in Pompeii until its destruction in A.D. 79, as the graffiti of election notices on Pompeian buildings testify.

There could be significant regional variations in the types of clubs that could be permitted. In many towns in Italy and the western provinces associations of smiths (*fabri*), rag dealers (*centonarii*), and timberworkers (*dendrophori*), or in certain areas combinations of these associations were permitted or encouraged to form fire brigades to fight the frequent fires that afflicted the poorer housing in ancient cities, and many inscriptions record their sense of civic importance. But when Pliny the Younger, then legate to Bithynia (in Asia Minor), asked Trajan whether on this model a collegium of smiths could be formed in Nicomedia (İzmit) after a serious fire, Trajan responded with great caution, arguing that the province had often been disturbed by the activities of such societies, and that whenever people assembled together there, they turned themselves into a political club (and Trajan used the latinized Greek term *hetaeria*); he advised encouraging the owners of properties to be in charge of fire-fighting equipment and to assemble assistants ad hoc. (Pliny the Younger, *Letters* 10.34, 10.35).

Similarly, Trajan agreed with Pliny that the "free city" of Amisus (Samsun, on the Black Sea) could be allowed to form "benefit societies" (*eranoi*) if provision for that existed in their laws, and added the proviso that "we should not interfere the more readily if they use the contributions not for crowds and illicit gatherings but for the alleviation of the hardship of the poor." Trajan also commented that this sort of body would be forbidden in cities subject to Roman laws (Pliny the Younger, *Letters* 10.93; 10.94). In the end Pliny was obliged to suppress all types of clubs because of political unrest.

The suspicion of new associations forms part of the background to the Roman persecution of the early Christian groups, which in some ways resembled other cult-based associations (with their shared meals and concern for the well-being and burial of members), although they differed significantly in their greater degree of exclusiveness, commitment, and hostility to traditional and civic religions. The points are well made by Tertullian in his *Apology* (38): "If I am not mistaken, the reason for prohibiting associations lay in the concern for public order, that the state should not be split into divisions, which is very likely to disrupt elections, public meetings, senates, assemblies, even the games through hostile clashing of partisans." He argued that Christians had no interest in politics, and that their corporate activities were calm, studious, disciplined, and supportive of the state and the public order.

The associations of the humbler people did indeed serve a variety of purposes; however, even the occupational collegia did not exist primarily to benefit their members economically. They were not at all like trade unions, since members were predominantly employers, not employees, and there are pitifully few cases—in the East and mostly during the later empire—when associations seem to have been seditious and refused to work. Nor were they like medieval guilds, given to activities designed to regulate or protect their economic interests; no proper guildhalls have been discovered (the so-called Piazza delle Corporazioni at Ostia seems to have been a collection of offices for a wide variety of private traders). Limited relations do seem to have developed in key areas between the central government and certain collegia. The major concern for the stability of the grain supply and the price of bread encouraged emperors and grain-supply officials to work with collegia of shippers, traders, and bakers, first to obtain lists of suitable operators to whom to offer long-term contracts, and second (perhaps from the time of Trajan) to offer them special licenses and tax privileges. The fire-fighting collegia of smiths or rag dealers were also offered tax privileges. All collegia naturally sought to increase their standing in their communities and to enhance their corporate properties and funds by attracting patrons from among the richest members of their cities and occasionally from relevant central government officials.

Although the collegia had religious functions, they were above all concerned with status, solidarity, sociability, and aspects of social security. It seems inaccurate, as has often been done, to classify a large number of collegia as specifically burial clubs (*collegia funeratica*), but it remains the case that perhaps a fifth of the collegia attested on inscriptions display a concern for the proper burial of their members. In an urban environment, where ties of kinship and of small-scale local communities were weaker or nonexistent, where death could be sudden, a pauper's grave horrid and degrading, and a decent burial costly, many will have found it easier to face the future with some burial insurance in the form of club membership. The collegium of Diana and Antinous from Lanuvium, for example, provides the fullest set of regulations, impressive in their formalism and detail, of a cult association in which provision of burial for its members is a major purpose and the object of a good deal of the members' contributions.

The regulations of the club of Diana and Antinous concern social life as well, as do all the others; they are designed to ensure proper celebration of the monthly club dinners, the provision of good wine, bread, and sardines, of oil for the bath before the dinner, the appointment and behavior of their various officials, and the avoidance of insults and disorder at their meetings. Club dinners, held in their clubhouses (*scholae*) with as much pomp, friendship, and luxury as members and patrons could provide, were no doubt for many the highlight of each month and a major feature of membership; some clubs even proclaimed their devotion to conviviality in their names, such as the "Late Drinkers" (*seri-bibi*) of Pompeii (*Corpus Inscriptionum Latinarum* 4.575). Jolly conviviality was thus a major feature of most collegia, and drunken revelry, with its subsequent insults, quarreling, and fighting, was by no means unknown. Constantly, regulations of the clubs seek to prevent it and to fine recalcitrant members, and these ten-

dencies provided further reasons for authorities and moralists to show concern. Cases include the attempts by a prefect of Egypt, Avillius Flaccus (A.D. 32–38), to discipline unruly clubs (actions approved by the Jewish Philo in *For Flaccus* 4ff., 135ff.) and the denunciations by the Christian polemicist Tertullian (in his *Apology*) 38–39.

Highly popular as these collegia clearly were in urban social life, their membership was not significantly drawn from the poorest of the city dwellers, although upper-class authorities classified the clubs as "of the lesser people" (*tenuiores*). The clubs of craftsmen and traders and the like were probably the most exclusive (although not all necessarily insisted on membership in the named occupation) and were predominantly made up of fairly prosperous workers, both freeborn and freedmen in varying proportions. The religious and social clubs were no doubt more mixed in their composition, but very few consisted mainly of the very poor. Women appear only rarely on membership lists, and very few women's cult associations are attested. Women appear rather more frequently as patrons and benefactors of male clubs, as in the famous case of Eumachia of Pompeii, who gave an impressive meeting hall to the fullers. Female slaves appear equally rarely (they are mentioned as possible members in the collegium of Diana and Antinous); the laws stated that no slave could join an association without the express permission of his or her master, and this regulation seems to have restricted slaves almost exclusively to social and religious clubs.

Conviviality of a more promiscuous type was readily available every day in the cities, in parks and baths, and above all in inns, restaurants, bars, and brothels, of which the excavations of Pompeii and Ostia have given us many vivid pictures. Less-favored collegia, such as the "Late Drinkers" of Pompeii, may have used rooms in hotels for their meetings, but more generally, one could say that inns and bars constituted the "clubs" for those too poor to join a proper collegium. Establishments catered to various tastes, and ranged from simple bars and fast-food shops on the streets to grander places with gardens, vegetable gardens, and many rooms. The more disreputable inns were doubtless the scene of regular brawls and fights (paintings on one tavern in Pompeii show fighting over dice, with the innkeeper saying, "Get out and quarrel outside"), and such places also encouraged (or forced) their staff to offer sexual services. Waitresses and barmaids tend to be presented in literature and on graffiti as prostitutes or witches, and the legal sources assert that intercourse with such women could not constitute adultery.

Emperors were frequently fearful of the dangers of seditious talk, drunken violence, or plots arising from gatherings in inns and bars, and measures restricting activities there often accompanied those restricting collegia. Claudius, for example, tried to close the inns where the collegia he was banning used to meet, and in general forbade the selling of cooked meats and hot drinks; Nero repeated the regulations restricting the ban on cooked meat. Such measures were doubtless hard to enforce, although it has been suggested by Hermansen that the absence of built-in food jars from Ostian bars, in contrast to those in Pompeii, indicates that gradually they ceased to offer cooked meals. Emperors failed to be consistent in these matters. According to Suetonius, Claudius rambled off during a senate debate into a reminiscence about the bars he had enjoyed in his youth, and the need for frequent snacks; and Nero's "slumming" revels naturally included a round of the bars.

An Ostian wine bar provides the scene of a final illustration of the extent to which the Greek tradition of the symposium and of the types of discussion appropriate to it per-

meated the daily life of the hellenized cities of Italy. The "wit and wisdom" of the archaic Greek lawgivers and thinkers collectively distinguished as the "Seven Wise Men" circulated for centuries at literary symposia as verses, mottoes, and moral statements that were used as the basis for verse or prose elaborations. At about the same time (*ca.* A.D. 100) that Plutarch, for example, wrote his lengthy elaboration, the "Symposium of the Seven Wise Men," a wine bar in Ostia decorated its walls with elegant portraits of these sages (the names of Chilon, Solon, and Thales survive under their pictures), with pithy sayings attached; below other paintings (obliterated, it seems, when the bar was changed to a bathhouse) is found the general message, "Have a good crap, and screw the doctors." Each sage offered specific advice on similar lines: for example, "Solon rubbed his stomach to get good motions," and "Thales advised the constipated to try hard." Like the amusements in "Dinner with Trimalchio" or a Lucian satire, this scene reveals both a popular, earthy concentration on the practical needs of the bowels, and also a widely disseminated desire to make reference to, and at times to poke fun at, the long-standing, leisure-class sympotic traditions of the Greeks, which were adopted and adapted throughout the urban cultures of the Hellenistic and Roman worlds.

BIBLIOGRAPHY

SOURCES

Cicero, *Pro Caelio* (*For Caelius*), R. Gardner, trans. (1958), *De Officiis* (*On Duty*), Walter Miller, trans. (1913), *Letters to Atticus*, D. R. Shackleton Bailey, ed., trans. (1964–1969), *Letters to Friends*, D. R. Shackleton Bailey, ed. (1977), *Pro Murena* (*For Murena*), and *In Catilinam* (*Against Catiline*), C. Macdonald, trans. (1977), *In Pisonem* (*Against*

Piso), and *Pro Milone* (*For Milo*) N. H. Watts, trans. (1931), and *Verrine Orations*, L. H. G. Greenwood, trans., 2 vols. (1928, 1935); Dio Cassius, *Dio's Roman History*, Earnest Cary, trans. (1914–1927); Macrobius, *Saturnalia*, J. Willis, ed. (1963); Martial, *Epigrams*, W. C. A. Ker, trans., 2 vols. (rev. ed. 1968); Ovid, *Art of Love*, J. H. Mozley, trans. (rev. ed. 1979), *Fasti* (*The Roman Calendar*) James G. Frazer, trans. (1931), and *Heroides, Amores*, Grant Showerman, trans. (1977); Petronius, *Satyricon*, J. P. Sullivan, trans. (1965); Pliny the Younger, *Letters and Panegyricus*, Betty Radice, trans., 2 vols. (1969); Plautus, *The Haunted House*, P. Nixon, trans. (1924); Statius, *Silvae*, J. H. Mozley, trans. (1928); Suetonius, *The Lives of the Caesars*, J. C. Rolfe, trans., 2 vols. (1914); Tacitus, *The Annals*, M. Grant, trans. (rev. ed. 1971); Tertullian, *Apologia*, T. R. Glover, trans. (1931).

SOURCE BOOKS

Mary Lefkowitz and Maureen B. Fant, *Women's Life in Greece and Rome* (1982); Naphtali Lewis and Meyer Reinhold, eds., *Roman Civilization, I: The Republic* (1951), and *II: The Empire* (1955).

STUDIES

Frank M. Ausbüttel, *Untersuchungen zu den Vereinen im Westen des römischen Reiches* (Frankfurter Althistorische Studien 11) (1982); J. P. V. D. Balsdon, *Life and Leisure in Ancient Rome* (1969); Larissa Bonfante, "Etruscan Couples and their Aristocratic Society," in Helene Foley, ed., *Reflections of Women in Antiquity* (1981); John D'Arms, *Romans on the Bay of Naples* (1970); Moses I. Finley, *Politics in the Ancient World* (1983), and *The Ancient Economy* (1973; 2d ed. 1985); Martin Frederiksen, *Campania* (1984); Ludwig Friedländer, *Roman Life and Manners under the Roman Empire*, 4 vols. (1908–1913); Michael Grant, *Cities of Vesuvius: Pompeii and Herculaneum* (1971), and *Erotic Art in Pompeii* (1975); Jasper Griffin, *Latin Poets and Roman Life* (1985); Miriam Griffin, *Nero: the End of a Dynasty* (1984); G. Hermansen, *Ostia: Aspects of Roman City Life* (1982); Keith Hopkins, *Death and Renewal* (1983); Wilhelmina L. Jashemski, *The Gardens of Pompeii* (1979); Natalie Kampen, *Image and Status: Roman Working Women in Ostia* (1981).

J. H. W. G. Liebeschuetz, *Continuity and Change in Roman Religion* (1979); Andrew W. Lintott, *Violence in Republican Rome* (1968); R. O. A. M. Lyne, *The Latin Love Poets* (1980); Alexander G. McKay, *Houses, Villas and Palaces in the Roman World* (1975); Ramsay MacMullen, *Enemies of the Roman Order* (1966; repr. 1975), and *Roman Social Relations, 50 B.C. to A.D. 284* (1974); Wayne Meeks, *The First Urban Christians* (1983); Russell Meiggs, *Roman Ostia*, 2d ed. (1973); Fergus Millar, "The Impact of Monarchy", in *Caesar Augustus, Seven Aspects* (1984); Oswyn Murray, "Symposium and Genre in the Poetry of Horace," in *Journal of Roman Studies*, **75** (1985); J. A. North, "Religious Toleration in Rome," in *Proceedings of the Cambridge Philological Society*, **25** (1979); S. E. Ostrow, "Augustales Along the Bay of Naples: A Case for Their Early Growth," in *Historia*, **34** (1985).

Geoffrey Rickman, *The Corn Supply of Ancient Rome* (1980); Ronald Syme, *History in Ovid* (1978); Susan Treggiari, *Roman Freedmen in the Late Republic* (1969); H. S. Versnel, "Historical Implications," in C. M. Stibbe *et al.*, *Lapis Satricanus*, Archeologische Studiën van het Nederlands Instituut te Rome, Scripta Minora 5 (1980); Andrew Wallace-Hadrill, "Family and Inheritance in the Augustan Marriage Laws," in *Proceedings of the Cambridge Philological Society*, **27** (1981), and *Suetonius* (1983); J.-P. Waltzing, *Étude historique sur les corporations professionelles chez les Romains*, 4 vols. (1895–); T. P. Wiseman, "*Pete nobiles amicos*: Poets and Patrons in Late Republican Rome," in *Literary and Artistic Patronage in Ancient Rome* (1982).

Medicine

JOHN SCARBOROUGH

IN LEADING AN ASSAULT on the main gate of Datos, Tychon the soldier had received an arrow in his back. The wound seemed quite minor, since the missile entered at a sharp angle, easily pulled out by a breathless companion as the mercenaries retreated from another unsuccessful attempt to gain entrance into Datos. Much grumbling followed this last failure, and Tychon occasionally reached over his right shoulder with his left hand to touch his wound, which had stopped bleeding. In the meantime, the company commander went among the dispirited troops, encouraging the mercenaries with talk of new plans for tomorrow's renewed attack on the stubborn town, and of the refurbished seige machinery that would make the crucial difference. Tychon sipped some freshly plundered Chian wine, and swapped tales of earlier campaigns with a grizzled veteran sitting beside him, who claimed to have fought with the great Spartan general Brasidas at the seige of Potidaea.

As dusk settled, the soldiers posted their pickets. The camp began to hear low moans from where Tychon had built his cooking fire; moans soon became grunts and what sounded like someone gnashing his teeth in a fury of rage. Rushing to see the cause of the trouble, the commander presumed that the noises were the usual preludes to a fight over some small bits of booty, seized the day before when the troops had sacked an outlying farmhouse. Tychon, however, was alone, moaning in a most curious posture: he was arched back in *opisthotonos,* and his jaws seemed locked together against his will. Shortly, he stumbled backwards and fell to the ground, still arched in pain. A friend forced some wine between his teeth, but Tychon could not swallow, and the liquid was expelled in spurts from his nostrils. Someone ran off to fetch an *iatros* (doctor), who had been seen in a small village three dozen *stades* (about five miles) away, and the rest of the small army settled into a troubled sleep while Tychon's struggles and grunts continued through the night.

In the late afternoon of the following day, the *iatros* Demosthenes arrived, and quickly hurried to Tychon, who was still in his arched posture, now and then on his side. His saliva had become frothy. Demosthenes observed that the arrow wound was hot, and there was a small amount of pus in the surface of the gash. In whispers, the *iatros* indicated that there was little he could do, with the exception of soothing plasters which might cool the wound and reduce the amount of yellow bile.

The next morning, as a cock crowed his welcome to the first rays of the dawn, Tychon died.

***

Tychon is recorded in one of the famous "case histories" found in the extant Hippocratic *Epidemics* (5.95) [Littré, V. pp. 254–257]); the unknown author relates how Tychon was at the seige of Datos and that he died, but the fictionalized account above compacts two "cases" into one (*Epidemics* 5.95 and 5.47 [Littré, V, pp. 234–235]). The soldier of *Epidemics* 5.47, who died after being wounded by an arrow in his upper right back, is not named, nor is the place of action. The Tychon of *Epidemics* 5.95 died from a wound in his chest from a missile hurled from a catapult, a day after being wounded, a rather compressed account of the actual, normal incubation period of five to ten days for tetanus. "Tychon" could as easily have died from the arrow. In Greek armies of the fifth and fourth centuries B.C., there was little provision for medical care among the common soldiers, so that the mercenary hurrying off to find an *iatros* would make historic sense. Moreover, once the physician arrived, he would bring with him a series of theoretical assumptions as he viewed the dying soldier: his term, *opisthotonos,* described a disease (*nosos*), not a symptom of tetanus. And if the *iatros* were well schooled in the various theories on *opisthotonos* current in the fourth century B.C., he would know that *opisthotonos* described "what happened when the tendons in the back of the neck are diseased," or what happened when someone fell on the back of his head, or simply what resulted "from a wound" (the Hippocratic *Internal Affections*

52–54, esp. 53 [Littré, VII, pp. 298–302]). Treatment for the varieties of *opisthotonos* was generally the injection of warm liquids through the nose, or cold water "if one desired" (the Hippocratic *Diseases* 3.12–13 [Littré, VII, pp. 132–135]). Underlying these practical actions were the physician's assumptions about humors, and about the functions of medical care in restoring the balance (*krasis*) of those basic liquids of the living human body. From his command of the theory of humors, *krasis,* and related notions, the doctor could then make a forecast (*prognosis*).

GREEK MEDICINE AND THE HIPPOCRATIC APPROACH

The Hippocratic corpus, a collection of works under the name of Hippocrates of Cos (*ca.* 425 B.C.), is a fundamental source for understanding ancient medicine. Even though none of the tracts was composed by Hippocrates, and although the surviving collection was compiled under the direction of scholars resident at the famous Museum and Library in Ptolemaic Alexandria (probably by 200 B.C. and later), the corpus records the state of medical practice and theory among the Greeks going back to at least the fifth century B.C. Within are numerous treatises on various subjects, including diseases, some anatomy, theoretical assumptions of causes, and hundreds of suggested drugs and treatments that occasionally owe their origins to venerated folk traditions, also recorded by Theophrastus (*ca.* 370–288 B.C.), Aristotle's most brilliant student. Thus the Hippocratic corpus is central in consideration of Greek medicine, but there are many other strands in the history of Greek science, philosophy, and medicine that aid comprehension of the essentials of a remarkable and satisfying system of medical theory and medical therapeutics.

Scholars argue fervently about the origins

of Greek medicine, which appears in striking contrast to the medical systems of the ancient Near East. Probably the initial germs of rational assumptions emerged with the pre-Socratic philosophers in the late seventh and early sixth centuries B.C., who began to perceive Nature (*physis*) in terms other than those of mythology or religion. The list of "nature-philosophers" is famous, beginning with Thales of Miletus (*ca.* 590 B.C.), who proposed that water was the primordial substance of all matter. Then followed Anaximander of Miletus (*ca.* 610–540 B.C.), who thought slime was a better candidate for the primordia of life; he was followed by Anaximines of Miletus (*ca.* 546 B.C.), who argued that air, not water, was primary. Greek Asia Minor produced these first philosophers, but the second phase of development in Greek philosophical thinking occurred in Greek southern Italy, where Pythagoras of Croton (*ca.* 530 B.C.) and his poorly known school defined Nature in terms of numbers. A younger contemporary of Pythagoras, Alcmaeon of Croton, was one of the first thinkers to apply the theory of opposites to medical matters, arguing that there must be a balance of opposing forces within the body to ensure health. Other philosophers were also important in gradually laying down a substructure of concepts from which fifth and fourth century B.C. Greek medicine would draw its basic vocabulary and essential suppositions. Empedocles of Acragas (Sicily), who probably lived from 493 to 433 B.C., taught that the "opposing forces" were "Love and Strife," which brought about opposite effects on the four "roots" (elements) of life: earth, air, fire, and water. Anaxagoras of Clazomenae, later a resident of Athens (*ca.* 500–428 B.C.), taught that there was an original mixture of things which encompassed various pairs of opposites, such as the wet and the dry, the hot and the cold, the light and the dark, namely qualities. Parmenides of Elea (*ca.* 470 B.C.) thought that position was also important—thus a child's sex would be determined by its position in the womb, right for males, left for females. By the fifth century B.C., physical and physiological theories depended heavily upon assumed notions of pairing, opposition, mixing, and balancing.

It is unclear how direct was the influence upon the Hippocratic writers of the pre-Socratic philosophers, but there are many common themes that appear in both the Hippocratic corpus and the extant remains of pre-Socratic writings. The Hippocratic physician knew that there were elementary forces (*dynameis*) that operated within the body, and that these forces might be infinite in number. But notions of forces and qualities were rather vague, and the Hippocratic doctor sought a more tangible manner of expressing what he knew about imbalances and balances of these qualities, elements, and forces. Observation showed that a primary substance for health and life was air, and therefore too much or too little air, or air of the wrong kind, or air that was polluted in some way, could be a major cause of disease. Then too there were the humors, known to everyone, and easily verified through observation and experience. In the human body, blood is everywhere; phlegm dribbles out of the nose and appears to keep the inner lining of the mouth moist; bile causes the bitter taste, sometimes mentioned by the ill; and one constantly saw escaping fluids in the urine and the feces. There was, however, uncertainty about the number of humors, even though there was general agreement that a perfect balancing or blending of them produced perfect health. Ill health and disease resulted if one humor increased too much because the patient had eaten something that promoted the overproduction of that humor, or if some action or ill-advised portion of the diet caused too much of a humor to escape from the body. Also, food that remained in a state of indigestion could produce a humor that rose into the head and there caused a discharge, or "flowing" (traditionally a "flux"), which, due to its heat or coolness, could affect any part of the body.

An unlimited number of humors, however, made the doctor's task of diagnosis and prognosis impossible, since each disease would have its own excess or reduction of a necessary humor. Because it had become a commonplace in Greek thinking to assume opposing pairs to explain natural phenomena, some Hippocratic physicians reduced the number of humors to four, but there was disagreement about which four. The Hippocratic *Diseases* (5.32 [Littré, VII, pp. 542–543]) states that the four are water, bile, blood, and phlegm, which become part of the male and female semen that produce the embryo (this in turn is why children have the identical humors of their parents, either healthily or badly proportioned); moreover, each humor in the body had to have an origin, and the Hippocratic writer of *Diseases* (4.33, [Littré, VII, pp. 542–545]) says that water comes from the spleen, bile from the gallbladder, phlegm from the head, and blood from the heart. And as much as Theophrastus' *History of Plants* (*Historia Plantarum*) and *Etiology of Plants* (*De Causis Plantarum*) record Greek theories on plant nutrition, so also the Hippocratic physician borrows long-standing ideas from agriculture to explain nutrition in the human body: the Hippocratic *Diseases* (4.34 [Littré, VII, pp. 545–549]) notes that since plants gain from the soil those materials necessary for their continued life, so also the human body nourishes itself with food and liquids appropriate for the maintenance of its life, and if the humors do not receive nourishment from the gastrointestinal tract, they renew themselves from the seats of their origins in the body itself. The full process of attempted renewal of the humors leads to an excess of one or a depletion of another, and any surplus or deficiency produces disease. Fever results if the body has a surplus of

digested food, especially when a patient has not eliminated the excess concurrently with the intake of fresh food into the digestive tract. The patient, in effect, is filled to overflowing with both old and new humors, and the body's response is inflammation (*phlegmone*), shown in fever. The Hippocratic physician used the terms *plethora* or *plerosis* to describe this accumulation of humors, and thought this was a major cause of disease. There were, of course, other causes: violence to the body, which could come from simple exhaustion; a blow to any part of the body; or a fall. And since man was an organism subject to the weather, as were other plants and animals, atmospheric conditions also produced diseases when they produced changes in the humors, causing them to thin or thicken or become altered in some way detrimental to health. The altered humor settled in a particular part of the body, and one named the consequent disease from the specifically affected organ or part (the Hippocratic *Diseases* 4.50 [Littré, VII, pp. 580–585]).

Observation suggested, however, that water was not a true humor. Although blood, phlegm, and bile were always seen in wounds, in runny noses, in vomit, and occasionally in the feces, water per se never appeared in either the vomit or the products of excretion. Urine was urine, not water, and water was one of the true elements, in company with fire, earth, and air. Omitting water from the list of humors left only three, which did not conform to the overriding desire for balancing pairs to explain disease and health, so that doctors were seeking another humor. With the composition of the Hippocratic *Nature of Man* (possibly written by Polybus, reputed to be the son-in-law of Hippocrates), one sees the new humor: black bile. Once the choice was made, clinical evidence seemed to confirm it. Physicians were familiar with the black feces of patients (who suffered from bleeding gastric ulcers), the black vomit of certain patients (who probably had some form of stomach cancer), and a curious form of fever that produced blackish or dark brown urine (the blackwater fever variety of malaria). After black bile became one of the four humors, it was assumed to cause many diseases that included afflictions of the kidneys, spleen, and liver, as well as quartan fever, headaches, epilepsy, dizziness, paralysis, spasms, and many others.

Physicians could presume connection of the four humors with the qualities (hot, dry, wet, cold), the four seasons, and the elements of Empedocles. Thus yellow bile was characterized by fire, and was most prominent in diseases that occurred in the summer; black bile was earthy, and appeared most often in diseases that arose in the autumn; phlegm was watery, and was seen in winter affections; and blood was associated with air, and an excess of blood was a mark of illnesses in the spring. The qualities also provide characteristics: the hot signified yellow bile and blood; the dry specified yellow bile and black bile; the wet indicated blood and phlegm; and the cold distinguished phlegm and black bile. Treatment with drugs was thereby established by contraries: plants and herbal remedies were perceived as having humors, elements, and qualities that indicated their therapeutic use in specific diseases. The whole system of humoral pathology brought the appearance of mathematical precision, which would become part of a diagnosis; the physician prescribed drugs, diet, exercise, or other treatments that would lessen or increase the humor or humors in question, attempting to restore the lost *krasis*. Moreover, the humoral theory was extended to make long-range prediction of diseases, in a manner that differed from astrological theories of disease predisposition. Individuals varied greatly from one another, and displayed "types" of physiognomy linked to a dominant humor, as a

student of Aristotle proposed for men of genius dominated by black bile, with a consequent "melancholic" personality (pseudo-Aristotle, *Problems* 953a–955a [30.1]).

Humors, however, were not enough to account fully for life in both health and disease. Something had to be present, an elementary potency that made humors from food, kept them moving, mixed them, cast out excesses, and maintained the necessary balance. Greek physicians, along with Aristotle, extended the concept of "innate heat," which had its seat in the left ventricle of the heart (the Hippocratic *On the Heart* 6 [Littré, IX, p. 84; Lloyd, *Hippocratic Writings* p. 349]). This is why the heart was so hot, and why it was cooled through respiration; babies had the most innate heat, because, in addition to their other living functions, they grew; the elderly had the least. Galen (A.D. 129–sometime after 200) helps us understand this difficult concept, as it would apply to medicine and therapeutics. In his *Mixtures and Properties of Simples* (3.2 [Kühn, XI, pp. 542–544]), Galen notes that pepper was "hot" and a rose was "cold," not in actuality or because they were "unmixed" or "simple," but because these characteristics were dominant (*epikrateia*) in them. He continues by saying that this is obvious by their actions in or on the human body: pepper is not as hot as fire, but will burn us when we eat it, or when it lodges in the eyes; the rose is not as cold as ice, but salves prepared from roses (rose-oil compounds and the like) are cooling and have a soothing effect on the skin, and are thus very useful in the treatment of burns (*Mixtures and Properties* 3.10 [Kühn, XI, p. 561]). Therefore, innate heat was a basic part of man's nature (*physis*), and the understanding of *physis* showed that diseases had their own *physeis*, since they occurred in Nature, and could be cured by comprehending their specific characteristics. Innate heat was basic in man, and any depletion would cause illness, due to the overpreponderance of the cold, and illnesses as they occurred in Nature indicated a natural course which could be recorded, for example, in the list of fevers that ran for four days. The natural course also included the development of symptoms over a set period of time, for example, in pneumonia where changes occurred in coughing, the consistency of the sputum, finally followed by a *krisis,* which stopped the coughing.

All the natural causes of disease produced an excess of a particular humor that had to be expelled in order to restore a proper balance. This bad humor had to undergo coction (*pepsis*), a kind of cooking, whereby the humor could be prepared for expulsion, either rapidly at a specific time (*krisis*), or gradually over a longer period of time (*lysis*). The *krisis,* of course, could lead to a worsening state (*katastasis*) as well as to the sudden change signaling the patient's recovery. Diseases could be classed as acute (*oxus*) or chronic (*chronios*), depending on their recurring nature. The concept of "critical days" had crucial importance in the diagnosis of most acute diseases, as vividly expressed by the author of the Hippocratic *Epidemics* (1 [Jones, I, pp. 147–211]), *Prognostic* (Jones, II, pp. 6–55), and the famous *Aphorisms* (Jones, IV, pp. 98–221).

Greek physicians gained their skills either by apprenticeships with experienced practitioners or through gradually accumulated expertise in drug lore, surgery, and medical theory. There were no teaching institutions in classical antiquity, so that a doctor could gain patients and a reputation only through his own successes and failures, not by any certificate attesting to his training. The philosophers sometimes employ medicine as an illustration in argument, and both Plato and Aristotle suggest how physicians functioned in Greek society. In the *Phaedrus* (270c–d) Plato cites Hippocrates as a physician who understands the necessity of knowing the "whole man" in order to perform good medicine, but in his *Laws* (4.720a–e) Plato makes a firm distinction (at least in his Ideal State) between the medical skills possessed by slaves and freemen: the slave has acquired skill derived from observation and practice, not by the study of nature, whereas the freeborn doctor has "learned his art by the observation of nature and in this he can instruct his students" (Scarborough, *Roman Medicine,* pp. 123–124). In his *Parva Naturalia* (436a.18–21) Aristotle notes that the "science of nature" forms the background of the education of a true physician, but in *Politics* (3.1282a.8) he makes a careful distinction among the medical craftsman, or ordinary practitioner (*demiourgos*), the specialist or scientist-physician (*architektonikos*), and the man who has studied the art (*ho pepaideumenos peri ten technen*). Thus, although there is good evidence from inscriptions about physicians being honored for their good works, there is almost no indication of the exact services for which these honorific memorials were erected. The best physicians were those who had studied the art of medicine, and if Plato and Aristotle are suggestive of actual regard for physicians in Greek antiquity, the "good doctors" (Hippocratic or otherwise) were well equipped with medical theory as well as lengthy experience.

POST-HIPPOCRATIC GREEK MEDICINE AND THE HELLENISTIC ERA

There are 500 years between the Hippocratic corpus and Galen, and numerous physicians, natural historians, and philosophers left their imprint upon the medical practice and theories summarized in the massive compilation under the name of Galen. In many cases, however, knowledge of particulars in this half-millennium is woefully fragmentary and incomplete. By contrast, the fourth century B.C. in Athens saw the towering intellects of Plato and Aristotle, whose philosophical systems not only raised issues that are still debated today, but who also became heavily influential in medical theories. Plato taught the existence of souls and said that man's intelligence was seated in the brain, while his student Aristotle formulated a carefully teleological Nature, gave numerous definitions for physiological functions in animals and man, and argued that man's intellect was seated in the heart. Aristotle's father was a Macedonian doctor, and there are many medical emphases in Aristotle's *History of Animals, Generation of Animals, Parva Naturalia,* and numerous other zoological tracts. He was famous for his investigations into animal functions in which he established classes of animals, performed fundamental research in avian and mammalian embryology, and made acute observations on the whole of the animal kingdom's myriad denizens, from bees and spiders to elephants and whales. The impact of Plato and Aristotle on Greco-Roman medicine is best seen in the adaptation of many of their theories by Galen.

The Hellenistic era (usually dated from the death of Alexander the Great in 323 B.C. to the death of Cleopatra VII of Egypt in 30 B.C.) was unusually rich in medical, pharmaceutical, surgical, and related activity. Diocles of Carystos (probably contemporary with Aristotle) was a wide-ranging authority on drugs and surgical technique. Theophrastus (*ca.* 370–288 B.C.) was one of several gifted students who studied with Aristotle, and Theophrastus' *History of Plants* set standards for botany and botanical classification until the publication of Linnaeus' *Species of Plants* in 1753. Another student of Aristotle, known as Meno, compiled the first history of medicine, which survives in part in the papyrus called the *Anonymus Londinensis.* Praxagoras of Cos (*ca.* 325 B.C.) made studies of the pulse and established a catalog for

diagnosis according to pulse rates and rhythms in various diseases. Under Ptolemy I and Ptolemy II Philadelphus, in the third century B.C. Alexandria became the mother city of the Hellenistic kingdoms and soon boasted the biggest collection of books and was the liveliest commercial center anywhere in the world. Ptolemy II established a library and a temple to the Muses (a *museon*), an idea that may have been inspired by Demetrius of Phaleron, another student of Aristotle, who had served for a time as tyrant of Athens, and who became Ptolemy I's chief adviser on cultural and intellectual matters after *ca.* 303 B.C. Thus the Aristotelian concept of "research" was paramount in the *museon,* and the collection of books pointed to the usual activity of the assembled savants: commentary on the Greek classics.

It was in this unusual setting that the work of Herophilus (*ca.* 280 B.C.) and Erasistratus (*ca.* 260 B.C.) took place. Only extracts survive of their writings, but later medical authorities (e.g., Soranus, Rufus, and Galen) excerpted enough from their lost works so that one can gain a reasonable view of their approaches, discoveries, and contributions in anatomy, physiology, therapeutics, and medical theory. If tradition records the chronological relationships accurately, Herophilus had been at one time a student of Praxagoras of Cos, and possibly of Theophrastus. There would be, consequently, a meld of the Peripatetic with the anatomical in the investigations of Herophilus at Alexandria. Even though Celsus (*ca.* A.D. 14–37) records the rumor that both Herophilus and Erasistratus performed vivisections on humans, one can dismiss this as a tale that encapsulated the reactions to the traditionally offensive activity of anatomical dissection. Herophilus and Erasistratus were the first to dissect human cadavers in a systematic way, although Aristotle had dissected (and vivisected) animals.

Herophilus made significant contributions to the knowledge of human internal anatomy, and enough is quoted from his major work, *On Dissections,* to show the results of his investigations of the brain, eye, and the nervous system. He disagreed with Aristotle's dictum that the heart was the seat of sensation, and asserted that the brain held control of sensate things. Herophilus was a gifted inventor of terms, which came from the available stock of Greek words and then applied by analogy to observed structures. For example, he used *neuron,* which could mean "ligament," "sandal-thong," or similar things, to refer to the "ligaments" that led from the brain—although there remained the confusion with the large tendons; in observing the confluences of the blood sinuses in the brain, he termed them the *lenos* (winepress), and this structure is still called the torcular Herophili; in the eye, he observed a "netlike" membrane, which retains his name, retina; and his most famous anatomical coinage is the duodenum, which is a Latin translation of his *dodekadaktylon* (twelve fingers), describing the length of this part of the small intestine in man. Herophilus discovered the ovaries, which he compared to the male testes. He followed humoral pathology bequeathed to him by earlier writers, but devised a theory of pulses that extended and elaborated Praxagoras' notions: Herophilus attempted to classify pulses according to their rates and rhythms, and recognized three basic types (pararhythmic, heterorhythmic, and ekrhythmic), dependent upon the age and constitution of the patient. His special terms for the pulses are sometimes vivid: one he called *myrmekizon* (crawling like an ant) and another *dorkadizon* (leaping like a gazelle). Galen also writes that Herophilus tried to apply theories of music in his work with the pulses, using the musicians' upward beat and downward beat (*arsis* and *thesis*) to describe the dilation and contraction of an artery (*Synopsis of the Books on Pulses* 12 [Kühn, IX, p. 464]).

Erasistratus represents another tradition in ancient medicine. Also reputed by later doxographers to have been a student of Theophrastus, Erasistratus may also have studied the works of Democritus of Abdera (*ca.* 400 B.C.), the most famous Greek exponent of the theory of "atoms." In his work at Alexandria, Erasistratus displayed great differences from Herophilus in his attempts to explain functions in the living human body: a basic dissimilarity was Erasistratus' theory that there were unnumbered empty spaces, interspersed with atoms. He observed that blood vessels divide and divide again and again to the point that they decrease in size beyond the limits of human vision. His theory of functions (moderns would label it physiology) contrasted starkly with those of his predecessors and most of his contemporaries. Generally it was argued that organs were nourished and life was sustained through a kind of specific *holke* (attractive power), but Erasistratus believed that Nature's tendency to fill up a vacuum was far more important to human physiology. Galen records a number of instances of Erasistratus' originality, especially in theory of growth and nourishment (*On the Natural Faculties* 2.3, 6 [Brock, pp. 136–137, 162–165; Kühn, II, pp. 87, 105]). He reports Erasistratus' effort to explain nourishment, and the consequent production of waste: "Nature has given a mechanism in the form of instincts [or appetites, *orexeis*], materials [or substances, *hyle*], and elementary forces [*dynameis*]. The main part of the *dynameis* is the *dynamis* of the *pneuma,* which transmutes the food into a form appropriate to take the place of the matter taken away" (*On the Natural Faculties* 2.6 [Brock, p. 164; Kühn, II, p. 105]). In fact, this quasi air that engendered life, *pneuma,* was the most important part of Erasistratus' views on human living functions, so much so that it was the basic force (or faculty, *dynamis*) that sustained life. He proved to his satisfaction that the arteries—in life—contained only *pneuma,* and the veins had blood. To explain why blood spurted forth from an artery when it was severed, he proposed the theoretical *synanastomoses,* which connected arteries with veins, and claimed that the blood from the veins rushed into the cut artery from the natural *horror vacui. Pneuma* also carried sensation through assumed tubes in the *neura,* and Erasistratus taught that those *neura* which were linked to the waking sensations (the modern sensory nerves) were always hollow. In his dissections, he traced the *neura* back to the brain (Galen, *On the Doctrines of Hippocrates and Plato* 7.3.10 [De Lacy, II, pp. 440–443]), while Herophilus had taught that some *neura* (not so hollow—perhaps the modern motor nerves) derived from both the brain and spinal column (Rufus of Ephesus, *Anatomy of Parts of the Body* 71–75 [Daremberg and Ruelle, pp. 184–185]). Erasistratus may have noted certain veins in the mesentery that ended in glands, but he seems to have concluded that these were arteries that first held *pneuma* and then *chylos,* a product of coction (here digestion). He appears to have been the first to demonstrate, through comparative anatomy, that man's cerebral cortex had greater complexity than other animals', and he inferred from this the reason that man had superior intelligence over the beasts (Galen, *Use of Parts* 8.13 [Helmreich, I, pp. 488–489; May, I, pp. 417–418]) and *Doctrines of Hippocrates and Plato* 7.3.10 [De Lacy, II, pp. 442–443]). In addition to his labors on the brain and the *neura,* Erasistratus made the important observation that bodily parts each have a vein, an artery, and a *neuron,* and that the part is nourished by the vein (Galen, *Use of Parts* 7.8 [Helmreich, I, p. 391; May, I, p. 345]). But it was the *pneuma* that was central: in digestion, the *pneuma* (coming into the stomach through the arteries) gave the stomach the

appropriate grinding motion, and Erasistratus rejected the theory of *pepsis* in digestion, noting that the heat of the body was insufficient to boil food (pseudo-Galen, *Commentary on Hippocrates' Book on Nourishment* 2.7. [Kühn, XV, p. 247]). In respiration, according to Erasistratus, outside air passed via the bronchi to the lungs, then to the left ventricle of the heart via the pulmonary vein, and then by way of the aorta and ascending arteries to the body and to the head (Galen, *Blood in the Arteries* 2 [Kühn, IV, p. 706] and *Doctrines of Hippocrates and Plato* 1.6.2 [De Lacy, II pp. 78–79]). In his notions of vascular function, he placed *pneuma* in the arteries and blood in the veins, which had been converted from the quasi-digested *chyle* of the intestine into the blood made in the liver (Galen, *Doctrines of Hippocrates and Plato* 6.6.13 [De Lacy, II, pp. 398–399]). Pathology was based on the fundamental notion that disease was caused generally by blood in the arteries, or by some mechanical cause impeding *pneuma* in the arteries, or related causes. Erasistratus' description of dropsy is illustrative: "Dropsy is a chronic and hardening inflammation of the liver or spleen which prevents the assimilation [*katergasia*] of the food in the intestines and its distribution throughout the body, but changes it to water, which is then cooled and settled between the peritoneum and intestines" (pseudo-Galen, *Introduction, or Doctor* 13 [Kühn, XIV, p. 746]). Erasistratus' entire system of medicine, a kind of "pneumatology," was unusual for classical antiquity, since he tried to give a mechanical explanation for observed phenomena.

Medical research in Alexandria apparently continued after the time of Erasistratus, but there is little specific information with the exception of truncated notices in later writers. Of greater importance than the steadily dwindling efforts at Alexandria are the treatises in medical botany, entomology, pharmacy, and toxicology, which had enormous influence. About a generation after Aristotle, an obscure Apollodorus wrote tracts on toxicology, perhaps borrowing some of his details from the earlier writings of Diocles of Carystos. Apollodorus' works are, in turn, lost except for infrequent quotations in later compilers, but the extant poems *Theriaca* and *Alexipharmaca* by Nicander of Colophon (prob. *ca.* 140 B.C., in Pergamon in western Asia Minor) are based directly upon Apollodorus. The incredibly obscure poems of Nicander formed the bridge between Hellenistic toxicology and later Roman works on the subject: here are poisonous creatures and substances, black widow spiders, cobras, scorpions, and other presumably dangerous animals and drugs, accompanied by purported remedies. Those recipes enjoyed a long history as evinced by their quotation by Pliny in his *Natural History,* by Galen, and by a host of authorities through the European Renaissance. In many ways, Apollodorus had expanded on a number of observations in Book Nine of Theophrastus' *History of Plants,* which is the first known Greek treatise on medical botany. In pharmacy, the work of Dioscorides stands as a landmark. He wrote the *Materia Medica* in Greek sometime around A.D. 65, after the Hellenistic world had passed almost completely under Roman dominion, but Dioscorides collects many details from earlier Greek works and adds his own system of drug classification as well as a multilingual nomenclature. Dioscorides' handbook (in its various forms) became the guidebook in medical botany and pharmacology, and remained an essential textbook well into the European Enlightenment.

ROMAN MEDICINE TO GALEN

Italic traditions of folk medicine had a hoary ancestry, but many are clouded in the early history of Roman civilization. Cato the Elder (234–149 B.C.) is the first extant Latin author who provides details of this long-lived approach. His *On Agriculture,* written about 160 B.C., sets down the multistranded combination of magic, folk medicine, and rural values that would mark Roman outlooks for the majority of the lengthy history of the Roman Republic and Empire. Cabbage is prescribed for many ailments, and there are rituals that had to accompany medical treatment, showing vividly how the Roman proudly bore his heritage, and could—as Pliny the Elder would write—easily do without doctors. After the appearance of the Greek god of medicine, Asclepius, in the Roman Republic (dated traditionally to 293 B.C.; the god's Latin name was Aesculapius), Roman awareness soon expanded from this god of medicine, imported from the Hellenistic world, into acquaintance with Greek and Hellenistic medicine and medical practitioners. According to the story, a certain Archagathus of Sparta arrived in Rome in 219 B.C. and set up a surgical practice, but shortly he earned the epithet *carnifex* (butcher). It would not be until the career of Asclepiades of Bithynia (*ca.* 120 B.C. in Rome) that Roman opinions of Greek medicine would shift from the negative to something closer to curiosity and occasional acceptance. Asclepiades was a careful judge of his patients' mores, and he prescribed mild remedies and little surgery, all packaged in the then-respectable philosophical structure of medical Epicureanism (later to be seen in *On the Nature of Things* by Lucretius).

The basic Roman approach to medicine that first appeared in Cato's writings is followed in the agricultural manuals of Varro (116–27 B.C.) and Columella (*ca.* A.D. 50). These compilations of knowledge had their inspiration in the encyclopedia first proposed in the school of Aristotle, but the Roman encyclopedists gave their own sense of organization to the compiled data. The Roman aristocrat knew his body of learning was competent in the four main activities that characterized a prominent Roman citizen: the arts of war, law, agriculture, and politics. By the age of Caesar and Augustus, Greek learning added oratory, rhetoric, philosophy, architecture and art, and medicine, so that the complete encyclopedia by Cornelius Celsus (*ca.* in the reign of Tiberius, A.D. 14–37) included all these areas as assumed aspects of the expertise of the Roman upper classes in the early Roman Empire. *On Medicine* of Celsus' encyclopedia has survived complete, and there are only short excerpts of the parts on law, oratory, and the rest in Pliny's *Natural History*, Quintilian's *Education of an Orator*, and the works of other later authors in Latin. It seems that Celsus had direct experience in the practice of surgery, while his sections on drugs and pharmaceuticals show close borrowing from Greek sources, many of which were also appropriated by Dioscorides and—a generation after Celsus—by Pliny. As a Roman aristocrat, Celsus either nursed slaves and sick members of his own family back to health in a sick bay (*valetudinarium*) or called in a medical specialist when he thought it proper. There is no trace of Celsus' *On Medicine* in any of the extant Greek medical sources from the Roman Empire, but Pliny the Elder uses Celsus, who is listed as one of the *auctores* in Book One of the *Natural History*. Pliny's marvelous hodgepodge includes animal lore, medical facts, botany, medical entomology, tales told from current gossip about the imperial family, art history and criticism, bits and pieces from Peripatetic zoology, meteorology, and physiognomy—plus a vast number of other subjects, related and unrelated, copied from many authorities, both Greek and Latin. It became one of the most widely read of all ancient books: only the Bible and Euclid's handbook of Greek mathematics surpassed Pliny in popularity throughout the Middle Ages and the European Renaissance.

The Roman context also left its mark on the development of medical practice among the Greek-speaking physicians plying their trade among the upper classes of the empire. Most of the doctors took Hippocrates as their patron saint, and they inherited the Greek predilection for theorizing. Consequently, Aretaeus of Cappadocia (prob. *ca.* A.D. 110), Rufus of Ephesus (*ca.* in the reign of Trajan, A.D. 98–117), and Soranus of Ephesus (*ca.* in the reigns of Trajan and Hadrian, A.D. 98–138) all based their conclusions upon assumptions that went with suitable branches of medical philosophy, often called "sects." Most prominent after late Hellenistic times were the Empirics, Dogmatists, and Pneumatics, each taking some philosophic principle and expanding it to encompass the whole of medicine. In the first and second centuries, the most vocal medical sect was Methodism, ultimately derived from the mechanical and atomistic principles laid down by Asclepiades of Bithynia. The *Gynecology* of Soranus, one of the best books on the subject written before the nineteenth century, was set within the precepts of Methodism, which suggests why there is little folklore or superstition in Soranus' medicine. Under Soranus' name, a compacted biography of Hippocrates has come down through the centuries in the manuscript tradition; this account is the earliest collection of presumed details on the life of the so-called father of medicine.

GALEN

The second great compilation of ancient medicine was performed by the polymathic philosopher-physician, Galen of Pergamon (A.D. 129–sometime after 200). Without the vague, impersonal quality dominating the works of the Hippocratic corpus, the tracts of Galen constantly strike the reader with the personality of their author, who reveals himself as something of a genius with all of the failings of a self-professed intellectual. Although there is little confirmation of Galen's life and career in contemporary sources, there are enough details in the huge corpus under his name that can be confirmed in other second-century writings, so that his autobiographical materials can be matched to contemporary events in the Roman Empire. Born in the prosperous Roman province of Asia (western Asia Minor), Galen was part of the upper class from his birth. His father, Nikon, was a prominent architect who had a hand in designing and building the imposing structures that dominated Roman Pergamon. The young Galen was schooled in Greek literature, art, language, and philosophy, and his father insisted that he study for a time with teachers of the various brands of philosophy then current. Galen continually reminds his readers of his expertise in philosophy, while favoring Plato, employing Aristotle's teleology, borrowing Stoic categories, and generally detesting anything that smacked of Epicureanism and its mechanistic world views. Sometime around A.D. 147, he began the serious study of medicine, having first listened to the medical lectures of Satyrus, who happened to be in Pergamon. Thereafter, Galen traveled to Smyrna, then to Corinth, and finally to Alexandria, where he spent time writing learned commentaries on Hippocrates, composing dialogues in the manner of Plato, and studying a few human bones. He returned to Pergamon (ca. A.D. 159) to become physician to the gladiators, and in this capacity he began to learn something about real human anatomy, the application of dietetics, and obviously self-taught surgical technique. By A.D. 162 he had made his way to Rome, shortly became part of the aristocratic circles, and ended up as personal physician to Marcus Aurelius and the imperial family by A.D. 169. It appears that he remained in Rome, except for journeys, until his death.

Galen's productivity is nothing short of phenomenal. Several of his works became landmarks in the history of medicine. One of the earliest surviving treatises is *On Anatomical Procedures,* in which Galen meticulously demonstrates dissecting technique, gained from numerous investigations of the Barbary ape (similar enough to the rhesus monkey that modern researchers can duplicate—and verify—Galen's observations). In *On Anatomical Procedures,* which has reached us only in part in an Arabic translation, he uses the simian structures as closely analogous to those of man, a system of anatomy that held until the Renaissance. In *On the Natural Faculties,* Galen canonized the old Hippocratic notion of powers (*dynameis*) and humors, and streamlined many physiological theories so well that these too became dominant in Western medicine for 1,500 years. The *Usefulness of the Parts of the Body* is an extended paean to Nature and observed structures and what they were meant to do, verifying the venerated Aristotelian notion that "Nature makes nothing in vain." *On Prognosis* is an eloquent autobiographical statement on the social verities of medicine in the Roman Empire, and his *On the Doctrines of Hippocrates and Plato* is a repository of quotations from Posidonius and many other Stoic philosophers, as well as an extended critique of Platonic and Hippocratic ideas, which could be used to refute Aristotle—if Aristotle disagreed with both Plato and Hippocrates. *On the Affected Parts* is a tart series of pronouncements and opinions on the "art" of therapeutics, and the *Institutio Logica* and *On the Passions and Errors of the Soul* suggest Galen's occasional originality in philosophy, as he sought an eclectic outlook. The *Hygiene* is an excellent handbook on how to stay healthy, and his shorter works on anatomy (e.g., *Bones for Beginners, Anatomy of the Uterus, Anatomy of the Neura, Anatomy of Arteries and Veins, Anatomy of Muscles for Beginners*) and physiology (e.g., *Movement of Muscles, Organ of Smell, On Spasm*) are in company with dozens of other titles on scattered topics (e.g., *On Habits, Medical Sects for Beginners, That the Mental Faculties Follow the Bodily Constitution, Exhortation to Study the Arts, That the Doctor Must Also Be a Philosopher*). His *Antidotes* and three long tracts *On Simples* are vast compendia of collected recipes, medical botany, toxicology, pharmaceutical poetry, and quoted authorities on drugs of all varieties. These titles represent only a fraction of the works in the standard, twenty-volume edition of Galen edited by C. G. Kühn, and does not include Galenic tracts that have survived in Arabic (e.g., *On Medical Experience, Anatomical Procedures* [books 9–15], *On the Parts of Medicine, On Cohesive Causes, On Regimen in Acute Diseases in Accordance with the Theories of Hippocrates, On the Variety of Similar Parts of the Body, Commentary on Hippocrates' "At the Surgery"*). It is little wonder that Galen's writings swamped those of his predecessors and became the standard authority (and quotable quarry) in Byzantine and Islamic medicine, as well as the absolute guide in Western medieval medicine from *ca.* 1250 until the publication of Vesalius' *On the Structure of the Human Body* in 1543.

One of the fruitless searches in medical history has been for Galen's "system" of medicine. He often changed his mind, even revising works already in circulation. There are, however, basic ideas that do characterize Galen's medical outlook, and some resemble, or are adapted from, long-accepted philosophical assumptions; the combination of Hippocrates, Plato, the Stoics, Aristotle, and the results of his own research in comparative anatomy, applied pharmacy, and therapeutics gives Galen's works a piquant, occasionally puzzling, but internally consistent tone.

Galen presumed that the ancient concept of four elements (fire, earth, air, and water) was essentially correct, and the blending (*krasis*) of the elements in the human body formed an underlying postulate in Galen's theories of health and disease. He accepted

the notion of the qualities (*poia*) as adapted by the Stoics, who had admitted *to poion* as one of the states of being. *Krasis* of *poia* was also necessary for health. He presumed that the four humors were fundamental in any medical analysis of human health, but Galen's assumptions about black bile, yellow bile, blood, and phlegm derived from an updated version of the Hippocratic humors. In a treatise called *Introduction, or Doctor*, which is in the Kühn collection but which is not by Galen, there is a clear expression of a revived nuance on the humors, derived ultimately from Plato's *Timaeus:* the humors "are four secondary substances, more closely resembling the human character or nature" (pseudo-Galen, *Introduction* 9 [Kühn, XIV, p. 696]). Galen adapted the Platonic idea of the three souls that simultaneously rule and serve the body, and these souls are called choleric, rational, and sensual. In Galen's refinements of the old Platonic doctrines, the rational soul had its seat in the brain, governing reason, motion, and sensation; the choleric soul resided in the heart, providing what Galen calls "vital force" for the body; and the sensual soul (also called the vegetative soul) in the liver directed the process of nutrition. All three souls were simply divisions of the one soul in the body, but Galen admits that he does not know the one soul's final substance or substances (*Formation of the Fetus* 6 [Kühn, IV, pp. 688–702]). In order for the souls to carry out their tasks, the one soul had agents serving it in its numerous living functions. Galen calls them all *pneumata*, and each *pneuma* engendered changes necessary for life. The *pneumata*, however, were fundamental for Galen's perceptions of the workings of the blood, and he extended and elaborated Erasistratus' concepts of the *pneuma*. Galen's ideas differed in one essential respect: there was blood in the arteries (he easily proved this with a simple double-ligation experiment on an artery in a living animal). Galen believed that the lungs prepared air to become *pneuma,* resulting in a proto-*pneuma,* which was altered air that then entered the veins and became mixed with blood; the proto-*pneuma* and the blood are then attracted (via the process called *holke*) to the left ventricle of the heart where more blood (seeping into the left ventricle through assumed pores in the intraventricular septum) combines with the proto-*pneuma* to transform it into "vital" *pneuma;* the transformed *pneuma* is now attracted (again via *holke*) into the arteries as well as being driven into them by the contraction of the ventricle; and more changes take place, once the *pneuma* enters the arterial system.

Part of the blood/*pneuma* is attracted into a complex retiform plexus at the base of the brain (the famous *rete mirabile*) where the *pneuma* is "delayed" to aid the brain in changing the *pneuma* (basic vital *pneuma*) into psychic *pneuma* (*Use of Parts* 9.4 [Helmreich, II, pp. 10–15; May, II, pp. 430–434]). The blood/*pneuma* from the *rete mirabile* is attracted through the carotid arteries to the brain, which changes the delayed *pneuma* into psychic *pneuma* with the aid of more air drawn into the brain via the olfactory bulbs. Once formed, the psychic *pneuma* is attracted into the invisible lumina of the *neura,* where psychic *pneuma* promotes sensation and motion, called by Galen "useful blood exhaled" (*Use of Parts* 6.17 [Helmreich, I, pp. 358–364; May, I, pp. 321–326]). Only one of the countless lumina is visible, Galen says, and this is the lumen of the *neuron* of the eye (the two lumina for the optic nerves); this is so because the need for *pneuma* by the eyes is enormous in comparison with other sensations (*Doctrines of Hippocrates and Plato* 7.3–4 [De Lacy, II, pp. 438–453], and *Use of Parts* VIII, 6 [Helmreich, I, pp. 461–472; May, I, pp. 398–407]). Basic for these theories was Galen's simple demonstration of blood in the arteries (*Blood in the Arteries* 5 and 6 [Kühn, IV, pp. 718–724]). A third *pneuma* functioned as the agent of the

vegetative souls, which had their seat in the liver, but Galen is quite vague about its transformations, saying that "if there is a natural [vegetative] *pneuma,* it would be contained in the liver and the veins" (*Method of Medicine* 12.5 [Kühn, X, pp. 839–840]).

In his *Natural Faculties,* Galen expounds a sixth fundamental functional concept: the *dynameis* (powers or faculties). Each part of the soul has a particular *dynamis* along with a *pneuma;* the liver, therefore, contains a natural (vegetative) *dynamis,* the brain a psychic *dynamis,* and the heart a vital *dynamis.* Liver, brain, and heart are the "ruling" organs, but Galen says that all parts of the body are endowed with their own particular *dynameis,* which allow the attraction of necessary and appropriate nourishment that will be particular for the part (e.g., *Use of Parts* 16.3 [Helmreich, II, p. 385; May, II, pp. 687–688]). This is the attractive *dynamis,* possessed by all parts, just as parts have a retentive or selective *dynamis* (enabling the part to keep nutriment until a point of satisfaction), and an expulsive *dynamis* that ejects superfluous nutriment. The proper mixture (*krasis*) of these three *dynameis* allowed the part to survive. There are other *dynameis,* explaining observed actions: a pulsation *dynamis* for the arteries, a contraction *dynamis* for muscles, and so on. Galen employs the concept of innate heat from Aristotle and the Hippocratics, and this adaptation is a complex of Galen's multistranded borrowing and refinement of earlier theories. Innate heat is the deathless substance in living beings that has intelligence (the Hippocratic *On Fleshes* 2 [Littré, VIII, pp. 584–585]), and respiration is necessary for the inner fire's nourishment (Aristotle, *Respiration* 473a.3 and 479a.7). These are but two sources of Galen's adapted notion, and a good illustration of how he goes about his involuted adaptations of earlier ideas of innate heat is in his *On Tremor, Rigor, Palpitation and Spasm,* 6 (Kühn, VII, pp. 614–616; David Sider and

Michael McVaugh, trans. [1979], pp. 183–210 [198–199]):

> Rigor is an affection of the natural heat so that no one may think that I am calling it an external affliction, and that I am falsely accusing Erasistratus, Praxagoras, Philotimus, Asclepiades, and unnumbered others, who all think that the heat of the body is not innate [*emphyton*] but acquired from without . . . rigor is a *pathos* of the natural heat in each animal . . . the argument will proceed from Hippocratic foundations . . . the heat [is] not acquired nor subsequent to the generation of the animal, but itself first and original and innate. This is nothing other than the nature of life.

Galen thus presents a system that has seven basic terms, presumed known to the reader: elements, qualities, humors, souls, *pneumata,* powers, and innate heat. To moderns used to the description of human physiology in terms of molecular biology, Galen's nomenclature may present some conceptual difficulties.

The murky organization of his multiple concepts led later scholars into attempts to provide precision and order in Galen's massive compendium of medical knowledge. Galen had no students, but by the mid fourth century there had emerged a definite "Galenism" as exemplified in the *Medical Collection* by Oribasius, physician to Julian the Apostate (A.D. 361–363). This systematic Galen became, for all practical purposes, the Galen of the Middle Ages (the Byzantine and Islamic East as well as the Latin West), and would be the Galen studied in the early Renaissance.

The heritages of Greco-Roman medicine, and especially the teachings and writings of the Hippocratic physicians, and the works of Galen, exercised a long-lasting influence on medicine and medical theory until well into the nineteenth century. As late as the 1880s and 1890s, physicians and their patients still spoke of humoral imbalances, and we yet occasionally describe someone as being in a "black humor," although such phrases are becoming part of an archaic English. Vesalius challenged Galen's anatomy by analogy in the sixteenth century, William Harvey overturned Galen's concept of vascular function in the early seventeenth century, but it was not until the development of chemistry in the late eighteenth century that the ancient ideas of elements, qualities, and humors began to be replaced. And it was not until dependable anesthetics were discovered in the mid nineteenth century that many of the surgical practices of the Hippocratics, Celsus, and other classical authorities were completely abandoned. Organic chemistry foreshadowed a new understanding of drugs, and by the 1880s, many of the "simple drugs" long known from the Hippocratics, Dioscorides, and Galen were replaced by laboratory products. One may, in conclusion, note that modern medicine is in its infancy, compared with the over two millennia in which Greco-Roman medical theory held dominance. Study of this long period of medical history suggests many reasons why such a medico-philosophical system should have been so satisfying for so long and should also remind the modern reader of how much medicine has changed since the days of our great-grandfathers, and how much change remains in store for the medicine of the future.

BIBLIOGRAPHY

GREEK MEDICINE: SOURCES

The basic collection of Greek texts (with French translations) of the Hippocratic corpus remains E. Littré, ed., *Oeuvres complètes d'Hippocrate,* 10 vols. (1839–1861; repr. 1973–1982). In English, most convenient are the Greek texts and translations by W. H. S. Jones and E. T. Withington, eds., *Hippocrates,* 4 vols. (1923–1931; repr. 1957–1962). A superb introductory volume of Hippocratic works in English (no Greek texts) is G. E. R. Lloyd, ed., *Hippocratic Writings* (1978, paper). Reedited Greek texts with French translations have begun appearing in the Budé series, and five volumes are now available, the first four edited by Robert Joly: *Hippocrate: Du régime* (1967); *Hippocrate, XI: De la génération. De la nature de l'enfant. Des maladies IV. Du foetus de huit mois* (1970); *Hippocrate, VI, pt. 2: Du régime des maladies aiguës. Appendice. De l'aliment. De l'usage des liquides* (1972); *Hippocrate, XIII: Des lieux dans l'homme. Du système des glandes. Des fistules. Des hémorroïdes. De la vision. Des chairs. De la dentition* (1978); and Jacques Jouanna, ed. and trans., *Hippocrate, X, pt. 2: Maladies II* (1983).

Several improved Greek texts (with German translations) of Hippocratic treatises have been published in the *Corpus Medicorum Graecorum* series (*CMG*), including: Hans Diller, ed., *Hippokrates: Über die Umwelt* (1970; *CMG* I 1, 2); Hermann Grensemann, ed., *Hippokrates: Über Achtmonatskinder. Über das Siebenmonatskind (Unecht)* (1968; *CMG* I 2, 1); Cay Lienau, ed., *Hippokrates: Über Nachempfängnis, Geburtshilfe und Schwangerschaftsleiden* (1973; *CMG* I 2, 2); and Paul Potter, ed., *Hippokrates: Über die Krankheiten III* (1980; *CMG* I 2, 3). Also available is the well-edited volume (with Italian translation) by Daniela Manetti and Amneris Roselli, *Ippocrate: Epidemie libro sesto* (1982).

Two extended commentaries by modern scholars have aided immeasurably the comprehension of Hippocratic medicine's role and relation to Greek medicine as a whole: Hermann Grensemann, *Hippokratische Gynäkologie . . . De mulieribus I, II und De sterilibus* (1982), and Iain M. Lonie, *The Hippocratic Treatises "On Generation," "On the Nature of the Child," "Diseases IV": A Commentary* (1981).

The standard edition (with German translations) of the remnants of the Greek texts of the pre-Socratic philosophers is Hermann Diels and Walther Kranz, eds., *Die Fragmente der Vorsokratiker,* 6th ed., 3 vols. (1952). An excellent selection of Greek texts with translations is G. S. Kirk, J. E. Raven, and M. Schofield, eds., *The Presocratic Philosophers,* 2nd ed. (1983); this volume has a superb running commentary. To find what is left of Empedocles' of Acragas writings, see pp. 280–321 of this work.

GREEK MEDICINE: STUDIES

The following is merely suggestive of the large literature on the topic: Dietrich Brandenburg, *Medizinisches bei Herodot* (1976). Ludwig Edelstein's papers have been reprinted in Owsei Temkin and C. Lilian Temkin, eds., *Ancient Medicine: Selected Papers of Ludwig Edelstein* (1967); included are "Hippocratic Prognosis," "The Hippocratic Physician," "The Genuine Works of Hippocrates," "The Role of Eryximachus in Plato's *Symposium,*" "The Methodists," "Empiricism and Skepticism in the Teaching of the Greek Empiricist School," "Greek Medicine in Its Relation to Religion and Magic," "The Professional Ethics of the Greek Physician," "The Relationship of Ancient Philosophy to Medicine," and *The Hippocratic Oath: Text, Translation and Interpretation.* A lucid amalgam of epidemiology, paleopathology, and classical philology characterizes Mirko D. Grmek, *Les maladies à l'aube de la civilisation occidentale* (1983); clear translations of often puzzling Greek mark the fine C. R. S. Harris, *The Heart and the Vascular System in Ancient Greek Medicine* (1973); William Arthur Heidel, *Hippocratic Medicine* (1941; repr. 1981) remains very useful; Robert Joly, *Hippocrate. Médecine grecque* (1964) suggests the range of Greek medical skills; Charles Lichtenthaeler, *Deux conférences* (1959) and *Der Eid des Hippokrates* (1984) indicate the long-lasting impact of Greek medical ethics.

G. E. R. Lloyd's published essays delineate a new awareness of Greek medicine's multilevel foundations, suggested by "Alcmaeon and the Early History of Dissection," in *Sudhoffs Archiv,* **59** (1975), "Aspects of the Interrelations of Medicine, Magic and Philosophy in Ancient Greece," in *Apeiron,* **9** (1975), "The Hippocratic Question," in *Classical Quarterly,* **25** (1975), "The Female Sex: Medical Treatment and Biological Theories in the Fifth and Fourth Centuries B.C.," in *Science, Folklore and Ideology* (1983), and the Cambridge inaugural lecture published as *Science and Morality in Greco-Roman Antiquity* (1985);

James Longrigg summarizes the curiously enormous literature on the famous Thucydidean plague in "The Great Plague of Athens," in *History of Science,* **18** (1980); various facets of Greek medicine and related matters receive detailed attention from a number of modern scholars, as suggested by titles: I. M. Lonie, "A Structural Pattern in Greek Dietetics and the Early History of Greek Medicine," in *Medical History,* **21** (1977); Guido Majno, "The Iatros," in *The Healing Hand: Man and Wound in the Ancient World* (1975); E. D. Phillips, *Greek Medicine* (1973); Jackie Pigeaud, *La maladie de l'âme* (1981); John Scarborough, "Thucydides, Greek Medicine and the Plague at Athens," in *Episteme,* **4** (1970), "Magic, Science, and Disease," in *Facets of Hellenistic Life* (1976), and "Beans, Pythagoras, Taboos and Ancient Dietetics," in *Classical World,* **75** (1982); Joseph Schumacher, *Antike Medizin* (1963); Henry E. Sigerist, "Archaic Medicine in Greece," and "The Golden Age of Greek Medicine," in *A History of Medicine,* II: *Early Greek, Hindu and Persian Medicine* (1961); Bennett Simon, *Mind and Madness in Ancient Greece* (1978); Owsei Temkin, "Greek Medicine as Science and Craft," in *Isis,* **44** (1953), and "Antiquity," in *The Falling Sickness,* 2nd rev. ed. (1971); Antoine Thivel, *Cnide et Cos?* (1981).

Hippocratic medicine has increasingly interested the international community of classical scholars and medical historians as indicated by the published proceedings of the triennial Colloque international hippocratique, e.g. M. D. Grmek, ed., *Hippocratica: actes du Colloque de Paris . . . 1978* (1980; 32 papers in French, German, Italian, and English), and F. Lasserre and P. Mudry, eds., *Formes de pensée dans la Collection hippocratique: actes du IVe Colloque international hippocratique Lausanne . . . 1981* (1983; 44 papers in French, Italian, English, and German); almost all aspects of Hippocratic medicine—from theory and practice to anatomy and pharmacology—are included.

HELLENISTIC MEDICINE AND RELATED TOPICS: SOURCES

ANONYMUS LONDINENSIS. Hermann Diels, ed., *Anonymi Londinensis ex Aristotelis iatricis Menoniis et aliis medicis eclogae* (1893), Greek text only; W. H. S. Jones, ed. and trans., *The Medical Writings of Anonymus Londinensis* (1947; repr. 1968), Greek text with English translation.

ARISTOTLE. W. S. Hett, ed. and trans., *Aristotle: Minor Works* (1936), *Aristotle: Problems,* 2 vols. (1936–1937), and *Aristotle: On the Soul. Parva Naturalia. On Breath* (1936), all with Greek texts and English translations; Martha Craven Nussbaum, ed. and trans., *Aristotle's De motu animalium* (1978), Greek text, English translation, and detailed commentary; A. L. Peck, ed. and trans., *Aristotle: Generation of Animals* (1943), and *Aristotle: Historia Animalium,* 2 vols. of 3, vol. 3 not published (1965–1970), all with Greek texts and English translations; A. L. Peck and E. L. Forster, eds. and trans., *Aristotle: Parts of Animals. Movement of Animals Progression of Animals* (1937), Greek texts and English translations; David Ross, ed., *Aristotle: De anima* (1961), and *Aristotle: Parva Naturalia* (1955), both Greek texts only, with commentary; D'Arcy Wentworth Thompson, trans., *The Works of Aristotle,* IV: *Historia Animalium* (1910), English translation only.

DIOCLES OF CARYSTOS. Max Wellmann, ed., *Die Fragmente der sikelischen Ärzte Akron, Philistion und des Diokles von Karystos* (1901), Greek texts only.

DIOSCORIDES. Max Wellmann, ed., *Pedanii Dioscuridis Anazarbei De materia medica,* 3 vols. (1906–1914; repr. 1958), Greek text only; John Scarborough and Vivian Nutton, "The *Preface* of Dioscorides' *Materia Medica:* Introduction, Translation, Commentary," in *Transactions and Studies of the College of Physicians of Philadelphia,* n.s. **4** (1982), English translation with detailed commentary of the *Preface* to Dioscorides.

ERASISTRATUS. No satisfactory collection of the fragments has been made, but useful are: J. F. Dobson, "Erasistratus," in *Proceedings of the Royal Society of Medicine,* sect. hist., **20** (1927), translation into English of scattered quotations of Erasistratus, generally from Galen in the Kühn edition; R. Fuchs, *Erasistratea,* Ph. D. diss., Berlin (1892), Greek texts with commentaries.

HEROPHILUS. No satisfactory collection of the fragments is available, but see the following: J. F. Dobson, "Herophilus of Alexandria," in *Proceedings of the Royal Society of Medicine,* sect. hist., **18** (1925), translation into English of about sixty quotations of Herophilus embedded in Galen, Rufus, and Soranus; F. H. Marx, *De Herophili celeberrimi medici vita* (1840), Latin translation and commentary with Greek texts.

NICANDER. A. S. F. Gow and A. F. Scholfield, eds. and trans., *Nicander: The Poems and Poetical Fragments* (1953), texts and translations into English of the *Theriaca* and *Alexipharmaca,* with occasional lexical, botanical, and zoological notes.

PRAXAGORAS. Fritz Steckerl, ed. and trans., *The Fragments of Praxagoras of Cos and his School* (1958), Greek and Latin texts with English translations.

THEOPHRASTUS. Benedict Einarson and G. K. K. Link, eds. and trans., *Theophrastus: De causis plantarum,* I (1976), Greek text and English translation of books one and two only, with a brilliant introduction by Einarson; Arthur Hort, ed. and trans., *Theophrastus: Enquiry into Plants and Minor Works On Odours and Weather Signs,* 2 vols. (1916), Greek texts and English translations, but the plant identifications by William Thiselton-Dyer in Vol. II cannot be trusted; F. Wimmer, ed., *Theophrasti Eresii Opera* (1866; repr. 1964), Greek texts with Latin translations, still the most complete edition of Theophrastus' works.

HELLENISTIC MEDICINE AND
RELATED TOPICS: STUDIES

P. M. Fraser, "Alexandrian Science: Medicine," in *Ptolemaic Alexandria,* 3 vols. (1972), one of the best all-around summaries, except that Erasistratus is omitted; Werner Jaeger, *Diokles von Karystos,* 2d ed. (1963); Fridolf Kudlien, *Die Sklaven in der griechischen Medizin der klassischen und hellenistischen Zeit* (1968), and *Der griechische Arzt im Zeitalter des Hellenismus* (1979), two good studies of the social contexts of Hellenistic medicine; James Longrigg, "Superlative Achievement and Comparative Neglect: Alexandrian Medicine and Modern Historical Research," in *History of Science,* 19 (1981), an excellent beginning essay.

Guido Majno, "Alexandria the Great," in *The Healing Hand: Man and Wound in the Ancient World* (1975), sprightly and a favorite of students; Markwart Michler, *Die hellenistische Chirurgie,* I: *Die alexandrinischen Chirurgen* (1968), and *Das Spezialisierungsproblem und die antike Chirurgie*

(1969), the first title a collection of literary fragments and commentary; John M. Riddle, *Dioscorides on Pharmacy and Medicine* (1985), a near-brilliant exposition of Dioscorides' drug affinity system, which gives Dioscorides long-overdue credit for his brilliance in pharmacology, medical botany, and diagnostics.

John Scarborough, "Diphilus of Siphnos and Hellenistic Medical Dietetics," in *Journal of the History of Medicine and Allied Sciences,* 25 (1970), "Nicander's Toxicology, I: Snakes," and "Nicander's Toxicology, II: Spiders, Scorpions, Insects and Myriapods," in *Pharmacy in History,* 19 (1977) and 21 (1979), and "Theophrastus on Herbals and Herbal Remedies," in *Journal of the History of Biology,* 11 (1978), "Erasistratus: Student of Theophrastus?," in *Bulletin of the History of Medicine,* 59 (1985), and *Pharmacy's Ancient Heritage: Theophrastus, Nicander and Dioscorides* (1985), a series of studies suggested by titles; Heinrich von Staden, "Experiment and Experience in Hellenistic Medicine," in *Institute of Classical Studies Bulletin,* 22 (1975), a lucid analysis of the intermeshing of scientific and philosophical assumptions.

ROMAN MEDICINE TO GALEN: SOURCES

ARETAEUS OF CAPPADOCIA. Francis Adams, ed. and trans., *The Extant Works of Aretaeus the Cappadocian* (1856), Greek text (now badly dated) and English translation; C. Hude, ed., *Aretaeus,* 2d ed. (1958; *CMG* II), the standard, revised and improved Greek text.

ASCLEPIAN TEMPLE MEDICINE. Emma J. Edelstein and Ludwig Edelstein, *Asclepius: A Collection and Interpretation of the Testimonies,* 2 vols. (1945), by far the best study of the topic; all Greek and Latin texts are translated, and many have extended commentaries.

CATO. William Davis Hooper, ed. and trans., *Marcus Porcius Cato: On Agriculture. Marcus Terentius Varro: On Agriculture* (1934), Latin texts with English translations.

CELSUS. F. Marx, ed., *A. Cornelii Celsi* (1915; *Corpus Medicorum Latinorum* [*CML*] I), Latin text only, with variants; Philippe Mudry, ed. and trans., *La préface du De medicina de Celse* (1982), lucid discussions of the famous Prooemium of Celsus' *De medicina,* one of the first extant "histories" of medicine; W. G. Spencer, ed. and trans., *Celsus: De medicina,* 3 vols. (1935–1938), Latin text, based on the Marx edition above, with English translation.

COLUMELLA. Harrison Boyd Ash, E. S. Forster, and Edward H. Heffner, eds. and trans., *Lucius Junius Moderatus Columella: On Agriculture. On Trees,* 3 vols. (1941–1955), Latin texts with English translations.

EMPIRIC PHYSICIANS. Karl Deichgräber, ed., *Die griechische Empirikerschule,* 2d ed. (1965), Greek and Latin texts with German commentary and occasional quoted translations in German and English; Michael Frede, trans., "Galen: An Outline of Empiricism," in Richard Walzer and Michael Frede, trans., *Galen: Three Treatises On the Nature of Science* (1985), English translation based on the Latin text edited by Deichgräber as transmitted by Niccolo da Reggio (1341).

PLINY THE ELDER. C. Mayhoff and L. Ian, eds., *C. Plini Secundi Naturalis historiae,* 6 vols. (1865–1898), Latin text only, still the best complete text of the *Natural History;* H. Rackham, W. H. S. Jones, and D. E. Eichholz, eds. and trans., *Pliny: Natural History,* 10 vols. (1938–1962), Latin text with a not always reliable English translation; Jean Beaujeu, *et al.,* eds. and trans., *Pline l'Ancien: Histoire naturelle,* 35 vols. to date (1950–1985), Latin texts, French translations, and commentaries, with the text generally that of Ian and Mayhoff plus important new readings from the manuscripts (this is the best edition and translation of Pliny currently available; in this Budé edition, each book of the *Natural History* is a separate volume, and of the thirty-seven books, the following have appeared: I–II, V, part 1, VI, part 2, and VII-XXXVII).

PNEUMATIC PHYSICIANS. Max Wellmann, *Die pneumatische Schule bis auf Archigenes* (1895), collection of fragments, with commentary.

RUFUS OF EPHESUS. C. Daremberg and C. E. Ruelle, eds. and trans., *Oeuvres de Rufus d'Éphèse* (1879; repr. 1963), Greek and Latin texts, Latin translations from the Arabic, with French translations, the most complete edition; Hans Gärtner, ed. and trans., *Rufus von Ephesos: Die Fragen des Arztes an den Kranken* (1962; *CMG* Supplementum IV), Greek text with German translation and commentary; Alexander Sideras, ed. and trans., *Rufus von Ephesos: Über die Nieren- und Blasenleiden* (1977; *CMG* III 1), Greek text and German translation of this important work on Roman urology; Manfred Ullmann, ed. and trans., *Die Schrift des Rufus von Ephesos Über die Gelbsucht* (1983), and *Rufus von Ephesos: Krankenjournale* (1978), Arabic texts with German translations and commentaries; these tracts by Rufus are known only in their Arabic versions.

SCRIBONIUS LARGUS. Sergio Sconocchia, ed., *Scribonii Largi Compositiones* (1983), the revised Latin text based on new manuscript readings; J. S. Hamilton, intro. and trans., "Scribonius Largus on the Medical Profession," in *Bulletin of the History of Medicine,* **60** (1986), a translation into English of Scribonius Largus' famous introduction to his drug manual of A.D. 43.

SORANUS. J. Ilberg, ed., *Sorani Gynaeciorum libri IV. De signis fracturarum. De fasciis. Vita Hippocratis secundum Soranum* (1927; *CMG* IV), the standard Greek texts of Soranus' *Gynecology, Fractures, Bandages,* and *Life of Hippocrates;* Owsei Temkin, trans., *Soranus' Gynecology* (1956), English translation based on Ilberg's Greek text.

VARRO. See CATO, above.

ROMAN MEDICINE TO GALEN: STUDIES

David Daube, "The Mediocrity of Celsus," in *Classical Journal,* **70** (1974), a terse essay showing how Celsus was *not* mediocre; I. E. Drabkin, "Soranus and his System of Medicine," in *Bulletin of the History of Medicine,* **25** (1951), a deft synopsis of the Roman medical sect called the Methodists; Hellmut Flashar, "Celsus, Aretaios und Soran," and "Rufus von Ephesos," in *Melancholie und Melancholiker in den medizinischen Theorien der Antike* (1966); George E. Gask and John Todd, "The Origin of Hospitals," and W. H. S. Jones, "Ancient Documents and Contemporary Life, with Special Reference to the Hippocratic *Corpus,* Celsus, and Pliny," both in E. A. Underwood, ed., *Science, Medicine and History: Essays . . . in honour of Charles Singer,* I, 2 vols. (1953); G. E. R. Lloyd, "Developments in Pharmacology,

Anatomy and Gynaecology," in *Science, Folklore and Ideology* (1983), a thought-provoking essay on the interlocking prejudices that encompassed drug lore, concepts of anatomy, and treatment of women's ailments in the Roman Empire; Guido Majno, "The Medicus," in *The Healing Hand: Man and Wound in the Ancient World* (1975).

Vivian Nutton, "Roman Oculists," in *Epigraphica*, **34** (1972), "Archiatri and the Medical Profession in Antiquity," in *Papers of the British School at Rome*, **45** (1977), "Murders and Miracles: Lay Attitudes towards Medicine in Classical Antiquity," in R. S. Porter, ed., *Patients and Practitioners: Lay Perceptions of Medicine in Pre-Industrial Society* (1985), and "The Perils of Patriotism: Pliny and Roman Medicine" in R. French and F. Greenaway, eds., *Science in the Early Roman Empire: Pliny the Elder, His Sources and Influence* (1986), articles by one of the most gifted scholars currently publishing in aspects of Roman medicine; Joanne H. Phillips, "The Emergence of the Greek Medical Profession in the Roman Republic," in *Transactions and Studies of the College of Physicians of Philadelphia*, n.s. **2** (1980); Elizabeth Rawson, "The Life and Death of Asclepiades of Bithynia," in *Classical Quarterly*, **32** (1982), and "Medicine," in *Intellectual Life in the Late Roman Republic* (1985) display brilliant philology applied to medicine in the republic.

John Scarborough, "Roman Medicine and the Legions," in *Medical History*, **12** (1968), *Roman Medicine* (1969; repr. 1976), "Some Notes on the Etruscan Heritage of Early Roman Medicine," in *Episteme*, **3** (1969), "Celsus on Human Vivisection at Ptolemaic Alexandria," in *Clio Medica*, **11** (1976), "On the Understanding of Medicine among the Romans," in *The Historian*, **39** (1977), "Some Beetles in Pliny's Natural History," in *Coleopterists Bulletin*, **31** (1977), "Roman Medicine and Public Health," in T. Ogawa, ed., *Public Health: Proceedings of the Fifth International Symposium on the Comparative History of Medicine 1980 . . . Shizuoka, Japan* (1981), "Roman Pharmacy and the Eastern Drug Trade," in *Pharmacy in History*, **24** (1982), and "Pharmacy in Pliny's Natural History: Some Observations on Substances and Sources," in R. French and F. Greenaway, eds.,

Science in the Early Roman Empire: Pliny the Elder, His Sources and Influences (1986); Jerry Stannard, "Pliny and Roman Botany," in *Isis*, **56** (1965), suggesting Pliny's expertise in Italian plant lore; Owsei Temkin, "Celsus' 'On Medicine' and the Ancient Medical Sects," in *Bulletin of the History of Medicine*, **3** (1935), still a standard synopsis of the problems; R. E. Walker, "Roman Veterinary Medicine" [Appendix], in J. M. C. Toynbee, *Animals in Roman Life and Art* (1973), a solid account unique in English; K. D. White, *Roman Farming* (1970), the best modern monograph on the subject.

GALEN: SOURCES

Both primary and secondary literature on Galen is enormous, so that the following merely suggests texts, translations, commentaries, and studies. The basic collection of Greek texts (with generally unreliable Latin translations) remains C. G. Kühn, ed., *Claudii Galeni Opera omnia*, 20 vols. in 22 parts (1821–1833; repr. 1964–1965). Unfortunately, the texts edited by Kühn are sometimes incomprehensible, so that one must always seek a more modern, well-edited Greek text whenever possible. Some are available in the *CMG* series and elsewhere, with several of these new texts accompanied by English translations.

Some modern editions of Galen's works with English translations, and some translations without Greek texts include: A. J. Brock, ed. and trans., *Galen On the Natural Faculties* (1916), Greek text and English translation; Phillip De Lacy, ed. and trans., *Galen On the Doctrines of Hippocrates and Plato*, 3 vols. (1978–1984; *CMG* V 4, 1.2), Greek text, English translation, and extended commentary; W. L. H. Duckworth, trans., ed. M. C. Lyons and B. Towers, *Galen On Anatomical Procedures: The Later Books* (1962), translated from the Arabic text edited by Max Simon as *Sieben Bücher Anatomie des Galen*, I (1906), books IX-XV of Galen's *Anatomical Procedures* have survived only in an Arabic translation; R. B. Edlow, ed. and trans., *Galen On Language and Ambiguity* (1977), Greek text, English translation, and commentary; C. M. Goss, translations from the Kühn Greek texts of five of Galen's shorter works on anatomy, "On

Anatomy of Veins and Arteries," in *Anatomical Record*, **141** (1961), "On the Anatomy of the Uterus," *ibid.*, **144** (1962), "On the Anatomy of Muscles for Beginners," *ibid.*, **145** (1963), "On Anatomy of the Nerves," in *American Journal of Anatomy*, **118** (1966), and "On Movement of Muscles," *ibid.*, **123** (1968).

R. M. Green, trans., *Galen's Hygiene* (1951), translated from the Greek text edited by K. Koch as *Galeni De sanitate tuenda* (1923; *CMG* V 4, 2); P. W. Harkins, trans., *Galen On the Passions and Errors of the Soul* (1963), translated from the Greek text edited by Wilko de Boer as *Galeni De propriorum animi cuiuslibet affectum dignotione et curatione. De animi cuiuslibet peccatorum dignotione et curatione* (1937; *CMG* V 4, 1.1); J. S. Kieffer, trans., *Galen's Institutio Logica* (1964), translated from the Greek text edited by C. Kalbfleisch as *Galeni Institutio logica* (1896); Malcolm Lyons, ed. and trans., *Galeni in Hippocratis de officina medici commentariorum versionem Arabicam et excerpta, quae ʿAlī Ibn Riḍwan ex eis sumpsit* (1963; *CMG* Supplementum Orientale I), and *Galen On the Parts of Medicine. On Cohesive Causes. On Regimen in Acute Diseases in Accordance with the Theories of Hippocrates* (1969; *CMG* Supplementum Orientale II), Arabic texts and English translations.

M. T. May, trans., *Galen On the Usefulness of the Parts of the Body*, 2 vols. (1968), translated from the Greek text edited by Georg Helmreich as *Galeni De usu partium*, 2 vols. (1907–1909; repr. 1968); Vivian Nutton, ed. and trans., *Galen On Prognosis* (1979; *CMG* V 8, 1), excellent text, good translation, and informative commentary; David Sider and Michael McVaugh, trans., "Galen On Tremor, Palpitation, Spasm, and Rigor," in *Transactions and Studies of the College of Physicians of Philadelphia*, n.s. 1 (1979), translated from newly edited series of manuscript readings; Charles Singer, trans., *Galen On Anatomical Procedures* (1956), translation of books one through eight that have survived in Greek, and "Galen's Elementary Course on Bones," in *Proceedings of the Royal Society of Medicine*, **45** (1952), both translated from Kühn, II; Owsei Temkin, trans., "Galen's Advice for an Epileptic Boy," in *Bulletin of the History of Medicine*, **2** (1934), translated from Kühn, XI; R. Walzer, ed. and trans., *Galen On*

Medical Experience (1944), Arabic text and English translation of a tract surviving only in Arabic.

Abraham Wasserstein, ed. and trans., *Galen's Commentary on the Hippocratic Treatise Airs, Waters, Places* (1982), Hebrew text (a truncated version of an unpublished Arabic text), English translation, and commentary; J. S. Wilkie and David J. Furley, eds. and trans., *Galen On Respiration and the Arteries* (1983), newly edited Greek and Arabic texts, English translations, and commentaries on *Use of Breathing, Blood in the Arteries, On the Use of the Pulse,* and *On the Causes of Breathing.*

GALEN: STUDIES

Phillip De Lacy, "Galen and the Greek Poets," in *Greek, Roman, and Byzantine Studies*, **7** (1966), and "Galen's Platonism," in *American Journal of Philology*, **93** (1972), two excellent studies of Galen's wide-ranging cultural knowledge; Georg Harig, "Verhältnis zwischen den Primär- und Sekundärqualitäten in der theoretischen Pharmakologie Galens," in *NTM*, **10** (1973), *Bestimmung der Intensität im medizinischen System Galens* (1974), and "Der Begriff der lauen Wärme in der theoretischen Pharmakologie Galens," in *NTM: Schriftenreihe für Geschichte der Naturwissenschaften, Technik und Medizin*, **13** (1976), astute studies of Galen's often muddled notions of drugs and drug properties; Elinor Lieber, "Galen on Contaminated Cereals as a Cause of Epidemics," in *Bulletin of the History of Medicine*, **44** (1970).

Vivian Nutton, "Galen and Medical Autobiography," in *Proceedings of the Cambridge Philological Society*, **18** (1972), "The Chronology of Galen's Early Career," in *Classical Quarterly*, **23** (1973), "Galen in the Eyes of His Contemporaries," in *Bulletin of the History of Medicine*, **58** (1984), and ed., *Galen: Problems and Prospects . . . the 1979 Cambridge Conference* (1981), the first three titles brilliant and fundamental essays on Galen's life and times (Nutton's research proves Galen was born in September of A.D. 129, and died sometime after A.D. 210, rendering all previous dating of Galen incorrect), and the *Problems* volume contains twelve excellent papers, seven in English; Steven M. Oberhelman, "Galen On Diagnosis from Dreams," in *Journal of the History of Medicine* *and Allied Sciences,* **38** (1983), a crucial study with translation of Galen's fragmentary treatise on the topic, demonstrating an aspect of the best diagnostics of the Roman Empire.

Donald W. Petersen, "Observations on the Chronology of the Galenic Corpus," in *Bulletin of the History of Medicine,* **51** (1977), a tightly argued essay on the thorny problems of when Galen wrote what; Anthony Preus, "Galen's Criticism of Aristotle's Conception Theory," in *Journal of the History of Biology,* **10** (1977), a vivid example of Galen's skills in comparative embryology; Emilie Savage-Smith, "Galen's Account of the Cranial Nerves and the Autonomic Nervous System," in *Clio Medica,* **6** (1971), a fine study based on Arabic texts of *Anatomical Procedures;* John Scarborough, "Galen and the Gladiators," in *Episteme,* **5** (1971), "Galen's Investigations of the Kidney," in *Clio Medica,* **11** (1976), "The Galenic Question," in *Sudhoffs Archiv,* **65** (1981), "Galen's Dissection of the Elephant," in *Koroth,* **8** (1985), and "Galen on Roman Amateur Athletics," in *Arete: Journal of Sport Literature,* **2** (1985); Wesley D. Smith, "Galen on Coans vs. Cnidians," in *Bulletin of the History of Medicine,* **47** (1973), and *The Hippocratic Tradition* (1979), the first title a pungent demonstration of how Galen —not the Greeks—posited the variations among Cnidian and Coan physicians, and the second a fundamental monograph on how Galen's views of earlier Greek, Hellenistic, and Roman medicine became canonical as the *real* story, bereft of historical truth; Owsei Temkin, *Galenism* (1973), by far the best study of the subject, which covers the long-range influence of Galen well into modern times; R. Walzer, *Galen on Jews and Christians* (1949), a splendid study of Galen's reflections on the vitriolic debates characteristic of the second-century Roman Empire.

GREEK AND ROMAN MEDICINE: BIBLIOGRAPHICAL GUIDES

Activity in this special facet of classical studies has increased markedly in the last decade, after being ignored for many years. There are few bibliographies available that are inclusive and reliable, but one may use the following with confidence: Gerhard Fichtner, *Corpus Galenicum: Verzeichnis der galenischen und pseudogalenischen Schriften* (1983), an extensive listing of 321 treatises available in Greek, Latin, Arabic, Syriac, and Hebrew, with indices for each language; Helmut Leitner, *Bibliography to the Ancient Medical Authors* (1973), does not include veterinary sources, listings of printed texts and editions to 1970 only, spotty for late Roman and early Byzantine sources, fundamental for listings of Hippocratic and Galenic works; Vivian Nutton, *Karl Gottlob Kühn and his Edition of the Works of Galen* (1976), good for various listings of secondary work that supplements Schubring (below).

John Scarborough, "Classical Antiquity: Medicine and Allied Sciences," in *Trends in History,* **1** (1979), "Ancient Medicine: Some Recent Books," in *Clio Medica,* **16** (1981), both listing and commentary on recently published materials, and ed., *Society for Ancient Medicine Newsletter,* nos. 3–14 (1978–1986; generally issued biannually [no. 14 issued as *Society for Ancient Medicine and Pharmacy Newsletter*]), each issue contains an annotated listing of recent publications ("Publications in Ancient Medicine") and newly published texts and translations into English, German, French, Italian, and occasionally other languages ("Supplements to Leitner"); Konrad Schubring, "Bemerkungen zur Galenausgabe von Karl Gottlob Kühn und zu ihrem Nachdruck," and "Bibliographische Hinweise zu Galen," in Kühn, XX.

Greek Attitudes Toward Sex

JEFFREY HENDERSON

DEFINITIONS

Sexuality is of fundamental importance to every individual and to every culture. Its regulation is necessary for cultural stability. Ideal norms and prohibitions define it and affect every aspect of life, yet they are different in each culture. The risk of ethnocentric misinterpretation by alien observers is exceptionally great. Investigators (there can be no observers) of the sexual mores of ancient Greece encounter additional and special difficulties. First, the evidence is scanty: written texts, artifacts, and other material remains. Examples are sporadic and of very uneven distribution: a disproportionately large amount was produced by tribes calling themselves "Ionian" and much of that by (or inspired by) fifth- and fourth-century Athenians. Virtually all of it was created by males belonging to the dominant classes of society. To make matters worse, males tended to be elaborately silent about those females who occupied their private worlds, and we hear mostly about homosexual relationships among men. And, since the Greeks placed far less value on one's individual character than on one's competence in a social role, their art and literature tended to be more idealizing and normative than ours. For us, Greek social realities must be inferred or extrapolated more often than they can be openly glimpsed. We know only what certain men publicly articulated and took for granted. It is a picture of a world where men appear in brilliant clarity but where women are all but invisible. Women were at once a public myth and a potent social reality.

It is an obscure picture, and a strange one. In the overview that follows an attempt has been made to keep these limitations in mind by asking of the evidence: Who made or wrote this? When, where, on what occasion, for what audience, and for what purpose? What is the reality that it symbolizes, and can we glimpse in it or infer from it the existing competitive realities? It is also assumed that none of the present author's own tribal dogmas, religious or otherwise, constitutes a panhuman norm. Mere coincidences aside, human sexuality is the creation of given cultural groups and, like all other kinds of social organization, evolves within a culture.

Those still inclined to appeal to religion

or philosophy for special sexual guidelines may find it strange that appeals are seldom made in this discussion to Greek religion and philosophy. There are two reasons. First, the Greek gods were merely superhuman Greeks whose sexual behavior differed from that of believers only in being less constrained by the threat of punishment. They were never morally superior; they could be superior only to people to whom believers themselves already felt superior, such as disqualified cultists or alien groups. Like all gods, they only ratified the believers' conception of reality, which they were then said to cause. When the reality changed, so did the gods. Second, the human sexual absolutes postulated through the ages by philosophers and religious apologists are merely expressions of this or that tribal rationale, adjusted (if they would succeed) for new trends or irrefutable new knowledge. Like religion, they are the product and the reflection of conventional versions of reality and are therefore merely a distinct, not a special, kind of evidence for that reality.

That the same two sexes occur in every society is a matter of biology: chromosome-patterning in individuals; gonadal production of eggs or sperm; external genital anatomy and internal, accessory reproductive mechanisms; and the more obvious mosaic of hormonal traits and characteristics that appear throughout life but most spectacularly at adolescence. That there is always sexuality is, however, a cultural matter, for the two sexes always occur in a culture. Sexuality is that complex of reactions, interpretations, definitions, prohibitions, and norms that is created and maintained by a given culture in response to the fact of the two biological sexes. It is wholly the prescription of given social groups and subgroups. In the case of the Greeks, what are now matters of biology were still largely matters of sexuality, for extensive or reliable biological knowledge was virtually nonexistent.

Masculinity and femininity are psychic traits. In combination with the approved behaviors associated with males and females, they are taught and learned within a social group. Sex is assigned by parents or parental figures to a child in the rearing process. Gender roles—what a group at a given time thinks males and females are like in nature and behavior—are learned through social processes. The individual, in response to prevailing stereotypes, develops perspectives on how he or she fits the approved model of expectations that constitute gender role, thus developing a gender orientation. But human beings are not uniform entities. No individual, save in fantasy, ever achieves an ideal dichotomy of traits. The range of biologically normal traits (height, shape, intelligence, dexterity, strength) always exceeds the prescribed norms of a given culture; so, too, with the normal range of ethologically possible behaviors, such as nurturing, aggression, co-operation, and competitiveness. In short, social, not biological, norms determine which individuals in a given society may achieve the status of admired role models.

Every human society thus invents the idea of male and female for itself and so defines a workable sexuality. Nevertheless, a society's sexual norms are always to some degree in flux. Each new generation reinvents and redefines them for itself in degrees ranging from the barely perceptible to the revolutionary. Moreover, radical changes may occur at any time as the result of internal (ecological, technical, or social) and external (contact with other groups) events. At such moments, a society discovers that fewer than an ideal number of individuals have actually been living up to the norm.

An example of the problems involved is the prohibition of sexual behavior between parent and child (incest)—the only prohibition found, as far as we know, in every human society. In order to understand this prohibition, however, we must realize that "prohibition," "sexual behavior," and therefore "incest" are culturally defined terms. A Manchu mother, for instance, would routinely suck her small son's penis in public but would never kiss his cheek. For, among the Manchus, fellatio is a form of sexual behavior except in the context of mother and small son, whereas kissing of any kind is always sexual. We are perplexed because, in our culture, fellatio is always sexual, whereas cheek-kissing among kin never is.

It is this kind of evidence that is often unavailable for Greece. In Aristophanes' *Wasps* (609), Philokleon says that (in addition to other fatherly pleasures) he routinely enjoys letting his daughter fish small coins from his mouth with her tongue. We know that tongue-kissing was a sexual behavior in fifth-century Athens, but no other reference to it is made in this context. Therefore we cannot know whether Philokleon's act indicated ordinary or extraordinary paternal affection, or whether the anticipated reaction was amusement or disgust. Our own feelings are irrelevant.

GENDER ROLES

The most salient feature of Greek sexuality, and the one that most differentiates it from ours, is the inseparably close connection of sexuality with social status. Social status defined one's sexual identity and determined the proper sexual behavior that one was allowed. Ideally at least, there could be no overlap: the nature of one's assigned status automatically ruled out characteristics and behavior associated with another status. One was defined both as what one was and as what one was not.

A Greek polis (city-state) was a tribal, legal, religious, and political alliance of *oikoi* (households). The goal of a polis vis-à-vis other city-states was to maintain and increase its safety and prosperity, and the goal of a household vis-à-vis other households was the same. These goals were pursued by competitions (warfare by poleis, politics by *oikoi*), and these competitions defined the public world of the Greeks. In this public world, male citizens were exclusively in charge. A male citizen was a warrior and head of an *oikos*. Both as an individual and in alliances with others, he competed in financing and conducting warfare, games, and religious and artistic festivals; in politics, business, and lawsuits; and in deliberation and decision on all issues affecting the polis as a whole. All positions of public attention were thus attained, and all were reserved for male citizens.

Inevitably, a citizen's character was defined by his success in these competitions, and his value was judged by his contribution to the survival and prosperity of the polis. A man was a good (if useful) or a bad (if deficient) object. How he performed in his role counted far more than his individual qualities, beliefs, or traits. Idiosyncratic virtues and vices that did not affect the polis were in fact publicly ignored: they were part of the private world of a citizen's *oikos,* which he jealously shielded from public view. Anyone who used an enemy's private behavior to discredit him had to show that it posed some kind of threat to the polis, that is, that it was actually a public matter. Since this kind of attack was made frequently, it is not surprising that a Greek citizen was extremely sensitive to any kind of public allusion whatsoever to his home life.

Noncitizens (resident aliens, slaves, and, as at Sparta, subject populations) and women (citizens and noncitizens alike) were, from the point of view of the polis, subordinate because they could not engage in any activity or display any behavior that would bring them into competition with male citizens; nor could a male citizen act or behave like a noncitizen or woman. Whatever these subordinate types contributed to the polis was considered less important and less demanding than what was expected of citizens. The virtues associated with their separate roles were correspondingly less admirable, and there was a tendency to believe that individuals were naturally incapable of anything greater. Their shortcomings were blamed on the male citizen in whose charge they were, and male citizens who could be assimilated to them in any way incurred tremendous ridicule and blame—even, in some cases, legal punishments of the utmost severity.

A female citizen occupied and dominated the private realm of the *oikos.* She was in fact a possession belonging to it, and throughout life she was in the charge of the male relative who was legally entitled to her. Before marriage she belonged to the *oikos* of her father and afterward to that of her husband. Marriage was arranged by the father, who put up a dowry commensurate with his wealth and status and intended to be passed on to her children. The woman had no say in any of this. Her duties in life were to manage her husband's *oikos* and to produce its male heirs, and her character and value were judged by her success in these roles.

But her success was not a matter for public comment, save in her epitaph. Pericles' notorious exhortation to war-bereaved citizen women "not to be worse than your nature" and his definition of the ideal female virtue as "to be least spoken of for good or ill among male citizens" (Thucydides, 2.45) can be paraphrased thus: "Your gender role is to manage your *oikos* so efficiently that we men will never have occasion to make it (and therefore your husband, father, etc.) the topic of public discussion. Silence is absence of blame and may therefore be construed as praise." Pericles was complimenting the women by announcing that he had nothing to say about their *oikoi;* it was as far as a

public speaker could go in consoling them on their sacrifice and loss.

Freedom of everyday movement by women varied from social class to social class and from polis to polis. In rural or lower-class households, paucity of slaves would often have made the segregation of women impracticable. In classical Athens, every effort was made to segregate citizen women, to restrict them to the *oikos,* and to conceal their features (they were covered and veiled). The public visibility in behavior and clothing of Spartan women was considered shocking by Athenians. In the archaic period and in the later Hellenistic period the situation was less restrictive: female freedom had much to do with the domination of noble or royal families, in which women assumed greater public roles. But the separateness of roles (women in the domestic, men in the military and political sphere) held everywhere, as did the fact that the roles required different virtues.

But because women had no legal or political power we must not assume that they lacked social power as well. In fact, both singly as wives and corporately with age-mates they exerted very substantial social power. Managing the *oikos* was a much more complex job than it is in our culture, for some households were busy centers of farming and craft activity that also served as the center of numerous public and private religious institutions. Wherever money and slaves allowed, males shopped and worked the fields. Everything else was run by the wife: preparing food; weaving, craftwork, and clothesmaking; managing household slaves and finances; providing medical care; rearing children; assisting pregnant women; supervising funerals and acting as mourner; teaching girls and helping them prepare for marriage; supervising domestic cults. She also participated in, or was priestess in charge of, many religious activities outside the *oikos,* some restricted to women, others jointly with men: processions, funerals, family celebrations, festivals (both as participants and as spectator). It was only on these occasions that male and female citizens publicly mingled, but it was precisely in this way that the importance of the *oikos* as a social and economic institution was demonstrated, and where the complementary nature of polis (male) and *oikos* (female) was enacted publicly. The cooperative (female) values of the *oikos* were seen to promote the welfare of the polis, and at such times there was a respite from the pressures associated with the competitive (male) values of warfare and politics.

No evidence suggests that women ever aspired to extend their competence into the male sphere, even though this possibility haunted men and inspired many colorful rituals, myths, and comic fictions, as Attic Old Comedy and tragedy attest. There could be no "women's liberation" in classical Greece; social status and gender role went hand in hand, and male and female roles were mutually exclusive as well as mutually defining. A woman competing in the male sphere would have had to abandon her gender entirely, and the men with whom she successfully competed would no longer be thought of as men. In any case, women had not only important functions of their own but also their own rich culture. Like men, they observed, defined, and transmitted cultural conventions and necessary skills; they supervised and took part in central religious activities; they educated; they sang, danced, and wrote poetry. That they considered these activities to be both essential and important, and that they felt their virtues to be comparable to men's, is evident in the speeches put into women's mouths by poets and dramatists (who also articulated the men's case). It is an unhappy consequence of Greek (and later Roman and Christian) concentration on masculine life that so little of women's culture survives. The pitiful scraps of Sappho's poetry reveal the magnitude of this loss.

GENDER ORIENTATION

Men and women occupied different and separate compartments of reality, each being what the other was not. Gender orientation was felt to be a growth that progressed in measurable stages from childhood to adulthood, the goal being to fulfill the requirements appropriate to one's social status. For boys it required that dependent (servile or feminine) status be converted into dominant (manly) status. Greek men tended to regard women as less endowed with those qualities upon which they prided themselves, and more endowed with those which they despised. Men were, ideally, physically strong, warlike, dominant, realistic, and intelligent; thrifty but generous with friends; capable of resisting strong emotions (sexual desire, fear, grief, pity, impulse); able to endure pain, fatigue, misfortune, hunger, and thirst; and reliable, straightforward, honest, brave, and informed in the ways of the world.

Men who failed to live up to these ideals were thought to be womanish or slavish, for women and slaves shared many attributes, though not the same status. Women were, by contrast, regarded as physically weak, unwarlike, submissive, credulous, and superstitious; artful, crafty, and cunning; spendthrift but selfish; unable to resist emotion and quick to display it; unable to endure discomfort; unreliable, deceitful, dishonest, cowardly, naive, and uninformed; and easily tempted by food, drink, and sexual desire. To be otherwise was to be threateningly mannish. These antitheses are partly a result and partly a rationalization of the segregation of women and the separation of their roles.

Myth and literature reveal a corresponding polarization in the way men and women were conceptualized. Men were associated with the sky, the sun, the city-state, society, and its institutions. Their space was outside, open, public, separate, and integral. Their time was eternity and immortality. Their motion was autonomous, kinetic, centrifugal, and direct. They counted, classified, and made hierarchies. They tamed, conquered, and penetrated. Their creations were verbal, spiritual, intellectual, and monumental. Women were associated with the earth, the moon, the home, the fields, and the uncultivated land beyond. Their space was inside, closed, private, communal, and secret. Their time was birth, life, and death. Their motion was centripetal and devious. They were irrational and inarticulate. They were tamed and penetrated. Their creations were children and other perishable things. Women occupied those parts of reality that men considered mysterious, dangerous, and even polluting.

THE SCOPE OF SEXUALITY

The Greeks regarded sexuality as a force of nature and therefore as divine. Sexual desire—on the same footing with, but stronger and more complex than, hunger, thirst, and fatigue—was the province of Eros, and sexual enjoyment that of Aphrodite. These were powerful and important gods who were seen at work in all natural phenomena. Every becoming was a birth or like a birth, and every god or goddess was expected to have, as well as to represent, human sexual attributes. The poets represented gods and heroes not only as enjoying the same sexual activities as human beings or animals but also as being allowed some that were normally forbidden to humans: adultery, rape, fornication, bestiality, sodomy, and even mutilation and incest. The gods of rulers will behave like rulers, only more so. The fact that systematic ethicists—poets and philosophers alike—debated or denounced this concept of the divine only demonstrates its strength among those of whom they disapproved. The gods were physically the same as human beings except for their immortality and superior strength and, at best, morally the same, too. We must remember that agriculture was still fundamental, animals had not yet been eliminated from everyday life, and knowledge about biological and natural phenomena was both rudimentary and unverifiable. In these conditions, it is not surprising that the scope of sexuality was much greater in Greek culture than it is in ours.

The enjoyment of sexuality in its proper contexts was not considered to be in itself dirty, shameful, embarrassing, obscene, or harmful. The Greek language possesses a vast sexual vocabulary that was technical, metaphorical, and obscene; it was used, even demanded, in many socially approved contexts, both public and private. Storytellers, playwrights, and even philosophers openly and frankly explored the sexual aspects of life. Some, like comic, iambic, and epigrammatic poets, used obscenities and the most direct possible descriptions of sexual acts. Vase painters, especially in the late archaic and early classical periods, routinely depicted all kinds of sexual intercourse, masturbation, and fellatio. Moreover, most Greek festivals and cults contained central sexual components. In the Dionysiac festivals at Athens, huge models of the penis were carried in procession and smaller ones worn by celebrants; ribald songs and farces were performed; and men could, like Dionysos himself, indulge in transvestism. Monumental phalluses were often used as boundary markers, and small ithyphallic herms (posts or pillars topped by heads of Hermes and equipped with erect penises) were as common in the streets as fire hydrants are today. Representations of male and female genitalia were used to promote

1254

fertility (human and otherwise) and also to scare away baneful influences. No evidence suggests that women and children were shielded from these activities or that participation was confined to particular social classes. Sexuality was present on too large a scale and was too important for anyone to think of trying to make it a secret.

Moreover, the Greeks considered it perfectly natural and normal that a man or youth would feel, and seek to gratify, sexual desire for other (usually younger) males. There is also strong evidence to suggest that a similar homosexual object choice was open to females. Aphrodite presided over both homosexual and heterosexual relations, and the same words were used to describe both. For example, males and females alike were "beautiful" (*kalos*) rather than the one "handsome" and the other "lovely"; and the statement, "I am in love," required the question, "With a boy or a woman?" (Aristophanes, *Frogs* 55 ff.). Not only was homosexual sentiment pervasive in Greek culture, but homosexuality, at least in the late archaic and early classical periods, also played an important role in the transition of boys (and probably girls, too) from childhood into adulthood. It was in no way felt to interfere with heterosexual enjoyment or with a happy marriage.

INHIBITION AND RELEASE

Although the range of sexual behavior considered to be normal and natural was wider in Greece than we are used to in our own world, and sexuality more openly acknowledged and celebrated, the Greeks were no less inhibited or less subject to feelings of shame and guilt than members of other cultures. Some kinds of sexual behavior, organs, and function are rarely if ever acknowledged: menstruation; cunnilingus (only in comic poetry, to vilify practitioners);

the clitoris (no slang or obscene term, only the technical one and otherwise only very indirect euphemisms); men, women, and slaves engaging in behavior inappropriate to their social status (again, only in comic vilification or fantasy). Uninhibited, direct sexual expression was always confined to certain permissible artistic, literary, and ritual or festive contexts and avoided in social conversation where individual propriety might be compromised. Sexual intercourse was always considered to be a private, although not secret, activity. There was a requirement of ritual purity in sanctuaries and chastity in many religious connections. Public urination and defecation were common sights but were conventionally "invisible" and not openly commented upon. Social and legal sanctions could be invoked against anyone whose desire for sexual gratification was felt to threaten the integrity of the household, the welfare of the polis, or the rights of citizens. Even slaves (damageable property) and noncitizens (contributing residents of the polis) enjoyed certain social, if not legal, protection. It was a commonplace that most of the sexual behavior of gods and heroes, and of their comic counterparts, would not be tolerated in a citizen.

In Greece, all poetry was public, and one of its functions was to provide or enhance opportunities for release from the inhibitions of everyday life. Art, poetry, and festival were rarely solemn activities; they encouraged wish fulfillment and merriment. Here one could experience life as both more and less pleasurable and exciting than it actually was. Obscene and otherwise uninhibited portrayals of sexuality were demanded in these contexts precisely because they allowed a safe and controlled rupture of ordinary restraints. By "obscene" is meant any linguistic, graphic, or mimetically enacted representation, in an explicit fashion, of those sexual or excremental organs and acts to which a community attaches powerful taboos and of which the representation itself is subject to social sanctions. Metaphors, puns, plays on words, or fortuitously overlapping symbolisms are less explicit in that they maintain an ambiguity into which innocent propriety may retreat, but they are still direct: the ambiguity itself reveals the inhibition.

Greek "four-letter words" referred to the same things that ours do, and the Greeks took even greater delight in discovering metaphorical and symbolic expressions of sexuality than we do. The latter are found particularly in the semantic and graphic areas of agriculture, horsemanship and hunting, seafaring, wrestling, warfare, and eating. The Greeks differed from us in their greater demand for occasions when these devices could be safely used and publicly enjoyed. Thus the pictorial conventions of artists are not documentary evidence for everyday life; nor are the obscenities, metaphors, stories, and fantasies of writers unambiguous evidence for everyday behavior. In this connection it might be added that, for the Greeks, words (and to a lesser degree, pictures) still possessed a kind of magical power. Thus we find that obscenity was very potent as a vehicle for curses, magical spells and charms, lampoons, and comic vilification. Poets like Archilochos and Hipponax used their special status as poets to discredit personal enemies by referring to their sexual misbehavior in public verses. This freedom of the iambist was continued and, in some measure, inherited by the comic poets of fifth-century Athens, especially Kratinos, Eupolis, and Aristophanes.

In all periods, the amount of festive and artistic license must have been inversely proportional to the degree of everyday restraint. In the Homeric age and again from the fourth century B.C. onward, considerably more restraint is evident than in the intervening period. It is always difficult to account for such changes in the pattern and

intensity of sexual inhibition, but it is surely no accident that in the sexually repressive society of late archaic and early democratic Athens, with its segregation of women and strict citizenship laws, people exalted and exaggerated sexuality in their festivals; made sexuality a central topic of ethical debate, notably in the Socratic "schools"; and prized dramas that portrayed individuals ruined by (tragedy) or evading (comedy) ideal norms of kinship, citizenship, the complementary natures of polis and *oikos,* and the behaviors assigned to men and women. Being adult meant learning, and living by, rules and limitations. Festive celebrants, like gods, heroes, and comic characters, were in a situation where they could afford to behave as if they had never had to become adults.

DESIRE AND PURSUIT

The characteristic Greek conception of sexuality was not as the reciprocated sentiment of equal participants but as a relationship between a pursuing senior partner and a pursued junior partner. Senior partners were usually older and always dominant in status and power, so that one could be pursuer and pursued at the same time but not with the same partner. The behaviors associated with pursuer and pursued depended entirely on gender and social status. Women could pursue other women but never men. A citizen male could pursue a citizen female only for the purposes of marriage, but he could pursue noncitizen and servile women for any purposes. A citizen male could pursue citizen males only in special circumstances, but he could pursue noncitizen and servile males without restraint. Noncitizens could pursue other noncitizens and slaves; slaves could pursue other slaves with the permission of masters. In all these relationships, care had to be taken to preserve the appearance—and as much of the reality as possible—of the gender roles conventionally assigned to males and females.

Physical beauty and other desirable attributes were much more important in the pursued than in the pursuer. Sexual desire was viewed as an external force acting upon the body and soul of the pursuer, and its source was located within the object of the pursuit. It was not essentially different from hunger, thirst, or fatigue, and it was up to the pursuer to know what was sufficient (normal) and what was excessive. The Greeks admired those who could resist desire of any kind by the manly virtues of endurance, pride, courage, reason, and sense of honor. Those unable to resist were thought to be "worsted" or "enslaved" by desire if their indulgence was perceived to threaten their socially important functions. Those like Socrates or the Spartan king Agesilaos whose ability to resist was abnormally great were thought to be extraordinarily manly. Thus it is not paradoxical to hear that one has been "captured" by the pursued object; in fact, this confession was virtually mandatory in the case of homosexual relationships among male citizens. Nor is it strange that women were thought to take more pleasure in sexual intercourse than men. Since they could only be sources, not victims, of eros, they were not expected to resist it; and those who did not resist were thought to be less resistant. In any case, responsibility rested with the male pursuer. A citizen male who was or could be enslaved by eros was suspected of being a potential lawbreaker, an unreliable friend, a dissipator of the resources of his *oikos,* and a threat to other households.

SEGREGATION OF CITIZEN FEMALES

The absence of effective contraception and a belief that a son inherits his qualities solely from his father (Aeschylus, *Eumenides* 655) greatly restricted the availability of citizen females as objects of pursuit. Where citizenship required that both parents be citizens (as in Athens after 451), pressure for segregation was great, as were penalties for rape and seduction. It was adultery to pursue the wife, widowed mother, unmarried daughter, sister, or niece of a citizen; and an adulterer could be killed, held for compensation, prosecuted, anally sodomized (actually or symbolically), or otherwise injured by the offended head of the *oikos.* Always he was shamed as having mistreated a fellow citizen. In Sparta, where women were less restricted, adultery seems to have been more a restriction on vaginal intercourse and, hence, on the risk of illicit pregnancy: males were expected to eschew it in favor of anal penetration (this custom underlies the humor of a scene in Aristophanes' *Lysistrata,* 1076–1107).

The sexual use of women of servile or foreign status was unrestricted and constituted the only licit heterosexual outlet apart from marriage. These women included prostitutes owned by a brothel keeper; courtesans (hetairai) financially supported by their clients; concubines owned, shared, hired out, or lent; and dancers, singers, and musicians who entertained men at drinking parties (symposia). These outlets were expected to be only physical ones and were not placed on a par with the emotional and familial satisfactions of marital intercourse, which fell under the heading of "love" (*philia*) rather than "mere lust." Comedy and other poetry glamorized extramarital activity of these sorts, but never at the expense of marital relations, unlike so much similar glamorization of today. A loving husband and wife were still the ideal of good sexual fortune, as the plot of *Lysistrata* and many a New Comedy reveal, and it was thought base to pursue other outlets and so shame a loyal wife. In the end, all other women were prostitutes, so that a pursuer could never know whether he was loved for himself or only for his money. Moreover, financial expense in the pursuit of women was always at the expense of the *oikos* and always demonstrated some lack of self-control. Eros was potentially a "disease" and "madness," a painful and a cruel affliction that forever threatened a man's integrity and safety.

In combination with the tendency to depersonalize women and to organize marriage as a mechanism for the inheritance of property and of male qualities, these restrictions on heterosexual relationships tended to produce a negative attitude to sexual response in philosophy and later in Christianity. Women were characteristically viewed as a temptation and thus as an assault on the male soul, as a costly luxury, and as an impediment to spiritual development. The self-sufficient man ought to be able to do without them, except for purposes of procreation; and from this idea it is a logical step to the notion that sexuality itself is harmful, dirty, and polluting. But there were sexual relationships much more rewarding and no less dangerous than those involving women, and it was these above all that give Greek sexuality its most characteristic features.

HOMOSEXUALITY

The most concentrated evidence of homosexual behavior is found in the late archaic and early classical period, and in the late Hellenistic period. It is preserved in vase paintings, the last 157 verses of the collection of poems attributed to Theognis, the poetry of Sappho, Old Comedy, Attic oratory (especially the speech *Against Timarchos* of Aischines), the writings of Plato and Xenophon, and in late archaic and late Hellenistic epigrams. These sources, taken to-

gether, reveal a pattern consistent with what was said above about Greek sexuality in general: a dominant pursuer tried to seduce a subordinate object. The virtues admired in the pursued (*eromenos*) were those approved by the pursuer (*erastes*) and were therefore submissive ones. Let us take male homosexuality first.

Homosexual relationships were not in any way a substitute for heterosexual contacts made difficult by the segregation of women. Quite the contrary: women were segregated not merely by sex but by gender role, so that males could not be substitutes for them. In any case, plenty of women of noncitizen status were available and were used alongside the relationships with males. Homosexual relationships took place on a grand public scale in male spheres and were based on the appropriate male gender roles. Men fell in love with boys and youths who were masculine in appearance and in behavior, and their relationship constituted part of a man's proper relationship to the polis. As always, sexual activity was linked to status. Free men (married and unmarried) could use servile and foreign boys as they pleased, but they were strictly restrained by custom and by law in their use of free boys; and no one but a citizen male could pursue citizen males. The special problem of Greek homosexuality was: How was a citizen *eromenos* to avoid behaving like, and being assimilated to, women and slaves?

Boyhood was an education and the teachers were older males. A boy was expected to become a brave soldier and a dependable citizen, eventually an *erastes* himself. This meant developing qualities that distinguished him absolutely from women and noncitizens. He was encouraged to model himself on older males, who in turn sought to be admirable models. The admiration and affection of boys and youths were earned by public displays of manly excellence, so that the educational and normative process took on sharply competitive aspects: fights between rival *erastai* were common, and *eromenoi* who were much in demand earned the envy of their age-mates. Divine (Zeus and Ganymede), heroic (Patroklos and Achilles), and historical (Harmodios and Aristogeiton) exemplars could be invoked, and the educational aspects could be idealized, as in the Socratic circles.

Mutual relationships (including sexual) thus evolved that were deeper, more complex, and more intense than the various relationships with women and slaves could be. There was an obvious narcissistic component, and the arena was that in which male citizens earned and enjoyed the honor that they had in all things reserved for themselves alone. But these relationships were also more poignant for being transitory. An aging *erastes* was less able to compete for the attentions of a new generation of youths, and when an *eromenos* grew a beard he not only changed his appearance but also his social status: now he was the competition, not the quarry. Youth was the best time of life and was idealized by Greek males. Just as our social ideal is the male whose assets and attributes attract beautiful young women, so for the Greeks it was the male who could attract beautiful young men. A married man's nostalgia for the freedoms and opportunities of his youth was directed this way. The envy and resentment felt by older men toward younger men can be seen frequently in Old Comedy, where the standpoint is: in my day men and boys were manlier than they are today, when *eromenoi* are like women and slaves and *erastai* don't know the difference!

The *erastes* was expected to pursue worthy *eromenoi* and could even boast to his friends of his successes, but the *eromenos* was expected to resist seduction and was reproached if it became known that he had submitted. The situation is similar to our own attitudes about premarital heterosexual relationships (see, for instance, Plato, *Symposium* 182a ff.). But whereas we consider seduced girls less reliable and valuable as candidates for marriage, the Greeks felt that seduced boys were less reliable and valuable candidates for citizenship. They had behaved like slaves or even prostitutes, and they had been defeated in a contest with an *erastes.* How were they to be trusted in battle or in deliberation, the occupations of men? For an *eromenos* to admit sexual desire for, or to flirt with, an *erastes* was just as bad: now he had assimilated himself to women. In Greek, *anteran* (to reciprocate eros) was used only of women; *anterastes* meant "rival *erastes.*" Proper behavior was strenuous pursuit met by strenuous flight, so that the manliness of both participants was maintained and enhanced. An *erastes* took care not to spoil an *eromenos,* and an *eromenos* had no wish to be spoiled. If it could be proved that a man had prostituted himself as a boy, or at any other time, he lost his citizen rights forever, just like a public debtor or military deserter. Now he was relegated to the status of the slaves and women with whom he had aligned himself. Thus fathers and the servile tutors assigned to supervise their sons kept a close watch on developments. A father was proud that his son attracted worthy *erastai* but also worried lest they succeed. As in all things manly, one had to maintain a position that malicious gossip could not change for the worse.

In every way, it was important to portray *eromenoi* as belonging to the class of male citizens, in spite of their submissive and subordinate position. The ideal "pinup" *eromenos* was a beardless, athletic-looking youth of good color, with broad shoulders, big muscles, big buttocks, and a short, thin penis with an elongated foreskin, behaving in a modest fashion. Pinup *erastai* were similar except that they were bearded and bulkier. Women, by contrast, were submissive, pale, and unmuscular, and had hairless or neatly depilated bodies. Slaves, barbarians, and comic types (like satyrs) were unmuscular, had large penises (circumcised if they were barbarian), and grotesque features. Being penetrated was unmanly, so that poets and artists avoid unseemly reference to oral, anal, and even intercrural penetration. Not only could women and slaves be penetrated; they were also made for penetration. At the extreme, oral and anal rape was a punishment meted out to trespassers, defeated enemies, and adulterers. This is part of the significance of phallic boundary-markers, herms, and statues of Priapos (who guarded gardens). Rape, like beating or depilation, turned a man into a womanish or slavish object. Masturbation, too, was avoided because it was characteristic of women (who used dildos), slaves, and barbarians. These latter types are depicted as indulging in all manner of sexual acts, but *eromenoi* as indulging only in acts appropriate to their special status. Women are shown in passive, often constrained, positions and seem to enjoy being penetrated; while *eromenoi* do not assume subordinate postures, do not have erections, and indeed show no sign of pleasure. In fact, it usually seems as if the *eromenos* is in control.

In short, citizen *eromenoi* were to be submissive and were in fact subordinate, but they were not to be passive. Every effort was made to de-emphasize or deny their subordination. In Athens, where the *oikos* was headed by an individual and where young boys were brought up alongside women and slaves, it was important that an adolescent be distinguished from the inhabitants of the *oikos* as dramatically as possible. But still, the transition had to be managed carefully, for the boys were in fact close to the women and slaves who had up to now provided their closest emotional ties. It was necessary to distinguish a *pais* (citizen male child) from a *pais* (slave). First, a boy passed from the *oikos* to the world of older males, but his subordinate position was infused with elements of

domination; he was a source of eros and admiration, older males fought for his attention, and he could choose among them. When he was no longer a *pais,* he competed with age-mates for *eromenoi* of his own. Finally, as an adult, he produced boys of his own, and the transition was complete.

In the fourth and later centuries the situation changes. Homosexuality is much less central and obsessive, and *eromenoi* are increasingly sensualized and assimilated to women in behavior and anatomy. Homosexual relationships become more mercenary, while heterosexual ones are both more common and less mercenary. More care is now taken to shield boys from any homosexual relationships, and we observe the onset of marked hostility toward "non-Platonic" homosexuality in general. As a major institutional vehicle for the acculturation of boys, homosexuality seems to be dying out. Possible contributing factors are a softer life (decreasing the need for rigorous exercise); a growing tendency for men to marry early; a relaxing of social boundaries between men and women, citizens and noncitizens; a relaxing of the ties between citizen status and land/property tenure; an educational system less restricted to and dominated by upper-class citizen males; the growing reliance on noncitizen and mercenary soldiers; and the increased decorum and politeness observable in other compartments of public life.

Sparta provides an interesting contrast. Notorious for the freedoms enjoyed by her women, who even took exercise publicly with males, Sparta was also notorious for her homosexual practices. Spartan institutions were fundamentally different from those of Athens, and the peculiarities of her sexual mores naturally reflect these differences. Because Sparta was a closed, secretive society that left behind virtually no information about itself, most of what we know is late and derives from non-Spartan sources heavily influenced by propaganda both pro and con and idealization, with few hard or undisputed facts.

Sparta was a monarchy in which citizens dominated not only the polis but also a subject population as well, and the threat of insurrection was constant. Life was organized around military training and warfare, with toughness and obedience to authority the main virtues. In dress, behavior, and appearance Spartans cultivated an image of straightforwardness and bellicosity. Age was authority, and it was institutionalized in the senate called the *gerousia*. An older person was always the superior of a younger person. Everyone wore uniforms appropriate to one's status, and passages in life were marked by a series of ranks. Boys and girls left the *oikos* at a very early age for life in the communal mess, and at that point they obeyed not only their father but also all superiors according to rank. The tribal elders in fact decided whether a child was to live, and the rearing was fixed by the constitution and regulated by the elders. Property and slaves were also regulated by the state, and no individual possessed absolute authority over them. Women could be shared among kinsmen and even with fellow citizens, with the offspring then considered to be in common.

Life was thus more communal and more regimented. Many of the functions exclusively belonging to the private *oikos* in Athens were in Sparta performed outside the *oikos* by tribal custom. Production and consumption, ownership and duties—these were constitutionally distributed in such a way that citizens were sharply distinguished from subjects and afforded every opportunity to devote their maximum effort to the maintainance of their precarious regime.

Thus boys had less experience of a prolonged, *oikos*-based childhood. They had little contact with slaves, *perioikoi* (the subject people of Laconia), and Helots, and the women were less drastically differentiated from men than was the case in Athens.

There was therefore less need to differentiate boys from others of lower status. Moreover, boyhood was a series of promotions in rank rather than a gradual transition supervised by one's father and other adult heads of *oikoi*. In Sparta, older males were of higher rank, and boys who survived the regimen could expect to attain these higher ranks in time. Less was left to the individual on either side of the age barrier. The attainment of adulthood was also a much longer process, usually lasting from early boyhood into one's thirties.

Homosexuality was similar to that in Athens with these main differences. The role of the *erastes* was quasi-official, and an *erastes* was held accountable for the performance of his *eromenoi*. The law required an *erastes* to have *eromenoi*, and an *eromenos* might stay under his influence for life. It may have been common to maintain the status of *eromenos* until around thirty, before one earned the right to have them himself. *Erastai* were not jealous rivals and pairing was not exclusive. An *erastes* could share his *eromenoi*, just as he could share his wife, and so help the community and strengthen friendships. Thus there was no counterpart to the Sacred Band in Thebes (a troop of lover-pairs who fought and died together). From the point of view of the *eromenos*, there was no point in being coy or elusive. An *erastes* was not going to fight over him, and finding one was part of the competitiveness that constituted his training. The regimen was strict, the rations meager, and age-mates were expected to acquire what they wanted by any means, including theft. Boys were therefore open and importunate in the quest for a worthy *erastes*. The nature and status of the sexual acts that took place are unclear and were disputed in antiquity. But if the caricatures of Old Comedy are any sort of indication, Spartan males were less restricted by social custom in their choice of sexual acts than were Athenians.

Female homosexuality is far more difficult to describe and evaluate because of the almost total lack of evidence. Sappho's poetry attests to it for archaic Lesbos; Plutarch mentions it in classical Sparta (*Parallel Lives,* "Lycurgus" 18.9), and Plato in classical Athens (*Symposium* 191e). In addition, there are a few vase paintings. The conspiracy of silence suggested by this lack of evidence need not be the result of the rarity of female homosexual relationships; more likely it reflects the confinement of such relationships to the private world of women. Since it did not affect any of the roles men expected of females with regard to marriage or procreation, it is not puzzling to find no mention of it in drama or in other kinds of literature written by men for public enjoyment.

Sappho's poetry reveals what we might have guessed: relationships between females occurred in girlhood and were expected to cease with marriage (frag. 31). The homosexual hetairai mentioned by Plato in his *Symposium* and by Anacreon (358) probably had nothing to do with female citizens, although they may be evidence of adult homosexuality in some form. The context of female homosexuality was, like male, the educational process in which young girls, under the tutelage of older women, were prepared for marriage, procreation, and household management. Opportunities for social contact included choral dancing and singing; women's cults (such as those surrounding Athena in Athens); participation in marriages; acquisition of skills in crafts such as cooking, weaving, and housework; and corporate entertainments, including making and performing poetry. The nature of the beauty contests attested for Lesbos (Alkaios, *Lyrics* 130.32 ff.), Elis (Theophrastos, frag. 111), and Sparta (Plutarch, *Parallel Lives,* "Lycurgus" 14.4), although problematical, falls into this category.

Female homosexual relationships cannot be expected to follow the patterns observable in those of males; they took place in the women's sphere and were contoured by the experiences of the women themselves. We have no way of knowing how women defined their separateness from males and the male public world, but we may suppose that there was no need for them—as there was for the males—to demonstrate and prove that they were separate. In fact, they probably could not have afforded to: whereas men could ignore the women's sphere and avoid knowledge of women's emotional lives, women by their very social definition had to pay attention to men and to the requirements of the men's public roles. They also had to supervise the rearing of their male children. In these circumstances we may suppose that women were less constrained in their emotional lives than were men.

Sappho's poems are the poetic projection of women's emotional life and social roles. Mention of bodily beauty, clitoral stimulation, and the use of dildos leaves no doubt that relationships could have a physical dimension; but, by contrast with men, the women seem less concerned about the relative status of participants and not at all concerned to define licit and illicit sexual behavior. Erotic experience is very closely connected with religious, natural, and communal experiences (Sappho, frag. 2), and there is a feeling of esprit de corps combined with expressions of foreboding with regard to the inevitability of marriage and nostalgia for the relationships that must then be ended. Hierarchical, competitive, and militaristic values are eschewed in preference for emotional and co-operative ones (Sappho, frag. 16). Myths, a common property of both men and women, are differently interpreted by Sappho to reflect a female view of life and behavior. Sappho belongs to a very old erotic-lyric tradition that drew from, but separately interpreted, the common matrix of cultural history.

Fragment 1 is a good example of these tendencies. The poet appeals to Aphrodite for help in an erotic pursuit. The goddess is asked to inspire in the pursued a reciprocal attraction: the poet wishes to appear more attractive and more lovely, so that the pursued may herself become a pursuer. Both parties may initiate; neither is seducer or rapist, but both may be equals in desire. The powerful emotions not only acknowledged but also particularized in the famous fragment 31 are expected to affect (afflict) both partners. In addition, there is a close personal and emotional relationship with the goddess that outweighs the poet's supplicant position. Such features of Sappho's poetry are fundamentally different from anything to be found in the erotic poetry of men, homosexual or heterosexual.

BIBLIOGRAPHY

Sexuality in antiquity has only recently become a respectable topic for serious scholarly investigation. Those interested in further reading can do no better than to consult the following for ideas, methodology, and bibliography Kenneth J. Dover, "Classical Greek Attitudes to Sexual Behavior," in *Arethusa,* **6** (1973), *Greek Popular Morality in the Time of Plato and Aristotle* (1975), a fundamental work, and *Greek Homosexuality* (1978), the standard treatment of the subject; Helene Foley, ed., *Reflections of Women in Antiquity* (1981), provides an excellent survey of heterosexual aspects of the field; Mark Golden, "Aspects of Childhood in Classical Athens," Ph. D. diss., University of Toronto (1981), a scholarly survey of the factors bearing upon the sexual habituation of individuals; Alick R. W. Harrison, *The Law of Athens: The Family and Property* (1968); Jeffrey Henderson, *The Maculate Muse: Obscene Language in Attic Comedy* (1975), a survey and lexicon of sexual language in the pre-Hellenistic period; Sarah Pomeroy, *Goddesses, Whores, Wives and Slaves: Women in Classical Antiquity* (1975), a more popular and general approach than that of the Foley collection; Amy Richlin, *The Garden of Priapus* (1983), includes a survey of Hellenistic Greek sexual language; David M. Schaps, *Economic Rights of Women in Ancient Greece* (1979); Philip Slater, *The Glory of Hera* (1968), an interesting and controversial approach, largely psychoanalytic and sociological, to the childhood experience of Greeks; J. A. Turner, *"Hiereiai: The Acquisition of Female Priesthoods in Classical Greece,"* Ph. D. diss., University of California at Santa Barbara (1983).

Roman Attitudes Toward Sex

JUDITH P. HALLETT

TWO DISTINCTLY DIFFERENT ATTITUDES toward what we would today define as "sex" emerge from a survey of ancient Roman sources. One of these attitudes is puritanical and repressive: it sanctions as acceptable sexual conduct only the lawful coupling of spouses, and deems that more of a duty than a pleasure. We find such an attitude voiced by the legendary Lucretia in Livy's well-known account of her tragedy (*History of Rome* 1.58). There, as she takes her own life—ashamed at her rape by Sextus Tarquinius, the son of Rome's last Etruscan king, impervious to the consolation and forgiveness proffered by her husband and father—Lucretia is portrayed as crying, "Though I absolve myself from sin, I do not except myself from punishment; nor shall any unchaste woman live hereafter with Lucretia as her model."

We also see such an attitude embodied in Plutarch's description of the behavior and proverbial remark of Julius Caesar when he divorced Pompeia in 61 B.C. (*Parallel Lives,* "Caesar" 10). As her affair with Publius Clodius was thought to have provoked the divorce, Caesar occasioned surprise when he not only spoke in Clodius' behalf at the subsequent trial, but even denied knowledge of Clodius' illicit liaisons with Pompeia or any other woman. Asked to explain how he could publicly declare his wife innocent of adultery and still repudiate her, Caesar is said to have stated, "I considered that my wife ought not to be even suspected of sexual impropriety." We observe this attitude as well in a philosophical poem roughly contemporary with Caesar's divorce. Lucretius in *On the Nature of Things* (4.1278 ff.) attributes sexual compatibility between a man and a woman to "long habit." In so doing, he likens the process of mutual sexual adjustment to the gradual erosion of rocks by falling drops of moisture.

Just as often, however, an antithetical attitude toward sex is expressed by or legitimately imputed to Romans of the classical era, a period stretching from *ca.* 220 B.C. to A.D. 150. This attitude is extremely permissive; it extols all manner of sexual self-expression and seeks the unbridled gratification of erotic appetites. Responsibility for and testimony to this outlook reside with several works of imaginative literature in

1265

particular: Petronius' *Satyricon,* which chronicles the escapades of four bisexually promiscuous main characters and an array of lust-ridden minor players; the epigrams of Catullus and Martial and the poems about Priapus, whose authors wittily celebrate the intense pursuit of sexual satisfaction with various partners of either sex; Ovid's poetic treatise, the *Art of Love,* an urbane manual to facilitate both pursuit and satisfaction by males and females alike. Ancient accounts of Roman comportment attest to this outlook and foster this image too. Suetonius' biographies of various emperors (*Lives of the Twelve Caesars*) document that charges of sexual misconduct were routinely leveled at his illustrious subjects: numerous extramarital affairs ("Julius" 50 ff.; "Augustus" 69), improper homoerotic entanglements ("Julius" 49; "Augustus" 68; "Nero" 28–29), bizarre and at times bestial forms of sexual entertainments ("Tiberius" 45; "Nero" 29). The physical remains of Roman civilization additionally contribute to Rome's reputation for sexual license and self-indulgence. One need only consider the material evidence of a sexual nature that abounds among artifacts from first-century A.D. Pompeii, a mere provincial city: ribald graffiti; phallic (and ithyphallic) images; and paintings, reliefs, statues, and metalwork with explicitly erotic scenes.

Yet even though both puritanical and permissive attitudes might be associated with the same individual, such as Julius Caesar or Augustus, for the most part they represent the views of different people, eras, circumstances, and literary genres. The fact that male writers supply nearly all of the ancient Roman testimony on sexual attitudes (as on everything else) complicates the picture further. Our evidence allows us to infer that Roman women of the classical era were as a rule held to much stricter standards of sexual conduct than were men.

FEMALE SEXUAL BEHAVIOR

All females were expected to be virgins when they married, ordinarily at the age of about thirteen or fourteen, in contrast to the average marrying age of twenty-two or twenty-three for men. Roman husbands were under no obligation to take paternal responsibility for children born to their wives but suspected to have been fathered by men other than themselves; according to Roman law, Roman men could even refuse to rear all but firstborn daughters; some were famous for having executed grown daughters for being judged unchaste, and by the Augustan period, all Roman fathers were legally empowered to do this (Suetonius, "Nero" 6.1; Ulpian, *Digest* 38.16.3, 9, 11; Dionysius of Halicarnassus, 2.15.2, 27; Valerius Maximus, 6.1, 3, 4, 6).

The homosexual liaisons of women never received as much attention as those of men. This disregard seems related to the Romans' much more negative assessment of female homosexual activity than of male homoeroticism, and to an idea that considered such behavior among women as "masculine" and "unnatural" (Ovid, *Metamorphoses* 9.666 ff.; Seneca the Elder, *Controversiae* 1.2.23; Martial, *Epigrams* 1.90; 7.67, 70). In contrast, male homosexual activity per se was not frowned upon as "feminine" or "perverted" among freeborn adult males as long as the man in question assumed the active, physically penetrating role with an adolescent passive partner, as long as that partner was not himself a freeborn Roman male, as long as the use of force or public funds did not facilitate the relationship, and as long as the liaison was conducted quietly and discreetly.

In consequence, Roman women may not have considered the satisfaction of their own sexual desires a tolerable or even a feasible aim. Their outlook on matters sexual may have been more straitlaced than the views frequently voiced by men, or at least lacking in the self-confidence bestowed by male sexual advantage. Even women cited in the ancient sources for multiple and extramarital sexual involvements may not have been pursuing or experiencing sexual pleasure. All the same, the extant testimony, given its masculine and overwhelmingly phallocentric perspective, makes it clear that eroticism and sexual self-expressiveness became increasingly visible and important as Rome evolved from rustic republic to cosmopolitan empire during the second century B.C., a time when Greek influence penetrated and transformed Roman civilization.

ETRUSCAN EROTICISM

The contrast between the Romans of the early republic, insofar as their attitudes may be recovered from later sources, and the Greeks of the same era is especially sharp in the area of sexual interest and self-expressiveness. But in this regard these Romans contrast no less sharply with the Etruscans of the same and an earlier period—although the Etruscans were a people with whom the Romans lived at close quarters and from whom Rome appropriated much of its emerging culture. A strikingly erotic element pervades much of extant Etruscan art, its funerary purpose notwithstanding; imported as well as indigenous artifacts vividly testify to the importance of the sexual in Etruscan society.

The sarcophagi of two married couples from the late sixth century B.C. (now in the Louvre, Paris, and the Villa Giulia Museum, Rome) serve as a case in point. They depict both pairs not only as reclining on banquet couches, and hence enjoying life's pleasures, but also as enjoying each other as

well; both husbands are bare-chested, and place their right hands on their wives' shoulders. Two sarcophagi of the same type from the mid fourth century B.C. (Boston, Museum of Fine Arts) place even greater emphasis on the sensual and sexual bond between the couples there portrayed. The lid of each sarcophagus depicts a marital bed; on one, man and wife are portrayed nude, and on both the couples lie in mutual embraces, making eye and body contact. The fresco of the Tomb of the Bulls in Tarquinii, dated to the mid sixth century B.C., contains two small erotic groups, each associated with an image of charging white bulls; one group is a pair of nude men engaged in anal intercourse. Fifth-century red-figure vases from the Etruscan cities of Tarquinii and Vulci, though of Attic provenance, also accord prominence to explicit depictions of sexual activity. Their scenes include portrayals of heterosexual anal congress as well as both rear-entry and frontal intravaginal intercourse (with the woman's legs atop her partner's shoulders); of a nude man brandishing a large erection and closely inspecting his female partner's genitals; of genital-touching by two nude females, one of whom sports a large and erect clitoris.

Roman lore about the Etruscan rulers at this time similarly stresses and negatively characterizes the Etruscans' erotic preoccupations. Livy's *History of Rome* (1.46) depicts King Tarquinius Superbus and his wife, Tullia, the parents of the Etruscan prince remembered for his lust for Lucretia, as having begun their relationship by an extramarital liaison, having wed after murdering their previous spouses (her sister and his brother), and having ascended to their monarchic posts after murdering the previous king, Tullia's father. Livy goes on (1.59.8 ff.) to link the couple's suffering upon their eventual ouster from Rome's throne with their earlier misconduct, implicitly contrasting the heinous Tullia with the virtuous Lucretia in the process.

THE EARLY ROMAN CONCEPT OF SEXUALITY

The earliest Romans do not even appear to have had a *numen* (divine spirit) of physical desire comparable to the Greek Eros. Purveyors of these same legends portray sexual appetites as exerting little effect on the Romans of these (and prior) times. In Livy's account (*History of Rome* 1.9), the need to repopulate an all-male settlement, and not the lustfulness of the men themselves, can be credited for the rape of the Sabine women; even Ovid's account of the episode (*The Roman Calendar* [*Fasti*] 3.187 ff.) stresses the men's eagerness to forge alliances with respectable fathers-in-law. Indeed, ideological legend characterizes sexual desire as a foe of Roman liberty and sound governance. Lucretia's suicide in shame, which allegedly roused the Roman people to overthrow its kings and institute a representative government, boasts a parallel in a politically significant deed movingly related by Livy (3.44 ff.) and dated to the mid fifth century: Verginius' slaying of his maiden daughter to protect her from the lust of a despotic decemvir, a heroic act that supposedly led to the downfall of the decemviri (the ten magistrates who were responsible for drawing up a code of laws).

What positive recognition of sexuality there was in earliest Rome seems to have focused on its procreative aspects. Some would argue that religious thought of that era assigned a symbolic sexual value to fire, as embodiment of male reproductive power. According to this view, Rome's most prestigious priestesses, the Vestal Virgins, originated as the prepubescent daughters of Rome's primitive priest-king; the Vestals'

time-honored task of guarding the state hearth is hence interpreted as an archaic and figurative mode of protecting a father's power to give life by female offspring capable of perpetuating, albeit not yet of an age to perpetuate, his bloodline themselves. It is maintained that an actual Roman *numen,* the *genius,* began as the representative of male familial reproductive power in earliest Roman times. Legends about early Rome even condone extramarital sex if it eventuates in issue. Livy depicts, for example, the raped Sabine women as heroic figures helping, through the agency of their young sons, to unite their fathers and abductors into one happy nation. Romulus, Rome's legendary founder, is himself said by Livy (1.4 ff.) and Ovid (*The Roman Calendar* 3. 11 ff.), among others, to have been sired illegitimately by Mars on the Vestal Virgin daughter of a deposed neighboring king, and not to have asserted his right to kingship of the new city until he had avenged the father of his unwed mother.

This view of acceptable sexual behavior as limited to heterosexual marital intercourse exhibits itself frequently in the earliest substantial body of contemporary evidence from the Romans themselves, the varied literary and inscriptional texts surviving from the late third and second centuries B.C. Several authors in this mid republican period use the noun *stuprum,* which apparently began as a term for "disgrace" in general, merely to describe disgrace of a sexual nature. To these sources, and to a host of later Latin writers as well, *stuprum* signifies any sexual act that brings shame to either or both of the partners, be it voluntary or forced, be it heterosexual—such as that involving an unmarried woman or that involving a married woman and a man not her husband—or homosexual, involving the assumption of the passive role by a mature and free Roman male.

VIEWS OF SEXUALITY IN THE SECOND CENTURY B.C.

In Livy's first-century B.C. eyes, one of the main events during this era was the Roman state's successful restraint of Bacchic worship in 186 B.C. Livy justifies such religious suppression by painting the orgiastic gatherings of cult followers as conspiratorial in character, meetings that already threatened—and if left unchecked stood to destroy—the very welfare of the body politic (39.9 ff.). Of special note is Livy's assertion that these orgies featured every kind of corruption, including promiscuous disgraceful sexual acts (*stupra*) of free men and women, and that more of these *stupra* were performed by men among themselves than performed by men and women together. To be sure, much in his account reeks of moralistic and dramatic exaggeration. Nonetheless, an inscription recording the decree of the Roman Senate on this occasion (*Corpus Inscriptionum Latinarum* I, 2d ed., 581.10.104) prohibits the exchange of oaths, vows, pledges, and promises by participants; requires that adult males—Roman citizens, allies, and Latins alike—obtain official authorization before attending a meeting of Bacchic women; and specifies that no more than two men and no more than three women may comprise a group of no more than five individuals allowed to hold Bacchic rites. This rule may therefore indicate that a gathering of more males than females was thought to provide the former with temptation to engage in homosexual acts, and hence was regarded as particularly undesirable; its recording may confirm Livy's claim that the sexual disgrace stemming from such worship disproportionately redounded to homosexually passive men. And this rule certainly indicates that disgraceful sexual conduct by women with men had been thought to characterize such worship, and was expected to abate by limiting the number of female Bacchic participants.

So, too, a widespread Roman concern over laxity in sexual and other moral conduct would appear to have resulted from the scandalous Bacchanalian episode in 186 B.C. and to have brought about the election of the elder Cato to the censorship two years later. Running on a platform proposing to eradicate luxury and restore sound morality against a field of popularity-seeking, lenient aristocrats, Cato—as his biographer Plutarch tells us (*Parallel Lives*, "Cato the Elder" 16 ff.)—made good his campaign promises by a number of official acts. Most notably, he is reported by Livy as well as Plutarch to have expelled from the senate a former consul who had indulged the bloodthirstiness of a lover—male in some accounts, female in others—when serving as a provincial governor; this the ex-consul did by ordering a man (and in some accounts an innocent seeker of asylum) slaughtered at a banquet before his lover's eyes.

Plutarch avers that Cato also expelled a strong consular contender for embracing his own wife in front of their daughter. Cato is additionally remembered for a speech he delivered, "On the Dowry," some time after his censorship; in it—Aulus Gellius relates in *Attic Nights* (10.23.4)—he claims:

> If you were to have caught your wife in an extramarital liaison, you would kill her without a trial and without penalty to yourself; but she, if you were to take the active or the passive role in an extramarital affair, would not dare lay a finger on you, nor is it lawful.

Along the same lines, Cato is said by Aulus Gellius in the same passage to have stated that in earliest Rome women received the same severe punishment for drinking wine that they suffered for adultery.

Yet the labeling of certain sexual activities

as disgraceful, the senatorial efforts to curb such activities, the censorial endeavors to punish individuals for failing to separate personal sexual passions from public and familial obligations, and even the claim of unreciprocated husbandly prerogative vis-à-vis a sexually misbehaving wife—these manifestations of moralistic sentiment and repressive conduct primarily serve as a reminder that the permissiveness and open sexual self-expressiveness also associated with classical Romans were already being manifested in the second century B.C. Many Romans themselves seem to have viewed this less rigid definition of what constituted proper sexual behavior and the greater freedom to search for erotic fulfillment, as new developments and as products of Greek influence. Still, Romans appear to have embraced this definition and availed themselves of the freedom it offered in large numbers; what is more, attempts to control and repress extramarital sexual involvements, especially by women, may have recurred in subsequent generations of the classical period, but they proved ineffectual, and often quite hypocritical.

SEX IN RELIGION

Sexually self-expressive behavior in the worship of a deity appears to have greatly disturbed Rome's leaders when it featured both passive homosexual conduct on the part of freeborn adult males and extramarital liaisons on the part of women, and when it threatened to undermine political order. Such conduct had implicitly and publicly received encouragement for several decades prior to the bacchanalian scandal by importation of erotically charged religious concepts and cults from the Greek world. Rome had acquired a divine personification of physical desire as a consequence of the First Punic War in the mid third century B.C. The

Greek cult of Aphrodite at Eryx (on Sicily)—which had absorbed that of the Phoenician Astarte and still practiced sacred prostitution—had won devotees among Roman soldiers fighting the Carthaginians in Greek Sicily. After the war, a suitable Roman *numen* with which to merge Aphrodite was needed, and was found in Venus, originally a sexless Italian spirit of well-tended herb gardens. Celebration of heterosexual union as embodied by this goddess became, as time went by, part of Roman religious devotion. In 215 B.C. a temple of Venus Erycina was reportedly constructed on the Capitoline Hill in Rome; after a second temple was dedicated to her on 23 April 181 B.C., prostitutes annually consecrated this date to her; by the Augustan era women partaking in Venus' festival on the first day of April were supposed to have supplicated Fortuna Virilis, goddess of the male reproductive organ. After the romanization of Aphrodite, and under the pressures of the Second Punic War, in 204 B.C. the Romans introduced the cult of the Great Mother Goddess, Magna Mater (also known as Cybele), from Asia Minor. Worship of this divinity was frenzied and was conducted by castrated male priests called *galli*. Although Roman citizens were forbidden to join this body, they did immediately establish an annual festival in honor of the Magna Mater. Called the Megalensia, its games included theatrical entertainments, performances of lascivious mimes, and salty Plautine comedies as well as less juicy fare.

SEXUALITY IN EARLY
LATIN LITERATURE

Mention of such entertainments reminds us that sexual topics and language figure, at times prominently, in Roman dramas and other works of literature that survive from this mid republican era. Such works, moreover, were created with (or written to at-tract) the support of the Roman state and Rome's citizens, although they pointedly de-rive from Greek models. One of Rome's first major literary figures, the poet Naevius, would seem to have alluded to sexual parts and acts so as to spice up his comedies (only the merest scraps of which survive). A pas-sage calling an aging male's penis a "little rake" (*rutabulum*) has been assigned by J. N. Adams (1982) to Naevius' comic fragments. Authorities on Roman literature interpret three verses by Naevius—which maintain that a celebrated Roman political leader had once been dragged, scantily clad in a single Greek garment, from his mistress by his fa-ther (Aulus Gellius, *Attic Nights* 7.8.5 ff.)—as referring to a youthful escapade of the illustrious conqueror of Carthage, Scipio Africanus.

We may also infer Naevius' penchant for humorous and metaphoric sexual descrip-tion in comic writings from the actual liter-ary practices of his successor Plautus, whose works are better preserved. Plautus may avoid "primary obscenities," explicit and (to the Roman taste) crude sexual terms, in his twenty-one extant comedies, all of which are set in the Greek world and based on Greek originals; still, he often treats sexual matters in euphemistic and figurative language. His sexual metaphors include one that plays on the humorous equation of the male organ with a sword or other military weapons of similar shape, one that has enjoyed a lasting impact on English sexual terminology: a metaphor likening the orifice penetrated by the male organ to a sheath, *vagina* (*Pseudolus* 1181). That the orifice so labeled in this pas-sage may well be the male anus is significant too, reminding us that a good deal of Plau-tine bawdy involves male homosexual activ-ity. To be sure, such conduct is not only portrayed as the interest of Greek individu-als, but also spoken of as specifically Greek in character: in Plautus' *Casina* (963), for ex-

ample, pederastic pursuits are called "cus-toms of the [Greek] colony of Massilia" (modern Marseilles); the word for sword figuratively employed along with *vagina* in what may well be a description of male ho-mosexual congress is a Greek one, *machaera*. It bears emphasis, however, that Plautus does not criticize such behavior provided that grown men of free birth limit them-selves to an active role and employ youthful slave partners; a recent study by Saara Lilja (1983) goes so far as to speculate that Plau-tus' allusions to homosexual master-slave relationships were his own additions to his Greek dramatic models. By contrast, in the prologue to *Casina* (82) Plautus brands as *stuprum* the assumption of the passive role by an adult male actor; that particular play proceeds to exploit the humorous potential of the disgrace incurred by both an elderly freeborn man and his male slave when they forcibly attempt genital contact with another mature male slave (played by a male actor in the disguise of a slave-girl bride).

Two generations after Plautus, the play-wright Afranius apparently allotted a con-spicuous place to sexual themes and lan-guage in his comedies, which—unlike those of Plautus—were performed in Roman dress. It may even have been Afranius' fail-ure to hellenize and hence distance his often homoerotic scenarios from his contempo-rary and later Roman audiences that drew strong and uncharacteristic criticism from the later literary authority Quintilian (1.10.100). After all, Quintilian qualifies his laudatory assertion that Afranius "excelled in the area of comedies in toga" by wishing that Afranius had not "defiled his stories with shameful passions for boys," and by judging Afranius' literary emphases to be "confes-sion of his own ways." Curiously, Quintil-ian's less favorable assessment of Plautus and other Roman comedies in Greek dress do not mention, much less try to account for, the sexual and homosexual elements in those works. Nor does Quintilian concern himself with such elements in the works of the late-second-century B.C. satirist Lucilius, although Lucilius resembles Afranius in writing about contemporary Rome and in his treatment of extramarital and homosexual activity. Quintilian's lack of comment may well reflect the fact that Lucilius, like Plautus, distanced and hellenized various types of sexual behavior: he is quick to fault what he regards as inappropriate sexual conduct, using straightforward Latin and mocking Greek terms, and he makes fun of major Hellenophilic personalities of his day.

The prominent Scipio Aemilianus—adopted by the son of the Scipio whom Naevius had earlier mocked, celebrated by his Greek historian friend Polybius for his distinctly un-Roman comportment (*Histories* 31.22 ff.), and a personal friend of Lucilius' as well—receives several sexually charged gibes in Lucilius' extant fragments. He is reviled for expelling men from his camp like dung, *stercus* (F. Marx, *C. Lucilii Carminum Reliquiae* [1904–1905], frags. 398–399). Lucilius here refers to Scipio as *spurcus ore*, "foul in the mouth," using a phrase later employed for those orally defiled by fellatio or cunnilingus. Lucilius later (Marx, frags. 1138–1140) seems to refer to a follower of Scipio with the term *cinaedus*, derived from a Greek word for an adult male whose conduct publicly and provocatively encourages homosexual advances.

HOMOSEXUALITY: "GREEK" SEX

The Greek origin of *cinaedus*, employed pejoratively by Latin authors from Plautus onward for an aggressively passive male homosexual, also testifies to the Roman propensity for distancing and hellenizing certain types of sexual behavior. By the early second century B.C., and throughout the classical period, in fact, numerous Latin writers appropriated various Greek terms to describe shameful homosexual conduct, and thereby to imply that it was alien as well as unacceptable in their society. The term *catamitus* appears in Plautus' *Menaechmi* (144) as the etruscanized and latinized form of the Greek name for Jupiter's boy *inamorato*, Ganymede; a century and a half later, moreover, Cicero uses the word in his Philippics (2.77) as a generalized term for a disgracefully passive male homosexual. *Pathicus*, an insulting Greek word for submitting to penile penetration, frequently figures in Catullus, Juvenal's satires, and the *Priapea*, (Catullus, 16.2; Juvenal, 2.99; and *Priapea* 25.3; 40.4; 73.1). Admittedly, several words of Latin pedigree are often employed for male homosexual activity in descriptions of both active and passive behavior. Foremost among them are *fellare* (fellatio), *irrumare* (to offer fellatio), and most likely *pedicare* (to penetrate the anus with a penis). It merits note, though, that these Latin terms can just as easily serve to delineate such forms of penetration when the passive partner is female. No less significantly, while these sources draw on both Greek and Latin terms for passive male homosexuals and their doings (with the Greek terms and what they describe carrying more negative connotations than the Latin), Roman authors utilize only a Greek word, *tribas*, for a female homosexual, and—on the few occasions when they even acknowledge the existence of women's homoerotic activities—tend to portray such comportment as occurring in Greek contexts and as involving phallically masculine as well as monstrously unnatural practices (Ovid, *Metamorphoses* 9.666 ff.; Seneca the Elder, *Controversiae* 1.2.23; Martial, *Epigrams* 1.90; 7.67, 70).

ROMAN SEXUAL EXPRESSION

Notwithstanding the Roman fondness for linguistically and culturally distancing various kinds of sexual conduct through the use of Greek terms (and often the context of Greek settings), the romanization of sexual self-expression in many forms increased as the classical era advanced. One might maintain as well that gradual romanization represented the only major change in attitude toward the male pursuit of sexual pleasure in various forms after the elder Cato's puritanical censorship, so widely had sexual permissiveness pervaded Roman life by that date. One may, with good reason, even dismiss Cato's puritanical repressiveness as misrepresentative of Roman social reality and as pretense belied by Cato's own ways. After all, when Aulus Gellius quotes Cato's claim that early Roman women suffered equally if convicted of alcohol consumption or adultery, he is quick to point out that Cato's claim is contradicted by testimony that women of that period could and did drink wine. Legal evidence challenges Cato's statement about a husband's right to kill an adulterous wife without trial or penalty (and suggests that Cato is describing a law he is proposing rather than one already on the books); until the late first century B.C., the law stipulates that a husband divorcing a wife for adultery could only keep one-twenty-fourth more of her dowry than if he divorced her for any other reason, and thus shows adultery to have ranked as a minor offense rather than a capital crime (Ulpian, *Regulae* 6.12). Cato's use—in his preserved remarks, "On the Dowry"—of subjunctive verb forms that denote a contrary-to-fact condition further indicates that he speaks of a hypothetical set of circumstances.

HYPOCRISY AND DEFAMATION

Cato's own biographers emphasize his hypocrisy in all matters, including sexual ones. According to Plutarch (*Parallel Lives,* "Cato

the Elder" 24), his sexual insatiability was such that, even in his widowed old age, he kept a female slave for libidinal refreshment and only disposed of her in favor of a young bride when his married son objected to his partaking of such refreshment in the small house he, his wife, and his father shared. Cato is also remembered by Horace (*Satires* 1.2.31–34) for congratulating a young man who emerged from a brothel on the grounds that the youth was thereby keeping away from other men's wives. Another source states, though, that after he later encountered the youth several times in the same place, Cato upbraided him with a rebuke: "I commended you for dropping in here occasionally, not for habituating the premises" (Rudd, 1966, p. 31). As Cato himself seems to have refrained from adulterous liaisons and thus expected respectable Roman males to do likewise, he also evidently tried to encourage if not personify sexual moderation.

The sources do not so much as hint at homosexual liaisons, active or passive, on Cato's part. Admittedly, Cato severely punished the wanton cruelty of an ex-consul; according to both Livy and Plutarch, this action was intended to gratify this man's male lover. Polybius, a contemporary writer and hence one of the earliest surviving authorities on Cato's life, also reports that Cato diagnosed as a sign of political decline the fact that a plot of land did not fetch as high a price as a pretty boy (*Histories* 31.25). Yet one cannot conclude from this evidence that Cato opposed homosexuality per se. For these authors do not suggest moral indignation at homosexual conduct on Cato's part, but rather outrage at the improper and excessive influence exerted by erotic bonds and attractions on political responsibilities and market values. A female, and not a male, courtesan is said in an account by Valerius Antias, cited by Livy, to have spurred the ex-consul's cruelty. So, too, when Polybius relates Cato's remark on the high price fetched by pretty boys, he also labels pederasty "Greek licentiousness and incontinence, resulting from an impulse towards the inferior," and hence further testifies that Roman society of the second century B.C. thought of male homosexuality as a Greek custom. But in this passage from *Histories* Polybius also classes socializing with female courtesans, musical entertainments, and drinking parties along with "loving boys physically" as striking manifestations of the same behavior. In addition, Polybius does not report that the elite youths who partook of such behavior were not allowed or permitted to act in this way. Indeed, he asserts that such youthful licentiousness was so prevalent that the contrasting conduct of his protégé, Scipio Aemilianus, soon earned Scipio more prominence and respect than others of his generation. And Lucilius' aforementioned gibe at Scipio for actively consorting with the *cinaedus* of a follower merely seems (the text is corrupt) to fault him for accepting excessive favors and fawning, and thus for indulging in questionable political practices; it does not employ the foul language, or imply the degradation, of the lines ascribing passive homosexual conduct to Scipio.

Lucilius' gibes, moreover, directly contradict Scipio's own surviving statements on this matter. In an oration of 129 B.C. (quoted by Macrobius, *Saturnalia* 3.14.7), Scipio Aemilianus attacked dancing schools attended by noble boys and girls as training them in "movements too disgraceful for a slave prone to sexually passive behavior," and as instructed by *cinaeduli*, "little male cock-teasers." An earlier speech nastily enumerated the effeminate traits of one Publius Sulpicius Galus, and concluded by asking if anyone could doubt that Galus did what *cinaedi* were accustomed to do (Aulus Gellius, *Attic Nights* 6.12.2). Although this discrepancy between the passive homosexual conduct imputed to Scipio and Scipio's

own disparagement of such conduct may well suggest the sort of hypocrisy on Scipio's part that we have detected in the pronouncements of the elder Cato, the fact that these imputations occur in the often abusive genre of satire and that the disparagement is found in the often abusive genre of oratory would allow another interpretation: that such homosexually passive conduct was not actually engaged in by Scipio but that it was ascribed to him because of the utter contempt in which Roman society held such conduct, and thus would strip him of any claim to moral worth and public respect.

Roman invective in satire, oratory, and other genres continues, in the centuries that follow, to lodge routine allegations of passive homosexuality against prominent, and politically powerful, males. Several of Cicero's orations, for example, attempt to discredit his foes Clodius and Mark Antony by accusing them of adopting the passive role in homosexual congress. Other evidence on the sexual behavior of both Clodius and Antony, however, recounts their aggressive heterosexual endeavors. As we have seen, Clodius' adulterous dalliances were thought to have precipitated Caesar's divorce from his wife, Pompeia; Plutarch's biography of Mark Antony abundantly attests to his reputation as a womanizer. Indeed, in these very same speeches Cicero himself attacks these same men for improper heterosexual entanglements (*For Milo* 73; *On His Home* 72 ff.; *Philippics* 2.77). Catullus' poems insult various political eminences of his (and Cicero's) day, among them Julius Caesar, who was charged with being both *cinaedus* and *pathicus.* Yet charges of brutal homosexual assault and heterosexual misdeeds figure no less prominently in Catullus' verses, and are leveled against some of the same men he denounces as passives. The abusive contexts of these allegations and the fact that other— and even the same—sources hurl other sexually insulting charges at the same men call the veracity of all such charges into question. Although authors like Cicero and Catullus can be used as valuable sources for what Romans regarded as inappropriate sexual behavior—and make it clear that homosexuality in and of itself did not fall into this category—we cannot rely upon their insulting allegations as proof that men so accused actually behaved as they were charged.

FICTION AND FACT
IN SEXUAL ACCOUNTS

Similar uncertainty has been voiced about the veracity of other ancient Roman sources, especially the poets of the Augustan era, on sexual behavior in the first centuries B.C. and A.D. Several scholars have attempted to distinguish "unreal" and "imaginary" Greek elements in these works from genuine Roman ones. They regard as a stylized literary convention the "life of luxury" that several Roman authors portray, and in particular deny the "Roman authenticity" of such elements of this existence as extramarital liaisons with women ranging in social class from slaves to cultivated courtesans (*meretrices*) to respectable matrons and love affairs between adult males and boys not of free birth; such a convention, they would say, was adapted in order to elevate various works of Latin literature to the level of their Greek models by rendering their settings as Greek as possible.

Yet a number of facts dispute such viewpoints and dispel such uncertainties, allowing the inference that while the sources may exaggerate Roman reality to some extent, inasmuch as they do not offer actual autobiographical or eyewitness accounts of personal experiences, they ultimately furnish realistic pictures of contemporary Roman society. For one thing, abundant material evidence establishes that Roman life itself had by the first century B.C. become so strongly hellenized in ambiance that a distinction between "Greek" and "Roman" elements therein is impossible. Second, most of these literary representations—most notably the odes of Horace and the love elegies of Propertius and Ovid—purport to describe contemporary people and events in Rome, and thus must at the very least feature a plausible portrait of this milieu. Moreover, numerous other sources corroborate details of these portraits. Some, such as Cicero in his invectives against Mark Antony and Clodius, and Lucretius in his attack on romantic love, testify to the cultural presence and even prevalence of extramarital hetero- and homosexual relationships by the mere vehemence of their negative remarks on specific and general manifestations of erotic pleasure-seeking. If this kind of behavior did not occur and flourish in their midst, why did Lucretius condemn it, or Cicero think it practical to defame individuals by imputing it to them (perhaps falsely)? As we have seen, too, others—such as even the moralistic Plutarch and the thorough researcher Suetonius—fill factual biographies of actual Roman luminaries such as Mark Antony, Caesar, and Augustus with details of their subjects' extramarital erotic activities, as if they thought such conduct at least plausible. Roman law—most obviously Augustus' legislation encouraging marriage and discouraging adultery—itself shows that extramarital sexual liaisons by wellborn men and women were common and perceived as a threat to the political and social order. Livy's moralistic glorification of the self-righteously chaste Lucretia and other early Romans must be understood as part of Augustus' effort to encourage marriage and female marital fidelity, an effort that, although given legal backing, was undermined by the attested behavior of elite Romans in subsequent generations.

Finally, evidence permits the conclusion that even those Romans of the first centuries B.C. and A.D. who stand on record as opposing and faulting others for sexual improprieties resemble the second-century B.C. Cato in being remembered for improprieties themselves. Suetonius relates (*Lives of the Twelve Caesars,* "Augustus" 68–71) various charges of homosexually passive behavior (including one of prostituting himself for political advancement) made against Augustus as a young man; he cites Augustus' own correspondence with Mark Antony to prove Augustus a proud practitioner of adultery, the very act Augustus later passed legislation to combat. So, too, Suetonius reports (*Lives of the Twelve Caesars,* "Julius" 49–52) that Caesar, who would not countenance suspicions of sexual misconduct by his wife, was widely suspected of and publicly teased for disgraceful sexual submission to the king of Bithynia. Such documentable hypocrisy (or at least inconsistency) should caution us against assuming that Roman utterances of moralistic sentiment automatically render Roman portrayals of sexual pleasure-seeking and sexual permissiveness less than credible.

THE CULTURAL BACKGROUND OF SEXUAL ATTITUDES

What cultural factors spawned these sexual attitudes among Romans during the mid republican to early imperial eras? First, there was the increasingly permissive outlook on sexual self-expression and the pursuit of sexual gratification, and in particular the tolerance of extramarital affairs and homosexual liaisons between freeborn males and lowly born boys. Second, there were the recurring, unsuccessful, and at times hypocritical attempts to deny and eradicate this permissiveness by the invocation of "traditional" moral excellence as well as by restrictive legislation. Let us begin by emphasizing that even the earliest Romans contrast with their Etruscan neighbors in placing little emphasis on the affective bond between husband and wife. The most archaic Roman laws contain provisions for both divorce and marital arrangements whereby women do not legally join their husbands' households; these laws also assign husbands total ownership of—and indeed life-and-death power over—children. Such legislation, along with the Roman practice of marrying girls in their early teens to men a decade their seniors, did nothing to encourage marital closeness and loyalty between spouses. That Roman society had traditionally felt a need to limit family size is implied by archaic laws permitting fathers to murder deformed infants (Cicero, *On Laws* 3.8.19) as well as those making only the rearing of the firstborn daughter obligatory. The concerted endeavors by Augustus to boost the birthrate by rewarding the production of offspring indicates that the custom of having relatively few children persisted even into the troubled times of the late first century B.C. Given the primitive nature of Roman contraception, this preference for small families would have discouraged marital intercourse, and hence marital physical intimacy as well. The minimal penalties for adultery prior to Augustus' reign and the widespread disregard for his legislation outlawing adultery thereafter warrant mention again in this context. Such factors help to explain not only how divorce and marriage for political reasons become so common among the upper class by the first century B.C., but also why love and sexual pleasure were so often sought and sanctioned outside of marriage.

Needless to say, the primitive nature of Roman contraception may have rendered intravaginal intercourse no less risky for extramarital sexual partners than for married couples eager to limit the number of their offspring. Their contraceptive reliability seems to have made the practices of anal and oral congress popular alternative modes whereby males might obtain orgasmic pleasure, particularly with lowborn or hired partners (Catullus 59.1; *Corpus Inscriptionum Latinarum* 4.2273; *Priapea* 3; Martial, *Epigrams* 11.99, 104). Furthermore, the popularity of anal and oral intercourse would have in turn caused both males and females to be regarded as similarly suitable sexual partners for men, and thus contributed to the acceptability of both homo- and heteroerotic extramarital liaisons. Other factors would seem to have contributed to the frequency of male homosexual affairs in Rome too. Esteem for and emulation of Greek culture, with which pederasty was closely identified, number among them; one might even argue that the pursuit of a beautiful boy had a certain cultivated cachet. When the younger Pliny writes of reading and imitating Cicero's bawdily playful poems to his freedman Tiro, he cites Cicero's effort as proof that the "minds of great and manly men take pleasure in human wit and much and varied charm" (*Letters* 7.4.6 ff.)

No less significant in this respect may be the Roman cultural potential for tensions in the bonds between kindred males. After all, Roman law allowed fathers to sell their sons thrice into slavery as well as to slay them outright (Dionysius of Halicarnassus, 2.27; Ulpian, *Tituli* 10.1). Ill will of sons toward fathers, and vice versa, figures as a key theme in sources from Plautine comedy to Valerius Maximus' collection of morally memorable deeds to accounts of the late republican proscriptions and of the Julio-Claudian principate (Valerius Maximus 5.8; Velleius Paterculus 2.67.2; and Tacitus, *Annals* 1.33, 52). Strains in the relationship be-tween brothers are equally commonplace in Roman culture, most memorably elaborated in the legend of Rome's founding by Romulus' fratricide (Valerius Maximus, 5.5; Horace, *Epodes* 7.17–20; Livy, 1.6 ff.). Such tensions may well have spurred elite Roman males to invest more emotions and ego in attachments to young and lowborn men outside of their families who did not present the threat of their male kinfolk. It warrants emphasis, however, that the Romans may have tolerated homoerotic and extramarital heteroerotic relationships, but did not glorify or for the most part celebrate (much less legalize) the former. Similarly, incestuous heterosexual relationships were consistently condemned; indeed, charges thereof were used much as charges of passive homosexual conduct were used in defamatory personal invective, and often used against the same individuals accused of passive homosexual conduct—Clodius, for one—in the very same speeches.

That Roman sexual permissiveness did not ever escalate into anything more than tolerance, that certain types of sexual behavior were not even tolerated, and that this permissiveness was itself denied and attacked by various moralists of different generations and literary genres can best be explained by the fact that sexual pleasure-seeking, especially outside of marriage and especially in the Romans' own eyes, did represent a break with their early past. The Roman tendency to idealize this past even enabled some of those discontented with sundry social phenomena of their day to portray whatever developments happened to irritate them as somehow sexually decadent, even when such phenomena—such as the appeal of Greek religious ritual or the growing economic power of women in times of high manpower loss or the declining population of the upper classes—did not primarily involve sexual behavior. A certain vagueness about how past Roman mores differed from those of later eras additionally allowed such individuals as the elder Cato to fabricate details of Roman's bygone moral superiority as well as to mask their own pursuit of sexual satisfaction outside of marriage by claiming their own reverence for and adherence to tradition. And inasmuch as Roman society had traditionally looked to its political leaders and laws for a sense of its earlier values, efforts to change sexual attitudes—like Cato's and Augustus' endeavors to stiffen the penalties for women's extramarital liaisons—sought to minimize their innovativeness by formulating them as legal provisions by political traditionalists.

In reflecting upon the sexual permissiveness of Rome in the classical era, we do well to remember that this period ends centuries before Rome itself falls. In fact, this era is succeeded by a period—that of the Antonine emperors—regarded by Edward Gibbon and others as Rome's finest years. In other words, no connection need be postulated between the tolerant sexual environment of classical Rome and the decline of Rome as a Mediterranean power; rather, this permissiveness merely ranks as a response to Rome's growing role as a cosmopolitan center and powerful presence in the Greek world.

BIBLIOGRAPHY

J. N. Adams, *The Latin Sexual Vocabulary* (1982); John Boardman and Eugenio La Rocca, *Eros in Greece* (1978); John Boswell, *Christianity, Social Tolerance, and Homosexuality* (1980); Otto J. Brendel, *Etruscan Art* (1978); Michael Grant, *Eros in Pompeii* (1975); Jasper Griffin, "Augustan Poetry and the Life of Luxury," in *Journal of Roman Studies*, **66** (1976); Judith P. Hallett, *Fathers and Daughters in Roman Society* (1984); Keith Hopkins, "The Age of Roman Girls at Marriage," in *Population Studies*, **18** (1965), and "Contraception in the Roman Empire," in *Comparative Studies in Society and History*, **8** (1965).

Saara Lilja, "Homosexuality in Republican and Augustan Rome", *Commentationes Humanarum Litterarum*, **74** (1983); Ramsay MacMullen, "Roman Attitudes to Greek Love," in *Historia*, **31** (1982); Sarah B. Pomeroy, *Goddesses, Whores, Wives, and Slaves: Women in Classical Antiquity* (1975); Amy Richlin, *The Garden of Priapus: Sexuality and Aggression in Roman Humor* (1983); Niall Rudd, *The Satires of Horace: A Study* (1966); Howard H. Scullard, *Festivals and Ceremonies of the Roman Republic* (1981).

Images of the Individual

PETER WALCOT

THE STUDY OF PERSONALITY remains a major area of research for the contemporary psychologist, so much so that, at the popular level, psychology can be thought to be little more than the description of personality and the assessment of those factors that determine the quality and development of personality. But particular problems bedevil both the description of personality and the assessment of determinants of personality. A statement of each problem and an initial consideration of the relevant evidence from antiquity will quickly reveal that the study of ancient images of personality is no academic exercise but rather offers an effective means of clarifying our own attitude toward these problems. And these are problems of special urgency today when we are all deeply conscious of the dangers inherent in racially or sexually inspired arguments that depend upon the proposition that genetic-physiological or hereditary factors have a greater influence on personality than sociocultural or environmental factors.

INDIVIDUAL VS. TYPE

What is the major problem that confronts those attempting to describe personality? The answer is clear: Which of the alternative research strategies that have been championed in the last fifty years as a means of describing personality is to be adopted? On the one hand, there are those psychologists, best represented by Gordon W. Allport, who maintain that a science of individual persons is practical and that we should, therefore, follow what is termed the idiographic approach, concentrating on the individual; more, however, would agree with Hans J. Eysenck in preferring the generalizing or nomothetic (rule-giving) methodology whereby what is unique in each individual is reckoned less significant than what is common to many individuals. Arguing in favor of the latter strategy, J. P. Guilford points out that "in every science, the individual case is properly regarded as merely an opportunity for making another observa-

1279

tion. The single case belongs to history, not to science. . . . In approaching a final goal, science aims at generalizations that apply to *classes* of phenomena, not at descriptions of particular events" (p. 24).

More than two thousand years before in his *Poetics,* Aristotle made a remarkably similar comment, stressing the importance of what is typical over that of what is unique, when he claimed that the poet's task was not to say what did happen but to indicate the kind of thing that might be expected to happen, given a strictly probable or necessary sequence. The essential difference between history and poetry, Aristotle argues, is not that one is written in prose and the other in verse but that the former tells us what took place whereas the latter tells us what might take place. "That," he adds, "is why poetry is at once something more scientific and more worthwhile than history, since poetry tends to make general statements, while those of history are particular" (*Poetics,* 1451b6–8). Aristotle is more celebrated as a philosopher and scientist than as a literary critic, and here he advances an argument which reflects his philosophical-scientific bias, declaring himself a forerunner of that majority of psychologists today which favors the nomothetic strategy when describing personality and, even more strikingly, justifying the adoption of such a strategy on the same basis as the modern psychologist. But Aristotle's position will cause no surprise when we remember how the Greek citizen found a meaningful existence essentially as a member of a group, whether the group was the family or, on a larger scale, the polis, so that Aristotle claims that the man who can exist outside the polis is either an animal or a god (*Politics* 1.1253a2–4).

In fact even the historians of antiquity tended to care more for the presentation of the type than for that of the individual, and so writers of biography might well produce accounts of the lives of a distinct cate-gory of person such as philosopher (for example, Diogenes Laertius) or literary figure or Roman emperor (for example, Suetonius). The same tendency is to be seen in "pure" history as early as Xenophon's *The March Up Country* (*Anabasis*) if we turn to his obituary notices for the three generals, Clearchus, Proxenus, and Menon, arrested and executed by the Persian king in the aftermath of the battle of Cunaxa (*The March Up Country* 2.6). A typological interest is clearly expressed when Xenophon says of Clearchus' career that his activities appear to be those of a man devoted to war (*The March Up Country* 2.6.6), while the picture of Menon seems to be grossly misrepresented, partly because of the personal animosity of Xenophon but also because the historian wished to contrast Proxenus, the good ambitious man, with Menon, the bad ambitious man. Again, character types have been readily identified in Tacitus' *Annals,* and to the type of the Tyrant—which, as we shall see, had long been established—Tacitus adds the Opportunist, the Victim, the Collaborator, the Noble Savage, and the Intransigent.

But to return to Aristotle, the philosopher also underlines for us the potential dangers of the nomothetic strategy when exploited by the unscrupulous. The results of its adoption are to be seen in Aristotle's handbook on the art of rhetoric or means of persuasion, as when Aristotle describes the characteristics of the young, the old, and those in the prime of life (*Rhetoric* 2.1388b–1390b). Each of these sketches of a type of personality depicts the general features of a group of persons. Why is such material included in a handbook of rhetoric? It is because we can hope to convince by argument only when we also take into account audience psychology. The nomothetic strategy enables us to exploit audience psychology, for it assumes, as its very name, "rule-giving," implies, that it is possible to formulate general rules about different types of personality; the formulation of such rules means that the behavior of groups may be predicted and so can be controlled by the skilled speaker. The study of what has aptly been called persuasive communication can obviously be directed to a political end and so persuasive communication degenerates into crude propaganda.

NATURE VS. NURTURE

But what of the relative influence of hereditary and environmental factors in shaping personality and its ancient background? The nature versus nurture (heredity versus culture/environment) controversy is an emotive issue, provoking especially strong passions when it is argued that there is a distinct and powerful genetic component that is responsible for differences in ability as well as in temperament between the races, or that woman's role as the bearer of children has so conditioned the female as to make her man's natural subordinate, or that "the male is better suited by nature to control than the female," a view endorsed in antiquity by Aristotle (*Politics* 1.1259b). Although Aristotle does reveal that there were Greeks who condemned slavery as contrary to nature (*Politics* 1.1253b20–22), that was not his own opinion (*Politics* 1.1255a2), and in a notorious passage he relates racial group traits to climatic conditions: Northerners, living in a cold region, possess spirit but lack intelligence and so political cohesion; Asiatics are intelligent but devoid of spirit and therefore remain subject peoples; Greeks, however, avoid both climatic extremes, occupying the geographic middle position, and are both spirited and intelligent (*Politics* 7.1327b21–30).

A more detailed correlation between the national characteristics of the peoples of Asia and Europe and their geographical location is offered by the unknown author of the Hippocratic treatise entitled *Airs, Waters, and Places*. A better-known explanation of personality associated with Greek medicine, however, is the theory of the four humors (blood, phlegm, yellow bile, black bile), to which correspond four types of constitution (sanguine, phlegmatic, choleric, melancholic). An example of how a humor could be thought to determine personality is presented in a work called *Problems,* which has come down to us under the name of Aristotle, although the philosopher is not its actual author. The thirtieth in this series of discussions of specific problems asks the question why all who are outstanding in philosophy, politics, poetry, or the arts are clearly of a melancholic or black-bile temperament. We are told that it is both the quantity and the type of black bile, whether it is cold or hot, that affects personality; for example, those who are naturally full of the cold variety become dull and stupid but those with an excess of hot black bile become mad, clever, passionate, and readily moved to anger and desire (*Problems* 30.954a). To sum up, our text states (30.955a), the melancholic temperament varies as the force of black bile varies; like wine mingling in the body in greater or lesser quantity, this humor gives us our own particular character and personality. All this is supported by a wealth of argument and analogy that is considerably less naive than is often supposed. Indeed it is not fanciful to see in the theory of the four humors an ancient equivalent of a modern biochemical theory of the etiology of affective disorders. At the same time the view that behavior is determined by the physical constituents of the body stresses the superiority of natural disposition, to the detriment of considering the role of cultural influences.

In the century before Aristotle the historian Thucydides claimed that he would be satisfied if his account of the Peloponnesian War was judged useful by those who wished to know clearly what had happened and what was likely to happen in the future, "human nature being what it is," in much the same form (*History of the Peloponnesian War* 1.22.4). Greek popular opinion, as illustrated by the fifth-century tragedians, appears to have supported the view that human nature was a constant and more important than culture in determining personality. In one fragment Euripides states that no one could ever make the bad good by careful rearing (frag. 810), while in a second he calls it the height of folly to want to overcome nature (frag. 904). In a snippet Sophocles is equally emphatic in claiming that one could never eliminate whatever nature gives a man (frag. 739). In Euripides' *Orestes* (126–129), Electra comments on the way in which Helen, for all her display of grief, remains the same wicked Helen, unaffected by experience. A desperate Hecuba, in Euripides' play of the same name, reckons it strange that poor soil blessed by heaven yields a good crop and good soil lacking what it needs yields a poor crop but, among men, the wicked are always wicked, the good always good (*Hecuba* 592–598). Yet, Hecuba proceeds to add (600–601), a noble upbringing does teach what is good. And the chorus in Euripides' *Iphigenia in Aulis* maintains (558–562) that although the natures and characters of men vary, true virtue is always clear and upbringing and education contribute much to virtue. Socrates, according to his biographer Xenophon (*Apology* 21), went much further, calling *paideia* (education) man's greatest blessing.

Experience of individuals shows that it is unwise to be too dogmatic, and in another of Euripides' plays, *Electra,* Orestes remarks (367–370) that human nature exhibits an element of confusion, for he has seen the son of a noble father to be worthless but the offspring of evil parents virtuous. A more searching assessment of the nature versus nurture controversy became possible when in the fourth century B.C. the collapse of the city-state system among the Greeks introduced an age of growing individualism, and we have already noted how Aristotle admits that there were those opposed to his own view that there was such a thing as a natural slave. One symptom of a new individualism was the further development of the biography, a historical genre whose most famous exponent in antiquity, Plutarch of Chaeronea, wrote his *Parallel Lives* of celebrated Greeks and Romans at the time of the early Roman Empire. The *Parallel Lives* includes a biography of the fifth-century B.C. Roman general Coriolanus, and Plutarch strikes a very modern note in the first chapter of this biography when, after observing that Coriolanus lost his father when young and was brought up by his widowed mother, he comments that the example of Coriolanus shows that the loss of a father does not prevent a man from achieving great distinction, and that it is only the worthless who cite parental neglect to excuse a deterioration of character. Coriolanus was grossly intolerant of others, and so Plutarch can go on to say that the hero's checkered career illustrates how a noble nature in need of *paideia* yields at the same time good and bad fruit just like fertile soil that lacks care and attention. Plutarch concludes that men receive no greater blessing from the kind Muses than the softening or humanizing of their nature by reason and education as they reject excess in favor of balance.

What is a passing reference in his biography of Coriolanus merits a detailed treatment in *The Education of Children* (*De Liberis Educandis*), the first of the essays by Plutarch that make up the collection we call *Moralia*. It is noticeable, however, that this program for the education of children opens by stressing the merits of good birth, and Plutarch draws another agricultural analogy, equating human nature with the soil, the teacher with the farmer, and instructions and precepts with seed. In fact the obsession throughout antiquity, among Greeks and Romans alike, with an individual's personal prestige or honor made it inevitable that good birth or nature was of a paramount importance, for honor was not only acquired by personal achievements, it was also a quality inherited from parents, as Plutarch demonstrates by two quotations from Euripides: "When the foundation of a family is not firmly laid, its offspring must be unfortunate" (*Hercules Furens* 1261–1262) and "Though of bold heart, the knowledge of his parents' shame makes a slave of a man" (*Hippolytus* 424–425). But there were dissentient voices, as we learn again from Aristotle, for according to a surviving fragment of Aristotle's *On Good Birth,* Lycophron the Sophist believed there was no difference between the lowborn and the wellborn (frag. 91 Rose; Stobaeus, 4.29.24). For Aristotle, however, there could be no dispute: good birth was excellence of stock, and stock was certain to be good when an original goodness was inherited over many generations, and what applied to men was similarly true of horses and other animals (frag. 94 Rose; Stobaeus, 4.29.52). A theory based in part on, or at least exemplified by, the breeding of animals is no less depressing than Plutarch's curt dismissal of parental deprivation or neglect as a possible explanation of deviant behavior, but we have as yet to turn from the theoretical discussion of personality and factors determining personality to actual case studies of personality types attempted by the ancient writers.

It must be stressed that our knowledge of such case studies is derived from texts not primarily devoted to the description and assessment of personality. Nor can we hope to find case studies based on experimental data or statistical analysis. Instead the ancients resorted to two forms of argumentation, illustrating rather than proving their views by the use of polarity and analogy, that is, con-

trast and comparison. Thus, as we have already noted, Xenophon contrasts two ambitious men, the generals Proxenus and Menon. In the best-known example of all, the Roman historian Sallust, toward the end of his monograph on the Catilinarian conspiracy, describes the "disposition and character" of two politicians of outstanding merit but contrasting character, Julius Caesar and the younger Cato (*The Catiline War* 54). As early as Homer the types of the brave warrior and the coward are defined by contrast: the latter changes color and has no control but shifts his weight from one foot to the other, as his heart pounds and his teeth clatter, whereas the former shows no physical sign of fear and if hit in battle receives the stroke on the front and not the rear of his body (*Iliad* 13.275–291). And, as we shall shortly see, the Homeric simile contributes much to argumentation by analogy, especially the simile comparing the deeds of the hero to the actions of an animal such as a lion, wolf, or boar or the simile comparing the emotional reaction of the hero and an animal, such as that equating the snarling of Odysseus' heart when he surveys the behavior of his unfaithful maidservants with the snarling of a bitch who feels her puppies to be threatened by a stranger (*Odyssey* 20.13–16).

IMAGES OF WOMEN

The ancient preoccupation with personal honor must similarly be stressed since this was of crucial importance in influencing the depiction of particular types of personality, and never more so than when the ancients attempted to describe types of female personality. As men of honor the ancients were obliged to protect women from injury and insult, whether real or anticipated, and the threat to honor posed by women's sexuality colored their whole concept of women's personalities. Although there was no standard account in Greek mythology of the origin of mankind, the story of the first woman, the notorious Pandora, was related by the poet Hesiod at the end of the eighth century B.C. in both his *Works and Days* (42 ff.) and his *Theogony* (535 ff.).

Hesiod's assessment of this first woman, and therefore of all women, is reinforced by the description of how Pandora was fashioned at the command of Zeus. In the story of the *Theogony*, the Titan Prometheus tricked Zeus into preferring the inferior portion of a sacrificed ox so carefully packaged that the bones appeared the better part of the offering (535–557). The god retaliated by denying fire to mankind. When this was recovered by Prometheus Zeus had the final word, deceiving his adversary by a repetition of the trickster's initial act of deceit: Zeus had Hephaestus and Athene prepare and adorn the first woman, Pandora (*Theogony* 570–584). Just as the inferior part of the sacrifice seemed splendid but was in fact useless, so too was Pandora a "beautiful evil" (585), having the face of a goddess but a personality clearly revealed in the *Works and Days* when Aphrodite and Hermes join in her preparation, the former giving her the capacity to arouse man's desire and limb-gnawing sorrows (66), and the latter the shameless disposition of a bitch and a deceitful pattern of behavior (67; 78). Such was the woman's sexuality that Epimetheus, the stupid brother of Prometheus, was persuaded to receive Pandora, who subsequently released from their jar the evils that now afflict mankind (*Works and Days* 83–104). Thus the story of Pandora, as understood by the ancients, vividly illustrates the destruction inevitably wrought when a man succumbs to a woman's attractions. A consequent fear of woman's sexuality is revealed that explains the ancient enthusiasm for the type of virgin or sexless goddess represented by Artemis or Athene and still exemplified today by the Mediterranean version of the Marian cult.

Pandora's bitchlike disposition and Homeric animal similes (e.g., the horse in the *Iliad* 6.506–511 and the donkey in the *Iliad* 11.558–562) help to explain the attempt made by the poet Semonides of Amorgos in the seventh century B.C. to define the personalities of various types of women by reference, in the main, to corresponding types of animals (Semonides, poem 7). This poem fragment of more than a hundred lines opens with a brief statement that in the beginning God made woman's disposition separately (1–2)—presumably the contrast here is with the disposition of man—and then proceeds to list ten types of female personality: the sluttish woman fashioned from the sow (2–6); the know-all, constantly changing, from the vixen (7–11); the ever-inquisitive and shameless woman from the bitch (12–20); the woman who only knows how to eat from earth (21–26); the changeable woman from the sea (27–42); the insensitive woman from the donkey (43–49); the repulsive, thieving woman from the ferret (50–56); the proud, disdainful woman from the horse (57–70); the ugly, spiteful woman from the monkey (71–82); and, finally, the good woman who increases her husband's prosperity from the proverbially chaste bee (83–93).

A two-line fragment of Semonides (poem 6) confirms that he agrees with Hesiod in thinking a man's best possession is a good wife and his worst a bad wife (cf. *Works and Days*, 702–703). Like Hesiod, Semonides displays throughout what is generally considered a satire on women a keen awareness of the dangers posed by a woman's sexuality. The donkey-woman accepts any man as lover (48–49), the ferret-woman is mad for sex (53), the horse-woman of aristocratic tastes tarts herself up lavishly (63–66), but, in stark contrast, the bee-woman finds no pleasure in sitting among women when they tell stories about sex (90–91).

Drawing analogies with animals seems at first sight a crude means of depicting human personality, since it assumes, for example, that all pigs are filthy and permanently filthy, and that the dirty woman must resemble the pig in all respects. Such equations persisted, even being given a pseudoscientific gloss at a later period of time by those we describe as physiognomists, for these writers, who explain mental character by physical appearance, argue that a particular animal form yields a particular mental character, and that a man resembling a particular animal physically shares that animal's mental characteristics. Thus, it was claimed (Aristotle, *Physiognomy* 806b) that timid animals (deer, hares, sheep) have soft coats and the bravest animals (lions, boars) the coarsest coats; similarly, Southerners are cowardly and soft-haired and Northerners brave and coarse-haired. In fact recent work by anthropologists has revealed how many preliterate societies pay special attention to animals as a means of defining norms and boundaries, so that the use of animal categories in an attempt to define types of human personality is to be thought standard rather than bizarre.

Semonides, moreover, does not allow analogy with an animal to control his material totally, remarking in the case of the horse-woman that while she is usually a curse to her husband, a tyrant or a king might approve of her extravagance. Fifth-century comedy confirms Semonides' general rule about such a woman in Aristophanes' portrayal of the aristocratic wife of the less-exalted Strepsiades in the *Clouds* (41–55), for this ill-matched couple consists of a husband with a peasant-farmer's tastes and a wife interested in a high life-style and sex. However, comedy describes but does not explain behavior, and so Theophrastus' *Characters*, a collection of brief sketches of types such as the talkative or superstitious man, apparently designed as a guide for the aspiring writer of comedy, is purely descriptive and lacks analysis. We must consult tragedy for any attempt at explanation, and here it is Euripides who offers the richest material. Indeed Euripides displays an insight into human motivation that has caused some to consider him virtually a psychologist, and the term "Electra complex" owes much to Euripides' presentation of that heroine in his play of the same name. In his version of the tragedy the aristocratic Electra is married to a mere farmer. Although her story forms the theme of extant plays by the three major Athenian tragedians of the fifth century B.C., it is in Euripides' play that her mother, Clytemnestra, tells Electra that from birth she has always adored her father, Agamemnon (*Electra* 1102). And it is in Euripides alone that Electra is married off to a social inferior to avoid her having offspring likely to avenge their murdered grandfather, as their status would hardly provide access to those on whom vengeance might be wreaked.

There can be no doubt that Euripides' princess bitterly resents her marriage to a farmer. Her sense of outrage at such a humiliation is illustrated by the way in which she takes the initiative in plotting her mother's death or gloats over her mother's slaughtered lover, Aegisthus. Unlike her brother, Orestes, Electra does not falter when Clytemnestra is to be slain. Her marriage to the farmer, although unconsummated, was like death (*Electra* 247), and she revels in her misery, appearing on stage dressed in rags and with shaven head. She is desperate that Orestes should appreciate her abject misery, and her apparent docility does not prevent her from a more than occasional exhibition of impatience, whether she converses with her husband (352; 404–405) or the old servant (534 ff.). Euripides, in short, both reveals Electra's ferocity of temper and also accounts for this by emphasizing an excessive affection for her father and an enforced and degrading marriage.

The sexuality of women in general and the pride of the aristocratic woman and her desire for revenge when humiliated are just as clearly illustrated by Queen Phaedra in Euripides' *Hippolytus.* In this play, Phaedra, having seen her stepson Hippolytus when he came to Athens, is seized by "devastating love" (24–28). Cruelly rejected by Hippolytus, Phaedra commits suicide, leaving, however, a note for her husband in order to protect both her own honor and that of her children, a note in which she accuses Hippolytus of rape (885–886). But Phaedra's suicide has another motive as well, and it is this revenge motive that stresses Euripides' understanding of human behavior. As Phaedra says herself (728–731), in dying she will become a cause of disaster for Hippolytus so that he may learn not to be haughty about her own disaster. In other words, we find here the typical suicide note so familiar to the modern psychologist, for as Erwin Stengel points out (1973, p. 44):

> [Modern suicide notes] usually contain expressions of love or hate. They certainly bear out the importance of aggression against others in the motivation of suicide, especially the revenge motive. . . . The writers appear to be profoundly interested in what is going to happen after their death. . . . Almost invariably, the writers of suicide notes aim at eliciting certain emotional responses from survivors who had been close to them.

Again, Euripides displays a deep insight into the human mind when, at the beginning of the *Hippolytus* (208 ff.), he depicts a starving and delirious Phaedra who indulges in sexual fantasies of a classic type in which her secret passion for her stepson "comes subconsciously to the surface in a series of wild wishes to be in the places where Hippolytus is and doing the things he does" (W. S. Barrett, trans. [1964], p. 200).

Euripides also explains why Phaedra is the victim of illicit but uncontrollable passion in terms of both nature and environment. Hers is an inherited curse, for her mother was Pasiphae of Crete and her sister Ariadne (337–343): the former fell in love with a bull and conceived the monstrous Minotaur, while the latter left Crete with Theseus, who abandoned her on Naxos, and then subsequently married Dionysus. Phaedra, therefore, is the third member of the family to experience a love that is sinful—such love is part of her blood or nature. Her behavior is also conditioned by her situation in two respects. First, she is a Cretan princess who becomes queen of Athens, and the burden of upholding honor is even heavier for her, for the rules of noblesse oblige require that the aristocrat must set the right example; when what is shameful appears acceptable to the noble, it will certainly seem to be so to the lowborn as well. Second, unlike Electra, she enjoys the life of the aristocratic lady on whose hands time lies heavily. In other words, Phaedra has the leisure and time during which neuroses and anxieties can develop and grow strong, and so when she lists (*Hippolytus* 381–385) the temptations that stand in the way of duty, her examples include laziness and the pleasures afforded by long hours of chatter and idleness. Thus Euripides demonstrates how both the sexuality intrinsic to her family and her enforced leisure contribute to Phaedra's collapse at the mere sight of her young stepson.

MOTHERS AND SONS

In a celebrated passage from his *Medea* (230–247), Euripides' heroine of that name stresses the tribulations of the wife in an arranged marriage: A woman first has to purchase her husband with a dowry, only to receive a master over her body; it is crucial whether her husband is good or bad, since divorce is a disgrace and a husband cannot be denied; the teenage girl is totally unequipped for marriage, and while a happy marriage is a joy, death is the only release from the unhappy union; a man can always find pleasure outside the family when bored, but woman has just one person, a husband, to whom she may turn. Such a picture of Greek marriage, even at its best, and the subordination demanded of a woman in marriage—she must simply reflect her husband's moods and fancies—have led to the argument that mothers played a particular part in shaping the personalities of their sons in Greek society. It has been suggested that a mother's attitude to her son was likely to be ambivalent: on the one hand, she transferred her resentment, and even hatred, of her husband to her more vulnerable son and, on the other, lavished attention on her son in the hope of realizing vicariously through him her own thwarted ambitions. Thus such an ambivalent attitude is thought to be represented by the meaning of the name of the greatest Greek hero, Herakles, "the glory of Hera"—who was, however, relentlessly persecuted by the wife of Zeus throughout his life on earth, a fact in seeming contradiction to the implications of his name. An overexposure to the sharply contrasting moods of an excessively attentive mother has been similarly held responsible for the cult of male beauty or narcissism among the Greeks and even seen as an explanation for Greek homosexuality. The tension between father and son that might arise from a mother's ambitions for her son is revealed, for example, by the relationship between the father Strepsiades and the son Pheidippides in Aristophanes' *Clouds*.

Remarkable confirmation of a mother's influence in determining her son's personality is offered by another attempt to define types of human personality on the basis of analogy. For Plato in his *Republic* the individual human soul and the state are analogous, each being compounded of three elements: reason paralleling the guardians, spirit paralleling the auxiliaries, and appetite paralleling the bulk of the population in the philosopher's ideal state. And so, when in the eighth and ninth books of the *Republic* Plato discusses inferior forms of government, he also sketches the characteristics of corresponding types of personality and, more important, describes how such types of personality developed. There are, according to Plato, four parallel forms of government and individuals: the timocratic state and individual, the oligarchic state and individual, the democratic state and individual, and the tyrannical state and individual. Much of the material here is traditional: thus the form of government and its exponent represented by tyranny had already been outlined in the fifth century B.C. by Herodotus (*Histories* 3.80.2–5), and the tyrant appears as a stock character exhibiting common characteristics in Greek tragedy. But with Plato's treatment of timocracy and the timocratic man we do see something new, a serious attempt to account for personality in terms of childhood experience, a feature missing from his following descriptions, which are vitiated because they are made to conform to a wholly artificial scheme of political development from timocracy through oligarchy and democracy eventually to tyranny.

The timocratic state is marked for Plato by rulers more interested in war than in peace, better trained in physical education than in cultural accomplishments, secretly greedy, and, above all, highly competitive in their pursuit of honor (*Republic* 8.547d–548d), the result being a state that is a mixture of good and evil. The timocratic man likewise enjoys an unbalanced education, is harsh to subordinates but obedient to authority, bases his claim to office on his military prowess, and, as he grows older, is less and less inclined to despise wealth (8.548d–549b). How does such a personality evolve? Such a man is the result of mixed parents. He is the son of a good father, who, living in a badly governed city, avoids honors, office, and litigation, wanting to keep clear of trouble and to live a private life; but the boy's mother is different, for she becomes annoyed that her husband is not one of the rulers and that she is therefore slighted by other women. When she sees that her husband is not serious about money and does not put up a fight in lawcourt or assembly but makes little of this, and that he is always self-absorbed and is indifferent to her as he is to public affairs, the mother gets upset and tells her son that his father is no man and too tolerant; she then adds—Plato remarks with a degree of familiarity that has made the great scholar Wilamowitz suspect that this is a portrait of Plato's own mother, Perictione—all the other complaints women are inclined to elaborate in such a situation. The opinion of the frustrated mother is endorsed by the servants and the son is urged to prove himself to be more of a man than his father. Pulled in contrary directions by his father's example and his mother's nagging, the son reaches a compromise and "delivers up the government of himself to the middle element, which is contentious and hot-tempered, and becomes a haughty man ambitious of honor" (Republic 8.549c–550c).

Timocracy as a mixture of good and bad must conform to the intermediate military element or the auxiliaries of Plato's ideal state, and conformity with that element finally spoils what is otherwise a penetrating appraisal of a mother's influence on her son. The mother of the timocratic man has been called Plato's only female character, and that this description of the son is a genuine—and valid—attempt to define and explain a personality type is confirmed by later evidence. Some four hundred years later the Roman philosopher Seneca the Younger wrote to his mother Helvia from exile a letter of consolation in which he sought to reconcile her to his fall from grace as chief minister to the emperor Nero. At one point in the letter Seneca says that Helvia is not like other mothers, the mothers who "because women are not permitted to enjoy office, seek power through their sons" (Moral Essays, "To Mother Helvia" 14.2). Helvia, it seems, was frugal in using her children's influence, as if it were the property of a stranger, and from their election to office she gained nothing but pleasure and expense; never did her tenderness consider self-interest ("To Mother Helvia" 14.3). Yet one might forgive Helvia if she had attempted to gratify her ambitions through her sons, for her husband, Seneca tells us, followed the custom of his ancestors and was a man of old-fashioned strictness who denied his wife the benefits of an education in philosophy ("To Mother Helvia" 17.3–4).

But, Seneca also relates, his mother's sister allowed affection to overcome modesty in the interests of her nephew, on whose behalf she became "even power-seeking" ("To Mother Helvia" 19.2). And Seneca's personal experience of the woman, all of whose hopes were centered on the advancement of her son, was considerable, since he had witnessed the machinations by which the emperor Claudius' wife Agrippina had engineered the succession of her son Nero to the imperial throne and had then seen Agrippina acting as coruler with her son. No less notorious was Livia, the wife of the emperor Augustus and the mother of his successor Tiberius, who was reputed not to have refrained even from murder in order to ensure that Tiberius became emperor. But the type of the resentful and therefore aggressive mother can be traced back as far as Homer's Thetis in the Iliad, and an obvious example, not neglected by modern psychologists, is Olympias, the mother of Alexander the Great.

But what of the son subjected to unrelenting pressure from a dominant mother? Here late antiquity offers unique evidence, the *Confessions* of St. Augustine, a profoundly introspective autobiography dating from the close of the fourth century A.D. In the *Confessions* Augustine's pagan father, Patricius, receives scant attention; his death when Augustine was seventeen is merely noted in passing (*Confessions* 3.4). However, the last days of the saint's mother, Monica, and Augustine's inconsolable anguish at her death form the climax of the strictly autobiographical part of the *Confessions* and are described in vivid detail that leaves the reader in no doubt as to her overriding influence (*Confessions* 9.11–13). Augustine presents a picture of a wife who bore her husband's hot temper and sexual adventures with a patience that Rebecca West (1933) suspects was guaranteed to irritate, and a picture of a mother whose love for her son was so suffocating that Augustine had to trick her before he could leave her at Carthage to go to Rome: "She loved to have me with her as mothers do but much more so than many mothers" (*Confessions* 5.8). Especially revealing are the very different reactions of father and mother when Patricius, having seen signs of his son's maturity at the baths, rejoices at the prospect of grandsons, whereas Monica on being informed "leapt up with a pious fear and trembling" (*Confessions* 2.3).

(MIS)UNDERSTANDING PERSONALITY

Another work by St. Augustine, *On Genesis against the Manichees,* illustrates the fundamental weakness in ancient attempts to explain the development of personality. For Plato, as we have already noted, states and in-

dividuals are made to conform to an identical scheme of development, and the development is predetermined by Plato's philosophical theorizing. Even Aristotle's descriptions in the *Rhetoric* (2.1388b–1390b) of the characteristics of the young, the old, and those in the prime of life are shaped by his philosophy, the young and the old being for the most part opposites, while those in the prime of life represent the Aristotelian mean between two extremes. Four ages of mankind are preferred by the Roman poets Horace and Ovid. Horace describes the behavior of the child, beardless youth, mature man, and old man (*The Art of Poetry* [*Epistles* 2.3] 158–176), but he is purely descriptive, presenting stereotypes suitable for the stage. In Ovid's *Metamorphoses* (15.199–213), it is the Greek philosopher Pythagoras who refers to the four stages of childhood, youth, maturity, and old age, each stage being compared to the appropriate season of the year, spring, summer, autumn, and winter. The use of analogy in a much more elaborate but even less convincing form is employed by Augustine in his *On Genesis against the Manichees,* for there Augustine lists six ages of mankind, adding infancy as a first stage and the age of the older man as the fifth stage, and relates these ages to the six periods of sacred history and the six days of the Creation. Such parallelism is totally distorted and owes nothing to a genuine understanding of the human personality.

At the same time, as we have seen, the significance of a child's experience and the role of the mother in the determination of personality traits were acknowledged. We may even detect echoes of procedure common in clinical psychology today. Thus Socrates' dialectic method by which truth is attained by a series of questions and answers may prefigure modern psychoanalysis, while the Socratic theory of recollection anticipates the discovery of the unconscious mind. Analysis, we hope, will lead to self-realization, and self-realization is not far distant from Plato's definition of *dikaiosune* (justice) as "doing that for which your nature is most suited" (*Republic* 4.433a). Finally, Aristotle's concept of catharsis, or relief from emotion by the intensification of emotion, suggests contemporary therapy. Thus we may trace back to antiquity not only the description of personality and factors determining personality, but also the means by which personality disorders may be alleviated. It is a failure of methodology, a dependence on argument based on either contrast or comparison, that limited the understanding of personality and was to continue to limit understanding in the absence of a genuinely scientific approach.

BIBLIOGRAPHY

SOURCES

Aristotle, *The Poetics*, William Hamilton Fyfe, trans. (1927; rev. ed. 1932), *Politics*, Harris Rackham, trans. (1932; rev. ed. 1944), *Problems* II, books 22–38, Walter S. Hett, trans. (1936–1937; rev. ed. 1963), and *The "Art" of Rhetoric*, John H. Freese, trans. (1926); St. Augustine, *Confessions*, William Watts, trans., 2 vols. (1912); Euripides, (*Works*), Arthur S. Way, trans., 4 vols. (1912), and *Hippolytus*, W. S. Barrett, ed. (1964); *Hesiod*, Hugh G. Evelyn-White, trans. (1914, rev. eds. 1920, 1936); Plato, *Republic*, Paul Shorey, trans., 2 vols. (1930; rev. ed. 1937); Plutarch, *Moralia* I, Frank C. Babbitt, trans. (1927), and *Parallel Lives*, vol. 4, Bernadotte Perrin, trans. (1916); Semonides, *Female of the Species: Semonides on Women*, Hugh Lloyd-Jones, ed. (1975); Seneca, *Moral Essays* II, John W. Basore, trans., 3 vols. (1928–1932).

STUDIES

A. MacC. Armstrong, "The Methods of the Greek Physiognomists," in *Greece and Rome*, **5** (1958); Joy Paul Guilford, *Personality* (1959); Richard S. Lazarus and Edward M. Opton, Jr., eds., *Personality: Selected Readings* (1967); Philip E. Slater, *The Glory of Hera: Greek Mythology and the Greek Family* (1968); Erwin Stengel, *Suicide and Attempted Suicide* (rev. ed. 1973); Rebecca West, *St. Augustine* (1933).

Prostitution

WERNER A. KRENKEL

PROSTITUTION, THE PROMISCUOUS BARTERING of sexual favors for money, is as old as civilization and urban life. Prostitution involves the treatment of human beings, female or male, as commodities. Although most organized prostitution takes place on an economic basis, there are examples in antiquity of the use of prostitution for religious purposes as well. The practice is virtually unknown among primitive peoples. Homer does not mention prostitutes, let alone organized prostitution. His heroes have recourse to female slaves (*Iliad* 1.111; 8.284; 9.449; *Odyssey* 1.433); later sources claim that Homeric warriors resorted to concubines or masturbation ("fought against Aphrodite with their hands": *Palatine Anthology* 1.22; Euboulos, *Fragments of Attic Comedy*, II, frag. 120.5–8). Archilochus (frags. 142, 184), a poet who flourished in the seventh century B.C., is the first Greek author to mention courtesans. But from his time on, the available Greek or Roman sources, which are written by men and reflect their biases, rarely record genuine verbatim accounts by female and male prostitutes. We therefore know little of what they thought about their situation.

In the following essay evidence from various periods and places in antiquity has been gathered together to give as full a picture as possible of the development and nature of ancient prostitution. Such a composite picture is necessary since the evidence we have is scanty and often difficult to interpret. The essay will examine the origins of prostitution in religious contexts, its organization in brothels, what we know of prostitutes' lives and the attitude toward them, and finally the phenomenon of male prostitution. In all these areas evidence from Greece and Rome and from various periods has been conflated to give a detailed account, although that account may not be accurate for any single period.

FEMALE PROSTITUTION

Commercial sex was the province of slaves, freed persons, and foreigners. Freeborn Greek and Roman citizens were protected against being forced to engage in prostitution (Aeschines, "Against Timarchus" 14; Plutarch, *Parallel Lives,* "Solon" 23; *Digest*

48.5.35). Individuals who were prostitutes ranged from people working for pimps to freelance courtesans and boys to de luxe paramours or "companions" (*hetairai*). Organized commercial sex is said to have originated in the temples of the Middle East. As towns, cities, and large temples first came into existence in Mesopotamia, it is perhaps not surprising that temple prostitution is first reported in Babylonia. According to Herodotus (1.199), "Every woman who is a native of the country must once in her life go and sit in the temple of Aphrodite and there give herself to a stranger." Rich and proud women, Herodotus continues, would drive to this temple in covered carriages and sit among the assembled throngs. Men would pass through the crowd and make their choices by throwing money into a woman's lap and saying, "I demand thee in the name of Mylitta" (the Assyrian Aphrodite); the couple would then leave the temple and have intercourse. Through this act a Babylonian woman made herself holy to the goddess; to refuse to participate was thought sinful. Similar customs are said to have prevailed in other parts of the ancient Mediterranean world.

The ancient sources portray fertility rites as common among primitive peoples: crops, cattle, and the human family had to be blessed by some deity. This god or goddess, in turn, would be offered compensation for his or her services: "I give so that you may give" (*do ut des*) the Latin formula runs. Men are claimed to have offered to the god or goddess as insurance for fertility and prosperity their daughters, spouses, and eventually slave women: one thousand women were supposedly pledged for a victory at the Greek Olympic Games (Pindar, *Olympian* 13). Such behavior was sanctified by pious-sounding justifications: "in the name of Mylitta," "refusal is sin," "money made sacred," "holy to the goddess." Women were indoctrinated with the idea that to refuse to

prostitute themselves was a sin and that prostitution was to be accepted as a form of consecration to the goddess. Still, prostitution in its various forms was recognized by males as existing for their own hedonistic pleasure (Demosthenes, "Against Neaira" 59.122; Plutarch, *Parallel Lives,* "Solon" 22.4). Women of wealthy families who could afford to speak their minds may have had some reservations about engaging in such conduct, but their elders no doubt instilled in them the belief that no matter what common sense and their own modesty dictated, only "virtuous, law-abiding" adherence to the rules could bring true happiness, as Plato argues in a different context. Men employed superstition to make a travesty out of morality (Tertullian, *On Spectacles* [*De Spectaculis*] 10 [6]). Temple prostitution could well be rooted in this "pious fiction."

According to Lucian (*On the Syrian Goddess* [*De Dea Syra*] 6), women at Byblos in Phoenicia (Jebeil, Lebanon) complied only unwillingly with this practice of consecrated male pleasure-seeking; hence the authorities assigned lengthier and more obvious obligations to women who refused to conform; those who did not prostitute themselves for a day to strangers in honor of Aphrodite had instead to have their hair cut at the rites mourning the death of Adonis.

The transition from temple prostitution as a form of consecration to earning a dowry (relieving paternal financial burdens) or a living through selling sexual favors in temples can be observed in ancient accounts of Lydia (Herodotus, 1.93), Carthage (Valerius Maximus, *Memorable Deeds and Sayings* 2.6.15), Armenia (Strabo, *Geography* 11.532 f.), and Cyprus (Justinus, *Epitome of the Philippic Histories of Pompeius Trogus* 18.5, 2.13). Freeborn girls in Italy were said to follow the Etruscan tradition by earning their dowries through prostitution (Plautus, *The Casket* [*Cistellaria*] 562 f.). Aphrodite—or Assyrian and Babylonian Ishtar, Phoenician Astarte,

Semitic Ashtoreth, Sumerian Inanna or Mylitta—changed from goddess of fertility and creation to a patroness of female prostitution (*Palatine Anthology* 7.222f.).

As a consequence of such changes, new social attitudes and a double standard of sexual morality came into being. A freeborn female had to be a virgin (*intacta*) at the time of her marriage. Until then she was isolated from society, living almost exclusively within the house. A freeborn male, on the other hand, sought premarital coitus from available females; the existence of prostitution guaranteed the accessibility of a variety of sexual partners. When Greeks and Romans married, the males between ages twenty-five and thirty, their inexperienced spouses between thirteen and sixteen, the husbands may often have been sexually and intellectually disappointed with their wives and hence may have returned to more worldly and erotically knowledgeable prostitutes for sexual satisfaction.

Women sometimes would enter the sexual market of their own accord, but more often than not they were motivated by dire need (Proverbs of Solomon 7.6–23; Suetonius, *Lives of the Twelve Caesars*, "Tiberius" 35.1; *Palatine Anthology* 6.47). Prostitution promised a way out of poverty (Herodotus, 1.196): "Since the conquest of Babylon made the Assyrians afflicted and poor, every common man lacking a livelihood makes his daughters into prostitutes." The prostitution of girls is also attested in later antiquity (Zosimus, 2.38). Lucian (*Dialogues of Courtesans* 6.1) depicts a mother telling her child, "There is no other means for us to make a living than this one [prostitution of the daughter]. Do you remember how wretchedly we have lived these past two years since your father died?" Thus economic motivation as well as pleasure-seeking can be seen to have kept prostitution alive in the ancient world. Poor families' economic needs, as well as masters' use of slaves for profit, by prostituting them in inns, bars, and public baths, provided the source to meet the demand created by the customs that fashioned sex and behavior in the ancient world.

Such behavior, according to Plato (*Laws* 841a–e), jeopardized familial ties, public health, morality, and the birth of offspring required for maintaining the community. To Dio Chrysostom, the popular philosopher of the first century A.D., prostitution was "sterile copulation." As prostitution was perceived as a threat to society, measures were taken to control its use. One measure was the creation of brothels, presumably to place prostitution under stark control. The following account illustrates how brothels were run and what attitudes they created.

The Athenian Solon, in 594 B.C., was said to have been the first to establish brothels (*porneia*) with prostitutes (*pornai*) purchased for this purpose (Athenaeus, *The Learned Banquet* [*Deipnosophistae*] 13.569d). Courtesans who populated brothels in antiquity often were foreign-born; sources mention Phoenicians, Lydians, Syrians, Thracians, and Ethiopians. A tax was paid on their importation (*Palatine Anthology* 9.415; Terence, *The Brothers* [*Adelphi*] 224–231). Other sources for populating brothels were exposed and abandoned children (Tertullian, *Apology* 9), women sold by their fathers or husbands for economic reasons, young girls inveigled by pimps (Seneca the Elder, *Controversiae* 10.4.11), and adulteresses, at least in Cyprus, where according to Dio Chrysostom (64.3), they were shaved and condemned to prostitute themselves in public houses. The Roman comedians suggest that girls of a lazy and lascivious disposition who preferred to be rich and infamous rather than modest and poor could easily be talked into the profession (Terence, *Girl of Andros* [*Andria*] 69–70; 797–980; Plautus, *A Comedy of Asses* [*Asinaria*] 504–544). In order to increase their value and the prices they could charge, young courtesans (*hetairai*) were trained in various skills. Aspasia, the famous mistress of Pericles, made the education given *hetairai* available to female citizens as well. She thereby made philosophers reassess the role of education and the status of women in the Athenian community (Aristotle, *Politics* 1260b15, 1269b17).

In Athens, prostitutes were controlled by the clerk of the market (*agoranomos*), who fixed the fee that they could charge for a single visit. In Rome, prostitutes had to register with the aedile who supervised markets, streets, and restaurants; he, we may assume, was also responsible for fixing their fees (Seneca the Elder, *Controversiae* 1.2.1). Brothel fees ranged from one obol, the sixth part of a drachma, to two drachmas, the maximum rate permitted officially. According to Juvenal's sixth satire, prostitutes had to be paid prior to intercourse. Some *hetairai*, however, commanded high fees from connoisseurs and steady lovers. Demosthenes, the famous orator, sailed to Corinth to meet the renowned courtesan Lais. For the rendezvous she demanded the breathtaking fee of 10,000 drachmas; according to Aulus Gellius (*Attic Nights* [*Noctes Atticae*] 1.8), Demosthenes did not pay it. In Rome cheap prostitutes received an as of brass, bronze, or copper, better ones a denarius or two (Martial, *Epigrams* 1.103.10; 9.32). Fees differed according to special circumstances: the defloration of a virgin drew one mina (100 drachmas) (Lucian, *Dialogues of Courtesans* 6.1–2) from a customer "who found the very virginity an attraction" (Seneca the Elder, *Controversiae* 1.22). Special services increased the fee as well, as noted in an epigram by Martial (9.4):

> Galla can be laid for two gold pieces, and she can be more than just laid, if you add this price again. Why, then, Aeschylus, do you give her ten gold pieces? Galla does not suck you dry for so much. What then?—She clams up.

In Roman times in particular the pleasure market was profitable, and fortunes could be amassed from brothel-keeping, so Plautus has a character say in *The Rope* (*Rudens*). Prostitutes followed Roman armies by the thousands. The market attracted landowners, and even emperors, who allegedly stocked their brothels with freeborn females and boys (Suetonius, *Lives of the Twelve Caesars*, "Gaius [Caligula]" 41). The clients were called "contributors to the imperial revenue."

Governments taxed prostitution, both in Greece and in Rome. The Roman system worked this way (Suetonius, *Lives of the Twelve Caesars*, "Gaius" 40, Robert Graves, trans. [1957]):

> Porters had to hand over an eighth part of their day's earnings and prostitutes their standard fee for a single act of intimacy even if they had quitted their profession and were respectably married; pimps and ex-pimps also became liable to this public tax.

Prostitutes were debased in many ways: by language, legal status, and the need for self-advertisement. To call someone the son of a prostitute was the worst kind of abuse (*Palatine Anthology* 11.363.3f.). It was employed against Jesus (Tertullian, *On Spectacles* 30.105) and the emperor Elagabalus (*Historia Augusta* 15.7.6, 17.2.1 f.). Brothel prostitutes were considered foul (*turpes*) and belonged to the lowest stratum of society. To attract customers, according to the converted Christian Clement of Alexandria (*Tutor* 2.116.1), they advertised their services by wearing shoes whose soles left the imprint "Follow me!" Agents would also bring visitors to their abodes (Petronius, *Satyricon* 6.4–8.4; Suetonius, *Lives of the Twelve Caesars*, "Gaius" 41.1).

Some information can be gathered about the conditions under which prostitutes worked. They tried to avoid conception by adopting a straddling position for intercourse or by making undulating movements, by rubbing cedar resin over the male organ as a prophylactic, or by inserting occlusive pessaries made of wool balls soaked in oil, honey, and vinegar (Soranus, *Gynaeceia* 1.61f.). Other contraceptive factors may have operated. If abortion were instrumentally induced, a chronic inflammation of the fallopian tubes inhibiting future pregnancies may have developed. Many prostitutes may not have been sexually aroused; in this case the Bartholin glands may not have yielded an alkaline secretion to neutralize the normal acidity of the vagina, and spermatozoa would have been naturally killed. Prostitutes are said to have sought sexual gratification from other women. One of the rhetoricians reported by Seneca the Elder (*Controversiae* 1.2.10) describes a woman as "sullied by the kisses of her companions," and other sources make similar suggestions (Lucian, *Dialogues of Courtesans* 5; Alciphron, *Letters* [*Epistulae Meretricium*] 14; Martial, *Epigrams* 1.90).

While prostitutes were on the whole scorned by society, the institution of prostitution was considered a necessity, at least by some male writers. "A girlfriend is better than a wife," says Eumolpus in the *Satyricon* (93.2.8 f.). Even Augustine recorded his support of prostitution (*On Order* 11.4.12): "Remove prostitution from human affairs and you will destroy everything with lust." The elder Cato phrased this in a different way when, as reported by Horace (*Satires* 1.2.28–35), he congratulated a young man who emerged from a brothel with the remark, "When sensual lust swells up the veins, it is better that young men come here rather than screw other men's wives." Horace, however, has suppressed the rest of the episode, provided to us by pseudo-Acro: "But later on, when Cato saw the man come frequently out of the bawdy house, he said, 'Young man, I praised you because you came here once in a while, but not because you lived here.' "

MALE PROSTITUTION

The phenomenon of male prostitution is rarely discussed. Male prostitutes catered to homosexual clients. Greek and Roman adolescents took homosexuality for granted; Minucius Felix (*Octavian* 28) accuses the Romans of projecting their own "worship" of pederasty onto the Christians. Aeschines, in fourth-century Athens, makes the distinction between a kept man who has only one lover and a man who sells his favor to many different men. The latter he calls a prostitute, and it is this state that was prohibited to freeborn boys and youths. The same law applied in Rome. Plautus has a character in *The Weevil* ([*Curculio*] 33–38) say:

> No one prohibits or forbids the purchase of what is for sale in public—provided you have got the money. No one prohibits anyone from going down the public way—as long as you do not take a shortcut cut through fenced-in land; as long as you stay away from married women, widows, virgins, from youths and freeborn boys—love anybody you please.

Nevertheless, there are cases in the *Digesta* (47.11.1.2; 48.5.35), the great compendium of Roman law, that suggest that the seduction of freeborn boys and girls was not unknown.

Slave boys were forced into prostitution; they would ply their trade in brothels and in private lodgings called *stegoi* by Aeschines (1.36). Phaidon, Socrates' disciple, had been purchased for an Athenian bawdy house, according to Gellius (*Attic Nights* 2.18.1–4). Through the aid of their lovers or their own earnings slaves could acquire the status of a freedman or even a citizen, although the possibility of this happening differed from period to period and place to place. Petronius satirizes such a situation in the *Satyricon* (81.4):

> A youth wallowing in every possible filth, who, on his own admission, deserved to be exiled, who achieved his status as a freedman through vice, his status as a Roman citizen through vice, whose young body was sold by tickets, and who had been hired as a girl even by someone who knew he was a man.

Young men would keep boys as concubines, putting them aside when they married, or continuing the liaison even after they had wed, just as the emperor Hadrian continued his relationship with Antinous. Intercourse between masters and their male slaves was normal and in accordance with the standards of a male-dominated society (Seneca the Elder, *Controversiae* 4 preface 10): "Sexual servicing is a crime for the freeborn, a necessity for a slave, and a duty for the freedman," a view that is echoed in the *Satyricon* (75.11).

Slave boys were sent out to attract customers, especially in harbor towns where they swarmed the dock areas like flies (Plautus, *The Little Carthaginian* [*Poenulus*] 688–691); they roamed cities (Seneca the Younger, *Dialogues* 1.5.3) and infested baths (Pliny the Elder, *Natural History* 33.40). Their fee in fourth-century Athens appears to have been four drachmas (Aeschines, 1.158), a minimum that was higher than the fee charged by female prostitutes. To meet the demand for male prostitutes, beautiful boys were captured, imported by carriage and ship (Juvenal, 9.132), sold (Aristophanes, *Knights* [*Equites*] 1069; Catullus, 106; Martial, 9.59), hired out (Plautus, *The Weevil* 382–384), and prostituted. Juvenal's ninth satire relates a conversation with a male prostitute, Naevolus, about his client Virro.

Despite laws and prohibitions designed to prevent it, freeborn youths of good families plied the trade of their own accord. Macrobius (*Saturnalia* 3.17.4), referring to a law of 161 B.C., reports: "Most of the freeborn youths sold their modesty and freedom." Close connections between a boy and an older man could exist without a sexual context. But a boy of good family was expected to start a political career: thus he had to find a patron under whose protection and guidance he could enter the realm of public life. If the relationship with his first patron did not work out, he then had to win a new protector; behavior to this end could, if misconstrued, earn him a reputation for being corruptible. Persius' fourth satire in fact likens a young politician to a prostitute. But Roman youngsters encountered homosexuality at school, long before they entered public life. Quintilian (*Education of an Orator* [*Institutio Oratoria*] 1.2.4; 2.2.1–5) advised parents not to send their boys to schools because pederasty flourished there.

Male prostitution also featured a double standard. Inasmuch as it was viewed as a sign of superior virility and power for one male to dominate another (thereby providing a rationale for pederasty), the reverse, to be the "beloved boy" after reaching adulthood, was frowned upon. Satirical inscriptions and graffiti make this clear: a sling bullet (*Corpus Inscriptionum Latinarum* 11.6721.9a) reads [S]ALVE OCTAVI FELAS, "Hi, Octavi(an), you fellate"; a Pompeian graffito (*Corpus Inscriptionum Latinarum* 4.1825) castigates "catamites" and "fellators," grown men who still lust after men. Men apparently had a deep sexual craving for being fellated (Suetonius, "Tiberius" 44); active fellatio, however, was the abyss of degradation for a mature male. This double standard is particularly obvious in Cicero's attempts to defame political opponents, where he makes vituperative attacks on the early sexual lives of his opponents, although their behavior as adults is not open to attack.

***

Judging by the evidence we can gather, prostitution was a common aspect of ancient life. It involved the exploitation of segments of the population who had the least protection under the law: women, children, and slaves. There is no record of the feelings of those who were thus exploited, but occasionally an ancient writer will reveal an understanding of the effect of prostitution on society and individuals. The elder Seneca's words describing prostitution may serve as a judgment: *infelix patientia*—unhappy and sterile submission.

BIBLIOGRAPHY

J. N. Adams, *The Latin Sexual Vocabulary* (1982), and "Words for 'Prostitute' in Latin," in *Rheinisches Museum für Philologie*, **12** (1984); John Boardman and Eugenio La Rocca, *Eros in Greece* (1975); John Boswell, *Christianity, Social Tolerance, and Homosexuality* (1980); Paul Brandt (Hans Licht, pseud.), *Sexual Life in Ancient Greece* (1932; repr. 1974); Kenneth J. Dover, *Greek Popular Morality in the Time of Plato and Aristotle* (1974), and *Greek Homosexuality* (1978); Emiel Eyben, "Family Planning in Graeco-Roman Antiquity," in *Ancient Society*, **11/12** (1980/1981); Michael Grant, *Eros in Pompeii* (1975); Jeffrey Henderson, *The Maculate Muse: Obscene Language in Attic Comedy* (1975); H. Herter, "Die Soziologie der antiken Prostitution im Lichte des heidnischen und christlichen Schrifttums," in *Jahrbuch für Antike und Christentum*, **3** (1960); Margaret C. Marks, "Heterosexual Coital Position as a Reflection of Ancient and Modern Cultural Attitudes," Ph.D. diss., State University of New York at Buffalo (1978); John Peradotto and J. P. Sullivan, eds., *Women in the Ancient World* (1984); Sarah B. Pomeroy, *Goddesses, Whores, Wives, and Slaves* (1975), and *Women in Hellenistic Egypt, from Alexander to Cleopatra* (1984); Amy Richlin, *The Garden of Priapus* (1983), and "Invective Against Women in Roman Satire," in *Arethusa*, **17** (1984); Robert F. Sutton, "The Interaction between Men and Women Portrayed on Attic Red-Figure Pottery," Ph.D. diss., University of North Carolina at Chapel Hill (1981); L. P. Wilkinson, *Classical Attitudes to Modern Issues* (1979).